Essays on Babylonian and Biblical Literature and Religion

# Harvard Museum of the Ancient Near East Publications

*Director of Publications*

Michael D. Coogan

*Editorial Board*


Gojko Barjamovic (Harvard University)
Alejandro Botta (Boston University)
Aaron A. Burke (University of California, Los Angeles)
Michael D. Coogan (Harvard University)
Katrien De Graef (Ghent University)
Paul Delnero (Johns Hopkins University)
Steven E. Fassberg (Hebrew University, Jerusalem)
Uri Gabbay (Hebrew University, Jerusalem)
W. Randall Garr (University of California, Santa Barbara)
Jonathan Greer (Cornerstone University)
Rebecca Hasselbach-Andee (University of Chicago)
Robert S. Homsher (Harvard University)
Jeremy M. Hutton (University of Wisconsin, Madison)
Enrique Jiménez (Universidad Complutense de Madrid)
Dan'el Kahn (University of Haifa)
Na'ama Pat-El (University of Texas, Austin)
Sara Milstein (University of British Columbia)
Francesca Rochberg (University of California, Berkeley)
Aaron Rubin (Pennsylvania State University)
Hervé Reculeau (University of Chicago)
Piotr Steinkeller (Harvard University)
Joshua Walton (Capital University)
Mark Weeden (University of London)
Christopher Woods (University of Chicago)


---

# Harvard Semitic Studies

VOLUME 65

The titles published in this series are listed at *brill.com/hvss*

# Essays on Babylonian and Biblical Literature and Religion

*By*

I. Tzvi Abusch

BRILL

LEIDEN | BOSTON

Library of Congress Cataloging-in-Publication Data

Names: Abusch, I. Tzvi, author.
Title: Essays on Babylonian and biblical literature and religion / by I. Tzvi Abusch.
Description: Leiden ; Boston : Brill, [2020] | Series: Harvard Semitic Museum publications | Includes bibliographical references and index. | Summary: "In this volume, I. Tzvi Abusch presents studies written over a span of forty years prior to his retirement from Brandeis University in 2019. They reflect several themes that he has pursued in addition to his work on witchcraft literature and the Epic of Gilgamesh. Part 1 includes general articles on Mesopotamian magic, religion, and mythology, followed by a set of articles on Akkadian prayers, especially šuillas, focusing on exegetical and linguistic (synchronic) studies and on diachronic analyses. Part 2 contains a series of literary studies of Mesopotamian and biblical classics. Part 3 is devoted to comparative studies of terms and phenomena. Part 4 examines legal texts"—Provided by publisher.
Identifiers: LCCN 2020022009 (print) | LCCN 2020022010 (ebook) | ISBN 9789004435179 (hardback) | ISBN 9789004435186 (ebook)
Subjects: LCSH: Assyro-Babylonian religion. | Magic, Assyro-Babylonian. | Mythology, Assyro-Babylonian. | Assyro-Babylonian religion—Prayers and devotions—History and criticism. | Incantations, Assyro-Babylonian. | Assyro-Babylonian literature—Relation to the Old Testament. | Assyria—Religious life and customs. | Babylonia—Religious life and customs.
Classification: LCC BL1620 .A28 2020 (print) | LCC BL1620 (ebook) | DDC 299/.21—dc23
LC record available at https://lccn.loc.gov/2020022009
LC ebook record available at https://lccn.loc.gov/2020022010

Typeface for the Latin, Greek, and Cyrillic scripts: "Brill". See and download: brill.com/brill-typeface.

ISSN 0147-9342
ISBN 978-90-04-43517-9 (hardback)
ISBN 978-90-04-43518-6 (e-book)



This book is printed on acid-free paper and produced in a sustainable manner.

*For My Students*

*Rabbi Hanina said:*
*Much have I learned from my Teachers,*
*Even more from my Colleagues,*
*But most of all from my Students.*

(TB Ta'anit 7a // TB Makkot 10a)

# Contents

Preface XI
Sources XIII
Abbreviations XVI

PART 1
*Magic and Religion*

*Overviews and Surveys*

1 **Mesopotamian Religion** 5
1 The Basis of Mesopotamian Religiosity 5
2 The Mesopotamian Pantheon 10
3 Magical Cult (Cult of the Individual) 14
4 The Epic of Gilgamesh 22

2 **Magic in Mesopotamia** 24
1 Introduction 24
2 Earlier Approaches to Mesopotamian Magic 24
3 Conceptions of the Universe and of Its Powers 27
4 Magical Texts 28
5 Ceremonies 31
6 Evil 35

3 **Sacrifice in Mesopotamia** 56
1 Mesopotamian Sacrifice: A Description 56
2 Blood in Mesopotamia and West Asia: A Hypothesis 60

*Ghosts and Gods*

4 **Ghost and God: Some Observations on a Babylonian Understanding of Human Nature** 67
1 Mythological Formulation 68
2 The Significance of Flesh as the Source of the Ghost 76
3 God, *ṭēmu*, and Personal God 81

5 **Etemmu אטים** 87
1 Name and Etymology 87
2 Character and History 87
3 Inside the Bible 91

6 **Ištar** 93
1 Name and Etymology 93
2 Character and History 93
3 Inside the Bible 98

7 **Marduk** 99
1 Name and Etymology 99
2 Character and History 99
3 Inside the Bible 107

*Talking to the Gods in Mesopotamia*

8 **Prayers and Incantations** 111
1 Prayers 111
2 Incantations 116

9 **The Promise to Praise the God in *šuilla* Prayers** 118

10 **The Form and Meaning of a Babylonian Prayer to Marduk** 126
1 The Hymnic Introduction 127
2 The Marduk *šuilla*: A New Form 136
3 A Prayer for Success and the Conclusion of the *šuilla* 140

11 **The Form and History of a Babylonian Prayer to Nabû** 149

12 **A Paean and Petition to a God of Death: Some Comments on a *šuilla* to Nergal** 163
1 Introduction 163
2 Hymnic Introduction 166
3 Petitioner's Justification and Description of His Approach to the God 169
4 Description of the Petitioner's Difficulties 170
5 Petitioner's Supplication 172
6 Conclusions 174

13 **The Reconciliation of Angry Personal Gods: A Revision of the *šuillas*** 176

14 **Two Versions of a *šuilla* to Gula** 206

PART 2
*Literary Studies*

15 **Fortune and Misfortune of the Individual: Some Observations on the Sufferer's Plaint in *Ludlul bēl nēmeqi* II 12–32** 217

16 **Kingship in Ancient Mesopotamia: The Case of *Enūma eliš*** 225
1 Divine Origin and Physical Features 227
2 Kingship over His Own Family 229
3 The Battle 229
4 Creation 230
5 Kingship over the Universe 230

17 **Some Observations on the Babylon Section of *Enūma eliš*** 233

18 **Biblical Accounts of Prehistory: Their Meaning and Formation** 238
1 Introduction 239
2 Mesopotamian Sources 239
3 Biblical Sources 241
4 Summary and Conclusions 251

19 **Two Passages in the Biblical Account of Prehistory** 255
1 The Creation of Man and Woman 255
2 The Tower of Babel 257

20 **Jonah and God: Plants, Beasts, and Humans in the Book of Jonah** 259

PART 3
*Comparative Studies*

21 ***alaktu* and *halakhah*: Oracular Decision, Divine Revelation** 269
1 *alaktu*: Mesopotamian Sources 270
2 *halakhah*: Jewish Sources and Mesopotamian Influence 290

22 **Blood in Israel and Mesopotamia** 299

23 **Cultures in Contact: Ancient Near Eastern and Jewish Magic** 308

**PART 4**
*Ancient Near Eastern Legal Practices and Thought*

24 **A Shepherd's Bulla and an Owner's Receipt: A Pair of Matching Texts in the Harvard Semitic Museum** 319

25 **"He Should Continue to Bear the Penalty of That Case": Some Observations on Codex Ḫammurabi §§3–4 and §13** 328
1 Introduction 329
2 Analysis and Translation 331
3 Meaning and Significance 338
4 Confirmation: Variant Readings and §13 341
5 Conclusion 345

**Bibliography** 347
**Index of Passages Quoted** 376

# Preface

The studies set out here were either published or accepted for publication prior to my retirement from Brandeis University in August 2019. They were written over a span of almost forty years and reflect several themes that I have pursued in addition to my work on witchcraft literature and the Epic of Gilgamesh. My studies on those topics have been collected in the following volumes: *Mesopotamian Witchcraft: Toward a History and Understanding of Babylonian Witchcraft Beliefs and Literature* (AMD 5), *Further Studies on Mesopotamian Witchcraft Beliefs and Literature* (AMD 17), and *Male and Female in the Epic of Gilgamesh*. The studies in the present volume illustrate my several interests and approaches; some are of a synchronic nature, others are diachronic. Some of the studies were developed as part of my course preparations, especially those that are exegetical and literary. Note that this volume is intended as a collection of previously published essays and not as a reasoned argument. Accordingly, there will be some duplication (occasionally even verbatim duplication, especially in overviews) between chapters. I should note that a phrase or argument has occasionally been clarified, and a uniform mode of bibliographical citation has been introduced throughout.

The first part of the volume begins with general articles ("Overviews and Surveys" and "Ghosts and Gods") on Mesopotamian magic, religion, and mythology written for handbooks and volumes intended for broad academic audiences. These are followed by a set of articles on Akkadian prayers, especially *šuilla*s ("Talking to the Gods in Mesopotamia"). In these articles I focus, first of all, on exegetical and linguistic (synchronic) analyses of *šuilla* prayers to Marduk, Nabû, and Nergal and follow these with diachronic analyses of prayers that also belong to the *šuilla* grouping. Part 2 contains a series of literary studies of Mesopotamian and biblical classics (*Ludlul bel nemeqi*, *Enūma eliš*, Genesis, and Jonah). Part 3 is devoted to comparative studies of terms and phenomena (*alaktu/halakhah*, blood, and magic). Finally, the fourth part takes up in detail texts that are of legal interest (Codex Ḫammurabi and a bulla/receipt from Nuzi).

I wish to thank those who have helped me put together this volume. PDFs of original publications were turned into Microsoft Word versions by Jared Pfost. Those versions were then corrected by Daniel Berman, who also sent out requests for permission to republish to the original publishers and/or editors. Eileen Xing read through the volume in search of errors and infelicities. Most of all, I thank Gene McGarry for unifying the bibliographical citations and correcting many inconsistencies. The funds for these activities were provided by the Department of Near Eastern and Judaic Studies and the School of Arts and Sciences of Brandeis University. I also wish to thank the original publishers and editors for permission to publish my studies here.

Finally, I would like to thank Michael Coogan for accepting the volume into the Harvard Semitic Studies series and for reviewing the volume. Publishing this collection in HSS is personally meaningful, as the essays of my teachers at Harvard University were also collected in this series.

# Sources

All articles are reprinted with permission.

1. "Mesopotamian Religion." To appear in *The Oxford Handbook of Ritual and Worship in the Hebrew Bible*, ed. Samuel Balentine (Oxford: Oxford University Press).
2. "Magic." To appear in *Handbook of Ancient Mesopotamia*, ed. Gonzalo Rubio, The Ancient Mesopotamian Civilization (Berlin: de Gruyter).
3. "Sacrifice in Mesopotamia," in *Sacrifice in Religious Experience*, ed. A. I. Baumgarten, Studies in the History of Religions 93 (Leiden: Brill, 2002), 39–48.
4. "Ghost and God: Some Observations on a Babylonian Understanding of Human Nature," in *Self, Soul and Body in Religious Experience*, ed. A. I. Baumgarten, J. Assmann, and G. G. Stroumsa, Studies in the History of Religions (*Numen* Book Series) 78 (Leiden: Brill, 1998), 363–383.
5. "Etemmu אטים," in *Dictionary of Deities and Demons in the Bible*, ed. K. van der Toorn, B. Becking, and P. W. van der Horst, 2nd ed. (Leiden, Brill: 1999), 309–312.
6. "Ishtar," in *Dictionary of Deities and Demons in the Bible*, ed. K. van der Toorn, B. Becking, and P. W. van der Horst, 2nd ed. (Leiden, Brill: 1999), 452–456.
7. "Marduk," in *Dictionary of Deities and Demons in the Bible*, ed. K. van der Toorn, B. Becking, and P. W. van der Horst, 2nd ed. (Leiden, Brill: 1999), 543–549.
8. "Prayers, Hymns, Incantations, and Curses: Mesopotamia," in *Religions of the Ancient World: A Guide*, ed. Sarah Iles Johnston, HUP Reference Library (Cambridge: The Belknap Press of Harvard University Press), 353–355. Copyright © 2004 by the President and Fellows of Harvard College.
9. "The Promise to Praise the God in *Šuilla* Prayers," in *Biblical and Oriental Essays in Memory of William L. Moran*, ed. Agustinus Gianto, Biblica et Orientalia 48 (Rome: Editrice Pontificio Istituto Biblico, 2005), 1–10.
10. "The Form and Meaning of a Babylonian Prayer to Marduk," *Journal of the American Oriental Society* 103 (1983): 3–15. (Also published as *Studies in Literature from the Ancient Near East*, ed. J. M. Sasson, American Oriental Series 65 [Ann Arbor: American Oriental Society, 1984].)
11. "The Form and History of a Babylonian Prayer to Nabû," in *"The Scaffolding of Our Thoughts": Essays on Assyriology and the History of Science in Honor of Francesca Rochberg*, ed. C. Jay Crisostomo, E. A. Escobar, T. Tanaka, and N. Veldhuis, Ancient Magic and Divination 13 (Leiden: Brill, 2018), 169–182.
12. "A Paean and Petition to a God of Death: Some Comments on a *Šuilla* to Nergal," in *From the Four Corners of the Earth: Studies in Iconography and Cultures of the Ancient Near East in Honour of F. A. M. Wiggermann*, ed. D. Kertai and O. Nieuwenhuyse, AOAT 441 (Muenster: Ugarit-Verlag, 2017), 15–28.

13. "The Reconciliation of Angry Personal Gods: A Revision of the *Šuillas*," in "Approaching a Critique of Mesopotamian Reason," ed. G. Gabriel, special issue, *JANEH* 5 (2018): 57–85. Republished with permission of *Journal of Ancient Near Eastern History*; permission conveyed through Copyright Clearance Center, Inc.
14. "Two Versions of a *Šuilla* to Gula," in "Altorientalische Gebetsliteratur: Form, außersprachlicher Kontext und interkulturelle Adaptionsprozesse," ed. A. Grund-Wittenberg and Elisabeth Rieken, special issue, *WO* 49/1 (2019): 6–13.
15. "Fortune and Misfortune of the Individual: Some Observations on the Sufferer's Plaint in *Ludlul bēl nēmeqi* II 12–32," in *Fortune and Misfortune in the Ancient Near East (Proceedings of the 60th Rencontre Assyriologique Internationale), Warsaw, 2014*, ed. O. Drewnowska and M. Sandowicz (Winona Lake, IN: Eisenbrauns, 2017), 51–57.
16. "Kingship in Ancient Mesopotamia: The Case of *Enūma Eliš*," in *The Body of the King: The Staging of the Body of the Institutional Leader from Antiquity to Middle Ages in East and West. Proceedings of the Meeting Held in Padova, July 6th–9th, 2011*, ed. G. B. Lanfranchi and R. Rollinger, History of the Ancient Near East/ Monographs 16 (Padua: S.A.R.G.O.N. Editrice e Libreria, 2016), 59–64.
17. "Some Observations on the Babylon Section of the *Enūma Eliš*." *Revue d'assyriologie et d'archéologie orientale* 113 (2019): 171–173.
18. "Biblical Accounts of Prehistory: Their Meaning and Formation," in *Bringing the Hidden to Light: The Process of Interpretation. Studies in Honor of Stephen A. Geller*, ed. K. Kravitz and D. M. Sharon (Winona Lake, IN: Eisenbrauns/JTS, 2007), 1–17.
19. "Two Passages in the Biblical Account of Prehistory," in *Studies in Hebrew and Arabic in Honor of Raymond P. Scheindlin*, ed. J. Decter and M. Rand (Piscataway, NJ: Gorgias Press, 2007), 1–5 (rights owned by Gorgias Press, NJ).
20. "Jonah and God: Plants, Beasts, and Humans in the Book of Jonah (An Essay in Interpretation)," *Journal of Ancient Near Eastern Religions* 13, no. 2 (2013): 146–152.
21. "*Alaktu* and *Halakhah*: Oracular Decision, Divine Revelation," *Harvard Theological Review* 80 (1987): 15–42. Reproduced with permission.
22. "Blood in Israel and Mesopotamia," in *Emanuel: Studies in Hebrew Bible, Septuagint and Dead Sea Scrolls in Honor of Emanuel Tov*, ed. S. M. Paul, R. A. Kraft, L. H. Schiffman, and W. S. Fields (Leiden: Brill, 2003), 675–684.
23. "Cultures in Contact: Ancient Near Eastern and Jewish Magic." To appear in *A Handbook of Jewish Magic*, ed. S. Bhayro and O.-P. Saar (Leiden: Brill).
24. "A Shepherd's Bulla and an Owner's Receipt: A Pair of Matching Texts in the Harvard Semitic Museum," in *Studies on the Civilization and Culture of Nuzi and the Hurrians in Honor of Ernest R. Lacheman*, ed. M. A. Morrison and D. I. Owen (Winona Lake, IN: Eisenbrauns, 1981), 1–9.

25. "'He Should Continue to Bear the Penalty of that Case': Some Observations on *Codex Ḫammurabi* parags. 3–4 and parag. 13," in *From Ancient Israel to Modern Judaism: Essays in Honor of Marvin Fox*, ed. J. Neusner, E. S. Frerichs, and N. M. Sarna, Brown Judaic Studies 159 (Atlanta: Scholars Press, 1989), 77–96.

# Abbreviations

## Bibliographical Abbreviations

| | |
|---|---|
| [[ ]] | Page and note numbers enclosed in double brackets indicate (1) cross-references to articles reprinted either in this volume or, if an abbreviation is included, in AMD 5, AMD 17, or *Gilgamesh*; and (2) cross-references to editions of texts in *CMAwR*. |
| 1*R* | H. C. Rawlinson, *The Cuneiform Inscriptions of Western Asia*, vol. 1. London: E. E. Bowler, 1861. |
| $4R^2$ | H. C. Rawlinson, G. Smith, and T. G. Pinches, *The Cuneiform Inscriptions of Western Asia*, vol. 4. 2nd ed. London: [British Museum], 1891. |
| AASOR | Annual of the American Schools of Oriental Research |
| AASOR 16 | R. H. Pfeiffer and E. A. Speiser, *One Hundred New Selected Nuzi Texts*. AASOR 16. New Haven: American Schools of Oriental Research, 1936. |
| AB | Anchor Bible |
| ABAW | Abhandlungen der Bayerischen Akademie der Wissenschaften |
| AbB | Altbabylonische Briefe in Umschrift und Übersetzung |
| *ABD* | D. N. Freedman, ed., *The Anchor Bible Dictionary*. 6 vols. New York: Doubleday, 1992. |
| ADFU | Ausgrabungen der Deutschen Forschungsgemeinschaft in Uruk-Warka |
| *AfO* | *Archiv für Orientforschung* |
| AfO Beih. | Archiv für Orientforschung Beiheft |
| *AGH* | E. Ebeling, *Die akkadische Gebetserie "Handerhebung" von neuem gesammelt und herausgegeben*. Berlin: Akademie-Verlag, 1953. |
| *AHw* | W. von Soden, *Akkadisches Handwörterbuch*. 3 vols. Wiesbaden: Harrassowitz, 1958–1981. |
| AIL | Ancient Israel and Its Literature |
| *AJA* | *American Journal of Archaeology* |
| AMD | Ancient Magic and Divination |
| AMD 3 | J. Scurlock, *Magico-Medical Means of Treating Ghost-Induced Illnesses in Ancient Mesopotamia*. AMD 3. Leiden: Brill/Styx, 2006. |
| AMD 5 | T. Abusch, *Mesopotamian Witchcraft: Toward a History and Understanding of Babylonian Witchcraft Beliefs and Literature*. AMD 5. Leiden: Brill/Styx, 2002. |

| | |
|---|---|
| AMD 17 | T. Abusch, *Further Studies on Mesopotamian Witchcraft Beliefs and Literature*. AMD 17. Leiden: Brill/Styx, 2020. |
| ANEM | Ancient Near Eastern Monographs |
| *ANET* | J. B. Pritchard, ed., *Ancient Near Eastern Texts Relating to the Old Testament*. 3rd ed. Princeton: Princeton University Press, 1969. |
| AnOr | Analecta Orientalia |
| *AnSt* | *Anatolian Studies* |
| *AO* | *Der Alte Orient* |
| AOAT | Alter Orient und Altes Testament |
| *AoF* | *Altorientalische Forschungen* |
| AOS | American Oriental Series |
| AOSTS | American Oriental Society Translation Series |
| AS | Assyriological Studies |
| ASSF | Acta Societatis Scientiarum Fennicae |
| *BA* | *Biblical Archaeologist* |
| BaF | Baghdader Forschungen |
| *BAM* | F. Köcher et al., *Die babylonisch-assyrische Medizin in Texten und Untersuchungen*. Berlin: de Gruyter, 1963–. |
| *BASOR* | *Bulletin of the American Schools of Oriental Research* |
| BBET | Beiträge zur biblischen Exegese und Theologie |
| *BBR* | H. Zimmern, *Beiträge zur Kenntnis der babylonischen Religion*. 2 vols. Assyriologische Bibliothek 12. Leipzig: Hinrichs, 1896–1901. |
| BBVO | Berliner Beiträge zum Vorderer Orient Texte |
| *Bib* | *Biblica* |
| BibOr | Biblica et Orientalia |
| BJS | Brown Judaic Studies |
| BMes | Bibliotheca Mesopotamica |
| *BMS* | W. L. King, *Babylonian Magic and Sorcery*. London: Luzac, 1896. |
| *BO* | *Bibliotheca Orientalis* |
| BPOA | Biblioteca del Próximo Oriente Antiguo |
| BRM | Babylonian Records in the Library of J. Pierpont Morgan |
| BSGW | Berichte über die Verhandlungen der Sachsischen Akademie der Wissenschaften zu Leipzig |
| *BSOAS* | *Bulletin of the School of Oriental and African Studies* |
| *BWL* | W. G. Lambert, *Babylonian Wisdom Literature*. Oxford: Clarendon, 1960. |
| *CAD* | A. L. Oppenheim et al., eds., *The Assyrian Dictionary of the Oriental Institute of the University of Chicago*. Chicago: The Oriental Institute of the University of Chicago, 1956–2006. |

| | |
|---|---|
| *CANE* | J. M. Sasson, ed., *Civilizations of the Ancient Near East*. 4 vols. New York: Scribner, 1995. |
| CBQMS | Catholic Biblical Quarterly Monograph Series |
| CD | Damascus Document |
| CḪ | Code of Ḫammurabi |
| CM | Cuneiform Monographs |
| *CMAwR* | T. Abusch et al., *Corpus of Mesopotamian Anti-witchcraft Rituals*. 3 vols. AMD 8/1–3. Leiden: Brill, 2011–2019. Vol. 1 coauthored with D. Schwemer; vol. 2 coauthored with D. Schwemer with the assistance of M. Luukko and G. Van Buylaere; vol. 3 coauthored with D. Schwemer, M. Luukko, and G. Van Buylaere. |
| CNIP | Carsten Niebuhr Institute Publications |
| CT | Cuneiform Texts from Babylonian Tablets in the British Museum |
| *CTH* | E. Laroche, *Catalogue des textes hittites*. Paris: Klincksieck, 1971. |
| CTN | Cuneiform Texts from Nimrud |
| CTN 4 | D. J. Wiseman and J. A. Black, *Literary Texts from the Temple of Nabû*. CTN 4. London: British School of Archaeology in Iraq, 1996. |
| DSS | Dead Sea Scrolls |
| FAS | Freiburger altorientalische Studien |
| FOTL | Forms of the Old Testament Literature |
| GAAL | Göttinger Arbeitshefte zur altorientalischen Literatur |
| *GAG* | W. von Soden, *Grundriss der Akkadischen Grammatik*. AnOr 33. Rome: Pontificium Institutum Biblicum, 1952. |
| GBS | Guides to Biblical Scholarship |
| *Gilgamesh* | T. Abusch, *Male and Female in the Epic of Gilgamesh: Encounters, Literary History, and Interpretation*. Winona Lake, IN: Eisenbrauns, 2015. |
| *HALAT* | L. Köhler and W. Baumgartner, *Hebräisches und aramäisches Lexikon zum Alten Testament*. 5 vols. 3rd ed. Leiden: E. J. Brill, 1967–1996. |
| HANE/M | History of the Ancient Near East/Monographs |
| HES | Heidelberger Emesal-Studien |
| HKAT | Handkommentar zum Alten Testament |
| *HR* | *History of Religions* |
| HSAO | Heidelberger Studien zum alten Orient |
| HSS | Harvard Semitic Studies |
| HSS 15 | E. R. Lacheman, *The Administrative Archives*. Vol. 6 of *Excavations at Nuzi*. HSS 15. Cambridge, MA: Harvard University Press, 1955. |

| | |
|---|---|
| HSS 16 | E. R. Lacheman, *Economic and Social Documents*. Vol. 7 of *Excavations at Nuzi*. HSS 16. Cambridge, MA: Harvard University Press, 1958. |
| HSS 19 | E. R. Lacheman, *Family Law Documents*. Vol. 8 of *Excavations at Nuzi*. HSS 19. Cambridge, MA: Harvard University Press, 1962. |
| HUCASup | Hebrew Union College Annual Supplements |
| JA | Jewish Aramaic |
| *JANEH* | *Journal of Ancient Near Eastern History* |
| *JANER* | *Journal of Ancient Near Eastern Religions* |
| *JAOS* | *Journal of the American Oriental Society* |
| *JBL* | *Journal of Biblical Literature* |
| *JCS* | *Journal of Cuneiform Studies* |
| *JHebS* | *Journal of Hebrew Scriptures* |
| *JJS* | *Journal of Jewish Studies* |
| *JMC* | *Journal des médecines cunéiformes* |
| *JNES* | *Journal of Near Eastern Studies* |
| *JQR* | *Jewish Quarterly Review* |
| *JRAS* | *Journal of the Royal Asiatic Society* |
| JSOTSup | Journal for the Study of the Old Testament Supplement Series |
| *JSP* | *Journal for the Study of the Pseudepigrapha* |
| JSRC | Jerusalem Studies in Religion and Culture |
| *JSS* | *Journal of Semitic Studies* |
| K | Tablets in the Collections of the British Museum from Kouyunjik |
| KALI | Keilschrifttexte aus Assur literarischen Inhalts |
| KALI 4 | S. M. Maul and R. Strauss, *Ritualbeschreibungen und Gebete I*. KALI 4, WVDOG 133. Wiesbaden: Harrassowitz, 2011. |
| *KAR* | E. Ebeling, *Keilschrifttexte aus Assur religiösen Inhalts*. 2 vols. Leipzig: J. C. Hinrichs, 1915–1923. |
| LAOS | Leipziger altorientalistische Studien |
| LAPO | Littératures anciennes du Proche-Orient |
| *LKA* | E. Ebeling, *Literarische Keilschrifttexte aus Assur*. Berlin: Akademie-Verlag, 1953. |
| LSS | Leipziger semitistische Studien |
| *MARI* | *Mari: Annales de recherches interdisciplinaires* |
| MC | Mesopotamian Civilizations |
| MCAAS | Memoirs of the Connecticut Academy of Arts and Sciences |
| Meier, *Maqlû* | G. Meier, *Die assyrische Beschwörungssammlung "Maqlû."* AfO Beih. 2. Berlin: Selbstverlag E. F. Weidner, 1937. |

| | |
|---|---|
| Meier, "Studien" | G. Meier, "Studien zur Beschwörungssammlung Maqlû." *AfO* 21 (1966): 70–81. |
| MVAG | Mitteilungen der Vorderasiatisch-ägyptischen Gesellschaft |
| NbK | Neubabylonischen Königsinschriften |
| NF | Neue Folge |
| NJPS | *Tanakh: The Holy Scriptures: The New JPS Translation according to the Traditional Hebrew Text*. Philadelphia: Jewish Publication Society, 1985. |
| *NPN* | I. J. Gelb, P. M. Purves, and A. A. Macrae, *Nuzi Personal Names*. OIP 57. Chicago: University of Chicago Press, 1943. |
| NS | New series |
| OBC | Orientalia Biblica et Christiana |
| OBO | Orbis Biblicus et Orientalis |
| OIP | Oriental Institute Publications |
| OLA | Orientalia Lovaniensia Analecta |
| OPSNKF | Occasional Publications of the Samuel Noah Kramer Fund |
| *Or* | *Orientalia* |
| ORA | Orientalische Religionen in der Antike |
| *ORACC* | *The Open Richly Annotated Cuneiform Corpus* (http://oracc.museum.upenn.edu/) |
| OtSt | Oudtestamentische Studiën |
| PBS | Publications of the Babylonian Section, University Museum, University of Pennsylvania |
| PBS I/1 | D. W. Myhrman, *Babylonian Humns and Prayers*. PBS I/1. Philadelphia: The University Museum, 1911. |
| PBS I/2 | H. F. Lutz, *Selected Sumerian and Babylonian Texts*. PBS I/2. Philadelphia: The University Museum, 1919. |
| *RA* | *Revue d'assyriologie et d'archéologie orientale* |
| *RB* | *Revue Biblique* |
| RIMB | The Royal Inscriptions of Mesopotamia, Babylonian Periods |
| RIMB 2 | G. Frame, *Rulers of Babylonia from the Second Dynasty of Isin to the End of the Assyrian Domination, 1157–612 BC*. RIMB 2. Toronto: University of Toronto Press, 1995. |
| RIME | The Royal Inscriptions of Mesopotamia, Early Periods |
| RIME 1 | D. R. Frayne, *Presargonic Period (2700–2350 BC)*. RIME 1. Toronto: University of Toronto Press, 2008. |
| *RlA* | E. Ebeling et al., eds., *Reallexikon der Assyriologie und vorderasiatischen Archäologie*. Berlin: de Gruyter, 1928–2018. |
| Rm | Tablets in the Collections of the British Museum (Rassam) |
| *RSO* | *Rivista degli studi orientali* |
| RT | Ritual Tablet (*Maqlû* IX) |

| | |
|---|---|
| SAA | State Archives of Assyria |
| SAACT | State Archives of Assyria Cuneiform Texts |
| SAALT | State Archives of Assyria Literary Texts |
| SAAS | State Archives of Assyria Studies |
| SANE | Sources from the Ancient Near East |
| SANER | Studies in Ancient Near Eastern Records |
| SBLDS | Society of Biblical Literature Dissertation Series |
| SBLMS | Society of Biblical Literature Monograph Series |
| SBLSymS | Society of Biblical Literature Symposium Series |
| SBT | Studies in Biblical Theology |
| SHCANE | Studies in the History and Culture of the Ancient Near East |
| SHR | Studies in the History of Religions |
| Si | Sippar Collection of the Istanbul Archaeological Museum |
| SJLA | Studies in Judaism in Late Antiquity |
| Sm | Tablets in the Collections of the British Museum (G. Smith) |
| SMN | Semitic Museum Nuzi |
| *SMS* | *Syro-Mesopotamian Studies* |
| *SMSR* | *Studi e materiali di storia delle religioni* |
| *SpBTU* | H. Hunger (vol. 1) and E. von Weiher (vols. 2–3), *Spätbabylonische Texte aus Uruk*. Ausgrabungen der Deutschen Forschungsgemeinschaft in Uruk-Warka, Endberichte, 9, 10, 12. Berlin: Gebr. Mann, 1976–1988. |
| SSN | Studia Semitica Neerlandica |
| StPohl | Studia Pohl |
| StSem | Studi semitici |
| *STT* | O. R. Gurney, J. J. Finkelstein, and P. Hulin, eds., *The Sultantepe Tablets*. 2 vols. Occasional Publications of the British Institute of Archaeology at Ankara 3, 7. London: British Institute of Archaeology at Ankara, 1957–1964. |
| *ŠU-ILA* | O. Loretz and W. R. Mayer, *ŠU-ILA-Gebete: Supplement zu L. W. King, "Babylonian Magic and Sorcery."* AOAT 34. Kevalaer: Butzon & Bercker, 1978. |
| TAPS | Transactions of the American Philosophical Society |
| TCS | Texts from Cuneiform Sources |
| TUAT | Texte aus der Umwelt des Alten Testaments |
| *UF* | *Ugarit-Forschungen* |
| UḪ | Udug-ḫul-a-kam |
| VAB | Vorderasiatische Bibliothek |
| VAB 4 | S. Langdon, *Die neubabylonischen Königsinschriften*. VAB 4. Leipzig: Hinrichs, 1912. |
| VTE | Vassal Treaties of Esarhaddon |

| | |
|---|---|
| VTSup | Supplements to Vetus Testamentum |
| WAW | Writings from the Ancient World |
| WMANT | Wissenschaftliche Monographien zum Alten und Neuen Testament |
| *WO* | *Die Welt des Orients* |
| WVDOG | Wissenschaftliche Veröffentlichungen der Deutschen Orient-Gesellschaft |
| YNER | Yale Near Eastern Researches |
| *ZA* | *Zeitschrift für Assyriologie* |
| *ZDMG* | *Zeitschrift der Deutschen Morgenländischen Gesellschaft* |
| *ZSS* | *Zeitschrift der Savigny-Stiftung für Rechtsgeschichte*, Romanistische Abteilung |

## Abbreviations of Biblical and Apocryphal Books

| | |
|---|---|
| Gen | Genesis |
| Exod | Exodus |
| Lev | Leviticus |
| Num | Numbers |
| Deut | Deuteronomy |
| Judg | Judges |
| 1–2 Sam | 1–2 Samuel |
| 1–2 Kgs | 1–2 Kings |
| Isa | Isaiah |
| Jer | Jeremiah |
| Jon | Jonah |
| Nah | Nahum |
| Hab | Habbakuk |
| Ps(s) | Psalm(s) |
| Dan | Daniel |
| Neh | Nehemiah |
| 1–2 Chr | 1–2 Chronicles |
| Bar | Baruch |

## Technical Abbreviations

| | |
|---|---|
| absol. | absolute |
| acc. | accusative |
| b. | Babylonian Talmud |

| | |
|---|---|
| BCE | Before the Common Era |
| CE | Common Era |
| ch(s). | chapter(s) |
| dupl(s). | duplicate(s) |
| ED | Early Dynastic |
| ed(s). | edition, editor(s), edited by |
| fem. | feminine |
| fig(s). | figure(s) |
| gen. | genitive |
| J | Yahwistic source of the Pentateuch |
| JA | Jewish Aramaic |
| lit. | literally |
| LXX | Septuagint |
| m. | Mishnah |
| masc. | masculine |
| mng. | meaning |
| ms(s). | manuscript(s) |
| MT | Masoretic Text |
| n(n). | note(s) |
| Nab. | Nabataean Aramaic |
| NB | Neo-Babylonian |
| no(s). | number(s) |
| obv. | obverse |
| P | Priestly source of the Pentateuch |
| p(p). | page(s) |
| Palm. | Palmyrene Aramaic |
| pers. | person |
| pl(s). | plate(s) |
| poss. | possessive |
| prep. | preposition |
| rev. | reverse |
| rev. ed. | revised edition |
| sing. | singular |
| suff. | suffix |
| Sum. | Sumerian |
| v(v). | verse(s) |
| var(s). | variant reading(s) |
| vol(s). | volume(s) |

# PART 1

## *Magic and Religion*

*Overviews and Surveys*

CHAPTER 1

# Mesopotamian Religion

## 1 The Basis of Mesopotamian Religiosity

Mesopotamian religion is attested in written texts for the first three thousand years of recorded history.* All the same we would begin with a few words about the early Mesopotamian view of human life, the gods, and the city. It should be noted that my understanding of early Mesopotamian religious history follows in the main the approach of Thorkild Jacobsen.[1]

The purpose of human life, the purpose of the community, was to serve the gods, to provide them with whatever needs a powerful ruling class, specifically a landed aristocracy, would require. Paramount forms of care are shelter and food. But this represents the developed or classical form of theology and was probably not the original ideology or theology of god and temple. For in the earliest periods, the divine powers were forces of nature, powers experienced in those natural phenomena that were of importance for the survival and growth of the settlers and settlements. In the main, in these early periods, the gods were not human in form.

Gods were linked to specific settlements, and the two, god and settlement, developed together. During the Ubaid period, that is, down till the end of the fifth millennium BCE, we have indications of cult places evolving in the midst of developing villages and towns. It is probable that these cult places served as storehouses for the community and as focal points for rituals directed to the aforementioned powers of nature: rituals of thanks and rituals of revitalization.

As noted, the gods in this period probably had not yet attained a predominantly human physical and social form. They were the forces of nature on which the original settlements had depended for their sustenance. The goal of the earlier rituals was to keep these forces present, vital, and productive. And the cult place would have served as the place where the rites centering

* My thanks to my student Anthony Lipscomb for his assistance, especially with notes regarding the Hebrew Bible. It should be noted that this essay is an attempt at synthesis and thus draws on material from my earlier publications, some of which are also reprinted in this volume.

1 See especially T. Jacobsen, *The Treasures of Darkness: A History of Mesopotamian Religion* (New Haven: Yale University Press, 1976); see also F. A. M. Wiggermann, "Theologies, Priests, and Worship in Ancient Mesopotamia," in *CANE* 3: 1857–1870.

 | DOI:10.1163/9789004435186_002

upon these forces were carried out. Some of these rites involved the bringing of offerings by the community as expressions of thanks, and perhaps even to allay communal guilt; others took the form of agricultural, magical rituals and served to revitalize nature. These expressions of thanks and magical rituals later became rites of offering and rites of the *hieros gamos* (sacred marriage), respectively.

Eventually, however, the powers in natural phenomena were anthropomorphized as the masters of the city, the ones who gave sustenance and care to the city and upon whom the city depended. (Of course, some of the most important original gods were females.) Certainly by the beginning of the third millennium, the characteristic and defining forms of classical Mesopotamian theology had emerged. This new theology was part of the evolution of early civilization and of the development of hierarchical structures within the cities. Naturalistic gods were now seen as manorial lords, as the divine equivalents to the newly emerging human chieftains and kings. Along with a human form, the gods were given families and households. Most important, their homes were now seen as manors or palaces, that is, the temples were now treated as the divine equivalent of the human ruler's abode. Hence, older cultic centers now became the classic Mesopotamian temples in which the god and his family were treated by his subjects as the ruling class of the city.

In the course of time, then, the nature of the temple and cult changed. There was a shift of emphasis from storage to presentation. The original temples may have served as communal storehouses. This economic function was never lost, and temples developed many rooms and buildings that served for production, storage, and distribution. But the central rooms of the temple were the god's cella; the temple developed from a locus for natural power to an abode for a divine ruler.

In Mesopotamia, then, by the third millennium the temple had evolved into the god's home. It was believed that the god had built the city for his or her own residence and sustenance. The god was now regarded as the primary owner of the city, and the city existed in order to support his or her needs. Thus, the temple was not simply a dwelling place to which a god repaired occasionally, but rather a permanent home in which the god and his family lived continually.

The earlier communal festivals, which derived from magical rites for prosperity, remained important for the cult. Communal religion now included a number of annual and ad hoc rituals. Mention should be made of the *hieros gamos* ritual, various divine processions, the Akitu New Year festival, and laments over dying gods. The king was involved in most, if not all, of these ceremonies; in addition, there were royal rituals, such as those that were performed on the occasion of the enthronement of a new ruler.

But let us focus here instead on the daily service of the god in his temple as reflected in sources from the first millennium BCE. The god sat in his cella in the form of a divine statue made of wood overlaid with precious materials and valuable garments. The statue was both alive and holy, having attained identity with a god by means of the "washing of the mouth" ritual. Each day the god and his family were awakened, bathed, clothed, fed, and entertained.[2] This daily regimen is nicely illustrated by temple ritual texts from Uruk: there were two main meals during the day, one in the morning and one in the evening, and each of these meals was divided into a lesser and greater course.[3] These meals included beer, wine, cereals, loaves of bread, cakes, meat, etc. Liquid offerings seem to have been poured out as libations. Food was treated differently; after being placed on the god's table and magically "eaten" by the god, it was distributed to the temple personnel and to the king.

It is important to note that the central act of the daily cult was not a sacrifice, in the sense of giving the food over to a fire that consumes it, nor was it the slaughtering of an animal and the pouring out of its blood. Rather, food was placed before the god and consumed by him through that mysterious act that characterizes Babylonian religiosity. As A. Leo Oppenheim noted,

> Looking at the sacrifice from the religious point of view, we find coming into focus another critical point in that circulatory system, the consumption of the sacrificial repast by the deity, the transubstantiation of the physical offerings into that source of strength and power the deity was thought to need for effective functioning. Exactly as, in the existence of the image, the critical point was its physical manufacture, so was the act of consumption of food in the sacrificial repast. It represents the central *mysterium* that provided the effective *ratio essendi* for the cult practice of the daily meals and all that it entailed in economic, social, and political respects.[4]

2 Images of the divine in human form and human activities in service of the divine in Mesopotamia find mention in the Hebrew Bible. Prophetic polemics assert that precious metals and wood, as well as stone, were used for fashioning a deity's image (see, e.g., Second Isaiah: Isa 40:19–20; 42:17; 45:20; 48:5; cf. Deut 29:17). Moreover, a deity's image received a wake-up call (see, e.g., Hab 2:19; cf. 1 Kgs 18:27) as well as food and libations (Jer 44:15–19) from its human attendants. Ezekiel 44:7 even describes the presentation of meat offerings to the God of Israel (by illicit foreigners) as a meal (בְּהַקְרִיבְכֶם אֶת־לַחְמִי חֵלֶב וָדָם), in contradistinction to the Priestly emphasis on burning and blood.

3 For the ritual texts, see, e.g., A. Sachs, "Daily Sacrifices to the Gods of the City of Uruk," in *ANET*, 343–345; M. J. H. Linssen, *The Cults of Uruk and Babylon: The Temple Ritual Texts as Evidence for Hellenistic Cult Practice*, CM 25 (Leiden: Brill/Styx, 2004).

4 A. L. Oppenheim, *Ancient Mesopotamia: Portrait of a Dead Civilization*, rev. ed. (Chicago: University of Chicago Press, 1977), 191.

The act of killing the animal that provides sustenance to the god is almost hidden behind the construct of feeding the god, a construct that emerges out of the earlier function of the temple as a place of offering and storage and the later image of feeding a divine king in his palace.

Liturgically, various Sumerian lamentations (mainly, *balag*s and *eršemma*s) formed the basis of the daily temple service in the first millennium BCE.[5] They focused on the anger of the god, gave expression to the fear of communal abandonment and destruction, and attempted to assuage the god so that he/she remain calm and relent.[6] Thus, for example, during the daily ceremony of "the awakening of the temple," a *balag* followed by an *eršemma* was recited.[7]

Basic to Mesopotamian religion is the belief not only that the human community must serve the gods, but also that even when it does so, the gods may still bring destruction upon it; the gods are capricious. (This mentality exists also on the level of the individual.) Mesopotamian civilization is pervaded with a sense of the uncertainty of life. Regardless of one's actions, the anger of gods could easily be aroused and could destroy individual or communal life. Hence, various rituals were performed prophylactically. Nonetheless, it is perplexing that the aforementioned laments served as the basis of the temple liturgy even when the city and the temple were not under actual threat. Clearly, Mesopotamian society was traumatized. This mentality may simply reflect the frequent periods of warfare and destruction endured by the country or perhaps its climatic conditions. But, the answer to this conundrum may possibly lie in the formative stages of Mesopotamian civilization rather than in its later history. Perhaps the fear of divine anger central to the daily cult and to so much else in Mesopotamian ritual life is a reflection of a fundamental anxiety

---

5 For a recent concise introduction to both city laments and cultic laments, see A. Löhnert, "Manipulating the Gods: Lamenting in Context," in *The Oxford Handbook of Cuneiform Culture*, ed. K. Radner and E. Robson (Oxford: Oxford University Press, 2011), 402–417. In ancient Israel and Judah, communal lament also arose amidst ongoing historical situations (e.g., Ps 137 and Lamentations). Moreover, Jer 9:17 seems to refer to a professional or dedicated ensemble of lamenters in Judah who performed during times of national tragedy (cf. 2 Chr 35:25).

6 For these laments see M. E. Cohen, *Sumerian Hymnology: The Eršemma*, HUCASup 2 (Cincinnati: Hebrew Union College Press, 1981); M. E. Cohen, *The Canonical Lamentations of Ancient Mesopotamia*, 2 vols. (Potomac, MD: CDL, 1988). More recently, see A. Löhnert, *"Wie die Sonne tritt heraus!" Eine Klage zum Auszug Enlils mit einer Untersuchung zu Komposition und Tradition sumerischer Klagelieder in altbabylonischer Zeit*, AOAT 365 (Münster: Ugarit-Verlag, 2009); U. Gabbay, *Pacifying the Hearts of the Gods: Sumerian Emesal Prayers of the First Millennium BC*, HES 1 (Wiesbaden: Harrassowitz, 2014); U. Gabbay, *The Eršema Prayers of the First Millennium BC*, HES 2 (Wiesbaden: Harrassowitz, 2014), and references there to the works of S. M. Maul.

7 For this ceremony, see Linssen, *Cults of Uruk and Babylon*, 27–36, esp. 27–30.

that came into being originally as part of the pioneering spirit of building cities and creating civilization in Mesopotamia. Here I follow the lead of Henri Frankfort. In discussing the birth of cities in Mesopotamia, Frankfort noted:

> Small wonder, then, that the boldness of those early people who undertook to found permanent settlements in the shifting plain had its obverse in anxiety; that the self-assertion which this city—its organization, its institutions, citizenship itself—implied was overshadowed by apprehension. The tension between courage and the awareness of man's dependence on superhuman power found a precarious equilibrium in a peculiarly Mesopotamian conception. It was a conception which was elaborated in theology, but which likewise informed the practical organization of society: the city was conceived to be ruled by a god.[8]

What Frankfort wrote about the founding of the Mesopotamian city might also explain, I think, the fundamental and ongoing apprehension and uncertainty that come to expression in so many areas of Mesopotamian cultural life and the manner in which religion attempted to deal with the underlying anxiety, anxiety that would likely have been aggravated by ongoing historical and ecological conditions.

In Mesopotamia, the city was required to care for its anthropomorphized divine rulers. A classical expression of this human responsibility to the gods is found in the story of Atraḫasīs.[9] The myth is made up of two originally separate parts; each part was an independent solution to the problem of the role of humans in the world. Originally, the gods created cities and lived there by themselves. Because humans had not yet been created, the gods themselves were required to do all the work necessary for their own survival. Not surprisingly, they found the labor of maintaining the cities and of producing and preparing food wearisome and burdensome. The worker gods rebelled and threw down their tools. This impasse was resolved by means of a solution devised by the god Ea (a not uncommon motif in Mesopotamian literature): humanity was created from clay mixed with the blood and flesh of the leader of the rebellion so that they might work and care for the gods. The act of creation was executed by Ea with the assistance of the mother-goddess. Humans now produced food for the gods. But, as we learn in the second part of the myth, humans also

8 H. Frankfort, *The Birth of Civilization in the Near East* (1951; repr., Garden City, NY: Doubleday, 1956), 54.

9 For an edition, see W. G. Lambert and A. R. Millard, *Atra-ḫasīs: The Babylonian Story of the Flood* (Oxford: Clarendon, 1969).

reproduced in larger numbers than expected and created a disturbance in the world (human numbers and noise probably reflect problems of city life), so that the great god Enlil, ruler of the earth, could not sleep peacefully. After trying unsuccessfully to decimate humanity, Enlil finally decided to exterminate them by means of a flood. As a consequence, the gods suffered from starvation, for there was no one to provide food for them. One man, Atraḫasīs by name, was saved by Ea, the god who had originally conceived the idea of creating humans. After the flood Atraḫasīs sacrificed food to the gods on the mountain on which his ark had landed. The gods were delighted with the offering, and their hunger was sated. And now, a new cosmic order was permanently instituted, for the gods realized their folly and recognized their need for human beings. Humanity would never again be destroyed and would permanently provide food for the gods in the form of offerings, but the cost of maintaining a human population would be reduced, for limits would now be placed on the ability of humans to reproduce as well as on the length of the human life span. Thus, humans were given a permanent place in the established order, but their numbers would be limited and death would be institutionalized.[10]

The city cult centered on its temples. Thus, the temple became the home of the god and his family just as the palace served those same purposes for the ruler; moreover, the rites of the temple reflected in part the way of life of the ruler. The temple is the center of an urban world. The temple and the feeding and care of its gods define the primary community of the dwellers in the land between the two rivers. To serve the god by supporting and participating in the economy of the temple constitutes the mark of membership in the urban community, a community which thus replaces or, at least, overshadows membership in one or another kinship community such as the family or clan.

## 2 The Mesopotamian Pantheon

The Mesopotamian pantheon derived from a series of local groupings of gods. These local pantheons reflected the natural forces of specific regions;

10 The unfolding drama of the Atraḫasīs story, that is, the creation of humankind, divine displeasure and retribution against humanity (centered on a flood), and a culminating settlement between the gods and humans, will be familiar to readers of the biblical Primeval History, which took over much of its structure and narrative content from the Mesopotamian myth. See, e.g., T. Abusch, "Biblical Accounts of Prehistory: Their Meaning and Formation," in *Bringing the Hidden to Light: The Process of Interpretation. Studies in Honor of Stephen A. Geller*, ed. K. F. Kravitz and D. Sharon (Winona Lake, IN: Eisenbrauns, 2007), 3–17 [[238–254]].

the natural forces represented especially those phenomena that were of economic significance to the local community. Thus, for example, the area of Eridu is marshland, and the native gods represent swamps, water, fish, and fowl. Similarly, the pantheon of Ur centers on ox-herding, that of Uruk on date orchards, that of the area north of Uruk in the Eden on shepherding. These phenomena were originally perceived as impersonal forces or numina; the god was perceived as being immanent in the phenomenon. With the development of city-states and the emergence of human rulers as central to their leadership, the gods were also perceived in human images—in anthropomorphic terms—and as transcendental powers behind various natural and cultural phenomena; they were treated and cared for in the same way as rulers. Each set of local gods was seen as the rulers/owners of a settlement. Thus, different city-states belonged to different gods, e.g., Enki/Ea was the chief god of Eridu; An and Inanna were in charge of Uruk; Nanna and his consort were responsible for Ur.[11]

Beginning as local groups, the organization of the gods and their leadership changed over the millennia. During the third millennium these newly anthropomorphized gods were integrated into a larger body and were organized into a regional pantheon centered in Nippur, perhaps in parallel to some form of unification or federation on the human level. In the course of time, the gods assumed first the form of a regional or ethnic pantheon, then that of a national pantheon; with the growth of imperialism, the gods became a universal pantheon with a single ruler. In the first millennium, the main imperial states prior to the Persian domination were the Assyrian empire and then the Babylonian one. But in spite of whatever changes took place on a regional level over the millennia, the local temples and cults remained viable and remained the center of religious life of the individual cities.

The Mesopotamian pantheon, already in the third millennium, comprised the gods of the Sumerian and of the Semitic populations, and even syncretized them. The main gods of Babylonia were An, Enlil, Enki/Ea, a mother-goddess, Nanna/Sîn, Utu/Šamaš, Inanna/Ištar, Ninurta, Nergal, Marduk, Nabû, and Aššur. Each individual god is associated with a specific locality, but by nature it is associated, even identified, with a cosmic and/or human area of activity. A city, a person, a text may at a certain moment focus on an individual god, but Mesopotamian religions always remain polytheistic. I should emphasize that even with the supremacy of Marduk during the

11 A polytheistic conception of divinity, which sometimes incorporates hierarchical, familial, and/or local features of the gods, appears also to have existed in ancient Israel, despite the monotheistic efforts of such biblical writers as Second Isaiah (Isa 40–55).

first millennium and the apparent existence of some henotheistic tendencies among some of the intellectuals, Mesopotamia remained polytheistic, with its several cities maintaining the cults of their gods.

Rather than discuss all the main gods of Mesopotamia,[12] we focus instead on Marduk, the divine ruler of the Neo-Babylonian empire, but also make some mention of Aššur, the supreme god of the Neo-Assyrian empire.

Marduk was the god of Babylon and the supreme ruler of the Mesopotamian universe. Beginning as the local god and patron of Babylon, Marduk became the master of the Babylonian national state, the king of the gods, and the absolute ruler of the universe.[13]

Marduk's ascension to the head of the pantheon and the expansion of his powers are related to the gradual elevation of Babylon to preeminence. During the Old Babylonian period, Marduk was incorporated into the Mesopotamian pantheon and considered to be the son of Enki/Ea and a member of the Eridu circle. The connection with Ea probably arose from the desire to link Babylon and Marduk with Eridu, its traditions, and its god Ea; the priests of Babylon were thus able to link Marduk to a major god other than Enlil and a venerable tradition other than Nippur. While there are indications that Marduk was emerging as supreme ruler already during the Kassite period and early in the second Isin period, Marduk seems neither to have replaced the high gods of Babylonia nor to have ascended to the head of the pantheon during most of the second millennium. His elevation seems to have been first publicly articulated only during the reign of Nebuchadnezzar I (1125–1104 BCE), when this king restored the plundered statue of Marduk to Babylon. Now, in addition to Marduk's rule over the city of Babylon, there was an open claim for Marduk's dominion over the gods and over the whole land. Thus, only late in the second millennium did Marduk take on many of Enlil's roles and become not only lord of the land but also king of the gods.

During the first millennium, culminating in the Neo-Babylonian empire, the notion of Marduk as king of the gods was systematically carried through to its logical conclusion. This is evident from first-millennium documents describing the Akitu New Year festival in the spring; for at that season, the gods all assembled in Babylon, where Marduk was declared king and destinies for the New Year were determined. Marduk's cult spread to Assyria before the Sargonids, but it was especially in the eighth–seventh centuries, when Assyria

12 For these gods, see, e.g., Jacobsen, *Treasures of Darkness*, ch. 4.

13 For a detailed and nuanced but perhaps somewhat dated understanding of Marduk, see T. Abusch, "Marduk," in *Dictionary of Deities and Demons in the Bible*, ed. K. van der Toorn et al., 2nd ed. (Leiden: Brill, 1999), 543–549 [[99–107]].

attempted to control Babylon, that interesting developments and conflicts surrounding Marduk and Babylon arose. The Assyrians had difficulty assimilating the Marduk cult or even defining an efficacious and stable relationship with Marduk and his city. An extreme form of the conflict is attested during the reign of Sennacherib (704–281 BCE), when Aššur was cast in the role of Marduk and assumed his deeds, or Marduk was made to function at the behest of Aššur/Anshar.

Here we should mention two relatively late documents that articulate Marduk's role as supreme god.

*Enūma eliš*, the so-called Babylonian Genesis, was recited before Marduk on the fourth day of the month of Nisannu during the Akitu New Year festival. Central themes of the work are the creation of the cosmos, the placement of Babylon in the center of the divine world, and the elevation of Marduk to the position of ruler of the gods. In addition, *Enūma eliš* also contains a Mesopotamian theory of the evolution of kingship and presents that theory through the story of Marduk.[14]

In the course of the last century, various dates have been suggested for *Enūma eliš*. In the first flush of rediscovery of the Old Babylonian period and the Code of Ḫammurabi, the composition of *Enūma eliš* was dated to that period. More recently, several dates in the latter half of the second millennium have been proposed. Most notably, W. G. Lambert has argued that *Enūma eliš* was composed during the reign of Nebuchadnezzar I as a work celebrating Marduk's official elevation to leadership of the pantheon. (For various reasons, I am not yet convinced of this date.)[15]

Another work that centers on Marduk is *Ludlul bēl nēmeqi*, the so-called Babylonian Job. The point of this composition is to convey the notion that everything—misfortune and fortune—comes from Marduk and that all other forces and considerations are secondary.[16] A traditional, or perhaps simply

14 For an edition of this text, see W. G. Lambert, *Babylonian Creation Myths*, MC 16 (Winona Lake, IN: Eisenbrauns, 2013).

15 *Enūma eliš* shares a number of features with the biblical account of creation in Gen 1. For example, to the primordial existence of principles of water—Tiāmat and Apsû in the Babylonian account—compare Gen 1:2: "the earth was a formless void and darkness covered the face of the deep, while a wind from God swept over the face of the waters." As Marduk creates the universe from his defeated enemy, so too does God create the universe by dividing the waters (Gen 1:6–7).

16 On the role of Marduk in *Ludlul bēl nēmeqi*, see, e.g., W. L. Moran, "The Babylonian Job," in *The Most Magic Word: Essays on Babylonian and Biblical Literature*, ed. R. S. Hendel, CBQMS 35 (Washington, DC: Catholic Biblical Association of America, 2002), 182–200, esp. 187, 193–195. Cf. T. Abusch, "Fortune and Misfortune of the Individual: Some Observations on the Sufferer's Plaint in *Ludlul bēl nēmeqi* II 12–32," in *Fortune and*

conventional, religious position is replaced by the all-encompassing Marduk theism. The speaker starts from the premise that his personal (or family) gods were the cause of his suffering, only to discover that, in fact, Marduk is responsible for both suffering and deliverance therefrom.[17]

Aššur was the chief god of the Neo-Assyrian empire. The Assyrian pantheon developed somewhat differently from its Babylonian counterpart. Aššur originally was the local numen of the city of that name. With the emergence of Assyrian kingship and the Assyrian state (in the fourteenth century BCE), the god Aššur took on the guise of a full Mesopotamian god and even became the supreme god at the time of the Assyrian empire. A number of Babylonian gods were imported into Assyria, most notably Enlil, Ninurta, and Nabû. During the time of the Sargonids, especially under Sennacherib, Babylonian mythology and rituals centering on Marduk were assigned to Aššur.

## 3 Magical Cult (Cult of the Individual)

In addition to the gods, there are, of course, other supernatural beings, the most important of which are the personal gods, demons, ghosts, and witches. The individual may be harmed by different supernatural powers or agencies. These are addressed primarily in the magical cult or cult of the individual and his family.

### 3.1 *Personal God*

The cult of the individual is directed to the service of the family or personal god. Stated succinctly, the personal god or the family god was the god of the individual as a social being. The personal god is the personification of the individual's powers of strength and effectiveness; he is also the personification of right and wrong action. He represents and rewards either effective/realistic actions or proper actions, or both. In the first place, the personal god is a projection of the individual's powers of effectiveness and procreation. In this role, he is an aspect of ego. But in a clan context, he also represents group or clan norms as well as the responsibility to maintain them. Hence, the personal god is also an aspect of superego or conscience. The personal god was thus an

---

*Misfortune in the Ancient Near East (Proceedings of the 60th Rencontre Assyriologique Internationale, Warsaw, 2014)*, ed. O. Drewnowska and M. Sandowicz (Winona Lake, IN: Eisenbrauns, 2017), 51–57 [[217–224]].

17 For the most recent edition of *Ludlul bēl nēmeqi*, see T. Oshima, *Babylonian Poems of Pious Sufferers*, ORA 14 (Tübingen: Mohr Siebeck, 2014).

externalization of both the ego and the superego, a representation of the self in the form of externalized, divinized figures, and was viewed as a divine parent.[18] As an example of the service required of the human and the help expected in return, note the following passage in *Ludlul bēl nēmeqi* Tablet II:

4 I called to (my) god, but he did not turn his face to me,
5 I prayed to (my) goddess, but she did not lift her head to me.
...
12 Like one who had not made libations for his god
13 And did not invoke his goddess at a meal,
...
19 Who did not invoke his god when he ate his food
20 And abandoned his goddess, did not bring a flour-offering.
...[19]

### 3.2 *Demons*

In the main, demons were regarded as evil and as wholly unsympathetic to human life.[20] They personified those destructive powers and events that were unpredictable, uncontrollable, and overwhelming. Originally, at least, they were not part of the cosmos and truly represented the "other." They were constrained neither by institutions nor by morals. Unlike the gods (who, admittedly, were occasionally demonic), most demons were barely anthropomorphic or anthropopathic (at least, they did not have those feelings that were regarded as humane and civilized). Especially in the early periods of

18 Biblical and extrabiblical onomastic data have been marshalled in support of the view that the veneration of a personal god was widespread in ancient Israel. Moreover, the patriarchal narratives, for example, portray the patriarch's god as a personal god: thus, Abraham's servant refers to "the God of my master Abraham" (Gen 24:12, 27, 42, 48), and God introduces himself with the words, "I am the God of your father Abraham" (Gen 26:24).

19 Translation based upon *BWL*, 39, and A. Annus and A. Lenzi, *"Ludlul bēl nēmeqi": The Standard Babylonian Poem of the Righteous Sufferer*, SAACT 7 (Helsinki: Neo Assyrian Text Corpus Project, 2010), 35, with minor modifications. Cf. Abusch, "Fortune and Misfortune," 52, 55 n. 10 [[218–219, 223 n. 7]].

20 Demons were well known to the authors of the Hebrew Bible. Note, for example, their depictions of desert wastes (see, e.g., Isa 34:14). By the way, in Exod 4:24, Yhwh's attack on Moses recalls the unpredictable and wild nature of demonic forces and reveals the demonic side of the deity. Witches are generally portrayed negatively (see, e.g., Exod 22:17; Deut 18:9–14; 2 Kgs 9:22). Witchcraft and consorting with the dead are on full display in 1 Sam 28, where Saul seeks assistance from a female medium to conjure up the ghost of Samuel, one of several divinatory and magical practices prohibited in Deut 18:10–11 and criticized elsewhere.

Mesopotamian civilization, demons were modeled upon irresistible natural forces, upon animals, upon external enemies and bandits, and upon the minions of newly emerging warlords or leaders trying to extend their rule. Initially they were even outside the control of the gods. But in the later periods, parallel to—or as a reflection of—the expansion of the powers and reach of the Mesopotamian state, areas and powers that earlier were uncontrollable now became part of an expanded cosmic structure. Demons, too, were integrated into the cosmos; they now came under the control of the gods, and whereas earlier demons lived mainly in the wild, now they lived in the netherworld together with the dead.

> 167 They are the Seven, they are the Seven,
> 168 they are the Seven from the source of the Apsû,
> 169 they are the Seven adorned in heaven,
> 170 they grew up in a cella in the source of the Apsû.
> 171 They are neither male nor female,
> 172 they are the wraiths who flit about,
> 173 they neither marry nor bear children.
> 174 They do not know how to spare or save (anyone),
> 175 nor do they heed prayer or supplication.
> 176 They are horses bred in the mountains,
> 177 they (are the) evil ones of Ea, the throne bearers of gods.
> 178 They always hang about in the street, to cause disruption in the thoroughfare.
> 179 They are evil, they are evil,
> 180 they are the Seven, they are the Seven, twice seven are they.
> 181 They were adjured by heaven, adjured by earth.[21]

### 3.3 *Ghosts*

*Eṭemmu* (Sumerian gidim) is a spirit, more properly a ghost. After death, what remained was the lifeless body and some form of intangible, but visible and audible "spirit." Wind imagery is associated with ghosts (and demons). Normally, the dead body was buried; moreover, the dead were to be the recipients of ongoing mortuary rites. The unburied or disinterred dead and even those who did not receive proper mortuary rites could become roaming and troublesome ghosts; some texts suggest that they could be relegated to the formless and chaotic world sometimes associated with steppe and winds and

21 Udug.ḫul v 167–181; translation: M. J. Geller, with the assistance of L. Vacín, *Healing Magic and Evil Demons: Canonical Udug-hul Incantations* (Boston: de Gruyter, 2016), 211–213.

could even become part of the demonic world that was neither human nor god, male nor female. (Hence, gidim/*eṭemmu* could become associated with the demonic class udug/*utukku* and even be designated as such.) Mention should also be made of the dead who had led unfulfilled lives and were drawn back to the world of the living, either out of envy or malice, or out of the desire to complete "unfinished business" (the líl group). Ghosts that plague the living may either belong to one's own family or be strangers who have attached themselves to the victim.

> The ghost which has set upon me, keeps harassing me, and [does not quit me] day or [nig]ht,
> Be it a stranger ghost,
> Be it a forgotten ghost,
> Be it a ghost without a name,
> Be it a ghost that has no one to provide for it,
> Be it a ghost of someone who [has no one to invoke his name],
> Be it a ghost of someone killed by a weapon,
> Be it a ghost of someone who died for a sin against a god or for a crime against a king,
> [Place] it [in the care of the ghosts of its family],
> May it accept this and let me go free![22]

### 3.4 *Witches*

Witchcraft in Mesopotamian sources normally refers to malevolent destructive magic performed usually, though not exclusively, by a human witch, *kaššāpu* (m.)/ *kaššāptu* (f.). These illegitimate practitioners of magic were motivated by malice and evil intent and used forms of destructive magic to harm other human beings. The belief in witchcraft reflected a feeling of human interdependence and a sense of vulnerability and was the personification of actual or perceived interhuman animosity and conflict. Although lists of witches include both male and female forms, the witch is usually depicted as a woman. The witch was able to control or harm her victim by means of indirect contact (reflecting the belief in the underlying principles of sympathetic magic [analogy and contiguity]): she could steal objects that had been in contact with and represented her victim, make an image in the likeness of her victim and then twist its limbs so that he suffered agony and debilitating disease, prepare figurines and bury them in holes in the wall or in the ground, feed statues

22 CT 23, 15: 6–9; translation: B. R. Foster, *Before the Muses: An Anthology of Akkadian Literature*, 3rd ed. (Bethesda, MD: CDL, 2005), 990.

to animals, or open up a grave and place the representation of her victim in the lap of a dead person, thus effecting a marriage of her victim and a corpse. Sometimes there was direct contact between victim and witch, for she was also said to cause her victim to incorporate witchcraft by means of food, drink, washing, and ointment; she was even described as one who could directly seize and harm the various parts of the victim's body, could even push, press, and strike his chest and back. In addition to such manipulations and activities, the witch could form an evil word in her heart and utter an incantation. She could even send signs that were thought to result in misfortune, evil omens that augured doom.

Though she had special powers, the witch was a human being, but as time went on she also developed a demonic form. Thus, eventually, the witch was also imagined as a demonic being who was even able to set other demons against her victim.

> The witch, she who roams the streets,
> Who continually intrudes into houses,
> Who prowls in alleys,
> Who spies about the broad ways—
> She keeps turning around from front to back,
> Standing, in the street she turns foot (progress) around,
> (And) in the broad way she cuts off (commercial) traffic.
> She robbed the fine young man of his virility,
> She carried off the attractiveness of the fine young woman,
> With her malignant stare she took away her charms.
> She looked at the young man and (thereby) robbed his vitality,
> She looked at the young woman and (thereby) carried off her attractiveness.
> The witch has seen me and has come after me,
> With her venom, she *has* cut off (commercial) traffic,
> With her spittle, she has cut off my trading,
> She has driven away my god and goddess from my person.[23]

### 3.5 *Manual and Oral Rites*

Having defined the causal agents and chains of causation, the exorcist would then undertake magical acts (that is, manual rites) and utter magical speeches (that is, oral rites); these manual and oral rites constituted *āšipūtu* (the exorcist's craft). Many of these acts and speeches were modeled on types of actions

23 *Maqlû* III 1–16; translation: T. Abusch, *The Magical Ceremony "Maqlû": A Critical Edition*, AMD 10 (Leiden: Brill, 2016), 305.

undertaken and types of speeches uttered in the everyday world to deal with actual beings and objects. Depending on the understanding of the cause of distress, the magical actions could take the form of acts of destruction, substitution, bribery and gift giving, burial, transference, binding and imprisonment, or expulsion. The addresses could be either incantations or prayers. These utterances could take the form of demand, request, praise, or other modes of address; these utterances would have been directed either to beneficent natural forces or ceremonial objects, or to the evil beings or forces themselves.

As examples of supplications of the individual, we may cite here two texts drawn from the Akkadian *šuilla* corpus. Nergal 2 and Marduk 2 are well-wrought invocations; they compare favorably with the finest examples of individual petitions in the biblical Psalter.[24]

The prayer Nergal 2 typifies the corpus of general *šuilla* prayers. It contains the three expected sections: (1) A hymnic introduction in which the god is invoked, described, and praised (1–10); (2) A supplication centering upon a petition to the god asking him or her to come to the aid of the petitioner. This central part of the prayer may also include a lament in which the supplicant describes his suffering and perhaps its cause (11–23); (3) Finally, a promise of praise should the deity grant the petition and allow the petitioner to regain a normal life (24). The sections are clearly articulated; they are thematically well developed and, in the main, have a formal shape.

1 Mighty lord, exalted son of Nunamnir,
2 Foremost among the Anunnaki, lord of battle,
3 Offspring of Kutušar, the great queen,
4 Nergal, all powerful among the gods, beloved of Ninmenna.

5 You are manifest in the bright heavens, your station is exalted,
6 You are great in the netherworld, you have no rival.
7 Together with Ea, your counsel is preeminent in the assembly of the gods.
8 Together with Sîn, you observe everything in the heavens.

9 Enlil, your father, gave to you the black-headed ones, all the living, and
10 He entrusted into your hands the herds, the animals.

24 The Hebrew Psalter is home to a relatively large corpus of individual laments (see, e.g., Pss 6, 13, 38, 69, 88) that share with the Akkadian *šuilla* the attributes of divine invocation, supplication, and the promise of praise to the deity.

11 I, So-and-so, son of So-and-so, your servant:
12 The anger of god and goddess has beset me so that
13 Expenses and losses befall my estate (and)
14 Giving orders but not being obeyed keep me awake.

15 Because you are sparing, my lord, I have turned toward your divinity,
16 Because you are compassionate, I have sought you,
17 Because you are merciful, I have stood before you,
18 Because you are favorably inclined, I have looked upon your face.
19 Regard me favorably and hear my supplication.
20 May your furious heart become calm toward me,
21 Pardon my sin, my error, and my misdeed,
22 May the wrath (lit., knots of your innards) of your great divinity speedily be appeased (lit., disentangled) for me,
23 May the offended, angry, and irate god and goddess be reconciled with me.

24 Then will I declare your great deeds and sing your praise![25]

In contrast to the *šuilla* to Nergal, the Marduk prayer does not follow the standard form of the type (Introductory Hymn, Prayer, Concluding Benediction); it displays a new pattern: Introductory Hymn (1–9); Capsule *šuilla* (10–12); Prayer for Success (13–21); Capsule *šuilla* (22–24); Concluding Benediction (25–27). The form of this *šuilla* was the result of innovation.

1 Famed mighty one, chieftain of Eridu,
2 Exalted prince, first-born of Nudimmud,
3 Raging Marduk, restorer of rejoicing to E'engura.

4 Lord of Esagila, hope of Babylon,
5 Lover of Ezida, preserver of life,
6 Lone one of Emahtila, multiplier of life.

25 Nergal *šuilla* no. 2; translation: T. Abusch, "A Paean and Petition to a God of Death: Some Comments on a *Šuilla* to Nergal," in *From the Four Corners of the Earth: Studies in Iconography and Cultures of the Ancient Near East in Honour of F. A. M. Wiggermann*, ed. D. Kertai and O. Nieuwenhuyse, AOAT 441 (Münster: Ugarit-Verlag, 2017), 16–17 [[165–166]].

7 Protection of the land, savior of the multitudes of people,
8 The single great one of chapels everywhere,
9 Your name is sweetly hymned by the people everywhere.

10 O Marduk, great lord,
11 By your affirmative decree, may I live and be well,
12 I will then constantly praise your godhead.

13 Whatsoever I seek may I attain,
14 Place effective speech in my mouth,
15 Fashion an agreeable word in my mind,
16 May courtier and attendant seek agreement on my behalf,
17 May my god stand at my right,
18 May my goddess stand at my left,
19 May the guardian-deity be constantly at my side,
20 Grant me (the power) to speak, to be heard, and to meet with consent (so that)
21 Whatsoever words I utter may meet with consent.

22 O Marduk, great lord, grant me my life,
23 Decree for me a healthy life,
24 In joyfully serving you regularly will I (then) find satisfaction.

25 May Enlil rejoice over you, may Ea exult over you,
26 May the gods of the universe bless you,
27 May the great gods make you happy.[26]

### 3.6 *Death and the Netherworld*

We would be remiss if we did not mention some Mesopotamian beliefs about death and the netherworld here in connection with our discussion of the religious life of the individual.

Death called forth a number of rituals. The body must be buried; otherwise, the ghost will have no rest and will not find its place in the community of the dead, usually associated with the netherworld. In addition, burial is crucial for future care: the dead are to be the recipients of ongoing mortuary rites, which include invocations of the name of the deceased, presentations of food,

26 Marduk *šuilla* no. 2; translation: T. Abusch, "The Form and Meaning of a Babylonian Prayer to Marduk," *JAOS* 103 (1983): 3–15 [[126–148]].

and libations of water. In this way the dead are cared for and their memory is preserved.[27]

Burial constitutes a rite of passage, both integrating the dead into the cosmic order and maintaining connections between the living and the dead. The living and dead maintain a permanent relationship and form an ongoing community, and thus burial was crucial because it allowed for the preservation and maintenance of the deceased's identity after death and for his continued connection with both the living and dead members of the family. Thus, whatever other purposes it served, burial of the body preserved the identity of the deceased and provided a focus and locus for the ghost's continued existence, for its relationship and place, that is, among the living and the dead. Of course, the conception of the netherworld changed in the course of time. Whereas in descriptions from the early second millennium, this realm is inhabited primarily by the dead (who are still human in form, though they lack animation and energy), later visions are more horrific and describe a netherworld inhabited by monsters and demons as well as by the dead (who no longer look human).

## 4 The Epic of Gilgamesh

We conclude our reflections on Mesopotamian religion with a short notice about the Epic of Gilgamesh, a profound Mesopotamian meditation on the meaning of life and death.[28]

There are at least three major versions of the Akkadian Epic of Gilgamesh. Around 1700 BCE, a Babylonian author created a unified epic about the hero Gilgamesh. This Old Babylonian (OB) account of Gilgamesh is the earliest, perhaps also the most immediately felt and compelling, version of the Akkadian epic. Subsequent to the OB period, the epic circulated throughout the ancient Near East. Not surprisingly, the work underwent many changes and developments, and a number of new versions took form in Akkadian as

27 A similar concern to provide for the deceased in the afterlife may very well have been a part of Israelite practice (Deut 26:13–14; the prescribed expression in this passage only rules out the offering of the "sacred portion" (קֹדֶשׁ) to the dead.). Along with the Priestly prohibition against certain mourning rites (Lev 19:28), the Bible also provides information about who performed burial rites (Gen 23:1–20; 25:7–11; 35:29), when (2 Sam 3:22–39), where (Gen 23:1–20; 35:8; 48:29–31; 1 Sam 31:13), and the importance one's burial may have on group and individual identity (Neh 2:1–5). See, e.g., R. Albertz and R. Schmitt, *Family and Household Religion in Ancient Israel and the Levant* (Winona Lake, IN: Eisenbrauns, 2012).

28 For an edition, see A. R. George, *The Babylonian Gilgamesh Epic*, 2 vols. (Oxford: Oxford University Press, 2003); for a collection of my studies of the epic, see T. Abusch, *Male and Female in the Epic of Gilgamesh* (Winona Lake, IN: Eisenbrauns, 2015).

well as in other languages. The Babylonian version(s) changed and developed during the course of the second and early first millennium. While a number of new recensions and versions took form, the Standard Babylonian eleven- and twelve-tablet versions represent without doubt the two most important post-Old Babylonian Akkadian versions that we possess.

Gilgamesh is presented to us as an individual who lives on a heroic plane and exists in spiritual isolation. But such a life is unbearable. Gilgamesh seeks immortality as a human being, and in all three versions of the text, he learns that this is impossible. In the Old Babylonian version, Gilgamesh finds a meaningful context within the bosom of the family, creating children who represent him in the future, and accepts the role of builder-king. In the eleven-tablet version, he becomes a responsible ruler who rules his community with wisdom and creates human cultural achievements that outlast his own reign and are passed down to future generations. In the twelve-tablet version, he readies himself to become a normal god who judges dead human beings for eternity.

The story draws together the many strands that make up the identity of Gilgamesh: man, hero, king, god. Gilgamesh must learn to live. He must find ways to express his tremendous personal energy but still act in a manner that accords with the limits and responsibilities imposed upon him by his society and universe. But the work emphasizes the theme of death and explores the realization that in spite of even the greatest achievements and powers, a human is nonetheless powerless against death. Thus, in the final analysis, Gilgamesh must also come to terms with his own nature and prepare for death, for he is both a man and a god, and as both he will experience loss and will die.

CHAPTER 2

# Magic in Mesopotamia

## 1 Introduction

A few words at the outset regarding what I term Mesopotamian magic. It is important to start out with definitions, because magic is treated somewhat differently in Mesopotamia (and the other areas of the ancient Near East) than in biblical and classical literatures (not to speak of modern Western thought); moreover, while Western thought (and scholarship) often draws a distinction between magic and religion (to the advantage of the latter), it is difficult to carry this distinction through in a wholly consistent manner in the study of the cultures of the ancient Near East.

Magic is here defined as those activities involving supernatural forces that are undertaken to serve the needs of the individual members of society, to deal with their difficulties, and to counter forces that bring evil upon them. Given that in many societies, especially in the West, the distinction between religion and magic is that one is legitimate, the other not, it must be stated at the outset that in Mesopotamia magic was regarded as legitimate and as part of the established religion. (Therefore, in a Mesopotamian context, terms usually translated as "witchcraft" [e.g., *kišpū*, *ruḫû*, *rusû*, and *upšāšû lemnūtu*] refer not to magical behavior as such, but to the practice of magic for antisocial and destructive purposes.)

## 2 Earlier Approaches to Mesopotamian Magic

The study of Mesopotamian magic has not been unaffected by the intellectual and religious developments of the last one hundred and fifty years. In the early period, magic was treated primarily as superstition, the beliefs of the lower parts of society. This view of magic was due to a number of factors. For some, magic was thought to have been replaced by religion, which was itself rendered obsolete by science. Enlightenment attitudes tended to carry with them negative valuations of institutional religion. Moreover, even those who valued religion often had negative outlooks on ritual (this was partly due to anti-Catholic prejudices); there was a sense that only belief and piety were true spiritual activities and that only sin and guilt, not demonic evil, were worthy causes of suffering. Given the prevalence of Protestant attitudes, the

 | DOI:10.1163/9789004435186_003

marginalization of magic, and the identification of magic with the beliefs of primitives in colonial societies, often the best we can hope for among scholars of that period is illustrated by the somewhat pejorative attitudes toward magic evident in the following remarks (presented in chronological order) made by scholars of the late nineteenth and early twentieth centuries:

> In order to realize the great number and variety of such beings [scil. demons] it would be necessary to turn to the spells and incantations and magical formulae which occupy so large a place in the religious literature of the Babylonians. To ignore this lower aspect of the belief of the Babylonians would be to give a one-sided and incomplete picture of their religion.[1]

> The Bab[ylonian] hymns and prayers to the gods reach a much higher religious level than the extensive literature of soothsaying and exorcism.[2]

> Magic may be said to be present wherever power over the unseen is believed to be inherent in the ritual, whereas, according to the religious concept, the seat of power is regarded as resting outside the sphere of man's deliberate control. When the term is used in this sense, it must be admitted that a great body of the religious beliefs and practices of the Babylonians and Assyrians should be more accurately described as falling under the category of magic.[3]

But, however one evaluates these attitudes, it should also be noted that the aforementioned scholars expressing these prejudices were among the great masters of and pioneers in the field of Mesopotamian magical activity and texts, and their opinions continued to carry weight in Assyriology.[4]

After the First World War, the approach to magic, certainly in anthropology, was transformed. Associated with the growth of form criticism, a change also began to take place in Assyriology. This change is especially evident in the work of Landsberger and his students; here I have in mind especially the Leipzig

1 L. W. King, *Babylonian Religion and Mythology* (London: K. Paul, Trench, Trübner, 1899), 202.

2 H. Zimmern, "Babylonians and Assyrians," in *Encyclopaedia of Religion and Ethics*, vol. 2, ed. J. Hastings (Edinburgh: T&T Clark; New York: Scribner, 1910), 317.

3 L. W. King, "Magic (Babylonian)," in *Encyclopaedia of Religion and Ethics*, vol. 8, ed. J. Hastings (Edinburgh: T&T Clark; New York: Scribner, 1916), 253.

4 E.g., L. W. King, *Babylonian Magic and Sorcery* (London: Luzac, 1896); H. Zimmern, *Beiträge zur Kenntnis der babylonischen Religion*, 2 vols., Assyriologische Bibliothek 12 (Leipzig: Hinrichs, 1896–1901).

dissertations of Falkenstein on Sumerian incantations (1931) and Kunstmann on the general and specific *šuillas* (1932).[5] This attention to literary form, mixed with a strain of Romanticism, and combined with the emphasis in Assyriology at that time on the Old Babylonian period, seems to have shifted the focus of interest from ritual to folkloristic themes that presumably derived from hoary antiquity (or, at least, from the Old Babylonian period).

In the fifties and sixties, exemplified especially in the work of Oppenheim, we begin to have a greater emphasis on the role of intellectuals in the formation of Babylonian religious thought and the important place of magic in the thought of the intelligentsia, but with this also came a de-emphasis of the "religious" and imaginative dimensions of magic.[6] Be that as it may, magic had, at least, regained its legitimacy.

Moreover, this period also saw a number of dissertations dedicated to reconstructing and analyzing individual corpora of magical literature, influenced perhaps by the achievements of the aforementioned Leipzig dissertations.[7]

More recently, a noteworthy attempt to understand the history of magic and its place in Mesopotamian society and culture is represented by a joint article of van Binsbergen and Wiggermann.[8] Much attention in recent decades has also been paid to the history of the creation and edition of series of magical texts, the revision and redaction of magical texts in antiquity, and the place of magic in Mesopotamian scribal history.[9]

---

5 A. Falkenstein, *Die Haupttypen der sumerischen Beschwörung literarisch untersucht*, LSS NF 1 (Leipzig: Hinrichs, 1931); W. G. Kunstmann, *Die babylonische Gebetsbeschwörung*, LSS NF 2 (Leipzig: Hinrichs, 1932).

6 E.g., A. L. Oppenheim, *Ancient Mesopotamia: Portrait of a Dead Civilization*, rev. ed. (Chicago: University of Chicago Press, 1977), 206–305.

7 See R. I. Caplice, "The Akkadian Text Genre Namburbi" (Ph.D. diss., University of Chicago, 1963); R. D. Biggs, *ŠÀ.ZI.GA: Ancient Mesopotamian Potency Incantations*, TCS 2 (Locust Valley, NY: J. J. Augustin, 1967); T. Abusch, "Studies in the History and Interpretation of Some Akkadian Incantations and Prayers Against Witchcraft" (Ph.D. diss., Harvard University, Cambridge, MA, 1972), published as T. Abusch, *Babylonian Witchcraft Literature: Case Studies*, BJS 132 (Atlanta: Scholars Press, 1987).

8 W. van Binsbergen and F. A. M. Wiggerman, "Magic in History: A Theoretical Perspective, and Its Application to Ancient Mesopotamia," in *Mesopotamian Magic: Textual, Historical, and Interpretive Perspectives*, ed. T. Abusch and K. van der Toorn, AMD 1 (Groningen: Styx, 1999), 3–34.

9 E.g., Abusch, *Babylonian Witchcraft Literature*, 7–82; T. Abusch, "The Revision of Babylonian Anti-Witchcraft Incantations: The Critical Analysis of Incantations in the Ceremonial Series *Maqlû*," in *Continuity and Innovation in the Magical Tradition*, ed. G. Bohak et al., JSRC 15 (Leiden: Brill, 2011), 11–41 [[AMD 17, 51–80]]; I. L. Finkel, "Adad-apla-iddina, Esagil-kīn-apli, and the Series SA.GIG," in *A Scientific Humanist: Studies in Memory of Abraham Sachs*,

## 3 Conceptions of the Universe and of Its Powers

Mesopotamian rites that address especially the human needs, crises, and desires of the individual, as well as of the king, are regarded as magical. Not all, but most magical rituals have as their focus the counteracting of evil. Our sources are the work of priests and scribes; they reflect the use of magic in the service of the elite and reflect elitist conceptions of magic. Mesopotamian magic may just as well be defined as *āšipūtu*—the field that the *āšipu* or "exorcist" mastered. But it should be noted that while our definition of magic covers most of the activities of the *āšipu*, it does not encompass all of his activities; moreover, our definition also includes some of the activities of the *asû* or "herbalist." (Note, therefore, that procedural texts prescribe the treatment of problems by means of either ritual therapy [*āšipūtu*], traditional herbal therapy [*asûtu*], or a combination of the two.)

For the individual Mesopotamian, magic remained the major means of asserting control over the uncertainties and vagaries of life. Accordingly, magic treats illness and other such life difficulties and transitions; these personal crises may manifest themselves in any area of human life and on a physical, psychological, psychosomatic, or socioeconomic plane. The principal agencies and causes of harm are gods, demons, tutelary (personal) gods, ghosts, witches, evil omens, curses, and sins. Magical activities may then be pursued in order to deal with the problem; it should be mentioned that these activities may be undertaken by an individual on his own behalf or (as is most often the case in our sources) by an exorcist (*āšipu*) on behalf of the individual in distress.

The exorcist tried to determine the cause of distress. He usually found this cause in the action or inaction of either personalistic or mechanistic powers within the supernatural universe. When these powers were viewed in personalistic terms, the universe would have been understood to be structured hierarchically and to be centered on divine powers. When viewed mechanistically, the world would have been understood holistically. (By this I mean that the world/reality was treated as if it were made up of organic wholes that were connected to each other, interconnections that underlie modes of magical

ed. Erle Leichty et al., OPSNKF 9 (Philadelphia: The University Museum, 1988), 143–159; N. P. Heeßel, "Neues von Esagil-kīn-apli," in *Assur-Forschungen*, ed. N. P. Heeßel and S. M. Maul (Wiesbaden: Harrassowitz, 2010), 139–187; N. P. Heeßel, "'Sieben Tafeln aus sieben Städten': Überlegungen zum Prozess der Serialisierung von Texten in Babylonien in der zweiten Hälfte des zweiten Jahrtausends v. Chr.," in *Babylon: Wissenskultur in Orient und Okzident*, ed. E. Cancik-Kirschbaum et al. (Berlin: de Gruyter, 2011), 171–195.

behavior such as sympathetic magic, a mode that is based upon the power of analogy and contiguity.) Thus, depending on the cosmological view and the ceremonial tradition, the exorcist would adopt (what we would consider) either a religio-magical, personalistic modus operandi, or a purely magical, mechanistic modus operandi. Although they are mixed together in *āšipūtu*, the personalistic, hierarchic approach seems to be later and to have emerged from, and to continually draw upon, the earlier mechanistic, holistic approach.

The earlier mechanistic magical universe reflected the social context of traditional society: the village and preurban settlement. Here, misfortune was due partly to irregularity, disorder, and chaos. This disorder was manifested in attacks by demons on individuals who were vulnerable; vulnerability was due to the lack of protection, only occasionally to culpability. This traditional worldview probably continued to remain operative for the mass of rural and urban dwellers. But alongside this worldview and based upon it, a new worldview arose in the late fourth or early third millennium BCE that reflected the values and interests of the emerging urban elite; in this new view, the gods increasingly gained more control over the world. This new worldview underwent changes of its own; different, emerging political-social contexts led to new ways through which to view and understand the travails of life. New successive contexts generated new causes of evil and placed the already existing ones into new settings and relationships. The sociopolitical contexts that underlay the new worldview were city, tribe, nation, and empire.

## 4 Magical Texts

I turn now to the ancient literature in which Mesopotamian magical activities are recorded. From almost the beginning of the cuneiform tradition down till the late first millennium BCE, texts written in both Sumerian and Akkadian prescribe and record various symbolic means of dealing with evil, suffering, and illness (of dealing, that is, with personal crises and difficulties) and of accomplishing personal goals. (I leave aside texts that are primarily diagnostic or speculative in intent.) These recipes include oral rites (prayers and incantations), ritual instructions, and medical prescriptions. Early text forms were already recorded on tablets from the mid-third millennium (coming from, e.g., Ebla, Abu Salabikh, Shuruppak). Many more texts (especially in Sumerian) are known from late third- and early second-millennia sites such as Nippur, Ur, and Meturan; some of these texts continue on into later periods. A significant number of texts (most in Akkadian) come from late second-millennium collections (mainly those of Boghazkoi and Assur); but by far, the greatest number come from first-millennium collections. Pride of place goes to the royal collections of seventh-century BCE Nineveh; but, in addition, major groups derive from both the Assyrian sites of Assur, Kalḫu (Nimrud), and Sultantepe, and the Babylonian ones of Uruk, Ur, Nippur, Babylon, and Sippar.

In the main, the texts are guides to actual performances that were consulted by magicians and herbalists and studied by scholars. The basic textual unit prescribes the performance of a discrete ritual. The texts usually present in varying combinations the elements crucial to the actual ritual activity or performance (oral and manual rites and the preparation or application of ceremonial/medical materials), as well as a statement describing the circumstance and purpose of the activity. At first, only the incantation was committed to writing; subsequently, instructions regarding the time, place, and manner of ritual performance, as well as other types of additional information, were added. This additional information in the form of introductory and concluding scribal statements could have included the following: (1) a statement of the problem in the form of an objective and/or subjective description (e.g., physical, psychological, and/or social symptoms); (2) an etiological or descriptive diagnosis; (3) a statement of the purpose of the ritual (e.g., "in order to undo witchcraft"); and (4) a prognosis (e.g., "the man will live").

Independent rites are the fundamental units of scribal composition. In the course of time, scribes attempted to organize the vast body of magical literature into coherent groups and collections. It is during the late period that most of the editing and serialization of the magical texts took place. Scribes differed in the way they organized these materials. Tablets often contained more than one ritual unit; moreover, the same ritual unit might appear in different religious, literary, or scribal contexts. These larger literary-editorial constructs might be either canonical or ad hoc compositions and might contain either a series of units that share some commonality (e.g., the evil addressed) or the text of a complex ritual.

Two typical ways of organizing and recording the contents of an individual ceremony may be cited: (1) the text of an incantation is presented, followed by a rubric (an ancient classificatory label) and ritual instructions; or (2) a description of a patient's symptoms (and often a diagnosis) is given, followed by ritual instructions (including instructions to recite oral rites), the text of the oral rite itself, and, finally, a prognosis. I cite here two texts from the anti-witchcraft corpus in order to provide examples of these formats and to acquaint the reader with magical texts.

1) Incantation, rubric, and ritual instructions:

14′ Incantation: “This is he, this is she:
15′ she runs after me,
16′ she strives to seize me!
17′ In her mouth she carries evil word(s),
18′ hateful magic she holds gathered in her hands,
19′ her arms are full of foul wash water.
20′ Having seen her the young man runs a mile (away),
21′ and even she, the girl, (runs) two-thirds of a mile.
22′ Who is this (woman) who runs after me
23′ (who) strives to seize me?
24′ I have seized you with the wisdom of Ea,
25′ I have stopped you with the magical procedures of the sage of the gods, Marduk.
26′ I have given you to drink spittle mixed with bile,
27′ like a spider I have covered your face with cobwebs.
28′ Cast away the evil spittle of your mouth
29′ throw down the hateful magic of your h[an]ds,
30′ May your arms be rendered slack!
31′ ... of the witch, the sorceress and the en[chant]ress,
32′ I have i[ntercepted] the passage of my sorceress,
33′ I have turned back the wi[tchcraft] of my enchantress.
34′ I am taking you and shutting you up with [...],
35′ I am entrusting you to the lock[ed] city gate—
36′ I have di[rected] your face to a hole toward sunset,
37′ I have put a weakling, a blind man, in charge of the city [gate].
38′ Because you keep pursuing me with evil intention,
39′ let the experts, the exorcists, (and) the snake-charmers
40′ dispel you, then I will undo your bond!” In[cantation (formula)].

---

41′ It is [the wo]rding (of the incantation) to undo witchcraft.

---

42′ Its ritual: <You make> a tongue of tallow, you drench (lit., “have it drink”) i[t] with bile, 43′ you cover its ‘face’ with cobwebs, 44′ you shut it up in a hole toward sunset; 45′ then you seal its opening with a seal of šubû-stone and (with a seal) of šadânu-stone.[10]

10 *CMAwR* 1, no. 7.8: 14′–45′.

2) Symptoms, ritual instructions, incantation, and prognosis:

47′ If a man is in constant fear of his palace, (if) he does not dare to speak, that man is bewitched; 48′ he has been anointed with oil of *questioning*. At night, you pinch off clay at the river. At his bedside you make a barge with this [cl]ay. 49′ You set up a censer with *burāšu*-juniper; you pour a libation of *miḫḫu*-beer. You have the man kneel down and speak thus:

---

50′ Incantation: "The one who performed sorcery against me,
who had sorcery performed against me,
who performed sorcery against me when the river was high,
51′ who performed sorcery against me when the river was low,
who (said) to the sorceress 'Perform sorcery against him!'
52′ who said to the enchantress 'Perform witchcraft against him!'—
53′ this is her barge:
Just as this (barge) turns over,
54′ let their witchcraft turn upon them
and go to their [he]ad and body!" Incantation formula.

---

55′ You recite this incantation three times and have the barge capsize. He *takes off the garment from his b*[*ody*] and 56′ throws (it) in the river. 'Cutting-of-the-throat' magic will not come near the man and [his] house.[11]

## 5 Ceremonies

Having reviewed several texts, we may now turn to their actual contents, that is, to the actual magical performance itself. Once the exorcist had defined the causal agents and chains of causation involved, he would undertake magical acts (i.e., manual rites) and utter magical speeches (i.e., oral rites); these constitute *āšipūtu* (the exorcist's craft). Many of these acts and speeches were modeled on types of actions undertaken and types of speeches uttered in the everyday world to deal with actual beings and objects.

### 5.1 *Manual Rites*

The actual ceremony might be either a relatively simple one or an extensive, elaborate performance; it might last anywhere from a few hours to a day or

---

11 *CMAwR* 2, no. 8.23: 47′–56′.

more. It often involved purification, food and drink offerings to the gods, the burning of incense, a central operation directed toward significant objects or symbols, the tying and untying of knots, washing, the setting up of protective devices, and the application of amulets. Depending on the understanding of the cause of distress, the central magical actions might take the form of acts of destruction, substitution, bribery and gift giving, burial, transference, binding and imprisonment, and expulsion. Some representative examples of manual rites drawn from various magical compositions are:

Introductory acts: preparation of a sacred space such as a reed hut or altar.
Central acts: destruction of objects representing evil forces by burning, burying, or drowning the representation.
Or: counteracting evil (through the elimination of forms of miasma) by washing or wiping off the patient.
Concluding apotropaic acts: the application of protective devices such as plants or amulets.
Medical preparations and treatments: the preparation and administration of salves, potions, or lotions.

### 5.2 *Oral Rites*

In the course of a ceremony, the *āšipu* would have recited one or more oral addresses. The addresses themselves might be either incantations or prayers. Here it should be noted that incantations and prayers are found in various written contexts: (1) as part of short rituals; (2) in short collections of incantations and prayers (with some ritual instructions); and (3) in standardized scribal series—some of which were collections, while others represented complex, lengthy ceremonies, such as *Maqlû*.

The aforementioned utterances might take the form of demand, request, praise, and so on, and would have been directed either to beneficent powers (gods, natural forces, ceremonial objects) or to the evil beings or forces themselves. The beneficent powers would be called upon to help the client; the evil would be expelled, chased away, or even destroyed. The most important themes contained in the magical utterances were legitimating the speaker (either priest or laity), calling upon and praising divine powers, identifying the evil force to be eliminated, identifying the purpose of the ritual, specifying the rites being performed, asking divine or other powers to help the speaker, and imposing an oath upon evil beings.

A few examples of addresses to beneficent powers should suffice as illustrations. The first comes from a *namburbi* ritual and is addressed to Šamaš; the rest are taken from the anti-witchcraft ceremony *Maqlû*.

*Namburbi* against a Monstrous Birth

15 Incantation: Šamaš, judge of heaven and earth, lord of justice and equity,
16 director of upper and lower regions.
17 Šamaš, it is in your power to bring the dead to life, to release the captive.
18 Šamaš, I have approached you! Šamaš, I have sought you out!
19 Šamaš, I have turned to you!
20 Avert from me the evil of this misborn creature!
21 May it not affect me! May its evil be far from my person,
22 that I may daily bless you (and) those who see me may forever [sing] your praise![12]

Girra, God of Fire

136 Incantation. O splendid Girra, scion of Anu,
137 Offspring of the pure one, the exalted Šalaš,
138 Splendid, ever-renewing, constant light of the gods,
139 Dispenser of cereal offerings to the gods, the Igigi,
140 Provider of illumination to the Anunnaki, the great gods.
141 Raging Girra, obliterator of reed marsh,
142 Mighty Girra, destroyer of (buildings of) wood and stones,
143 Burner of the evildoers, seed of warlock and witch,
144 Annihilator of the wicked, seed of warlock and witch,
145 On this day, stand by me at my judgment,
146 And vanquish the rebel, the one who changes, the evil one!

12 R. I. Caplice, *The Akkadian Namburbi Texts: An Introduction*, SANE 1/1 (Los Angeles: Undena, 1974), 16. I have split up Caplice's running translation according to the line division of the original edition. For an edition, see Caplice, "Namburbi Texts in the British Museum I," *Or* NS 34 (1965): 126, 128. For a more recent edition and translation, see S. M. Maul, *Zukunftsbewältigung: Eine Untersuchung altorientalischen Denkens anhand der babylonisch-assyrischen Lösrituale (Namburbi)*, BaF 18 (Mainz am Rhein: Phillip von Zabern, 1994), 338–339, 342.

147 As these figurines dissolve, melt, and drip ever away,
148 So may my[!] warlock and witch dissolve, melt, and drip ever away.[13]

## Salt

119″ Incantation. You, Salt, who were created in a pure place,
120″ For food of the great gods did Enlil destine you.
121″ Without you a meal would not be set out in Ekur,
122″ Without you god, king, noble, and prince would not smell incense.
123″ I am So-and-so, the son of So-and-so, whom witchcraft holds captive,
124″ Whom machinations hold in (the form of a skin) disease.
125″ Release my witchcraft, O Salt, dispel my spittle,
126″ Take over from me the machinations, then will I constantly praise you as (I praise) my creator god.[14]

## Oil

29 Incantation. Pure oil, clear oil, bright oil,
30 Oil that purifies the body of the gods,
31 Oil that soothes the sinews of mankind,
32 Oil of the incantation of Ea, oil of the incantation of Asalluḫi.
33 I coat you with soothing oil
34 That Ea granted for soothing,
35 I anoint you with the oil of healing,
36 I cast upon you the incantation of Ea, lord of Eridu, Ninšiku.
37 I expel Asakku, *ahhāzu*-jaundice, chills of your body (*zumru*),
38 I remove dumbness, torpor, (and) misery of your body (*pagru*),
39 I soothe the sick sinews of your limbs.
40 By the command of Ea, king of the *apsû*,
41 By the spell of Ea, by the incantation of Asalluḫi,
42 By the soft bandage of Gula,
43 By the soothing hands of Nintinugga
44 And Ningirima, mistress of incantation.
45 On So-and-so, Ea cast[15] the incantation of the word of healing
46 That the seven sages of Eridu soothe his body. TU$_6$.ÉN[16]

13 *Maqlû* II 136–148; T. Abusch, *The Magical Ceremony "Maqlû": A Critical Edition*, AMD 10 (Leiden: Brill, 2016), 299.

14 *Maqlû* VI 119″–126″; Abusch, *Magical Ceremony "Maqlû,"* 345.

15 Possible var.: "O Ea, cast" (imperative); if so, perhaps read: "your incantation of healing," instead of "the incantation of the word of healing."

16 *Maqlû* VII 29–46; Abusch, *Magical Ceremony "Maqlû,"* 350–351.

## 6 Evil

Magic stepped in when the individual suffered misfortune. Under the best of circumstances, life was uncertain and unpredictable and humans were vulnerable. Misfortune was often understood to be a consequence of human misdeed or failure, but it often seemed to be unrelated to one's deeds and to come arbitrarily. Significant agencies or causes of misfortune were demons, ghosts, tutelary (personal) gods, witches, evil omens, curses, and sins. Even those among these forces that were often favorable to humans would occasionally harm them. The aforementioned forces and their nefarious deeds are described in detail in the oral rites that were recited to rid oneself of or protect oneself against these evils. Moving from forces that are more anthropomorphic to those that are more mechanistic, I shall define each of the forces and then provide examples of their nature and activities from the oral rites themselves.

### 6.1 *Demons*

In the main, demons were regarded as evil and as wholly unsympathetic to human life. They were the least "human" of the supernatural forces that threatened the lives of Mesopotamians. They personified those destructive powers and events that were unpredictable, uncontrollable, and overwhelming. Originally, at least, they were not part of the cosmos and truly represented the "other." They were constrained neither by institutions nor by morals. Unlike the gods (who, admittedly, were occasionally demonic), most demons were barely anthropomorphic or anthropopathic (at least, they did not have those feelings that were regarded as humane and civilized). Especially in the early periods of Mesopotamian civilization, demons were modeled upon irresistible natural forces, upon animals, upon external enemies and bandits, and upon the minions of newly emerging warlords or leaders trying to extend their rule. Initially they were even outside the control of the gods. But in the later periods—parallel to, or as a reflection of, the expansion of the powers and reach of the Mesopotamian state—areas and powers that earlier were uncontrollable now became part of an expanded cosmic structure. Demons, too, were integrated into the cosmos; they now came under the control of the gods, and whereas earlier demons lived mainly in the wild, now they lived in the netherworld together with the dead.[17]

17 Of course, the netherworld itself changed; whereas in descriptions from the early second millennium BCE, this realm is inhabited primarily by the dead (who are still human in form, though they lack animation and energy), later visions are more horrific and describe a netherworld inhabited by monsters and demons as well as by the dead (who no longer look human).

Udug.hul V 167–182

167 They are the Seven, they are the Seven,
168 they are the Seven from the source of the Apsû,
169 they are the Seven adorned in heaven,
170 they grew up in a cella in the source of the Apsû.
171 They are neither male nor female,
172 they are the wraiths who flit about,
173 they neither marry nor bear children.
174 They do not know how to spare or save (anyone),
175 nor do they heed prayer or supplication.
176 They are horses bred in the mountains,
177 they (are the) evil ones of Ea, the throne bearers of gods.
178 They always hang about in the street, to cause disruption in the thoroughfare.
179 They are evil, they are evil,
180 they are the Seven, they are the Seven, twice seven are they.
181 They were adjured by heaven, adjured by earth.

---

182 It is an Udug-hul incantation.[18]

Udug.hul V 1–20

1 While cold and chills weaken everything,
2 the evil Utukku-demons are spawned from the seed of Anu;
3 Namtaru (Fate), beloved son of Enlil, is born of Ereškigal.
4 Above (the demons) were snarling, while below they donned mourning-clothes,
5 they are the product of the netherworld,
6 above they roar, but below they twitter,
7 they are the poisonous spittle of the gods.
8 They are huge storms which are released from heaven,
9 they are the owl which screeches in the city,
10 they are the offspring of earth spawned by the seed of Anu.
11 They circle the high, broad roofs like waves,
12 and constantly cross over from house to house.
13 They are the ones which no door can hold back nor any lock can turn away,

18 M. J. Geller, with the assistance of L. Vacín, *Healing Magic and Evil Demons: Canonical Udug-hul Incantations* (Boston: de Gruyter, 2016), 211–213.

14 they always slip through the doorway like a snake
15 and blow through the door-hinge like the wind.
16 They turn the wife away from the husband's lap,
17 make the son get up from his father's knee,
18 and oust the groom from his father-in-law's house.
19 They are the stupor and depression which are attached behind a man.
20 The (personal) god of the man is a shepherd seeking pasture for (his) human client, but whose (personal) god (the demons) have attacked for (his) food offering.[19]

Lamaštu II 152–166

152 Spell: She is monstrous, the Daughter-of-Anu, who wreaks havoc among the babies.
153 Her paws are a snare net, her bosom (hold?) spells death.
154 Cruel, raging, malicious, rapacious, violent,
155 destructive, *aggressive* is the Daughter-of-Anu.
156 She lays hands on the womb(s) of women in labor,
157 she pulls the babies from (the hold of) the nannies,
158 suckles (them), sings (to them), and covers (them) with kisses.
159 The weapons she uses are powerful, (and) her muscles are very agile.
160 The Daughter-of-Anu acts as the *wet-nursing priestess/nun* of the gods, her brothers.
161 Her head is a lion's head, donkey's teeth are [her] teeth
162 Her lips are a gale and spread death.
163 From deep in the mountains she came down,
164 roaring like a lion,
165 *whimpering* all the time like a bitch.
166 She leans over one window crosspiece after the other.[20]

### 6.2 *Ghosts*

The *eṭemmu* (Sum. gidim) is a spirit, more properly a ghost. After death, what remained was the lifeless body and some form of intangible, but visible and audible "spirit." Wind imagery is associated with ghosts (and demons). Ghosts were heard, felt, and, most of all, seen, particularly in dreams. Normally, the dead body was buried; moreover, the dead were to be the recipients of ongoing

19 Geller, *Healing Magic*, 175–180.
20 W. Farber, *Lamaštu: An Edition of the Canonical Series of Lamaštu Incantations and Rituals and Related Texts from the Second and First Millennia B.C.*, MC 17 (Winona Lake, IN: Eisenbrauns, 2014), 179. For an edition, see ibid., 120–122, 178.

mortuary rites, which included invocations of the name of the deceased, presentations of food, and libations of water. Mesopotamians believed that burial allowed for the preservation and maintenance of the deceased's identity after death and for the deceased's continued connection with both the living and dead members of the family.

The unburied or disinterred dead, and even those who did not receive proper mortuary rites, could become roaming and troublesome ghosts; some texts suggest that they could be relegated to the formless and chaotic world sometimes associated with steppe and winds and could even become part of the demonic world that was neither human nor god, male nor female. (Hence the gidim/*eṭemmu* could become associated with the demonic class udug/*utukku* and even be designated as such.) Mention should also be made of the dead who had led unfulfilled lives and were drawn back to the world of the living, either out of envy or malice, or out of the desire to complete "unfinished business" (the líl group).

Magical and medical texts that deal with ghosts usually focus on those that plague the living, though some ghosts—usually the family *manes* (*eṭem kimti*)—are invoked to help the living by taking one or another form of evil down to the netherworld. Ghosts that plague the living may either belong to one's own family or be strangers who have attached themselves to the victim. Some therapeutic texts prescribe material cures (e.g., potions, salves); others operate more in the magical and symbolic realms and try to rid the victim of the ghost either by providing the ghost with proper burial and/or mortuary treatment or by performing some other form of expulsion.

CT 23, 15: 6–9

> The ghost which has set upon me, keeps harassing me, and [does not quit me] day or [nig]ht,
> Be it a stranger ghost,
> Be it a forgotten ghost,
> Be it a ghost without a name,
> Be it a ghost that has no one to provide for it,
> Be it a ghost of someone who [has no one to invoke his name],
> Be it a ghost of someone killed by a weapon,
> Be it a ghost of someone who died for a sin against a god or for a crime against a king,
> [Place] it [in the care of the ghosts of its family],
> May it accept this and let me go free![21]

21 B. R. Foster, *Before the Muses: An Anthology of Akkadian Literature*, 3rd ed. (Bethesda, MD: CDL, 2005), 990. For an edition and another translation, see J. Scurlock, *Magico-Medical*

AMD 3, no. 10: 1–7

1 [Recitation]: "Šamaš, you are the king of heaven and earth [who] makes the things above and the things below go aright, who loosens what is bound.

2 A ghost (or) *mukil rēš lemutti* which was set on me and so continually pursues me—I am continually frightened and terrified (about him)—

3 he continually sets about oppressing and murdering me. Whether he be an evil *utukku*-demon or an evil *alû*-demon or an evil ghost

4 or an evil *gallû*-demon, whether he be a buried (person's) ghost or an unburied (person's) ghost or a ghost who has no brother or sister,

5 or a ghost who has no one to invoke his name or the roving ghost of (one of) his family, or a ghost (of one) who was abandoned in the steppe and thus

6 his spirit was not blown away (and) his name was not invoked, entrust him to his family ghost(s)."

---

7 Recitation (to be used when) one continually sees dead persons.[22]

## 6.3 *Tutelary (Personal) Gods*

The personal god or the family god was the god of the individual as a social being (originally, the personal god was the god of a family group and belonged to the male head of the family). In the first place, it was the personification of the individual's powers of strength, effectiveness, and procreation. In this role, it was an aspect of ego. But it was also the personification of the individual's responsibility with respect to right and wrong actions. It represented group norms as well as the responsibility to maintain them. Thus, it was not only an aspect of ego, but also an aspect of superego or conscience; in that capacity it punished the self. The personal god was thus an externalization of both the ego and the superego, a representation of the self in the form of externalized, divinized figures, and was viewed as a divine parent.

Success was construed as the presence and support of the personal god. Misfortune, on the other hand, was experienced as the loss of the personal god, or as the god's punitive actions, or both. To deal with this misfortune one

---

*Means of Treating Ghost-Induced Illnesses in Ancient Mesopotamia*, AMD 3 (Leiden: Brill/Styx, 2006), 183–184.

22 Scurlock, *Magico-Medical Means*, 198–199. For the edition, see ibid., 197–198. In line 1, I have altered Scurlock's "looses" to "loosens.".

had to reengage the god and convince it to forgive the human client and give up its anger. The Shadibba prayers exemplify such a situation.

Anger of the personal god

1 Incantation: My god, I did not know your punishment was (so) severe!
2 I repeatedly swore a solemn oath on your life in vain.
3 I repeatedly neglected your ordinances. I went too far.
4 I repeatedly skirted(?) your work in (times of) difficulty.
5 I repeatedly trespassed well beyond your boundary.
6 I did not know, I … in excess.
7 My sins are (so) many! I do not know what I did.
8 O my god, annul, release, relax the anger of your heart.
9 Disregard my transgressions, accept my prayer.
10 Turn my errors into virtues.
11 Your hand is (so) severe! I have experienced your punishment.
12 Let the one who does not revere his god and goddess learn from me.
13 My god, be at peace, my goddess, be reconciled.
14 Turn your faces toward (i.e., take notice of) the petition of my upraised hands.
15 Let your furious hearts calm down.
16 Let your feelings be soothed, grant me reconciliation,
17 (That) I may without forgetting constantly sing your praises to the widespread people.[23]

Anger of the personal god

18 Incantation: My god, my lord, who created my name,
19 Who guards my life, who creates my progeny,
20 O (my) furious god, let your furious heart calm down.
21 O (my) angry goddess, be at peace with me.

---

22 Who knows, O my god, your dwelling?

23 A. Lenzi, "Dingirshadibbas to Personal Deities," in *Reading Akkadian Prayers and Hymns: An Introduction*, ANEM 3 (Atlanta: Society of Biblical Literature, 2011), 443. For Lenzi's edition see ibid., 434–438. For an earlier edition, see W. G. Lambert, "Dingir.šà.dib. ba Incantations," *JNES* 33 (1974): 274–277: 23–39; for a more recent one, see M. Jaques, *Mon dieu qu'ai-je fait? Les diĝir-šà-dab*$_{(5)}$*-ba et la piété privée en Mésopotamie*, OBO 273 (Fribourg: Academic Press; Göttingen: Vandenhoeck & Ruprecht, 2015).

23 Your holy abode, your shrine I never saw.
24 Constantly I am despondent. My god, where are you?
25 Turn back your anger against me.
26 Turn your face toward the pure divine meal of choice oil,
27 That your lips may receive the goodness. Speak that I may prosper.
28 With your holy mouth speak (long) life!
29 Take me away from the evil that I may be rescued with you (i.e., under your protection).
30 Decree for me a destiny of (long) life!
31 Lengthen my days, give to me (long) life!

---

32 It is an incantation for appeasing the angry heart of a god.[24]

## 6.4 *Witches*

Therapeutic texts directed against witchcraft attribute misfortune and ill health to the machinations of people designated as witches and prescribe the means of combating the witch and witchcraft. They set out the various ceremonies, devices, and treatments that are to be used to dispel witchcraft, to destroy the witch (symbolically), and to protect and cure the patient. Personal distress ascribed to witchcraft includes the individual's experience of physical, psychological, and/or social difficulties.

Witchcraft in Mesopotamian sources normally refers to malevolent destructive magic performed usually, though not exclusively, by a human witch, *kaššāpu* (m.)/ *kaššāptu* (f.). These illegitimate practitioners of magic were motivated by malice and evil intent and used forms of destructive magic to harm other human beings. The belief in witchcraft reflected a feeling of human interdependence and a sense of vulnerability and was the personification of actual or perceived interhuman animosity and conflict. Although lists of witches include both male and female entries, the witch is usually depicted as a woman. The witch was able to control or harm her victim by means of indirect contact (reflecting the belief in the underlying principles of sympathetic magic [analogy and contiguity]): she could steal objects that had been in contact with and represented her victim, make an image in the likeness of her victim and then twist its limbs so that he suffered agony and debilitating disease, prepare figurines and bury them in holes in the wall or in the ground, feed statues to animals, or open up a grave and place the representation of

24 Lenzi, "Dingirshadibbas," 443–444. For Lenzi's edition, see ibid., 438–441. For an earlier edition, see Lambert, "Dingir.šà.dib.ba," 276–77: 40–54; for a more recent one, see Jaques, *Mon dieu qu'ai-je fait?*

her victim in the lap of a dead person, thus effecting a marriage of her victim and a corpse. Sometimes there was direct contact between victim and witch, for she was also said to cause her victim to incorporate witchcraft by means of food, drink, washing, and ointment; she was even described as one who could directly seize and harm the various parts of the victim's body, could even push, press, and strike his chest and back. In addition to such manipulations and activities, the witch could form an evil word in her heart and utter an incantation. She could even send signs that were thought to result in misfortune, evil omens that augured doom.

Though she had special powers, the witch was a human being, but as time went on she also developed a demonic form. Thus, eventually, the witch was also imagined as a demonic being who was even able to set other demons against her victim.

*Maqlû* III 1–16

1 Incantation. The witch, she who roams the streets,
2 Who continually intrudes into houses,
3 Who prowls in alleys,
4 Who spies about the broad ways—
5 She keeps turning around from front to back,
6 Standing, in the street she turns foot (progress) around,[25]
7 (And) in the broad way she cuts off (commercial) traffic.
8 She robbed the fine young man of his virility,
9 She carried off the attractiveness of the fine young woman,
10 With her malignant stare she took away her charms.
11 She looked at the young man and (thereby) robbed his vitality,
12 She looked at the young woman and (thereby) carried off her attractiveness.
13 The witch has seen me and has come after me,
14 With her venom, she *has* cut off (commercial) traffic,
15 With her spittle, she has cut off my trading,
16 She has driven away my god and goddess from my person.[26]

25 Lit., she turns (others') feet around.
26 Abusch, *Magical Ceremony "Maqlû,"* 305.

*Maqlû* II 183–204

183 Incantation. Whoever you are, O witch, who has taken out clay (for a figurine) of me from the river,
184 Buried my figurines in a dark house,
185 Buried my (funerary) water in a grave,
186 Collected my leavings from a garbage pit,
187 Cut off my hem in the house of a launderer,
188 Collected the dust from [my fe]et at the threshold.
189 I have sent to the gate of the quay—they have bought for me tallow (for) your (figurine),
190 I have sent to the city ditch—they have pinched off for me the clay (for) your (figurine).
191 I am sending against you a burning oven, flaring Girra,
192 Ever-renewing Girra, constant light of the gods,
193 [Sîn] from Ur, Šamaš from Larsa,
194 Nergal with his troops,
195 Ištar of Agade together with her sanctuary,
196 To collect the seed of my warlock and my witch, as much as there is.
197 May they kill the witch, but may I live,
198 Because I![27] have not performed sorcery against her, but she has performed sorcery against me,
199 Because I have not sought (to perform witchcraft against) her, but she has sought (to perform witchcraft against) me.
200 She relies on her scheming witchcraft,
201 But I (rely) on the con[stant] light <of the gods>, Girra, the Judge.
202 Girra, bur[n her, Gi]rra, scorch her,
203 Girra, vanquish her. TU$_6$.ÉN

---

204 It is the wording (of the incantation) to undo witchcraft: a figurine of clay mixed with tallow.[28]

## 6.5 *Evil Omens*

The Mesopotamians often understood present events and phenomena as signs of what might happen in the future. That is, they believed that ominous chains of events proceeded on predetermined courses to outcomes that could be predicted by the reading of signs in the present. (As in a mechanical

27 Text: she.
28 Abusch, *Magical Ceremony "Maqlû,"* 301–302.

universe, the sequence did not require a human or divine deed or intention for its inception, though it might have one.) Of course, the signs could augur either a good or a bad outcome. But since signs are to be understood less as unalterable predictions than as early manifestations of an ominous chain of events, an evil outcome could be changed either by divine decree and/or by a redirection of the chain of events. And this was the purpose of the nam.bur$_2$.bi rituals, an example of which is the following:

*Namburbi* no. 7, obv. 10–rev. 3

10 *Namburbi* for the evil of a dog which howls (and) moans in a man's house, or spatters its urine upon a man. Three times you recite (the incantation), then the evil of that dog will not approach the man and his house.

14 Its ritual: you make a clay image of a dog. You place cedar wood upon its neck. You sprinkle oil upon its head. You clothe it in goat's hair. You set horse bristles in its tail. At the river bank you set up a reed altar before Shamash. You arrange twelve emmer loaves. You heap up dates and fine flour. You set out confections of honey and ghee. You set up a jug, (and) fill two bottles with fine beer and set them out. You set out a censer of juniper. You libate fine beer. You have that man kneel and raise that figurine, and he recites as follows.

24 Incantation: Shamash, king of heaven (and) earth, judge of the upper and lower regions, light of the gods, governor of mankind, pronouncer of judgement on the great gods, I turn to you, seek you out. Among the gods, command that I live! May the gods who are with you command my prosperity! Because of this dog, which has voided its urine upon me, I am frightened, alarmed, and terrified. Avert from me the evil of this dog, that I may sing your praise!

34 When he has recited this before Shamash, you recite as follows over that figurine.

36 I have given you as a [replacemen]t for myself, I have given you as a substitute for myself. [I have stripped off all the evil] of my body upon you. I have stripped off, I have stripped off all the evil of my flesh upon you. I have stripped off all the evil of my figure upon you. I have stripped off all the evil before me and behind me upon you.[29]

29 Caplice, *Akkadian Namburbi Texts*, 17. For an edition, see R. I. Caplice, "Namburbi Texts in the British Museum II," *Or* NS 36 (1967): 2–3. For a more recent edition, see Maul, *Zukunftsbewältigung*, 314–318, and for a translation, ibid., 172.

### 6.6 *Oath/Curse*

The oath (*māmītu*) invoked a power and threatened a curse or a punishment authorized by the gods as well as by other powers of nature, society, and culture. The oath was meant to deter its subjects from breaking the terms of an agreement and was taken in support of and as a guarantee for a statement (an asseverative oath) or a promise (a promissory oath) made. By threatening to bring curses on those who do not fulfill the terms of the oath, the oath ensured that statements (or words of testimony) were true and guaranteed that promises (or words of agreement) were upheld. But humans make mistakes and cannot always live up to their promises. Moreover, one might not even realize that one had taken an oath either verbally or symbolically; and, in any case, supernatural powers may behave in unexpected ways.

*Šurpu* V–VI 1–16

1/2 An evil curse like a *gallû*-demon has come upon (this) man,
3/4 dumbness (and) daze have come upon him,
5/6 an unwholesome dumbness has come upon him,
7/8 evil curse, oath, headache.
9/10 An evil curse has slaughtered this man like a sheep,
11/12 his god left his body,
13/14 his goddess (Sumerian adds: his mother), usually full of concern for him, has stepped aside.
15/16 Dumbness (and) daze have covered him like a cloak and over whelm him incessantly.[30]

*Šurpu* V–VI 144–172

144/145 Incantion. [Uttu] took the thread into her [hand],
146/147 Ištar made the thread of [Uttu] ready,
148/149 made the skillful woman sit down to its tot (?);
150/151 she spun with a spindle white wool, bl[ack] wool, a double thread,
152/153 a mighty thread, a great thread, a multicolored thread, a thread that cuts the oath,
154/155 against the words of bad portent, an 'oath' (caused) by men,
156/157 against the curses of the gods,
158/159 a curse that cuts the oath;
160/161 she tied the head, the hands, the feet of this man,

30 E. Reiner, *Šurpu: A Collection of Sumerian and Akkadian Incantations*, AfO Beih. 11 (Graz: Im Selbstverlage des Herausgebers, 1958), 30, with edition.

162/163 so that Marduk, son of Eridu, the prince, could rip it off with his pure hands.
164/165 May he remove the thread (representing) the oath into the field, the pure place,
166/167 may the evil oath step aside,
168/169 may this man be purified, cleaned,
170/171 may he be entrusted into the propitious hands of his god.

---

172 Conjuration to undo the oath.[31]

## 6.7 *Sin*

The failure to perform a required deed, an incorrect performance thereof, or the performance of a prohibited act constituted a sin.[32] Certain infractions were treated as acts of sacrilege and taboo. Adherence to these rules was necessary for the maintenance of an orderly human and divine society. But, as already expressed in the prayers to the personal gods, people sin knowingly or unknowingly, by omission or by commission, and they deal with the consequences of sin by means of petition and magic.

*Lipšur* Litanies Type II 7′–22′

7′ may my sin rise skyward like smoke,
8′ may my sin recede like the water from my body,
9′ may my sin, like a drifting cloud, rain down into another field,
10′ may my sin be consumed like a flame,
11′ may my sin fly away like a flickering flame,
12′ may my sin be peeled off like an onion,
13′ may my sin be stripped off like dates,
14′ may my sin be unraveled like a matting,
15′ may my sin, like a potter's broken pot, never return to its former state,
16′ may my sin be shattered like a potsherd,
17′ may my sin, like silver and gold brought from its mine, never return to its home,

31 Reiner, *Šurpu*, 34–35, with edition.

32 For the sake of simplicity, I have treated "sin" and "oath/curse" separately. Note that they often occur alongside each other; this is not the place to try to define their relationship, but for the conjunction see K. van der Toorn, *Sin and Sanction in Israel and Mesopotamia: A Comparative Study*, SSN 22 (Assen: Van Gorcum, 1985), esp. 52–53, and J. Bottéro's study of *Šurpu* cited there: "Antiquités assyro-babyloniennes," in *École pratique des hautes études. $4^{e}$ section, Sciences historiques et philologiques. Annuaire 1976–1977* (Paris: La Sorbonne, 1977), 183 n. 158.

18′ may my sin, like meteoric (?) iron, never return to its home,
19′ may my sin, like fresh water, never return to its source,
20′ may my sin, like an uprooted tamarisk, never return to its place,
21′ may my sin, like falling rain, never return to its origin,
22′ may a bird take my sin up to the sky, may a fish take my sin down to the abyss![33]

*Lipšur* Litanies Type I 81–95

81 If So-and-so, son of So-and-so, has sinned, may he be absolved, may he be wiped clean;
82 if he was negligent, if he committed errors, same (= may he be absolved, may he be wiped clean); if he committed an assault,
83 if he committed murder, same (= may he be absolved, may he be wiped clean); if he ate unwittingly what is taboo to his god,
84 if he had intercourse with the priestess of his god, same (= may he be absolved, may he be wiped clean); if he had intercourse with the wife of his friend,
85 if his actions were displeasing to his god, same (= may he be absolved, may he be wiped clean); if he talked to an accursed man,
86 if he ate the food of an accursed man, if he drank the water of an accursed man,
87 if he drank the leftovers of an accursed man, if he talked to a sinner,
88 if he ate the food of a sinner, if he drank the water of a sinner, if he interceded for a sinner,
89 if he committed grievous sins, if he sinned against his father,
90 if he sinned against his mother, if he sinned against his god, if he sinned against his goddess,
91 if he swore (many) oaths, if he was ... by oaths,
92 if he swore by his god, if he brought up trifles before his god,
93 if he violated an interdict, if he brought his washwater before his god,
94 if he swore (friendship) to friend and companion, if he swore true and false oaths,
95 if he swore heavy and light oaths, if he swore aware of what he was doing or swore unwittingly.[34]

33 E. Reiner, "Lipšur Litanies," *JNES* 15 (1956): 141. For an edition, see ibid., 140. For a recent translation, see Foster, *Before the Muses*, 1004.

34 Reiner, "Lipšur Litanies," 137. For an edition, see ibid., 136. I have replaced Reiner's "NN" with "So-and-so."

In conclusion, I should emphasize that the study of Mesopotamian magical beliefs and rituals is more than just an exposition of esoterica. It is important not least because the relevant texts address physical, psychological, existential, and social difficulties that not infrequently formed the center of concern of Mesopotamian life. But in addition to shedding light on problems that the Mesopotamian shared with general humanity, with us, Mesopotamian magical beliefs and rituals are an integral part of the larger system of religious belief and of the broader cultural cosmology of that civilization and, thus, are a source of information regarding its history and culture.

In spite of the significant progress that has been made, the study of Mesopotamian magic is still very much in its infancy, and much remains to be done with respect to establishing the text corpus and to interpreting the texts. Many different approaches and foci will prove useful; based on their personal styles, scholars will pursue whatever attracts their interest.[35] I would draw attention to two modalities of study that I personally have found very important and useful: the search for literary, logical, and structural forms; and the reconstruction of textual and literary history (I include here also the study of redaction, revision, and transmission) based upon both manuscript evidence and internal critical analysis. But, more broadly, we have barely scraped the surface as regards the historical and cultural contexts of our materials; beyond enhancing our understanding of the magical materials, such studies would surely open new vistas, enrich our understanding of Mesopotamian society, religion, and thought, and enhance our attempts at reconstructing the history of that civilization.

## Bibliographical Essay

In the listing of readings for individual Mesopotamian texts and topics, this essay generally contains only recent treatments and thus omits some important older studies and editions.

### *Magic, in General*

In studying Mesopotamian magic, I have found it very useful to consult anthropological literature on magic as well as studies of European magic. I list here a few general studies and collections: A. F. C. Wallace, *Religion: An Anthropological View* (New York:

35 See, e.g., T. Abusch, "Alternative Models for the Development of Some Incantations," in *Sources of Evil: Studies in Mesopotamian Exorcistic Lore*, ed. G. Van Buylaere et al., AMD 15 (Leiden: Brill, 2018), 223–234 [[AMD 17, 146–156]].

Random House, 1966); D. L. O'Keefe, *Stolen Magic: The Social History of Magic* (New York: Random House, 1983); B. P. Levack, ed., *Anthropological Studies of Witchcraft, Magic, and Religion*, vol. 1 of *Articles on Witchcraft, Magic, and Demonology: A Twelve-Volume Anthology of Scholarly Articles* (New York: Garland, 1992); A. Glucklich, *The End of Magic* (New York: Oxford University Press, 1997); B. Ankerloo and S. Clark, eds., *Witchcraft and Magic in Europe*, 6 vols. (Philadelphia: University of Pennsylvania Press, 1999–2002).

### *Ancient Near Eastern Magical Thought*

For an understanding of the mentality or point of view of ancient Near Eastern magical thought, I recommend: H. Frankfort et al., *The Intellectual Adventure of Ancient Man: An Essay on Speculative Thought in the Ancient Near East*, rev. ed. (Chicago: University of Chicago Press, 1977); for Mesopotamia, see T. Jacobsen, "Mesopotamia: The Cosmos as a State," ibid., 125–219, especially his remarks on 130–135.

### *Magic in Mesopotamia*

There are a number of good overviews on and general studies of magic in Mesopotamia. The following are highly recommended: C. Fossey, *La magie assyrienne: Étude suivie de textes magiques transcrits, traduits, et commentés* (Paris: Ernest Leroux, 1902); R. C. Thompson, *Semitic Magic* (London: Luzac, 1908); W. Farber, "Witchcraft, Magic, and Divination in Ancient Mesopotamia," in *CANE* 3:1895–1909; E. Reiner, *Astral Magic in Babylonia*, TAPS NS 85/4 (Philadelphia: American Philosophical Society, 1995); G. Cunningham, *"Deliver Me From Evil": Mesopotamian Incantations, 2500–1500 BC*, StPohl, series maior 17 (Rome: Pontifico Istituto Biblico, 1997); T. Abusch and K. van der Toorn, eds., *Mesopotamian Magic: Textual, Historical, and Interpretive Perspectives*, AMD 1 (Groningen: Styx, 1999); van Binsbergen and Wiggerman, "Magic in History"; F. H. Cryer and M.-L. Thomsen, *Biblical and Pagan Societies*, vol. 1 of Ankerloo and Clark, *Witchcraft and Magic in Europe*; C. Jean, *La magie néo-assyrienne en contexte: Recherches sur le métier d'exorciste et le concept d'āšipūtu*, SAAS 17 (Helsinki: Neo-Assyrian Text Corpus Project, 2006); D. Schwemer, "Magic Rituals: Conceptualization and Performance," in *The Oxford Handbook of Cuneiform Culture*, ed. K. Radner and E. Robson (Oxford: Oxford University Press, 2011), 418–442.

### *Corpora of Magical Texts*

Mesopotamian magical literature may be divided into groups of texts that focus on different types of problems or evils (the divisions are already ancient). Studies that try to analyze and reconstruct the several corpora are:

**Demons:** Falkenstein, *Haupttypen*; F. A. M. Wiggermann, "Lamaštu, Daughter of Anu. A Profile," in *Birth in Babylonia and the Bible: Its Mediterranean Setting*, by M. Stol,

CM 14 (Groningen: Styx, 2000), 217–252; N. P. Heeßel, *Pazuzu: Archäologische und philologische Studien zu einem altorientalischen Dämon*, AMD 4 (Leiden: Brill/Styx, 2002); F. A. M. Wiggermann, "The Four Winds and the Origins of Pazuzu," in *Das geistige Erfassen der Welt im Alten Orient: Sprache, Religion, Kultur und Gesellschaft*, ed. C. Wilcke (Wiesbaden: Harrassowitz, 2007), 125–165; F. A. M. Wiggermann, "Some Demons of Time and Their Functions in Mesopotamian Iconography," in *Die Welt der Götterbilder*, ed. B. Groneberg and H. Spieckermann (Berlin: de Gruyter, 2007), 103–116; Farber, *Lamaštu*; E. Frahm, "A Tale of Two Lands and Two Thousand Years: The Origins of Pazuzu," in *Mesopotamian Medicine and Magic: Studies in Honor of Markham J. Geller*, ed. S. V. Panayotov and L. Vacín, AMD 14 (Leiden: Brill, 2018), 272–291.

**Witches:** T. Abusch, *Babylonian Witchcraft Literature*; T. Abusch, *Mesopotamian Witchcraft: Toward a History and Understanding of Babylonian Witchcraft Beliefs and Literature*, AMD 5 (Leiden: Brill/Styx, 2002); D. Schwemer, *Abwehrzauber und Behexung: Studien zum Schadenzauberglauben im alten Mesopotamien (Unter Benutzung von Tzvi Abuschs Kritischem Katalog und Sammlungen im Rahmen des Kooperationsprojektes Corpus of Mesopotamian Anti-witchcraft Rituals)* (Wiesbaden: Harrassowitz, 2007); T. Abusch et al., *Corpus of Mesopotamian Anti-witchcraft Rituals*, 3 vols., AMD 8/1–3 (Leiden: Brill, 2011–2019); D. Schwemer, "Evil Helpers: Instrumentalizing Agents of Evil in Anti-witchcraft Rituals," in Van Buylaere et al., *Sources of Evil*, 173–191.

**Sexual and Related Difficulties:** Biggs, *ŠÀ.ZI.GA*.

**Ghosts:** J. Bottéro, "Les morts et l'au-delà dans les rituels en accadien contre l'action des 'revenants,'" *ZA* 73 (1983): 153–203; Scurlock, *Magico-Medical Means*.

**Dreams:** A. L. Oppenheim, *The Interpretation of Dreams in the Ancient Near East. With a Translation of an Assyrian Dream-Book*, TAPS NS 46/3 (Philadelphia: American Philosophical Society, 1956); S. Butler, *Mesopotamian Conceptions of Dreams and Dream Rituals*, AOAT 258 (Münster: Ugarit-Verlag, 1998).

**Evil Omens:** Caplice, "Akkadian Text Genre Namburbi"; Caplice, *Akkadian Namburbi Texts*; Maul, *Zukunftsbewältigung*.

**General and Specific *šuillas*:** King, *Babylonian Magic and Sorcery*; Kunstmann, *Die babylonische Gebetsbeschwörung*; E. Ebeling, *Die akkadische Gebetsserie "Handerhebung" von neuem gesammelt und herausgegeben* (Berlin: Akademie-Verlag, 1953); W. Mayer, *Untersuchungen zur Formensprache der babylonischen "Gebetsbeschwörungen,"* StPohl, series maior 5 (Rome: Pontifical Biblical Institute, 1976); M.-J. Seux, *Hymnes et prières aux dieux de Babylonie et d'Assyrie*, LAPO 8 (Paris: Éditions du Cerf, 1976); O. Loretz and W. R. Mayer, *ŠU-ILA-Gebete: Supplement zu L. W. King, "Babylonian Magic and Sorcery,"* AOAT 34 (Kevalaer: Butzon & Bercker, 1978); W. R. Mayer, "Sechs Šu-ila-Gebete," *Or* NS 59 (1990): 449–490; W. R. Mayer, "Das Bussgebet an Marduk von BMS 11," *Or* NS 73 (2004): 198–214; A. Zgoll, *Die Kunst des Betens: Form und Funktion, Theologie und Psychagogik in babylonisch-assyrischen Handerhebungsgebeten zu Ištar*, AOAT 308 (Münster: Ugarit-Verlag, 2003); T. Abusch, "Prayers, Hymns, Incantations, and Curses:

Mesopotamia," in *Religions of the Ancient World: A Guide*, ed. S. I. Johnston (Cambridge, MA: Belknap Press of Harvard University Press, 2004), 353–355 [[111–117]]; C. Frechette, *Mesopotamian Ritual-prayers of "Hand-lifting" (Akkadian Šuillas): An Investigation of Function in Light of the Idiomatic Meaning of the Rubric*, AOAT 379 (Münster: Ugarit-Verlag, 2012); T. Abusch, "The Reconciliation of Angry Personal Gods: A Revision of the Šuillas," in "Approaching a Critique of Mesopotamian Reason," ed. G. Gabriel, special issue, *JANEH* 5 (2018): 57–85 [[176–205]].

**Other Incantations and Rituals:** Reiner, "Lipšur Litanies"; W. Farber, *Beschwörungsrituale an Ištar und Dumuzi: Attī Ištar ša Ḫarmaša Dumuzi* (Wiesbaden: Franz Steiner, 1977); A. Schuster-Brandis, *Steine als Schutz- und Heilmittel: Untersuchung zu ihrer Verwendung in der Beschwörungskunst Mesopotamiens im 1. Jt. v. Chr.*, AOAT 46 (Münster: Ugarit-Verlag, 2008).

### *Magical Series*

Although they are part of the corpora just detailed, one should pay particular attention to individual magical series and be mindful of their text editions. Here I will mention a few of the more important ones:

**Udug.hul:** M. J. Geller, *Forerunners to Udug-hul*, FAS 12 (Stuttgart: Franz Steiner Verlag Wiesbaden GMBH, 1985); M. J. Geller, *Evil Demons: Canonical* Utukkū Lemnūtu *Incantations*, SAACT 5 (Helsinki: Neo-Assyrian Text Corpus Project, 2007); Geller, *Healing Magic and Evil Demons.*

**Other Sumerian Incantation Series:** W. Schramm, *Bann, Bann! Eine Sumerisch-Akkadische Beschwörungsserie*, GAAL 2 (Göttingen: Seminar für Keilschriftforschung, 2001); W. Schramm, *Ein Compendium sumerisch-akkadischer Beschwörungen*, Göttinger Beiträge zum Alten Orient 2 (Göttingen: Universitätsverlag Göttingen, 2008).

***Maqlû*:** T. Abusch, "The Revision of Babylonian Anti-Witchcraft Incantations: The Critical Analysis of Incantations in the Ceremonial Series *Maqlû*," in *Continuity and Innovation in the Magical Tradition*, ed. G. Bohak et al., JSRC 15 (Leiden: Brill, 2011), 11–41 [[AMD 17, 51–80]]; T. Abusch, *The Witchcraft Series "Maqlû,"* WAW 37 (Atlanta: Society of Biblical Literature, 2015); Abusch, *Magical Ceremony "Maqlû"*; Abusch, "Alternative Models"; D. Schwemer, *The Anti-Witchcraft Ritual "Maqlû": The Cuneiform Sources of a Magic Ceremony from Ancient Mesopotamia* (Wiesbaden: Harrassowitz, 2017).

***Šurpu*:** Reiner, *Šurpu*; R. Borger, "*Šurpu* II, III, IV und VIII in 'Partitur,'" in *Wisdom, Gods and Literature: Studies in Assyriology in Honour of W. G. Lambert*, ed. A. R. George and I. L. Finkel (Winona Lake, IN: Eisenbrauns, 2000), 15–90; F. Simons, "Burn Your Way to Success: Studies in the Mesopotamian Ritual and Incantation Series *Šurpu*" (Ph.D. diss., University of Birmingham, 2017).

**Dingir Šà.dib.ba:** Lambert, "Dingir.šà.dib.ba Incantations"; Jaques, *Mon dieu qu'ai-je fait?*

***Bīt rimki***: J. Laessøe, *Studies on the Assyrian Ritual and Series "bît rimki"* (Copenhagen: Munksgaard, 1955); C. Ambos, "Rites of Passage in Ancient Mesopotamia: Changing Status by Moving Through Space: *Bīt rimki* and the Ritual of the Substitute King," in *Approaching Rituals in Ancient Cultures*, ed. C. Ambos and L. Verderame, *RSO* NS 86, Supplement 2 (Pisa: Fabrizio Serra, 2013), 39–54.

***Muššu'u***: B. Böck, *Das Handbuch Muššu'u "Einreibung": Eine Serie sumerischer und akkadischer Beschwörungen aus dem 1. Jt. vor Chr.*, BPOA 3 (Madrid: Consejo Superior de Investigaciones Científicas, 2007).

***Bīt salā' mê***: C. Ambos, *Der König im Gefängnis und das Neujahrsfest im Herbst: Mechanismen der Legitimation des babylonischen Herrschers im 1. Jahrtausend v. Chr. und ihre Geschichte* (Dresden: Islet, 2013).

***Lamaštu***: Farber, *Lamaštu*.

***Mīs Pî***: C. Walker and M. Dick, *The Induction of the Cult Image in Ancient Mesopotamia: The Mesopotamian "Mīs Pî" Ritual*, SAALT 1 (Helsinki: Neo-Assyrian Text Corpus Project, 2001).

### *Selected Topics*

But no less should one pay attention to the many good studies of individual topics related to the texts and text groups listed above. A few of those not mentioned thus far are:

**Catalogues**: M. J. Geller, "Incipits and Rubrics," in *Wisdom, Gods and Literature: Studies in Assyriology in Honour of W. G. Lambert*, ed. A. R. George and I. L. Finkel (Winona Lake, IN: Eisenbrauns, 2000), 225–258; Jean, *La magie néo-assyrienne en contexte*, 62–82; E. Frahm, "The Exorcist's Manual: Structure, Language, *Sitz im Leben*," in Van Buylaere et al., *Sources of Evil*, 9–47; U. Steinert, "Catalogues, Texts, and Specialists: Some Thoughts on the Aššur Medical Catalogue and Mesopotamian Healing Professions," in Van Buylaere et al., *Sources of Evil*, 48–132.

**Collections of Pre-First-Millennium BCE Incantations**: Cunningham, *"Deliver Me From Evil"*; N. Wasserman, *Akkadian Love Literature of the Third and Second Millennium BCE*, LAOS 4 (Wiesbaden: Harrassowitz, 2016); E. Zomer, *Corpus of Middle Babylonian and Middle Assyrian Incantations*, LAOS 9 (Wiesbaden: Harrassowitz, 2018).

**Curses, Sins, and Oaths:** van der Toorn, *Sin and Sanction*.

**Demons:** F. A. M. Wiggermann, *Mesopotamian Protective Spirits: The Ritual Texts*, CM 1 (Groningen: Styx, 1992); Wiggermann, "Lamaštu, Daughter of Anu"; F. A. M. Wiggermann, "The Mesopotamian Pandemonium. A Provisional Census," *SMSR* 77, no. 2 (2011): 298–322; K. van der Toorn, "The Theology of Demons in Mesopotamia and Israel. Popular Belief and Scholarly Speculation," in *Die Dämonen: Die Dämonologie der israelitisch-jüdischen und frühchristlichen Literatur im Kontext ihrer*

*Umwelt*, ed. A. Lange et al. (Tübingen: Mohr Siebeck, 2003), 61–83; A.-C. Rendu Loisel, "Gods, Demons, and Anger in the Akkadian Literature," *SMSR* 77, no. 2 (2011): 323–332.

**Divination:** A. L. Oppenheim, "Divination and Celestial Observation in the Last Assyrian Empire," *Centaurus* 14, no. 1 (1969): 97–135; S. M. Maul, *The Art of Divination in the Ancient Near East: Reading the Signs of Heaven and Earth*, trans. B. McNeil and A. J. Edmonds (Waco, TX: Baylor University Press, 2018).

**Evil Omens:** Caplice, "Akkadian Text Genre Namburbi"; S. M. Maul, "How the Babylonians Protected Themselves against Calamities Announced by Omens," in *Mesopotamian Magic: Textual, Historical, and Interpretive Perspectives*, ed. T. Abusch and K. van der Toorn, AMD 1 (Groningen: Styx, 1999), 123–129.

**Ghosts:** Bottéro, "Les morts"; J. Bottéro, *Mesopotamia: Writing, Reasoning, and the Gods* (Chicago: University of Chicago Press, 1992), 268–286; T. Abusch, "Ghost and God: Some Observations on a Babylonian Understanding of Human Nature," in *Self, Soul and Body in Religious Experience*, ed. A. I. Baumgarten et al., SHR 78 (Leiden: Brill, 1998), 363–383 [[67–86]]; D. Katz, *The Image of the Netherworld in the Sumerian Sources* (Bethesda, MD: CDL, 2003); M. Stol, "Ghosts at the Table," in *From the Four Corners of the Earth: Studies in Iconography and Cultures of the Ancient Near East in Honour of F. A. M. Wiggerman*, ed. D. Kertai and O. Nieuwenhuyse, AOAT 441 (Münster: Ugarit-Verlag, 2017), 259–281.

**The Human Being**: U. Steinert, *Aspekte des Menschseins im Alten Mesopotamien: Eine Studie zu Person und Identität im 2. und 1. Jt. v. Chr.*, CM 44 (Leiden: Brill, 2012).

**Intelligentsia and magic:** Oppenheim, *Ancient Mesopotamia*; Oppenheim, "Divination and Celestial Observation"; S. Parpola, *Letters from Assyrian Scholars to the Kings Esarhaddon and Assurbanipal*, 2 vols., AOAT 5/1–2 (Kevelaer: Butzon & Bercker; Neukirchen-Vluyn: Neukirchener Verlag, 1970–1983); N. P. Heeßel, "The Babylonian Physician Rabâ-ša-Marduk: Another Look at Physicians and Exorcists in the Ancient Near East," in *Advances in Mesopotamian Medicine from Hammurabi to Hippocrates*, ed. A. Attia and G. Buisson, CM 37 (Leiden: Brill, 2009), 13–28; Heeßel, "Neues von Esagil-kīn-apli."

**Medicine:** J. V. Kinnier Wilson, "An Introduction to Babylonian Psychiatry," in *Studies in Honor of Benno Landsberger on His Seventy-Fifth Birthday, April 21, 1965*, ed. H. G. Güterbock and T. Jacobsen, AS 16 (Chicago: University of Chicago Press, 1965), 289–298; J. V. Kinnier Wilson, "Mental Diseases of Ancient Mesopotamia," in *Diseases in Antiquity*, ed. D. Brothwell and A. T. Sandison (Springfield, IL: C. C. Thomas, 1967), 723–733; J. V. Kinnier Wilson, "Organic Diseases of Ancient Mesopotamia," in ibid., 191–208; E. K. Ritter, "Magical-Expert (= *āšipu*) and Physician (= *asû*): Notes on Two Complementary Professions in Babylonian Medicine," in *Studies in Honor of Benno Landsberger on His Seventy-fifth Birthday, April 21, 1965*, ed. H. G. Güterbock and T. Jacobsen, AS 16 (Chicago: University of Chicago Press, 1965), 299–321; R. D. Biggs,

"Medizin. A. In Mesopotamien," *RlA* 7 (1987–1990): 623–629; M. Stol, *Epilepsy in Babylonia*, CM 2 (Groningen: Styx, 1993); T. Abusch, "Illnesses and Other Crises: Mesopotamia," in Johnston, *Religions of the Ancient World*, 456–459 [[AMD 17, 203–208]]; J. Scurlock and B. R. Andersen, *Diagnoses in Assyrian and Babylonian Medicine: Ancient Sources, Translations, and Modern Medical Analyses* (Urbana: University of Illinois Press, 2005); M. J. Geller, *Ancient Babylonian Medicine: Theory and Practice* (Chichester: Wiley-Blackwell, 2010); J. Scurlock, *Sourcebook for Ancient Mesopotamian Medicine*, WAW 36 (Atlanta: SBL Press, 2014).

**Prayers:** T. Abusch, "The Form and Meaning of a Babylonian Prayer to Marduk," *JAOS* 103 (1983): 3–15 [[126–148]]; Zgoll, *Die Kunst des Betens*; A. Lenzi, ed., *Reading Akkadian Prayers and Hymns: An Introduction*, ANEM 3 (Atlanta: Society of Biblical Literature, 2011); A. Lenzi, "Invoking the God: Interpreting Invocations in Mesopotamian Prayers and Biblical Laments of the Individual," *JBL* 129 (2010): 303–315; A. Lenzi, "Scribal Revision and Textual Variation in Akkadian *Šuila*-prayers: Two Case Studies in Ritual Adaptation," in *Empirical Models Challenging Biblical Criticism*, ed. R. F. Person and R. Rezetko, AIL 25 (Atlanta: SBL Press, 2016), 63–108; T. Abusch, "A Paean and Petition to a God of Death: Some Comments on a *Šuilla* to Nergal," in *From the Four Corners of the Earth: Studies in Iconography and Cultures of the Ancient Near East in Honour of F. A. M. Wiggermann*, ed. D. Kertai and O. Nieuwenhuyse, AOAT 441 (Münster: Ugarit-Verlag, 2017), 15–28 [[163–175]]; T. Abusch, "The Form and History of a Babylonian Prayer to Nabû," in *"The Scaffolding of Our Thoughts": Essays on Assyriology and the History of Science in Honor of Francesca Rochberg*, ed. C. Jay Crisostomo et al., AMD 13 (Leiden: Brill, 2018), 169–182 [[149–162]].

**Tutelary (Personal) Gods:** Jacobsen, "Mesopotamia," 212–216; T. Jacobsen, *The Treasures of Darkness: A History of Mesopotamian Religion* (New Haven: Yale University Press, 1976), 152–164; Oppenheim, *Ancient Mesopotamia*, 198–206; J. Klein, "'Personal God' and Individual Prayer in Sumerian Religion," in *Vorträge gehalten auf der 28. Rencontre Assyriologique Internationale in Wien 6.–10. Juli 1981*, AfO Beih. 19 (Horn: Berger, 1982), 295–306; K. van der Toorn, *Family Religion in Babylonia, Syria, and Israel: Continuity and Change in the Forms of Religious Life*, SHCANE 7 (Leiden: Brill, 1996), 66–93; Abusch, "Ghost and God," 378–383 [[81–86]]; Abusch, *Mesopotamian Witchcraft*, 48–50.

**Witches:** S. Rollin, "Women and Witchcraft in Ancient Assyria," in *Images of Women in Antiquity*, ed. A. Cameron and A. Kuhrt (Detroit: Wayne State University Press, 1983), 34–45; M.-L. Thomsen, *Zauberdiagnose und schwarze Magie in Mesopotamien*, CNIP 2 (Copenhagen: Museum Tusculanum Press, 1987); D. Schwemer, "'Forerunners' of *Maqlû*: A New *Maqlû*-Related Fragment from Assur," in *Gazing on the Deep: Ancient Near Eastern and Other Studies in Honor of Tzvi Abusch*, ed. J. Stackert et al. (Bethesda, MD: CDL, 2010), 201–220; Schwemer, "Evil Helpers."

**Women:** Stol, *Birth in Babylonia and the Bible*; U. Steinert, "K. 263+10934, A Tablet with Recipes against the Abnormal Flow of a Woman's Blood," *Sudhoff's Archive* 96 (2012): 64–94; U. Steinert, "Fluids, Rivers, and Vessels: Metaphors and Body Concepts in Mesopotamian Gynaecological Texts," *JMC* 22 (2013): 1–23.

CHAPTER 3

# Sacrifice in Mesopotamia

This paper treats the topic of sacrifice in Mesopotamia. It focuses on sacrifice as it was performed in the public or temple realm and places the topic in a broad Mesopotamian context. The paper is divided into two sections—one informational, the other argumentative. In the informational section, I have presented a synthesis of our general understanding of the topic. In the argumentative section, I take up one theme and develop it.[1]

## 1 Mesopotamian Sacrifice: A Description

When we think of sacrifice we tend to think of slaughtering animals or consuming an offering by means of fire. But we must imagine sacrifice a bit differently when we approach the topic in Mesopotamia. For our Mesopotamian religious sources emphasize neither the slaughter of animals nor the process of consumption. Rather, they usually focus on presentation. To understand the Mesopotamian view of sacrifice, it is important that we constantly keep this perspective in mind.

Before approaching the topic of sacrifice, however, we do well to understand the Mesopotamian and, in particular, the Sumerian view of human life, the gods, and the city.[2]

1 This essay is a slightly revised version of the first part of the presentation on sacrifice in Mesopotamia that I delivered in Israel in February 1998 at the conference "Sacrifice: A Comparative Inquiry," sponsored by the Jacob Taubes Minerva Center of Bar Ilan University. (The second part dealt with sacrifice in the private realm.) I am grateful to the Center and its director Prof. A. I. Baumgarten for the invitation and for their kind hospitality on that occasion. The explanation of the difference between Israel and Mesopotamia as regards the use of blood in the sacrificial cult also formed part of an invited address, "Blood in Mesopotamia and Israel" [[299–307]], delivered later that spring at the session "Cult in the Temple: Blood" during a conference sponsored by the Center for Judaic Studies of the University of Pennsylvania. I wish to thank Kathryn Kravitz for her helpful comments on this paper and to express my gratitude to Lucio Milano and Marcel Sigrist, with whom I enjoyed conversations on the topic of sacrifice in Mesopotamia while preparing the conference version of this paper.

2 In this context, I should mention that my understanding of early Mesopotamian religious history follows in the tradition of several scholars, most notably that of my teacher Thorkild Jacobsen; see especially T. Jacobsen, *The Treasures of Darkness: A History of Mesopotamian Religion* (New Haven: Yale University Press, 1976). On the topic of temple and sacrifice

 | DOI:10.1163/9789004435186_004

The purpose of human life, the purpose of the community, was to serve the gods, to provide them with whatever care a powerful ruling class, a landed aristocracy, would require. Paramount among these needs are shelter and food. But this represents the developed or classical form of theology and was probably not the original ideology or theology of god and temple. For in the earliest periods, the divine powers were forces of nature, powers experienced in those natural phenomena that were of importance for the survival and growth of the settlers and settlements. In the main, in these early periods, the gods were not human in form.

Gods were linked to specific settlements, and the two, god and settlement, developed together. During the Ubaid period, that is down till the end of the fifth millennium BCE, we have indications of cult places evolving in the midst of developing villages and towns. It is probable that these cult places served as storehouses for the community and focal points for rituals directed to the aforementioned powers of nature, rituals of thanks and rituals of revitalization.

As noted, the gods in this period probably had not yet attained a predominantly human physical and social form. Upon these forces of nature the original settlements had depended for their sustenance. The goal of the earlier ritual was to keep these forces present, vital, and productive. And the cult place would have served as the place where the rites centering upon these forces were carried out. Some of these rites involved the bringing of offerings by the community as expressions of thanks, and perhaps even to allay communal guilt; others took the form of agricultural, magical rituals and served to revitalize nature. Here I have in mind rites that later became rites of offering and rites of the *hieros gamos* (sacred marriage).

But eventually, the powers in natural phenomena were anthropomorphized as the masters of the city, the ones who gave sustenance and care to the city and upon whom the city depended. The form of their presence was that of a lord in his home. Certainly by the beginning of the third millennium, the characteristic and defining forms of classical Mesopotamian theology had emerged. This new ideology was part of the evolution of early civilization and of the development of hierarchical structures within the cities. Naturalistic gods were now seen as manorial lords, as the divine equivalents to the newly emerging human

in Mesopotamia, see, e.g., W. G. Lambert, "Donations of Food and Drink to the Gods in Ancient Mesopotamia," in *Ritual and Sacrifice in the Ancient Near East: Proceedings of the International Conference Organized by the Katholieke Universiteit Leuven from the 17th to the 20th of April 1991*, ed. J. Quaegebeur (Leuven: Peeters, 1993), 191–201; M. Roaf, "Palaces and Temples in Ancient Mesopotamia," in *CANE* 1:423–441; F. A. M. Wiggermann, "Theologies, Priests, and Worship in Ancient Mesopotamia," in *CANE* 3:1857–1870.

chieftains and kings.[3] Along with a human form, the gods were given families and households. Most important, their homes were now seen as manors or palaces, that is, the temples were now treated as the divine equivalent of the human ruler's abode. Hence, older cultic centers now became the classic Mesopotamian temples in which the god and his family were treated by his subjects as the ruling class of the city.

In Mesopotamia, then, by the third millennium the temple had evolved into the god's home. It was believed that the god had built the city for his or her own residence and sustenance. The god was now regarded as the primary owner of the city, and the city existed in order to support his or her needs. Thus, the temple was not simply a dwelling place to which a god repaired occasionally, but rather a permanent home in which the god and his family lived continually.

For its part, the city was required to care for these anthropomorphized deities. A classical expression of this human responsibility to the gods is found in the *Atraḫasīs* myth. The myth is made up of two originally separate parts; each part was an independent solution to the problem of the role of humans in the world. Originally, the gods created cities and lived there by themselves. Because humans had not yet been created, the gods themselves were required to do all the work necessary for their own survival. Not surprisingly, they found the labor of maintaining the cities and of producing and preparing food wearisome and burdensome. The worker gods rebelled and threw down their tools. As a solution, humanity was created from clay mixed with the blood and flesh of the leader of the rebellion in order to work and care for the gods. Man now produced food for the gods, but, as we learn in the second part, humans also reproduced and created a disturbance in the world. After trying unsuccessfully to decimate humanity, the great god Enlil finally decided to exterminate them by means of a flood. As a consequence, the gods suffered from starvation, for there was no one to provide food for them. One man, Atraḫasīs by name, was saved. After the flood he sacrificed food to the gods on the mountain on which his ark had landed. This mountain becomes a new exemplar of the temple.[4] The gods were delighted with the offering, and their hunger was sated. Now, a new cosmic order was permanently instituted. The gods realized their folly

3 We imagine that this development took place in the early third millennium partly because this is the time when a prominent human ruling class with its own special domiciles emerges, and partly because the evidence suggests that it was only then that the gods attained full human form. Prior to the Early Dynastic II period (ca. 2700–2600 BCE), there seem to be no unambiguous anthropomorphic representations of deities. It is from this period onward that in visual representations, deities in human form were distinguished from mortals by being shown wearing special headgear with horns.

4 So I understand *ziqqurrat šadê* in the Epic of Gilgamesh XI 156.

and recognized their need for human beings. Humanity would never again be destroyed and would permanently provide food for the gods in the form of offerings.

In the course of time, then, the nature of the temple and cult changed. There was a shift of emphasis from storage to presentation. The original temples may have served as communal storehouses. The economic function was never lost and temples developed many rooms and buildings that served for production, storage, and distribution. But the central rooms of the temple were the god's cella, and the development that we have noted of the temple from a locus for natural power to an abode for a divine ruler is evident, for example, in the addition of a reception room to the cella.

The earlier communal festivals which derived from magical rites for prosperity remained important for the cult. But here I shall take further note only of the daily service of the god. The god sat in his cella in the form of a divine statue made of wood overlaid with precious materials and valuable garments. The statue was both alive and holy, having attained identity with a god by means of the ritual of the washing of the mouth. Each day the god and his family were awakened, bathed, clothed, fed, and entertained. We learn from temple ritual texts[5] that there were two main meals during the day, one in the morning and one in the evening, and each of these meals was divided into a lesser and greater course. These meals included beer, wine, cereals, loaves of bread, cakes, meat, etc.

Libations seem to have been poured out. Food was treated differently; after being placed on the god's table and somehow magically eaten by the god, it was distributed to the temple personnel and to the king. This was not the only food slaughtered and prepared in the temple. The temple was a major storehouse and economic center, and therein took place the secular preparation and butchering of food for distribution to those who were temple dependents.[6]

The central act of the daily cult is not sacrifice in the sense of giving the food over to a fire which consumes it, nor is it acts of slaughter and the pouring out of blood. Food was placed before the god and consumed by him through that mysterious act that characterizes Babylonian religiosity. As A. Leo Oppenheim noted,

5 This regime is nicely illustrated by first-millennium BCE ritual texts from Uruk; see, e.g., A. Sachs, "Daily Sacrifices to the Gods of the City of Uruk," in *ANET*, 343–345.

6 Animals were slaughtered also for other reasons. Here mention should be made, for example, of extispicy; in this classical form of Babylonian divination, sheep were slaughtered so that their innards could be inspected in order to determine the will of the gods.

> Looking at the sacrifice from the religious point of view, we find coming into focus another critical point in that circulatory system, the consumption of the sacrificial repast by the deity, the transubstantiation of the physical offerings into that source of strength and power the deity was thought to need for effective functioning. Exactly as, in the existence of the image, the critical point was its physical manufacture, so was the act of consumption of food in the sacrificial repast. It represents the central *mysterium* that provided the effective *ratio essendi* for the cult practice of the daily meals and all that it entailed in economic, social, and political respects.[7]

The act of killing the animal is almost hidden behind the construct of feeding the god, a construct which emerges out of a combination of the earlier function of the temple as a place of offering and storage and the later image of feeding a divine king in his palace.

The temple is the center of an urban world. The temple and the feeding and care of its gods define the primary community of the dwellers in the land between the two rivers. To serve the god by supporting and participating in the economy of the temple constitutes the mark of membership in the urban community, a community which thus replaces or, at least, overshadows membership in one or another kinship community such as the family or clan.

## 2 Blood in Mesopotamia and West Asia: A Hypothesis

I turn now to a phenomenon that has been previously noticed but not explained. It is not my intention to propose definitive answers, but, rather, to suggest a tentative hypothesis that will surely require further testing and modification. It has been noted, again by Oppenheim, that a "difference that separates the sacrificial rituals in the two cultures [scil. Mesopotamia and the West, represented best by the Old Testament] is the 'blood consciousness' of the West, its awareness of the magic power of blood, which is not paralleled in Mesopotamia."[8]

7 A. L. Oppenheim, *Ancient Mesopotamia: Portrait of a Dead Civilization*, rev. ed. (Chicago: University of Chicago Press, 1977), 191.

8 Oppenheim, *Ancient Mesopotamia*, 192. In his discussion of the "deep-seated differences between the West—represented best by the Old Testament—and Mesopotamia with regard to the concept of the sacrifice," Oppenheim notes that in addition to blood, "The Old Testament concept is best expressed by the burning of the offered food, a practice which had the purpose of transforming it from one dimension—that of physical existence—into another, in

This observation seems to be correct so far as the major urban temples are concerned. And yet one can find an important place where blood does play a role in Mesopotamia, and this place may provide a clue to the significance of the emphasis on blood in the Semitic West and its apparent absence in Mesopotamia. Actually, this can be found, I think, in texts that tell the story of the creation of man for the service of the gods. For example, in the *Atraḫasīs* myth, discussed earlier, the god who led the rebellion was slaughtered and his flesh and blood mixed together with clay in order to create the human creature necessary for the welfare of the gods. The use of flesh and blood in addition to clay in the formation of humanity represents a *novum*. The flesh and blood are actually unnecessary, for the original model for the creation of humanity in this mythological tradition is that of a potter who creates statues by forming them out of wet clay. In fact, we even possess a Sumerian myth, "Enki and Ninmah," which describes the discontent of the divine workers and the subsequent creation of human beings from clay.[9] The killing of the god and the use of his flesh and blood to create humanity are an intrusion into the Mesopotamian system of thought, an intrusion which affects two major early Mesopotamian mythological traditions, those of Eridu and Nippur. Hence, gods are killed in order to create human beings not only in *Atraḫasīs* and texts related to it, like *Enūma eliš*, but also in KAR 4, which belongs to the Nippur text-tradition.

In the new construct, the clay still serves to form the physical person, while the flesh and blood of the slaughtered god add qualities to the clay and to the human that is created therefrom. The addition of the flesh and blood reflects a new point of view. While the flesh is the source of the human ghost, the blood,

which the food became assimilable by the deity through its scent" (192). Oppenheim also notes that, "There is no trace in Mesopotamia of that *communio* between the deity and its worshippers that finds expression in the several forms of commensality observed in the sacrificial practices of circum-Mediterranean civilizations, as shown by the Old Testament in certain early instances and observed in Hittite and Greek customs" (191). These observations support the explanation presented in this paper for the presence of blood-consciousness in the West and its general absence in the Mesopotamian temple cult.

9 But see now W. G. Lambert, "The Relationship of Sumerian and Babylonian Myth as Seen in Accounts of Creation," in *La circulation des biens, des personnes et des idées dans le Proche-Orient ancien, XXXVIII^e R.A.I.*, ed. D. Charpin and F. Joannès (Paris: Éditions Recherche sur les Civilisations, 1992), 129–135. Basing himself upon a bilingual version of "Enki and Ninmah," Lambert argues that Enki created man by mixing clay and blood. If Lambert's understanding also applied to the original Sumerian text, the episode in "Enki and Ninmah" might then represent an earlier example of the mixing of blood and clay; however, if "Enki and Ninmah" is dependent upon *Atraḫasīs*, as has also been suggested, the occurrence of blood in "Enki and Ninmah" may be no more than a carryover from *Atraḫasīs*.

as I have argued elsewhere,[10] is the origin of an ability to plan, that is, of human intelligence, and is, ultimately, the source and etiology of the personal god or, rather, the family god who is passed down from generation to generation by the male progenitor. The personal god is not simply the god of an isolated individual; rather, he is the god of the individual as a social being. He is both the divine personification of individual procreation and achievement and the god of the family or tribal group.[11] It is the god of the family who finds expression first of all in the act of reproduction, an act basic to the continuation of the god's group. The god is the blood, or is in the blood, and his transmission from father to son creates a relationship of kinship between generations of men by the emphasis on the tie of blood.

This intrusion into the Mesopotamian mythological tradition and into its understanding of the nature of humanity is probably due to Western Semitic influences.[12] The killing of a god seems to be depicted already on seals dating to the Old Akkadian period;[13] but it entered the literary tradition in the Old Babylonian Period possibly as a consequence of the settlement of the tribal Amorites in Mesopotamia. Certainly, the family god, a god represented by blood, was important for the Western Semites; it is they who created and cemented alliances by means of the bloody splitting of animals and to whom we owe the image of divine blood in the *Atraḫasīs* epic.

Turning back to sacrifice, let me generalize in an attempt to formulate a possible solution to our problem. Sacrifice may serve to maintain a group that is drawn together by, or whose identity is based on, some common characteristic. One may consider the possibility that those systems of sacrifice that emphasize blood serve to maintain family groups, groups which are organized

---

10 T. Abusch, "Ghost and God: Some Observations on a Babylonian Understanding of Human Nature," in *Self, Soul and Body in Religious Experience*, ed. A. I. Baumgarten et al., SHR 78 (Leiden: Brill, 1998), 363–383 [[67–86]].

11 For my understanding of the personal god, see T. Abusch, "Ghost and God," 378–383 [[81–86]], and T. Abusch, "Witchcraft and the Anger of the Personal God," in *Mesopotamian Magic: Textual, Historical, and Interpretive Perspectives*, ed. T. Abusch and K. van der Toorn, AMD 1 (Groningen: Styx, 1999), 105–107, 109–110 [[AMD 5, 48–50, 52–53]], as well as the literature cited in "Ghost and God," 379 n. 35 [[82 n. 35]], and "Witchcraft and Anger," 106 n. 62 [[AMD 5, 49 n. 62]].

12 Cf. also T. Frymer-Kensky, "The Atrahasis Epic and Its Significance for Our Understanding of Genesis 1–9," *BA* 40 (1977): 155, where Frymer-Kensky suggests that "Considering the special notion of blood that we find in the Bible, it seems likely that the blood motif in Atrahasis and in Enuma Elish may be a West Semitic idea, and may have entered Mesopotamian mythology with the coming of the West Semites."

13 See F. A. M. Wiggermann, "Discussion," in E. Porada, *Man and Images in the Ancient Near East*, Anshen Transdisciplinary Lectureships in Art, Science, and the Philosophy of Culture 4 (Wakefield, RI: Moyer Bell, 1995), 78–79.

along common blood lines that are usually, though not necessarily, tribal and patrilineal. That is, blood sacrifice maintains a relationship of kinship between men by the emphasis on a tie of blood and would agree with the emphasis on blood in a clan context.[14]

This function of sacrifice surely applies to the tribal shepherds and herdsmen who spread out over the ancient Near East and entered Palestine and Mesopotamia during the middle and late Bronze Age and who were primarily organized according to family and clan. Accordingly, we may suggest that the importance of blood in the West reflects the fact that an important element in Israelite (as well as in Hittite and Greek) society derived from a semi-nomadic element which defined itself in tribal terms. And it is significant, moreover, that the livelihood of this group was involved in the flesh and blood of animals of the herd. Moreover, at least in the case of the Israelites, this semi-nomadic element saw itself as different from the indigenous, autochthonous element of the population and tried to maintain that separateness by means of blood rituals.

For the Semites, then, it was the family, the tribe, and the wider tribal territory that defined identity and power. This remained true even of the Semites of northern Babylonia and northeastern Syria. For while they absorbed the culture of the urban Mesopotamians of the south, they did not fully give up their own identities; rather, they transformed the culture that they had assimilated, introducing new images into it that were consonant with their own background and social situation—images such as the image of blood that they introduced into the Mesopotamian mythological tradition of the creation of man.

14 I owe some of my understanding of blood sacrifice to the recent work of Nancy Jay, *Throughout Your Generations Forever: Sacrifice, Religion, and Paternity* (Chicago: University of Chicago Press, 1992). Among other things, she develops and modifies some of the insights of W. Robertson Smith along lines suggested by modern gender studies. According to Jay, "sacrifice is at home in societies where families are integrated into extended kin groups of various kinds" (so K. E. Fields in her foreword to the book, p. xxiv). Jay notes that while sacrifice may serve to define both matrilineal and patrilineal descent systems, it is especially prevalent and significant in patrilineal societies, where "sacrificing orders relations within and between lines of human fathers and sons, between men and men, at least as effectively as it does relations between men and their divinities" (34). Sacrifice establishes blood ties among men that supersede the natural blood ties produced through women's childbirth (cf. pp. 30–40). Jay does not distinguish between animal sacrifice that emphasizes blood and animal sacrifice that does not; that distinction is mine, as are my application of some of her gender-based insights to the tribal Semites (but not to the urban Mesopotamians) and my attempt to explain Western blood consciousness thereby.

But the image of blood could not dominate the Mesopotamian cultic landscape, whose form was and remained fundamentally urban. For the classical Mesopotamian city defined itself not as a community of kinsmen, but rather as a community of service which had grown out of and around a female center, the fertility of the earth. Its admission rules were based on a willingness to serve the city god, not on family ties. In Mesopotamia, the basic form was created in Sumer: that society seems to have descended directly from the Neolithic villages of the same area where the Sumerians lived in historical times, and saw itself as indigenous to the land. Hence, the central forms of the Mesopotamian temple had little use for blood.[15]

It is in the context, then, of a contrast between kin-based and temple-based communities that we should view the blood-consciousness in the Israelite cult and its apparent absence in the Mesopotamian temple.

15 The fact that, in contrast to the tribal world, the distribution and consumption of meat in these cities were several steps removed from the process of slaughter undoubtedly contributed to the relative unimportance of blood in the Mesopotamian sacrificial cult.

# *Ghosts and Gods*

CHAPTER 4

# Ghost and God: Some Observations on a Babylonian Understanding of Human Nature

In the present essay, I shall take up some questions associated with the understanding of body, soul, and self in ancient Mesopotamia.[1] I shall do so first by examining a specific formulation of the Babylonian understanding of the nature of man, and then by exploring some relevant issues according to categories suggested by the text itself. The text that I propose to start from is a mythological passage that deals with the creation and composition of man. The passage will be seen to focus on two components: flesh and intellect; these constitute, respectively, the ghost and god of the individual human being. I shall then take up each of the components in turn: (1) Having noticed that in the aforementioned text, man's ghost derives from the flesh of the god, we will turn our attention to rituals that treat the end of human life and comment on the nature of the ghost and the treatment of the corpse. It should come as no surprise that we will notice some relationship between birth and death, between myths of creation and rituals of death. (2) And having observed, moreover, that the god from whom man is created possessed intelligence, we will suggest a connection between this intelligence and everyman's personal god and thereby try to understand something about Mesopotamian psychology.

Some of what I will say has already been noticed by others, but I hope here and there to have added something new to the mix. Still I must emphasize that some of my observations are speculative and provisional and that the treatment as a whole should be regarded as a work in progress, a work stimulated by the challenge of the conference theme: Body, Soul, and Self in Religious Experience.

1 Some of the ideas in this paper were worked out, and a draft written for the conference "Self, Soul and Body in Religious Experience," held in Israel in February 1995, while I was a Fellow of the Netherlands Institute for Advanced Study in the Humanities and Social Sciences during the academic year 1994–1995. I should like to thank Shaul Shaked, Karel van der Toorn, and especially Frans Wiggermann for discussing the topic with me while I was preparing that draft, and the whole NIAS research theme group "Magic and Religion in the Ancient Near East" for discussing the draft subsequent to its presentation in Israel. I wish also to thank Ra'anan Abusch, Stephen A. Geller, Laurie Pearce, and especially Kathryn Kravitz for critiquing drafts of this paper. I am grateful to the conference organizers for the opportunity to take up the problem, and to the staff of NIAS for the wonderful working conditions that allowed me to write this essay.

 | DOI:10.1163/9789004435186_005

## 1 Mythological Formulation

We turn now to the account of the creation of human beings found in the mythological story of Atraḫasīs, the Babylonian Noah. The *Atraḫasīs* narrative was probably composed during the Old Babylonian period (ca. 2000–1600 BCE). In any case, the oldest version of the text is preserved in a copy that dates to that period; more precisely, it was found at Sippar and is dated to the reign of Ammiṣaduqa, a seventeenth-century BCE monarch of Babylon.[2]

The *Atraḫasīs* myth deals with the human order, with problems of human reproduction and death. It tells of the creation of humans, but it also recounts how the Flood came about because the newly created human population had increased without limits because death due to illness and old age did not yet exist; subsequent to the Flood, the gods deal with the problem in a more permanent manner: they curtail human reproduction and mark a normal limit to the days of human life. This myth preserves ancient traditions while also presenting an individual articulation of Mesopotamian theology and anthropology.

The myth recounts that before the creation of man, the gods were men; more precisely, they possessed human and divine characteristics and functions. The mass of gods served as workers for and servants to the few. The mass of gods dug and maintained the irrigation canals that, on the human plane, made Mesopotamia a wealthy country and the cradle of civilization. The very tasks that the gods performed were those that human beings actually performed in order to maintain the human community and to uphold the temple regime. The work was onerous and the mass of gods, the workers, rebelled, refused to continue working, and went out on strike. The social and natural order was threatened. Finally, a solution was worked out, namely, to kill the god who had led the rebellion and to create humanity from his body in order to provide a source of labor that would free the gods from their toil.

Let us now examine portions of the passage (I 192–230) that tells of the killing of the god and the creation of humanity.[3]

---

2 For editions of *Atraḫasīs*, see W. G. Lambert and A. R. Millard, *Atra-ḫasīs: The Babylonian Story of the Flood* (Oxford: Clarendon, 1969), and W. von Soden, "Die erste Tafel des altbabylonischen Atramḫasīs-Mythus. 'Haupttext' und Parallelversionen," *ZA* 68 (1978): 50–94. For translations, see also S. Dalley, *Myths from Mesopotamia: Creation, The Flood, Gilgamesh, and Others*, rev. ed. (Oxford: Oxford University Press, 2000), 1–38; B. R. Foster, *Before the Muses: An Anthology of Akkadian Literature*, 3rd ed. (Bethesda, MD: CDL, 2005), 227–280, with bibliography on 278; and W. von Soden, "Der altbabylonische Atramchasis-Mythos," in K. Hecker et al., *Mythen und Epen II*, ed. O. Kaiser, TUAT NF 3/4 (Gütersloh: Gütersloher Verlagshaus, 1994), 612–645. See now also A. R. George, *Babylonian Literary Texts in the Schøyen Collection*, CUSAS 10 (Bethesda, MD: CDL, 2019), 16–27.

3 For the text, see Lambert and Millard, *Atra-ḫasīs*, 56–59; for recent translations, see Foster, *Before the Muses*, 235–236, and S. A. Geller, "Some Sound and Word Plays in the First Tablet of

They summoned and asked the goddess,
The midwife of the gods, wise Mami:
"You are the womb-goddess, (to be the) creator of mankind!
195 Create a human being that he may bear the yoke!
Let him bear the yoke, the work of Enlil,
Let man assume the load of the god!"
Nintu made her voice heard
And spoke to the great gods:
200 "By me alone he cannot be fashioned.
Only together with Enki can the task be done;
He alone makes everything pure!
Let him give me the clay that I may do the task."
Enki made his voice heard
205 And spoke to the great gods:
"……………………
……………………
Let the leader-god[4] be slaughtered,
……………………
210 With his flesh and his blood
Let Nintu mix clay
That both the god himself and man
May be mixed together in the clay.
214 For all days to come let us hear the drum [= heart(beat)],
215 From[5] the god's flesh let there be a ghost,[6]
216 To the living creature, let it make known its sign,
217 That there be no forgetting let there be a ghost."
(They) answered "yes" in the assembly
219 The great Anunnaki,
220 who assign the fates.
……………………
……………………
$^{d}$We-ila (or We, the god) who has Intelligence
They slaughtered in their assembly.
225 With his flesh and his blood
Nintu mixed the clay

the Old Babylonian *Atramḫasīs* Epic," in *The Frank Talmage Memorial Volume*, ed. B. Walfish, 2 vols. (Haifa: Haifa University Press, 1993), 1:63–64. I omit several lines which might confuse the issue and divert our attention.

4 With W. L. Moran, "The Creation of Man in Atrahasis I 192–248," *BASOR* 200 (1970): 50.

5 Or, "in."

6 Or, perhaps better, "let a ghost come into being."

<So that both the god himself and man
Were mixed together in the clay>.
……………………
From[7] the god's flesh there was a ghost,[8]
To the living creature, it made known its sign,
The ghost existed so that there be no forgetting.

The *Atraḫasīs* text is one of the main sources of the biblical account of creation and of the Flood and, like the biblical account, tells about the creation of humanity and the origin of human knowledge and mortality. But in this text, mankind is created by the mixing of divine flesh and blood with/in clay. Thus, our Babylonian text is also quite different from the biblical one. For unlike the Yahwistic account where man is created from earth enlivened by the divine breath (see Gen 2:7), in *Atraḫasīs*, man is created from the mixing in clay of the blood and flesh of a slain god.

The god is slain and his flesh is the source of the human ghost, a derivation that remains true whether the *eṭemmu*, "ghost," was originally the god's own ghost or, rather, a human ghost that came into existence only after the god's flesh (*šīru*) was used to form the human being.[9] Here, then, I should comment that the creation of the human being from a slain god imparts not only immortality or divinity to man but also mortality. Mortality is inherited with the flesh

7 Or, "in."

8 Or, "a ghost came into being."

9 Lines 214–217 (// 227–230) pose some serious problems. I cannot take up all of them here. I would note, however, that in my opinion, line 215 does not continue line 214, and line 217 does not continue line 216; rather, 216 develops the thought of 214, and 217 that of 215. I arrived at this conclusion recently while struggling over the passage; I am therefore all the more pleased to note that I. M. Kikawada already arrived at a similar conclusion many years ago, for he "points out that the *uppu* line, Atrahasis I 214 (and 227) belongs to a quatrain of the ABAB pattern." See I. M. Kikawada, apud A. D. Kilmer, "Notes on Akkadian *uppu*," in *Essays on the Ancient Near East in Memory of Jacob Joel Finkelstein*, ed. M. de Jong Ellis, Memoirs of the Connecticut Academy of Arts and Sciences 19 (Hamden: Archon Books, 1977), 130 n. 4, and earlier, A. D. Kilmer, "The Mesopotamian Concept of Overpopulation and Its Solution as Reflected in the Mythology," *Or* NS 41 (1972): 163, where Kilmer sets out the interpretive context for that observation. I accept the suggestion that *uppu* is the heart(beat) ("drum" = "beating heart")—see Kilmer, "Mesopotamian Concept of Overpopulation," 163, and "Notes on Akkadian *uppu*," and cf. T. Jacobsen, apud Moran, "Creation of Man," 56. (The form here—A1 + B1; A2 + B2—may be explained as either a conflation, a mistake, or [since these lines differ in form from the surrounding ones, which are organized either in consecutive narration and/or the poetic form A1 // A2 : B1 // B2] a change of form due to the incorporation of a traditional utterance from another context. Further support for this position may perhaps be found in the omission of line 228 in one of the manuscripts; see Lambert and Millard, *Atra-ḫasīs*, 58, variant to line 228.) Thus, I understand lines 214 and 216 as developing the issue of heart-blood and lines 215 and 217 as developing that of flesh.

itself. But in this strain of Mesopotamian mythology (in contrast perhaps to that earlier one that deals with fertility), gods do not age and die in the natural course of events; they die only as a result of violence. And thus, originally, human mortality is a mortality derived from a slain god. Initially, human death, then, comes only from violence, though subsequently, at the end of *Atraḫasīs* and in related Flood accounts, natural death is introduced and, thereby, the human mortality that initially derived from the slaying of a god is redefined.

There are some interesting concepts here that deserve our attention. As noted, mankind is created from a mixture of the flesh and blood of a slain god. But creation in this text is achieved not only by means of action. Also language, more precisely, linguistic plays assume and produce a form of reality. Let us begin, then, with the linguistic plays, some of which have already been noticed by others, but especially by Jean Bottéro and Stephen Geller,[10] for they constitute an important form of thought and, in any case, point clearly

10 See, e.g., J. Bottéro, "La création de l'homme et son nature dans le poème d'*Atraḫasîs*," in *Societies and Languages of the Ancient Near East: Studies in Honour of I. M. Diakonoff*, ed. M. A. Dandamayev et al. (Warminster: Aris & Phillips, 1982), 24–32, and for a summary statement, J. Bottéro, *Mesopotamia: Writing, Reasoning, and the Gods* (Chicago: University of Chicago Press, 1992), 241; Geller, "Some Sound and Word Plays"; Kilmer, "Mesopotamian Concept of Overpopulation," 163–165; Lambert and Millard, *Atra-ḫasīs*, 21–22 and 153; K. Oberhuber, "Ein Versuch zum Verständnis von Atra-Hasīs," in *Zikir Šumim: Studies Presented to F. R. Kraus on the Occasion of His Seventieth Birthday*, ed. G. van Driel et al. (Leiden: Brill, 1982), 279–281.

It is apparent that I do not follow W. von Soden's reading Widimmu/Edimmu for *eṭemmu*, for which see W. von Soden, "Der Mensch bescheidet sich nicht: Überlegungen zu Schöpfungserzählungen in Babylonien und Israel," in *Symbolae Biblicae et Mesopotamicae Francisco Mario Theodoro de Liagre Böhl Dedicatae*, ed. M. A. Beek et al. (Leiden: Brill, 1973), 350–353, and more recently in W. von Soden, "Der Urmensch im Atramḫasīs-Mythos," in *Mésopotamie et Elam: Actes de la XXXVI*ème *Rencontre Assryriologique Internationale*, ed. L. de Meyer and H. Gasche, Mesopotamian History and Environment, Series 4: Occasional Publications 1 (Ghent: Universiteit Ghent, 1991), 47–51; W. von Soden, "Die Igigu-Götter in altbabylonischer Zeit und Edimmu im Atramḫasīs-Mythos," in *Aus Sprache, Geschichte und Religion Babyloniens: Gesammelte Aufsätze*, ed. L. Cagni and H.-P. Müller, Dipartimento di studi asiatici Series Minor 32 (Naples: Istituto Universitario Orientale, Dipartimento di Studi Asiatici, 1989), 339–349; and W. von Soden, "Altbabylonische Atramchasis-Mythos," 614 615 and 623 624. Regarding von Soden's objection to the use of <we> in the writing *we-ṭe-em-mu* in manuscript E ("Erstens ist *eṭemmu* aus sum. *gidim* entlehnt. Ein *w*-Anlaut ist daher undenkbar, weil das Sumerische kein w-Phonem kennt" ["Urmensch," 48]), note that the writing is intended as a way of combining the name of the god and *ṭēmu*, and therefore objections based upon the absence of the /w/ phoneme in Sumerian are irrelevant (see below).

For a recent discussion of scholarly opinion on *Atraḫasīs* I 214–217 // 227–230 and an understanding of these lines that is different from the one suggested in this paper, see J. Tropper, *Nekromantie: Totenbefragung im Alten Orient und im Alten Testament*, AOAT 223 (Kevelaer: Butzon & Bercker; Neukirchen-Vluyn: Neukirchener Verlag, 1989), 49–55.

to the fundamental ideas and expressive power of the composition. Recall that the common nouns in Akkadian for "god" and "man," respectively, are *ilu* and *awīlu*; the name of the god who is killed so that man might be created is *Wê-ila*, and he is characterized as the god *ša išu ṭēma*, "the god who possesses *ṭēmu*" (that is, "understanding," "intelligence," "deliberation"); and, finally, the word for "blood" is *damu*, for "intelligence" *ṭēmu*, for "ghost" *eṭemmu*.

Note, then, the similarity in sound and the punning between *awīlu*, "man," and the god's name *wê*(-)*ila*. Thus, when alive, mankind receives both its life and its name *awīlu*, "man" from this god ((*a*)*wê-ilu*). One scholar has gone so far as to claim that "the god Wê(ila) was chosen to be slaughtered because his name contained the phoneme /w/ through which the new creature, man (*awīlum*), was to be distinguished from divinity (*ilum*). In the first line of the epic the phrase *ilu-awīlum* is to be regarded as a compound term.... It reflects an original unity of humanity and divinity that was sundered by slaughter of the god and the resulting differentiation of *ilum* and *awīlum*."[11]

Note further the similarity in sound between *ṭēmu*, "intelligence," and *damu*, "blood," a word-play that seems not to have been previously noticed.[12] What does this homophony accomplish? In this creation myth, man's composition includes divine blood. The homophony of *damu*/*ṭēmu* highlights the source of human intelligence: intelligence has been imparted to mankind through the god's blood. By the homophony, the slaughtered god characterized as possessing *ṭēmu* imparts his intellectual quality to human beings.

But the linguistic play or punning goes beyond this. Man lives on after death, and this, too, is signaled by the name. Note, then, also the similarity in sound between the god's name and characterization "*we-e ila* who possesses *ṭēma*," on the one side, and the Babylonian word *eṭemmu*, "ghost," on the other. The text, thus, implicitly treats *eṭemmu*, "ghost," as having been formed from (or in some way related to) the combination of the *Wê* of the god's name and his *ṭēmu*. Thus, because of man's origin from a particular divinity and the nature of the god from whom he derives, mankind possesses not only intelligence but also a ghost and survives after death in the form of that ghost. And it is the *ṭēmu*, "intelligence," that unites the two periods of human existence, for it is exercised during life in daily actions and is present after death phonetically as part of *eṭemmu*.

11 I quote from Geller's summary of his "Some Sound and Word Plays," 1:41.

12 Note that emphatic /ṭ/ and /d/ were probably even more alike in pronunciation than /t/ and /d/.

It is possible that one manuscript (Lambert/Millard, ms. E, lines 215 and 217) even renders the combination of the *Wê* of the god's name and his *ṭēmu* explicit by representing the beginning of the word *eṭemmu* by means of the <*we*> sign instead of the normal <*e*> of the other manuscripts. Moreover, I should note that although the god's name and the mention of the *eṭemmu* are several lines apart, support for the correctness of treating *we-e ... ṭēma* as an exegesis or etymology of *eṭemmu* is provided by a late commentary text, where in the course of explicating a magical text and explaining and providing etymologies for *eṭemmu*, the commentary states:

36 ... *e-*[*ṭe*]*m-me* : *qa-bu-ú ṭè-e-me*
37 E : *qa-bu-ú* : K[A$^{\text{de-e}}$]$\text{m}_4^{\text{-ma}}$ḪI : *ṭè-e-me*.[13]

There is more to be learned from *Atraḫasīs*, and several additional features of this text may serve to advance the argument of this paper. Let us take a closer look at the creation of both man's life force and his ghost. In Mesopotamia, there is a tradition reflected in such other creation accounts as *KAR* 4 and *Enūma eliš* that man is created from the remains of a slain god and thus, for better and for worse, contains divine elements.[14] On the face of it, then, it is not terribly surprising that also in our *Atraḫasīs* text, man is created from the flesh and blood of a god. Divine and human are thus joined up in what we call the human being.[15]

But our text is clear that mankind is created not only from a mixture of the flesh and blood of the slain god, but also from the mixture of these with clay. And with this observation we are immediately sensitized to an apparent

13 H. Hunger, *Spätbabylonische Texte aus Uruk*, Teil 1, ADFU 9 (Berlin: Mann, 1976), no. 49, rev. 36b–37; transliterated and translated on pp. 58–60. (I owe this reference to Frans Wiggermann.) Hunger (p. 59) translates these lines: "*eṭemmu* (= Totengeist) heisst 'der Befehl gibt', denn e heisst sagen, und demma heisst Befehl," and comments, "ein weiteres Beispiel für Erklärung durch Wortzerlegung: *eṭemmu* wird in *e-ṭemmu* zerteilt und dadurch als *qabû ṭemu* verstanden" (p. 60).

14 For discussions of these texts and the tradition, see, e.g., G. Pettinato, *Das altorientalische Menschenbild und die sumerischen und akkadischen Schöpfungsmythen* (Heidelberg: Carl Winter, 1971), esp. 39–46, and, more recently, M. Dietrich, "Die Tötung einer Gottheit in der Eridu-Babylon-Mythologie," in *Ernten, was man sät: Festschrift für Klaus Koch zu seinem 65. Geburtstag*, ed. D. R. Daniels et al. (Neukirchen-Vluyn: Neukirchener Verlag, 1991), 49–73, and W. G. Lambert, "Myth and Mythmaking in Sumer and Akkad," in *CANE* 3:1832–1834.

15 Of course, a usage such as the Akkadian idiom *šīru u damu*, which literally means "flesh and blood" and conveys as in English a sense of kinship or family, may well have contributed to the formulation of our text.

discrepancy in the account, one which accentuates or highlights our text's understanding of aspects of the human constitution or condition that might otherwise have gone unremarked. I note that either the flesh or the clay, one or the other, would seem to be superfluous, a point that is made abundantly clear by a further comparison with the related early Sumerian text "Enki and Ninmah," on the one side, and the later Babylonian text *Enūma eliš*, on the other. In the former, man is created from clay and water, in the latter from the blood of a slain god who had incited a war against Marduk's lineage ("he created mankind from his blood").

Properly speaking, then, it would have sufficed if there had been no mention of the flesh and if the blood of the god had simply been mixed with the clay, for the blood and clay are like the breath of God and the clods of earth in Genesis, with the blood surely representing the life principle; see, e.g., Gen 9:4–5, Lev 17:11 and 14, and Deut 12:23, where "the life is in the blood."

We thus see how very special the particular articulation of our passage is. (Here I underscore especially the fact that according to this text the god's flesh serves as the source of the human ghost. Others have already noted this derivation; one of the goals of this paper is to explore further the significance of the fact that the ghost adheres to the human body and the paradox that the apparently insubstantial ghost derives from flesh—even divine flesh.) Our passage represents a conflation of, or an overlay upon, an earlier craftsman story which told of the creation of man by the mixing of clay and water. But the conflation is more than just a historical vestige and accidental overlay; rather it serves a pronounced purpose, for it formulates and presents a particular understanding of man. For while the clay retains the older function of matter, the god's blood and flesh represent the divine sources from which, respectively, the life force and nature of man, on the one side, and the body and ghost, on the other, are created.[16]

The passage expresses the notion that the mind and body derive from the god. As noted above, I understand lines 214 and 216 as developing the theme of heart-blood and lines 215 and 217 as developing that of flesh. Assuming, then, that *uppu* refers to the heartbeat, the ABAB structure of lines 214–217 (// 227–230)[17] allows us to expand the *damu–šīru* pair into the following structure:[18]

16 See Lambert and Millard, *Atra-ḫasīs*, 22, for a discussion of the blood and flesh.

17 I translate line 216 as follows: "To the living creature (or, While alive), let it (= the heart/blood) make known to him (= the human being) his (= the human being's) sign (= the personal god) /or his (= the god's) sign (= *ṭēmu* = personal god)." For a discussion of the blood/intelligence/personal god, see below, Part 3.

18 I owe the category inner/outer to an observation by Julia Asher-Greve.

| | | | | | |
|---|---|---|---|---|---|
| *Mind* | inner | heart (*uppu*/*libbu*) | blood (*damu*) | intelligence (*ṭēmu*) |
| *Body* | outer | body (*zumru*) | flesh (*šīru*) | ghost (*eṭemmu*) |

The blood is the dynamic quality of intelligence, and the flesh is the form of the body that is imposed on the clay. The *ṭēmu* reflects the blood, the *eṭemmu* the body. The human being combines the qualities of intelligence and physical form derived from the god. And now *damu* transmits human life and intelligence (*ṭēmu*), and *šīru* provides bodily form, a form which is preserved and continued by the *eṭemmu*. With death the blood is gone, but the form remains and continues into the hereafter.

Thus, while the clay represents the material form of man and serves as a base, the blood and flesh transmit respectively the life and kinship of the god. That is to say, the blood serves as the force which preserves and imparts to the living the characteristic quality "god who had a plan" and thereby provides the life principle and intelligence, while the flesh brings forth both the mortal and immortal ghost, the ghost of man and the memorial to the god who had been slain.[19] From the god's blood comes the person, the self;[20] from the god's body, the ghost.

And one is thus tempted to equate the flesh and ghost with the physical image of God (of Genesis) and the blood and intelligence with the soul. But, in any case, it would be remiss of me to pass on to the next part of my exposition without relating our discussion, if only cursorily, to a different approach to, or perhaps just a different terminology for, the concept of the soul(s) in some primitive and early societies. We might say that the god in *Atraḫasīs* serves, first of all, as the source of that soul which elsewhere has been described as the "body soul," a soul which is often divided into such parts as the "life soul" and the "ego soul"; in a Semitic context, it is perhaps best treated as a soul that imbues the individual with life and consciousness, or, in modern terminology, with "ego" or the "self." But the god is also the source of the other soul, the death soul, the soul of the individual after death, a soul that gradually loses individuality until it becomes part of the collectivity of the ancestors.[21]

---

19 I regret that I cannot accept W. L. Moran's argument ("Creation of Man," 54) that the *eṭemmu* belongs to the god alone, though I do concede many of his objections. The ghost may belong to both the god and the human.

20 For the notion of person or self, see especially M. Mauss, "A Category of the Human Mind: The Notion of Person, the Notion of 'Self,'" in *Sociology and Psychology: Essays*, trans. B. Brewster (London: Routledge & Kegan Paul, 1979), 57–94.

21 For a recent discussion of some of these concepts and especially their application to ancient Greek understanding, see J. M. Bremmer, *The Early Greek Concept of the Soul* (Princeton: Princeton University Press, 1983), and J. M. Bremmer, "The Soul, Death and

## 2 The Significance of Flesh as the Source of the Ghost

We have seen in the *Atraḫasīs* creation account, firstly, that the god who has *ṭēmu* serves as the source of the human life force or identity. This point, namely that the aforementioned god imparts and defines human life, will eventually be our jumping-off point for a discussion of the self and of the personal god. But we have also seen that the flesh of the god who has *ṭēmu* is the source of the human ghost. And here we shall start with this latter point and elaborate, if only briefly, on the "ghost," *eṭemmu*,[22] in order to notice some of the implications of the creation account's contention that the god's flesh is the source of the human ghost.

The *Atraḫasīs* text recounts that human beings derive from an admixture of the divine with clay; it not only informs us that the live human derives from the divine, but also explains how it is that while the human being is mortal, having been created from a slain god, part of him is also immortal and exists or appears in the form of an *eṭemmu*, a ghost which exists apparently during life as well as after death.

*Eṭemmu*, the term used in our own text, is the main term for "ghost" in Akkadian. It is the primary Akkadian equivalent or translation of Sumerian gidim, from which word it probably derives. Moreover, I accept the recent suggestion (Frans Wiggermann, orally) that the Sumerian term itself derives in turn from the Semitic *qādīm*, "ancestor." Ghosts are also designated by or associated with "divinity."[23]

the Afterlife in Early and Classical Greece," in *Hidden Futures: Death and Immortality in Ancient Egypt, Anatolia, the Classical, Biblical and Arabic-Islamic World*, ed. J. M. Bremer et al. (Amsterdam: Amsterdam University Press, 1994), 77–106. The limits of this paper do not allow a discussion of the conceptually related terms *napištu* (Hebrew *nephesh*) / *zaqīqu* / líl = breath, wind. Thus, I have also not discussed the relationship of the free or dream soul to the death soul.

22 For the Mesopotamian conception of *eṭemmu*, "ghost," and the care of the dead, see T. Abusch, "Etemmu אטים," in *Dictionary of Deities and Demons in the Bible* (*DDD*), ed. K. van der Toorn et al., 2nd ed. (Leiden: Brill, 1999), 309–312 [[87–92]], and bibliography there (to the bibliography, add Tropper, *Nekromantie*, 47–109).

23 Note also that wind imagery is associated with the ghost—cf. simply the use of líl, wind, for "ghost." The association of ghost and wind in Mesopotamia may be reminiscent of the association of *nephesh* and breath in the Hebrew Bible, especially if we accept the view that West Semitic *nephesh* may sometimes be the equivalent of *eṭemmu*, "ghost"; see J. C. Greenfield, "Un rite religieux araméen et ses parallèles," *RB* 80 (1973): 46–50. And we may wonder whether, like the *nephesh* in the live human, the *eṭemmu* may not also exist during life. I note here only that it is certainly possible to interpret *Atraḫasīs* I 215–216 // 228–229 in this manner.

In Mesopotamian thought, what remains after death is the lifeless body and some form of intangible, but visible and audible *eṭemmu*. The body must be buried; otherwise, the ghost will have no rest and will not find its place in the community of the dead, usually associated with the netherworld. In addition, burial is crucial for future care, for the dead are to be the recipients of ongoing mortuary rites, which include invocations of the name of the deceased, presentation of food, and libation of water. In this way, the dead are cared for and kept (alive) in memory. The dead may be remembered as individuals for up to several generations and then become part of the ancestral family.

Here burial constitutes a rite of passage, both integrating the dead into the cosmic order and maintaining connections between the living and the dead. The living and dead maintain a permanent relationship and form an ongoing community, and thus burial was crucial because it allowed for the preservation and maintenance of the deceased's identity after death and for his continued connection with both the living and dead members of the family. Thus, whatever other purposes it served, burial of the body preserved the identity of the deceased and provided a focus and locus for the ghost's continued existence, for its relationship and place, that is, among the living and the dead.

Thus, when one wishes to deprive the recent dead of the possibility of retaining their individual and/or social identity, one must destroy their body/corpse. In light of our discussion of *šīru*, "flesh," in *Atraḫasīs* and our recognition that the *eṭemmu* is in the flesh of the dead, it comes as no surprise that the destruction of the dead is sometimes described in terms of the destruction of their flesh: the flesh is fed to animals and, thereby, both the individuality and even the very humanity of the dead are destroyed. There are many examples of this kind of treatment in historical texts,[24] but one of the most evocative examples that I know comes from the world of ritual. The concluding section of the anti-witchcraft ritual *Maqlû*[25] indicates that the witch's body is not to be buried; rather her corpse is to be devoured by animals. The penultimate incantation and ritual in *Maqlû* (VIII 108″–128‴ // RT 170′–174′) describe how the

24 See, e.g., A. Westenholz, "*berūtum, damtum*, and Old Akkadian KI.GAL: Burial of Dead Enemies in Ancient Mesopotamia," *AfO* 23 (1970): 29–30; R. Borger, *Die Inschriften Asarhaddons, Königs von Assyrien*, AfO Beih. 9 (Graz: Selbstverlag des Herausgebers, 1956), 57–58: Episode 18, v 6; S. Parpola, "The Murder of Sennacherib," in *Death in Mesopotamia*, ed. B. Alster, Mesopotamia 8 (Copenhagen: Akademisk Forlag, 1980), 175. Cf. E. Cassin, "Le mort: valeur et représentation en Mésopotamie ancienne," in *La mort, les morts dans les sociétés anciennes*, ed. G. Gnoli and J.-P. Vernant (Cambridge: Cambridge University Press; Paris: Éditions de la Maison des sciences de l'homme, 1982), 355–372.

25 For a general overview of *Maqlû*, see T. Abusch, "*Maqlû*," in *RlA* 7 (1987–1990): 346–351. For the text of *Maqlû*, see provisionally Meier, *Maqlû*, and Meier, "Studien," and now T. Abusch, *The Magical Ceremony "Maqlû": A Critical Edition*, AMD 10 (Leiden: Brill, 2016).

witch is fed to eagles, vultures, and dogs. Note the reference there, in line 127'''', to the destruction of the witch's flesh, her *šīru*. A portion of the incantation (VIII 124''''–127'''') reads:

> May eagle and vulture prey on your corpse,
> May silence and shivering fall upon you,
> May dog and bitch tear you apart,
> May dog and bitch tear apart your flesh (*šīrīk*[*i*]).

In ritual practice, images made of dough embedded in bread are fed to dogs (RT 171'–174'). By feeding the witch to animals, she is executed, her corpse is destroyed, and she herself is deprived of any possibility of burial. Thereby, the ritual achieves its purpose of destroying the body and ghost of the witch.

Moreover, the body may also be burned, for burning the body makes it impossible to give it proper burial rites, and its ghost will not be found in the netherworld: thus, fittingly, in "Gilgamesh, Enkidu, and the Netherworld," Gilgamesh asks, "Did you see him who was set on fire?" And Enkidu answers, "I did not see him. His smoke went up to the sky and his ghost does not live in the netherworld."[26]

Normally, then, the dead body was buried. But when a corpse was left unburied and/or was destroyed by animals, fire, or the like, the dead person would lose his human identity and human community. He could no longer be integrated into the structured community of the dead and thereby into the ongoing and continuous community of the living and the dead. In some cases, the remains are so totally transformed and disintegrated that the dead lose all vestiges of human identity. Some texts suggest that those dead who were left unburied and had their corpses destroyed are relegated to the formless and chaotic world sometimes associated with steppe and winds, may even become part of the demonic world that is neither human nor god, male nor

26 See A. Shaffer, "Sumerian Sources of Tablet XII of the Epic of Gilgameš" (Ph.D. diss., University of Pennsylvania, 1963), 121: 3–4 (variant from Ur); cf. 119: 302–203: "'Did you see him who was set on fire?' 'I saw.' 'How does he fare?' 'His spirit is not about. His smoke went up to the sky.'" Similarly, in *Maqlû*, the witch is addressed and told: "Dissolve, melt, drip ever away! / May your smoke rise ever heavenward, / May the sun extinguish your embers, / May the son of Ea (Asalluḫi), the exorcist, cut off your emanations" (I 140–143 // V 145–148). Especially in the first part of *Maqlû*—see especially I 73–IV 106—emphasis is placed upon and importance accorded to burning the witch and destroying her body. In the *Maqlû* passages just quoted, the witch's being rises up as smoke into the sky and is there scattered; now her ghost cannot enter the netherworld. Thus, by burning her body or feeding it to animals, the witch is deprived of burial and is annihilated; her body is destroyed, and her ghost is no more.

female, and/or may even lose all semblance of existence and be transformed into formlessness and even nothingness. Put differently, even the actual ghost thus loses its human identity and existence.[27]

To be sure, *Atraḫasīs* is a unique creation text insofar as it informs us about the origin of the ghost and therefore about the creation of an afterlife. One might have thought that the flesh was chosen simply because the author needed to provide for the creation of the ghost, and narrative logic presented the flesh as a convenient vehicle for this purpose. Perhaps, but it now seems to me that the flesh is more than just an author's fanciful "excuse" for, or explanation of, the creation of the ghost. First and foremost, the choice of flesh reflected the belief that the human ghost and human flesh are closely linked, at least prior to burial. Just as in Gen 1:27 the physical image of God gives form to the human being/body, so in *Atraḫasīs* the outward physical body, the flesh, gives form to the human being in life, to the corpse in death, and to the ghost that inheres in that body. Hence, destruction of the body rather than its inhumation constitutes, in effect, the destruction of the ghost.

Whether or not the text constitutes an aetiology, one may reasonably surmise that the origin of the ghost in the god's flesh reflects the Semitic practice of burial and provides one particular understanding of the importance accorded to burial of the body. Thus, if the flesh is the source of the ghost, this belief would provide one explanation—perhaps a historically valid one, perhaps just an aetiology—why in contrast to some Indo-Europeans, the Semites, and the Mesopotamians among them, abhorred cremation. Whereas among the Greeks cremation rendered the body *hagnos*, "pure," and freed the ghost or, rather, allowed the *psyche* to enter the netherworld, among the Semites

27 Such is the fate not only of those who do not receive burial immediately after death. The same awaits the dead who are disinterred and whose skeletal remains are destroyed. See T. Abusch, "The Socio-Religious Framework of the Babylonian Witchcraft Ceremony *Maqlû*: Some Observations on the Introductory Section of the Text, Part I," in *Riches Hidden in Secret Places: Ancient Near Eastern Studies in Memory of Thorkild Jacobsen*, ed. T. Abusch (Winona Lake, IN: Eisenbrauns, 2002), 1–34 [[AMD 5, 219–247]], and Cassin, "Le mort," 358–359, 362, as well as J.-P. Vernant, "India, Mesopotamia, Greece: Three Ideologies of Death," in *Mortals and Immortals: Collected Essays*, ed. F. Zeitlin (Princeton: Princeton University Press, 1991), 78 (Vernant's article originally formed the introduction to the conference volume in which Cassin's essay appeared).

Some historical and magical texts go so far as to suggest that a transgressor may never escape retribution and can be punished even if he has already died. Thus, the criminal who had died prior to being punished for his crimes may be deprived of mortuary rites; moreover, his burial may be reversed by exhumation and, occasionally, his remains destroyed. His ghost, too, is thus excluded from the community of the dead. Even the actual ghost, then, does not escape punishment and may even lose its human identity.

cremation destroyed the ghost, for the ghost attached itself in some peculiar way to the body.[28]

I note, somewhat ironically, that some of what I have said regarding the burial of the body as a transfer or translation of the living to the dead is not all that dissimilar from what has been said on the Greek side about the burning of the body. Thus, for example, Jean-Pierre Vernant:

> What does it mean to enter into the furthest reaches of death? The fatal blow that strikes the hero liberates his *psuchē*, which flees the limbs, leaving behind its strength and youth. Yet for all that, it has not passed through the gates of death. Death is not a simple demise, a privation of life; it is a transformation of which the corpse is both the instrument and the object, a transmutation of the subject that functions in and through the body. Funerary rites actualize this change of condition; at their conclusion, the individual has left the realm of the living, in the same way as his cremated body has vanished into the hereafter, and as his *psuchē* has reached the shores of Hades, never to return.... [There] he continues to exist on another plane, in a form of being that is released from the attrition of time and destruction.[29]

And a bit later in the same essay:

> The fire of the funerary pyre, by contrast, consumes and sends into the realm of the invisible, along with the perishable flesh and blood, a person's entire physical appearance and the attributes that can be seen on

28 To be sure, the flesh rots after burial. At that point, the identity of the individual is associated with his skeleton or bones. The destruction of the bones, then, constitutes the complete destruction of the individual (see, e.g., Cassin, "Le mort," and Vernant, "India, Mesopotamia, Greece," 77–79). Here, therefore, we may wonder how the Babylonians understood or construed the relationship of the flesh and bones of the dead. Perhaps immediately after death, the flesh or fresh corpse represented the individual but, at a later stage in the process of disintegration, it was the bones that came to represent the individual. Returning to our *Atraḫasīs* text, we may expand the question and suggest the following scheme, one which is rather obvious and is made up of three stages: blood represents the life force of the live individual, flesh (and bodily shape) the individual at death, and bones the permanently dead individual. The significance of the skeleton or bones as the permanent repository of the human soul may well attain mythological formulation in *Enūma eliš* VI 5–6, when Marduk says: "I shall compact blood, I shall cause bones to be, I shall make stand a human being, let 'Man' be its name," and then uses the blood of the slain leader of the rebel gods. Translation: Foster, *Before the Muses*, 469.

29 J. P. Vernant, "A 'Beautiful Death' and the Disfigured Corpse in Homeric Epic," in Vernant, *Mortals and Immortals*, 68.

> the body.... The visible form of the body, such as is displayed when it is laid out for viewing at the beginning of the funeral rites, can only be saved from corruption by disappearing into the invisible.[30]

But the ghost retains the visible form of the body.[31] And we would conclude this section by emphasizing again that for the Mesopotamians (as sometimes for ourselves) the body itself gives form to the perception of the self and of the other and provides the image under which the deceased and his ghost remain in the mind of the living: a human form or body. The *eṭemmu* derives from the body and preserves the body image.

## 3 God, *ṭēmu*, and Personal God

We noticed that the ghost is of divine origin and derives from the god's flesh; accordingly, we discussed the flesh, the corpse, and the ghost. We noticed, in addition, that also the life force is divine or of divine origin. Thus, we should now turn to a consideration of the human being during his lifetime.

The god's blood is the source of man's life force; it is the channel through which certain divine qualities enter into man. As noted earlier, it is of particular interest that the god to be slain is characterized as one who possesses *ṭēmu* and that his blood (*damu*) is the channel through which intelligence (*ṭēmu*) is imparted to humanity. Therefore, we should here pay some attention to the intellectual quality of the slain god. The possession of *ṭēmu* is crucial for this god and for humanity. So before even exploring any further the concepts about this god that define the human (or, rather, the reverse, the concepts about the human that define the god), we should say a word or two about *ṭēmu*. *ṭēmu* is plan, inspiration, or intelligence as well as the verbal formulation that conveys or expresses these. In the context of *Atraḫasīs*, the use of *ṭēmu* is the act of deliberation about the slave condition of the worker gods in an irrigation economy, the formulation of a plan of rebellion, and its execution.[32] The god who hit upon and developed the idea of the rebellion and who worked out the plan of execution serves as the progenitor of humanity.

30 Vernant, "'Beautiful Death,'" 70.

31 Cf., e.g., J. P. Vernant again, but this time in the essay "Psuche: Simulacrum of the Body or Image of the Divine?" (*Mortals and Immortals*, 189): "The *psuchē* is like a body; as shown on works of art, on vases, it is represented like a miniature body, a *corpusculum*; it is the double of the living body, a replica that can be taken for the body itself that has the same appearance, clothing, gestures, and voice."

32 Cf., e.g., Moran, "Creation of Man," 52.

The early Mesopotamian is an organizer, an innovator, who struggles to understand and control his environment and must put his mind to the future in order to create and maintain a system of intense irrigation. The concept of *ṭēmu* is an important component in that civilization's understanding of man and in the Mesopotamian concept of the personal god, who is, I believe, a personification of the self.

Mesopotamian *ṭēmu* is strikingly similar to John Dewey's understanding of mind (which influenced American interactionism and, particularly, the thought of George Herbert Mead and thereby the concept of the "self" in the social sciences):

> What is unique to humans, Dewey argued, is their capacity for thinking. Mind is not a structure but a process that emerges out of efforts by humans to adjust to their environment. Moreover, mind is the unique capacity that allows humans to deal with conditions around them....
>
> Mind for Dewey is the process of denoting objects in the environment, ascertaining potential lines of conduct, imagining the consequences of pursuing each line, inhibiting inappropriate responses, and then selecting a line of conduct that will facilitate adjustment. Mind is thus the process of thinking, and thinking involves deliberation.[33]

Dewey's understanding seems very much in line with our understanding of the Mesopotamian definition of man and represents a set of notions that the Babylonians would have associated with *ṭēmu*. These concepts of human life and mind coincide to some extent with the concept of the personal god, and thus we may now take up some further implications of the *Atraḫasīs* passage for an understanding of man. For it is possible that the *Atraḫasīs* passage even intends to provide an aetiology for the existence of the personal god and for his acquisition by man.[34] The personal god, to quote Thorkild Jacobsen, is "clearly a power for effective thinking, planning, and inspiration, and this is the central element in the concept."[35] The significance of the *Atraḫasīs* passage thus

33 J. H. Turner, *The Structure of Sociological Theory*, rev. ed. (Homewood, IL: Dorsey, 1978), 314.

34 Perhaps indirectly it also provides an aetiology for the relationship of man to his personal god.

35 T. Jacobsen, *The Treasures of Darkness: A History of Mesopotamian Religion* (New Haven: Yale University Press, 1976), 156. For Jacobsen's understanding of the personal god, see T. Jacobsen, "Mesopotamia: The Cosmos as a State," in H. Frankfort et al., *The Intellectual Adventure of Ancient Man: An Essay on Speculative Thought in the Ancient Near East*, rev. ed. (Chicago: University of Chicago Press, 1977), 202–208, as well as *Treasures of Darkness*, 152–164.

seems clear. Man's life force derives directly from a god who possessed and is characterized in terms of the powers of intelligence and deliberation. Thus, just as the slain god possessed the power of deliberation, so man who incorporated the god's blood now possesses that power. And with that power, man also possesses a personal god or rather the potential to acquire a personal god. For the personal god is a projection or personification of the human power of deliberation, decision, and planning. When man exercises his powers of deliberation, he acquires its personification in the form of his personal god. As the Mesopotamian bilingual proverb states, "when you plan ahead your god is yours, when you do not plan ahead your god is not yours."[36]

Later parts of *Atraḫasīs* lend support to my contention that, among other things, the creation account at the beginning of the work dealt with the personal god and provided for his acquisition by man. That our *Atraḫasīs* passage recounts how humans first acquired a personal god may find confirmation in the fact that, and explain why, the existence of service to personal gods is already taken for granted as a basic fact of religious life later in the myth, when, as each catastrophe took place, Enki advised Atraḫasīs to command that the people cease providing service to their personal gods and instead serve the god responsible for the destruction:

> Do not reverence your gods.
> Do not pray to your goddess(es).
> Namtar (Adad, resp.), seek his gate,
> Bring a baked-loaf before it,
> Let the meal-offering please him,
> So that, embarrassed at the gifts,
> He will raise his hand.[37]

Here, I should perhaps place the concept of the personal god into a clearer Mesopotamian context. The Mesopotamian did not formulate his own personal psychology primarily in the form of internal categories; rather he objectified and externalized major aspects of self. He could thus be surrounded

36 For the text of the proverb, see *BWL*, 227: 23–26; for its interpretation, see Jacobsen, "Mesopotamia," 204, and Jacobsen, *Treasures of Darkness*, 156.

37 Namtar: I 378–383 // I 393–398, cf. I 405–410 (Lambert and Millard, *Atra-ḫasīs*, 68–71); Adad: II, col. ii (Lambert and Millard, *Atra-ḫasīs*, 74–77). Translation: W. L. Moran, "Atrahasis: The Babylonian Story of the Flood," *Bib* 52 (1971): 54. That the gods to be neglected were the personal gods, and not simply gods and goddesses, was argued convincingly by Moran (55).

by a series of divine beings[38] who represented aspects of self or perhaps even different life- or body-souls.[39] Among these divine beings are the *ilu* and *ištaru*, the personal god and goddess.[40] One may surmise that this god and goddess are no more than psychologically internalized father and mother figures that find expression among the Babylonians in the form of externalized, divinized figures.[41] Here, I limit myself to the *ilu*. It is possible that the god (*ilu*) originally represented the family or clan, but perhaps because of the individual's close connection to his group, the god also became the personal god of the individual, especially as that individual related to the world, to the present, and to the future. Most of all, the god was evident in social success and in the ability to have children.[42]

It should now be recalled that god and ghost serve many of the same functions. First of all, the personal god and the ghosts of the family belong together in the sense that they both represent parents: the one represents and preserves the norms of the family among the living; the other represents and preserves the norms of the family among and from the dead. Human beings attain their identity in no small measure from their social contexts; these connections extend over both space and time, i.e., over the here-and-now and through time.

---

38 Such as *ilu, ištaru, utukku, lamassu, šēdu, bāštu, dūtu*.

39 Cf. A. L. Oppenheim, *Ancient Mesopotamia: Portrait of a Dead Civilization*, rev. ed. (Chicago: University of Chicago Press, 1977), 198–206.

40 By the second millennium BCE, individuals seem to have had both a personal god and a personal goddess (*ištaru*).

41 If for the Mesopotamians, the father is a force for action or doing and the mother a force for socialization, it is perhaps not a coincidence that a late commentary text explains the illness "hand of the god" as "he curses the gods, he speaks insolence, he hits whom(ever) he sees," and the illness "hand of the goddess" as "he has … of heart-break, time and again, and forgets his (own) words, time and again"; text: A. T. Clay, *Epics, Hymns, Omens, and Other Texts*, BRM 4 (New Haven: Yale University Press, 1923), no. 32, obv. 2–3; translation: M. Stol, *Epilepsy in Babylonia*, CM 2 (Groningen: Styx, 1993), 25. The illness "hand of the god" seems to be the transformation of energy that cannot be turned to constructive purposes into anger and aggression against others, while the illness "hand of the goddess" seems to represent the turning of a feeling of not belonging, or of not being cared for, into anger against the self and thereby into a state of anxiety and depression. The loss of the father is the loss of a sense of constructive action in society, the loss of the mother is the loss of a social sense of belonging and feeling that others care for one.

42 Again to quote Jacobsen: "In a sense, and probably this is the original aspect, the personal god appears as the personification of a man's luck and success. Success is interpreted as an outside power which infuses itself into a man's doings and makes them produce results" ("Mesopotamia," 203). "As a divine power dwelling in the man and causing him to succeed, the god would naturally be present and active in the most decisive and necessary achievement of fulfilment for the ancient Mesopotamian, that of engendering a son" (*Treasures of Darkness*, 158).

Identity is derived from the contemporary living context but also from ancestors and progeny. In both dimensions, the Mesopotamians encounter the numinous other, the divine. The ghost represents the ancestral kinship group, while the god who inhabits the living body—the personal god—represents the living family and the actual or daily social world. Ghost and personal god represent aspects of both individual and group ego and superego.

The ancestral ghost requires continued honor and care and may become a hostile presence if disregarded. Not only the ghost but also the personal god may make demands of the living person and punish or reward him, accordingly, so that this god is undoubtedly an aspect of superego or conscience.[43] But the personal god is also certainly an aspect of ego. He belongs to the clan, but through the corporate identity of individuals as well as the identification of the god with the power of procreation, the personal god became the personification of the luck and fortune, the well-being, the effectiveness, accomplishment, and success of the individual member of the group. Perhaps the personal god even amounts to a sense of self, for he is the power for thought, the ability of the individual to plan and deliberate so that he may act effectively and achieve success. The personal god is something like an externalized ego, if by ego we understand that which "brings into being the conscious sense of self. The ego engages in secondary process thinking, or the remembering, planning, and weighing of circumstances that permit us to mediate between the fantasies of the id and the realities of the outer world."[44] For it is through the sense of identification with the personal god that man acquires a sense of self as an intelligent and effective being.

Just as the *ṭēmu*, "intelligence," of the god imparts to collective mankind the ability to work as a society and serve the gods of the state, so *ṭēmu* also imparts to the single man the ability to work as an individual and thereby serve his personal god.[45]

43 This is exemplified nicely by a reference to *ilu* in an Old Assyrian letter: "Your god (and mine) would want you to act in such a way."

44 S. A. Rathus and J. S. Nevid, *Abnormal Psychology*, instructor's ed. (Englewood Cliffs, NJ: Prentice Hall, 1991), 37.

45 The fact that *ṭēmu*, "intelligence," derives from a "rebel" god does not disqualify the claim that the aforementioned power or quality allows the individual human to be successful and to possess a personal god. Put differently, the fact that *ṭēmu* allows humans to be effective and serve the god in no way requires or even suggests that the *ṭēmu* must derive from an "innocent" god. Rather than detracting from human ability to provide service to the god(s), if anything, the origin of human intelligence in the "rebel" god enhances it. For just as the human community in *Atraḫasīs* makes use of the *ṭēmu* of the leader of the striking gods to assume the work of the gods and to serve the divine community, so the individual human makes use of this *ṭēmu* to serve his personal god.

Just as the early Mesopotamians regarded the human city as created by and belonging to the gods, human society as existing for the sake of the gods, and human actions as deeds in the service of the gods, in part in order to allay the anxieties aroused by their own collective daring and the precarious nature of their existence,[46] so perhaps also their own individual attempts at imposing control over their environment led them to project their own rationality and achievements onto a divine other, the personal god.

In *Atraḫasīs* the flesh defines physical identity, the body, and therewith the ghost, and places the human being in relationship to the past, while the blood, and therewith the intelligence, defines the personality or living identity and continues into the future through the blood (seed). Thus, the personal god and ghost may be drawn together for purposes of understanding a Mesopotamian construction of human nature.[47]

---

46 See H. Frankfort, *The Birth of Civilization in the Near East* (1951; repr., Garden City, NY: Doubleday, 1956), ch. 3, esp. 52–54, 63–64.

47 For a recent treatment of the creation of man in "Enki and Ninmah," which escaped my attention during the writing of this essay, see W. G. Lambert, "The Relationship of Sumerian and Babylonian Myth as Seen in Accounts of Creation," in *La circulation des biens, des personnes et des idées dans le Proche-Orient ancien, XXXVIII*$^{e}$ *R.A.I.*, ed. D. Charpin and F. Joannès (Paris: Éditions Recherche sur les Civilisations, 1992), 129–135. Basing himself upon a bilingual version, Lambert argues that Enki created man by mixing clay and blood (Lambert leaves open the question whether it is Enki's blood or his mother's). If correct, this contention (which differs in its construction of the text from previous translations) would require that the statement (above, p. 74) that man was created from clay and water in "Enki and Ninmah" be modified; but it in no way disqualifies the argument (above, p. 74) that the mention of flesh alongside clay in *Atraḫasīs* was significant, for that argument depends not on the absence of blood in "Enki and Ninmah," but rather on the presence of flesh and clay in *Atraḫasīs* and the absence of the former in "Enki and Ninmah."

CHAPTER 5

# Etemmu אטים

## 1 Name and Etymology

*Eṭemmu* is the main term for "ghost" in Akkadian. It is the primary Akkadian equivalent or translation of Sumerian gidim, from which word it may derive. The term *eṭemmu* seems to underlie the biblical *ʾiṭṭîm* in Isa 19:3, where, however, the final *mem* is treated as if it were the Hebrew marker of the masculine plural.

## 2 Character and History

*Eṭemmu* is a spirit, more properly a ghost. Wind imagery is associated with ghosts (and demons)—note the use of líl for "ghost." Ghosts are heard, felt, and especially seen, particularly in dreams. Ghosts are also designated by or associated with "divinity." Of particular significance is the etiology of *eṭemmu* found in the Old Babylonian *Atraḫasīs* epic (I 206–230). There, mankind is created from a mixture of clay and the flesh and blood of a slain god. This god's name is *Wê-ilu*, and he is characterized as one who has *ṭēmu*, "understanding, intelligence" or perhaps even "psyche." Note the similarity in sound and the punning between *awīlu* and *wê(-)ila* and between *we-e ... ṭēma* and *eṭemmu*. Thus, when alive, mankind receives both its life and the name *awīlu*, "man," from this god *(a)wê-ilu*. But also because of this god and man's divine origin, mankind survives after death in the form of a ghost, and this too is signaled by a name; for this text implicitly treats *eṭemmu*, "ghost," as having been formed from the combination of the *Wê* of the god's name and his *ṭēmu*.

After death, what remains is the lifeless body and some form of intangible, but visible and audible "spirit." The body must be buried; otherwise, the ghost will have no rest and will not find its place in the community of the dead, usually associated with the netherworld. In addition, the dead are to be the recipients of ongoing mortuary rites, which include invocations of the name of the deceased, presentation of food, and libation of water. In this way the dead are cared for and their memory is preserved. The dead may be remembered as individuals for up to several generations and then become part of the ancestral family (*eṭem kimti*). It needs always to be emphasized that Mesopotamian burial and mortuary rituals as well as beliefs about the dead are not simply an

 | DOI:10.1163/9789004435186_006

autonomous area of religious life; they also reflect social structure and psychological experience. In any case, care for the dead may provide an occasion for the maintenance of social bonds. The living and dead maintain a permanent relationship and form an ongoing community. Dead and living kin in Mesopotamia are dependent upon each other and therefore their relationship will naturally reflect or express both hostility and love.

Normally the dead body was buried, and burial allowed for the preservation and maintenance of the deceased's identity after death and for his continued connection with both the living and dead members of the family. Burial is crucial, for if a corpse is left unburied and/or is destroyed by animals, fire, or the like, the dead person cannot be integrated into the structured community of the dead and thereby into the ongoing and continuous community of the living and the dead. He loses his human community and human identity. This is not only the fate of those who do not receive burial immediately after death. The same fate awaits the dead who are disinterred and whose skeletal remains are destroyed. In some cases, the remains are so totally transformed and disintegrated that the dead lose all vestiges of human identity.

The unburied or disinterred may become roaming and troublesome ghosts; more important, some texts suggest that they are relegated to the formless and chaotic world sometimes associated with steppe and winds, and may even become part of the demonic world that is neither human nor god, male nor female. Hence the gidim/*eṭemmu* may become associated with the demonic class udug/*utukku* and even be so designated.

Lack of burial and/or destruction of the body will often occur accidentally and belongs psychologically together with the fear of premature death; such treatment of the body may also be imposed as a punishment for a crime. It is among the most dreadful sanctions of Mesopotamian society.

Information about the condition of the dead is found in a variety of sources. Particularly worthy of note are (a) rituals, especially therapeutic ones, that deal with ghosts and their effects on humans; (b) "descents" to the netherworld; and (c) curses that describe the various evils which may befall human beings.

a) Magical and medical texts that deal with ghosts usually focus on those ghosts who plague the living. The topos of a restless and troublesome ghost is particularly prevalent. Ghosts who plague the living may either belong to one's own family or be strangers who have attached themselves to the victim. These ghosts are often said to have not been provided with mortuary rites or, even worse, to have not received a proper burial in the first place. Mention must also be made of the dead who had led unfulfilled lives and are drawn back to the world of the living, either out of envy or malice, or out of the desire to complete "unfinished business." Various physical and psychological symptoms are attributed to ghostly seizures in therapeutic texts. Notable, in addition, is the frequent mention of visions of the dead, often in dreams. Some therapeutic texts prescribe material cures (e.g., potions, salves); others operate more in the magical and symbolic realms and try to rid the victim of the ghost either by providing the ghost with proper burial and/or mortuary treatment or by performing some other form of expulsion.

In other instances, ghosts—usually the family manes (*eṭem kimti*)—are invoked to help the living by taking one or another form of evil down to the netherworld. Of great interest, especially in view of the aforementioned biblical passage (and similar passages which mention the *ʾôb* and *yiddĕʿōnî* though not the *ʾiṭṭîm*), are attempts to raise the dead for purposes of necromancy. One designation of the necromancer is *mušēli eṭemmi*.

b) Among the "descents," pride of place should perhaps go to the descent of Enkidu to the netherworld in the Sumerian "Gilgamesh, Enkidu, and the Netherworld" (// Epic of Gilgamesh, Tablet XII) and in the later Epic of Gilgamesh (Tablet VII). In the former—which represents an early text—the state of the dead is described in terms of and related to the human support system (e.g., number of children), the manner of death, and the treatment of the body. In the main, the dead are pale imitations of the living—they are human in form but seem to lack animation and energy. In later descriptions, by contrast, the vision of the dead is more horrific and shows us a netherworld inhabited by monsters and demons and dead who no longer look human. Here, mention should be made especially of "The Netherworld Vision of an Assyrian Prince," a late text which exhibits this horrific vision of the netherworld.[1]

Equally illuminating historically as regards changes in the idea of the netherworld is the graphic description of the dead and of the netherworld in the opening lines of the "Descent of Ištar":

> The daughter of Sin was determined to go
> To the dark house, dwelling of Erkalla's god,
> To the house which those who enter cannot leave,
> On the road where travelling is one-way only,
> To the house where those who enter are deprived of light,
> Where dust is their food, clay their bread.
> They see no light, they dwell in darkness,
> They are clothed like birds, with feathers.
> Over the door and the bolt, dust has settled.[2]

1 A. Livingstone, *Court Poetry and Literary Miscellanea*, SAA 3 (Helsinki: Helsinki University Press, 1989), no. 32.

2 S. Dalley, *Myths from Mesopotamia: Creation, The Flood, Gilgamesh, and Others*, rev. ed. (Oxford: Oxford University Press, 2000), 155: 3–11.

Here I would make several historical observations. Firstly, it is significant that the older "Descent of Inanna" (from which the "Descent of Ištar" derives) does not focus upon or even contain this type of description. Moreover, in the later text, the dead are described as birds and not humans. Furthermore, the description of the netherworld in the later text is itself a later image, one that has been superimposed upon the earlier vision of the netherworld as a city which is entered through gates and in which the dead are housed or even imprisoned. Its secondary nature is clear from the fact that the house of the dead is here described as one whose door and bolt are covered with dust, for the earlier image—an image which is even used of Ištar's own descent later in the text—is that of gates through which the dead constantly go and which therefore would not be covered by dust. This image of the dusty netherworld and with it the image of the dead as birds would seem to derive from that of a tomb or even a ruin and/or a cave. More than the earlier texts, these later visions serve to draw a sharper line and a greater contrast between the living and the dead.

c) Often, texts whose purpose is to maintain or protect the "status quo" (e.g., boundary stones, treaties, laws, building and tomb inscriptions, etc.) include sanctions in the form of curses. Notable among these curses are various threats associated with death: death itself, denial of burial, destruction of the corpse, deprivation of rites which provide care for the dead. Most powerful are those curses which seem to suggest that the transgressor will not only suffer death but will also be excluded, one way or another, from the organized community of the dead. On occasion, it appears that the transgressor is punished whether he is dead or alive: he does not escape retribution. Thus, the living criminal is killed, his ghost made to wander, and even his remains destroyed. For his part, the criminal who had died before being punished is deprived of mortuary rites; moreover, his burial may be reversed by exhumation and, occasionally, his remains destroyed. His ghost, too, is thus excluded from the community of the dead and made to wander. (Passages such as CḪ rev. xxvii, 34–40 and VTE 476–477—"above, among the living, may he (Šamaš)/they (the great gods) uproot him/you; below, in the earth, may he/they deprive his/your ghost of water"—may stipulate not only two sequential punishments for the same person, but also two separate, parallel punishments for either eventuality). The *eṭemmu*, then, does not escape punishment and may even lose its human identity. In this construction, as I understand it, the criminal must not only be killed but must also be kept from being integrated or reintegrated into the netherworld. For the netherworld and the heavens form a connected structure or even continuum, and if the criminal were allowed to remain in the netherworld, he would find a place in the cosmic state.

This approach to sanction involves the exclusion of the transgressor from the organized cosmos of the divine, the living, and the dead. It forms one of the underlying principles of Sargonid treaty ideology and explains the "vengeful" behavior of Esarhaddon and Assurbanipal to the corpses and skeletons of those who violated their treaty obligations. It operates no less in the symbolic sphere as evidenced, for example, by the anti-witchcraft ceremony *Maqlû* ("Burning"). *Maqlû* took place at the time of the annual reappearance of ghosts in Abu. One of its central purposes was to ensure that all witches be expelled and kept outside the organized social and cosmic community. "Live" witches were judged and destroyed; "dead" witches were captured and expelled. Thus, all witches were to be prevented from having a proper burial. They were deprived of burial in order to prevent them from finding a place in the netherworld and consequently in the cosmic state.

## 3 Inside the Bible

In the Hebrew Bible the *ʾiṭṭîm* are mentioned only in Isa 19:3: in an oracle against Egypt it is stated that Yhwh will "frustrate the spirit of Egypt and destroy their plans." In reaction to this prophecy of doom the Egyptians are expected to intensify their divinatory practices, among which are "the consulting of mediums and the asking of *ʾiṭṭîm* for advice."[3]

3 In addition to the literature cited in the preceding notes, see the following: T. Abusch, "Mesopotamian Anti-Witchcraft Literature: Texts and Studies. Part I: The Nature of *Maqlû*: Its Character, Divisions, and Calendrical Setting," *JNES* 33 (1974): 251–262, esp. 259–261 [[AMD 5, 99–111, esp. 108–110]]; T. Abusch, "Ishtar's Proposal and Gilgamesh's Refusal: An Interpretation of the *Gilgamesh Epic*, Tablet 6, Lines 1–79," *HR* 26 (1986): 143–187 [[*Gilgamesh*, 11–57]]; T. Abusch, "The Socio-Religious Framework of the Babylonian Witchcraft Ceremony *Maqlû*: Some Observations on the Introductory Section of the Text, Part I," in *Riches Hidden in Secret Places: Ancient Near Eastern Studies in Memory of Thorkild Jacobsen*, ed. T. Abusch (Winona Lake, IN: Eisenbrauns, 2002), 1–34 [[AMD 5, 219–247]]; M. Bayliss, "The Cult of Dead Kin in Assyria and Babylonia," *Iraq* 35 (1973): 115–125; J. Bottéro, "La mythologie de la mort en Mésopotamie ancienne," in *Death in Mesopotamia*, ed. B. Alster, Mesopotamia 8 (Copenhagen: Akademisk, 1980), 25–52; J. Bottéro, "La création de l'homme et son nature dans le poème d'*Atraḫasîs*," in *Societies and Languages of the Ancient Near East: Studies in Honour of I. M. Diakonoff*, ed. M. A. Dandamayev et al. (Warminster: Aris & Phillips, 1982), 24–32; J. Bottéro, "Les morts et l'au-delà dans les rituels en accadien contre l'action des 'revenants,'" *ZA* 73 (1983): 153–203; E. Cassin, "Le mort: valeur et représentation en Mésopotamie ancienne," in *La mort, les morts dans les sociétés anciennes*, ed. G. Gnoli and J.-P. Vernant (Cambridge: Cambridge University Press; Paris: Éditions de la Maison des sciences de l'homme, 1982), 355–372; H. R. Cohen, *Biblical Hapax Legomena in the Light of Akkadian and Ugaritic*, SBLDS 37 (Missoula, MT: Scholars Press, 1978), 42; I. L. Finkel, "Necromancy in

Ancient Mesopotamia," *AfO* 29–30 (1983–1984): 1–17; S. A. Geller, "Some Sound and Word Plays in the First Tablet of the Old Babylonian *Atramḫasīs* Epic," in *The Frank Talmage Memorial Volume*, ed. B. Walfish, 2 vols. (Haifa: Haifa University Press, 1993), 1:63–70; B. Groneberg, "Zu den mesopotamischen Unterweltsvorstellungen: Das Jenseits als Fortsetzung des Diesseits," *AoF* 17 (1990): 244–261; T. Jacobsen, "The lil$_2$ of $^{d}$En-lil$_2$," in *DUMU-E$_2$-DUB-BA-A. Studies in Honor of Åke W. Sjöberg*, ed. H. Behrens et al. (Philadelphia: University of Pennsylvania Museum of Archaeology, 1989), 267–276, esp. 271–275; J. Scurlock, "Magical Means of Dealing with Ghosts in Ancient Mesopotamia" (Ph.D. diss., University of Chicago, 1988); K. Spronk, *Beatific Afterlife in Ancient Israel and in the Ancient Near East*, AOAT 219 (Neukirchen-Vluyn: Neukirchener Verlag, 1986), 96–125; A. Tsukimoto, *Untersuchungen zur Totenpflege (kispum) im alten Mesopotamien*, AOAT 216 (Kevelaer: Butzen & Bercker; Neukirchen-Vluyn: Neukirchener Verlag, 1985).

CHAPTER 6

# Ištar

## 1 Name and Etymology

The major Mesopotamian goddess of love, war, and the planet Venus is known primarily by the Sumerian name Inanna and the Akkadian name Ištar. Although the name Inanna is usually translated as "Lady of Heaven" (nin.an.ak), the alternative translation "Lady of the date clusters" (nin.ana.ak), suggested by Jacobsen, seems preferable.[1] The name Ištar is Semitic and earlier was pronounced Eshtar. Ištar is not simply a Semitic name brought in and applied without further change to a preexisting Sumerian goddess, but rather represents an independent Semitic deity who helped shape the personality of the Mesopotamian goddess. Ištar derives from common Semitic *ʿaṯtar*. (A masculine god with this name appears in Southern Arabia and Ugarit [*ʿaṯtar*], though a feminine form [Astarte] is also attested in Canaanite literature and in the Bible.) In the course of time, Ištar became the generic name for goddess and *ištarātu*, a plural form of her name, the term for goddesses. Sometimes the name is superimposed upon other goddesses without, however, necessarily changing the separate identity of the underlying god (e.g., the use of the name Ištar for the mother-goddess in the Epic of Gilgamesh, Tablet XI).

There are a few oblique references to Ištar in the Bible.

## 2 Character and History

Though she has other filiations, Inanna is best known as the daughter of the moon god Nanna/Sîn and his wife Ningal and as the sister of Utu/Šamaš, the sun god. In the Sumerian literary traditions reflecting fertility rituals, especially those rooted in Uruk, the goddess is depicted as the wife of various Dumuzi/Tammuz figures, fertility gods who are the power for new life and growth. She is also the wife of An, the god of the sky. This latter association may be a late development, but it seems more likely that here is preserved an older tradition in which Inanna/Ištar represents a variant of the earth: Ki ("earth"), the wife

1 T. Jacobsen, *The Treasures of Darkness: A History of Mesopotamian Religion* (New Haven: Yale University Press, 1976), 36.

 | DOI:10.1163/9789004435186_007

of An, or Ereshkigal ("mistress of the great earth"), the goddess of the netherworld who was the wife of An in his bull form, Gugalanna.

The goddess Inanna/Ištar seems to exhibit a greater variety of (perhaps inconsistent) traits and qualities than most other deities and plays a wide variety of roles. She is a goddess of sexual love and possesses strong powers of sexual attraction. In the fertility cult, she receives foodstuffs and appears to be the numen of the communal storehouse. In addition, Inanna/Ištar is a rain goddess who, like other storm gods, is also a war goddess and personifies the battle-line. She is also the patroness of prostitutes and other independent women as well as the goddess of the morning and evening star (Venus). The character of the goddess is arresting: "love and sensuality alongside battle and victory. On the one hand, therefore, Ištar was depicted as hierodule (naked goddess) and on the other as heroine and queen."[2]

The goddess is the spouse and lover of the king, with whom she participates in the ritual of the sacred marriage. She provides the king with economic blessings as well as power and victory in war. Inanna/Ištar is associated with the cults of many cities; she is particularly prominent in Uruk, Akkad, Kish, Nineveh, and Arbela. In Uruk, but particularly in Akkad and Assyria, she is a goddess of war and victory.

In Mesopotamian literary texts, Inanna/Ištar has a coherent and believable, if complex, personality. Inanna/Ištar is a young, independent, and willful woman of the upper class. She is a product of an urban world and is closely associated with cities more than with cosmic functions. She seems to be constantly on the move, perhaps because of her association with heavenly bodies and unencumbered women; in any case, her movement expresses and enhances a quality of discontent and restlessness that characterizes her. Inanna/Ištar often appears as a sexually attractive being, but she remains unsatisfied and is constantly "injured," striving, and contentious. She tends toward anger and rage and "troubles heaven and earth." (One is tempted to talk of early "psychic wounds.") Her roles (as wife, mother, etc.) are not fully realized; she behaves as if she were incomplete. Yet there is also sometimes real loss; thus, for example, her husband dies prematurely. But while the death of Tammuz reflects the cycle of fertility and is understandably emphasized in her cult and related myths, this loss remains determinative in the formation of her personality even when her personality and story are freed from the fertility context. Ištar reminds us of Gilgamesh, a powerful individual with great energy who always

2 W. H. P. Römer, "Religion of Ancient Mesopotamia," in *Historia Religionum: Handbook for the History of Religion*, ed. C. J. Bleeker and G. Widengren, 2 vols. (Leiden: Brill, 1969), 1:132.

remains dissatisfied with the allotted role or portion and is constantly driven to go beyond. They seem to be male and female counterparts.

The figure who appears under the name of Inanna or Ištar possesses a number of sharply delineated characteristics. The goddess seems even to exhibit contradictory or conflicting traits. She seems to encompass polar opposites: she is death and life, male and female, she is a female who does not nurture nor have a permanent partner, a sexual woman who is warlike and glories in aggression and destruction, etc. She is glorified but frightening, exalted but also intimidating. Moreover, a number of possibly separate goddesses appear under the name Ištar of a particular place (e.g., Ištar of Nineveh). In view of her diversity, several questions about the goddess should be asked. In simplified form, these questions are: (1) Is the Inanna/Ištar of Mesopotamia a single goddess, a conflation of several goddesses, or separate goddesses under a single name? (2) As a single goddess or a conflation of several, did she possess a coherent personality? Recent attempts to understand the nature of Inanna/Ištar have emphasized either the continued existence of separate goddesses of love and of war, or the existence of a single goddess whose nature is in fact expressed by or related to the very quality of variety or even contradiction.

1) It is likely that Inanna-Ištar is an amalgam of several different Sumerian, or southern Mesopotamian, goddesses as well as a fusion of this amalgam with a Semitic goddess, Ištar. Inanna and Ištar seem already to be identified early in Mesopotamian history. But although the goddess has evolved from different figures, she nevertheless seems to possess a believable, even coherent personality. While it is tempting to believe that this persona constituted a new entity, formed by the merger of separate goddesses, it is equally possible, perhaps more reasonable, to suppose that it was the similarities between goddesses that led to the original merger. While different traits or configurations of traits may originally have been associated, respectively, with the Semitic and the Sumerian goddesses, it is likely that the two were identified because they, in fact, resembled each other and contained features associated both with sexual love as well as with military (Semitic) or social (Sumerian) conflict.

2) Various explanations for the occurrence in one persona of the aforementioned contradictory traits have been offered. Thus, for example, it has been suggested that the goddess is the embodiment of qualities or lifestyles that seem contradictory and paradoxical and call into question the categories or values of the society and thus confirm their existence; an embodiment, that is, of figures who are marginal (e.g., a prostitute), bisexual, or anomalous (e.g., a woman of the respectable upper class who, however, is powerful, free, and undomesticated). Alternatively, it has been suggested that she is the embodiment of strife.

Without wishing to suggest that these issues are anything but complex, I shall offer a somewhat subjective and simplifying hypothetical construction. I would suggest that under the figure of the goddess Inanna/Ištar there originally existed a unitary power that encompassed an extensive range of continuous, if diverse, qualities and activities, and that later the goddess drew to herself different characteristics and roles that were then perceived as conflicting.

This original power was, in effect, an earth goddess who partook of and generated both death and life. To use an evocative, if hackneyed, phrase, the goddess was both womb and tomb. Her nature and behavior are characteristic of a type of early earth goddess who was both the source of fertility and life as well as the cause of death. She is the receiver of the dead and the mother of the living. Ištar gives and takes life-force and power. She embodies the female principle. But as with other primitive earth or mother-goddesses, she did not need a male and contained within herself all forms and stages of life and death. She projects or personifies both the fear of death and sexual interest and arousal.

For our purposes here, it suffices simply to note several indications of Inanna/Ištar's association with death/life and the chthonic realm in the myth(s) known as the "Descent of Inanna/Ištar." They are: her very descent to the netherworld; her threat to bring up the dead to eat the living; her own death there; and with her death, the absence of human and animal fertility as a consequence of the loss of sexual attraction, drive, and activity. Even as the dead goddess is brought back to life, it is at the price of another's death as her substitute. Inanna/Ištar is thus also the cause of death to others as well as the one who brings back fertility and sexual interest when she returns to this world.

The figure of Ereshkigal, the mistress of the netherworld and Inanna's elder sister, is informative here, for Ereshkigal represents death, but yet gives birth to young who die before their time; she is a mother, but also a virgin. (It is only the later mythological tradition that cannot understand the virgin mother and thus represents her as a girl who, before the appearance of Nergal, had yet to enjoy a male and needs one.) Similarly, Ištar spends most of her life without a husband or children, for her husbands change their nature almost immediately after consummation or die before their time. Everything is premature, aborted, embryonic.

Inanna/Ištar is a goddess of life and death; but unlike Ereshkigal, she is not rooted in a single realm or cut off from the living world. She is peripheral and moves between the dead and the living. She is concurrently central and marginal to the living community. Moreover, she is not static; in fact, she is the principle of movement and dynamism that is used to explain the interchange of death and life. Where Ereshkigal is static, Inanna/Ištar is the dynamic principle of change. She is movement and change, hence also insatiability and discontent. Most of all, she represents transformation and unpredictability. Hence, also, her power of attraction and repulsion, even aggression.

Her underlying power acts in the life–death and dynamic fashion described above in many of the natural and social forms associated with the goddess. This is especially true of the numen of the underground storehouse, for in it is found food that has been buried in the earth and that could either spoil or provide life-giving sustenance. (The underground house is similar to, or perhaps identical with, a place of burial.) In fact, the location of this storehouse (and of burials) further contributes to the formation of the character of Inanna/Ištar, for as an underground place of death and life, it is central (to the community), yet set apart (from its living or social space). Like the goddess, it is both marginal and unpredictable.

In the course of societal development, perhaps already in the late fourth millennium BCE, the type of earth goddess that stood behind the historical Inanna/Ištar became less understandable and acceptable. Qualities that were a natural part of one unified power began to fragment, for they seemed disparate, even mutually exclusive. The goddess was seen to possess unrelated features, for how could one goddess be a power for both life and death? When it was felt that one character could no longer contain all these features, a reconceptualization of the older form occurred; the goddess was now redefined in terms of sets of characteristics that were seen as culturally connected, if opposite, to each other and could therefore be imposed on the older form. Thus, on the original death–life continuum were imposed new polar opposites: love/death; sex/war; male/female; upper-class establishment/social fringe, opponent of convention. The new sets of opposing characteristics were now united in a newly formed character whose opposing sides were construed as a meaningful construction of opposites. Accordingly, the fragmentation of the original goddess led to the attraction of qualities of a bipolar nature and the creation of what seems to be a conflicted personality, a personality of contraries. As part of this process of re-constitution, other gods were introduced and identified with the original goddess. Hence, Inanna/Ištar grows out of an earlier goddess and is formed by a concomitant redefinition of that goddess and syncretism with various other Sumerian goddesses and a Semitic god of war and of the planet Venus.

## 3 Inside the Bible

As a deity, Ištar is not mentioned in the Bible. Commonly, the name *ʾestēr*, Esther, has been interpreted as derived from Ištar,[3] although other interpretations have been proposed: J. Sheftelowitz suggested a derivation from Old Indian *strī*, "young woman,"[4] the Rabbis connected the name with the Persian noun *stāreh*, "star,"[5] while A. S. Yahuda proposed a relation with an alleged Old Median noun **astra*, "myrtle tree."[6]

M. Delcor vocalized the enigmatic *huṣab* in Nah 2:8 as *haṣṣēbi*, "ornament; glory," interpreting the noun as an epithet for Ištar.[7]

It is possible that the Queen of Heaven mentioned in Jer 7:18 and 44:17–19:25 refers to Ištar.[8]

---

3 M. Noth, *Die israelitischen Personennamen im Rahmen der gemeinsemitischen Nemengebung* (Stuttgart: Kohlhammer, 1928), 11; *HALAT*, 73.

4 I. Scheftelowitz, *Arisches im Alten Testament, I* (Königsberg: Hartungsche Buchdruckerei, 1901), 39.

5 *HALAT*, 73.

6 A. S. Yahuda, "The Meaning of the Name Esther," *JRAS* 8 (1946): 174–178.

7 M. Delcor, "Allusions à la déesse Ištar en Nahum 2,8?," *Bib* 58 (1977): 73–83.

8 In addition to the literature cited in the preceding notes, see the following: T. Abusch, "Ishtar's Proposal and Gilgamesh's Refusal: An Interpretation of *The Gilgamesh Epic*, Tablet 6, Lines 1–79," *HR* 26 (1986): 143–187 [[*Gilgamesh*, 11–57]]; T. Frymer-Kensky, *In the Wake of the Goddesses* (New York: Fawcett Columbine, 1992), 25–31, 45–69, 222; B. Groneberg, "Die sumerisch-akkadische Inanna/Ištar: Hermaphroditos?," *WO* 17 (1986): 25–46; R. Harris, "Inanna-Ishtar as Paradox and a Coincidence of Opposites," *HR* 31 (1991): 261–278; W. Heimpel, "A Catalog of Near Eastern Venus Deities," *SMS* 4 (1982): 59–72; T. Jacobsen, "Mesopotamian Religions," *Encyclopedia of Religion* (New York: Macmillan; London: Collier Macmillan, 1987), 9:458–461; W. G. Lambert, "The Cult of Ištar of Babylon," in *Le Temple et le Culte: Compte rendu de la vingtième Rencontre Assyriologique Internationale, organisée à Leiden du 3 au 7 juillet 1972* (Istanbul: Nederlands Historisch-Archeologisch Instituut, 1975), 104–106; J. J. M. Roberts, *The Earliest Semitic Pantheon* (Baltimore: Johns Hopkins University Press, 1972), 37–40; H. L. J. Vanstiphout, "Inanna/Ishtar as a Figure of Controversy," in *Struggles of Gods: Papers of the Groningen Work Group for the Study of the History of Religions*, ed. H. G. Kippenberg et al., Religion and Reason 31 (Berlin: Mouton, 1984), 225–238; C. Wilcke, "Inanna/Ištar," *RlA* 5 (1976): 74–87.

CHAPTER 7

# Marduk

## 1 Name and Etymology

Marduk was the god of Babylon and the supreme ruler of the Mesopotamian universe. Normally, the name Marduk is written $^{d}$AMAR.UD. The name has been treated by some as pre-Sumerian and the writing understood as a folk etymology, whereby an unintelligible name is rendered understandable in Sumerian. It seems better, however, to treat the name as an original Sumerian name: amar.uda.ak. This agrees with the fact that the name possesses a long form: (*A*)*marut/duk* (= MT: *Mĕrōdāk*, LXX: *Marōdak*) in addition to its short form Marduk. While the name is usually interpreted as "calf/son of the sun," the interpretation "calf of the storm" is to be preferred, especially since Marduk is not a solar deity. There are other ancient interpretations of the name (e.g., *Enūma eliš* I 101–102).

With his exaltation, Marduk assumed the name *Bēl* (= "Lord," from the title *bēlu*; cf. Canaanite *Baʿal* as well as Heb *ʾĂdōnāy* = Gk *Kurios*) as his proper name.

## 2 Character and History

Marduk's earliest beginnings seem to be as the local god and patron of Babylon. Already in the Old Babylonian period, he was incorporated into the Mesopotamian pantheon and considered to be the son of Enki/Ea and a member of the Eridu circle. It has been argued that Marduk became the son of Ea because both he and Asalluḫi were gods of exorcism. Especially since Asalluḫi seems originally to have been the messenger of Ea and not a god of exorcism as such, it is more reasonable to assume that the connection with Ea arose from the desire to link Babylon and Marduk with Eridu, its traditions, and its god Ea. Continuing the tradition of the kings of Isin-Larsa, who also had a special relationship to Eridu, the priests of Babylon were thus able to link Marduk to a major god other than Enlil and a venerable tradition other than Nippur. The subsequent identification of Marduk with Asalluḫi came about because both Marduk and Asalluḫi were associated with rain clouds and water and, as sons of Ea, both functioned as his messengers, agents, and executors. Eventually, Asalluḫi/Marduk indeed became an exorcist, perhaps because the human *āšipu*, who was the messenger of Ea and identified with Asalluḫi, preferred

 | DOI:10.1163/9789004435186_008

to assume an identification with a divine exorcist rather than remaining only a messenger, thus enhancing his power. (This development was part of the expanding role and status of this class of exorcists.)

As Babylon developed and grew in significance, Marduk's natural features were overlaid by characteristics and roles he assumed as the god of the city, and he himself incorporated features and identities of other gods (e.g., Tutu of Borsippa). Marduk is often treated as if he were a political construct lacking in natural features. This approach is understandable, given that, on the one hand, we have no early mythic materials which present him as a natural force or as a developed personality, and that, on the other hand, texts that provide a detailed picture seem to reflect a time when as the supreme god he had taken over many roles and identities. Still, it seems preferable to follow T. Jacobsen's assessment and to treat Marduk as a god who was originally associated with thunderstorms and brought natural abundance by means of water. Accordingly, we should not explain all of Marduk's associations with water and vegetation as simply having been taken over from Ea and his circle. Note, especially, the identification of Marduk with Enbilulu in *Enūma eliš* VII and the emphasis in hymns and prayers upon Marduk's power to bring water and nourishment in abundance (sometimes in conjunction with the rendering of decisions and determination of destinies at the New Year).[1] Also suited to (or derived from) his natural character are some of the storm-like (and hence war-like) features and deeds attributed to him in his fight against Tiāmat in *Enūma eliš* and the use there of Ninurta traditions. In texts from the first millennium BCE, Marduk's astral identification is especially with Jupiter.

The history of the god is of importance for an understanding of Mesopotamian religion and thought. We turn now, therefore, to that topic. Marduk has a more textured personality than simply that of the god of the expanded Babylon, and his full character and deeds should not be seen only as a projection of political developments. Still, his ascension to the head of the pantheon and the expansion of his powers are surely related to the gradual elevation of Babylon to preeminence.

Although mentioned as early as the Early Dynastic period (ca. 2900–2350 BCE; perhaps even ED II, ca. 2700–2600 BCE), it is only during the Old Babylonian period under Ḫammurabi—who for the first time made Babylon an important city and the capital of an extended state—that Marduk emerges as a significant god and a member of the Sumero-Akkadian pantheon. Thus the Code of Ḫammurabi begins: "When lofty Anum, king of the Anunnaki, (and) Enlil,

1 See, for example, A. Livingstone, *Court Poetry and Literary Miscellanea*, SAA 3 (Helsinki: Helsinki University Press, 1989), 21–23, and *BMS* 12 (and dupls.): 24–31.

lord of heaven and earth, the determiner of the destinies of the land, determined for Marduk, the first-born of Enki, the Enlil functions over all mankind, made him great among the Igigi, called Babylon by its exalted name, made it supreme in the world, established for him in its midst an enduring kingship, whose foundations are as firm as heaven and earth …"[2] Even here, Marduk's election is still the continuation of an older Mesopotamian tradition. In that tradition, the god of the politically dominant city ruled the land, but the central meeting place or assembly of the gods remains Nippur and ultimate power resides with the divine assembly and its leaders. One difference, however, from some earlier formulations seems to be the treatment of Marduk's kingship in Babylon as eternal. All the same, Marduk in the Old Babylonian period seems to be no more than a junior member of the pantheon; he is a local god but he is now a permanent member of the pantheon and god of a city that has become a permanent part of the ideological landscape.

As Babylon developed, so did the god. Beginning as the local god and patron of Babylon, Marduk became the god and master of the Babylonian national state and the supreme god and absolute ruler of the universe. However, during most of the second millennium, Marduk seems neither to have replaced the high gods of Babylonia nor to have ascended to the head of the pantheon. Only late in the second millennium does he take on many of Enlil's roles and become not only lord of the land but also king of the gods.

While there are indications that Marduk was emerging as supreme ruler already during the Kassite period[3] and early in the second Isin period, his elevation seems to have been first publicly articulated only during the reign of Nebuchadnezzar I (1125–1104 BCE). This king defeated the Elamites and restored the plundered statue of Marduk to Babylon. Now, in addition to Marduk's rule over the city of Babylon, there was an open claim for Marduk's dominion over the gods and over the whole land. He takes on some of the roles of Enlil and occasionally even replaces him. Generally speaking, however, the other major gods are not replaced by or made simply subservient to Marduk (especially in texts from cities other than Babylon). Rather, Marduk, no longer a junior, is now ranked with the supreme gods of the pantheon.

By the end of the second millennium, a Babylonian nation-state seems to have been created with the city of Babylon as its center and Marduk as its god. As mentioned above, Marduk is now even referred to occasionally as king of

2 CḪ I 1–21; translation: T. J. Meek, "The Code of Hammurabi," in *ANET*, 163–180.

3 Cf., e.g., the events associated with Adad-shuma-uṣur in A. K. Grayson, *Babylonian Historical-Literary Texts* (Toronto: University of Toronto Press, 1975), 56–77 (but note that this text contains anachronisms and was probably composed well after that reign).

the gods, but it is only during the first millennium BCE, culminating in the Neo-Babylonian empire, that we find this idea systematically carried through to its logical conclusion. This is evident from first-millennium documents describing the Akitu New Year festival; for at that season, the gods all assembled in Babylon, where Marduk was declared king and where destinies for the New Year were determined. Certainly, during the Neo-Babylonian empire, Marduk was the supreme god of a universal empire ruled from Babylon.

The date of the elevation of Marduk has occasioned a variety of scholarly opinions. The problem is a knotty one and requires a nuanced approach. It is likely that the perception of Marduk as head of the pantheon was already developing even before the time of Nebuchadnezzar I. Already in the Kassite period, Babylonia became a national state with Babylon as its capital. But the conception of Marduk as king of the gods in the form known to us, for example, from *Enūma eliš*, could not be fully articulated until at least two conditions were met: (1) Babylon had to replace Nippur as the divine locus of power upon which the world, the nation, and the monarchy were based; and (2) a new model of world organization had to be available.

1) Nippur/Babylon: Even though the Kassite kings ruled the country from Babylon, they followed the older Nippur-Anu-Enlil construction of government and, in addition to being kings of Babylon, were kings of Sumer and Akkad. The nation, in accordance with the traditional cosmology, was imagined as being governed by the divine assembly in Nippur under Enlil. The nation/country of Babylonia and the city of Babylon were kept conceptually separate, with the kingdom of "Sumer and Akkad"—not the royal capital—being perceived as the primary unit of government and source of power. Marduk was god of the city of Babylon, the capital, and god of the royal family, but Enlil remained lord of the land.

Naturally, as the god of Babylon and of the royal family, Marduk's position continued to evolve. For residents of Babylon, for its priests and theologians, and even for the kings in their role of rulers of Babylon, Marduk might have been perceived as king of the gods even before Nebuchadnezzar I. However, as long as the Nippurian conception of governance of the Mesopotamian cosmos and territory remained operative, the concept of the nation and the role of Enlil would remain the same, and developments in Babylon would not initially have affected them. Thus, until the replacement of the political framework that had Nippur as its center by a different framework centering on Babylon, Marduk's supremacy would not be expressed in political documents. Official recognition of Babylon as the permanent capital and source of legitimacy was a precondition to the public, official exaltation of Marduk as the supreme god.

2) World organization: But more was required than just the replacement of Nippur with Babylon to bring about such a change in the conception of Marduk. The recognition of Marduk as the supreme god was a new religious idea that depended upon a radical shift in thinking about the state. What was required was not only a different center, but also a new conception of the cosmic and political world as a world empire revolving around one central city. In this divine empire, everything revolves around the god of the central city; at home in their own cities, the other gods pay homage to the supreme god and also journey to the center to do obeisance: their relationship to the supreme god defines the character of the divine world and their role within it. Such a conception depends not only on the existence of absolute kingship, but even more upon an imperial form of government. It is for this reason that Marduk's elevation to full divine supremacy could only take place in the first millennium BCE at a time of world empire. (Compare, perhaps, Marduk's replacement of the divine assembly with developments in Egypt under Akhnaten.)

But regardless of how one assesses the evidence from/about the latter half of the second millennium and what one concludes regarding the date of Marduk's elevation, it is clear that in the first millennium the new image of Marduk as world ruler dominated Babylonian thinking. Marduk and Babylon have become the primordial god and city; the *Erra* poem can present Marduk as the god who ruled before the Flood and whose temporary absence brought about the Flood, and in this new antediluvian tradition, Marduk replaces the older gods Enlil and Ea. Nevertheless, despite the new supremacy of Marduk and the apparent existence of henotheistic tendencies, Mesopotamia remained polytheistic, with its several cities maintaining the cults of their gods.

Marduk's cult spread to Assyria before the Sargonids, but it was especially in the eighth–seventh centuries BCE, when Assyria attempted to control Babylon, that interesting developments and conflicts surrounding Marduk and Babylon arose. The Assyrians had difficulty assimilating the Marduk cult or even defining an efficacious and stable relationship with Marduk and his city. An extreme form of the conflict is attested during the reign of Sennacherib when, alternatively, Aššur was cast in the role of Marduk and assumed his deeds or Marduk was made to function at the behest of Aššur/Anšar.

During the late seventh and first half of the sixth century, under the Neo-Babylonian kings, Marduk was regarded as the principal god of the empire. Apparent threats to the prerogatives of the Marduk cult led the priests of Babylon to welcome and justify Cyrus's conquest.

Apparently, the events of the reign of Nebuchadnezzar I—especially the return of the statue of Marduk—occasioned the composition of literary works revolving around Marduk, his experiences and deeds, and his new exalted position of power and rank. In such texts as the Marduk *šuilla BMS* 9, obv. (and dupls.), Marduk is shown outgrowing the role of son of Enki and young prince of Eridu (a role in which he was comparable to Ninurta as son of Enlil and young prince in Nippur) and assuming the role of master of Babylon and of the whole land. While recognizing that Babylon is the center of the world, this text does not focus only on the city. Rather, it uses Babylon as a stepping-off point to the rest of the world. *BMS* 9, obv. is to be dated, I believe, to the reign of Nebuchadnezzar I.

A somewhat different situation obtains, however, in *Enūma eliš*, for in addition to describing Marduk's ascendancy to the kingship of the gods, it focuses narrowly on Babylon, on its creation as the first city and designation as the center of the world of the gods, and thus also displays an inward turning. For other reasons as well, *Enūma eliš* should perhaps not be dated to the time of Nebuchadnezzar I. We should now, therefore, discuss this document.

*Enūma eliš* ("When On High"), a seven-tablet work, is certainly the most important document defining Marduk's elevation. It describes his rise to permanent and absolute kingship over the gods. His ascendancy is expressed not only by the recognition of his kingship over the gods but also by the naming of his fifty names, for by this naming many gods are identified with Marduk or are made aspects of him. In this work, the idea of an assembly ruled by Marduk from the Esagila in Babylon is clearly envisaged and worked out, and the earlier structure of a national assembly of the gods in Nippur (led by Enlil and Anu) is, by implication, replaced.

While various documents composed under Nebuchadnezzar I reflected the ascendancy of Marduk, it may be a mistake to include *Enūma eliš* among them. The date of composition of *Enūma eliš* is not without historical significance; moreover, the date has a bearing on the interpretation of the work and its relationship to other literatures. In the course of the last sixty or seventy years, various dates have been suggested for *Enūma eliš*. In the first flush of rediscovery of the Old Babylonian period and the Code of Ḫammurabi, the composition of *Enūma eliš* was dated to that period. (Such passages as the above-quoted passage from the prologue to the Code of Ḫammurabi were used to support this notion.) More recently, dates in the latter half of the second millennium have been proposed. While W. von Soden suggests a date of composition around 1400 BCE, W. G. Lambert argues for the composition of *Enūma eliš* during the reign of Nebuchadnezzar I as a work celebrating Marduk's official elevation to leadership of the pantheon.[4] T. Jacobsen, on the other hand, introduces a

4 W. G. Lambert, "The Reign of Nebuchadnezzar I: A Turning Point in the History of Ancient Mesopotamian Religion," in *The Seed of Wisdom: Essays in Honour of T. J. Meek*, ed.

number of subtle distinctions and argues that the work dealt with issues surrounding Babylonia's reconquest of the Sealand and national unification and should be dated subsequent to that event (after Ulamburiash) in the early part of the second half of the second millennium.[5]

Previous attempts at dating and interpretation have assumed that the work reflects a period of ascendancy of the city Babylon and the Babylonian kingdom. If this were the case, we would expect our text to evidence characteristics of a work written either by temple circles or by palace circles and to support the interests of one or the other. Rather, it exhibits a mixed set of features with regard to temple and palace. This mixture can be explained if we assume that *Enūma eliš* was written not at a time of ascendancy, but rather at a time when the interests of temple and palace had coalesced because the seat of power had shifted elsewhere and it had become necessary to reassert the central importance of the god, his temple, and his city. Thus, rather than viewing *Enūma eliš* as a work composed during a period of Babylonian political ascendancy and as a reflection of the city's attainment of increasing power, I would suggest that we instead view *Enūma eliš* as having been composed at a time when it was necessary to preserve the memory of Babylon's ascendancy and to assert its claim to be a world capital on the grounds that it had been so since the beginning of time. It was composed some time during the early first millennium BCE in a period of weakness of the city Babylon and served to bolster the city's claim to cultural prestige and privilege at a time when it was coping with the loss of political power and centrality. While supporting political aspirations, the work reflects even more the need of a major temple organization to preserve its religious and cultural significance and may well have been composed in temple circles.

Thus, while *BMS* 9, obv. (and dupls.) is a more natural example of increasing strength, *Enūma eliš* is a conservative attempt to preserve something that was threatened with loss. The emphases and approach of *Enūma eliš* would agree with composition in the first millennium at a point when Babylon's ascendancy was threatened either by the Aramaeans or the Assyrians. Certainly, *Enūma eliš* exhibits a pronounced baroque style characteristic of late periods.

Moreover, while the universalistic worldview implicit in *Enūma eliš* is not consonant with the second millennium, when the concept of world empire had not yet become part of the Mesopotamian political and religious imagination, it does fit with the thought and experiences of the first millennium. *Enūma eliš* is rooted in the notion of Marduk as king of the gods; while the

W. S. McCullough (Toronto: University of Toronto Press, 1964), 3–13.

5 T. Jacobsen, *The Treasures of Darkness: A History of Mesopotamian Religion* (New Haven: Yale University Press, 1976), 190.

earlier period may have already articulated this idea, the vision of *Enūma eliš* reflects a radical extension of it, perhaps in reaction to the Assyrians and under the influence of the model provided by the Assyrian world empire. It reflects the cultural needs of first-millennium Babylon. For the time being, then, *Enūma eliš* should not be called upon to give testimony to the ascendancy of Marduk at the end of the second millennium.

Marduk's main sanctuary was located in the center of Babylon and comprised a group of buildings, most notably the low temple Esagila and the temple tower (ziggurat) Etemenanki. Between these two complexes ran the main processional street. Esagila contained the major shrines of Marduk and his wife Zarpanītu as well as a number of chapels dedicated to other gods. On the top of the ziggurat, which was located within an enclosure, stood the high temple of Marduk, with rooms of worship for other gods. Among the gods who had chapels in these complexes special mention should be made of Marduk's son Nabû, the scribe of the gods and god of Borsippa. Nabû, too, eventually attains high eminence among the gods alongside his father Marduk.

The Akitu New Year festival in Babylon was based in Marduk's temple complex and centered on his cult. Comprising several separate strands which were joined together over time, the rites of the festival, which took place in the spring during the first twelve days of the first month (Nisannu), center upon the god, city, and king of Babylon. But although the Akitu festival had several originally independent dimensions (natural, cosmological, and political), it nevertheless remains true that *Enūma eliš* gives expression to some of the same basic issues and narrative themes as the late festival and corresponds to several of its major ritual enactments. *Enūma eliš* (probably our text, but possibly some other version or retelling of the story) was recited before Marduk on the fourth day of the month (it may well have been recited in other months as well). Principal among the ritual events that should be mentioned here are prayers for Babylon; divesting and reinvesting the king before Marduk; ingathering of the gods from various cities to Babylon; gathering of the gods in assembly on two separate occasions in the shrine of destinies of the Nabû sanctuary for the purpose of determining destinies (parallel to the two assemblies in *Enūma eliš*, before and after the battle); procession of Marduk and the other gods (with the king taking Marduk's hand) by way of the processional way and Ištar's gate, and travel on the river to the Akitu house, where a banquet takes place. Sitting down in the Akitu house has been taken as representing the victorious battle over Tiāmat, though this battle may be equally or better represented by the voyage on the river to the Akitu house. Thus, evidently battle, enthronement, and determining destinies are among the many acts that are celebrated during the Akitu festival.

## 3 Inside the Bible

*Merodach* is mentioned in Jer 50:2, where he is the god of Babylon and is referred to also under the name Bel. As Bel he occurs also in Jer 51:44 and Is 46:1; in the latter passage he appears together with his son Nebo = Nabû. For Bel in the OT Apocrypha, see Letter of Jeremiah (= Bar 6) 40 and Bel and the Dragon (= LXX Dan 14) 3–22. All biblical references allude to the Marduk cult of the Neo-Babylonian period. Several Babylonian names with Marduk as the theophoric element appear in the Bible: Evil-merodach, Merodach-baladan, and perhaps Mordechai.[6]

---

6 D. J. A. Clines, "Mordechai," *ABD* 4:902–904, esp. 902; C. A. Moore, "Esther, Book of," *ABD* 2:633–643, esp. 633. In addition to the literature already cited, see the following: T. Abusch, "The Form and Meaning of a Babylonian Prayer to Marduk," *JAOS* 103 (1983): 3–15 [[126–148]]; J. A. Black, "The New Year Ceremonies in Ancient Babylon: 'Taking Bel by the Hand' and a Cultic Picnic," *Religion* 11 (1981): 39–59; M. J. Geller, *Forerunners to Udug-ḫul*, FAS 12 (Stuttgart: Franz Steiner Verlag Wiesbaden GMBH, 1985), 12–15; T. Jacobsen, "Babylonia and Assyria, Part V. Religion," *Encyclopedia Britannica* (1963) 2:972–978, esp. 977 (= "Mesopotamian Gods and Pantheons," in *Toward the Image of Tammuz*, ed. W. L. Moran, HSS 21 [Cambridge, MA: Harvard University Press, 1970], 16–38, esp. 35–36); T. Jacobsen, "The Battle between Marduk and Tiamat," *JAOS* 88 (1968): 104–108; T. Jacobsen, "Religious Drama in Ancient Mesopotamia," in *Unity and Diversity*, ed. H. Goedicke and J. J. M. Roberts (Baltimore: Johns Hopkins University Press, 1975), 65–97, esp. 72–76; W. G. Lambert, "The Great Battle of the Mesopotamian Religious Year: The Conflict in the Akītu House," *Iraq* 25 (1963): 189–190; W. G. Lambert, "Studies in Marduk," *BSOAS* 47 (1984): 1–9; W. G. Lambert, "Ninurta Mythology in the Babylonian Epic of Creation," in *Keilinschriftliche Literaturen*, ed. K. Hecker and W. Sommerfeld, BBVO 6 (Berlin: Dietrich Reimer, 1986), 55–60; J. J. M. Roberts, "Nebuchadnezzar I's Elamite Crisis in Theological Perspective," in *Essays on the Ancient Near East in Memory of Jacob Joel Finkelstein*, ed. M. de Jong Ellis (Hamden, CT: Archon, 1977), 183–187; J. Z. Smith, *Imagining Religion: From Babylon to Jonestown* (Chicago: University of Chicago Press, 1982), 90–96; W. Sommerfeld, *Der Aufstieg Marduks*, AOAT 213 (Kevalaer: Butzon & Bercker; Neukirchen-Vluyn: Neukirchener Verlag, 1982); W. Sommerfeld, "Marduk," *RlA* 7 (1987–1990): 360–370.

*Talking to the Gods in Mesopotamia*

CHAPTER 8

# Prayers and Incantations

Akkadian prayers and incantations composed in Standard Babylonian during the post-Old Babylonian period are known from first-millennium BCE copies found in libraries or collections in such Assyrian and Babylonian cities as Nineveh, Aššur, Nimrud, Sultantepe, Sippar, Babylon, Ur, and Uruk. In Mesopotamia, there was a range of sacred speech forms that included lengthy literary hymns and prayers, royal prayers (especially of the kings of the Neo-Assyrian and Neo-Babylonian periods), prayers of diviners, lamentations, penitential psalms, folkloristic and learned incantations, and so on. Here, however, we pay particular attention to some of the major types of prayers and incantations of the *āšipu* (exorcist), over against those of the diviner or temple lamentation priest. The oral rites of the exorcist are invocations to gods and addresses to evil forces.

## 1 Prayers

Of special interest are laments or prayers of the individual known as *šuilla*s, according to the native designations found especially in their rubrics. The *šuilla*s are directed to many of the gods of the Babylonian pantheon, but most often to Marduk, Šamaš, and Ištar. The *šuilla*s are often referred to as *Gebetsbeschwörungen* (incantation prayers) because they have the form and thematic makeup of prayers, but open with the designation ÉN (incantation), are identified by rubrics normally found with incantations, and are linked to ritual activities that are referred to within the prayer and/or in ritual instructions that accompany the prayer. This terminology reflects a modern Western and often artificial distinction between magic and religion. Assyriological scholarship distinguishes, furthermore, between general and special *Gebetsbeschwörung*. The former carries the designation *šuilla* in at least some of its manuscripts; the latter has the form of a *šuilla* but does not carry that designation. The special *šuilla*, moreover, is often directed against specific types of evil and is recited as part of a magical ritual.

The basic format of the Akkadian *šuilla* contains three elements:

1. An address to and praise of the god by means of epithets and whole sentences. This part of the *šuilla* prayer will often provide a laudatory description

 | DOI:10.1163/9789004435186_009

of the god, first in terms of his/her place within the divine community and then in terms of his/her relationship to earth and the human world. This descriptive praise, particularly the description of the god's relationship to humanity, provides the backdrop and jumping-off point for the request to the god to listen to and help the petitioner. It warrants the human address to the god and explains in very general terms why the supplicant turns to the god for help. Even more, praise here elicits the power that inheres in the addressee; it activates the god by reminding him/her of his/her powers and functions and perhaps by flattering him/her.

2. A supplication centering upon a petition to the god asking him/her to come to his aid. Usually this central part of the prayer also includes an introductory lament in which the supplicant describes his/her suffering and perhaps its cause. Personal suffering may include the individual's experience of physical and/or psychological illness or difficulties and/or socioeconomic crises such as the loss of wealth and status, breakup of family, and social isolation. This part of the prayer may also contain an explicit presentation of the supplicant and a mention of the ritual act(s) accompanying the recitation.

3. Finally, a promise of praise should the petition be granted and the deity allow the supplicant to regain a normal life. In the most common form of promise, this praise serves to express thanksgiving, to affirm the individual's loyalty to this god, to give honor to the god, and to publicize the god's saving deeds so as to attract other loyal followers to his/her service.

The following prayer to Nergal, a god of war and pestilence and ruler of the netherworld, is an excellent example of a general *šuilla*:

> Mighty lord, exalted son of Nunammir,
> foremost among the Anunnaki, lord of battle,
> offspring of Kutušar, the great queen,
> Nergal, all powerful among the gods, beloved of Ninmenna.
>
> You are manifest in the bright heavens, your station is exalted,
> you are great in the netherworld, you have no rival.
> Together with Anu (variant: Ea), your counsel is preeminent in the assembly of the gods.
> Together with Sîn, you observe everything in the heavens (variant: and earth/netherworld).
>
> Enlil, your father, gave to you the black-headed ones, all the living,
> he entrusted into your hands the herds, the animals.

I am So-and-so, son of So-and-so, your servant.
The anger of god and goddess has beset me so that
expenses and losses befall my estate (and)
giving orders but not being obeyed keep me awake.

Because you save, my lord, I have turned toward your divinity,
because you are compassionate, I have sought you,
because you are merciful, I have stood before you,
because you are favorably inclined, I have looked upon your face.

Favorably look upon me and hear my supplication.
May your furious heart become calm toward me,
pardon my crime, my sin, and my misdeed,
may the indignation of your great divinity be appeased for me.
May the offended, angry, and irate god and goddess be reconciled with me.

Then will I declare your great deeds and sing your praise![1]

The *šuilla* type may be used to invoke not only anthropomorphic gods and stars, but also materials used in magical rituals such as amulets, salt, oil (the so-called *Kultmittelbeschwörung* or *Kultmittelgebet*). An excellent example of this type is the following *šuilla*:

O Salt, created in a clean place
for food of gods did Enlil destine you.
Without you no meal is set out in Ekur,
without you god, king, nobleman, and prince do not smell incense.
I am So-and-so, the son of So-and-so, whom witchcraft holds captive,
whom bewitchment holds by means of [a skin] disease.
O Salt, break my witchcraft! Loosen my spell!
Receive from me the bewitchment so that, as my creator, I may praise you.[2]

1 L. W. King, *Babylonian Magic and Sorcery* (London: Luzac, 1896), no. 27 and dupls. = W. Mayer, *Untersuchungen zur Formensprache der babylonischen "Gebetsbeschwörungen,"* StPohl, series maior 5 (Rome: Pontifical Biblical Institute, 1976), 478–481, Nergal 2.

2 *Maqlû* VI 119″–126″.

There are variations on the basic pattern of the *šuilla*. Some deviate from the norm and represent creative innovations. An excellent example of this is a twenty-seven-line *šuilla* addressed to Marduk.[3] It exhibits a new design that is created by the inclusion of two related summary statements of invocation, prayer, and thanksgiving, with the first being placed between the hymnic introduction and the prayer, and the second between the prayer and the concluding benediction. Although deviating from the usual liturgical pattern, this *šuilla* does not lack a meaningful order and creates a new religious effect.

Other *šuilla*s are longer and less orderly than these three. An example drawn from among the most important *šuilla*s is the famous Great Prayer to Ištar known from both second- and first-millennium copies. The later version runs to about 110 lines and while thematically very rich and powerful and dynamic in its representation, its *šuilla* structure is less clear, as its sections of praise, complaint, and prayer are somewhat jumbled and repetitive.

Here we turn to some general problems relating to the makeup of the *šuilla* corpus. But first, we recall that the *šuilla* is not part of the temple liturgy; rather, it is to be compared to the biblical laments of the individual, the most prevalent type of prayer in the Hebrew Psalms. The *šuilla* was part of a ceremony meant to heal or protect an individual and was recited at the home of the supplicant (or palace of the king) or in a secluded outdoor area. Originally, the magician viewed natural and material powers holistically. But although the *āšipu*'s activities on behalf of supplicants were not part of the temple cult and took place outside the temple, it seems that he increasingly thought in terms drawn from the urban temple as he became a servant and representative of the elite. He thus came to address both natural forces and material objects in forms drawn from the temple cult, that is, modeled on the image of the god in the temple, who himself/herself was conceived in accordance with the image of the human ruler. The evolution of the *šuilla* reflects this suggested development.

This perspective may help to explain the use of a temple-oriented text for home service, the place of the personal god in the *šuilla*, and the wide variety of texts that are designated as *šuilla*s. In addition, it may help to understand the formation and existence of the special *šuilla*.

Composers of *šuilla*s did not simply compose their works on the basis of one design. The development of this body of material is complicated. The sources upon which the composers drew were various, and some of the same tendencies apply to both general and special *šuilla*s.

3 King, *Babylonian Magic and Sorcery*, no. 9, obv. and dupls.

The *šuilla* type as well as many of its actual examples seem to have their origin in prayers that were recited on behalf of individuals and did not contain developed hymnic introductions. These supplications for the individual derived from various sources; but prayers to the personal god or, more properly, the god of the family were a particularly important source (but see now "The Reconciliation of Angry Personal Gods: A Revision of the *šuillas*" [[176–205]]). Prayers to the personal god were recited originally in a family context; they reflect the problems of the individual householder or family head and represent an attempt to rectify personal or family problems caused by a rupture of relations between this person and the god—a rupture that led to abandonment and suffering and a rectification that involved forgiveness and reconciliation. That originally these supplications did not contain extended praise is supported by biblical laments of the individual; many of these laments seem to have been recited to the family or clan-god in a nontemple context and call directly upon the god for help without first offering significant praise (cf., e.g., Pss 6, 13, 35, 38). Not infrequently, the divine recipient was identified with a cosmic or urban deity normally worshiped in a temple, and the address was modeled on temple liturgies by *āšipu*s with a temple orientation. A hymnic introduction of praise would then have been added to the supplication; for the new praise section, the composer drew upon temple imagery and experiences associated with gods of the temple. (This suggestion regarding the development of the *šuilla* explains, by the way, why the biblical and Mesopotamian laments of the individual, two obviously related literary corpora, are both similar and different.)

The family background of the original prayers explains the frequent mention of the personal god in many *šuilla*s. Of course, the social location of many of the *šuilla*s was now changed; concerns internal to the family are sometimes found alongside or even replaced by the court concerns of the elite members of society for whom the developed *šuilla*s were composed or adapted. This development may also explain some of the different roles of the personal god in this body of literature. Sometimes the role of the personal god is taken over by the urban god to whom the *šuilla* is addressed; at other times, the family god is mentioned in the text, but has been transformed into a mere reflection or manifestation of the major god, on the model of the royal court with its king (temple god) and courtiers (personal gods), in which circles the elite moved. (The earlier role of the personal god as an intercessor may also have been colored by the image of the courtier; but this role seems to recede in the developed *šuilla* and is replaced by the model of the courtier who simply reflects the disposition and moods of the king.)

The special *šuilla* is often recited as part of a magical ceremony, and the ritual as well as the prayer, the *Gebetsbeschwörung*, focus on the specific evil to be combated by the ceremony, evils such as roaming ghosts, witchcraft, *māmīt* (oath), evil omens, demons. Šamaš is the most common addressee of the special *šuillas*.[4]

The formation of the special *Gebetsbeschwörung* type is a result of the transformation of magical incantations to divine forces into prayers with hymnic introductions. As I have argued elsewhere, the different forms of a text may attest to this development. Thus, for example, manuscript variations of a Šamaš incantation seem to reflect the exorcist's attempt to transform an incantation rooted in nature and ritual into a hymn and prayer to the god. The incantation is thus transformed into a *Gebetsbeschworung*, taking on the form of the standard *šuilla* prayer type. This development reflects a similar process whereby popular material, in this case magical, is transformed into the literary form of a centrist institution, that is, a temple, by a literate clergy, knowledgeable in the forms of temple imagery and worship. A further example, perhaps, of the same general process is the use of forms derived from juridical practice in the prayers, thus turning the encounter with an evil force into a case at law and the prayer itself into an address to a judge.

## 2 Incantations

There are many different kinds of incantations; in the main, they address evil forces as well as beneficent forces that are meant to aid in the fight against evil forces. Such causes of suffering as demons, witchcraft, evil omens, roaming ghosts, and so on are confronted so as either to expel them or to keep them at a distance. Originally, incantations were recorded only in part as an *aide-mémoire*, but eventually the entire incantation was committed to writing, and instructions regarding the time, place, and manner of ritual performance as well as other types of information (particularly an objective description of the problem, a diagnosis, and a statement of purpose) were subsequently added. Incantations are found in various written contexts: (1) individual incantations as part of short rituals; (2) short collections of incantations (with some ritual instructions); and (3) standardized scribal series—some were collections, others represented complex, lengthy ceremonies such as *Šurpu* and *Maqlû*. Among the themes in which incantations are particularly rich are the

4 See *KAR* 80, obv. 12–rev. 14 and dupls. [[*CMAwR* 1, no. 8.4]], and *BAM* 323, obv. 19–35 and dupls.

imagery used to depict evil beings; the nature and cause of the suffering; and, finally, the ritual acts that are performed alongside the recitation and are often reflected in one way or another in the incantation itself.[5]

5 In addition to the literature cited in the preceding notes, see the following: T. Abusch, "Blessing and Praise in Ancient Mesopotamian Incantations," in *Literatur, Politik und Recht in Mesopotamien: Festschrift für Claus Wilcke*, ed. W. Sallaberger, K. Volk, and A. Zgoll, OBC 14 (Wiesbaden: Harrassowitz, 2003), 1–14 [[AMD 17, 94–109]]; T. Abusch, "The Demonic Image of the Witch in Standard Babylonian Literature: The Reworking of Popular Conceptions by Learned Exorcists," in *Religion, Science, and Magic in Concert and in Conflict*, ed. J. Neusner, E. Frerichs, and P. Flesher (New York: Oxford University Press, 1989), 27–58 [[AMD 5, 3–25]]; T. Abusch, "The Form and Meaning of a Babylonian Prayer to Marduk," *JAOS* 103 (1983): 3–15 [[126–148]]; T. Abusch, *Mesopotamian Witchcraft: Toward a History and Understanding of Babylonian Witchcraft Beliefs and Literature*, AMD 5 (Leiden: Brill/Styx, 2002); W. G. Kunstmann, *Die babylonische Gebetsbeschwörung*, LSS NF 2 (Leipzig: Hinrichs, 1932); M.-J. Seux, *Hymnes et prières aux dieux de Babylonie et d'Assyrie*, LAPO 8 (Paris: Éditions du Cerf, 1976).

CHAPTER 9

# The Promise to Praise the God in *šuilla* Prayers

In his posthumously published article entitled "The Babylonian Job," William L. Moran made the following observation concerning the well-known Babylonian wisdom poem *Ludlul bēl nēmeqi*:

> In the many prayers we have in which a suffering penitent bewails his situation, confesses his sins, known and unknown, and begs for a god or goddess to heal him, a very common conclusion is the promise that, if healed, the penitent will sing to the world the praises of the healing god or goddess. Our text [scil. *Ludlul*] should be seen as the fulfillment of such a promise.[1]

It affords me all the more satisfaction, therefore, to dedicate this study to the memory of Bill Moran, teacher and friend, who embodied the rabbinic dictum עשה לך רב וקנה לך חבר.[2]

In a recently published study about praise in the Wilcke Festschrift,[3] I focused on incantations, particularly *Kultmittelbeschwörungen*, and studied the development of addresses to live but impersonal materials into addresses to materials and forces that have been given human physical, psychological, and social form. Here, I turn to the praise of gods and examine some aspects of praise in prayers addressed to fully anthropomorphized divinities.

Having seen how a numinous force may assume the characteristics and personality of an anthropomorphic deity, we may now begin to think about praise as a human phenomenon. For it is the human quality of the praise that completes the transformation of the addressee from object to god; conversely, and perhaps more important, the fact that the god now has the form of a human being allows for and even promotes the full use of images of praise that derive from human models. For now, in contrast to addresses to material objects, we

1 W. L. Moran, "The Babylonian Job," in *The Most Magic Word: Essays on Babylonian and Biblical Literature*, ed. R. S. Hendel, CBQMS 35 (Washington: Catholic Biblical Association of America, 2002), 191.

2 m. Avot 1:6.

3 See T. Abusch, "Blessing and Praise in Ancient Mesopotamian Incantations," in *Literatur, Politik und Recht in Mesopotamien: Festschrift für Claus Wilcke*, ed. W. Sallaberger et al., OBC 14 (Wiesbaden: Harrassowitz, 2003), 1–14 [[AMD 17, 94–109]]. Earlier versions of both papers were first presented at the conference on "Blessings and Curses" sponsored by the American Academy in Rome in March 2001.

 | DOI:10.1163/9789004435186_010

are not only dealing with a form of word magic that brings something into being by its utterance, but with the approach to a god by means of the full panoply of psychological and social images and resonances drawn from individual, family, and communal life.

We have seen how powers and qualities of material objects are enhanced and elicited. Praise serves similarly to activate the fully anthropomorphized divinity. Gods, no less than people, often fall into a mode of passivity and must be aroused. An example of this is provided by the well-known contest between Elijah and the prophets of Baal in 1 Kgs 18:26–27:

> [The prophets of Baal] took the bull that was given them; they prepared it, and invoked Baal by name from morning until noon, shouting, "O Baal, answer us!" But there was no sound, and none who responded; so they performed a hopping dance about the altar that had been set up. When noon came, Elijah mocked them, saying, "Shout louder! After all, he is a god. But he may be in conversation, he may be detained, or he may be on a journey, or perhaps he is asleep and will wake up."[4]

Gods, no less than human beings, must have their sleep. But a good thing can sometimes be taken too far. And, in the myth of Erra, a god of war and pestilence, the god is described as one who is inactive and must be roused to activity.[5] But activation is only one, albeit the most important, function of praise.

To grasp more fully the nature of praise, we will now examine its place in developed liturgical prayer. For this purpose, I have chosen Akkadian texts that were designated by the ancients, or that may be regarded on typological grounds, as *šuilla*s (either general or specific) and hope to make a specific contribution to our understanding of the meaning of the promise of praise. The basic format of the Akkadian *šuilla* is: (1) an address to and praise of the god by means of epithets and whole sentences; (2) a supplication which centers upon a petition to the god but usually also includes an introductory lament, and may contain an explicit presentation of the supplicant; and (3) finally, a promise of praise should the petition be granted.[6] This structure is consistent with the

4 Translation: NJPS.

5 See, e.g., Erra I 15–93. Translation: S. Dalley, *Myths from Mesopotamia: Creation, The Flood, Gilgamesh, and Others*, rev. ed. (Oxford: Oxford University Press, 2000), 285–288.

6 For detailed discussion of *šuilla* texts and of their structure, see W. G. Kunstmann, *Die babylonische Gebetsbeschwörung*, LSS NF 2 (Leipzig: Hinrichs, 1932), and W. Mayer, *Untersuchungen zur Formensprache der babylonische "Gebetsbeschwörungen,"* StPohl, series maior 5 (Rome: Pontifical Biblical Institute, 1976). For an observation on some developments in the type, see also T. Abusch, "The Demonic Image of the Witch in Standard Babylonian Literature: The

nature of praise as both a means to elicit or activate the power that inheres in the addressee as well as a means of thanksgiving.

## 1 Address: Activation

By means of the address to and statements about the god, the first part of the *šuilla* prayer will often provide a laudatory description of the god, first in terms of his/her place within the divine community and then in terms of his/her relationship to earth and the human world. This descriptive praise, particularly the description of the god's relationship to humanity, provides the backdrop and jumping-off point for the request to the god to listen to and help the petitioner. It warrants the human address to the god and explains in very general terms why the supplicant turns to the god for help. Even more, praise here elicits the power that inheres in the addressee; it activates the god by reminding him/her of his/her powers and functions, and perhaps by flattering him/her.

## 2 Thanksgiving: Devotion and Public Acclaim

But in this paper, I should like to pay particular attention to part three of the prayer-type under consideration. Part three also may be regarded as referring to praise. This part of the prayer will often assume one of two forms. It may appear as a request that the community of the gods greet and salute the god being addressed.[7] For example:

> Grant me my life; decree for me a healthy life,
> In joyfully serving you regularly will I then find satisfaction,
> May Enlil rejoice because of you, may Ea be joyful because of you,
> May the gods of the universe bless you,
> May the great gods satisfy your heart (i.e., please you). (*AGH* 64: 21–25)[8]

---

Reworking of Popular Conceptions by Learned Exorcists," in *Religion, Science, and Magic in Concert and in Conflict*, ed. J. Neusner et al. (New York: Oxford University Press, 1989), 35–36 [[AMD 5, 11–12]]; and for a detailed analysis of an individual *šuilla*, see T. Abusch, "The Form and Meaning of a Babylonian Prayer to Marduk," *JAOS* 103 (1983): 3–15 [[126–148]].

7 See Kunstmann, *Gebetsbeschwörung*, 40, and Mayer, *Untersuchungen*, 331–332 and 336–337.

8 For a minor variation of the divine greeting, see, e.g.:
> May heaven rejoice because of you, may the depths rejoice because of you,
> May the gods of the universe bless you,
> May the great gods satisfy your heart (i.e., please you).
> (*AGH* 62: 37b–38)

It is not, however, this formulation of the end of the prayer that I wish to focus on primarily, although we will return to it later in the paper.

The more common ending to a prayer is a promise by the human supplicant to praise the god should he/she heal the speaker or otherwise fulfill his desires. A simple and typical form is:[9]

> *lubluṭ lušlimma*
> *narbîka lušāpi dalīlīka ludlul*

> May I have health and well-being,
> That I may declare your great deeds and sing your praise!

Man will give praise should the deity save him and allow him to resume a healthy life. A passage like the following suggests one form that the praise might take.

> May your furious heart be calmed,
> And your feelings be eased, have mercy!
> Let me endow your temple richly, and anoint your door bolt with oil,
> Let me sound my lord's praises,
> Let me ever exalt the greatness of your great divinity! (Anu: *AGH* 36: 18–25 [*BMS* 6 and dupls.])[10]

The conjunction of the hope to get well and the hope to declare the god's praise, and the parallelism of the latter with a promise to endow the temple, suggest that the praise serves as a form of thanks to the deity that is to be given when the supplicant's wish has been granted. We might presume that the praise consists of statements that recite the god's deeds and in some way refer to the god's actions on behalf of the speaker.

But in the *šuillas*, we are usually not told what the content of the praise will be, since most texts do no more than promise to declare the god's deeds or greatness should the supplicant be healed, and we are still left wondering what precise form the promised thanksgiving praise will take. Fortunately,

---

9 For this and related forms and examples, see Kunstmann, *Gebetsbeschwörung*, 40–41, and Mayer, *Untersuchungen*, 312 n. 16, 319–325. For a slightly expanded version of the form given here, see, e.g., *BMS* 12 [[*CMAwR* 2, no. 8.28]]: 90–91:
> May I, your servant, So-and-so, son of So-and-so, have health and well-being,
> That I may exalt your divinity and sing your praise!

10 Translation: B. R. Foster, *Before the Muses: An Anthology of Akkadian Literature*, 3rd ed. (Bethesda, MD: CDL, 2005), 640.

then, there are a few texts that deviate from the norm.[11] I will here take up one of these texts because I think that it provides an answer to our question and because I believe that I can adduce some further evidence in support of understanding this text as containing the aforementioned praise. I have in mind *Maqlû* II 77–103,[12] an incantation to the fire god Girra. The incantation ends (98–103) on the following note:

> *ᵈGirra šarḫu ṣīru ša ilī*
> *kāšid lemni u ayyābi kušussunūtima anāku lā aḫḫabbil*
> *anāku aradka lubluṭ lušlimma maḫarka luzziz*
> *attāma ilī attāma bēlī*
> *attāma dayyānī attāma rēṣu'a*
> *attāma mutirru ša gimilliya* TU$_6$ ÉN

> O stately Girra, eminent one of the gods,
> Conqueror of the wicked and the enemy, overwhelm them so I not be wronged.
> May I, your servant, have health and well-being that I may serve you (lit., stand before you).
> You alone are my god, you alone are my lord,
> You alone are my judge, you alone are my aid,
> You alone are my champion!

That the declaration "You alone are my god, you alone are my lord, you alone are my judge, you alone are my aid, you alone are my champion!" at the very end of this prayer (101–103) is the equivalent of the praise[13] promised in the

11 That a *šuilla*-type prayer occasionally ends with praise, sometimes following and sometimes in place of the promise of praise, has already been noted in the literature; see Mayer, *Untersuchungen*, 318 n. 29 and especially 350–353 and 350 n. 53 for references to several prayers and to secondary literature.

12 For lines 77–89, the first half of the incantation, see Abusch, "Blessing and Praise," 10–11 [[AMD 17, 104–105]]; for the latter half (lines 90–103), see T. Abusch, "Considerations when Killing a Witch: Developments in Exorcistic Attitudes to Witchcraft," in *The Dynamics of Changing Rituals*, ed. J. Kreinath et al., Toronto Studies in Religion 29 (New York: Peter Lang, 2005), 198–201 [[AMD 5, 70–72]]. For a recent analysis of this incantation, see now Abusch, "Alternative Models for the Development of Some Incantations," in *Sources of Evil: Studies in Mesopotamian Exorcistic Lore*, AMD 15 (Leiden: Brill, 2018), 223–234 [[AMD 17, 146–156]].

13 I do not mean to suggest that in all cases the praise promised was identical with the statement contained in *Maqlû* II 101–103; but that passage provides an exemplary and typical formulation.

other prayers may be inferred from a prayer contained in *LKA* 154 + 155 and dupls. [[*CMAwR* 1, no. 8.2]]. Our incantation, *Maqlû* II 77–103, is a judgment and destruction incantation addressed to Girra; it is derived typologically from the same incantation type found in *LKA* 154 + 155; more specifically, lines 89–102 of the *Maqlû* incantation are similar to *LKA* 154, rev. 9′b–16′.[14] In *LKA* 154, rev. 14′–15′, we find the line "May I, your servant, have health and well-being, that I may declare your great deeds and sing your praise" (*ana-ku* ARAD-*ka lu-ub-luṭ lu-uš-lim-ma nar-bi-ka lu-ša-pi* ⌜*dà*⌝-*lí-lí-ka lud*-⌜*lul*⌝).[15] This line stands in the same position as lines 100–103 of the *Maqlû* incantation. Accordingly, if the two texts are typologically related, the two passages should be functionally equivalent, and the replacement of the promise with the declaration surely tells us what the content of the praise was to be.[16] Even so, we might have expected the *Maqlû* incantation to introduce the declaration with the statement: "I will declare …"; instead, it simply gives the declaration itself. The omission of the promise and its replacement by the praise itself are due probably to the fact that, in the *Maqlû* context, the closing lines of the incantation do not refer to what will be said in the future, but instead are the realization of the actual act of praise itself, praise that in other texts is simply promised. For whereas a simple prayer with accompanying offering represents a static situation and looks toward the future for its fulfillment, a *Maqlû*-type ritual was a dramatic progression,[17] and the experience of setting images of the witch on fire and watching them burn may have caused the speaker to feel that by means of the ritual burning, the fire god Girra had already achieved his goal for him and, therefore, was already deserving of his praise.[18]

---

14 For the relationship of the two texts, see Abusch, "Considerations When Killing a Witch," 198–201 [[AMD 5, 70–72]].

15 For a transliteration and translations of *LKA* 154, rev. 9′b–16′, see Abusch, "Considerations When Killing a Witch," 199 n. 16 [[AMD 5, 71 n. 16)]].

16 Does 4*R*[2] 29/1 (= UḪ II), rev. 1–18 shed any light on, or possibly even contradict, this conclusion?

17 Cf., e.g., T. Abusch, *Babylonian Witchcraft Literature: Case Studies*, BJS 132 (Atlanta: Scholars Press, 1987), 85–147, where I explicated *Maqlû* I 1–36 and demonstrated its dynamic and progressive nature.

18 For a different opinion, see Mayer, *Untersuchungen*, 355–357. Generally speaking, Mayer doubts that we have the actual wording of the promised praise in our incantation and in others that contain concluding praise (355–356). On the basis of considerations stated there, he concludes (356): "möchte ich annehmen, dass das Lob in allen Fällen nicht der Vollzug des versprochenen bzw. gewünschten Lobens ist, sondern als selbständiges Element danebensteht; somit darf in der Uebersetzung kein Doppelpunkt nach dem eventuell vorausgehenden Lobversprechen bzw. -wunsch gesetzt werden."

I should note that when reflecting on the sense of the praise at the end of the prayer, Mayer seems to consider something not wholly unlike my suggestion that the utterance

It is interesting that this statement focuses upon the relationship of the man and the god. It suggests that the god, in his capacity as god, lord, judge, aid, champion, has rescued the man. It thus expresses the speaker's gratitude, for the speaker has been the recipient of the action. But even more, it recognizes the existence of a mutual relationship, for the god has judged or championed the supplicant, and thereby has either fulfilled the terms of an already existing relationship or created a new one. In return, the human recipient asserts his thanks and recognition in the form of a statement of allegiance and devotion. Given this context, as well as other formulations, his statement that he stands before the god signifies a commitment to service. This is in agreement with a recent observation regarding the vow of praise in the Psalms:

> [T]o praise God is ... a kind of *prise de position*, a formal setting up of the worshiper as subject to God (one might almost say, in the royal sense, a subject of God, dependent, indebted), in every sense a devotee. Hence the significance of the vow of praise, which was akin to a vow of subservience, a transfer of personal glory and honor to Israel's God and a public identification of oneself as a devotee of that deity.[19]

Praise and thanksgiving are a pledge of loyalty, a promise to serve the god. It is no different, for example, than the following definition of what belief meant to Chaucer: "for Chaucer it was 'to pledge loyalty.' Belief in God was ... a promise to live one's life in the service of God, like a bondsman to his lord."[20]

of praise in *Maqlû* II 99–102 is a reflection of the fact that the speaker is in the midst of and experiencing an ongoing ceremony, for he considers the possibility that perhaps the praise reflects the following situation (356): "Da der Grund für solches Preisen nicht gut die Verwirklichung all dessen sein kann, um was in dem Gebet gebeten wurde, wird er wohl darin zu suchen sein, dass der Beter der Erhörung gewiss ist, dass er nunmehr überzeugt sein kann, der Gott habe sich ihm zugeneigt und die Beseitigung der Not werde daraus notwendig folgen—wohl deswegen, weil er im Vollzug des Ritus und Rezitieren des Gebetes (mit der Vergegenwärtigung der Macht des Gottes, der Darstellung der Hilfsbedürftigkeit, der flehentlichen Bitte) all das getan hat, was ihn in den Schutz des Gottes stellt und ihm so dessen Hilfe garantiert." He cites Gula 4 as the clearest example of this phenomenon (357). I would only note that in an emotion-laden and dramatic ceremonial situation, the ancient Mesopotamian might indeed experience "die Verwirklichung all dessen ..., um was in dem Gebet gebeten wurde," and that we should beware of confusing experience with theological constructions, especially those which agree with later religious thinking.

19 J. L. Kugel, "Topics in the History of the Spirituality of the Psalms," in *Jewish Spirituality I: From the Bible through the Middle Ages*, ed. A. Green (New York: Crossroad, 1986), 127.

20 F. Bowie, *The Anthropology of Religion: An Introduction* (Oxford: Blackwell, 2000), 245.

But the thanksgiving expressed in relational terms goes beyond a private statement between the speaker and his god; rather, it is a statement to the public by the speaker declaring the god's ability and willingness to help. Texts often describe the praise as being uttered in the presence of a public.[21] It is a statement of personal allegiance that is intended to draw others to the service of the god.

Like the alternative ending that calls for the blessing of the other gods, the promise of human praise probably has a primitive aristocratic world as its setting. But whereas the divine blessing is set in the divine realm and is directed to a returning warrior, the human praise is set in the human world, where the gods are seen as competing chieftains; and the praise is an invitation, a call, to serve a newly emergent leader. It declares why one should place one's trust in one leader over another. The call appears to have its *Sitz im Leben* in the competition between heroes for the office of chieftain and may go back to the early emergence of the institution of primitive kingship. Perhaps the call is now in the service of the late tendency to divine supersessionism, that is, the movement of an individual god to eclipse all others and become the most important in the pantheon and eventually the sole god.

On this note, I shall draw this paper to a close. But I should mention that the promise of human praise surely also plays upon the desire of the gods for honor and glory. One recalls Walter Burkert's observation that "Archaic society is based on honor, and 'gods too rejoice when they are honored by men.'"[22] The psychology of the gods is no different from Yhwh's, as reflected in the dialogue between Moses and the deity in Num 14. There Moses uses as the basis of his argument the assumed concern of the deity for what others may think of his capability:

> "If then you slay this people to a man, the nations who have heard Your fame will say, 'It must be because the Lord was powerless to bring that people into the land He had promised them on oath that He slaughtered them in the wilderness.' Therefore, I pray, let my Lord's forbearance be great." ... And the Lord said, "I pardon, as you have asked."[23]

---

21 For examples, see Mayer, *Untersuchungen*, 340–342; cf., e.g., Ps 22:23.

22 W. Burkert, *Creation of the Sacred: Tracks of Biology in Early Religions* (Cambridge, MA: Harvard University Press, 1996), 81.

23 Num 14:15–17, 20. Translation: NJPS. Cf. Exod 32:11–14.

CHAPTER 10

# The Form and Meaning of a Babylonian Prayer to Marduk

Mesopotamian hymns and prayers often evoke a response of boredom; more than one reader has found himself wondering whether these texts are not simply collections of phrases that were strung out indiscriminately.[*,1] Perhaps; still it is no less possible that the sense of meaninglessness and dreariness is due to mechanical reading and presentation. Understanding the artistry and thought of a Babylonian psalm—especially one which represents a new form and thus gives evidence of creativity—underscores the vitality of Mesopotamian psalmody; this study of the poetic form and theological meaning of a well-known and relatively simple prayer, the Marduk *šuilla BMS* 9, obv. and dupls.,[2] may serve, then, as an appropriate tribute to Professor Samuel Noah Kramer: for Kramer has sought repeatedly to draw the attention of scholars and general readers alike to the vigor and excitement of Mesopotamian literature.

The composition will be treated as a self-contained unit. First the introductory hymn (1–9) will be explicated, particular attention being paid to some of the techniques used by the composer and the ideas he wished to convey

* I have enjoyed conversations with M. Brettler, S. Kaufman, W. L. Moran, and P. Stark on various aspects of the text.

1 Cf. W. W. Hallo, review of *Hymnes et prières aux dieux de Babylonie et d'Assyrie*, by M.-J. Seux, *JAOS* 97 (1977): 582–585, esp. 582–583.

2 This *šuilla* is cited as Marduk 2 in the lists of *šuilla*s compiled by W. Kunstmann, *Die babylonische Gebetsbeschwörung*, LSS NF 2 (Leipzig: Hinrichs, 1932), 94, and W. Mayer, *Untersuchungen zur Formensprache der babylonischen "Gebetsbeschwörungen,"* StPohl, series maior 5 (Rome: Pontifical Biblical Institute, 1976), 395. For a list of exemplars and other bibliographical information, see Mayer, *Untersuchungen*, 395; the unpublished British Museum duplicates listed there have since appeared in copy in *ŠU-ILA*, nos. 26–29. This *šuilla* was known by its opening line: *gašru šūpû etel* (var. *etelli*) *Eridu*. This incipit is cited in line 11 of the list K 2832 + 6680 col. I (L. W. King, *Babylonian Magic and Sorcery* [London: Luzac, 1896], xix, and Mayer, *Untersuchungen*, 399) and follows there immediately upon the entry: *gašru šūpû ilitti Eridu* (9). Kunstmann (*Gebetsbeschwörung*, 95) and Mayer (*Untersuchungen*, 399) take line 9 as referring to an otherwise unattested or unidentified prayer (Kunstmann: Marduk 7; Mayer: Marduk (?) x). However, since one ms. of Marduk 2 (*ŠU-ILA*, nos. 28 (+) 29: 3′) preserves the reading *gašru šūpû ilitti Eridu* (the better reading is *etelli*; *ilitti* is due to an auditory error which resulted in metathesis: *etelli* → *ilitti*), the incipit *gašru šūpû ilitti Eridu* in K 2832 + 6680 I 9 may simply refer to a version of Marduk 2 that had *ilitti* instead of *etelli* in its opening line. If such is indeed the case, it might explain why the scribe of K 2832 + 6680 associated the two incipits and entered them together.

 | DOI:10.1163/9789004435186_011

thereby (1). Then several irregularities in the remainder of the text (10–27) will be noted, and the sections (10–12; 22–24) responsible for these irregularities will be studied (2). A consideration of lines 10–12 and 22–24 suggests the possibility that the composition is arranged concentrically. This possibility is examined: the central prayer (13–21) is analyzed, the relation of lines 13–21 to 10–12 and 22–24 explored, and the introductory hymn and concluding benediction drawn together. The structure of the text is presented in diagram form (3). A historical observation concludes the discussion.

## 1 The Hymnic Introduction

The *šuilla* begins with a hymn of praise to Marduk:

1. *gašru šūpû etel Eridug*
2. *rubû tizqāru bukur* ᵈ*Nudimmud*
3. ᵈ*Marduk šalbābu murīš E'engura*
4. *bēl Esağila tukulti Bābili*
5. *rā'im Ezida mušallim napišti*
6. *ašarēd Emaḫtila mudeššû balāṭi*
7. *ṣulūl māti gāmil nišī rapšāti*
8. *ušumgal kalîš parakkī*
9. *šumka kalîš ina pī nišī ṭāb*

These nine lines[3] constitute a distinct unit. The unit opens with the invocation *gašru šūpû etel Eridug* (1) and ends with the statement *šumka kalîš ina pī nišī ṭāb* (9). To be sure, line 10 also contains an invocation: *Marduk bēlu rabû*; but this invocation recurs in line 22. It is the opening of a summary statement (10–12; 22–24) recited once between the introductory hymn (1–9) and the prayer

3 The division into nine lines is supported by almost all mss. On two points do we encounter variation: line 8 is joined with line 9 in *STT* 55 and with line 7 in the *bīt mēseri* version $4R^2$ 21* no. 1(c), rev. (= G. Meier, "Die zweite Tafel der Serie *bīt mēseri*," *AfO* 14 [1941–1944]: 140–143); this is due to the brevity of line 8. More significant, $4R^2$ 21* splits up line 5 and joins 5a with 4 and 5b with 6. Besides destroying the parallelism of lines 4, 5, and 6, this division obscures the scholastic wordplays upon which our text turns (see below). One must assume that the scribe of $4R^2$ 21* was unaware of, or had no regard for, the devices used to convey the meaning and was more concerned with compressing the text into a smaller number of lines. It is unfortunate that the line division of $4R^2$ 21* has been perpetuated by *BMS* 9, obv., F. Delitzsch, *Assyrische Lesestücke mit grammatischen Tabellen und vollständigem Glossar: Einführung in die assyrische und babylonische Keilschriftliteratur bis hinauf zu Hammurabi*, 5th ed., Assyrische Bibliothek 16 (Leipzig: Hinrichs, 1912), 85, and K. K. Riemschneider, *Lehrbuch des Akkadischen* (Leipzig: VEB Verlag Enzyklopaedie, 1969), 155–156.

and again between the prayer and the concluding benediction.[4] Line 10, then, begins a new section and is not part of the introductory hymn. Besides, line 9 is itself bound up with what immediately precedes it. Lines 8 and 9 are bound together by their content:

> The single great one of chapels everywhere,
> Your name is lovingly hymned by the people everywhere.

They are bound even more closely by their sound; note the alliteration of the first two words of 8 and of 9: *ušumgal kalîš* ...; *šumka kalîš* .... And we may even wonder whether the play does not extend backward from *ušumgal* of line 8 to *gāmil* of line 7. It is possible, moreover, that the boundaries of the hymn are signaled by its first and last lines:

> *gašru šūpû etel Eridug* (1)
> *šumka kalîš ina pī nišī ṭāb* (9)

*gašru* at the beginning of line 1 and *šumka* at the beginning of line 9 call to mind *gašru* at the beginning and *gašru lū šumka* at the end of the speech to enlist aid in *Anzu*.[5] Furthermore, the occurrence of Eridug[6] at the end of line 1 and of *nišī ṭāb* at the end of line 9 appears to be more than just a coincidence: dùg and *ṭāb* are, respectively, the Sumerian and Akkadian words for "good"; eri, "city," and *nišī*, "people," encapsulate the two poles of Marduk's activities in the poem: in the first stanza the focus is on the city of his youth, and in the third stanza it is on the people for whom he cares and who admire him in his maturity. Other Sumero-Akkadian wordplays in the hymn[7] lend credence to this observation. However, we need not belabor these uncertain boundary markers, for the definition and unity of the hymn are rendered sufficiently clear by the thematic makeup and structure of lines 1–9.

---

4 For this characterization of lines 10–12 and 22–24, see below, section 2.

5 For *Anzu*, see J. S. Cooper, "Symmetry and Repetition in Akkadian Narrative," *JAOS* 97 (1977): 508–511 (example A); W. W. Hallo and W. L. Moran, "The First Tablet of the SB Recension of the Anzu-Myth," *JCS* 31 (1979): 82–87, lines 37–44, 58–65, 79–86.

6 For a discussion of the form and meaning of the name "Eridug," see T. Jacobsen, "Some Sumerian City-Names," *JCS* 21 (1967): 102 n. 14. It is of no consequence for our interpretation of *BMS* 9 whether "the good city" is the original meaning of the name or the result of ancient etymologizing.

7 See below.

The hymn comprises nine poetic lines. These nine lines are to be arranged into three-line stanzas;[8] the basic unit is the triplet.

I. Famed mighty one, chieftain of Eridu,
Exalted prince, first-born of Nudimmud,
Raging Marduk, restorer of rejoicing to E'engura.
II. Lord of Esağila, hope of Babylon,
Lover of Ezida, preserver of life,
Lone one of Emaḫtila, multiplier of living.
III. Protection of the land, savior of the multitudes of people,
The single great one of chapels everywhere,
Your name is sweetly hymned by the people everywhere.

Each stanza conveys a picture of Marduk. Each picture is full-blown and self-contained, and yet each differs from the others. Marduk's actions and concerns, the groups with which he interacts, and the areas in which he operates change from one stanza to the next. But the hymn is not a series of disjointed images. It retains a sense of constancy while portraying a changing figure. This is all the more impressive in view of the brevity of the hymn and the static form of description. The hymn integrates a series of different pictures and tells a story of the expansion of the activities and concerns of a single god. Earlier roles presage later ones; later roles do not require the rejection of earlier ones; rather, they incorporate and expand them.

To understand how the composer has achieved his goal, we must take note of the picture and thought of each stanza, see some of the ways in which the stanzas are joined together, and try to imagine the progression of images and the overarching conception of the hymn.

In the first stanza Marduk is presented as a young aristocrat residing in his parents' estate and acting on their behalf. He is a warrior-prince, a well-endowed son who is accorded social prerogatives and placed under filial obligations. He performs heroically in the service of his family; still, he remains a local figure. He serves his family within the confines of his ancestral town and home. Yet the way forth is prepared by his role as *murīš E'engura* (3). The third stanza presents a very different scene: here Marduk is the supreme god. He takes care of the land and its people and is rewarded for his care. The first and third stanzas seem to clash. But for all their differences, they also balance and parallel each other. Both operate within the bounds of the concrete. The

8 For a different stanza arrangement, see A. Falkenstein and W. von Soden, *Sumerische und akkadische Hymnen und Gebete* (Zurich: Artemis, 1953), 297–298.

first describes Marduk's place in a specific city, family, and temple; the third describes Marduk's relation to the land, its people, and its sanctuaries.[9] All the same, the universalism of the third stanza contrasts with the particularism of the first, and Marduk's domination of the country in the third contrasts with his dependent status in the first.

The third stanza is obviously an outgrowth and widening of the first one. But how was the transition achieved? The connecting piece is provided by lines 4–6: this stanza constitutes the pivot of the text; it draws the first and third stanzas together and creates a whole. In the second stanza, Marduk is presented as the god of Babylon and its environs. The role of lord of Babylon, Esağila, Ezida, and Emaḫtila forms a crucial episode in his life. It fits nicely between his role in the first stanza as the young god of Eridu and his role in the third as supreme god of the land. This does not exhaust the meaning and function of the second stanza: this stanza gives the hymn a distinct slant. But to understand the stanza and its place in the poem, we must first take note of a series of anomalies in lines 4–6 and explain them. The stanza reads:

4. *bēl Esağila tukulti Bābili*
5. *rā'im Ezida mušallim napišti*
6. *ašarēd Emaḫtila mudeššû balāṭi*

The epithets are standard enough; yet the sequence and conjunction are striking and unexpected. It is sufficient to take note of a similar section of a Nabû *šuilla* to appreciate our own stanza:

14. *ašarēd Bābili rā'im Esağila*
15. *ṣulūl Barsip tukulti Ezida*
16. *šā'imu šīmāti mušallim napišti*
17. *murrik ūmī qā'išu balāṭi*[10]

This address to Nabû shares many elements with our stanza but orders them in a more conventional way: Epithets describing the god's relation to city and temple are joined together and appear in the order city-temple (14–15); these epithets are followed by epithets describing the god's relation to human life (16–17). These two distinct sets of epithets are presented separately and are

9 More specifically, note the city in line 1, the country in line 7; elevated princely status in line 2, elevated divine station in line 8; the applause of the family in line 3, the applause of all people in line 9.
10 *AGH*, 110: 14–17.

not mixed together. Turning back to our own stanza, we now note the following: Line 4: The expected and logical procedure would have been to mention first the city Babylon and then the temple Esağila. Certainly, the first stanza has prepared us for the order city-temple by presenting Marduk first as *etel Eridu* and then as *murīš E'engura*. Instead, line 4 presents Marduk first as *bēl Esağila* and only then as *tukulti Bābili*. Lines 5–6: Coming to these lines from line 4, we notice immediately the absence of a city name. Moreover it would have been more usual and natural for the two epithets describing the god's relation to temples of Borsippa to be joined together in one line and the two describing his relation to human life to be joined together in another. Instead, the sets of epithets are split up, and epithets describing his relation to temples in Borsippa are juxtaposed to those describing his care for human life.

Far from being mere hackwork, the second stanza is tightly knit and ingeniously constructed. The order is intentional and expresses the central notion of the hymn. The purpose of the stanza is not simply to depict Marduk as the lord of Babylon. Even more it serves as a transition and provides the vehicle for Marduk's development from the local god of Eridu into the supreme caretaker of mankind, and it does so by expressing a thought basic to the composer's theology and art: the god's place in the temple is intimately related to his ability to care for the people; his power to care for human life derives from his rootedness in the temple. The connection between the god's relation to temple and his relation to people is expressed first of all by the juxtaposition of temple and mankind:

> Lover of Ezida, preserver of life,
> Lone one of Emaḫtila, multiplier of living.

The two are thus put on a par. But the connection is more than just mechanical. There is an internal, organic connection, and here a mere scholastic play serves to draw together god, temple, and man. The composer relies on a knowledge of the equations zi : *napištu* and ti.la : *balāṭu* to convey his meaning. Here, far from being an orthographic convention that obscures the Akkadian text, the use of Sumerograms is a literary device meant to express or, at least, enhance the composer's message.[11] *napišti* translates and is written in all but

11 The literary use of ideograms might suggest a written—rather than an oral—form of composition. Note, however, that a learned composer could certainly see and exploit the connection between Ezida and *napištu* and between Emaḫtila and *balāṭu* without recourse to writing. If this *šuilla* was originally composed orally, the scribe who introduced the writing ZI for *napišti* in line 5 and TI.LA for *balāṭi* in line 6 is to be credited with preserving and rendering explicit the aforementioned connections.

one manuscript with ZI[12] and plays on the temple name "Ezida," a name translated elsewhere as *bīt napišti māti*.[13] *balāṭi* translates and is written in almost all manuscripts with TI.LA[14] and plays on the temple name "Emaḫtila."[15] Thus in line 5 Ezida shares zi with *napišti* and in line 6 Emaḫtila shares ti.la with *balāṭi*:

> *rā'im Ezida mušallim napišti* (ZI[D])
> *ašarēd Emaḫtila mudeššû balāṭi* (TI.LA)[16]

---

12 + *ti*/*tì*; *STT* 55: *na-piš-ti*.

13 For this translation, see E. Unger, "Aššur, Stadt," *RlA* 1 (1928): 188; cf. *AGH* 124: 8: *zēr Ezida bīt šikin napišti ša ilī rabûti*.

14 The exceptions are *ŠU-ILA*, no. 26: TIN and *KAR* 59: *ba-l*[*á*?-*ṭi*].

15 While completing this study, I located E. Lehmann and H. Haas, eds., *Textbuch zur Religionsgeschichte*, 2nd ed. (Leipzig: Deichert, 1922), and noted that whereas in the first (1912) edition B. Landsberger ("Babylonisch-assyrische Texte," in *Textbuch zur Religionsgeschichte*, ed. E. Lehmann and H. Haas [Leipzig: Deichert, 1912], 101–102) had apparently not noticed any wordplays, in the second (1922) edition (307–308) he comments on 6b: "Anspielungen auf die vorangehenden Tempelnamen" (307 n. 7).

16 The use of Sumero-Akkadian equations as a poetic device and as a way of expressing thought is not particularly surprising in this hymn; the composer seems to have been acquainted with bilingual literature. Note, for example, that whereas the combination Babylon, Esağila, Ezida, and Emaḫtila in our text is relatively uncommon in Akkadian prayers, it occurs with greater frequency in Sumerian and bilingual liturgies. See, for example, the Sumerian Marduk *šuilla* published by J. S. Cooper, "A Sumerian ŠU-ÍL-LA from Nimrud with a Prayer for Sin-šar-iškun," *Iraq* 32 (1970): 58–59: 5–8 (disregard the additions of the Nabû adaptation ms. D) and the Marduk Kiutukam 4$R^2$ 29/1, obv. 27–30 // *STT* 182 (+) 183, obv. 6′–7′: lugal tin.tir.KI lugal é.sağ.il.la : *šar* (*STT*: [x]x) *ba-bi-lì* (*STT*: KÁ.DI[INGIR.RA.KI]) *be-el é-sağ-íla*; lugal é.zi.da lugal é.maḫ.ti.la : *šar* (*STT*: xx) *é-zi-da be-el é-maḫ-ti-la*. Babylon—Esağila—Ezida—Emaḫtila formed the original kernel out of which was constructed the expanded and convoluted Babylon section (Babylon, Esağila, Borsippa, Ezida, Emaḫtila, Etemenanki, Edaranna) of such *eršemma*s and *balag*s as M. E. Cohen, *Sumerian Hymnology: The Eršemma*, HUCASup 2 (Cincinnati: Hebrew Union College Press, 1981), 29: 7–13; 118b: 8–14; 127: 12–18; 113–114: 21–25 (= R. Kutscher, *Oh Angry Sea: The History of a Sumerian Congregational Lament*, YNER 6 [New Haven: Yale University Press, 1975], 63: 26–30 [Kutscher's ms. Haa = Cohen's ms. B]; Eturkalama in line 27 between Esağila and Borsippa must be misplaced; elsewhere, it occurs before Babylon [e.g., Cohen, *Eršemma*, 133: 37; 144: 22; 147: 17; 148: 21]); M. E. Cohen, *Balag-Compositions: Sumerian Lamentation Liturgies of the Second and First Millennium B.C.*, SANE 1/2 (Malibu, CA: Undena, 1974), 18: 88–92; 19: 134–138; 30: 17–21 (cf. S. Langdon, *Sumerian and Babylonian Psalms* [Paris: Geuthner; New York: G. E. Stechert, 1909], 104, 108, 120). In these lists, Borsippa introduces Ezida and Emaḫtila; it is set on a level with Babylon and introduces its temples as Babylon introduces Esağila. The secondary nature of this longer list is suggested by the separation of the Babylonian Etemenanki and Edaranna from Esağila and their citation after Ezida and Emaḫtila, by the joining together of Esağila and Borsippa in one line in the *balag*s cited above (Babylon // Esağila—Borsippa // Ezida—Emaḫtila, etc.), and by such adaptations as Cooper, "Sumerian ŠU-ÍL-LA," 58 ms. D, which attest directly to the insertion of Borsippa (6a) between Esağila (6) and Ezida—Emaḫtila (7–8).

The placing of the temple name in first position in lines 5 and 6 explains furthermore the order of line 4: *bēl Esağila tukulti Bābili*.[17] Esağila is placed before Babylon in order to open the stanza with a line beginning with a temple, a stratagem facilitated by the mention of the temple E'engura at the end of line 3. By placing the temple first and city second in line 4, the composer both provides a precedent for beginning lines 5–6 with a temple name, as well as cushions the shock of these lines, for not only do lines 5–6 begin with temples, but they also replace references to cities with references to mankind.

The second stanza presents an important episode in the life of Marduk and sets forth a period of growth and transition. It plays a special role in the poem. It links the first and third stanzas and creates a unity. The first stanza leads into it; the third emerges out of it. The second stanza is a center: it draws the text to itself and then sets in motion the progressive loosening of tightly knit connections. The tightening and loosening, the narrowing and widening come to expression not only in the choice and order of themes but also in the choice and order of metrical and grammatical units. These forms arrange themselves into concentric patterns with the second stanza forming the center. A primitive count of the number of syllables in each stanza indicates that whereas the first and third stanzas contain approximately the same number of syllables, ca. 30, the second has a different number, ca. 35. This pattern sets off the second stanza by giving it special marking and balances the first and third stanzas. On a grammatical level, too, we find a marking off of stanzas. But the grammatical structure does more; it is more flexible and therefore able to convey the meaning of the text. The grammatical units form a concentric pattern. The second stanza is more tightly drawn than the first and third, and it forms a center. The first is relatively loose at the beginning; it tightens up and becomes more particular as it approaches and links up with the second. The third becomes looser and less particular as it moves away from the second, until at the end it is looser and more general even than the first line of the poem. A diagram of the text demonstrates this point. A characterization of the syntactic structures encountered in the hymn should make clear our interpretation. a construct chain is the tightest form of linking two words; a

17 I do not wish to imply that the order Esağila—Bābili is found only in this hymn; see simply *AGH* 68: 5–6: *šarrat Esağila ... bēlet Bābili ...* and 54: 3 // 112a: 4: *Esağila liḫdūka Bābili lirīška* (corrected reading: M.-J. Seux, *Hymnes et prières aux dieux de Babylonie et d'Assyrie*, LAPO 8 [Paris: Éditions du Cerf, 1976], 304 and n. 26, and Mayer, *Untersuchungen*, 336, 1c). The first example is addressed to Zarpanītu and is found on the reverse of *BMS* 9; the second is part of the concluding benediction of the prayer to Nabû from whose introduction we cited an example of the more usual order! For Marduk, see G. Wilhelm, "Ein neues Lamaštu-Amulett," *ZA* 69 (1979): 39: *ina qibīt* ᵈ*Marduk āšib Esağila u Bābili*.

noun plus attributive adjective is a looser form; a sentence with an adjective in predicate position is the loosest form. A proper noun is the most particularizing substantive; a general noun is less particularizing; an adjective is the least particularizing. The grammatical scheme is as follows:

| | | | | |
|---|---|---|---|---|
| Stanza I | 1a | nominalized adjective + adjective | 1b | construct chain |
| | 2a | general noun + adjective | 2b | construct chain |
| | 3a | proper noun + adjective | 3b | construct chain |
| Stanza II | 4a | construct chain | 5b | construct chain |
| | 5a | construct chain | 5b | construct chain |
| | 6a | construct chain | 6b | construct chain |
| Stanza III | 7a | construct chain | 7b | construct chain augmented by adjective modifying 2nd member of chain, *nišī* |
| | 8 | construct chain expanded by a second bound form, *kalîš*, before the *nomen rectum* | | |
| | 9 | stative sentence composed of nominal subject and adjectival predicate, separated by adverb, *kalîš*, and prepositional phrase (preposition + construct chain whose second member is *nišī*) | | |

The last line is the only real sentence; it is the most expansive form in the hymn and describes the delights of praising the god, thus stating the essence of a hymn: *šumka kalîš ina pī nišī ṭāb*.

We have witnessed the loosening of Marduk's local ties and the widening of his orbit, his change from a local to a national god, from a god who serves his divine parents to one who cares for the people of the land. We watch the broadening of Marduk's scope and note that the composer has managed to preserve the god's connections with the concrete. A desirable and even necessary achievement: while extending his care to more and more people, Marduk must remain rooted, for only thus can he remain the master of his home, the object of a cult, and the possessor of the power to help people. But seeing all this only makes us more aware of the difficulties that faced the poet. To describe a god's growth and not to let go of the link between the god and the concrete world and to manage even to extend the god's links are not easy tasks. For our poet the difficulty was if possible even greater. Locality, temple, and community were connected in the first stanza; but locality then served as a stepping stone to the temple and receded into the distance. Temple then served as a stepping stone for reaching the people and then began slipping away. The second stanza asserted that temple and human life were connected but conveyed this thought by means of an interlocking structure which could easily fly apart. The third stanza provides a climax and the poet's solution: the first stanza emphasized city and temple; the second, temple and human life; the third stanza serves both to broaden Marduk's focus of concern and action as well as to bring together again locality, temple, and human community—but this time on a higher level of generalization: Marduk is the supreme god; he takes care of the land and its people and is rewarded for this care. This is expressed clearly in the wording and structure of this last stanza. Line 7 is composed of two distinct halves and these two parallel each other:

| | | |
|---|---|---|
| 7a. | *ṣulūl māti* | Protection of the land, |
| 7b. | *gāmil nišī rapšāti* | Savior of the multitudes of the people |

Lines 8 and 9, for their part, also parallel each other:

| | | |
|---|---|---|
| 8. | *ušumgal kalîš parakkī* | The single great one of chapels everywhere, |
| 9. | *šumka kalîš ina pī nišī ṭāb* | Your name is sweetly hymned by the people everywhere. |

What draws the stanza together and brings together the loose pieces of the poem is the relationship of line 7 to lines 8 and 9: each half of line 7 stands in direct relation to one of the two following lines: 7a to 8, 7b to 9: he who covers the land (7a *ṣulūl māti*) attains dominion over all chapels therein (8 *ušumgal kalîš parakkī*); he who saves the widespread people (7b *gāmil nišī rapšāti*) is joyfully praised by the people everywhere (9 *šumka kalîš ina pī nišī ṭāb*).

Marduk is the shelter of the land and protector of the people; as his due for being caretaker of the land, he becomes the single great one of chapels everywhere; as his due for being the protector of the people, his name is lovingly hymned by people everywhere. A climax worthy of Marduk. Instead of living in only one temple and being a subordinate member of a group of gods, he has become master of all sanctuaries and the object of praise of diverse human constituencies. Marduk has changed, but always the new has been drawn back into an original if constantly widening circle of places, temples, and communities. True, he has had to extend his care to the whole land and to more and more people. The power to care derives from his place in the temple; but his desire to care may be motivated by the knowledge that in this way he will acquire more chapels and more veneration. In any case, Marduk has been provided with the elements that comprise the identity of a national god: land, people, residences, and service. One may even consider the possibility that what Marduk is to the gods in *Enūma eliš*, he is to mankind in our hymn. But then there is the expected reversal: in *Enūma eliš*, the gods receive *parakku*s in Babylon; in our hymn Marduk receives *parakku*s all over the land. He has been transformed into a great god who grants life and receives homage in return. And this thought, we shall see, is not restricted to the hymnic introduction; it is taken up and developed in later sections of the prayer.

## 2 The Marduk *šuilla*: A New Form

In explicating the hymn, we discerned thematic and formal levels of expression and saw how the composer merged the various modes of expression to convey meaning. Not surprisingly, his art and thought extend beyond the hymn; especially in its later portions, the composition shows a number of innovations and forms a new structure.

Following the hymnic introduction, the remainder of the *šuilla* reads:[18]

10. $^{d}$*Marduk bēlu rabû* (*ilu rēmēnû* →) Ø
11. *ina qibītika* (*kītti* → *kabitti* →) *ṣīrti lubluṭ lušlimma*
12. *luštammar ilūtka*
13. *ēma uṣammaru lukšud*
14. *šuškin kīttu ina pīya*
15. *šubši amāt damiqti ina libbiya*
16. *tīru u nanzāzu liqbû damiqtī*
17. *ilī lizziz ina imniya*
18. *ištarī lizziz ina šumēliya*
19. *ilu mušallimu idāya* / *ina idīya lū kayān*
20. *šurkamma qabâ šemâ u magāru*

18 Phonetic variations and standard *attalû*-insertions (*BMS* 54: 1′–4′; PBS 1/2, no. 108, obv. 1′–8′; *ŠU-ILA*, no. 27, obv. 11–14) are ignored. The few variants that require mention in the context of the present study are included in the transcription and discussed at appropriate places below. Contrary to the impression given by some editions, manuscripts are often internally consistent in their treatment of case endings; others represent definite stages of transition. I follow the mss. that have merged sing. nominative and accusative and have retained a separate genitive; the forms *qabâ* and *šemâ* are found even in those mss. that read *magāru* (*STT* 55, *KAR* 23 + 25, PBS 1/2, no. 108). The claim that “in the literary dialect these CVC signs [i.e., CVM] are used only for forms in which the /m/ ending is historically correct” (E. Reiner, *A Linguistic Analysis of Akkadian* [The Hague: Mouton, 1966], 60) requires modification in light of such writings as SIG$_5$-TIM (*KAR* 59) / MÍ.SIG$_5$-TIM (*KAR* 23 + 25) for *damiqtī* (acc. + 1. sing. poss. suff.; cf. SIG$_5$.MU [*STT* 55]) in line 16 and ZI-TIM (*BMS* 9, PBS 1/2, no. 108) for *napištī* (acc. + 1. sing. poss. suff.) in line 22; cf. ZI-TIM-*ia* (*BMS* 9) / ZI-TIM-MU (PBS 1/2, no. 108) for *napištiya* (gen. + 1. sing. poss. suff.; cf. *na-píš-ti-ia* [*KAR* 23 + 25], ZI-*ti-ia* [*STT* 55], ZI-*ia* [$4R^2$ 21*]) in line 23.

21. *amāt aqabbû (kīma →) ēma aqabbû lū magrat*
22. [d]*Marduk bēlu rabû napištī qīša*
23. *balāṭ napištiya qibi*
24. *maḫarka namriš atalluka lušbi*
25. [d]*Enlil liḫdūka* [d]*Ea lirīška*
26. *ilū ša kiššati likrubūka*
27. *ilū rabûtu libbaka liṭibbū*

The text deviates from the norm and in so doing poses some difficulties of interpretation. The normal structure of a *šuilla* is (a) introduction: hymn; (b) body: prayer; (c) conclusion: promise of thanksgiving or divine benediction.[19] In the main, our *šuilla* follows this form: it contains an introductory hymn (1–9), a prayer (13–21), and a concluding benediction (25–27). However, some elements are repeated and do not appear where expected. Thus in addition to the hymn, prayer, and benediction, the text also contains two other invocations (10; 22a), two other prayers (11; 22b–23), and two other concluding promises of thanksgiving or service (12;[20] 24). And the arrangement of these duplicate elements seems to give the text a somewhat confused and disjointed appearance: the second invocation (22a) appears after the main prayer and is separated from the hymnic introduction (1–9) and the first invocation (10);[21] the prayer in lines 13–21 is separated from the prayer in line 11 by a promise (12) and from the prayer in lines 22b–23 by an invocation (22a); the first promise (12) appears surprisingly before the main prayer (13–21) and is separated from the second promise (24) and final benediction (25–27).[22] Furthermore, the prayer in lines 13–21 seems to differ in tone and purpose from the prayer in lines 11 and 22b–23: lines 13–21 present a request for success; lines 11 and 22b–23 contain the request for life itself. Even on formal grounds, the prayer in lines 13–21 is set off from the preceding and following sections. It begins and ends with a similar theme and identical words—*ēma uṣammaru lukšud … amāt aqabbû ēma* (←*kīma*) *aqabbû lū magrat*; these lines thus form a border and mark the outer limits of the segment.

Noting seemingly divergent themes and structural irregularities may on occasion lead to the identification of a new pattern. Such is the case here. The

19 See Kunstmann, *Gebetsbeschwörung*, 7–42.

20 The occasional occurrence of a thanksgiving formula in a prayer that concludes with a benediction is noted and line 12 cited by Kunstmann, *Gebetsbeschwörung*, 40 and n. 4; cf. Mayer, *Untersuchungen*, 331 and n. 42, 347–348.

21 The first invocation (10) is not cited here because it follows immediately upon the hymn.

22 The second promise (24) is not cited here because it immediately precedes the benediction.

difficulties are the result of innovation. Although the text deviates from the usual liturgical pattern, it does not lack a meaningful order. We have here a new form, the recognition of which resolves the very difficulties which led to its recognition. Examining the list of difficulties, we note that the source of the formal and thematic incongruities is located in lines 10–12 and 22–24. This is hardly fortuitous. Each of these sections constitutes a capsulated *šuilla*, and the two sections parallel each other to the extent even of playing on the same words and sharing identical forms:

| | | | |
|---|---|---|---|
| Invocation: | 10 | // | 22a |
| $^{d}$*Marduk bēlu rabû* (*ilu rēmēnû*) | | // | $^{d}$*Marduk bēlu rabû* |
| Prayer for life: | 11 | // | 22b–23 |
| *ina qibītika kītti*[23] *lubluṭ lušlimma* | | // | *napištī qīš, balāṭ napištiya qibi* |
| Promise of Service: | 12 | // | 24 |
| *luštammar ilūtka* | | // | *maḫarka namriš atalluka lušbi* |

Each set of consecutive lines constitutes a summary statement. These statements, moreover, form discrete units and are set off from the introductory hymn and concluding benediction, on the one side, and the core prayer on the other. The structure of the text seems to be:

23 On grounds of usage, *kītti* and *ṣīrti* are to be preferred over *kabitti*. On the whole, *kītti* appears to be the original reading: (a) whereas *ka-bit-ti* (4$R^2$ 21*) and *ṣir-ti* (*BMS* 9) are found only in Nineveh, *kit-ti* is found in mss. from Babylonia (PBS 1/2, no. 108; *ŠU-ILA*, no. 26: *kit-tú*), Aššur (*KAR* 59; *KAR* 23 + 25: *kit-*[*ti*]), Sultantepe (*STT* 55), and Nineveh (*BMS* 54). (b) It is easier to explain the development of *kabitti* from *kītti* than from *ṣīrti*. Limiting ourselves to simple linear models, we suggest the development 1. *kītti* → 2. *kabitti* → 3. *ṣīrti*: (1) *kītti* is chosen perhaps under the influence of *kīttu* in line 14. (2) *kit-ti* → *ka-bit-ti*: we note (a) *qibītika* is written several ways in our mss. including *qí-biti-ka* (*KAR* 23 + 25: [*q*]*í-biti-ka*; *STT* 55: [*qí*]*-biti-ka*). The signs KIT and BIT are similar and can be identical in NB; and (b) *ka* of *kabitti* is easily explained as a dittography of the suffix *-ka* of *qibītika*. Accordingly, the development *kītti* → *kabitti* requires only the repetition of *ka* and the misreading of *kit* as *bit*, perhaps under the influence of a preceding BIT: *qí-biti-ka ka-bit-ti*.

(3) *kabitti* is hypercorrected to *ṣīrti*. Note, however, that this reconstruction remains provisional; a final assessment must await the determination of the precise nature and direction of the relation between our text and the genetically related Nabû *šuilla BMS* 22: 1–29 and dupls. Compare the variant readings *ina qibītika kītti* / *kabitti* / *ṣīrti* of our text with the parallel lines (9–10) of the Nabû text: *ina amātika kītti ina siqirka kabitti ina qibītika rabīti*; if the Marduk composition is dependent on the Nabû one, our variants may reflect the breakup of a ἓν διὰ τριῶν and the preservation of its parts in different mss.; if, on the other hand, the Nabû composition is dependent upon the Marduk one, the ἓν διὰ τριῶν may simply be the result of a conflation of several variants.

| | | |
|---|---|---|
| 1–9 | I | Introductory Hymn |
| 10–12 | A | Capsule *šuilla*: (a) invocation; (b) prayer for life; (c) promise |
| 13–21 | II | Prayer for Success |
| 22–24 | A′ | Capsule *šuilla*: (a′) invocation; (b′) prayer for life; (c′) promise |
| 25–27 | III | Concluding Benediction |

What seems to be emerging is a different *šuilla* design, a design created by the inclusion of two related summary statements of invocation, prayer, and thanksgiving, the first placed between the hymnic introduction and the prayer, the second between the prayer and the concluding benediction. We may account, then, for the present form of the text by assuming that the (original) prayer (13–21) was (secondarily) framed by two related summary statements.

But having recognized that lines 10–12 and 22–24 form an envelope construction, we must still ask: Why were these summary statements included? This question gains in significance to the extent that the inclusion constitutes the creation of a new pattern or, at the very least, the use of an unconventional one. It may be easier to find an answer if the question is rephrased: What purpose do the summary statements serve? A partial answer is provided by the observation that the summary statements repeat the central thought of the hymn—the greatness of Marduk and the reciprocal relationship between the god and mankind. If anything, the summary seems to carry the thought even further; by the very baldness of its formulation, the summary articulates this thought in sharper terms and renders it more explicit than does the hymn itself:

> O Marduk great lord,
> By your affirmative decree may I live and be well,
> I will then constantly praise your godhead. (lines 10–12)
>
> O Marduk great lord,
> Grant me my life; decree for me a healthy life,
> In joyfully serving you regularly will I then find satisfaction. (lines 22–24)

The summary links up with the hymn; one may even go so far as to state that each set of parallel lines of the summary statements corresponds to one of the three stanzas of the hymn:

| *Hymn* | | *Summary A* | | *Summary A′* | |
|---|---|---|---|---|---|
| 1–3 | // | 10 | // | 22a | the person of Marduk |
| 4–6 | // | 11 | // | 22b–23 | the granting of life (*balāṭu*, *napištu*) by Marduk |
| 7–9 | // | 12 | // | 24 | the praise of Marduk |

The summary statements draw together the introductory hymn and the body of the prayer.

## 3 A Prayer for Success and the Conclusion of the *šuilla*

Lines 10–12 and 22–24 carry forward the thought of the hymn: Marduk is the great god who grants life and receives homage in return. These lines are important for the ideas they convey; they are no less important for the place they occupy in and the effect they have on the composition. They form a circle: on its inner side (12 + 22), this circle surrounds the core prayer—the center of the text (13–21); on its outer side (10 + 24), it runs along the inner border of the introductory hymn (1–9) and of the concluding benediction (25–27). The circle affects the meaning of the parts it touches and forms a bridge between the outer hymn and benediction and the inner prayer, thus drawing the parts of the composition together and creating a circular structure. For once the frame has been set in place, the text no longer follows a linear design but is arranged concentrically. Ring composition becomes the architectonic principle of the text, and the world of gods and the world of men touch and interact where the movement inward from an outer divine orb and outward from a human center attain equilibrium and meet.

This characterization is in line with observations made in our analysis of the hymn and summary statements. 1. Cohesion and integrity. The hymn and the two summary statements parallel each other and share a common theme. Furthermore, each summary constitutes a miniature *šuilla* (invocation // hymn; prayer // prayer; promise // benediction); by linking up with and recapitulating the crucial parts of the *šuilla*, each summary signals a joining together of the parts of the whole *šuilla* and suggests the notion of unity. 2. Circular structure: the introductory hymn (1–9) follows a concentric pattern. The same pattern obtains in the body of the *šuilla* (10–24) in that the summary statements form a frame around a core prayer (13–21) which itself begins and ends with a similar line (13 : 21). At this stage of exposition, however, the value of these earlier observations is presumptive, not demonstrative. Thus for the above characterization to be more than just an assertion, we must now try to set out the structure in some detail and understand how it gives direction to the movement of ideas and shapes new images. We start at the center and work our way outward. We begin by asking what is achieved by the innovative technique of constructing a frame and setting the core prayer within it. This question may be answered by forming some impression of the core prayer as an independent entity and then noticing the nature and consequence of the interaction of core and frame.

In lines 13–21, the petitioner sets out his requests:

13. Whatsoever I seek may I attain,
14. Ordain (the response) "done!" to my speech,
15. Fashion (the response) "agreed!" to my thought,
16. May courtier and attendant seek agreement on my behalf,
17. May my god stand at my right,
18. May my goddess stand at my left,
19. May the guardian-deity be constantly at my side,
20. Grant me (the power) to speak, to be heard, and to meet with consent (so that)
21. Whatsoever words I utter may meet with consent.

Though not ordered sequentially, his wishes form more than just a random list of requests. The common concern is achievement and success. This text-segment conveys a picture of effective behavior, a picture which possesses scenic (though not yet dramatic) coherence. To what shall we ascribe the coherence? Certainly the existence of a common theme contributes to the creation of a structured scene, but if there were nothing more than this common theme, the text would probably just ramble and give the impression of discontinuity. Thus alongside a common theme there must be a structural principle giving form to the segment. The occurrence of a frame (10–12; 22–24) around the section, the similarity of the first and last lines (13 : 21), and their possession of features found nowhere else in the segment[24] suggest that even if there is a linear stanza arrangement we also have a concentric structure.

Support for seeing a concentric arrangement in our text is provided by the observation that ancient readers also seem to have understood the text in this way. This is suggested by two variants: line 10: $^{d}$*Marduk bēlu rabû ilu rēmēnû* is read by all mss. except the *bīt mēseri* text $4R^2$ 21*, which deletes *ilu rēmēnû*; line 21: *amāt aqabbû kīma uqabbû* is read by all mss. except $4R^2$ 21* and *ŠU-ILA*, no. 26, which replaces *kīma* with *ēma*. The minority readings $^{d}$*Marduk bēlu rabû* and *amāt aqabbû ēma uqabbû* are secondary. They reflect an attempt to harmonize, and thereby emphasize the relation of, the parallel lines 10 // 22a and 13 // 21: by the deletion of *ilu rēmēnû*, the invocation $^{d}$*Marduk bēlu rabû* of line 10 is rendered identical with the parallel invocation $^{d}$*Marduk bēlu rabû* of

24 Subjunctive and first-person verb forms.

line 22;[25] by the replacement of *kīma* with *ēma*, the first (13) and last (21) lines of the core prayer are rendered even more alike (*ēma uṣammaru … ēma aqabbû …*).

But however welcome such supporting testimony is, we need not rely on it, for the demonstration of concentric symmetry here is simple enough. If the text is unfolded from its outer edge inward and corresponding lines are placed alongside each other, corresponding lines are seen to be essentially identical in meaning and structure, and to parallel each other and form segments of the same circle.

| | | | |
|---|---|---|---|
| 13 : 21 | *ēma uṣammaru lukšud* | : | *amāt aqabbû ēma* (←*kīma*) *aqabbû lū magrat* |
| 14–15 : 20 | *šuškin kīttu ina pīya, šubši amāt damiqti ina libbiya* | : | *šurkamma qabâ šemâ u magāru*[26] |
| 16 : 19 | *tīru u nanzāzu liqbû damiqtī* | : | *ilu mušallimu idāya / ina idīya lū kayān* |
| 17 : 18 | *ilī lizziz ina imniya* | : | *ištarī lizziz ina šumēliya* |

An outer ring (13 : 21)[27] encircles an inner ring (14–15 : 20) which in turn encircles a chiastic staircase quatrain (16–19).[28] In lines 13 : 21, the petitioner

25 I cannot exclude the possibility that the shorter form is due to haplography: … GAL <-*ú*/*u* DINGIR *réme*/*re-mé-nu*>-*ú*/*u*. The original, longer form of the line may derive from a prayer which begins with the invocation ᵈ*Marduk bēlu rabû ilu rēmēnû*. Note that a Marduk *šuilla* with this opening line is attested in all its occurrences immediately after our *šuilla* (cf. Kunstmann, *Gebetsbeschwörung*, 95, no. 8; Mayer, *Untersuchungen*, 397, no. 18); in view of the observation made below that line 10 is part of a written equivalent of a "presentation scene," see also the inscribed prayer cited below, n. 34.

26 Note that all finite verb forms in lines 14–15 and 20 begin with /š/: *šuškin, šubši, šurkamma*.

27 Various translators (Landsberger, "Babylonisch-assyrische Texte," 1st ed. [1912], 102; 2nd ed. [1922], 308; Falkenstein and von Soden, *Hymnen und Gebete*, 298; Seux, *Hymnes*, 291; and Mayer, *Untersuchungen*, 348) separate line 13 from line 14 and connect it to line 12. However, the concentric structure of lines 13–21, the parallelism of lines 13 and 21, the fact that line 12 constitutes a promise and forms a proper ending of the statement in lines 10–12, and the parallelism of lines 12 and 24 all indicate that line 13 is joined to lines 14–21. Furthermore, an occurrence such as *AGH* 62: 37a does not contradict—rather it seems to confirm—this conclusion. This Ištar *šuilla* (*AGH* 60–63) also contains a line identical with our line 21: 34 (…) 37a: *amāt aqabbû kīma aqabbû lū magrat* (…) *ēma uṣammaru lukšud*. The composer of this *šuilla* has reversed the order of lines identical with the opening and closing lines of our core prayer. This reversal indicates, I believe, that lines 13 and 21 belong together and form a single circle and that the circle may be rotated 180°. This Ištar *šuilla* also contains a promise and benediction and displays some affinity with the Marduk *šuilla*.

28 The connection of line 16 with line 19 and the unity of lines 16–19 are underscored by such a passage as *AGH* 22: 5–8: *ilī lizziz ina imniya, ištarī lizziz ina šumēliya, ilu mušallimu ina idīya lū kayān, tīru manzāzu liqbû damiqtī*.

himself is the actor; in lines 14–15 : 20, he shares the role of actor; in lines 16–19, the role of actor is assumed by divine guardians. Lines 17–18 form the actual center. Each line is more nearly identical with the other than are any other two adjoining or concentrically balanced lines. Jointly they share features with the two surrounding lines. The form *lizziz* in lines 17–18 both draws on the same root as *nanzāzu* of line 16 and concretizes and specifies the general and non-transitive *lū kayān* of line 19. Lines 16–19 are drawn together by these shared features and by the studied contrast of single members in lines 17–18 with groups of two in lines 16 and 19. Lines 17–18 have single subjects and single indirect/locative objects, while line 16 has two subjects and line 19 has a dual indirect/locative object:

| | | |
|---|---|---|
| *tīru u nanzāzu* | | *liqbû damiqtī* |
| *ilī* | *lizziz ina imniya* | |
| *ištarī* | *lizziz ina šumēliya* | |
| *ilu mušallimu* | *ina idīya* | *lū kayān* |
| | *idāya* | |

Lines 17–18 separate entities which appear in groups of two in lines 16 and 19: *ilī* and *ištarī* (17–18) individualize (and define the divine nature of[29]) the preceding *tīru u nanzāzu* (16), and *ina imniya* and *ina šumēliya* (17–18) split *idāya* (19) into its two component parts. By associating each of the "sides" with a single god, the subsequent joining of the two sides in the dual *idāya* then allows and renders credible the merging of the individual *ilu* and *ištaru* into the group concept *ilu mušallimu* in a picture which would be spatially impossible—*ilu mušallimu idāya lū kayān*—were the speaker (and the modern reader) not caught up in the transformation. Fused together in this way, lines 16–19 form a scene of divine guardians surrounding a petitioner on all sides.[30]

29 A decision whether the *tīru* and *nanzāzu* refer to palace officials or to divine figures is not cut and dried: note, for example, that Landsberger treated them as "untergeordnete Götter" in the 1912 version of "Babylonisch-assyrische Texte" (102 n. 1), but as "Palastbeamte" in the 1922 version (308 n. 1). I prefer the former characterization; cf. Mayer, *Untersuchungen*, 255 n. 56: "Da dieser Wunsch [i.e., *tīru u nanzāzu liqbû damiqtī*] jeweils neben Bitten steht, die sich auf 'Schutzgeister' beziehen ... hat man vermutet, *tīru* und *nanzāzu* seien hier ebenfalls der Kategorie der Schutzgottheiten zuzurechnen.... Wenn das zutrifft, wäre hier das Modell des königlichen Hofstaates auf die Welt der Götter übertragen."

30 Note that a verbal strand seems to run through our passage: ... *kīttu* (14) ... *amāt damiqti* (15) ... *liqbû damiqtī* (16) ... *kayān* (19) ... *qabâ* (20) ... *amāt aqabbû* ... *aqabbû* (21).

The core prayer may be diagrammed as follows:

13 21

14–15 20

16 19

17–18

This analysis of lines 13–21 is confirmed by the grammatical structure of the segment. Note especially that every line contains a form of the "volitive" mood; the concentric structure finds expressions in the pattern of distribution of precatives and imperatives.

| | | | | | |
|---|---|---|---|---|---|
| 13 : 21 | *lukšud* | : | *lū magrat* | precative | *lu-*/*lū* |
| 14–15 : 20 | *šuškin, šubši* | : | *šurkamma* | imperative | |
| 16 : 19 | *liqbû* | : | *lū kayān* | precative | *li-*/*lū* |
| 17 : 18 | *lizziz* | : | *lizziz* | precative | *li-*[31] |

13 *luprus* *lū parsat* 21[32]

14–15 *purus* *purus* 20

16 *liprus* *lū parrās* 19

17 *liprus* *liprus* 18

The use of the techniques of ring composition and hysteron proteron result in the creation of a concentrically symmetrical form. Circles are balanced in an inverted order around a still point, and our attention is directed first inward toward the center and then back to the border (13 : 21) and beyond, to lines 10–12 and 22–24. Around the prayer, lines 10–12 and 22–24 form a further circle. This outer frame accentuates the concentric structure of the core prayer. It also changes the meaning of the prayer for success and itself receives a definite setting. In lines 10–12 and 22–24, a suppliant petitions Marduk for the gift of life. In this setting, the core prayer is transformed into a request for the kind of assistance, skills, and reception that the suppliant imagines he

31 For other grammatical features that are shared by corresponding lines, note 13 : 21: conjunction + 1st pers. subjunctive verb form, and 17 : 18: preposition + noun + 1 sing. poss. suff.

32 Note the gradual loosening of grammatical structure: *lu-*… … *li-*… *li-*… *li-*… *lū* + masc. absol. … *lū* + fem. absol. It almost appears as if each side is building up one difference: 17–13: *u* (*li-* → *lu-*), 18–21: independent form (*li-* → *lū* + predicative stative); the segment would thus form a circle that begins and ends with *lu-*/*lū* + (13/21).

needs to present his petition effectively and to be granted whatever he asks for; a prayer for mundane success becomes a prayer that prepares the suppliant for a successful audience with Marduk. What previously only possessed scenic coherence now possesses dramatic coherence. From being a snapshot, the core prayer is transformed into a story, a description of movement toward a journey's end. The meeting of petitioner and god is that end, and this meeting takes the form of the petitioner's address to Marduk in lines 10–12 and 22–24.

By joining together (1) scenes of meeting and addressing Marduk (10–12 : 22–24) with (2) those of preparation and introduction (13–21), the composer creates a scene comparable to the "presentation scene"[33] so often represented on cylinder seals, and it is hardly a coincidence that the most common and basic wish expressed in prayers engraved on Kassite seals is the wish for a long life.[34] We now have a scene with a frame and an apex. The frame—10–12 : 22–24—represents both culmination and context, and the apex—16–19—represents the point from which the action moves. The petitioner asks that protective, minor gods accompany him and speak well of him to the god (16–19), that he himself be granted the ability to address the god convincingly (14–15 : 20), and that whatever he requests from the god be granted him (13 : 21). Standing before Marduk and surrounded by his gods, he then presents his petition (10–12 : 22–24): he addresses Marduk respectfully, as a loyal subject addresses his overlord (10 : 22a); he asks Marduk to grant him the boon of life (11 : 22b–23); and he declares his personal allegiance to Marduk and his desire to continue serving the god faithfully (12 : 24).

Minor gods give way to the great god; intimacy with interceding guardians is replaced by the feeling of majesty and the call to praise that Marduk inspires. The suppliant has drawn near to Marduk and asked for life. We witness the direct meeting of man and god. But now we have reached the introductory hymn (1–9) and concluding benediction (25–27) and the god disengages and draws away. The conflict between divine involvement and separateness is recognized and resolved. The distancing allows man and god to retain their

33 Cf. the characterization of this scene by H. A. Groenewegen-Frankfort, *Arrest and Movement: An Essay on Space and Time in the Representational Art of the Ancient Near East* (Chicago: University of Chicago Press, 1951), 166.

34 Cf. H. Limet, *Les légendes des sceaux cassites* (Brussels: Palais des Académies, 1971), 46; furthermore, compare lines 10–12 with such inscribed prayers as Limet, *Légendes*, 83, no. 6.5. (As an aside, note that *a-mi-ri* of 95, no. 7.9: 2 does not refer back to Marduk; it is the subject of the following *liqbi*: "May the one who beholds me speak well of me.")

separate identities and thus preserves the possibility of an ongoing relationship. However much Marduk cares for man, he is finally a member of a different community. At the moment of direct contact, the text looks outward and beyond the world of man and reasserts the god's divine nature.

The first-person voice of the suppliant is silenced. The introduction and conclusion present Marduk's withdrawal from man and his reentry into the world of the gods. Human praise gives way to divine praise in hymn and benediction. The praise of the individual man in lines 10–12 is replaced with that of mankind in general. Marduk then draws back from caring for and being praised by men everywhere (7–9) and turns first to his cities Borsippa and Babylon (4–6) and returns finally to his family and home in Eridu (1–3). Care of the god and the joy man feels in his service (22–24) are replaced by the joy Marduk feels when he returns to his own world and receives the greeting and praise of Enlil and Ea, the gods of the heaven and the abyss (25), of the gods of the universe (26), and of the great gods (27).

Forming the outer ring, hymn and benediction, though internally concentric, stand in parallel symmetry to each other, a symmetry best exemplified by shared words:[35]

| | | | |
|---|---|---|---|
| 1–3 | // | 25 | $^{d}$*Marduk ... murīš E'engura* (3); ... $^{d}$*Ea lirīška* (25) |
| 4–6 | // | 26[36] | |
| 7–9 | // | 27 | *šumka ... ina pī nišī ṭāb* (9); *ilū rabûtu libbaka liṭibbū* (27)[37] |

Moving from the center, we have made our way to the outer edge of the composition. The following diagram sets out in schematic form the structure of the text and may serve to summarize and conclude this last portion of our exposition:

35 What looks like a standard benediction is only one variation among many (see Mayer, *Untersuchungen*, 336–337); if it is granted that intention and choice played some part in the formulation, then the connections between hymn and benediction are all the more striking.

36 The parallelism of lines 4–6 and 26 is posited for systematic reasons; I am unable to isolate specific points of contact between lines 4–6 and 26.

37 Cf. lines 14–15: ... *ina pīya, ... ina libbiya.*

| | | | | | | | | | | lines |
|---|---|---|---|---|---|---|---|---|---|---|
| | | 1 | | | | | | | | 1–3 |
| Hymn | A | | 2 | | | | | | | 4–6 |
| | | 3 | | | | | | | | 7–9 |
| | | | | | 1 | | | | | 10 |
| Meeting with Marduk | | | | B | 2 | | | | | 11 |
| | | | | | 3 | | | | | 12 |
| | | | | | | 1 | | | | 13 |
| | | | | | | | 2 | | | 14–15 |
| | | | | | | | | 3 | | 16 |
| Preparation for meeting | | | | | | C | | | X | 17–18 |
| | | | | | | | | 3′ | | 19 |
| | | | | | | | 2′ | | | 20 |
| | | | | | | 1′ | | | | 21 |
| | | | | | 1′ | | | | | 22a |
| Meeting with Marduk | | | | B′ | 2′ | | | | | 22b–23 |
| | | | | | 3′ | | | | | 24 |
| | | 1′ | | | | | | | | 25 |
| Benediction | A′ | | 2′ | | | | | | | 26 |
| | | 3′ | | | | | | | | 27 |

•••

The way we chose to study the Marduk *šuilla* was determined, in the first instance, by several difficulties which we encountered in the text itself, and this approach has served us well. But there is more than one way of reading a text, and much has also been left unsaid. Our composition, as we have noted, has a form different from most other *šuillas*. Precisely because we have eschewed historical questions and modes of inquiry and have treated the composition as an independent creation, it is necessary to remark at this point that our study also suggests that the composition did not stand in isolation. Some of the compositional features that characterize our text and distinguish it from other *šuillas* are also found in various degrees of development in prayers to other members of Marduk's circle.[38] The composition, moreover, is genetically related to the Nabû *šuilla BMS* 22: 1–29.[39] The Marduk *šuilla* was composed, I should guess,

38 Cf. *AGH* 60–63; 68–71; 106–109.

39 See Kunstmann, *Gebetsbeschwörung*, 99 s.v. Nabû 2: "Stilistisch auf das engste verwandt mit dem Gebete Marduk 2." For a new edition, see Mayer, *Untersuchungen*, 473–475. For the relationship between the two compositions, see T. Abusch, "The Form and History of

sometime before the reign of Adad-apla-iddina;[40] it appears to have been a product of a theological and literary movement that centered around the figure of Marduk. Such questions, though, are best left for another occasion; here, we must be satisfied with having recovered an aspect of the form and a fragment of the meaning of a prayer.

a Babylonian Prayer to Nabû," in *"The Scaffolding of Our Thoughts": Essays on Assyriology and the History of Science in Honor of Francesca Rochberg*, ed. C. Jay Crisostomo et al., AMD 13 (Leiden: Brill, 2018), 169–182 [[149–162]].

40 But now see Abusch, "Form and History of a Babylonian Prayer to Nabû," 180 n. 29 [[160 n. 29]].

CHAPTER 11

# The Form and History of a Babylonian Prayer to Nabû

In an earlier study, I examined the *šuilla* Marduk 2.[*,1] I demonstrated there, I believe, that this prayer did not follow the standard form of the *šuilla* type (Introductory Hymn, Prayer, Concluding Benediction[2]) and that it displayed a new pattern:

> Introductory Hymn (1–9)
> Capsule *šuilla* (10–12)
> Prayer for Success (13–21)
> Capsule *šuilla* (22–24)
> Concluding Benediction (25–27).

Thus, the form of this *šuilla* was the result of innovation. But this Marduk *šuilla* does not stand in isolation. Some of its compositional features are found elsewhere.[3] Moreover, it is genetically related to Nabû 3.[4] The purpose of the present article is to examine this Nabû *šuilla* in light of this genetic relationship

---

* Professor Francesca Rochberg has devoted much of her scholarly attention and gifts to the study of Mesopotamian science, astronomy, and astrology. These fields border and often overlap those of Mesopotamian religion, and thus I hope that Chessie will receive this study of an Akkadian prayer in the spirit of respect and friendship in which it is offered.

1 T. Abusch, "The Form and Meaning of a Babylonian Prayer to Marduk," *JAOS* 103 (1983): 3–15 [[126–148]].

2 For this standard form, see W. G. Kunstmann, *Die babylonische Gebetsbeschwörung*, LSS NF 2 (Leipzig: Hinrichs, 1932), 7–42; cf. W. Mayer, *Untersuchungen zur Formensprache der babylonischen "Gebetsbeschwörungen,"* StPohl, series maior 5 (Rome: Pontifical Biblical Institute, 1976), 34–37.

3 See Abusch, "Form and Meaning," 14 and n. 38 [[147 and n. 38]].

4 See already Kunstmann, *Gebetsbeschwörung*, 99 s.v. Nabû 2: "Stilistisch auf das engste verwandt mit dem Gebete Marduk 2." Note that Kunstmann's Nabû 2 = Nabû 3 in W. R. Mayer's system of enumeration, which I follow here; see Mayer, *Untersuchungen*, 400–401. For an edition of Nabû 3, see Mayer, *Untersuchungen*, 473–475. For copies of mss. A–D, see *ŠU-ILA*, nos. 54–57. For a new copy and edition of Mayer's ms. E (= *LKA* 56), see S. M. Maul and R. Strauss, *Ritualbeschreibungen und Gebete I*, KALI 4, WVDOG 133 (Wiesbaden: Harrassowitz, 2011), no. 64 (transliteration and translation, pp. 120–122; copy, p. 228). For a recent English translation, see B. R. Foster, *Before the Muses: An Anthology of Akkadian Literature*, 3rd ed. (Bethesda, MD: CDL, 2005), 695–696.

 | DOI:10.1163/9789004435186_012

in order to work out its structure, history of composition, and relationship to Marduk 2.

Let us begin with a presentation of the two compositions in parallel columns. Variants deemed significant for our discussion are given on the line in round brackets.

| | **Marduk 2** | | **Nabû 3** |
|---|---|---|---|
| 1. | ÉN *gašru šūpû etel Eridug* | 1. | ÉN *rubû ašarēdu bukur* $^{d}$*Tutu* |
| 2. | *rubû tizqāru bukur* $^{d}$*Nudimmud* | 2. | *massû itepšu ilitti* $^{d}$*Papnunanki* |
| 3. | $^{d}$*Marduk šalbābu murīš Eʾengura* | 3. | $^{d}$*Nabû nāš ṭup šīmāt ilī āšir Esaĝila* |
| 4. | *bēl Esaĝila tukulti Bābili* | 4. | *bēl Ezida ṣulūl Barsipa* |
| 5. | *rāʾim Ezida mušallim napišti* | 5. | *narām* $^{d}$*Nudimmud* (var. $^{d}$*Papnunanki*) *qāʾišu balāṭi* |
| 6. | *ašarēd Emaḫtila mudeššû balāṭi* | 6. | *ašarēd Bābili nāṣiru napišti* |
| 7. | *ṣulūl māti gāmil nišī rapšāti* | 7. | *andul dadmi ēṭir nišī bēl ešrēti* |
| 8. | *ušumgal kalîš parakkī* | | |
| 9. | *šumka kalîš ina pī nišī ṭāb* | 8. | *zikirka ina pī nišī šuṭubba* $^{d}$*lamassi* |
| 10. | $^{d}$*Marduk bēlu rabû ilu rēmēnû* (var. Ø) | 9. | *mār rubê rabî* $^{d}$*Marduk ina amātika kītti* |
| 11. | *ina qibītika kītti* (vars. *ṣērti* / *kabitti*) *lubluṭ lušlimma* | 10. | *ina siqrika kabti ina qibīt ilūtika rabīti* (var. *ina qibītika* [*rabīti*]) |
| | | 11. | *anāku annanna mār annanna marṣu šumruṣu aradka* (var. lines 11–12 absent) |
| | | 12. | *ša qāt eṭemmi ušburrudâ*(sic) *māmītu iṣbatūnima irteneddûni* |
| | | 13a. | *lubluṭ lušlimma* |
| 12. | *luštammar ilūtka* | | |
| 13. | *ēma uṣammaru lukšud* | 13b. | *ēma akappudu lukšud* |
| 14. | *šuškin kīttu ina pîya* | 14. | *šuškin kīttu ina pîya* |
| 15. | *šubši amāt damiqti ina libbiya* | 15. | *šubši amāt damiqti ina libbiya* |
| 16. | *tīru u nanzāzu liqbû damiqtī* | 16. | *tīru u manzāzu liqbû damiqtī* |
| 17. | *ilī lizziz ina imniya* | 17. | *lizziz ilī ina imniya* |
| 18. | *ištarī lizziz ina šumēliya* | 18. | *lizziz ištarī ina šumēliya* |
| 19. | *ilu mušallimu idāya* (var. *ina idīya*) *lū kayān* | 19. | *šēdu damqu lamassu damiqtu lirrakis*$^{\text{(sic)}}$ *ittiya* |
| 20. | *šurkamma qabâ šemâ u magāru* | 20. | *šutlimamma tašmâ u magāra* |
| 21. | *amāt aqabbû ēma* (var. *kīma*) *aqabbû lū magrat* | 21. | *zikir atammû qibītī lišl*[*im*] |

*(cont.)*

| Marduk 2 | | Nabû 3 | |
|---|---|---|---|
| 22. | *Marduk bēlu rabû napištī qīša* | 22. | *mār rubê rabî $^{d}$Marduk [bal]āṭa qīša* |
| 23. | *balāṭ napištiya qibi* | | |
| 24. | *maḫarka namriš atalluka lušbi* | 23. | *maḫarka kīniš atalluka lušbi* |
| 25. | *$^{d}$Enlil liḫdūka $^{d}$Ea lirīška* | 24. | *$^{d}$Šazu liḫdūka [$^{d}$Nudimmu]d lirīška* |
| 26. | *ilū ša kiššati likrubūka* | 25. | *ilū ša šamê u erṣeti likrubūka* |
| | | 26. | *šamû [(u) erṣetu … l]išālilūka* |
| 27. | *ilū rabûtu libbaka liṭibbū* | 27. | *ilū rabûtu libbaka liṭibbū* |
| | | 28. | *$^{d}$Taš[mētu ḫērtu narāmtaka]* |
| | | 29. | *ina Ez[ida bīt ši]kin napišti š[a ilī (rabûti) damiqti?] liqb[īka]* |

We may now turn to an analysis of the two texts. We first set out the textual segments and structures that the two *šuilla*s share, citing for each corresponding section the Akkadian text and its English translation.[5] Only after establishing the parallel structures will we point to some imperfections in the Nabû text and consider some of their implications.

**1) Hymnic Introduction:** Both *šuilla*s begin with hymnic introductions. The hymnic introduction of Marduk 2 is made up of three stanzas.

1. ÉN *gašru šūpû etel Eridug*
2. *rubû tizqāru bukur $^{d}$Nudimmud*
3. *$^{d}$Marduk šalbābu murīš E'engura*

4. *bēl Esaĝila tukulti Bābili*
5. *rā'im Ezida mušallim napišti*
6. *ašared Emaḫtila mudeššû balaṭi*

7. *ṣulul mati gamil niši rapšati*
8. *ušumgal kalîš parakkī*
9. *šumka kalîš ina pī nišī ṭāb*

5 I assume that the reader is familiar with my study of the text of Marduk 2 [[126–148]]; I will repeat as little as possible from that earlier study.

1. Famed mighty one, chieftain of Eridu,
2. Exalted prince, first-born of Nudimmud,
3. Raging Marduk, restorer of rejoicing in E'engura

4. Lord of Esagila, hope of Babylon,
5. Lover of Ezida, preserver of life,
6. Lone one of Emaḫtila, multiplier of living.

7. Protection of the land, savior of the multitudes of people,
8. The single great one of chapels everywhere,
9. Your name is sweetly hymned by the people everywhere.

The first stanza (1–3) presents Marduk as the young hero of Eridu. The focus is upon his relationship to his parents and his actions on their behalf (*murīš E'engura*). The second stanza (4–6) presents Marduk as the god of Babylon and its environs: in line 4, he is the lord of Esaĝila and the trust of Babylon (note the order temple–city); in lines 5–6, epithets describing Marduk's relation to temples in Borsippa are juxtaposed to those describing his care for human life. The third stanza (7–9) presents Marduk in relationship to land, people, and sanctuaries, and ends with a declaration that his praise is sung by people everywhere.

We find a similar structure in Nabû 3, for here too the hymnic introduction is made up of three stanzas that seem to parallel those of the Marduk text:

1. ÉN *rubû ašarēdu bukur* $^{d}$*Tutu*[6]
2. *massû itepšu ilitti* $^{d}$*Papnunanki*
3. $^{d}$*Nabû nāš ṭup šīmāt ilī āšir Esaĝila*

4. *bēl Ezida ṣulūl Barsipa*
5. *narām* $^{d}$*Nudimmud* (var. ms. E: $^{d}$*Papnunanki*) *qā'išu balāṭi*
6. *ašarēd Bābili nāṣiru napišti*

7. *andul dadmi ēṭir nišī bēl ešrēti*
8. *zikirka ina pī nišī šuṭubba* $^{d}$*lamassi*

6 My transcription generally follows the main text in Mayer's edition, which is usually based on the Nineveh mss. Note that the Aššur ms. *LKA* 56 = KALI 4, no. 64 (= Mayer's ms. E) has a number of earlier and better readings than the Nineveh mss.

1. O Preeminent prince, scion of Tutu,
2. Accomplished leader, offspring of Papnunanki
3. Nabû, bearer of the tablet of destinies of the gods, supervisor of Esagila.

4. Lord of Ezida, protection of Babylon,
5. Beloved of Nudimmud (var.: Papnunanki), bestower of life,
6. Preeminent one of Babylon, protector of life.

7. Shelter of settlements, savior of the people, lord of shrines,
8. Your mention is sweeter in the mouth of the people than that of their own protective spirit.[7]

The first stanza (1–3) places Nabû in relationship to his parents and sets out his activities in his native home: He is the son of Marduk (under the name Tutu, the original god of Borsippa) and Zarpanītu (under the name Papnunanki, originally the wife of Asalluḫi) and administrator of Esagila (the temple of Marduk in Babylon). The second stanza (4–6) presents Nabû as the god of Borsippa and its environs: in line 4, he is the lord of Ezida and the protector of Borsippa (note the order temple–city); in lines 5–6, epithets describing his relationships are juxtaposed to those describing his care for human life. The third stanza (7–8) presents Nabû in relationship to land, people, and sanctuaries, and ends with a declaration that his praise is sung by people everywhere.

2) **Capsule *šuilla*:** Marduk 2 has a capsule *šuilla* in lines 10–12, immediately following the hymnic introduction:

10. *dMarduk bēlu rabû*
11. *ina qibītika kītti* (vars.: *ṣērti* / *kabitti*) *lubluṭ lušlimma*
12. *luštammar ilūtka*

10. O Marduk, great lord,
11. By your affirmative decree, may I live and be well,
12. I will then constantly praise your godhead.

Marduk 2 has a second capsule *šuilla* in lines 22–24, immediately preceding the concluding benediction:

7 Cf. *CAD* L, 62b.

22. $^{d}$*Marduk bēlu rabû napištī qīša*
23. *balāṭ napištiya qibi*
24. *maḫarka namriš atalluka lušbi*

22. O Marduk, great lord, grant me my life,
23. Decree for me a healthy life,
24. In joyfully serving you regularly will I (then) find satisfaction.

Each of these summaries contains (a) an invocation; (b) a prayer for life; and (c) a promise of praise or service. The two summary *šuilla*s in lines 10–12 and 22–24 serve as a frame for the prayer for success with Marduk in lines 13–21.

Similarly, Nabû 3 contains two summary *šuilla*s, one after the hymnic introduction (9–13a), the other before the concluding benediction (22–23):

9. *mār rubê rabî* $^{d}$*Marduk ina amātika kītti*
10. *ina siqirka kabti ina qibīt ilūtika rabīti* (var. ms. E: *ina qibītika* [*rabīti*])
11. *anāku annanna mār annanna marṣu šumruṣu aradka* (var. ms. E: lines 11–12 absent)
12. *ša qāt eṭemmi*[8] *ušburruddâ*(sic)[9] *māmītu iṣbatūnima irteneddûni*
13a. *lubluṭ lušlimma* (13b *ēma akappudu lukšud*)
……
22. *mār rubê rabî* $^{d}$*Marduk* [*bal*]*āṭa qīša*
23. *maḫarka kīniš atalluka lušbi*

9. O Son of the great prince Marduk, by your affirmative decree,
10. By your honored command, by the command of your great godhead (var.: by your great command)—
11. I, So-and-so, the son of So-and-so, your sick, suffering servant
12. Whom the Hand of a Ghost, Witchcraft, Hand of a Curse have seized and constantly persecute (var.: lines 11–12 absent)—
13a. May I live and be well.
……
22. O Son of the great prince Marduk, grant me life,
23. In faithfully serving you regularly will I (then) find satisfaction.

Each of the capsule *šuilla*s in Nabû 3 contains an invocation of the god and a prayer for life; the latter one concludes with a promise of service.

8 Or *šugidimmakku*.

9 UŠ$_{11}$.BÚR.RU.DA is a mistake for "witchcraft" = *kišpū* (UŠ$_{11}$ or UŠ$_{11}$.ZU). UŠ$_{11}$.BÚR.RU.DA refers to a ritual to undo witchcraft.

**3) Prayer for Success:** The prayer for success in Marduk 2 reads:

13. *ēma uṣammaru lukšud*
14. *šuškin kīttu ina pîya*
15. *šubši amāt damiqti ina libbiya*
16. *tīru u nanzāzu liqbû damqtī*
17. *ilī lizziz ina imniya*
18. *ištarī lizziz ina šumēliya*
19 *ilu mušallimu idāya* (var. *ina idīya*) *lū kayān*
20. *šurkamma qabâ šemâ u magāru*
21. *amāt aqabbû ēma* (var. *kīma*) *aqabbû lū magrat*

13. Whatsoever I seek may I attain,
14. Place effective speech in my mouth,
15. Fashion an agreeable word in my mind,
16. May courtier and attendant seek agreement on my behalf,
17. May my god stand at my right,
18. May my goddess stand at my left,
19. May the guardian deity be constantly at my side,
20. Grant me (the power) to speak, to be heard, and to meet with consent (so that)
21. Whatsoever words I utter may meet with consent.

As noted above, the capsule *šuilla*s in Marduk 2 serve as a frame for the prayer for success in the audience before the deity (13–21). Similarly, the capsule *šuilla*s in Nabû 3 serve as a frame for the prayers for success (13b–21) in that *šuilla*:

13b. ... *ēma akappudu lukšud*
14. *šuškin kīttu ina pîya*
15. *šubši amāti damiqti*[10]
16. *tīru u manzāzu liqbû damiqtī*
17. *lizziz ilī ina imniya*
18. *lizziz ištarī ina šumēliya*
19. *šēdu damqu*[11] *lamassu damiqtu lirrukis*[12] *ittiya*

10 Text: *damiqtu*.

11 Perhaps, rather, *šēd dumqi lamassi dumqi*. See Mayer, *Untersuchungen*, 245 and n. 43, 247. I choose *damqu* and *damiqtu* because of a writing cited there in n. 43: $^{d}$LAMMA SIG$_6$-*tú*/*tu*$_4$—see *BMS* 12 [[*CMAwR* 2, no. 8.28]]: 110, and *KAR* 298: 36, cited in *CAD* L, 64a. But note that Mayer (*Untersuchungen*, 247) reads our passage as *šēd dumqi lamassi dumqi*.

12 We expect a plural verb; but see F. Köcher, A. L. Oppenheim, and H. G. Güterbock, "The Old Babylonian Omen Text VAT 7525," *AfO* 18 (1957–1958): 67 iii 30, cited in *CAD* Š/2, 258b.

20. *šutlimamma tašmâ u magāra*
21. *zikir atammû qibītī lišl[im]*

13b. ... Whatsoever I seek may I attain,
14. Place effective speech in my mouth,
15. Fashion an agreeable word in my mind,
16. May courtier and attendant seek agreement on my behalf,
17. May my god stand at my right,
18. May my goddess stand at my left,
19. May a protective spirit and a spirit of vitality be bound to my side.
20. Accord me (the power) to speak and to meet with consent (so that)
21. My command be fulfilled as I pronounce it.

Even a cursory examination of the prayers for success in the two *šuilla*s will indicate their likeness. Note the virtual identity of the central part of the prayers for success: Marduk 2, lines 14–18 = Nabû 3, lines 14–18; note also that while the opening and closing lines (Marduk 2, lines 13, 20–21 // Nabû 3, lines 13, 20–21) of the prayers for success are not identical, they are structurally parallel and quite similar:

**Marduk:**

13. *ēma uṣammaru lukšud*
...
20. *šurkamma qabâ šemâ u magāru*
21. *amāt aqabbû ēma aqabbû lū magrat*

13. Whatsoever I seek, may I attain,
...
20. Grant me (the power) to speak, to be heard, and to meet with consent (so that)
21. Whatsoever words I utter may meet with consent.

**Nabû:**

13b. *ēma akappudu lukšud*
...
20. *šutlimamma tašmâ u magāra*
21. *zikir atammû qibītī lišl[im]*

13b. ... Whatsoever I seek may I attain,
...
20. Accord me (the power) to speak and to meet with consent (so that)
21. My command be fulfilled as I pronounce it.

**4) Concluding Benediction:** Finally, both *šuilla*s end with similar benedictions (Marduk: lines 25–27; Nabû: lines 24–29). The benediction in Marduk 2 reads:

25. $^{d}$*Enlil liḫdūka* $^{d}$*Ea lirīška*
26. *ilū ša kiššati likrubūka*
27. *ilū rabûtu libbaka liṭibbū*

25. May Enlil rejoice over you, may Ea exult over you,
26. May the gods of the universe bless you,
27. May the great gods make you happy.

The benediction in Nabû 3 reads:

24. $^{d}$*Šazu*[13] *liḫdūka* [$^{d}$*Nudimmu*]*d*[14] *lirīška*
25. *ilū ša šamê u erṣeti likrubūka*
26. *šamû* [(*u*) *erṣetu* ... *l*]*išālilūka*
27. *ilū rabûtu libbaka liṭibbū*
28. $^{d}$*Taš*[*mētu ḫērtu narāmtaka*]
29. *ina Ez*[*ida bīt ši*]*kin napišti š*[*a ilī* (*rabûti*) *damiqti*?] *liqb*[*īka*].[15]

24. May Šazu rejoice over you, may [Nudimmu]d exult over you,
25. May the gods of heaven and the netherworld bless you.
26. May heaven [and the netherworld ...] celebrate you.
27. May the great gods make you happy.
28. May Taš[mētu, your beloved wife]
29. Speak [well of me to you] in Ez[ida, the house of the Grant]ing of life o[f the (great) gods].

---

13 A name of Marduk.

14 Originally probably $^{d}$Papnunanki or the like, a reading that I imagine ms. E had; unfortunately, ms. E is broken at this point.

15 For the reading of the last two lines, see P.-A. Beaulieu and W. R. Mayer, "Akkadische Lexikographie: CAD Š$_2$ und Š$_3$," *Or* NS 66 (1997): 174; for a different reading, see Maul and Strauss, *Ritualbeschreibungen*, 121–122.

The first part of the Nabû benediction is quite similar to the benediction in Marduk 2;[16] the last two lines of the Nabû benediction are a special addition to the Nabû composition.[17]

• • •

Overall, the two *šuilla*s parallel each other. But while the Marduk one seems to have attained a new form that is complete and as free as possible from flaws, this cannot be said of the Nabû one. There are a number of imperfections in our Nabû prayer, the most significant of which is found in line 13. For there, the expected promise of praise is absent, and the present text juxtaposes *lubluṭ lušlimma*, the request for life, with the beginning of the prayer for success.[18] Contrast the absence here of the promise of praise with the closing summary *šuilla* in this text (22–23), but especially with the first summary *šuilla* in Marduk 2, which ends with *luštammar ilūtka*. There, this phrase occurs immediately after *lubluṭ lušlimma* and just before the beginning of the prayer for success. In our Nabû *šuilla*, the phrase *luštammar ilūtka* is missing in line 13 between *lubluṭ lušlimma* and *ēma akappudu lukšud*.[19]

The absence—which reflects either a textual omission or a failure to provide the correct form in the process of composition—is not unrelated to other problems in this part of the text, difficulties which may be at least partially responsible for the absence:

> (1) Lines 9–10 and 13a are separated from each other by 11–12, where the speaker introduces himself and asserts that various evils have seized him (*anāku annanna mār annanna marṣu šumruṣu aradka / ša qāt eṭemmi ušburruddâ*^(sic) *māmītu iṣbatūnima irteneddûni*). Lines 11–12 have no correspondence in Marduk 2,[20] and should be treated as an insertion that breaks up the segment 9–10 + 13a; in fact, it is absent in ms. E.[21]

16 Marduk 25 // Nabû 24; Marduk 26 // Nabû 25; Marduk 27 = Nabû 27.

17 Cf. Mayer, *Untersuchungen*, 348.

18 This has led translators to erroneously connect the two; see, for example, A. Falkenstein and W. von Soden, *Sumerische und akkadische Hymnen und Gebete* (Zurich: Artemis, 1953), 312: "möge ich … zu Leben und Gesundheit kommen und es so, wie ich es erstrebe, (auch) erreichen!"; M.-J. Seux, *Hymnes et prières aux dieux de Babylonie et d'Assyrie*, LAPO 8 (Paris: Éditions du Cerf, 1976), 298: "Que je vive, que je sois sauf et que je réalise tout ce que je projette."

19 Further support that the two half lines 13a and 13b are separate and are not to be connected is provided by ms. E, which "verteilt 13 auf 2 Zeilen" (Mayer, *Untersuchungen*, 473).

20 Marduk 2 does have the inserted *attalû* formula before line 11 in *BMS* 54: 1′–4′; *ŠU-ILA*, no. 27, obv. 11–14; and PBS 1/2, no. 108, obv. 1′–8′.

21 Cf. Mayer, *Untersuchungen*, 473: "E: lässt den Einschub 11f weg."

(2) Lines 9b–10 essentially say the same thing three times and parallel the variants in Marduk 2: 11: *ina qibītika kītti* / *ṣērti* / *kabitti*. That is to say, the three variants in different manuscripts of Marduk 2 are preserved in Nabû 3 as three parallel phrases.[22] Leaving for later the question as to which of our two compositions preserves the more original text, it is clear that *ina qibīt ilūtika rabīti* in Nabû 3, line 10b is a corrupt form of the expected *ina qibītika rabīti*,[23] which, in fact, is preserved in ms. E. *ilūtka* belongs in line 13. This corruption is perhaps due to the insertion of lines 11–12, which caused the displacement of *ilūtka*[24] from line 13 to line 10. (We should probably move *ilūtka* down from line 10 to line 13 and supply *luštammar*, thus reconstructing the expected <*ilūtka luštammar*>.)

Other imperfections in our text agree with the inelegant, actually clumsy or maladroit, form of the summary *šuilla* in lines 19–10 + 13a of our main text. Here I would simply turn back to the hymnic introduction and take note of the text of lines 5–6: the Marduk *šuilla* suggests that there should be a connection between 5a and 5b and between 6a and 6b—but I, for one, do not see a connection here in the Nabû composition. In 5a (and 6a) we expect a temple (or city) name, instead we have the name Nudimmud (= Ea); Nudimmud is Nabû's grandfather (according to the Eridu-Babylon lineage),[25] but following *narām* we expect a female name, a reading that is actually found in ms. E.[26]

• • •

There can be no doubt that a relationship exists between Nabû 3 and Marduk 2, though it should be clear by now that while the Marduk composition is a consummately executed example of a new form, the Nabû composition is an imperfect, perhaps second-rate, example of the form. But now we must face a difficult question: which of the two is earlier and which is constructed using the other as a model? To rephrase the question: is the Nabû composition dependent on the Marduk one or is the Marduk composition dependent on the Nabû one? We can simplify the problem by noting that ms. E, the Aššur version of

22 See Abusch, "Form and Meaning," 9–10, n. 23 [[138 n. 23]]. In place of *ṣērti*, Nabû 3 has *rabīti*.

23 But note *ina qibīt ilūtika rabīti* in Nabû 4, rev. 25, edited by Mayer, *Untersuchungen*, 476–477 and cited at 304.

24 And the change of form from DINGIR(-*ut*)-*ka* = *ilūtka* to DINGIR-*ti*-*ka* = *ilūtika*.

25 For Nabû in association with Ea, see F. Pomponio, *Nabû: Il culto e la figura di un dio del Pantheon babilonese ed assiro*, StSem 51 (Rome: Istituto di Studi del Vicino Oriente, Università di Roma, 1978), 165–168.

26 Thus, the reading [d]Papnunanki in E is to be preferred.

Nabû 3, represents an earlier version of the text than do the Nineveh mss. A–D; thus, in determining dependency, we may ignore the textual problems and corruptions in A–D and compare only ms. E. Nevertheless, even without the textual problems of Nabû 3, mss. A–D, the text preserved in Nabû 3, ms. E is still not as well formed as that in Marduk 2.

I imagine that ancient composers/scribes would appreciate a newly worked out text form and, without good reason, would hesitate to alter or damage the form. This being the case, we may well conclude that a new literary form would not immediately degenerate[27] and that an imperfect example of a new form might well be earlier than a fully formed example. Accordingly, we may treat Nabû 3 (ms. E) as the precursor—a trial run or an early draft—of a new form and Marduk 2 as the more developed creation.

Against this conclusion is the observation that the Nabû composition seems to reflect a later stage of history than Marduk 2. For while in Marduk 2, Marduk is associated with the main temples of Borsippa (lines 5–6), in Nabû 3, Nabû is the protector of Borsippa (line 4) and the master of Ezida (line 4; cf. line 29).[28] Since historically Nabû replaces Marduk as the god of Borsippa (as earlier Marduk took over this role from Tutu),[29] Marduk's connections with Borsippa in Marduk 2, but Nabû's connections with it in Nabû 3 suggest that the Nabû *šuilla* is later than the Marduk one. Thus, given the shared forms, we should conclude that the Nabû composition is dependent on the Marduk one, that it is inferior, and that it does represent a deterioration or degeneration in form.[30]

We thus have arguments in support of the priority of each of the texts, though the latter argument in favor of the priority of Marduk 2 and the dependence thereupon of Nabû 3 undoubtedly carries much more weight. But it would be best if we could decide which is earlier on the basis of a parallel passage in the

27 I can see no reason why the composer of Nabû 3 would wish to alter the form.

28 This is not to deny that Nabû had several important functions in Babylon (cf. lines 3 and 6) even after he took over Borsippa; compare, for example, his roles in the Akitu festival in Babylon and statements about him in other texts such as *kudurrus*.

29 See Pomponio, *Nabû*, 63–65, and F. Pomponio, "Nabû. A. Philologisch," *RlA* 9 (1998): 19. In the last paragraph of Abusch, "Form and Meaning" [[147–148]], I noted: "The Marduk *šuilla* was composed, I should guess, sometime before the reign of Adad-apla-iddina." In view of the inscription of Marduk-šāpik-zēri (RIMB 2 B.2.7.2, pp. 47–48), cited by Pomponio, "Nabû," 19, I would now change my estimate of the date of composition to "before the reign of Marduk-šāpik-zēri."

30 This conclusion would agree with my supposition that an original composition usually coheres better than its descendent. Of course, texts undergo change (additions and reformulations) because of ritual or conceptual changes (not to mention mistakes in transmission) and may become less coherent in the process of transmission.

two texts. I would suggest, therefore, that we turn back to a passage mentioned earlier, the invocation of the god's decree in the first summary *šuilla*.

In Nabû 3, ms. E, the invocation reads: *ina amātika kītti, ina siqrika kabti, ina qibītika* [*rabīti*]; in Marduk 2, the equivalent passage reads: *ina qibītika kītti* (vars.: *ṣērti*; *kabitti*). If the Marduk composition is dependent on the Nabû one, the variant readings in the Marduk text would reflect the breakup of a ἓν διὰ τριῶν (*hendiatrion*) in the Nabû text and the preservation of synonymous variant readings in different manuscripts of the Marduk composition; if, on the other hand, the Nabû composition is dependent on the Marduk one, then the *hendiatrion* may be the result of the conflation of several variants and should be regarded as a triple reading or triplet.[31]

It is possible that it is easier to imagine the breakup of an expansive *hendiatrion* into three synonymous variant readings rather than the reverse (in which case our Nabû text would be the earlier of the texts); but this is a subjective (aesthetic) judgment. And, for purposes of a decision regarding priority, it would be better to ascertain whether or not there are other examples of similar *hendiatrions* or triplets used as invocations of a god's decree. If there are, then this passage in the Nabû prayer need not be dependent on the Marduk prayer. But if such a usage is rare, this anomaly would suggest that the formulation in the Nabû text is the result of a particular circumstance and would support the proposition that the Nabû text is dependent on the Marduk one. A perusal of the examples collected by Mayer reveals that our passage is the only one in this function that is made up of three elements (all others have one or two).[32] Given the uniqueness or, at least, oddity of the repetition of a similar phrase three times in the invocation of the god's decree, I surmise that our Nabû prayer represents an attempt to preserve earlier synonymous variants (found in the Marduk *šuilla*) by conflating them into the present triplet.[33]

31 See already my comment in Abusch, "Form and Meaning," 10 n. 23 [[138 n. 23]].

32 For the examples collected by Mayer, see *Untersuchungen*, 300–306; for our passage, see 304; cf. 301–302.

33 I have modeled my understanding of triple readings and triplets on the phenomena of double readings and doublets. The phenomenon of preserving variant readings by creating doublets is well known in biblical text criticism. For double readings there, see especially S. Talmon, "Double Readings in the Massoretic Text," *Textus* 1 (1960): 143–184 (= S. Talmon, *Text and Canon of the Hebrew Bible: Collected Studies* [Winona Lake, IN: Eisenbrauns, 2010], 217–266), and S. Talmon, "The Textual Study of the Bible: A New Outlook," in S. Talmon, *Text and Canon of the Hebrew Bible: Collected Studies*, 35–46. Cf. also S. Talmon, "Conflate Readings (OT)," in *Interpreter's Dictionary of the Bible: Supplementary Volume* (New York: Abingdon Press, 1976), 170–173; for purposes of the comparison of Marduk 2 and Nabû 3, note Talmon's comment on p. 171: "The recognition of a doublet in the MT or in a version usually arises from a comparison of two or more

Accordingly, I feel compelled to conclude that our Nabû *šuilla* is dependent upon Marduk 2 and made use of it.[34] To be sure, not only is Nabû 3 not an improvement on Marduk 2, but it also seems to be a degraded form. Why this should be the case is certainly worthy of further study.

witnesses to the text. A simple or short reading in one indicates that an expanded reading in the other may constitute a doublet, if the assumedly redundant component is but a reiteration of what already is expressed in the other textual component."

For a concise treatment of doublets and synonymous readings in the Bible, see E. Tov, *Textual Criticism of the Hebrew Bible*, 3rd ed. (Minneapolis: Fortress, 2012), 225–227, 257–258, and for the preservation of variant readings in different manuscripts (as in Marduk 2: 11), see S. Talmon, "Synonymous Readings in the Textual Traditions of the Old Testament," *Scripta Hierosolymitana* 8 (1961): 335–383 (= Talmon, *Text and Canon of the Hebrew Bible: Collected Studies*, 171–216).

34 Here, then, I should mention that the corruptions in Nabû 3, mss. A–D are later developments of the Nabû text, changes that are independent of Marduk 2, and may have been introduced into the text either in Nineveh or whence the Nineveh tradition derived.

CHAPTER 12

# A Paean and Petition to a God of Death: Some Comments on a *šuilla* to Nergal

## 1 Introduction

Nergal 2 is an excellent example of a general *šuilla* prayer.[*,1] As *šuilla*s go, it is relatively simple. It contains the expected sections:

1. A hymnic introduction in which the god is invoked and described (lines 1–10);
2. A supplication containing the self-presentation of the petitioner, a description of his difficulty, his approach to the god, and his request (lines 11–23);
3. A promise of praise (line 24).

* Frans Wiggermann is an erudite and discerning scholar of ancient Mesopotamia. What distinguishes Frans is his masterful command of both texts and visual images and their interconnections. Frans loves to study details, but he also knows how to use them to create comprehensive and meaningful constructs. Frans has an acute appreciation of artistic form. It is a great pleasure, therefore, to dedicate to a dear friend this study of some forms in a text addressed to a god in whom he has shown much interest (for example in "Nergal," *RlA* 9 [1998]: 215–226).

Parts of this study have appeared in an earlier pedagogical form; see T. Abusch, "A Shuilla: Nergal 2," in *Reading Akkadian Prayers and Hymns: An Introduction*, ed. A. Lenzi, ANEM 3 (Atlanta: Society of Biblical Literature, 2011), 339–349. My interest in this Nergal prayer and in the mode of analysis presented here goes back to the first time that I taught Akkadian literary texts (Jerusalem 1974). I have since taught the text several times, and I thank my students for their observations and questions. I thank particularly my student Bronson Brown-deVost, with whom I have recently had several enjoyable and productive discussions about this text. This study was submitted in 2011.

1 For a recent and reliable edition of this text and a listing of manuscripts, see W. Mayer, *Untersuchungen zur Formensprache der babylonischen "Gebetsbeschwörungen,"* StPohl, series maior 5 (Rome: Pontifical Biblical Institute, 1976), 478–481. In the main, I have followed Mayer's edition. The unpublished texts used there have since been published in copy by O. Loretz and W. R. Mayer, *ŠU-ILA*, nos. 60–63. A manuscript of this text has just been published by S. M. Maul and R. Strauss, *Ritualbeschreibungen und Gebete I*, KALI 4, WVDOG 133 (Wiesbaden: Harrassowitz, 2011), no. 65, transliteration and translation: 122–123, copy: 229. For an earlier edition and translation, see *AGH*, 112–115. The text has been translated a number of times; see especially A. Falkenstein and W. von Soden, *Sumerische und akkadische Hymnen und Gebete* (Zurich: Artemis, 1953), 313–314; R. Labat, A. Caquot, and M. Sznycer, *Les religions du Proche-Orient asiatique: Textes babyloniens, ougaritiques, hittites* (Paris: Fayard-Denoël, 1970), 113–114; M.-J. Seux, *Hymnes et prières aux dieux de Babylonie et d'Assyrie*, LAPO 8 (Paris: Éditions du Cerf, 1976), 312–314.

 | DOI:10.1163/9789004435186_013

The sections are clearly articulated and generally coherent; they are thematically well developed and, in the main, have a formal shape.

Actually, formal patterns define a significant part of this prayer. Not surprisingly, therefore, certain sections of the text are amenable to a meaningful formal analysis. Thus, my first purpose in this study is to point to some of the patterns (morphological, syntactic, and poetic) displayed by the prayer and thereby to explicate major portions of the text; though somewhat formalistic in nature, this explication will, of course, touch on issues of meaning. But there are sections of the text that, while displaying some formal patterns, remain conceptually problematic. My second purpose, then, is to take up those sections that are not immediately amenable to a meaningful formalistic analysis and to try to make some sense of them.

In transcription and translation, the text reads:

1. ÉN *bēlu gašru tizqāru bukur* $^{d}$*Nunamnir*
2. *ašarēd* $^{d}$*Anunnakkī bēl tamḫāri*
3. *ilitti* $^{d}$*Kutušar šarrati rabīti*
4. $^{d}$*Nergal kaškaš ilī narām* $^{d}$*Ninmenna*

5. *šūpâta ina šamê ellūti šaqu manzāzka*
6. *rabâta ina arallî māḫira lā tīšu*
7. *itti* $^{d}$*Ea*[2] *ina puḫur ilī milikka šūtur*
8. *itti* $^{d}$*Sîn ina šamê*[3] *taše’’i gimri*

9. *iddinka-ma* $^{d}$*Enlil abuka ṣalmāt qaqqadi puḫur napišti*
10. *būl* $^{d}$*Šakkan nammaššê qātukka ipqid*

11. *anāku annanna mār annanna aradka*
12. *šibsāt ili u* $^{d}$*ištari iššaknūnim-ma*
13. *ṣītu u ḫuluqqû ibbašû ina bītiya*
14. *qabû u lā šemû iddalpūninni*

15. *aššum gammalāta bēlī Nergal assaḫur ilūtka*
16. *aššum tayyārāta ešteʾēka*
17. *aššum rēmēnêta attaziz maḫarka*
18. *aššum muppalsāta ātamar pānīka*

2 Variant: *Ani*.

3 Variant: + *u erṣeti*.

19. *kīniš naplisanni-ma šime teslītī*
20. *aggu libbaka linūḫa*
21. *puṭur annī ḫiṭītī u gillatī*
22. *kiṣir libbi ilūtika rabīti zamar lippašra*[4]
23. *ilu u ištaru zenûtu šabsūtu kitmulūtu lislimū ittiya*

24. *narbîka lušāpi dalīlīka ludlul*

Mighty lord, exalted son of Nunamnir,
foremost among the Anunnaki, lord of battle,
offspring of Kutušar, the great queen,
Nergal, all powerful among the gods, beloved of Ninmenna.

You are manifest in the bright heavens, your station is exalted,
you are great in the netherworld, you have no rival.
Together with Ea,[5] your counsel is preeminent in the assembly of the gods.
Together with Sîn, you observe everything in the heavens.[6]

Enlil, your father, gave to you the black-headed ones, all the living, and
he entrusted into your hands the herds, the animals.

I, So-and-so, son of So-and-so, your servant:
The anger of god and goddess has beset me so that
expenses and losses befall my estate (and)
giving orders but not being obeyed keep me awake.

Because you save, my lord Nergal, I have turned toward your divinity,
because you are compassionate, I have sought you,
because you are merciful, I have stood before you,
because you are one who views with regard, I have looked upon your face.

4 Variant: *lippaṭ(a)ram-ma*.
5 Variant: Anu.
6 Variant: + and the netherworld (lit., earth).

Regard me favorably and hear my supplication.
May your furious heart become calm toward me,
pardon my sin, my error, and my misdeed,
may the wrath (lit., knots of your innards) of your great divinity speedily be appeased (lit., disentangled)[7] for me (so that)
the offended, angry, and irate god and goddess may be reconciled with me.

Then will I declare your great deeds and sing your praise!

The sections most amenable to formal analysis are the hymnic introduction and the petitioner's justification and description of his approach to the god, and we turn to these sections first.

## 2 Hymnic Introduction

The hymnic introduction is devoted to the descriptive praise of Nergal. It contains three stanzas that are syntactically linked together; they treat (1) the god's nature and place in a divine family (lines 1–4); (2) his place in the cosmos (lines 5–8); and (3) his relationship to the world of humans and animals (lines 9–10). Each of these is formally structured, though, occasionally, the artistry shows itself to be somewhat mechanical.

*The first stanza* treats two themes: the god's nature as a warrior (a), and his place in a divine family (b). Each line is made up of two half-lines; the lines form couplets and the two couplets form a stanza. The two aforementioned themes are integrated and laid out chiastically:

| | | |
|---|---|---|
| 1. | a *bēlu gašru* | b *tizqāru bukur* $^{d}$*Nunamnir*[8] |
| 2. | b′ *ašarēd* $^{d}$*Anunnakkī* | a′ *bēl tamḫāri* |
| 3. | b *ilitti* $^{d}$*Kutušar* | (= *šarrati rabīti*) |
| 4. | a′ $^{d}$*Nergal kaškaš ilī* | b′ *narām* $^{d}$*Ninmenna* |

7 Variant: "unknotted."
8 The thematic pattern warrior/status thus indicates that the first line is divided into two segments and that *tizqāru* is part of the second half of the line (pace Labat et al., *Religions*, and Falkenstein and von Soden, *Hymnen und Gebete*).

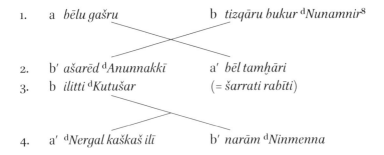

Note that the chiasm is reversed in the second couplet; however, the composer did deviate from this chiastic pattern in the second part of line 3, where instead of presenting a feature of Nergal's power (theme a), he provides an epithet of Kutušar, Nergal's mother, thus explicating and expanding on the first half of the line.[9] Even so, the half-lines, or hemistichs, form basic separate units; each unit is made up of either a noun + adjective, a construct chain, or a construct chain + adjective. The name Nergal in line 4 stands outside the unit.

*The second stanza* describes the god's place in the cosmos. Here, again, the composer follows a formal structure. Each couplet contains two parallel lines. Yet, here, the form is different from that of lines 1–4. There, the stanza was made up of eight hemistichs, none of which formed an independent grammatical clause. Here, on the other hand, lines 5–6 are each made up of two independent (though obviously associated) clauses, whereas both lines 7 and 8 form single clauses. Common themes (Nergal's preeminence in the cosmos and among the gods) draw together each of the individual subsections and, then, the stanza as a whole. But, certainly, the distribution of grammatical forms between lines and between couplets serves these purposes as well. That is, grammatically, line 5a parallels line 6a, and line 7a parallels line 8a; moreover, whereas the first half-lines draw together each of the two subsections (lines 5–6 and 7–8), the latter halves draw together the stanza as a whole, for the corresponding half-lines 5b // 7b and 6b // 8b share syntactic forms:

| | | | |
|---|---|---|---|
| 5a. | stative-2ms + prep. (*ina*) + region | 5b. | stative + subject with 2ms poss. suff. |
| 6a. | stative-2ms + prep. (*ina*) + region | 6b. | object + prefixed verb (2ms) |
| 7a. | prep (*itti*) DN + prep (*ina*) + region | 7b. | subject with 2ms poss. suff. + stative |
| 8a. | prep (*itti*) DN + prep (*ina*) + region | 8b. | prefixed verb (2ms) + object |

Whereas the parallel lines of each couplet have the same syntax and grammatical word order in their first half, the latter halves of these lines correspond in respect to their syntax not with each other, but rather with those of the other couplet: 5b // 7b, 6b // 8b. Note, moreover, the chiastic arrangement of

9 Line 3 is omitted in PBS 1/2, no. 119 (Mayer, *Untersuchungen*, ms. G). Given the deviant form of the line and its omission in one ms., it is possible that the line is not part of the original text. However, this inference is probably incorrect, since all other considerations indicate that this stanza originally contained not three but four lines.

the grammatical forms in the corresponding lines of the two couplets: 5b × 7b, 6b × 8b.

| | |
|---|---|
| 5bα. stative | 5bβ. subject with 2ms poss. suff. |
| 7bα. subject with 2ms poss. suff. | 7bβ. stative |
| 6bα. object | 6bβ. prefixed verb (2ms) |
| 8bα. prefixed verb (2ms) | 8bβ. object |

Thus, the first half-lines define and draw together the individual couplets, and the final half-lines define and draw together the stanza as a whole.[10] The word order is clearly intentional; the structured variation in pattern provides the literary form for the stanza and shapes its meaning.

As the god of death and of war (that is, the one who inflicts death in war), Nergal has a preeminent place in heaven, in the netherworld, and among the gods. Whereas lines 9–10 transport Nergal to earth, among the living animals and humans (see below), lines 5–6 emphasize his preeminence in the two cosmic regions ruled by the gods (heaven/netherworld) and lines 7–8 emphasize his importance by making him an equal with Ea regarding the power of his advice in the divine council and an equal with Sîn regarding the breadth of his vision in the heavens. Thus in lines 5–8, we have a chiastic arrangement a–b–b′–a′.

a. heaven (5)
  b. institution, i.e., netherworld (6)
  b′. institution, i.e., council (7)
a′. heaven (8)

Whereas in lines 5–6 Nergal is viewed not anthropomorphically but rather naturalistically in terms of his heavenly and infernal manifestations, lines 7–8 view him anthropomorphically and emphasize his role in divine institutions (in preparation for his role in the world of animals and humans). This pattern is that of our main text. But the pattern suggested by the variant readings in

10 Note, moreover, that all verbs in the second half of the lines contain /š/.

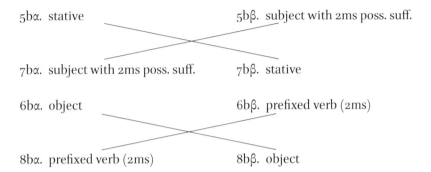

lines 7–8 (*Ani* instead of *Ea*, and especially *šamê u erṣeti* instead of *šamê* alone) seems to be different.[11]

*The third stanza* describes the god's relationship to humans and animals, thus bringing the god down to earth and serving as a prelude to the petitioner's call upon the god in the next section. This stanza is made up of two clauses, each of which extends over a whole poetic line. Lines 7–8 also contain clauses that extend over whole lines. But while those clauses are grammatically (not thematically) independent of each other, the clauses in lines 9–10 are connected by the enclitic *-ma* attached to *iddinka-ma* of line 9 and thus form a longer sentence.

From section to section, the elements of the hymn both grow and become more interrelated syntactically. Thus, lines 1–4 comprise a series of hemistichs where each half contrasts with the other, lines 5–6 comprise a series of hemistichs where each half supplements the other, lines 7–8 comprise full clauses, and finally lines 9–10 have two full clauses that are connected with each other. The types of clauses form a sequence that unify the hymn and move from an arena where the gods alone exist to areas of concern to humans, from the poetic divine to the prosaic human, from the world of the divine alluded to by compact poetic images to the world of the human depicted in drawn-out prosaic descriptions.

## 3 Petitioner's Justification and Description of His Approach to the God

In lines 15–18 the speaker then points to the features of Nergal that have encouraged him to approach the god. Before laying out the structure and form of these lines, I should first note that against the majority of witnesses, I follow K 2836 (Mayer, *Untersuchungen*, ms. B) in placing our line 17 before our line 18. (Contrary to this order, these lines are transposed in the other mss. and in Mayer's edition.) I place line 17 before line 18 because *muppalsāta* of our

11 If we follow the variant readings instead, we seem to have not so much a chiastic pattern, but one that runs through the different parts of the world, then draws them together: heaven (5), netherworld (6), earth (where the gods of heaven and the netherworld meet in council; cf. *ubšukkina*) (7), the universe (lit., heaven and earth, where Sîn and Nergal appear in both the heaven and the netherworld) (8). Of course, the variant *šamê u erṣerti* may simply represent an expansion of *šamê* using a standard formula. (Personally, I would have preferred the simple pattern heaven–netherworld–netherworld–heaven, but have desisted because of *puḫru* in line 7 [but perhaps *puḫru* should be associated with the netherworld].)

line 18 should, I think, lead directly into *naplisanni-ma* of line 19; cf. *AGH* 26: 37 (Ninurta *šuilla* no. 1), where we read *muppalsāta kīniš naplisanni*, "You are one who views with regard, regard me favorably."[12] Moreover, the supplicant's action *attaziz maḫarka*, "I have stood before you," of our line 17 should precede his action *ātamar pānīka*, "I have looked upon your face," of our line 18.[13]

Lines 15, 16, 17, 18 (as I number them in the present treatment) parallel each other. More specifically, the opening hemistichs of lines 15–18 all contain: *aššum* + a predicative adjectival form which describes a permanent feature of the divine addressee + a 2ms subject pronominal suffix (*gammalāta // tayyārāta // rēmēnêta // muppalsāta*). The second hemistichs of these lines all contain verbs in the same grammatical form: 1cs perfect + either a 2ms object pronominal suffix or an accusative noun + a 2ms possessive pronominal suffix. The predicative adjectives in the opening halves of these lines appear to describe a positive feature of the god and seem simply to be synonymous; while it may be the case that also the verbs in the latter halves of the lines are in synonymous parallelism, I think rather that they represent a meaningful sequence or progression of movement toward the presence of the god: searching for him, focusing upon him, standing before him, looking at him, all done in preparation for making a request of him (lines 19–23).[14]

We turn now to two sections of the text that seem to us to be problematical on an interpretive level. They are the description of the petitioner's difficulties (lines 12–14) and his supplication (lines 19–23).

## 4 Description of the Petitioner's Difficulties

In line 11 the supplicant or petitioner identifies himself.[15] Following his self-presentation, he gives voice to his lament, that is, he describes his difficulties:

12 This *šuilla* shares other motifs with our composition; compare, e.g., *AGH* 26: 15–18 with our lines 5–6 and 9–10.

13 In support of this, perhaps note that *azziz* precedes the other actions in the sequence *Maqlû* II 87–89 (… *maḫarka azziz* / … *allika ana maḫrika* / … *šapalka akmis*).

14 That is, the suppliant searches for the temple, seeks the god or his chapel, comes into his presence, looks at his face.

15 The main text has *anāku annanna mār annanna aradka*. This has been expanded in two mss. by the identification of the petitioner as Assurbanipal in one (K 2836+ [Mayer, *Untersuchungen*: ms. B]), and Šamaš-šum-ukīn in the other (PBS 1/2, no. 119 [Mayer, *Untersuchungen*: ms. G]).

*šibsāt ili u ᵈištari iššaknūnim-ma*
*ṣītu u ḫuluqqû ibbašû ina bītiya*
*qabû u lā šemû iddalpūninni*

The lines that make up the lament (lines 12–14) show some grammatical similarity with each other, though not on the order of that found in the hymnic introduction or in the description of the petitioner's approach to the god. Each line is a clause. The first hemistich of each line represents the subject of the clause and contains two items joined together by the copula *u*. The second hemistich of each line represents the predicate;[16] two or perhaps three of these predicates are in the N-stem.[17] Line 12 is the cause of misfortune ("The anger of god and goddess has beset me so that"),[18] and lines 13–14 the actual misfortune itself; hence line 12 ends with *-ma*, "with the consequence that," in order to make the causal connection explicit.

But why are his god and goddess angry with him? That is, what is the ultimate cause of the misfortune? Has he ignored his god and goddess or committed a cultic sin against them, or has he perhaps shown disrespect to the public cult

16 Lines 12 and 14 have a verb + pronominal suffix. Line 13 has added the adverbial *ina bītiya*; this addition is meant to compensate for the absence of a pronominal suffix on the verb in this line and to maintain the balance of the line.

17 The verbs in lines 12 and 13 are unambiguously in the N-stem (correct, accordingly, the transcription of *ibbašû*, an N preterite, as a G durative *ibaššû* in *CAD* Ṣ, 220, s.v. *ṣītu* 4b–2′); the verb *id-dal-pu-nin-ni*/*id-dal-pu-in-ni* in line 14 presents some difficulties in classification. Formally, it can be a G perfect or an N preterite (note that *AHw* does not recognize a Gt-stem for this verb). While *CAD* does not recognize an N-stem for the verb *dalāpu*, *AHw* does. All the same, both *CAD* and *AHw* cite our line together with *BMS* 11: 3, classify them as G-stem verbs, and thus presumably understand them as G perfects. Our verb in *BMS* 11: 3 does indeed seem to be a G perfect (compare line 4 there), but here in our text where the verbs in the preceding two lines of the complaint are clearly preterites, it is difficult to understand why the verb in line 14 would be in the perfect. However, as a preterite our verb cannot be a G-stem, but should be an N preterite like the verbs in the preceding two lines. Of course, this conclusion is not certain, for it is possible that line 14 is a stock phrase and was carried over mechanically from another text such as *BMS* 11, in which case the verb here in line 14 might also be a G perfect. Accordingly, my note in Abusch, "A Shuilla: Nergal 2" (345) on the verb in line 14 should be read with some qualification.

18 Line 12 is omitted in PBS 1/2, no. 119 (Mayer, *Untersuchungen*: ms. G). The omission comes immediately after the introduction of Šamaš-šum-ukīn as the speaker of the text and the request that the evil portended by signs not affect the palace and land. The omission may be due to the fact that when the scribe introduced these matters in place of line 11, he dropped line 12 accidentally—if so, then lines 11 and 12 were probably written on one line in his *Vorlage*. (A less likely explanation is that the evil signs mentioned in this insertion were meant to replace "the anger of the god and goddess" as the cause of the difficulties described in lines 13 and 14.)

or damaged the fabric of society? The text is silent on this matter. What is clear is that the anger of the personal gods must in some way be related to Nergal, for the supplicant turns to Nergal to solve the problem. Does he turn to Nergal because that god is the actual source or cause of the anger and the personal gods simply reflect that anger, or because the beneficence of a powerful god will convince the personal gods to forgive their human protégé?

## 5 Petitioner's Supplication

For answers, we must, in any case, turn to the supplication or petition itself. The petitioner's request reads:

> Regard me favorably and hear my supplication.
> May your furious heart become calm toward me,
> pardon my sin, my error, and my misdeed,
> may the wrath (lit., knots of your innards) of your great divinity speedily be appeased (lit., disentangled)[19] for me (so that)
> the offended, angry, and irate god and goddess may be reconciled with me.

In line 19, he asks (imperatives [2×]) Nergal to pay heed to his request; in line 20, he expresses the wish (precative [1×]) that the god's raging heart be calmed toward him; in line 21, he asks (imperative [1×]) the god to release various sins; in line 22, he expresses the wish (precative [1×]) that the god's bound heart be released toward him; finally in line 23, he expresses the wish (precative [1×]) that the personal gods give up their anger and reconcile with him.

There is no obvious formal pattern in these lines. And one is left with such questions as: Why is the calming of Nergal's heart mentioned twice (lines 20 and 22), but not in contiguity? What is the relationship between Nergal and the personal gods? The nature of this relationship is still not clear, though the contiguity of the requests in lines 22 and 23 (and the occurrence of a variant verb *lippaṭ(a)ram-ma* at the end of line 22 with enclitic *-ma*) suggests that appeasing Nergal's anger can lead to reconciliation with the personal gods. It is possible, therefore, that we have here the same dynamic described, for example, in *Ludlul bēl nēmeqi* I 41–48:

19 Variant: "unknotted."

Fr[om] the day Bel punished me,
And the hero Marduk was angry [wi]th me,
My god rejected me, he disappeared,
My goddess left, she departed from *my* side.
[The protec]tive spirit of good fortune who *was* at my side [spl]it off,
My divine guardian became terrified and was seeking out another.
My dignity was taken, my masculine features obscured,
My characteristic manner was cut off, it jumped for cover.[20]

In that case, the anger of the personal gods mentioned in line 12 as the cause of the petitioner's misfortune would probably be no more than a reflection of Nergal's anger. If so, we might suggest that the two occurrences of the calming of Nergal's heart (lines 20 and 22) would each serve a different function. The first puts Nergal into a frame of mind where he is willing to release the sins of the petitioner (line 21), the second leads to the reconciliation of the personal gods with the supplicant (line 23). If so, then, the sins mentioned in line 21 would seem to be the ultimate cause of misfortune, for they led to Nergal's anger and consequently to the anger of the personal gods.

Given the state of the present text, this interpretation is not unreasonable and is perhaps correct. But it is not at all certain; it remains possible that the anger of the personal gods and the anger of Nergal are independent phenomena, that the personal gods and Nergal are separate powers, and that the personal gods allow themselves to be reconciled once they see that a great god such as Nergal has forgiven the supplicant, or when Nergal forgives the supplicant and intercedes for him. (It is also possible that the personal gods incite the high god's anger; the supplicant would then request forgiveness from the high god, a forgiveness which leads somehow to reconciliation with the personal gods.) Moreover, given the predominance of formal patterns in our text, we may wonder at their apparent absence in the actual supplication. That absence raises the possibility that the concluding section of our text might have once had a different form[21] or might originally have belonged to a different *šuilla* prayer or tradition of composition.

20 Translation: A. Annus and A. Lenzi, *"Ludlul bēl nēmeqi": The Standard Babylonian Poem of the Righteous Sufferer*, SAACT 7 (Helsinki: Neo-Assyrian Text Corpus Project, 2010), 32. For the dynamic that exists between Marduk and the personal gods in *Ludlul*, see W. L. Moran, "The Babylonian Job," in *The Most Magic Word: Essays on Babylonian and Biblical Literature*, ed. R. S. Hendel, CBQMS 35 (Washington, DC: Catholic Biblical Association of America, 2002), 195.

21 There are several other possible ways to analyze and reconstruct this portion of the text (none of which is entirely convincing); three examples may be given here: (1) the original

## 6 Conclusions

In view of the understanding of the development of *šuillas* that I have noted elsewhere[22] and given the difficulties in reconciling the roles of Nergal and

text was lines 19–20 and 23, to which lines 21–22 were added (thus eliminating the only occurrence of sin in this text [line 21], and note that *paṭāru* in line 21 and in a variant form in line 22 links these two lines together); (2) the original text was lines 19–20, to which lines 21–23 were added (thus the text revolves around the anger of Nergal and neither mentions sin nor resumes the topic of the personal god); (3) the original text was lines 19–20 and 22–23 to which line 21 was added (again removing sin and producing a pattern of imperatives followed by precatives).

22 Elsewhere, I have argued that the creation of a *šuilla* sometimes involved the addition of a hymnic introduction to a basic incantation or to a basic request to the personal god. See especially my comments in T. Abusch, "Prayers, Hymns, Incantations, and Curses: Mesopotamia," in *Religions of the Ancient World: A Guide*, ed. S. I. Johnston (Cambridge: Belknap Press of Harvard University Press, 2004), 354 [[115]]: "The *šuilla* type as well as many of its actual examples seem to have their origin in prayers that were recited on behalf of individuals and did not contain developed hymnic introductions. These supplications for the individual derived from various sources; but prayers to the personal god or, more properly, the god of the family were a particularly important source. Prayers to the personal god were recited originally in a family context; they reflect the problems of the individual householder or family head and represent an attempt to rectify personal or family problems caused by a rupture of relations between this person and the god." Sometimes the prayer was readdressed to "a cosmic or urban deity normally worshipped in a temple, and the address was modeled on temple liturgies by *āšipu*s with a temple orientation. An hymnic introduction of praise would then have been added to the supplication; for the new praise section, the composer drew upon temple imagery and experiences associated with gods of the temple." While sometimes the personal god disappeared, often the original address to the personal god and the personal god himself did not disappear completely but remained part of the prayer.

C. Frechette argues that "a defining purpose of Akkadian Šuillas was to gain a favorable reception by the high-ranking deity addressed with a view toward gaining that deity's aid," for example, "in reconciling the speaker with his or her angry personal gods." See C. Frechette and I. Hrůša, "The Ritual-Prayer Nisaba 1 and Its Function," *JANER* 11 (2011): 73. Similarly, Frechette states that "[i]t is widely recognized that shuillas in monolingual Akkadian ... in many cases explicitly request one of the 'high gods' to intercede with the speaker's angry personal gods"; so C. Frechette, "Shuillas," in *Reading Akkadian Prayers and Hymns: An Introduction*, ed. A. Lenzi, ANEM 3 (Atlanta: Society of Biblical Literature, 2011), 27; cf. 33. Recently, C. Ambos in his study of the *bīt salāʾ mê* ritual has argued that the purpose of the *šuilla*s in that ritual is not only to seek the favor of the higher gods addressed but mainly to convince them to intercede with the king's alienated personal gods and reconcile them with the king; see C. Ambos, *Der König im Gefängnis und das Neujahrsfest im Herbst: Mechanismen der Legitimation des babylonischen Herrschers im 1. Jahrtausend v. Chr. und ihre Geschichte* (Dresden: Islet, 2013), especially sections II.3.3.8–II.3.3.9; cf. C. Frechette, *Mesopotamian Ritual-prayers of "Hand-lifting" (Akkadian Šuillas): An Investigation of Function in Light of the Idiomatic Meaning of the*

the personal gods in our Nergal *šuilla,* I would ascribe significance to the existence of marked sections defined by formal patterns alongside relatively unstructured sections in this text. Since the passages that have formal patterns, that is, the hymnic introduction (lines 1–10) and the statement of seeking the presence of the god (lines 15–18), focus on Nergal, I would suggest that these lines were composed separately from the less structured prayer to the personal gods (lines 12–14 and 23) that was the original kernel of this text. The composer tried to integrate these disparate parts by adding the supplication to Nergal in lines 19–22 (and the obligatory line 24).[23]

Be that as it may, the consistent use of morphological and syntactic patterns in earlier sections of the text does indeed characterize this Nergal prayer. These phenomena are surely the result not of coincidence, but of a deliberate mode of composition. Its style gives our text a formal design and enabled the composer to develop complex thoughts succinctly.

*Rubric,* AOAT 379 (Münster: Ugarit-Verlag, 2012), 166–176. If his interpretation is correct, Ambos has provided the contextual explanation of the relationship between the higher gods and the personal gods in the *šuillas* for which I was searching.

23 But note that in a later study I reached a different conclusion. See T. Abusch, "The Reconciliation of Angry Personal Gods: A Revision of the Šuillas," in "Approaching a Critique of Mesopotamian Reason," ed. G. Gabriel, special issue, *JANEH* 5 (2018): 79 n. 56 [[200–201 n. 64]].

CHAPTER 13

# The Reconciliation of Angry Personal Gods: A Revision of the *šuilla*s

In my youth I tended to try to understand the world by thinking in broad strokes—deductively and ideologically.* When I became a scholar of texts, I learned to think inductively, to have ideas emerge from the close reading of the texts themselves. Close reading came naturally to me as a result of my Jewish education, for that education emphasized close reading of texts as well as the notion that all texts have meaning and express ideas. So generally, I have worked from details, though I hope that I have not turned into a positivist. I have studied individual texts or groups of texts and have tried to work on those details that did not make sense to me initially. Admittedly, I have combined my inferences with intuition.

As a scholar, I have devoted most of my energies to text genres that treat existential and intellectual issues. The texts I study partake of the fantastic. Their study requires that one open oneself up to the belief system of the texts, and perhaps their study forms a sort of escape from the real world. From my work, one would hardly know that I am sympathetic to a Marxist approach. Even prayers, incantations, and rituals may be studied from such an approach, though I cannot claim to have done so. And even if on occasion I regret this failure, I still believe that it is of profound importance that in our study we emphasize the spiritual and intellectual world of antiquity.

Since our broader interest in this volume is intellectual history, it is not inappropriate that I deal with a crucial preliminary question: How can we understand the main source of ancient intellectual history, namely, texts? The main problem is the issue of finding coherence in these texts. I will not deal with the nature of ancient mythological thinking. Rather, I limit myself to a narrower focus: how can we approach the issue of coherence in a specific genre of prayers, the *šuilla* prayers? Prayers are speeches. A prayer or incantation contains an underlying or organizing situation or narrative. It has a narrative

* I read the texts that form the basis of this paper with my Advanced Akkadian class in Fall 2016; I thank Dan Berman, Noam Cohen, Justin Huegenin, Anthony Lipscomb, and Jared Pfost. I am especially grateful to Jared Pfost, my research assistant in 2016–2017, for his assistance and suggestions while I composed this paper. I thank Stephen A. Geller for commenting on an early draft and David P. Wright for discussing the Hittite prayers with me.

 | DOI:10.1163/9789004435186_014

flow, but while an incantation may reflect a dynamic story, a prayer usually represents a static one. The prayer has scenic unity and does not progress from one situation to another. That is, the situation at the conclusion of the speech is not different from what it was at the beginning. As a speech, the prayer may contain various rhetorical devices, but it should convey a clear message—one without blatant gaps, inconsistencies, contradictions, etc. No less than a legal speech, a prayer is an address that tries to convince and to make a persuasive case. Coherence is required to achieve the immediate aim of the prayer, that of attaining a specific request or goal. If some element of the text seems to interfere with or contradict this pressing and immediate aim, one must raise an objection and rethink the issue in terms of coherence.

I expect a text—perhaps any text—to be coherent. It is true that different scholars have different expectations and that our expectations may be different with different types or genres of texts. A word or two, then, about my expectations. A text should possess the quality of being logical and consistent and of forming a unified whole. Of course, one can overlook internal discrepancies in pursuit of understanding, but I believe that one should not do so or should do so only to a measured degree, for by overlooking too many difficulties, the pursuit of understanding will result in various forms of harmonization that distort meaning. In truth, we uncover the conventions and structure of a text type and then judge its exemplars by whether they live up to our expectations. But actually, there is nothing wrong with a certain amount of circular reasoning as long as it does not form a vicious circle.

I use the criterion of coherence in this study and elsewhere.[1] There are basically three approaches to the issue of coherence. One approach is to declare that ancient thinking is so different from ours that to use logical criteria is mistaken. A second approach is to look for some principle of internal coherence in the text; sometimes this is not immediately apprehensible because of our own ignorance of the context but can be discovered or hypothesized on the basis of a closer examination of the culture. Occasionally, this second approach does not succeed; when this happens we may—and perhaps should—take a third approach: to view the text as being composed of discordant elements as a result of a process of revision and to seek a source-critical answer to the problems of the text. (Even here one should still look for the notion of coherence in the mind[s] of the editor[s].) I exclude the first approach, but we will examine the second and third approaches in this study of the *šuilla*s.

1 I have been concerned with the issue of coherence from the very beginning of my work on Mesopotamian literature; see, for example, T. Abusch, *Babylonian Witchcraft Literature: Case Studies*, BJS 132 (Atlanta: Scholars Press, 1987), 5.

Let me therefore begin with a few words about coherence and cohesion. I draw here on some recent text linguistic studies.[2] A quote from Jeffery Stackert's recent study of coherence as it applies to the Pentateuch should serve to introduce us to the topic: "*Cohesion* refers to … the internal semantic linkages between sentence elements.… As a characteristic of the text itself, cohesion may be distinguished from *coherence*, which is properly an achievement of the reader, even as it is highly dependent upon a text's cohesive ties."[3] A text is a structure, and coherence, then, is a meaningful relationship that we see between and amongst the elements of the text—whether contiguous or not. Coherence involves concepts and links between concepts. Some of the most important links are causality relations and time relations.[4] Rather than emphasizing the role of the reader in creating coherence, I prefer to follow a recent statement of I. Abushihab:

> [C]ohesion refers to connectivity in terms of surface structure while coherence refers to connectivity in terms of content and organization.… Coherence refers to the understandability of text and the functioning of that text as a unified whole. Coherence also refers to the relationships of ideas and the ability of those ideas to function together for the purpose of conveying meaning. When coherence is lacking, the ideas in the text are difficult or impossible for the reader to comprehend.[5]

More than most other genres, a prayer should be coherent. As stated earlier, I decided, therefore, to take up a problem that recurs in some of the *šuilla*s and have tried to look at some broad issues from the perspective of details. I should

2 I refer the reader to M. Z. Brettler, "The 'Coherence' of Ancient Texts," in *Gazing on the Deep: Ancient Near Eastern and Other Studies in Honor of Tzvi Abusch*, ed. J. Stackert et al. (Bethesda, MD: CDL, 2010), 411–419, and J. Stackert, "Pentateuchal Coherence and the Science of Reading," in *The Formation of the Pentateuch: Bridging the Academic Cultures of Europe, Israel, and North America*, ed. J. C. Gertz et al. (Tübingen: Mohr Siebeck, 2016), 253–268. See also K. Malmkjaer, "Text Linguistics," in *The Linguistics Encyclopedia*, ed. K. Malmkjaer (London: Routledge, 1991), 461–471, and I. Abushihab, "The Role of Lexical Cohesion and Coherence in Promoting Reading Comprehension," *Ekev Akademi Dergisi* 12/35 (2008): 333–342 (I owe my knowledge of Abushihab's article to Jeffrey Stackert, who kindly sent me a copy thereof).

3 Stackert, "Pentateuchal Coherence," 254.

4 See Malmkjaer, "Text Linguistics," 465.

5 Abushihab, "Lexical Cohesion and Coherence," 335.

begin by introducing the genre that we will be examining.[6] The basic format of the Akkadian *šuilla* is:

1) A hymnic introduction in which the god is invoked, described, and praised.
2) A supplication centering upon a petition to the god asking him/her to come to the aid of the petitioner. Usually this central part of the prayer also includes a lament in which the supplicant describes his suffering and perhaps its cause.
3) Finally, a promise of praise should the deity grant the petition and allow the petitioner to regain a normal life.

I begin my exposition here with an attempt to articulate the underlying worldview of a number of the compositions that we will be looking at, one worldview among several that existed in ancient Mesopotamia.[7] The world is divided between the speaker and the Other. The Other comprises other humans and non-humans; the non-humans are made up of the gods and nature.[8] Occasionally, the latter two are identical, but in the main the gods are separate from and in control of nature.[9] These texts see the world as would a member of the elite. Accordingly, the world forms a structure, and that structure is hierarchical. The world was certainly not an organic whole; the worldview was surely not holistic.

Moreover, the gods are seen in human form. To be sure, the vantage point of the speech is that of a human who is addressing the gods but who stands at a much lower rung of existence than the high gods. To give a few examples,

6 The designation of the *šuillas* by number follows that of W. Mayer, *Untersuchungen zur Formensprache der babylonischen "Gebetsbeschwörungen,"* StPohl, series maior 5 (Rome: Pontifical Biblical Institute, 1976).

7 For an understanding of worldview, or *Weltanschauung*, see R. Redfield, *The Primitive World and Its Transformations* (Ithaca, NY: Cornell University Press, 1953), esp. ch. 3, and M. Kearney, *World View* (Novato, CA: Chandler and Sharp, 1984). For the differentiation between worldview and philosophy, see G. Gabriel, "Introduction," in "Approaching a Critique of Mesopotamian Reason," ed. G. Gabriel, special issue, *JANEH* 5 (2018): 1–14.

8 See H. Frankfort et al., *The Intellectual Adventure of Ancient Man: An Essay on Speculative Thought in the Ancient Near East*, rev. ed. (Chicago: University of Chicago Press, 1977), esp. ch. 1. See also M. Van De Mieroop, "Theses on Babylonian Philosophy," in "Approaching a Critique of Mesopotamian Reason," ed. G. Gabriel, special issue, *JANEH* 5 (2018): 15–39, esp. Thesis 1.

9 That there could be limits to this dominance is discussed in G. Gabriel, "An Exemplificational Critique of Violence: Re-Reading the Old Babylonian Epic *Inūma ilū awīlum* (a.k.a. *Epic of Atramḫasīs*)," in "Approaching a Critique of Mesopotamian Reason," ed. G. Gabriel, special issue, *JANEH* 5 (2018): 179–213.

allow me to quote from the hymnic introduction of two *šuilla*s, one to Nergal, the other to Marduk.

Nergal 2: 1–10

1. ÉN *bēlu gašru tizqāru bukur* $^{d}$*Nunamnir*
2. *ašarēd* $^{d}$*Anunnakkī bēl tamḫāri*
3. *ilitti* $^{d}$*Kutušar šarrati rabīti*
4. $^{d}$*Nergal kaškaš ilī narām* $^{d}$*Ninmenna*
5. *šūpâta ina šamê ellūti šaqu manzāzka*
6. *rabâta ina arallî māḫira lā tīšu*
7. *itti* $^{d}$*Ea* (var.: *Ani*) *ina puḫur ilī milikka šūtur*
8. *itti* $^{d}$*Sîn ina šamê* (var.: + *u erṣeti*) *taše''i gimri*
9. *iddinkama* $^{d}$*Enlil abuka ṣalmāt qaqqadi puḫur napišti*
10. *būl* $^{d}$*Šakkan nammaššê qātukka ipqid*

1. Mighty lord, exalted son of Nunamnir,
2. Foremost among the Anunnaki, lord of battle,
3. Offspring of Kutušar, the great queen,
4. Nergal, all powerful among the gods, beloved of Ninmenna.
5. You are manifest in the bright heavens, your station is exalted,
6. You are great in the netherworld, you have no rival.
7. Together with Ea (var.: Anu), your counsel is preeminent in the assembly of the gods.
8. Together with Sîn, you observe everything in the heavens (var.: + and the netherworld).
9. Enlil, your father, gave to you the black-headed ones, all the living, and
10. He entrusted into your hands the herds, the animals.[10]

10 For an analysis of this prayer as a whole and of the hymnic introduction, see T. Abusch, "A Paean and Petition to a God of Death: Some Comments on a *Šuilla* to Nergal," in *From the Four Corners of the Earth: Studies in Iconography and Cultures of the Ancient Near East in Honour of F. A. M. Wiggermann*, ed. D. Kertai and O. Nieuwenhuyse, AOAT 441 (Münster: Ugarit-Verlag, 2017), 15–28 [[163–175]].

Marduk 2: 1–9

1. ÉN *gašru šūpû etel Eridug*
2. *rubû tizqāru bukur* $^{d}$*Nudimmud*
3. $^{d}$*Marduk šalbābu murīš E'engura*
4. *bēl Esaĝila tukulti Bābili*
5. *rā'im Ezida mušallim napišti*
6. *ašarēd Emaḫtila mudeššû balāṭi*
7. *ṣulūl māti gāmil nišī rapšāti*
8. *ušumgal kalîš parakkī*
9. *šumka kalîš ina pī nišī ṭāb*

1. Famed mighty one, chieftain of Eridu,
2. Exalted prince, first-born of Nudimmud,
3. Raging Marduk, restorer of rejoicing to E'engura.
4. Lord of Esagila, hope of Babylon,
5. Lover of Ezida, preserver of life,
6. Lone one of Emahtila, multiplier of living.
7. Protection of the land, savior of the multitudes of people,
8. The single great one of chapels everywhere,
9. Your name is sweetly hymned by the people everywhere.[11]

As mentioned, the worldview is hierarchical, and there is a distance between the "I" of the speaker and the high gods. The self is in a distant relationship to the high gods in terms both of space and of separation (i.e., detachment). But some of the texts speak not only of the relationship of the self with the high god, but also of the relationship of the self with personal gods. For there are some texts where also an angry personal god is mentioned specifically in the context of a request to the high god to reconcile the personal god(s) with the petitioner. The introduction of the personal god reflects a change of orientation in, at least, that section of the prayer: from focusing on the gods, albeit from a distance, the text turns back to the petitioner and places him at the center, for the personal god is the personification of the self and of the family.

To exemplify this, allow me therefore to quote a few examples from texts in which the high god is asked to intercede with the petitioner's angry personal gods.

11 For an analysis of this prayer as a whole and of the hymnic introduction, see T. Abusch, "The Form and Meaning of a Babylonian Prayer to Marduk," *JAOS* 103 (1983): 3–15 [[126–148]].

Anu 1: 9–13

9. *... ina tēka [ša balāṭi] luptaṭṭirū*
10. *mimmû mala ana iliya [u ištariya] aḫṭû lipp[ašra]*
11. *libbi iliya u [ištariya] zenûte ana ašrišu l[itūr]*
12. *aggu libbaka li[nūḫa]*
13. *lippašra kabtat[ka] rišâ rēm[u]*

9. ... be absolved with your [life-giving] incantation,
10. And all that I have committed or neglected against my (personal) god [and my (personal) goddess be absolved.
11. May the heart(s) of my angry (personal) god and [(personal) goddess] be re[conciled to me],
12. May your furious heart b[e calmed],
13. And [your] feelings be eased, have mercy![12]

Nergal 2: 19–24

19. *kīniš naplisannima šime teslītī*
20. *aggu libbaka linūḫa*
21. *puṭur annī ḫiṭītī u gillatī*
22. *kiṣir libbi ilūtika rabīti zamar lippašra*
23. *ilu u ištaru zenûtu šabsūtu kitmulūtu lislimū ittiya*
24. *narbîka lušāpi dalīlīka ludlul*

19. Regard me favorably and hear my supplication.
20. May your furious heart become calm toward me,
21. Pardon my sin, my error, and my misdeed,
22. May the wrath (lit., knots of your innards) of your great divinity speedily be appeased (lit., disentangled) for me,
23. May the angry, irate, and furious god and goddess be reconciled with me.
24. Then will I declare your great deeds and sing your praise!

12 For editions of these lines, see *AGH*, 36, lines 12–20, and C. Ambos, *Der König im Gefängnis und das Neujahrsfest im Herbst: Mechanismen der Legitimation des babylonischen Herrschers im 1. Jahrtausend v. Chr. und ihre Geschichte* (Dresden: Islet, 2013), 204, lines 9–13 (I follow Ambos's line count and line divisions); the translation is that of B. R. Foster, *Before the Muses: An Anthology of Akkadian Literature*, 3rd ed. (Bethesda, MD: CDL, 2005), 640. But note that his "angry hearts" in line 11 should be corrected to "the heart(s) of my angry...."

Sîn 1: 21–24b

21. *kamsāku azzaz ašēʾʾe kâša*
22. *egerrê dumqi u mīšari šukun eliya*
23. *ilī u ištarī ša ištu ūmī maʾdūtu isbusū eliya*
24a. *ina kītti u mīšari lislimū ittiya*
24b. *urḫī lidmiq padānī līšir*

21. Kneeling (and) standing, I (hereby) seek you.
22. Establish for me a propitious and just oracular utterance.
23. My god and my goddess, who have been angry with me for many days,
24a. Through truth and justice, may they be at peace with me,
24b. May my path be favorable, may my way be straight.[13]

The introduction of the personal god is strange, for it transforms a hierarchical structure with the human at its bottom to one in which the human is central at least for the nonce. To understand why this is a serious reorientation of a text that views the world hierarchically, we must remember what the personal god represents. As I wrote years ago:

> Stated succinctly, the personal god is the personification of the individual's powers of strength and effectiveness; he is also the personification of right and wrong action. He represents and rewards either effective/realistic actions or proper actions, or both. First of all, the personal god is a projection of the individual's powers of effectiveness and procreation. In this role, he is an aspect of ego. But in a clan context, he also represents group or clan norms as well as the responsibility to maintain them. Thus the personal god is also an aspect of superego or conscience.... He is thus an externalization of the ego and superego, a representation of the self in the form of externalized, divinized figures.[14]

The request of the high god to reconcile the personal god is problematic for a number of reasons: We have already mentioned the change of orientation and

13 Edition: Mayer, *Untersuchungen*, 493–494, lines 21–24b; the translation is that of A. Lenzi, "A Shuilla: Sin 1," in *Reading Akkadian Prayers and Hymns: An Introduction*, ed. A. Lenzi, ANEM 3 (Atlanta: Society of Biblical Literature, 2011), 400, lines 27–31.

14 T. Abusch, "Witchcraft and the Anger of the Personal God," in *Mesopotamian Magic: Textual, Historical, and Interpretive Perspectives*, ed. T. Abusch and K. van der Toorn, AMD 1 (Groningen: Styx, 1999), 105–107 [[AMD 5, 48–49]].

the new centrality of the petitioner. Moreover, it is normal in earlier periods to observe the opposite, that is, the personal god serving as an intermediary to the high god.[15] Thus, the request of the high god to act as an intermediary so as to reconcile the personal god is a reversal of what we would have expected of the traditional form. Older seals, for example, usually show the personal god bringing his client before and introducing him to the high god. Hermann Vorländer comments on the request addressed to the high god to reconcile the angry personal god, though as far as I can see he does not see any problem: "Während also sonst der persönliche Gott als Fürsprecher gegenüber dem anderen Göttern fungiert, liegt hier der umgekehrte Fall vor."[16] I should mention that I have not found early examples (e.g., Old Babylonian) of requests to the high god asking him/her to bring about reconciliation between the petitioner and his personal god.[17] Rather, as mentioned above, in earlier texts the

15 See, e.g., H. Vorländer, *Mein Gott: Die Vorstellungen vom persönlichen Gott im Alten Orient und im Alten Testament*, AOAT 23 (Kevelaer: Butzon & Bercker; Neukirchen-Vluyn: Neukirchener Verlag, 1975), 87–90, and K. van der Toorn, *Family Religion in Babylonia, Syria, and Israel: Continuity and Change in the Forms of Religious Life*, SHCANE 7 (Leiden: Brill, 1996), 136–138.

16 Vorländer, *Mein Gott*, 112.

17 Could the shift away from the image of the personal god as an intercessor before higher gods to the present image of the high god as the one who reconciles the personal god be the consequence of the experience of Šamaš as the god who travels the world and can reach all powers?

In any case, following my paper on versions of a *šuilla* to Gula at the 2017 Rencontre Assyriologique Internationale, Gernot Wilhelm noted that the phenomenon of asking a high god to cause a personal god to relent and to give up his anger already existed in Hittite prayers. He was referring to prayers to the Sun-god for appeasing an angry god (*CTH* 372–374), translated as no. 4 in I. Singer, *Hittite Prayers*, WAW 11 (Atlanta: Society of Biblical Literature, 2002), and recently reedited by D. Schwemer, "Hittite Prayers to the Sun-God for Appeasing an Angry Personal God: A Critical Edition of *CTH* 372–74," in M. Jaques, *Mon dieu qu'ai-je fait? Les diĝir-šà-dab$_{(5)}$-ba et la piété privée en Mésopotamie*, OBO 273 (Fribourg: Academic Press; Göttingen: Vandenhoeck & Ruprecht, 2015), 349–393 (cf. C. Steitler's glossary of *CTH* 372–374 in the same volume, pp. 421–457). In these prayers, the Sun-god "is asked to intercede with the supplicant's angry personal god. This is followed by a plea that in the main addresses the angry god directly—thus spelling out the message the Sun-god is asked to transmit" (Schwemer, "Hittite Prayers," 349).

Accordingly, it is not impossible that the request that the personal god be reconciled with his protégé in the Akkadian *šuilla*s be due to the influence of the Hittite tradition (or reflect an earlier Babylonian tradition that also influenced the Hittite prayers). Against this conclusion, however, stand several differences between the two traditions.

(1) The Hittite texts take the form of addresses to the Sun-god, who is asked to function as a messenger and is given the message that he is to convey verbatim to the personal god. The Akkadian texts are different; they are prayers, though on a few occasions the god is asked to be a messenger (see Gula 1a, Gula 1b, and Nisaba 1), yet even in those instances the prayer does not contain the wording to be passed on to the personal god.

petitioner requested the personal god to intercede with the high god.[18] Note, for example, the following well-known Old Babylonian letter to a personal god:

---

(2) In line with the form, both the high god and the personal god are addressed in the second person in the Hittite prayers; in contrast, in the *šuillas* the high god is addressed in the second person and the personal gods are referred to in the third person.

(3) In contrast to the *šuillas*, the Hittite texts seem to comprise four sections: (1) first address to the Sun-god (= high god); (2) first address to the personal god; (3) second address to the Sun-god; and (4) second address to the personal god. Note that G. Wilhelm argues that *CTH* 373 (Kantuzzili), probably the earliest of the three prayers, may be a conflation of two separate prayers, each with two parts; see G. Wilhelm, "Zur Struktur des hethitischen 'Kantuzzili-Gebets,'" in *Kulte, Priester, Rituale: Beiträge zu Kult und Kultkritik im Alten Testament und Alten Orient (Festschrift für Theodor Seidl zum 65. Geburtstag)*, ed. S. Ernst and M. Häusl, Arbeiten zu Text und Sprache im Alten Testament 89 (Erzabtei St. Ottilien: EOS, 2010), 36–38.

The identification of the textual segments in which the Sun-god and the personal god are addressed is far from simple, in part because of the fragmentary state of the texts. Using Schwemer's editions, the layout of the three Hittite texts seems to be as follows:

| | | |
|---|---|---|
| *CTH* 373: | First address to the Sun-god | ] 1′–5′ |
| | First address to the personal god | 6′–29′ |
| | Second address to the Sun-god | 30′–39′ |
| | Second address to the personal god | 40′–56′ [ |
| *CTH* 374: | Address to the Sun-god | 0′–56″ |
| | Address to the personal god | 56″– (The latter part of the text is too fragmentary to know where this address ends and whether a following address is preserved.) |
| *CTH* 372: | First address to the Sun-god | 1–83 |
| | First address to the personal god | 84–129 |
| | Second address to the Sun-god | 129–149 |
| | Second address to the personal god | 150–226 |

(4) While the Sun-god and the personal god are often addressed in the second person in the Hittite texts, there are sections in *CTH* 373 and *CTH* 372 where the personal god is referred to in the third person (in *CTH* 374 there are no exceptions to the rule of addressing the relevant god in the second person); see, for example, *CTH* 373, lines 24–28, 31–36, and *CTH* 372, lines 119–127, 131–135. While it is possible that in some cases the third-person references to the personal god are simply part of the address to the Sun-god (e.g., *CTH* 373, lines 31–36), in a number of cases they seem rather to be part of an address to the personal god (e.g., *CTH* 373, lines 24–28). Occasionally, the shift to third person may represent redactional changes in the text. (Is it possible, for example, that lines 19 and 29 of *CTH* 373 were originally contiguous and that lines 20–28 were later insertions?) This feature suggests that the Hittite texts may be in the process of development.

For some of the reasons given in my main text, especially the dissonance of the *šuillas* noted in my discussion, I still feel that the theme of the anger of the personal gods was added secondarily to the *šuillas*. But I would note that since I have not found actual manuscript evidence (see below) for the absence of this theme in variant manuscripts, I cannot exclude the possibility that a literary form containing the theme already existed at an early period and might conceivably derive from the Hittite materials.

18 See, e.g., van der Toorn, *Family Religion*, 136–138 ("Family God as Intercessor").

> Speak to the god, my father: Thus says Apil-Adad, your servant. Why have you become (so) indifferent to me? Who could give you one like me? Write to Marduk, who loves you, so that he may break my bondage. May I see your face, may I kiss your feet. Also, look after my family, old and young; have mercy upon me because of them. May your help reach me.[19]

In addition, it seems a bit strange to go to a higher divine authority in order to attain reconciliation with a lower one. Rather, one would seek reconciliation directly with the personal god; and if that failed, one might ask a power on the same level as or lower than the personal god to speak on one's behalf.

Finally, the presence of the personal god(s) in the *šuilla*s occasionally introduces a note of dissonance into the texts. A few examples:[20]

(a) Sîn 1: 20b–24b[21]

20b. *alsīka bēlī ina qereb šamê ellūti*
21. *kamsāku azzaz ašē'e kâša*
22. *egerrê dumqi u mīšari šukun eliya*
23. *ilī u ištarī ša ištu ūmī ma'dūtu isbusū eliya*
24a. *ina kītti u mīšari lislimū ittiya*
24b. *urḫī lidmiq padānī līšir*

20b. I (hereby) call out to you, my lord, in the midst of the pure heavens.
21. Kneeling (and) standing, I (hereby) seek you.
22. Establish for me a propitious and just oracular utterance.
23. My god and my goddess, who have been angry with me for many days,
24a. Through truth and justice, may they be at peace with me,
24b. May my path be favorable, may my way be straight.[22]

Lines 23–24a ask that the personal gods who have been angry for many days be reconciled. Lines 23–24a disrupt the thought of lines 22 and 24b and seem to be an addition. In support, note the occurrence in both lines 22 (*egerrû dumqi*)

19 M. Stol, *Letters from Yale*, AbB 9 (Leiden: Brill, 1981), 88–91, no. 141.

20 See Appendix A for more examples.

21 For an edition of this composition, see Mayer, *Untersuchungen*, 490–495; a further manuscript is published by S. M. Maul and R. Strauss, *Ritualbeschreibungen und Gebete I*, KALI 4, WVDOG 133 (Wiesbaden: Harrassowitz, 2011), no. 66.

22 Mayer, *Untersuchungen*, 493–494, lines 20b–24b; translation: Lenzi, "Sin 1," 400, lines 26–31.

and 24b (*urḫī lidmiq*) of forms of *damāqu* and that line 24b appears to be a continuation of line 22.[23]

(b) Sîn 3: 55–60, 66–68[24]

55. *ša ilšu zenû* (var. *iznû*) *ittišu tusallam arḫiš*
56. *enūma ilī zenû ittiya*
57. *ištarī nesât eliya*
58. *ištu ullâ ašaddad ilū tamṭâti emūqī iškunū eliya*
59. *ṣīti ḫuluqqû butuqqû nušurrû magal šaknūnimma*
60. *ītašuš libbī iktūru napištī*

66. *ša lā mašê* $^{d}$*Sîn lā tamaššânni sullim*$^{!}$ (text: *si-lim*)[25] *ittiya*
67. *ilī u ištarī zenûti šabsūti u kummulūti*
68. *ilūtka rabīta ittiya sullimamma*

55. The one whose god is angry with him you reconcile (the god with him) speedily,
56. Since my god became angry with me,
57. My goddess abandoned me,
58. Since then I bear (the following): the gods have imposed decrease of strength on me,
59. Exceedingly, expenses, losses, shortages, diminution have befallen me,
60. I myself have suffered great distress, and my life has been shortened.

66. The one who does not forget, O Sîn, do not forget me. Reconcile with me
67. My angry, irate, and furious god and goddess,
68. Reconcile your great divinity with me.

The anger of the personal gods finds mention in lines 55, 56–60, and 67 (perhaps also line 66[c]). Line 55 is the last line of the hymnic introduction (for a similar line at the end of a hymnic introduction, see Ninurta 1: 24). This line is immediately followed by lines 56–60 in which the speaker presents his

23 As regards lines 23–24b, cf. Ištar 11: 23–25 (Ištar 11 seems to be dependent on Sîn 1). See Appendix A: Ištar 11.

24 For an edition of this composition, see Mayer, *Untersuchungen*, 495–502.

25 I take *si-lim* as an error for *sullim*: SILIM-*lim*; see below.

complaint regarding the anger of the personal god.[26] Thus, line 55, the last entry in the hymnic introduction, leads right into the description of the problem caused by the anger of the personal gods (56–60). A similar phenomenon occurs in Ištar 11 (though there the introduction leads right into the petition rather than into a description of the problem). The juxtaposition of the last line of the hymnic introduction with a new section dealing with the personal gods might allow also here for the same possible explanations as those suggested in our analysis of Ištar 11 (see Appendix A). However, in Sîn 3 the section immediately following the hymnic introduction seems to be secondary on thematic as well as on syntactic (*enūma* …) grounds. It is therefore more likely that line 55 was part of the original text, and its occurrence at the end of the hymnic introduction allowed the secondary inclusion of lines 56–60 in their present position in Sîn 3.

We now turn to the last part of the request itself, lines 66–68. Also lines 66$^{c}$–67 can be treated as secondary: perhaps *sullim*$^{!}$ *ittiya* at the end of line 66 should be attached to line 67 (and not to line 66), with line 67 forming its direct object. In support of attaching line 66$^{c}$ to line 67 (and of the emendation), note that line 66$^{a-b}$ (*ša lā mašê* $^{d}$*Sîn lā tamaššânni*) matches the pattern of lines 64 and 65 (*eṭērēta* $^{d}$*Sîn eṭer napištī* / *gammalāta* $^{d}$*Sîn ina ilī gimilla šukna*) insofar as each line begins with an attribution of a quality to the deity and ends with the request that the deity act toward the petitioner in accordance with that quality. Thus, line 66$^{c}$ does not belong to 66$^{a-b}$ and may be connected with the following line. The verb at the end of line 68 would then apply only to that line; note also that line 68 (anger of the high god) can form a continuation of line 66$^{b}$. Alternatively, lines 67–68 may have to be taken together, and the request for reconciliation at the end of line 68 would then apply to both the high god of line 68 and the personal gods of line 67; in this context, also note Enlil 1b where *ittiya sullimamma* in rev. 14 applies to both the anger of the personal gods and the anger of the high god.[27]

26 We include line 60 in the secondary personal god section because it is connected by *-ma* to line 59. Perhaps lines 58–60 are borrowed from another text.

27 Sîn 3: 66$^{c}$ [or 67]–68 are equivalent to *KAR* 68 (Enlil 1b) rev. 10–14. Does this suggest that the whole segment (Sîn 3: 66$^{c}$ [or 67]–68 and Enlil 1b: [*KAR* 68] rev. 10–14) is an addition in both texts, or perhaps that the whole segment is original in both? For a discussion of Enlil 1b, see below.

(c) Madānu 1 (= Nusku 1): 13–19 // KALI 4, no. 59, obv. 14′–rev. 1[28]

13. *ṣābit qātī naski ina dannati muballiṭ mīti*
14. [*ta*]*yyārāta ina ilī šime teslītī*
15. [*ana* ᵈ*Marduk bēli rēšt*]*î ili rēmēnî ṣabat abbūtī qibi dumqīya*
16. [*sullim*]*amma ilī zenâ ištarī zenītu*
17. *ilu u ištaru lištēšerūninni alaktī lidmiq*
18. *asḫurka ina ilī rišâ rēmu*
19. *aṣbat sissiktaka balāṭa qīša*

13. The one who takes the hand of the cast down when (he is) in difficulty, the reviver of the dying.
14. You are the (most) compassionate one among the gods, hear my prayer,
15. Intercede for me [before Marduk, the foremost lor]d, the merciful god, speak a good word for me.
16. [Reconcile] with me my angry god and goddess,
17. May god and goddess cause me to be successful, (and) may my (oracular) decision be favorable.
18. I turn to you among the gods, have mercy on me,
19. I seize your hem, grant me life.

The personal god section (16–17) seems out of place because it comes right after the hymnic introduction and the beginning of the request to Madānu to intercede with Marduk but before the section where the speaker (18–19) states the reason for turning to Madānu with a request. Actually, lines 18–19 may be an appropriate continuation of line 14 (or 14–15).

(d) In several prayers[29] (Ištar 4: 15′: *lissaḫra ilī ša iznû ittiya* "May my god who is angry with me turn back to me"; Tašmētu 1 [CTN 4, no. 168, rev. i 32]: *ilu u ištaru lislimū ittiya* "May god and goddess be reconciled with me"; Ninurta 4 [[*CMAwR* 2, no. 10.8]]: 19: *sullim(am)ma ittiya ila u ištara zenûti* "Reconcile with me the angry god and goddess"), the anger of the personal god stands at the head of a series of afflictions and seems to be discordant. Here, the anger of the personal god may have been introduced in order to provide an explanation for the petitioner's sufferings, which are enumerated by means of the aforementioned list of afflictions. See also Marduk 24 [[*CMAwR* 2, no. 8.27]]: 35–36,

28 In addition to the edition prepared by Mayer, *Untersuchungen*, 459–465, see Maul and Strauss, *Ritualbeschreibungen*, no. 59. I follow Mayer's line count.

29 See Appendix A for references to the editions of these prayers.

which lines I deemed secondary many years ago, when examining this composition with a different problem in mind, and I determined that the insertion of these lines is an "expression of an attempt to make the anger of the god primarily responsible for the various evils encountered in the text."[30]

(e) Ištar 2: 67–68, 75–78, 85–90[31]

67. *mīnâ ēpuš ilī u ištarī anāku*
68. *kī lā pāliḫ iliya u ištariya anāku epšēk*

75. *šuḫarrur sagêya šuḫarrurat aširtī*
76. *eli bītī bābī qarbātīya šaqummati tabkat*
77. *ilī ana ašaršanimma suḫḫurū pānūšu*
78. *sapḫat illatī tabīnī purrur*

85. *qibîma ina qibītīki ilu zenû lislim*
86. *ištaru ša isbusa litūra*
87. *eṭû qatru limmir kinūnī*
88. *belīti linnapiḫ dipārī*
89. *sapiḫtu illatī lipḫur*
90. *tarbaṣu lirpiš lištamdilu supūrī*

67. I, O my god, O my goddess, what have I done?
68. I am dealt with as if I did not revere my god and my goddess.

75. My chapel is deathly still, my sanctuary is deathly still,
76. A ghastly stillness has fallen upon my household, my courtyard, and my fields,
77. My god's face is turned to some other place,
78. My relations are scattered, my fold dispersed.

85. Speak, that from your speaking the angry god be reconciled,
86. That the goddess who became furious relent!
87. May my dark and smoky hearth burn clear,

30 Abusch, *Babylonian Witchcraft Literature*, 55.

31 For an edition of this composition, see A. Zgoll, *Die Kunst des Betens: Form und Funktion, Theologie und Psychagogik in babylonisch-assyrischen Handerhebungsgebeten zu Ištar*, AOAT 308 (Münster: Ugarit-Verlag, 2003), 41–67; the translation is that of Foster, *Before the Muses*, 604.

88. May my snuffed-out torch burst into flames,
89. May my scattered relations regroup themselves,
90. May my paddock enlarge, my fold expand.

Lines 67–68, 75–78, 85–90 focus on the petitioner's relationship to his personal gods. These lines seem to be discreet and to be separate from the surrounding context, for the statement that the supplicant has been abandoned by his personal gods and that as a consequence his household has been destroyed (lines 67–68, 75–78, 85–90) seems to be indiscriminately interspersed with the description of his suffering and failure (lines 56–66, 69–74) and his prayer to Ištar (lines 53–54, 79–80, 91–92). It would seem, therefore, that the sections treating the personal gods are secondary.

•••

Having noted several reasons why the theme of alienation of the personal god and the request of the high god to reconcile the personal god(s) are at variance with and seem out of place in the *šuillas* to high gods, we would now try to provide an explanation for the occurrence of this discordant note. Several explanations regarding the theme of alienation of the personal god in specific texts might meet some of these objections and might provide an explanation for this anomaly. In general terms, it is possible that the juxtaposition of a major god of nature and/or of a polity and the family god may have been meant to resolve the problem of the relationship of major gods and personal gods and to answer the questions of who is actually responsible for the suffering of the individual,[32] to whom should one turn for help, and who will ultimately restore the sufferer to a normal life. But this does not eliminate the impression that the theme of alienation of the personal god seems to be disconnected and to be an insertion.

A second explanation was suggested in conversation by William L. Moran on the basis of *Ludlul bēl nēmeqi* I, 41–48, to wit, that the personal god has become simply a manifestation of the high god and the anger of the personal god is simply a reflex of the anger of the high god; therefore, one might first ask the high god to calm down so that the personal god might then also be

32 The sufferings of humankind as a whole are discussed in Gabriel, "Exemplificational Critique of Violence."

pacified.[33] Moran's explanation is most insightful, but the scenario that he suggests fits some but not all of the contexts.

Another approach is suggested implicitly by Claus Ambos in his recent study of *bīt salāʾ mê*.[34] He has argued that the purpose of the *šuilla*s in that ritual is not only to seek the favor of the high gods addressed, but mainly to convince them to intercede with the king's alienated personal gods and to reconcile them with the king. The personal god is addressed in that ritual because he represents the individual personhood of the king (the absence of the personal god reflects the vulnerability of the king). The ritual was directed in part to the personal god of the king because the ritual is concerned not only with the human being in his role as king but also with the king as an individual person; therefore, there is a need to strengthen and protect not only kingship but also the individual himself.

Ambos provides a historical context in which to understand the occurrence of the personal gods in these texts and the request of the high god that they reconcile the personal gods with the king. But even with the new contextual explanation suggested by Ambos's work, the texts often seem not to be coherent. And we should in any case not ignore the fact that the occurrence of the personal god disrupts the flow or coherence of the prayers.

This lack of coherence suggests that the portion of the prayer focusing on the anger of the personal god and/or on the request that the high god reconcile the angry personal god with his protégé is an insertion into a prayer addressed to a high god. Actually, Ambos's suggestion of a historical or cultural context for the use of the texts provides an explanation and justification for the addition of the request that the high god reconcile the personal god(s) with the petitioner. Previously, I held the opinion that some *šuilla*s grew out of prayers to the personal god,[35] but at this point I think that my earlier attempt must be bracketed.

33 W. L. Moran, "The Babylonian Job," in *The Most Magic Word: Essays on Babylonian and Biblical Literature*, ed. R. S. Hendel, CBQMS 35 (Washington, DC: Catholic Biblical Association of America, 2002), 195 (the original paper was delivered in 1992).

34 Ambos, *König*, esp. sections II.3.3.8–II.3.3.9.

35 See T. Abusch, "Prayers, Hymns, Incantations, and Curses: Mesopotamia," in *Religions of the Ancient World: A Guide*, ed. S. I. Johnston (Cambridge: Belknap Press of Harvard University Press, 2004), 353–355 [[111–117]]. Let me briefly explain this earlier thesis: Prayers to the personal god were recited originally in a family context; they reflect the problems of the individual householder or family head. These prayers represent an attempt to rectify personal or family problems caused by a rupture of relations between the man and his god—a rupture that led to abandonment and suffering; the rectification of the rupture thus involved forgiveness and reconciliation. Prayers to the personal god were subsequently directed to one of the cosmic or urban deities normally worshipped in a temple, and the address was then modeled on temple liturgies by *āšipu*s with a temple

For it now seems to me that my earlier suggestion was probably wrong and that the request of the high gods that they reconcile the personal gods with the petitioner might be a secondary addition to many of the texts, especially in those texts where it introduces a discordant note into the prayer. It may be that the presence of the anger of the high god in some of these compositions serves as a point of attraction for the mention of the anger of the personal gods, but I should also note here that the anger of the high god itself may possibly be a secondary development in the *šuillas*, a theme taken over perhaps from the *eršahungas*. It is possible that Old Babylonian or even Middle Babylonian juridical administration served as a model for going directly to the high god. Already in the Old Babylonian period, letters from Ḫammurabi indicate that he had received complaints or petitions and was himself dealing with the problem and ordering a lower official to rectify the situation.[36]

When I formulated this hypothesis, to wit, that occasionally the portion of the prayer focusing on the anger of the personal god is an insertion into the prayer addressed to a high god, I expected to find that the texts were more coherent without the section mentioning the alienation of the personal god and that there were manuscript variations among the exemplars of individual prayers—that is, variant manuscripts that do not mention the personal god.

The first expectation was realized, and perhaps it was the occasional absence of coherence that led me to formulate the hypothesis in the first place. The second expectation did not materialize, or, rather, I did not find the evidence in the simple form that I expected—the straightforward absence of a line or two in a variant manuscript of a prayer. But when comparing versions of a prayer—not manuscripts—I noticed that whereas one version did not contain the section requesting that the high god cause the angry personal god to be reconciled, the other version did. I have in mind particularly versions of a prayer to Enlil, designated Enlil 1a and Enlil 1b by Walter Kunstmann and Werner Mayer.

There is a close relationship between Enlil 1a (PBS 1/1, no. 17 // *BMS* 19) and Enlil 1b (*KAR* 68 // *KAR* 25 iii 21′–31′, iv 1′–2′). As noted already by previous scholars, Enlil 1b is dependent on Enlil 1a.[37] The first part of the hymnic

orientation. A hymnic introduction of praise was added to the supplication, and composers drew upon temple imagery and experiences associated with gods of the temple in the preparation of this new praise section; however, the prayer itself seems still to be an attempt to deal with individual or family (and not communal) problems.

36 My purpose in mentioning the judicial administration is not to propose a specific date but rather to provide some possible background for the development under consideration.

37 See W. G. Kunstmann, *Die babylonische Gebetsbeschwörung*, LSS NF 2 (Leipzig: Hinrichs, 1932), 88: "Dieses Gebet [scil. Enlil 1b] stimmt im grossen und ganzen von Z. 10 [sic.,

introduction in Enlil 1b (lines 1–6[38]) is not found in Enlil 1a. In fact, the prayer in Enlil 1b seems to contain a double introduction. Lines 7ff. in Enlil 1b (// Enlil 1a: 1ff.[39]) are the more original hymnic introduction; the opening lines in Enlil 1b are an addition and should not be viewed as an accidental omission in Enlil 1a.

The lines dealing with the anger of the personal gods in Enlil 1b, *KAR* 68, rev. 10–12, seem to be an addition. *KAR* 68, rev. 9–14 read:

9. *naplisannima bēlī leqe unnīnīya*
10. *libbi iliya u* ${}^{d}$*ištariya zenûti*
11. *šabsūti u kummulūti*
12. *ša ittiya zenû šabsu u kamlu*
13. *libbi ilūtika rabīti*
14. *ittiya sullimamma*

9. Look upon me, my lord, and accept my prayer.
10–12. The heart(s)[40] of my angry, irate, furious (personal) god and (personal) goddess that are angry, irate, and furious with me,
13. The heart of your great divinity,
14. Reconcile with me.

It seems that once lines 10–12 are removed, the preceding line, rev. line 9, in which the petitioner requests that Enlil accept the prayer, leads right into lines 13–14, the request that Enlil reconcile his angry heart with the petitioner.[41] It might appear that the other version of this prayer, Enlil 1a, also makes

correct to Z. 8] ab mit 1a überein, Z. 1–9 [sic., correct to Z. 1–7] sind Zusatz"; Mayer, *Untersuchungen*, 384: "Das Gebet [scil. Enlil 1b] stimmt von *KAR* 25 iii 27 // 68, Vs 8 ab ungefähr mit 'Enlil 1a' überein; die Zeilen davor sind Zusatz. Das Ende (*KAR* 68 Rs.) weicht wieder stark ab."

38 I treat *KAR* 68, obv. 6–7 as one line: 6 and 6b.

39 *bēlu šurbû šadû* ${}^{d}$*Igigī*
*malku* ${}^{d}$*Anunnakkī rubû muštālu*
${}^{d}$*Enlil bēlu šurbû šadû* ${}^{d}$*Igigī*
*malku* ${}^{d}$*Anunnakkī rubû muštālu*, etc.

40 Cf. M.-J. Seux, *Hymnes et prières aux dieux de Babylonie et d'Assyrie*, LAPO 8 (Paris: Éditions du Cerf, 1976), 273. Seux in his main translation also takes *libbi* of line 10 as the subject of the relative clause in line 12 (in n. 24 he offers an alternative).

41 Note also that *KAR* 68 (Enlil 1b), rev. 10–14 seem to be equivalent to Sîn 3: 66$^{c}$ [or 67]–68. Does this suggest that the whole segment (Enlil 1b [*KAR* 68], rev. 10–14 and Sîn 3: 66$^{c}$ [or 67]–68) is an addition in both texts, or perhaps that the whole segment is original? If *KAR* 68, rev. 13–14 in Enlil 1b is part of the addition, lines 10–14 would thus express the request for reconciliation with both the high god and the personal god.

mention of the personal gods in PBS 1/1, 17: 30: DINGIR [*liš*]-[*t*]*am-mar-ka* ᵈ15 *liš-te-ʾ-e-ka*.[42] But note that the line there deals not with the relation of the personal gods to the petitioner but rather with their relation to the high god. This line contrasts with the lines in Enlil 1b (*KAR* 68, rev. 5–8) which might have been regarded as its functional equivalent, for the lines in Enlil 1b request that the personal gods be at the petitioner's side and help him.[43] In effect, we have no section in Enlil 1a that treats the personal god.

The opening part of the text indicates that Enlil 1b is a development of Enlil 1a. Not only the opening part but also the mention of the anger of the personal gods (as well as the request that they help the petitioner) may be regarded as a new development in Enlil 1b and may constitute textual evidence of insertion. Whereas Enlil 1a is concerned with the request that the god grant the petitioner a successful life among the elite (PBS 1/1, no. 17, obv. 16–rev. 5 // *BMS* 19, obv. 18′–rev. 9b [I treat *BMS* 19 rev. 29–30 as one line: 9 and 9b][44]), Enlil 1b asks for the same (*KAR* 68, obv. 19–25, rev. 1–4 [*KAR* 25 is broken here]) but adds on a section (*KAR* 68, rev. 5–16) that focuses on the role of the personal gods as intermediaries and the petitioner's reconciliation with his personal gods and the high god Enlil.

•••

I believe that the request that the high god intercede and reconcile the angry personal god(s) with the petitioner is a secondary addition to the *šuilla*s. At the very least, I trust that I have shown that this theme constitutes a problem in the *šuilla*s and presents us with a difficulty when we read these texts. It may be possible, by means of detailed (and sometimes forced) exegesis of the individual passages, to justify some of the occurrences. This approach would be a mistake. Rather than explicate each individual occurrence, I would suggest, especially in view of the fact that some of the occurrences are similar,[45] that

42 This line was read correctly by W. Mayer, review of *Hymnes et prières aux dieux de Babylonie et d'Assyrie*, by M.-J. Seux, *Or* NS 46 (1977): 389, "[Que] (mon) dieu te célèbre, que (ma) déesse te cherche."

43 These four lines in Enlil 1b (*KAR* 68, rev. 5–8) are virtually identical with Marduk 2: 15–18 (lines 16–19 in my study); cf. Šamaš 1: 122–125.

44 Of no significance in this discussion is the occurrence of the *attallû*-formula in *BMS* 19, obv. 10′–12′.

45 For example, compare Sîn 3: 66ᶜ [or 67]–68 with *KAR* 68 (Enlil 1b), rev. 10–14 and Ištar 11: 22–25 with Sîn 1: 22–24b.

these passages are related, and that we are dealing with a revision or rewrite of a body of literature to give expression to a new theology.[46]

To return to my introductory comments about coherence: even in simple genres, one is faced with the possibility of at least two different approaches. We can try to explicate the text and/or subject it to a critical appraisal. How much more so in more complex genres and texts! And lest the reader think that I am confident about my conclusion regarding the secondary nature of the material in the *šuillas*, I should emphasize my own uncertainty. Should my construction of the evidence be wrong, then we must seek another hypothesis to explain the data. I myself do not know how else to construe the evidence.

## Appendices

Appendices A and B are lists of *šuilla*s that contain the mention of the anger of the personal god in its request section. In compiling these lists, I have drawn upon my memory, but mainly upon C. Frechette, *Mesopotamian Ritual-prayers of "Hand-lifting" (Akkadian Šuillas): An Investigation of Function in Light of the Idiomatic Meaning of the Rubric*, AOAT 379 (Münster: Ugarit-Verlag, 2012), appendix 4, "Comparison of features in šuilla prayers," col. 4a (= pp. 277–282); and Mayer, *Untersuchungen*, 94–98, 242–243. When possible, I cite only one edition, usually the most recent one. These lists are not intended to be exhaustive. Appendix C lists a few prayers that are not *šuilla*s. The mention therein of the anger of the personal gods may be an original part of the prayer.

### *Appendix A*

The texts cited here contain references to the anger of the personal god(s) that seem to be secondary additions. In some of the cases, the prayer becomes significantly more coherent with the elimination of the lines dealing with the personal god.

**Adad 1b** Edition: *CMAwR* 2, no. 8.43
Lines 34 and 36 ([*ilī*] *u ištarī sullima*[47] *ittiy*[*a*] / … / [*ilī l*]*irēmanni* [*iš*]*tarī liršâ rē*[*ma*]) are secondary. It is not certain whether line 35 ([*aggu li*]*bbaka linūḫa lippašr*[*a k*]*abattaka salīma šukn*[*a*]) should be regarded so as well. Line 30 connects nicely to line 33 (lines 31–32, the lines dealing with witchcraft, are probably secondary [cf. *CMAwR* 2, p. 319, "Content"]), but note that line 35 does not follow naturally on line 33. Because

46 Cf. P. Steinkeller, "The Reluctant En of Inana—or the Persona of Gilgameš in the Perspective of Babylonian Political Philosophy," in "Approaching a Critique of Mesopotamian Reason," ed. G. Gabriel, special issue, *JANEH* 5 (2018): 149–177.

47 This may also be read *lislimūma*; see *CMAwR* 2, no. 8.43, note to line 34′.

of the uncertainty, we are left with three alternative reconstructions: (1) The original text had lines 30 and 33; then lines 34–36 were added, followed later by the addition of lines 31–32. (2) Lines 34–36 were part of the original text and only lines 31–32 are additions. (3) The original text contained lines 30, 33, and 35; then lines 34 and 36 were added, followed later by the addition of lines 31–32.

The anger of the high god in line 35 may not have been part of the original text and may have only been introduced alongside the anger of the personal gods. The problem in our text is that the anger of the high god is sandwiched between statements regarding the anger of the personal gods. Even when the two themes are in proximity to each other, they are usually juxtaposed and not interwoven. See, e.g., Nergal 2: 19–23, where the request to the high god to give up his anger (19–22) is followed by the request that the angry personal gods be reconciled with the petitioner (23); but cf. Anu 1: 10–13 and Sîn 3: 66ᶜ–68, where reconciliation of the anger of the personal gods (Anu 1: 10–11 and Sîn 3: 66ᶜ–67) is followed by reconciliation of the anger of the high god (Anu 1: 12–13 and Sîn 3: 68).[48] Finally, in Madānu 1, we again find sandwiching, but here the request that Madānu bring about the reconciliation of the angry personal gods (16–17) comes right after the request to Madānu to intercede with Marduk (15), and immediately before the request to Madānu to have mercy on the petitioner (18); that is to say, in contrast to Adad 1b, the anger of the personal gods occurs between statements asking the high god to perform his normal activities.

**Anu 1** Edition: *AGH*, 34–37.

This text occurs as the first prayer in the ninth *Abschnitt* of *bīt salā'mê* (following *BMS* 6 and Ambos, *König*, 203–205). Lines 10–11 (*mimmû mala ana iliya* [*u ištariya*] *aḫṭû lipp*[*ašra*] / *libbi iliya u* [*ištariya*] *zenûte ana ašrišu l*[*itūr*])[49] deal with the personal gods and can easily be an addition.[50] Removing lines 10–11 about the personal gods does not detract from the coherence of the prayer and, if anything, adds to its coherence. This conclusion appears valid despite the fragmentary quality of this part of the composition. These two lines (10–11) are part of a section that starts in line 8 (line 8 is largely a restoration; it is partially preserved in *BMS* 6, line 8) and ends in lines 12–13[51]

48 But, in the case of Sîn 3, if line 66ᶜ is read *silim ittiya* rather than *sullim*! *ittiya* and Sîn is the addressee of the imperative, then Sîn 3 might also be an example of sandwiching, but here the anger of the personal gods (67) would be sandwiched between statements regarding the anger of the high god (66 and 68).

49 Lines 10–11 are drawn from *LKA* 50, obv. 13–rev. 2 and *BMS* 6, obv. 10–11; they are lines 13–17 in *AGH*.

50 CT 51, 211 contains significant variants but still has the lines that deal with the personal gods.

51 For these lines, cf. Nergal 2: 20 and 22.

where the petitioner asks Anu to give up his anger and expresses the wish that Anu show compassion to him.[52]

**Enlil 1b** (*KAR* 68 // *KAR* 25 iii 21′–31′, iv 1′–2′)[53]
The lines dealing with the anger of the personal gods, *KAR* 68, rev. 10–11, seem to be an addition. For a fuller discussion of Enlil 1b and for further details on the relationship of Enlil 1b and Enlil 1a, see the body of the paper.

**Gula 1a/1b** Edition: Mayer, *Untersuchungen*, 450–457.
The two texts (1a and 1b) are clearly related. It appears that Gula 1a developed out of Gula 1b. In any case, both texts have parallel sections on the anger of the personal gods:

Gula 1a: 81–82 // Gula 1b: 22–23:

> *lušpurki ana iliya zenî ištariya zenīti*
> *ana il āliya ša šabsuma kamlu ittiya* (so 1a; 1b variant: *ša šabsu kamlu libbašu it*[*tiya*]).

Gula 1a: 87–89 // Gula 1b: 31–33a:

> *ilī šabsu litūru* ^d^*ištarī zenītu lissaḫr*[*a*]
> *il āliya ša šabsuma kamlu ittiya* (so 1a; 1b variant: *il āliya* ^d^*Marduk*)

The fact that both versions have almost identical sections dealing with personal gods does not prove that these sections originated in the Gula text. In my estimation, the sections in which the petitioner states that he wishes to send the goddess Gula to his angry personal gods so that they relent and turn back to him were not an original part of either version of the Gula *šuilla*[54] but were inserted into the prayer from which the two versions (Gula 1a and 1b) derive. I would guess that the theme of reconciliation was taken up originally by the Gula Ur-text from a prayer such as Nisaba 1.[55]

52 For variations and restorations of lines 8–13, see Ambos, *König*, 204 and "Kommentar" on p. 205, and Seux, *Hymnes*, 271 and nn. 11–14 there. Given the state of the text, it is possible that the section under study begins at line 10 and runs through line 13. Our argument is not materially affected should this be the case.

53 The edition in *AGH*, 20–23 is much too confusing. In the meantime, see the translation in Foster, *Before the Muses*, 652–653. My line count follows *KAR* 68.

54 Cf. my comments on Šamaš 23 below.

55 For a detailed analysis of the two versions of this prayer, see "Two Versions of a Šuilla to Gula," in "Altorientalische Gebetsliteratur: Form, außersprachlicher Kontext und interkulturelle Adaptionsprozesse," ed. A. Grund-Wittenberg and Elisabeth Rieken, special issue, *WO* 49/1 (2019): 6–13 [[206–214]].

**Ištar 2** Edition: Zgoll, *Kunst*, 41–67.
Lines 67–68, 75–78, 85–90 focus on the petitioner's relationship to his personal gods. For a fuller discussion, see the body of the paper.

**Ištar 4** Edition: Zgoll, *Kunst*, 183–190.
Line 15′ (*lissaḫra ilī ša iznû ittiya*) is probably an addition; the other harmful phenomena mentioned in lines 16b–18 are afflictions or results,[56] not causes of harm. Hence, *ilī ša iznû ittiya* stands out. It seems that the request for reconciliation with the personal god stands at the beginning of the list of requests for elimination of evils. In this sense it is similar to Tašmētu 1 and Ninurta 4.

**Ištar 11** Edition: *AGH*, 128–129. Translation: Seux, *Hymnes*, 323–325.
The relevant lines are:

22. *sullimīmma ila z*[*enâ u ištara zenīta*]
23. *ilī u ištarī* [*ša ištu ūmī ma'dūti išbusū eliya*]
24. *ina kītti u mīš*[*ari lislimū ittiya*]
25. *urḫī līšir* [*padānī lidmiq*]

Compare lines 22–25 with Sîn 1: 22–24b.[57] Perhaps Ištar 11: 23–25 is dependent on Sîn 1: 23–24b (this explains the occurrence in Ištar 11: 25 of *urḫī līšir* [*padānī lidmiq*] without the earlier mention of *dumqi* of Sîn 1: 22).[58]

The line preceding the aforementioned section, Ištar 11: 21 (*musallimat ili z*[*enâ u ištari zenīta*]), is the last entry in the hymnic introduction[59] and leads right into the request that the personal gods be reconciled. The same phenomenon occurs in Sîn 3: 55–60. It seems to me that there are three alternative reconstructions from which we can choose to explain this situation:

1. Lines 21–25 are original.
2. Line 21 was secondarily inserted in order to connect the request for reconciliation of the personal gods in lines 22–25 with the hymnic introduction. Under these circumstances, the request can either be primary or secondary. If lines 22–25 are

56 With the possible exception of *ennettu* (wr. *inninti*) in line 16a.

57 Probably restore Ištar 11: 23 on the basis of Sîn 1: 23; so already Seux, *Hymnes*, 325, note to line 23, as well as Mayer, *Untersuchungen*, 96, 243.

58 In comparison with Sîn 1, Ištar 11 may represent an attempt to more fully integrate the theme of the anger of the personal god by the addition of lines 21–22 (and the elimination of a line comparable to Sîn 1: 22).

59 I should mention that in the hymnic section of Nabû 1, there is an important statement (9–10: *ša ilšu isbusu tusaḫḫar kišāssu / ša zenât šīmtašu tusallam ittišu*) that gives clear expression to the high god's power to bring about reconciliation.

secondary, then line 21 was probably added at the same time as they were and is also secondary.

3. Line 21 at the end of the hymnic introduction was part of the original text. It existed prior to the insertion of lines 22–25 and allowed the addition of lines 22–25.

Note that the dependence of lines 23–25 on Sîn 1 (see above) seems to exclude the first possibility. If we use Sîn 3 as a way to decide, then we might prefer option 3 because in Sîn 3 the lament (55–60) certainly looks secondary while the immediately preceding entry in the hymnic introduction may or may not be secondary. On the other hand, since we do not often have a close relationship of praise and request as regards personal gods such as the one we find here, the occurrence here might argue for the secondary nature of both line 21 and lines 22–25 (option 2 above).

**Madānu 1 (= Nusku 1)** Edition: Mayer, *Untersuchungen*, 459–465.
The section dealing with the personal gods (16–17) may be extraneous. For a fuller discussion, see the body of the paper.

**Marduk 24** Edition: *CMAwR* 2, no. 8.27.
Lines 35–36 (*s*[*allim*] *ilī zenî u ištarī zenītu ša kamlu libbašunu zenû ittiya* / *ina suḫḫur pānī u malê libbāte irteneddûni* "Re[concile] my angry god and my angry goddess / whose hearts have become furious and angry with me, they keep chasing me with rejection and with great fury.") are secondary and are "the expression of an attempt to make the anger of the god primarily responsible for the various evils encountered in the text."[60]

**Nergal 2** Edition: Mayer, *Untersuchungen*, 478–481.[61]
Line 23 relates to the personal gods and looks like an addition. The version of line 22 with *lippaṭ*(*a*)*ram-ma* suggests a connection between lines 22 and 23 (because of the *-ma*). On the other hand, the version of line 22 with *lippašra* could easily be attached to lines 19–22 and be part of the original text.[62]

If the request in line 23 that the personal gods be reconciled with the petitioner is treated as an addition and separated from the request that the anger of the high god be pacified (lines 20–22),[63] it would follow that the lament in lines 11–14 should also be treated as secondary; accordingly, all sections of the text addressing Nergal would

60 Abusch, *Babylonian Witchcraft Literature*, 55; cf. 47: "*KAR* 26, a prayer originally concerned with the effects of witchcraft, has been changed into one which has universal applicability and which regards the anger of the gods as the source of the sufferer's difficulty."

61 A further manuscript is published by Maul and Strauss, *Ritualbeschreibungen*, no. 65.

62 We are far from certain whether or not to treat also line 22 as an addition.

63 If this is so, then the variant without *-ma* is to be preferred; *-ma* then is secondary.

be treated as primary (lines 1–10, 15–22, 24). In any case, I regard line 23 as a late addition separate from the preceding lines.[64]

**Ninurta 4** = **Kaksisa 2** Edition: *CMAwR* 2, no. 10.8.
Line 19 (*sullim(am)-ma ittiya ila u ištara zenûti*) is perhaps an addition. It seems to me that line 19 begins a list of problems to be dealt with. Note the similarity to Ištar 4 and Tašmētu 1; see comments there and comparison.[65]

**Nisaba 1** Edition: C. Frechette and I. Hrůša, "The Ritual-Prayer Nisaba 1 and Its Function," *JANER* 11 (2011): 71–72, 90–93.

**Sîn 1** Edition: Mayer, *Untersuchungen*, 490–495.[66]
Lines 23–24a seem to be an addition. As regards lines 23–24b, cf. Ištar 11: 23–25. For a fuller discussion, see the body of the paper.

**Sîn 3** Edition: Mayer, *Untersuchungen*, 495–502.
The anger of the personal gods finds mention in lines 55, 56–60, and 67 (perhaps also line 66$^c$). For a fuller discussion of these lines, see the body of the paper.[67]

**Šamaš 23** Edition: E. Ebeling, "Beiträge zur Kenntnis der Beschwörungsserie Namburbi," *RA* 49 (1955): 36–40, no. 20. Translation: Seux, *Hymnes*, 354–356.
Mayer (*Untersuchungen*, 97) reads 4$R^2$ 60, obv. 42–43 as: *ilī iznû ittiya ištarī isbusa eliya*. The text may be too broken for use in our study and is, in any case, a *namburbi*.

64 In regard to the Nergal prayer, I have here come to a conclusion opposite to the one stated in the penultimate paragraph of Abusch, "Paean and Petition" (pp. 22–23 [[174–175]]). There I concluded that the "less structured prayer to the personal gods (lines 12–14 and 23)" was "the original kernel of this text." Though I still "ascribe significance to the existence of marked sections defined by formal patterns" in this Nergal text, I would now conclude that "the passages that have formal patterns," that is, the sections that focus on Nergal (lines 1–10, 15–18) were the original kernel, and the sections dealing with the personal gods were secondary. (Although the aforementioned article was published in 2017, it was submitted years earlier and represented work done prior to the work underlying the present study.)

65 All the same, I do not yet see a clear justification for treating either line 19 or lines 19–20 as secondary. They are part of a larger section of requests in this text and should probably not be removed without further justification.

66 For another edition, see S. Butler, *Mesopotamian Conceptions of Dreams and Dream Rituals*, AOAT 258 (Münster: Ugarit-Verlag, 1998), 379–396; a further manuscript is published by Maul and Strauss, *Ritualbeschreibungen*, no. 66.

67 Note also that Sîn 3: 66$^c$ [or 67]–68 is equivalent to *KAR* 68 (Enlil 1b), rev. 10–14. Does this suggest that the whole segment (Sîn 3: 66$^c$ [or 67]–68 and Enlil 1b: [*KAR* 68] rev. 10–14) is an addition in both texts, or perhaps that the whole segment is original in both?

However, it is worth listing here and not in Appendix C below because of the following: If Ebeling's ("Beitrage," 40) restoration of lines 42–43 ([*lu-uš-pur-ka ana ili šá*] *zi-nu-ú itti-ia*$_5$ / [*ana* $^{d}$*ištari šá is*]-*bu-sa muḫḫi-ia*$_5$) is approximately correct (followed by Seux, *Hymnes*, 355), then Šamaš is being sent to reconcile the angry personal gods; note the similarity with Gula and Nisaba who are similarly sent. Perhaps, therefore, the notion of the reconciliation of the personal gods by the intercession of the high gods derives from the image of sending cultic material (or something/someone similar) to the personal gods (cf. prayers to Gula and Nisaba). Note also the Hittite materials cited in n. 17 above.

**Tašmētu 1** Edition: CTN 4, no. 168, rev. i, 3–43 // *AGH*, 124–127.[68]
Rev. i, line 32 (*ilu u ištaru lislimū ittiya*) is part of the petition in this prayer; it is the first entry of a list of evils that the speaker seeks to eliminate. The absence of the personal gods is part of a series of problems, including witchcraft (32–39); perhaps the anger of the personal gods here is intended as an explanation for the different evils. The personal god entry is also the first entry in the list of requests in Ninurta 4: 19–25 and Ištar 4: 15–19.[69]

The reconciliation of the personal gods in Tašmētu differs from the requests that come after it, for whereas the request for reconciliation tries to bring the personal gods close, the other requests try to distance the evils. This seems also to be true in Ninurta 4 and Ištar 4. Note also that the lists in Tašmētu 1 and Ninurta 4 include witchcraft, the *asakku*-illness, and NAM.TAR.

## *Appendix B*

The texts in this list mention the anger of the personal gods but are not cited as evidence for the secondary nature of the relevant lines. The reasons they are not cited as evidence include: the present evidence does not allow a decision, the relevant line does not refer simply to the anger of the personal god and its reconciliation, etc.

**Ea 1a** Edition: *CMAwR* 2, no. 9.6
Lines 18–19 mention the personal god (*ilu*), but request that this god and the king be amenable to the man. This passage is therefore not relevant.

68 For the purposes of this study, the manuscript of this composition that I have utilized is D. J. Wiseman and J. A. Black, *Literary Texts from the Temple of Nabû*, CTN 4 (London: British School of Archaeology in Iraq, 1996), no. 168, photograph plates nos. 149 and 150, as well as the transliteration and translation prepared by G. Van Buylaere, "CTN 4, 168," *ORACC*, 2010, http://oracc.museum.upenn.edu/cams/gkab/P363582/html (accessed September 6, 2016).

69 See my comments on Ištar 4, Ninurta 4, and Tašmētu 1 in the body of the paper and here in Appendix A.

**Ea, Šamaš, Marduk** 9 (*LKA* 86 // *LKA* 88)
The relevant lines for our purposes are *LKA* 86, rev. 4 // *LKA* 88, obv. 32: ... *ša ištu ūme pānī isbusu eliya*, and *LKA* 86, rev. 13–15 // *LKA* 88, rev. 9–11: *ina ūme annê lizzizū ina maḫrikunu / lislimū ittiya*.... But the meaning of the text is not clear, and the text is somewhat broken as well; accordingly, this prayer cannot be used in our study.

**Ištar** 10 Edition: Zgoll, *Kunst*, 107–126.
One would have liked to include line 11 in this study, but Ištar in mss. A and D refers also to the goddess Ištar; but see *ilī bāniy*[*a* ...] $^{d}$*ištarī bānīt*[*iya* ...] in ms. C. For the variants of this line, see Zgoll, *Kunst*, 110 and especially line 11 in the chart on p. 126.

**Ištar** 25 Edition: C. J. Mullo-Weir, "Fragment of an Expiation-Ritual against Sickness," *JRAS* 2 (1929): 281–284 (= Rm 2, 160, rev.) lines 1–13.
Lines 9–10 (*ila zenâ ištar zenītu sullimīm*[*ma*] / *kimilti ili u ištari šupṭirī yâ*[*ši*]) deal with the anger of the personal gods and request their release. Lines 3–8 seem to describe negative manifestations (i.e., physical and psychological problems, including in line 3 the mention that the personal gods have been made angry with the petitioner); lines 9–12 seem to represent the cause of the problems (lines 9–10: request for reconciliation and release of anger of the personal gods; lines 11–12: request for release of the sin of the curse of relatives and friends). I am unsure about the relation between lines 9–10 and 11–12 and therefore cannot simply treat lines 9–10 as secondary at this time.

**Marduk** 4 Edition: T. Oshima, *Babylonian Prayers to Marduk*, ORA 7 (Tübingen: Mohr Siebeck, 2011), 346–353.[70]
That line 25 refers to the personal god is not at all clear. I follow A. Lenzi ("A Shuilla: Marduk 4," in *Reading Akkadian Prayers and Hymns: An Introduction*, ed. A. Lenzi, ANEM 3 [Atlanta: Society of Biblical Literature, 2011], 302 ad line 25) in taking *ilī* in this line as referring to Marduk, though W. Mayer ("Das Bussgebet an Marduk von BMS 11," *Or* NS 73 [2004]: 206) and Oshima (*Babylonian Prayers*, 351) take it as referring to the personal god.

**Marduk** 5 Edition: *CMAwR* 2, no. 8.28.
Anger of the (personal) god is alluded to in line 41 and implied in line 61. It is mentioned explicitly in line 57, but note the argument in favor of treating line 57 as original to the composition in Abusch, *Babylonian Witchcraft Literature*, 67–73.

70 For bibliographical information, see Oshima, *Babylonian Prayers*, 111–112.

**Marduk 16** Edition: W. Mayer, "Sechs Šu-ila-Gebete," *Or* NS 59 (1990): 455–459.
Line 12 treats the anger of the personal gods and the city gods (*ilī ištarī il āliya ištar āliya*). This line is attached to lines 13–14. The latter lines are difficult to understand, and therefore we cannot use this passage.

**Ninurta 1** Edition: *AGH*, 24–27.
Line 24 (*ša ilšu ittišu zenû tusallam arḫiš*), the last line in the hymnic introduction, does treat the angry personal god, but line 40 (*ilī u ištarī lišāqirū'innima liqbû damiqtī*), the one mention of the personal gods in the petition, asks not for the reconciliation of angry personal gods but rather that the personal gods value the petitioner and speak well of him.

**Šamaš 3** Edition: *AGH*, 50–53.
The one line that might be relevant for our investigation is p. 52, rev. 2a, but this line is unclear (see Mayer, *Untersuchungen*, 243 [bottom line of page]).

**Šibzianna 1** Edition: *CMAwR* 2, no. 9.8.
The text deals in the main with witchcraft; only line 24 (*ilu ištaru amēlūtu salīmu liršûni*) deals with the anger of the personal gods, but in conjunction with humans as well.

**Zarpanītu 2** Edition: *AGH*, 138–141.
Page 140a, rev. 5 ( ] *bēlti ilī ištarī šabbāsūti* [ ) certainly deals with the anger of the personal gods, but p. 140a rev. 3 indicates that Zarpanītu is also angry at the petitioner. The text is too broken to be used in this study.

### *Appendix C*

The texts cited here are not *šuilla*s. Additionally, the anger of the personal gods in these texts may be an original part of the prayer.

**Šamaš 6** Edition: Ebeling, "Beiträge," 144–147, no. 25. Translation: Seux, *Hymnes*, 410–412.
This text is probably not a *šuilla* but rather a *namburbi* or *namerimburuda* (see also Mayer, *Untersuchungen*, 411). Lines 12–13 (*libbi ilūtika lippašra libbi iliya u ištariya lippašir*) and line 17 ({*anāku*}… *ša ilšu ištaršu ittišu zenû*) deal with the personal gods. These lines are perhaps not original but are too uncertain for use in our investigation.[71]

71 See *CAD* Ṣ, 165–166: "may your divine heart be appeased (with respect to) the seizure caused by the curse and by (the oath sworn by) the touching of my breast, which my good friend did, whether he lifted his hand or pronounced the words" (*KAR* 228, line 7 [actually

Note that in this text the anger of the personal gods is linked (i.e., juxtaposed) with the anger of the high god.

**Šamaš** 73 Edition: J. Scurlock, *Magico-Medical Means of Treating Ghost-Induced Illnesses in Ancient Mesopotamia*, AMD 3 (Leiden: Brill/Styx, 2006), 530–535, no. 226. This is a ritual and prayer against ghosts and is not part of the basic *šuilla* corpus. The line mentioning the anger of the personal gods, (*anāku* ...) *ša ina šibsāt ili u ištari iʾiltu īʾilanni* (p. 531: obv. 28), is the first item in the list of afflictions and may be an original part of the prayer. But note that while the anger of the god finds mention in the lament, the gods' reconciliation is not mentioned in the request.

**Šamaš and Marduk** 2 Edition: S. M. Maul, *Zukunftsbewältigung: Eine Untersuchung altorientalischen Denkens anhand der babylonisch-assyrischen Lösrituale* (*Namburbi*), BaF 18 (Mainz am Rhein: Phillip von Zabern, 1994), 409–414.
The prayer, a *namburbi*, is edited on pp. 411: 10–413: 31 and 414 of Maul's edition. The section that is relevant to the present investigation is p. 412, lines 21–30. This prayer seems unique, not formulaic; therefore, I view the theme of the "anger of the god" here as original to the text and thus do not include it as an example of a secondary addition.

lines 6–12], var. from Sm 1155); "against the evil caused by the touching of my breast, when PN touched me on the breast" (line 14). But the translation should also include line 13; lines 12–13 should read something like: "may your divine heart be appeased, may the heart of my god and goddess be appeased (with respect to) ..."

CHAPTER 14

# Two Versions of a *šuilla* to Gula

This paper is a by-product of a larger investigation—an examination of all *šuilla* prayers in which the high god to whom the prayer is addressed is asked to bring about reconciliation between the petitioner and his angry personal gods.* The appearance of the angry personal gods in the *šuilla*s is problematic for a number of reasons. I detail these reasons elsewhere (see note 2) and will therefore not repeat them, but I note here that the occurrence of the aforementioned request calls for an explanation.

An explanation is suggested implicitly by Claus Ambos in his recent study of *bīt salāʾ mê*.[1] Ambos has argued that the purpose of the *šuilla*s in that ritual is not only to seek the favor of the high gods addressed, but also to convince them to intercede with the king's alienated personal gods and to reconcile them with the king. The personal god is addressed in that ritual because he represents the individual personhood of the king and his absence reflects the vulnerability of the king. The ritual was directed in part to the personal god of the king because the ritual is concerned not only with the human being in his role as king but also with the king as an individual person; therefore, there is a need to strengthen and protect not only kingship but also the individual himself.

We understand Ambos's work as providing a historical context in which to understand the occurrence of the personal gods in these texts and the request addressed to the high gods that they reconcile the personal gods with the king. But even with this new contextual explanation, the texts sometimes seem not to be coherent. In any case, we should not ignore the fact that the occurrence of the personal god occasionally disrupts the flow or coherence of the prayers. This lack of coherence suggests that the portion of the prayer focusing on the anger of the personal god and/or on the request that the high god reconcile the angry personal god with his protégé is an insertion into a prayer addressed to a high god. Actually, our proposal probably applies to a body of prayers and, at the very least, suggests a broad revision of a number of *šuilla*s and the

* My thanks to the students in my Advanced Akkadian class in fall 2016 with whom I read the prayers to Gula. I am especially grateful to Jared Pfost, my research assistant in 2016–2017, for his suggestions.

1 C. Ambos, *Der König im Gefängnis und das Neujahrsfest im Herbst: Mechanismen der Legitimation des babylonischen Herrschers im 1. Jahrtausend v. Chr. und ihre Geschichte* (Dresden: Islet, 2013); see especially sections 11.3.3.8–11.3.3.9.

 | DOI:10.1163/9789004435186_015

addition to them of the request that the high god reconcile the personal god(s) with the petitioner.

I discussed the general problem in a paper delivered in April 2017 at Harvard University, at a workshop entitled "Approaching a Critique of Mesopotamian Reason" and organized by Gösta Gabriel.[2] In the context of the aforementioned investigation, I compared the manuscripts of all relevant individual *šuilla*s. I also examined related compositions addressed to the same god to see if all versions of a prayer contained the theme of reconciliation. Here I should like to discuss some of the results of my examination of versions of *šuilla* prayers to Gula and to make some observations regarding the relationship of the versions of this prayer to each other. I should begin by noting that the two versions of the *šuilla* to the goddess Gula (1a and 1b) both contain the theme of reconciliation. This theme is secondary to both prayers.

There are several first-millennium BCE Akkadian *šuilla*s addressed to the goddess Gula. In the texts to be examined here, Gula 1a and Gula 1b, the goddess is presented less as a goddess of healing and more as a goddess able to carry out intercessions.[3] The two *šuilla*s are related to each other, a fact that was noted previously by Cecil J. Mullo-Weir, Walter Kunstmann, and Werner Mayer.[4] The similarities between Gula 1a and Gula 1b are overwhelming. The two prayers will be treated here as versions of one composition.

Let us begin with a presentation of the two compositions in parallel columns:

---

2 The conference proceedings are published in a special issue of the *Journal of Ancient Near Eastern History*. See T. Abusch, "Reconciliation of Angry Personal Gods." In light of my discussion there (64–65 n. 12 [[184–185 n. 17]]) of the possibility that the theme "the request to a high god to bring about reconciliation with the personal god" in the *šuillas* is derived from an earlier second-millennium BCE source, as well as my examination there of *CTH* 372–374, see C. Metcalf, "New Parallels in Hittite and Sumerian Praise of the Sun," *WO* 41 (2011): 168–176; C. Metcalf, "Old Babylonian Religious Poetry in Anatolia: From Solar Hymn to Plague Prayer," *ZA* 105 (2015): 42–53 (my thanks to D. Schwemer for these two references).

3 Actually, in several manuscripts of one of our texts, Gula 1a, she is referred to not as Gula but as *bēlet ilī* "mistress of the gods," a birthing goddess.

4 See C. J. Mullo-Weir, "Four Hymns to Gula," *JRAS* 1 (1929): 4; W. G. Kunstmann, *Die babylonische Gebetsbeschwörung*, LSS NF 2 (Leipzig: Hinrichs, 1932), 89–90; W. R. Mayer, *Untersuchungen zur Formensprache der babylonischen "Gebetsbeschwörungen,"* StPohl, series maior 5 (Rome: Pontifical Biblical Institute, 1976), 455. For editions of the two texts, see Mayer, *Untersuchungen*, 450–457.

| Gula 1a | Gula 1b |
| --- | --- |
| 71. ÉN *Gula bēltu šurbūtu ummu rēmēnītu āšibat šamê ellūti* | 10. ÉN *Gula bēltu šurbūtu āšibat šamê Anim* |
| | 11. *[ilt]u rēmēnītu qāišat bal[āṭi]* |
| | 12. *ša naplussa tašmû qibīssa šu[lmu]* |
| 72. *alsīki bēltī izizzīmma šimî yâti* | 13. *alsīki bēltī izizzīmma šimî qabâ[ya]* |
| | 14. *ana dīni dâni purussâ parāsi ḫibilti šullumi* |
| 73. *ešēki asḫurki kīma sissikti iliya u ištariya sissiktaki aṣbat* | 15. *asḫurki ašēki sissiktaki aṣbat kīma sissikti iliya u iš[tariya]* |
| 74. *aššum dīni dâni purussâ parāsi* | 16. *dīni dīnī purussâya pursī alaktī lim[dī]* |
| 75. *aššum bulluṭu u šullumu bašû ittiki* | 17. *aššum eṭēra gamāla šūzuba tīd[e/ê]* |
| 76. *aššum eṭēra gamāla u šūzuba tīde/ê* | 18. *aššum bulluṭu šullumu bašû ittik[i]* |
| ——————— | ——————— |
| 77. *Gula bēltu šaqūtu ummu rēmēnītu* | |
| 78. *ina ma'dūti kakkabī šamāmī* | |
| 79. *bēltu kâši asḫurki ibšâki uznāya* | 19. *bēltu ana kâši atkalki šumki azk[ur]* |
| | 20. *ibšâki uznāya eṭrīnnima ilūtki lud[lul]* |
| 80. *masḫata muḫrīnnima liqê unnīnīya* | 21. *nīš qātāya muḫrīma liqê unnīn[īya]* |
| 81. *lušpurki ana iliya zenî ištariya zenīti* | 22. *lušpurki ana iliya zenî ištariya zenī[ti]* |
| 82. *ana ili āliya ša šabsuma kamlu ittiya* | 23. *ana ili āliya ša šabsu kamlu libbašu itt[iya]* |
| 83. *ina bīri u šutti ittanaškanamma* | 24. *ina šutti u bīri ittanaškan[amma]* |
| | 25. *ina lumun attalî Sîn ša ina arḫi annanna ūmi annanna šak[na]* |
| | 26. *lumun idāti ittāti lemnēti lā ṭā[bāti]* |
| | 27. *ša ina ekalliya u mātiya ibš[â]* |

| | | | |
|---|---|---|---|
| 84. | *palḫākuma atanamdaru* | 28. | *palḫāku adrāku u šutādurā[ku]* |
| 85. | *Gula bēltu šurbūtu ina amat qibītiki ṣīrti ša ina Ekur šurbât* | 29. | *ina amat qibītiki ṣīrti ša ina Ekur šu[rbât]* |
| 86. | *u anniki kīni ša lā enû* | 30. | *u anniki kīni ša lā en[û]* |
| 87. | *ilī šabsu litūra ištarī zenītu lissaḫr[a]* | 31. | *ilī šabsu litūra ištarī zenītu [lissaḫra]* |
| 88. | *il āliya ša šabsuma kamlu ittiya* | 32. | *il āliya Marduk ša īguga l[inūḫa]* |
| 89. | *ša īziza linūḫa ša īguga lippašra* | 33a. | *[š]a īzizu lipp[ašra]* |
| 90. | *Gula bēltu šurbūtu ṣābitat abbūt enši* | 33b. | *Gula bēltu šurbūtu um[mu rēmēnītu]* |
| 91a. | *ana Marduk šarri ilī bēlu rēmēnû* | 34. | *ana Marduk bēli r[ēmēnî mā]r rēštê ša [Ea]* |
| 91b. | *abbūtī ṣabtī qibî dameqt[ī]* | 35. | *abbūtī ṣabtī qibî [damiqtī]* |
| | | 36. | *šu-uš-ki-ni DA-[xxx] ...* |
| 92. | *ṣulūlki rapšu tayyārātūki kabt[ātu libš]ânimm[a]* | 37. | *ṣulūlki rapšu tayy[ārātūki kabtātu libšânimma]* |
| 93. | *gimil dumqi u balāṭi el[i]ya [šuknī]ma* | 38. | *gimil dumqi u ba[lāṭi eliya šuknīma]* |
| | | 39. | *dalīl ilūtiki [(...) ludlul]* |
| 94. | *narbîki lušāpi dalīlīki [ludlu]l* | 40. | *narbî ilūtiki [(...) lušāpi]* |

Translation:[5]

| **Gula 1a** | | **Gula 1b** | |
|---|---|---|---|
| 71. | Incantation: O Gula, supreme mistress, merciful mother who dwells in the pure heavens, | 10. | Incantation: O Gula, supreme mistress who dwells in the heavens of Anu, |
| | | 11. | Merciful goddess who bestows life, |

5 For recent translations of both versions, see M.-J. Seux, *Hymnes et prières aux dieux de Babylonie et d'Assyrie*, LAPO 8 (Paris: Éditions du Cerf, 1976), 337–339, for Gula 1a ("À Gula, 2, ou à Belet-ili"), and 335–337, for Gula 1b ("À Gula, 1"); for Gula 1a see also B. R. Foster, *Before the Muses: An Anthology of Akkadian Literature*, 3rd ed. (Bethesda, MD: CDL, 2005), 671–672.

| | |
|---|---|
| | 12. Whose glance is acquiescence, whose command is well-being, |
| 72. I call upon you, my mistress, stand by me and listen to me, | 13. I call upon you, my mistress, stand by me, listen to my utterance, |
| | 14. To judge the case, to render the verdict, to repair the damage, |
| 73. I seek you, I turn to you, like the hem of my (personal) god and my (personal) goddess I seize your hem, | 15. I turn to you, I seek you, I seize your hem like the hem of my (personal) god and (personal) goddess, |
| 74. Because judging the case, rendering the verdict | 16. Judge my case, render my verdict, grant me an (oracular) decision |
| 75. Because reviving and granting well-being are yours (to grant), | 17. Because you know how to save, spare, and rescue |
| 76. Because you know how to save, spare, and rescue, | 18. Because reviving and granting well-being are yours (to grant), |
| ——————— | ——————— |
| 77. O Gula, most elevated mistress, merciful mother, | |
| 78. Among the numerous stars of heaven, | |
| 79. O mistress, I turn to you, I am attentive to you | 19. O mistress, I trust you, I invoke your name, |
| | 20. I am attentive to you; save me so that I may praise your divinity, |
| 80. Accept from me a flour offering, receive my supplications, | 21. Accept my prayer and receive my supplications. |
| 81. Let me send you to my angry (personal) god and my angry (personal) goddess | 22. Let me send you to my angry (personal) god and my angry (personal) goddess, |
| 82. To the god of my city who is irate and furious with me, | 23. To the god of my city whose heart is irate and furious with me, |

| | |
|---|---|
| 83. On account of omens and dreams that constantly beset me, | 24. On account of dreams and omens that constantly beset me, |
| | 25. Because of the ominous eclipse of the moon that occurred in such-and-such a month, on such-and-such a day, |
| | 26. The evil outcome of evil, unfavorable signs and portents, |
| | 27. Which occurred in my palace and my land, |
| 84. I am fearful and continually troubled. | 28. I am fearful, troubled, and terrified. |
| ——————— | ——————— |
| 85. O Gula, supreme mistress, at the utterance of your exalted command which is supreme in Ekur | 29. At the utterance of your exalted command which is supreme in Ekur |
| 86. And of your assured approval which cannot be changed, | 30. And of your assured approval which cannot be changed |
| 87. May my irate (personal) god return to me, may my angry (personal) goddess turn back to me, | 31. May my irate (personal) god return to me, may my angry (personal) goddess turn back to me, |
| 88. May the god of my city who is irate and furious with me, | 32. May the god of my city, Marduk, who is incensed, become calm, |
| 89. Who is enraged, become calm, who is incensed, be soothed. | 33a. Who is enraged, be soothed. |
| ——————— | ——————— |
| 90. O Gula, supreme mistress, who intercedes for the weak, | 33b. O Gula, supreme mistress, merciful mother, |
| 91a. With Marduk, king of the gods, merciful lord, | 34. With Marduk, merciful lord, firstborn son of Ea, |
| 91b. intercede! Speak a favorable word! | 35. intercede! Speak a favorable word! |
| | 36. ... [ ] |
| 92. May your broad protection and your weighty forgiveness be upon me, | 37. May your broad protection and your weighty forgiveness be upon me, |

| Gula 1a | Gula 1b |
|---|---|
| 93. Accord me reward and life, | 38. Accord me reward and life, |
| | 39. Then will I sing the praise of your divinity |
| 94. Then will I declare your great deeds and sing your praise. | 40. And declare the great deeds of your divinity. |

The differences between Gula 1a and Gula 1b aside, the address to Gula may be summarized as follows: After invoking the goddess and asking her to heed him, the petitioner explains why he has turned to Gula. He affirms that she has the abilities to give judgment, to heal, and to save. After stating that he is turning to her, he asks her to attend to his request. He states that he wishes to send her to his angry personal gods and to the angry god of his city and asks that she cause all these gods to be reconciled with him by means of her powerful word. Invoking her again, the petitioner asks her to intercede on his behalf with Marduk. He ends with a general request for the goddess's help and a promise of praise.

The relationship of the two versions is not simply one of free variation wherein the person who recited the text felt free to introduce changes. Rather, the differences are deliberate, and the changes seem to be intentional. The issue before us is the nature of the relationship between Gula 1a and Gula 1b. Which of the two texts is the earlier and more original version?

The text of Gula 1a is more formal and more clearly articulated than that of Gula 1b. This includes the leveling through of significant elements. For example, the invocation: *Gula bēltu šurbūtu*, "Gula supreme mistress," occurs four times in Gula 1a, at the beginning of each section, whereas it occurs only twice in Gula 1b. Although these considerations suggest that Gula 1a is the later version, we need not rely on this feature alone to make our decision. I note that Gula 1a contains several formulations that reveal themselves as errors and/or as secondary, thus indicating that Gula 1a is the more developed version. Thus, before we assess the issue of the invocations in and the structure of the two versions, let us examine the other passages that point in this direction.

I begin with the phrase *dīna dânu purussâ parāsu*. It occurs in both versions: in Gula 1a it occurs once, in line 74; in Gula 1b, it occurs twice, in lines 14 and 16. Gula 1a has eliminated the duplication of *dīna dânu purussâ parāsu* found presently in Gula 1b 14 and 16 and has used only one of the occurrences; 1a joins the phrase to the two lines that begin with *aššum* and prefixes it with *aššum*:

74. *aššum dīni dâni purussâ parāsi*
75. *aššum bulluṭu u šullumu bašû ittiki*
76. *aššum eṭēra gamāla u šūzuba tīdê*

74. Because judging the case, rendering the verdict,
75. Because reviving and granting well-being are yours (to grant),
76. Because you know how to save, spare, and rescue.

That line 74 has been relocated is suggested by the fact that in contrast to the following two lines, both of which have a subject and a predicate, line 74 lacks the predicate.

There are at least two other indications that Gula 1a is a later development than Gula 1b. First, Gula 1a 79 has eliminated *šumki azkur*, "I invoke your name," found in Gula 1b 19 and has replaced *atkalki*, "I trust you," of that text with *asḫurki*, "I turn to you." The secondary nature of *asḫurki* in Gula 1a is indicated by the fact that *asḫurki* has already occurred in line 73 and by the fact that two of the manuscripts of Gula 1a (Mayer's mss. E [= Rm 96] and H [= Si 6]) have the same reading as Gula 1b (*at-kal-ki*). Second, it is possible that Gula 1a 90b *ṣābitat abbūt enši* is secondary because that quality is repeated as a request in Gula 1a 91b.[6]

We turn now to an examination of the invocation of the goddess and its implications. The specific arguments enumerated above in favor of Gula 1a representing a later development than Gula 1b are supported by the observation that Gula 1a is more formal, more clearly articulated and structured.[7] We note that Gula 1a 77–78 is absent in Gula 1b. That line 77 (*Gula bēltu šurbūtu ummu rēmēnītu*) in Gula 1a is an addition is indicated by the fact that *bēltu* is repeated in line 79 (note that Gula 1b has the equivalent of line 79 but not of lines 77–78). Similarly, the invocation occurs again in Gula 1a in line 85a but is absent in Gula 1b. The invocations in Gula 1a 77 and 85 are additions that agree with the structural formality of Gula 1a. That is to say, the prayer in Gula 1a begins each of its four sections with an invocation of Gula: *Gula bēltu šurbūtu* in lines 71, 77, 85, 90.

The invocation occurred originally only at the beginning of the prayer at Gula 1b 10 (= 1a 71) and at the beginning of the last part of the prayer at Gula 1b 33b (= 1a 90). The secondary presence of invocations in Gula 1a at lines 77 and 85 and their absence in Gula 1b support the impression that the prayer did not originally contain four sections. The two original parts of this prayer in both versions are the hymnic introduction (1a 71–76; 1b 10–18) and the request that Gula intercede with Marduk on behalf of the petitioner (1a 90–94; 1b 33b–40). Accordingly, the last part of the prayer would have been the original

6 It is more than possible that the restoration in Mayer's edition of Gula 1b (*um*[*mu rēmēnītu*]), if proven to be correct, is a better reading than Gula 1a's *ṣābitat abbūt enši*.

7 Thus, contrary to expectation, the more structured text is not the earlier version.

purpose of the prayer. Thus, a text with two sections has been expanded to four. The sections that are later developments are (1) the section that centers upon the statements that the petitioner is sending the goddess to his angry personal gods (and his city god) (1a 81–84; 1b 22–28 and the variants of the *attalû*-formula) and (2) the section asking that the alienated personal gods be reconciled (1a 85–89; 1b 29–33a).[8]

•••

In my estimation, the sections in which the petitioner states that he wishes to send the goddess Gula to his angry personal gods so that they relent and turn back to him were not an original part of either version of the Gula *šuilla* but were inserted into the prayer from which the two versions (Gula 1a and 1b) derive. I would guess that the theme of reconciliation was drawn by the original text of the Gula prayer from a text such as the *šuilla* Nisaba 1.[9]

By way of conclusion, I would bring our discussion back to the broader problem that precipitated my examination of Gula 1a and Gula 1b and suggest that the two versions of the prayer to Gula derive from a composition that did not contain sections dealing with the angry personal gods. These sections were secondarily inserted into the Gula Ur-text, one more indication that the statements about the anger of the personal gods in prayers to a high god are oftentimes secondary.

8 I should mention here that A. Lenzi recently published a text-critical study of the manuscripts of Gula 1a in "Scribal Revision and Textual Variation in Akkadian *Šuila*-Prayers: Two Case Studies in Ritual Adaptation," in *Empirical Models Challenging Biblical Criticism*, ed. R. F. Person and R. Rezetko, AIL 25 (Atlanta: SBL Press, 2016), 63–108. I agree with many of his specific observations, but find that I must disagree with his more general statement that "we cannot establish the chronological priority of specific variants to retrace the genealogy of revision. And yet these are the very kinds of things scholars often do with the biblical text" (107). He might have reached a different conclusion both for the Mesopotamian text and for the implications of his study for the history of the biblical text if he had also considered Gula 1b in his study.

9 For the text of Nisaba 1, see C. Frechette and I. Hrůša, "The Ritual-Prayer Nisaba 1 and Its Function," *JANER* 11 (2011): 70–93.

# PART 2

## *Literary Studies*

CHAPTER 15

# Fortune and Misfortune of the Individual: Some Observations on the Sufferer's Plaint in *Ludlul bēl nēmeqi* II 12–32

To address the topic of fortune and misfortune, I choose a text that protests against misfortune on the grounds that it is not deserved.[1] I have in mind the first part of *Ludlul bēl nēmeqi* Tablet II, where the speaker states that he has been beset with misfortune (line 11) as if he were one who was not observant and pious (lines 12–22), although in fact he is observant (lines 23–28) and even teaches the people to follow this example (lines 29–32). In this paper I am concerned with understanding only this part of his speech and the belief system conveyed by this section.

Of course, the point of *Ludlul* is to convey the notion that everything—misfortune and fortune—comes from Marduk and that all other forces and considerations are secondary.[2] Still, the sufferer's claim—even if it only represents a conventional position that is rendered obsolete by the end of the work—is of importance and is one that we must grasp if we are to understand the religious position replaced by the all-encompassing Marduk theism. The speaker starts from the premise that private behavior vis-à-vis one's personal gods (that is, one's family gods) is the cause of suffering. Our passage, as we shall see, expands this purview to include public behavior in regard to the cult of the city gods (that is, the public cult) and even to the king. The universal gods, generally, and Marduk, specifically, are not part of the purview of this passage. But when the work expands its outlook, focusing on Marduk and

1 Text and translation are based upon *BWL*, 38–41, and A. Annus and A. Lenzi, "*Ludlul bēl nēmeqi*": *The Standard Babylonian Poem of the Righteous Sufferer*, SAACT 7 (Helsinki: Neo-Assyrian Text Corpus Project, 2010), 19–20, 35, with modification. (This paper was written prior to the appearance of T. Oshima, *Babylonian Poems of Pious Sufferers*, ORA 14 [Tübingen: Mohr Siebeck, 2014]. As far as I can see, nothing there affects the observations and argumentation in this paper.)

2 On the role of Marduk in *Ludlul*, see, e.g., W. L. Moran, "The Babylonian Job," in *The Most Magic Word: Essays on Babylonian and Biblical Literature*, ed. R. S. Hendel, CBQMS 35 (Washington, DC: Catholic Biblical Association of America, 2002), 187, 193–195, and R. Albertz, "*Ludlul bēl nēmeqi*—eine Lehrdichtung zur Ausbreitung und Vertiefung der persönlichen Mardukfrömmigkeit," in *Ad bene et fideliter seminandum: Festgabe für Karlheinz Deller zum 21. Februar 1987*, ed. G. Mauer and U. Magen, AOAT 220 (Kevelaer: Butzon & Bercker; Neukirchen-Vluyn: Neukirchener Verlag, 1988), 34–35.

 | DOI:10.1163/9789004435186_016

treating him as the cause of suffering (in the introductory hymn) and deliverance from suffering (in Tablets III–IV), the place of the personal god does indeed change. But rather than Marduk becoming the personal god of the land (as Albertz has argued) and the personal gods disappearing, the personal gods remain but are seen as subservient to Marduk. The position of the work in this regard is similar to what we find stated in lines 28′–31′ of the Marduk prayer from Ugarit:

28′ [*ad*]*allal adallal š*[*a b*]*ēli*
29′ [(*ša*)] $^{d}$*Marduk adallal*
30′ [*ša i*]*li šabši adallal*
31′ [*ša*] $^{d}$*ištar zenīti adallal*

28′ I will praise, I will praise the (deeds) of the lord,
29′ [the (deeds) of] Marduk I will praise,
30′ [the (deeds) of] the angry (personal) god I will praise,
31′ [the (deeds) of] the irate (personal) goddess I will praise.[3]

We turn now to the text of *Ludlul*. The speech referred to earlier, lines 12–32, begins with the speaker's statement in lines 12–22 that he is being treated as if he were a person who is not observant and pious:

12 *kī ša tamqītu ana ili lā uktinnu*
13 *u ina mākālê* $^{d}$*ištari lā zakru*
14 *appi lā enû šukenni lā amru*
15 *ina pîšu ipparkû suppê u teslīti*
16 *ibṭilu ūmu ilī išēṭu eššēši*
17 *iddû ahšuma mêšunu imēšu*
18 *palāḫu u it'udu lā ušalmedu nišīšu*
19 *ilšu lā izkuru* (var. *izkur*) *īkulu* (var. *ēkul*) *akalšu*
20 *īzbu* (var. *īzib*) $^{d}$*ištartašu maṣḫatu lā ūbla* (var. *ūblu*)
21 *ana ša imḫû bēlšu imšû*
22[a] *nīš ilišu kabti qalliš izkuru*
22[b] *anāku amšal* (or possibly: *amrāk*)

3 For Nougayrol's copy of the text, see J. Nougayrol et al., eds., *Ugaritica* 5 (Paris: Paul Geuthner, 1968), 435, no. 162; for his transliteration and translation of lines 28′–31′, see 268–269. Nougayrol restores *ša* in the break at the beginning of line 29′, but if we follow W. von Soden, "Bemerkungen zu einigen literarischen Texten in akkadischer Sprache aus Ugarit," *UF* 1 (1969): 191 (for his translation, see 192), who assumes that nothing is missing at the beginning of line 29′, we would then translate lines 28′–29′: "I will praise, I will praise, the (deeds) of the lord Marduk I will praise."

12 Like one who had not made libations for (his) god,
13 And did not invoke (his) goddess at a meal,
14 Who did not engage in prostration, was not practiced in bowing down,
15 From whose mouth supplication and prayer had ceased,
16 Who abandoned the day of the gods, disregarded the festival,
17 Became negligent and despised their rites,
18 Did not teach his people to reverence and to pay heed,
19 Who did not invoke his god when he ate his food,
20 And abandoned his goddess, did not bring a flour-offering,
21 Like one who raved(?) and forgot his lord,
22a And invoked the solemn oath of his god in vain,
22b (Like such a one) do I appear.

Problems in this portion of text render it difficult to determine the ideational structure of lines 12–22, to determine, that is, the specific ideas conveyed by the ordering of these lines.

Lines 12–22 depend on the opening *kī* of line 12, and we immediately notice that lines 12–13 and 19–20 seem to be saying the same thing.[4]

12–13 *kī ša tamqītu ana ili lā uktinnu / u ina mākālê* $^{d}$*ištari lā zakru //*
19–20 *ilšu lā izkuru īkulu akalšu / īzbu* $^{d}$*ištartašu maṣḫatu lā ūbla*

12–13 Like one who had not made libations for (his) god / And did not invoke (his) goddess at a meal //
19–20 Who did not invoke his god when he ate his food / And abandoned his goddess, did not bring a flour-offering

4 As an aside, I should mention that lines 12–13 and 19–20 are excellent exemplifications of one of the functions of synonymous parallelism. They demonstrate how "synonymous" parallelism may serve not simply to represent the same thing twice or to repeat something and emphasize it, but rather to create a fuller picture by associating different parts of a scene with the different subjects. Libation/offering and invocation of the deity's name at a meal are the two modes of service for both the male and the female personal gods; the different aspects of service are split between the god and goddess in these two passages as a way of presenting a picture of the whole service, and not because each of the two deities receives only one or another part of the service. This use of parallelism is especially clear here: for while libation is associated with the male deity and invocation with the female deity in lines 12–13, the reverse is the case in lines 19–20, where invocation is associated with the male and offering with the female. Note especially the association of the verb *zakāru* with the goddess in line 13 but with the god in line 19.

On closer observation, we notice that lines 12–13 and 19–20 form what seems to be a frame around lines 14–18. But we also notice that the frame is unbalanced. For while, as expected, its beginning opens the section of comparisons, its end does not close it, but is itself followed by lines 21–22. Additionally, while both lines in the couplet 12–13 contain a single clause, the immediately following couplet, lines 14–15, begins with a line that contains two clauses. Moreover, and more generally, the poetic and syntactic pattern of lines 14–22a is contradicted by lines 12–13: For while lines 12–13 form a couplet, each line containing a single clause, lines 14–22a represent an expansion of verse types, with a concomitant increase of clause types.[5] Thus, whereas lines 12–13 simply parallel each other, the poetic and syntactic structure of lines 14–22a create a progression of sorts.

The imbalance of lines 12–13 // 19–20 and the poetic and syntactic contradiction between lines 12–13 and lines 14–22a suggest that portions of lines 14–22 were added to the text. We must determine which lines were added to lines 14–22; moreover, the imbalance of the frame requires that we also ask: Why and when was the frame set into our text? Were both couplets of the frame inserts, or was one an insert and the other part of the "original" text?

To confirm our original impression and to answer these questions, we must subject our text to a closer examination. A solution is perhaps forthcoming from a comparison of lines 12–22 with lines 23–28 and 29–32. For the segments comprising lines 23–28 and 29–32 are paralleled to a large extent by those in lines 14–18. But before making use of lines 14–18, we should first comment further on their poetic and grammatical form.[6] As noted above, these five lines should probably be divided into two poetic verses: 14–15 and 16–18—a couplet

5 Thus, lines 14–15 form a couplet: line 14 contains two clauses, line 15 contains a single clause. Lines 16–18 form a triplet: line 16 contains two clauses, line 17 contains two connected clauses, line 18 contains a single clause. Lines 19–22 seem to form a quatrain: line 19 contains two clauses, line 20 contains two clauses, line 21 contains two clauses (one independent and one subordinate), line 22a contains a single clause.

6 One of the first times that I taught *Ludlul* II—probably in the mid-1980s—I noticed and worked out the complex grammatical and poetic structure of the first part of the tablet. Very soon thereafter I discovered E. Reiner's detailed formalistic analysis of the grammatical form of the text in *Your Thwarts in Pieces, Your Mooring Rope Cut: Poetry from Babylonia and Assyria*, Michigan Studies in the Humanities 5 (Ann Arbor: University of Michigan Press, 1985), 106–108. Reiner concludes her study of the first part of *Ludlul* II with the statement: "To sum up, in this strophe each line contains at least one verbal predicate, and some lines contain two, one in each hemistich. It is the placement of the predicate within the line and in relation to the predicates of the other lines that gives variety to the diction. That this variety is not an accident, nor required by the syntactic structure of the language, becomes apparent when we look ..." (107–108). What is missing, of course, is some explanation of the form, beyond an observation about linguistic variety. I would like here to suggest some thoughts

followed by a triplet. But the expansion is not created simply by the addition of a single line to the second verse. Rather, while each verse starts with a line containing two grammatically short clauses, i.e., two hemistichs (14 *appi lā enû šukenni lā amru*; 16 *ibṭilu ūmu ilī išēṭu eššēši*), and ends with a line containing one grammatically long clause (15 *ina pîšu ipparkû suppê u teslīti*; 18 *palāḫu u itʾudu lā ušalmedu nišīšu*), at the center of the second verse a line is added that contains two clauses that are connected by an enclitic *-ma* (17 *iddû aḫšuma mêšunu imēšu*). Thus, line 17 is tighter than line 16, a line that like line 17 contains two clauses, but looser than line 18, a line with one clause. The pattern seems to represent a buildup of thought. The form of lines 14–18 seems to represent, or to suggest, a movement and buildup from personal gods to city gods to king.

We may now turn to the comparison of lines 12–22 with lines 23–28 and 29–32. Lines 23–28 read:

23 *aḫsusma ramāni suppê u teslīti*
24 *teslītu tašīmat niqû sakkûʾa*
25 *ūmu palāḫ ilī ṭūb libbiya*
26 *ūmu ridûti ištar nēmeli tatturru*
27 *ikribi šarri šī ḫidûti*
28 *u nigûtašu ana dameqti šumma*

23 But I, for my part, was attentive to supplication and prayer,
24 Prayer was common sense, sacrifice my rule.
25 The day to reverence the gods was a delight to my heart,
26 The day of the goddess's procession was profit and gain.
27 The king's prayer: it was a pleasure,
28 And his fanfare was truly a delight.

Lines 29–32 read:

29 *ušāri ana matiya mê ili naṣari*
30 *šūmi ištari šūquru nišīya uštāhiz*
31 *tanadāti šarri iliš umaššil*
32 *u puluḫti ekalli ummān ušalmid*

about what the form of the text conveys as well as to speculate about how the text took on its present form.

29 I taught my land to observe the rites of the god,
30 I instructed my people to esteem the name of the goddess.
31 I made my praises of the king like those of a god,
32 And taught the masses reverence for the palace.

While in lines 12–22 the sufferer states that he is treated as one who is not observant and pious, in lines 23–32 he asserts that, to the contrary, he is observant and pious—that is, in lines 23–28 he states that his actions are those of one who is observant and pious and in lines 29–32 he states that he teaches this behavior to his people. The sufferer serves his personal gods, his "city" gods, and his king. Many of the same themes and terms recur in lines 14–18, 23–28, and 29–32. Thus, as regards identical or near identical terms, note *suppê teslīti* in lines 15 and 23 (and *teslīti* in line 24); *tamqītu* in line 12 and *niqû* in line 24; *ūmu ilī* in line 16 and *ūmu palāḫ ilī* in line 25; *mêšunu* in line 17 and *mê ilī* in line 29; *palāḫu* in line 18 and *puluḫti* in line 32; *ušalmedu* in line 18 and *ušalmid* in line 32.

A comparison of the three segments yields, in tabular form, the (tentative) results as regards their relationship:

| | **Sufferer's personal actions (23–28)** | **Sufferer's teaching (29–32)** | **Sufferer's treatment (14–18)**[a] |
|---|---|---|---|
| Service to personal gods/personal piety | 23–24[b] | —— | 14–15 |
| Service to city gods | 25–26 | 29–30 | 16–17 |
| Service to king | 27–28 | 31–32 | 18[c] |

a It appears that the composer here combined in one section (lines 14–18) the themes of the sufferer's actions and teaching, for while lines 14–17 compare him to one who has not performed the correct actions, line 18 compares him to one who has not taught reverence for the palace (see below). Thus, the speaker emphasizes that he is treated as one who neither acts nor teaches properly.

b I take lines 14–15 and 23–24 as referring to the service of the personal god. If, instead, these lines refer to the city cult, then the city cult and the palace are the referents of lines 14–18 and 23–28 // 29–32 (and this would explain why the segment 29–32 makes no mention of the personal god). See below.

c That line 18 deals with the palace is indicated by the verbal parallels between lines 18 and 32 (that is to say: line 32 clearly deals with the palace; accordingly, line 18 should probably be understood in the same way). But if line 18 is part of a poetic verse (lines 16–18) dealing with the public cult, perhaps the composer intended to combine the public cult and reverence for the king by combining line 18 with lines 16–17.

Notice the horizontal and vertical axes on the chart. On the horizontal axis, lines 23–28 deal with the sufferer's personal actions, lines 29–32 deal with the sufferer's teaching, and lines 14–18 deal with the sufferer's treatment. On the vertical axis, each segment treats in order the several themes of service: lines 23–24 // —— // 14–15 treat service to the personal gods/personal piety; lines 25–26 // 29–30 // 16–17 treat service to the city gods; lines 27–28 // 31–32 // 18 treat service to the king.

It is reasonable to suppose that some of the problems in our text, especially the imbalance of the two halves of the frame in lines 12–20 and the differences between the syntactic structures of lines 12–13 and 14–22, are indicators of change in the text. The parallel structures of lines 14–18 // 23–28 // 29–32 and, specifically, the pattern (most clear in lines 23–28) of personal god–city god–king suggest that the same pattern existed in lines 12–22 and that the repetition of the personal god theme in lines 19–20 is secondary, for it disrupts this pattern. Accordingly, we may suggest the following stages of development for our passage: Lines 4–5,[7] 12–13, and 22b (or 22), treating the issue of the personal gods, were an original part of the text; subsequently, lines 14–18[8] (and possibly also line 21) were introduced into the text on the model of lines 23–28 and 29–32; thereafter, a section dealing with the personal gods (lines 19–20 [or 19–22a]) was added in order to refocus attention on the personal gods—gods who had already been introduced in lines 4–5 and 12–13—thereby creating the frame 12–13 // 19–20.[9]

Further support for the supposition that the latter part of the frame (lines 19–20), rather than its first part (lines 12–13), was secondary is suggested by the way the gods are mentioned in these lines: Whereas lines 4–5 and 12–13 have in common the usage *ilu* and *ištaru* without pronominal suffixes when referring to the personal gods, lines 19–20 add third-person pronominal suffixes to both and have *ištartu* instead of *ištaru*, and thus differ from both lines 4–5 and 12–13. It is true that often personal gods are specified by means of

7 Lines 4–5 read: *ila alsīma ul iddina pānīšu / usalli ištari ul ušaqqâ rēšīša*, "I called to (my) god, but he did not turn his face to me / I prayed to (my) goddess, but she did not lift her head to me."

8 The poetic/syntactic form of lines 14–18 represents the movement and buildup from personal gods to city gods to king.

9 Our conclusion emerges even stronger if we take lines 14–15 and 23–24 as referring to the city cult. If so, the theme of the personal god in lines 4–5 and 12–13 was extended to include the city god and the king by the addition of lines 23–28 // 29–32, and then by the addition of lines 14–18 as a parallel to lines 23–28 // 29–32. After expanding its purview to include the city gods and the king, the text added a section dealing with the personal gods (19–20 or 19–22a) in order to refocus on the personal gods. But note that our conclusion remains valid whether or not lines 14–15 and 23–24 refer to the personal gods or to the city gods.

pronominal suffixes. But if, as I have argued, lines 4–5 and 12–13 were original to the text, there would have been no need to include suffixes because no other gods were mentioned (and this might be further support for the originality of these lines). The personal gods in lines 19–20, on the other hand, were mentioned only after the introduction of other gods in lines 14–18 and therefore required specification.

Furthermore, some of the manuscripts of lines 19–20 do not have the expected subjunctive ending—suggesting that these lines were added and were only later integrated into the text (by the addition of the required subjunctive ending). Line 22a may well have been added together with or after lines 19–20—their connection is signaled by the occurrence of *izkuru* in lines 19 and 22. Line 21 also seems to have been a later addition in view of *ana ša*; given *kī ša* in line 12, *ana ša* is superfluous and makes the line appear as if it derived from a different source.[10]

We have analyzed the passage and tried to trace its history. But, by way of conclusion, we may now ask: If the original text dealt with the personal gods, why were the city gods and the king added first in lines 23–28 and 29–32 and then carried over to lines 14–18? Certainly, the addition indicates that it is not sufficient to serve only one's personal god, but service of the city god and even of the king does not solve the problem of the sufferer. There is, I think, a further and more important purpose behind this portion of text. The service of Marduk takes precedence over all other forms of service. The text adds the images of city gods and royalty to those of the personal gods in order to add greater nuance and complexity to the character of Marduk. Marduk will now possess the features not only of personal gods but also of city/national gods and kings. As I stated earlier, Marduk was not simply turned into the personal god of the land by our text. Whatever religious and theological developments and changes accompany the elevation of Marduk, the personal god, the city god, and human government remain and do not disappear. Rather, Marduk now subsumes all authorities in his person and rule, and the personal god, the city god, and the human king become embodiments of aspects of Marduk's nature.

10 But note that *bēlšu* in this line could refer either to a personal god or to a king. If I am right that lines 19–20 are secondary, the possible contiguity of lines 21 and 18 at an earlier stage of the text and the reference of line 18 to the palace (of the king) would suggest that *bēl* in line 21 also refers to a king. At the risk of circular reasoning, I would only add that the inference that both lines 18 and 21 seem to refer to the king suggests that line 21 was part of the text prior to the addition of lines 19–20.

CHAPTER 16

# Kingship in Ancient Mesopotamia: The Case of *Enūma eliš*

At the conference "The Body of the 'King,'" which was devoted to the study of the image and institution of the king in Europe and Asia, I reviewed the papers on kingship in Mesopotamia and Egypt.* In addition, I decided to take up a well-known Mesopotamian treatment of kingship to see if the reading of that text in the kind of sophisticated intellectual context created by this conference on kingship (with its emphasis on the body of the king) might not enhance our understanding of such a treatment. Accordingly, I shall comment here in general terms on the well-known composition *Enūma eliš*, "When on High." This composition is surely one of the major statements of Mesopotamian mythology, religion, and political thought. It was written either in the early first millennium BCE (as I have previously argued)[1] or perhaps earlier in the late second millennium, but drew on older traditions.

*Enūma eliš* is usually viewed as a work focusing upon the creation of the cosmos, the placement of Babylon in the center of the divine world, and the elevation of Marduk to the position of ruler of the gods. Of course, the work legitimates the rule of both the divine and the human king.[2] So, here,

---

* This essay was presented at the conference in 2011 and submitted in 2012; I have not been able to take account of recent publications on *Enūma eliš* such as W. G. Lambert's important new edition in *Babylonian Creation Myths*, MC 16 (Winona Lake, IN: Eisenbrauns, 2013). For the review of papers on kingship in Mesopotamia and Egypt mentioned in the first sentence of the essay, see T. Abusch, "Comments on the Opening Session: Ancient Mesopotamia and Egypt," in *The Body of the King: The Staging of the Body of the Institutional Leader from Antiquity to Middle Ages in East and West. Proceedings of the Meeting Held in Padova, July 6th–9th, 2011*, ed. G. B. Lanfranchi and R. Rollinger, HANE/M 16 (Padua: S.A.R.G.O.N. Editrice e Libreria, 2016), 65–68.

1 See T. Abusch, "Marduk," in *Dictionary of Deities and Demons in the Bible*, ed. K. van der Toorn et al., 2nd ed. (Leiden: Brill, 1999), 543–549, esp. 547–548 [[99–107, esp. 104–106]].

2 Cf., e.g., A. Annus, *The Standard Babylonian Epic of Anzu: Introduction, Cuneiform Text, Transliteration, Score, Glossary, Indices and Sign List*, SAACT 3 (Helsinki: Neo-Assyrian Text Corpus Project, 2001), xxxiii, with reference to N. Wyatt, "Arms and the King: The Earliest Allusions to the *Chaoskampf* Motif and their Implications for the Interpretation of the Ugaritic and Biblical Traditions," in *"Und Mose schreib dieses Lied auf": Studien zum Alten Testament und zum alten Orient. Festschrift für Oswald Loretz zur Vollendung seines 70. Lebensjahres*, ed. M. Dietrich and I. Kottsieper, AOAT 250 (Münster: Ugarit-Verlag, 1998), 839–841, 848–849.

 | DOI:10.1163/9789004435186_017

I should like to look at it in terms of kingship; for in addition to everything else, it contains a Mesopotamian theory of the evolution of kingship and presents that theory through the story of Marduk. It is a monument to kingship, certainly one of the most important formulations of the Mesopotamian understanding of the person and role of the king.

The identification of the Mesopotamian king with Marduk is not simply a construct of the modern imagination; in antiquity the king was already identified with Marduk and even with his battle against Tiāmat. This identification is evident from various rituals and commentaries (e.g., SAA 3, no. 37); yet one of the more interesting reflexes of this identification is found in an account of Sennacherib's eighth campaign, for there the composer of this inscription drew some of his descriptions from *Enūma eliš*, and the king was identified with Marduk (or, more probably, Aššur in this instance), and his enemies with the opponents of this god.[3]

What I should like to do here, then, is follow the story of Marduk as it pertains to the birth, body, personality, role, behavior, and office of a king, for through this story *Enūma eliš* educated the king and his subjects. In terms of the education of a king, this work serves purposes that are not so very different from those of the Epic of Gilgamesh. Elsewhere, I have argued that the story underlying the Epic of Gilgamesh is that of a hunter; the values and characteristics exemplified thereby are those that need to be conveyed to and embodied by a king. There the images and experiences of hunting serve to educate a crown prince and to teach him how to act as a king.[4] To a similar end, *Enūma eliš* invites the identification of the king with the god Marduk; the story and qualities of Marduk are meant to be conveyed to and embodied by a Mesopotamian king.

I shall first outline the overall story of *Enūma eliš* and then look in more depth at the story of Marduk. Beginning with a formless world in which only the principles of water—Tiāmat and Apsû—existed, the text first describes the emergence of the generation of one family or succession of gods—the line from Laḫmu to Ea. Apsû finds their activities burdensome and wishes to destroy his offspring. Instead Ea overcomes him and establishes his home

3 See E. Weissert, "Creating a Political Climate: Literary Allusions to *Enūma Eliš* in Sennacherib's Account of the Battle of Halule," in *Assyrien im Wandel der Zeiten: XXXIX^e Rencontre Assyriologique Internationale, Heidelberg 6.–10. Juli 1992*, ed. H. Waetzoldt and H. Hauptmann, HSAO 6 (Heidelberg: Heidelberger Orientverlag, 1997), 191–202.

4 See T. Abusch, "Hunting in the Epic of Gilgamesh: Speculations on the Education of a Prince," in *Treasures on Camels' Humps: Historical and Literary Studies from the Ancient Near East Presented to Israel Eph'al*, ed. M. Cogan and D. Kahn (Jerusalem: Magnes, 2008), 11–20 [[*Gilgamesh*, 166–176]].

upon Apsû. In his new home, Ea fathers Marduk. Marduk is a precocious and active child and causes turmoil around him. The unnamed other gods, those gods who are outside the line of Marduk's direct ancestors, are bothered and approach Tiāmat with the demand that she take up arms. She acquiesces with alacrity to their request and mounts an army of gods and newly created monsters. She declares war on the aforementioned line of gods. First Ea, and then Anu are sent by Anšar to subdue Tiāmat, but are unable to do so. Ea enjoins his son Marduk to volunteer to serve as the champion of the gods. This he does, but he also sets the condition that the assembly of the gods give him the power of supreme command, the power to ordain destiny. Marduk is hailed as king and goes forth in battle. He overcomes Tiāmat and her host. He then creates the universe from his defeated enemies and organizes the gods. The gods build Babylon and Esağila for Marduk and make it into the center of the universe. They now declare Marduk to be lugal.dimmer.an.ki.a, "king of the gods of the heavens and the netherworld."

Turning now to an examination of the image of Marduk himself, I believe that we may read the office of kingship and the person of the king in the description and the story of the god, though to be sure it is the institutional figure that is represented, not the person of an individual king. From his birth on, the text presents Marduk as if he were a king, that is, in terms of the Mesopotamian conception of kingship. It thereby intends to present a set of values regarding kingship and the king, to educate the king and community in those values, and to cause the prince and king to identify with the role of king as represented by the god. Allow me, therefore, to set out the main terms in which kingship is presented.[5]

## 1 Divine Origin and Physical Features

In the dwelling that Ea created upon Apsû, Marduk is born to Ea and Damkina:

> In the cella of destinies, the abode of designs,
> The most capable, the sage of the gods, the Lord was begotten,
> In the midst of Apsû Marduk was formed,
> In the midst of holy Apsû was Marduk formed!
> Ea his father begot him,
> Damkina his mother was confined with him.

5 I cite the translation of *Enūma eliš* in B. R. Foster, *Before the Muses: An Anthology of Akkadian Literature*, 3rd ed. (Bethesda, MD: CDL, 2005), 436–486.

He suckled at the breast of goddesses,
The attendant who raised him endowed him well with glories.
His body was magnificent, fiery his glance,
He was a hero at birth, he was a mighty one from the beginning!
When Anu his grandfather saw him,
He was happy, he beamed, his heart was filled with joy.
He perfected him, so that his divinity was strange,
He was much greater, he surpassed them in every way.
His members were fashioned with cunning beyond comprehension,
Impossible to conceive, too difficult to visualize:
Fourfold his vision, fourfold his hearing,
When he moved his lips a fire broke out.
Formidable his fourfold perception,
And his eyes, in like number, saw in every direction.
He was tallest of the gods, surpassing in form,
His limbs enormous, he was surpassing at birth. (I 79–100)

Similar to descriptions of kings, Marduk is here presented as being of divine birth, having been raised by divine nurses, and having superlative physical and emotional qualities. One recalls the description of Eanatum from the third millennium in the Stele of the Vultures:

> [The god Ni]n[ĝir]su [imp]lanted the [semen] for E-[a]natum in the [wom]b.... The goddess Inanna ... set him on the special knee of the goddess Ninḫursaĝ. The goddess Ninḫursaĝ [offered him] her wholesome breast. The god Ninĝirsu rejoiced over E-anatum, semen implanted in the womb by the god Ninĝirsu. The god Ninĝirsu laid his span upon him, for (a length of) five forearms he set his forearm upon him: (he measured) five forearms (cubits), one span! The god Ninĝirsu, with great joy, [gave him] the kin[gship of Lagaš].[6]

According to this description, Eanatum was of divine origin, suckled by a goddess, and 2.75 m or 9′2″ tall.[7] It is of interest to notice that in the Israelite accounts of the emergence of kingship, it is said of the first king, Saul, that "no

6 RIME 1.9.3.1: iv 9–v 17 (pp. 129–130).

7 For the birth of kings in the third millennium, see C. Wilcke, "Vom göttlichen Wesen des Königtums und seinem Ursprung im Himmel," in *Die Sakralität von Herrschaft: Herrschaftslegitimierung im Wechsel der Zeiten und Räume*, ed. F.-R. Erkens (Berlin: Akadamie, 2002), 70. For the measurement, see J. S. Cooper, *Presargonic Inscriptions*, vol. 1 of *Sumerian and Akkadian Royal Inscriptions*, AOSTS 1 (New Haven: American Oriental Society, 1986), 38 n. 7.

one among the Israelites was handsomer than he; he was a head taller than any of the people" (1 Sam 9:2). This description is repeated even in a parallel text that seems to be anti-monarchic (1 Sam 10:23).

## 2 Kingship over His Own Family

Prior to going to battle against Tiāmat, Marduk is chosen as king:

> When the gods his fathers saw what he had commanded,
> Joyfully they hailed, "Marduk is king!"
> They bestowed in full measure scepter, throne, and reign. (IV 27–29)

This account parallels third-millennium accounts of kings who are of divine birth but only become king when they are chosen from among the people: for example, Enmetena, Uruinimgina, Gudea, and Urnammu.[8] Marduk has been chosen by his fathers and becomes king of a clan of gods.

## 3 The Battle

Marduk confronts his enemies in battle:

> The Lord drew near to see the battle of Tiāmat,
> He was looking for the stratagem of Qingu her spouse.
> As he[9] looked, his tactic turned to confusion,
> His reason was overthrown, his actions panicky,
> And as for the gods his allies, who went at his side,
> When they saw the valiant vanguard, their sight failed them. (IV 65–70)

But Tiāmat does not fear:

> She was beside herself, she turned into a maniac.
> Tiāmat shrieked loud, in a passion,
> Her frame shook all over, down to the ground. (IV 88–90)

8 For the choice of these men as king, see the texts cited by Wilcke, "Vom göttlichen Wesen," 68–69, and his discussion there; cf. J. N. Postgate, *Early Mesopotamia: Society and Economy at the Dawn of History*, rev. ed. (London: Routledge, 1994), 268–270. For editions of the texts referring to Enmetena and Uruinimgina, see now also RIME 1.9.5.18: i 1″–8″ (p. 222), and RIME 1.9.9.1: vii 29–viii 9 (pp. 261–262) (as well as RIME 1.9.9.2: iv 1–8 [p. 267]).

9 According to Foster, *Before the Muses*, 459 n. 3, "presumably Qingu is meant."

When Tiāmat becomes enraged, she opens herself up to attack. Attack her Marduk does. And he is victorious.

In contrast to Qingu, Marduk is courageous. But to be victorious, it is not enough to be courageous, one must also remain free from agitation. Thus, in contrast to Tiāmat, Marduk remains calm and collected. He is an effective fighter. The values of a heroic warrior are conveyed by Marduk's stance and disposition. Marduk is the heroic warrior and the model for the king as hero and warrior.

## 4 Creation

Subsequent to his victory, Marduk builds and organizes the cosmos and the gods. For example:

> The Lord calmed down, he began inspecting her carcass,
> That he might divide(?) the monstrous lump and fashion artful things.
> He split her in two, like a fish for drying,
> Half of her he set up and made as a cover, heaven.
> He stretched out the hide and assigned watchmen,
> And ordered them not to let her waters escape.
> He crossed heaven, he inspected (its) firmament,
> He made a counterpart to Apsû, the dwelling of Nudimmud. (IV 135–141)

The king must also deal with that which he has conquered. Here, too, Marduk is a model for human kingship, the king as builder.

## 5 Kingship over the Universe

After building and organizing the universe, Marduk is again declared king:

> Laḫmu and Laḫamu [ ]
> Made ready to speak and [said to] the Igigi-gods,
> "Formerly [Mar]duk was 'our beloved son,'
> Now he is your king, pay heed to his command."
> Next all of them spoke and said,
> "'Lugaldimmerankia' is his name, trust in him!" (V 107–112)

> Then the great gods convened,
> They made Marduk's destiny highest, they prostrated themselves.
> They laid upon themselves a curse (if they broke the oath),
> With water and oil they swore, they touched their throats.
> They granted him exercise of kingship over the gods,
> They established him forever for lordship of heaven and netherworld. (VI 95–100)

Marduk was required to defeat Tiāmat and her armies in order to carry out the mandate of the kingship given to him prior to the battle. But that earlier kingship was awarded without a temporal limitation. Why was it then necessary for him to be awarded kingship a second time?[10] What is the difference between the two kingships? A solution to the problem of Marduk's two kingships is suggested, I think, by the fact that with his victory and ordering of the universe, he has created an empire that differs in essence and extent from the realm that he was initially given. The kingship bestowed upon him prior to the battle was a local or ethnic kingship; earlier he had assumed no more than the leadership of one group of gods, not of all the gods. He has now become the ruler of a universe, a universe that encompasses not only the ethnic center but also all known areas and all gods; he is now ruler of all the gods. This is the meaning of the second kingship that he assumes. Marduk goes from being king for a reign (*palû*) of a limited realm to being permanent (and therefore eternal) king of the gods of heaven and earth. He has become lugal.dimmer.an.ki.a, "king of the gods of the heavens and the netherworld." Marduk serves as a model here for

10 I am not the first to ask this question. This question is implicit in Thorkild Jacobsen's treatment of *Enūma eliš*; see, e.g., T. Jacobsen, *The Treasures of Darkness: A History of Mesopotamian Religion* (New Haven: Yale University Press, 1976), 180, 185. Jacobsen thought that while the first kingship was represented by the formula "security and obedience," and was no more than an emergency authority yielded by the gods under threat of attack, the second kingship bore the formula "benefits and obedience," and was granted to Marduk so that the gods might benefit from a permanent, true monarchy. As always, Jacobsen's reading is insightful. But his solution answers the question only partially. For, as I read the text, there are no temporal or situational limitations on the initial kingship. Marduk was not required, or even asked, to yield up the kingship. For him to remain king after the death of Tiāmat, neither a new declaration of allegiance nor a grant of a new mandate was required. Certainly the gods did not have to give him the kingship one more time. (I have not dealt in this essay with the "permanent kingship" of VI 92–100; see now T. Abusch, "Some Observations on the Babylon Section of the *Enūma Eliš*," *RA* 113 (2019): 171–173 [[233–237]].)

those Mesopotamian kings who were not only rulers of city-states, but also rulers of empires.

Marduk embodies the power and responsibility of kingship as well as the form, the disposition, and the emotions of the ideal king. By identifying with Marduk, the king learns and assumes these features and embodies the kingship of a permanent and enduring empire. An immortal god, Marduk, serves here as the exemplar for the human king, and his kingship serves as the exemplar for kingship. This ideal exists from generation to generation: The king is dead; long live the king!

CHAPTER 17

# Some Observations on the Babylon Section of *Enūma eliš*

In this note, I wish to make a few observations regarding the possibility that the text of *Enūma eliš* has undergone revision and to lay out the possible sections in the latter part of the epic that may be considered additions or "insertions."[1] My central contention here is that sections of the text dealing with the construction of the city Babylon (and related themes) were secondarily added to the text of *Enūma eliš*. I base this suggestion first and foremost on inconsistencies and unnecessary repetitions within the text. But allow me to note, here, that even with Lambert's new erudite edition, the text of *Enūma eliš* remains incomplete and, therefore, new textual finds may demonstrate that parts or the whole of the present suggestion is incorrect.

1 I decided to investigate the Babylon sections of *Enūma eliš* in the context of discussions regarding the intellectual life of Assyria with Eva Cancik-Kirschbaum in 2011 and 2012 (following the conference in Padua on "The Body of the King," in which we both participated). I have of course consulted the literature that has appeared since, especially W. G. Lambert, *Babylonian Creation Myths*, MC 16 (Winona Lake, IN: Eisenbrauns, 2013). This study makes use of Professor Lambert's last great work with great respect, even if occasionally I take a different approach to literary history. His mastery, erudition, and contribution to the field of Assyriology will be profoundly missed.

I began to give thought to the question of insertions at a time when I was contemplating the possibility that *Enūma eliš* might have been composed in Assyria. The obvious difficulty with any such reconstruction is the emphasis in *Enūma eliš* on the construction of the city Babylon; for that reason, I reexamined the relevant sections of *Enūma eliš*. I should emphasize here that my intention in this essay is to argue for the addition of the section dealing with the city Babylon and not to treat the question of Assyrian composition or redaction at all. For my previous attempts to understand the *Enūma eliš*, see T. Abusch, "Marduk," in *Dictionary of Deities and Demons in the Bible*, ed. K. van der Toorn et al., 2nd ed. (Leiden: Brill, 1999), 543–549, esp. 547–548 [[99–107, esp. 104–106]] (here, I would correct the impression given in Lambert, *Creation Myths*, 441 n. 10 that I favored a late second-millennium BCE date in that article, when in fact I was arguing for an early first-millennium BCE date), and T. Abusch, "Kingship in Ancient Mesopotamia: The Case of *Enūma Eliš*," in *The Body of the King: The Staging of the Body of the Institutional Leader from Antiquity to Middle Ages in East and West. Proceedings of the Meeting Held in Padova, July 6th–9th, 2011*, ed. G. B. Lanfranchi and R. Rollinger, HANE/M 16 (Padova: S.A.R.G.O.N. Editrice e Libreria, 2016), 59–64 [[225–232]].

 | DOI:10.1163/9789004435186_018

Lines giving expression to the intention to build Babylon occur twice, once in V 117–130, a second time in VI 47–64.[2] Scrutinizing these lines, one immediately notes a discrepancy. Whereas it is Marduk's idea to build Babylon in Tablet V, it is the idea of the Anunnaki in Tablet VI. Additionally, we note that the ziggurat of Babylon is intended in VI 64 ("And for Anu, Enlil, Ea and him they established it as a dwelling"[3]) not simply for Marduk but also for Anu, Enlil, and Ea.

Moreover, especially if we accept Landsberger's and Kinnier Wilson's reconstruction of the latter part of Tablet V,[4] it is difficult to understand how the end of Tablet V leads to Marduk's decision to create humanity at the beginning of Tablet VI.[5] In addition, the section dealing with the creation of humanity (VI 1–38) does not lead smoothly into the following VI 39–46, for we should probably distinguish between VI 1–38, a section dealing with the liberation of the gods (and the creation of humanity), and VI 39–46, a section dealing with the division of the gods. Furthermore, the statement regarding Marduk's division of the gods in VI 39–46 disagrees with the number of the gods given in VI 69;[6] and the statement that the Anunnaki constructed their own shrines in VI 68 seems to go against the impression that Marduk constructed them (cf., e.g., V 122–130).

We can explain the aforementioned discrepancies if V 117–VI 92 is treated as an insertion.[7] This conclusion is supported by the similarity of and connection between V 115 (*ul-tu* $u_4$*-me at-ta lu za-ni-nu pa-rak-ki-ni* "Henceforth you are the caretaker of our shrines") and VI 110 (*za-ni-nu-us-su-un li-pu-šá li-pa-qí-da*

2 For recent editions and translations of *Enūma eliš*, see P. Talon, *The Standard Babylonian Creation Myth Enūma Eliš*, SAACT 4 (Helsinki: Neo-Assyrian Text Corpus Project, 2005); B. R. Foster, *Before the Muses: An Anthology of Akkadian Literature*, 3rd ed. (Bethesda, MD: CDL, 2005), 436–486; T. R. Kämmerer and K. A. Metzler, *Das babylonische Weltschöpfungsepos Enūma eliš*, AOAT 375 (Münster: Ugarit-Verlag, 2012), 81–360; Lambert, *Creation Myths*, 45–134; G. Gabriel, *enūma eliš—Weg zu einer globalen Weltordnung. Pragmatik, Struktur und Semantik des babylonischen "Lieds auf Marduk,"* ORA 12 (Tübingen: Mohr Siebeck, 2014), 419–447 (selections).

3 Translation: Lambert, *Creation Myths*, 113.

4 B. Landsberger and J. V. Kinnier Wilson, "The Fifth Tablet of *Enuma Eliš*," *JNES* 20 (1961): 154–179, especially 166–169 (lines 131–156). I note that Lambert has chosen not to restore the relevant breaks.

5 Thus I do not find convincing the connections explicated in Gabriel, *enūma eliš*, 160–162, 165.

6 See Lambert, *Creation Myths*, 464 and 479, note to VI 69: "This line ... contradicts the figures in lines 41–44 above and disrupts the couplet structure of the passage. It is an addition to be excised."

7 It is possible that the section dealing with the bow of Marduk (VI 82–92) is not part of the insertion but belongs to the earlier text.

*eš-re-es-su-un* "Let him provide for their maintenance and be caretaker of their sanctuaries"),[8] and the repetition of the word *zāninu* in both passages.

Of course, the block v 117–vi 92 is made of up several sections and should perhaps not be treated as a unified section. Originally then, the text comprised: –v 116 + vi 93–120, to which were added:

1. A section dealing with the construction of Babylon: iv 142–146, v 117–156, vi 47–92 (or vi 81);
2. A section dealing with the creation of humanity and the liberation of the captive gods: vi 1–38;
3. A section dealing with the division of the gods: vi 39–46.

Accordingly, I would suggest that an early version of *Enūma eliš* did not include a section dealing with Babylon—something not necessitated by the plot.[9] We should not be at all surprised that there may have existed a version of *Enūma eliš* without the Babylon section, for such a version would have been the story of Marduk, a conclusion that agrees with the view that Ninurta source material provided many of Marduk's heroic deeds/exploits narrated in the work.[10]

There is one other difficulty of plot in this section that this hypothesis allows us to explain. I have explained elsewhere why Marduk must be declared king a second time in v 107–116, subsequent to his defeat of Tiāmat and her hosts and his creation of the cosmos.[11] But why must he be granted the kingship a third time in vi 93ff.?[12] By linking v 116 with vi 93–120, we eliminate the repetitive and unnecessary third bestowal of kingship upon Marduk; vi 93ff. is simply a

8 Text and translation: Lambert, *Creation Myths*, with one modification: in view of the close association of v 115 and vi 110 and the occurrence of *ešrēssun* in vi 110, I construe *pa-rak-ki-ni* in v 115 as a plural (*parakkīni*) and translate it as "our shrines."

9 I acknowledge that the building of an abode for a victorious god seems to have been part of a pattern in which the battle of a storm god with the sea led to the building of a palace for the newly acknowledged leader of the gods (see the Canaanite Baal Cycle, where Baal receives a palace after defeating Yamm; a similar pattern has been seen in the culmination of Yhwh's conflicts with the building of the temple in Jerusalem).

10 See W. G. Lambert, "Ninurta Mythology in the Babylonian Epic of Creation," in *Keilschriftliche Literaturen*, ed. K. Hecker and W. Sommerfeld, BBVO 6 (Berlin: Dietrich Reimer, 1986), 55–60; Lambert, *Creation Myths*, 202–247.

11 See Abusch, "Kingship," 63–64 [[230–232]].

12 Cf. Abusch, "Kingship," 63 n. 10 [[231 n. 10]].

continuation of the original text up through V 116[13] and forms part of the second bestowal of kingship.

My statements thus far do not exhaust the number of sections that may have been added to the epic. Even W. G. Lambert, the most recent editor of *Enūma eliš*, viewed at least two sections of *Enūma eliš* as secondary: the creation of the monsters in Tablet I and the section that listed and explicated Marduk's fifty names (VI 121–VII 145), a section that he thought derived from a separate document.[14] With these exceptions, Lambert believed that "the text as it stands came from a single hand."[15] But it should be evident from the preceding arguments that I think that the text should be approached not only synchronically but also diachronically. In my estimation, it is a composite formed over time rather than a composite text that was put together at one time by a single composer using different traditions and documents. By suggesting that the sections dealing with Babylon (and related sections) are secondary, I do hope that I have pointed to solutions to some difficulties in the work and have shown that the remaining sections of text adhere and produce a more coherent text.

But the question still remains: why were the insertions added to a work that was about Marduk, and do they tell us anything about the date of composition of *Enūma eliš* and of the additions concerning the city Babylon? Here I would speculate that perhaps Lambert was right to think that *Enūma eliš* was composed to honor Nebuchadnezzar I's liberation of the statue of Marduk.[16] But,

13 Of course, there might be additions to earlier parts of the text; with the exception of IV 142–146, I am not addressing that question here.

14 See, e.g., Lambert, *Creation Myths*, 456 and 463. Note that he thought that the list of fifty names existed before the composition of *Enūma eliš* and was incorporated into it by the composer. At the very least, treating the list of names in that section (VI 121–VII 145) as secondary explains why Marduk is given the name Asalluḫi both in VI 101 and once again as the seventh name of the fifty in VI 147. For a study of the list of fifty names, see recently A. Seri, "The Fifty Names of Marduk in *Enūma eliš*," *JAOS* 126 (2006): 507–519. Note, for example, that S. Dalley thinks that Tablets VI and VII are not essential to the epic and are later additions to the earlier main epic comprising Tablets I–V; see S. Dalley, *Myths from Mesopotamia*, rev. ed. (Oxford: Oxford University Press, 2000), 230.

15 Lambert, *Creation Myths*, 463. Lambert accepts, of course, that the "author made abundant use of traditional materials" (ibid.). I should note that Lambert was of the opinion that "a study of the variant readings reveals only little evidence of recensions or a prehistory" (4) and that "the MSS offer no evidence of recensional changes" (6). It seems to me that the argument he presents against the presence of redaction is of a piece with his later assertion that all copies "go back to a single archetype from a period later than the composition of the text" (464).

16 See W. G. Lambert, "The Reign of Nebuchadnezzar I: A Turning Point in the History of Ancient Mesopotamian Religion," in *The Seed of Wisdom: Essays in Honour of T. J. Meek*, ed. W. S. McCullough (Toronto: University of Toronto Press, 1964), 3–13; Lambert, *Creation Myths*, 271–274. There are, of course, other opinions regarding the date of composition

in my estimation, this is a version without the Babylon section. Why and when, then, was the Babylon section added? I would think that it would be in the early first millennium BCE that the sections on Babylon were added, perhaps, as I have argued previously in regard to the epic as a whole, in order to emphasize the importance of the city Babylon at a time when the significance of the city was threatened. But I cannot prove this historical reconstruction, for such reconstruction requires evidence different from that produced strictly by literary analysis. By way of conclusion, then, I can only express my hope that I have made a reasonable and responsible case for the secondary nature of sections of the epic.

of *Enūma eliš*: see, e.g., T. Jacobsen, "The Battle Between Marduk and Tiamat," *JAOS* 88 (1968): 104–108; T. Jacobsen, *The Treasures of Darkness: A History of Mesopotamian Religion* (New Haven: Yale University Press, 1976), 189–190; W. Sommerfeld, *Der Aufstieg Marduks: Die Stellung Marduks in der babylonischen Religion des zweiten Jahrtausends v. Chr.*, AOAT 213 (Kevelaer: Butzon & Bercker; Neukirchen-Vluyn: Neukirchener Verlag, 1982), 174–176; Dalley, *Myths from Mesopotamia*, 228–230; J.-M. Durand, "Le mythologème du combat entre le dieu de l'orage et la mer en Mésopotamie," *MARI* 7 (1993): 41–61; S. Dalley, "Statues of Marduk and the Date of Enūma Eliš," *AoF* 24 (1997): 163–171; Kämmerer and Metzler, *Das babylonische Weltschöpfungsepos Enūma eliš*, 16–21. For recent surveys of possible dates for the composition of *Enūma eliš*, see, e.g., E. Frahm, "Counter-texts, Commentaries, and Adaptations: Politically Motivated Responses to the Babylonian Epic of Creation in Mesopotamia, the Biblical World, and Elsewhere," *Orient: Reports of the Society for Near Eastern Studies in Japan* 45 (2010): 5–6; S. Flynn, *YHWH Is King: The Development of Divine Kingship in Ancient Israel*, VTSup 159 (Leiden: Brill, 2014), 99–105; J. Finn, *Much Ado about Marduk: Questioning Discourses of Royalty in First Millennium Mesopotamian Literature*, SANER 16 (Boston: de Gruyter, 2017), 46–47; R. D. Miller II, *The Dragon, the Mountain, and the Nations: An Old Testament Myth, Its Origins, and Its Afterlives*, Explorations in Ancient Near Eastern Civilizations 6 (University Park, PA: Eisenbrauns, 2018), 124.

CHAPTER 18

# Biblical Accounts of Prehistory: Their Meaning and Formation

In this essay, I will present some thoughts about the biblical account of prehistory.[1] By prehistory, I mean the stories in the book of Genesis that precede the accounts of the patriarchs and that tell the story of early humanity in mythic terms. I shall treat these texts as a mythological account with the hope of entering its inner world and understanding its metaphors and meaning. Any interpretation of such a long and complex myth can only focus on a limited line of thought. Thus, I do not claim exclusivity for my interpretation, for surely there are many aspects of the text that I have not taken up. A mythic text—especially one that has gone through several revisions—operates on more than one level and treats more than one set of issues. I have focused on the line of thought that seemed to me to be central when I worked out my original analysis, and I have emphasized one set of components more than others.

---

1 This essay originated as a lecture that I was privileged to deliver over the course of some twenty years to several audiences, both academic and lay. Among the most stimulating occasions were the Colloquium in the History of Psychiatry, Harvard Medical School, 1984; the Inaugural Potts Lecture in Cosmology, Johns Hopkins University, 1997; and a lecture to the Department of Bible, Jewish Theological Seminary of America, 2003. On the last of these occasions, I dedicated the lecture to the presiding chair, Professor Stephen Geller, one of my oldest and dearest friends. Steve is among the foremost practitioners of the literary approach to the interpretation of the biblical text, and it is, therefore, a profound pleasure to dedicate this literary and psychological interpretation of a biblical text to him.

This contribution is intended as an essay in interpretation and not as a work of research. I have retained the original informal lecture style; moreover, I have neither searched out nor provided bibliographical information. I would emphasize that most of the conclusions were arrived at independently by me and that the overall interpretation is mine, though I have no doubt that many of the individual points made in this essay may already be found in the voluminous secondary literature. The analysis of J was worked out in the late 1970s; that of P and the relation of the two sources in the early 1980s. The work has taken as its presumption the existence of biblical documentary sources and the dependence of the biblical text on Mesopotamian literary sources. The biblical translations follow the translations of E. A. Speiser except insofar as I have replaced his use of "Yahweh" with "Yhwh"; see E. A. Speiser, *Genesis*, 3rd ed., AB 1 (Garden City, NY: Doubleday, 1981).

 | DOI:10.1163/9789004435186_019

## 1 Introduction

The biblical stories explain how humans in their most fundamental sense came into being and how human institutions emerged. These are stories of creation, yet humanity is not immediately created in its fullness; for, just as a child is born but is not immediately part of the world, so too humans were not immediately part of the world at their creation. Thus, the biblical story of creation first describes the physical creation of the universe and of humanity and then tells us how people came to be part of the world. It defines their place in the universe by telling how they were accepted into the world and attained a stable place therein.

The main actors in this dynamic story are human beings and God. In contrast to polytheistic creation accounts in which several gods function as peers, in the biblical monotheistic account, the protagonists are God and mankind. God is presented as an adult, while humans are presented as children; the biblical story is an account of the interaction of this adult and these children and of the development of their relationship. In other words, the emergence of the present order is told in terms of the development of the relationship between humankind and God. Accordingly, we are primarily interested in the first nine chapters of Genesis, for only after the Flood do we observe the emergence of the order in which we live. These chapters allow us to see how humankind came about, how human nature evolved, how also God changed, and how, through a new resolution of their relationship, the two created a form of coexistence that is the world order in which we live. Accordingly, we must enter into the story in order to identify the issues with which it is concerned as well as the nature of the characters.

Turning to the story, we note that its scheme is very simple. At first, an order is established. But this order does not work out and gradually, through intervening generations, the situation becomes more and more intolerable—so intolerable that God must bring the Flood. The aftermath of the Flood is the creation of a new order.

To understand this account, we should first realize that the account is not made of whole cloth. First, the writers have drawn on ancient Near Eastern sources, and second, the biblical story itself is not unitary, for there are two separate sources or documentary strands that run through chapters 1–9.

## 2 Mesopotamian Sources

With regard to ancient Near Eastern sources, it suffices to recall the well-known story of Atraḫasīs, the Babylonian Noah. The story begins before the creation of man, when only the gods existed. The gods worked within an organized administration in which some were administrators and others did the actual physical work of digging canals and maintaining the irrigation system that was necessary for agriculture. The worker-gods found the work heavy and burdensome and went on strike; they burned their tools and threw up a picket line around the temple, the home of the god Enlil, the chief executive officer of the earth. At the suggestion of Enki, the god of water, the administrator-gods decided to create humankind as a replacement for the worker-gods.

Humans were created as the replacement for the worker-gods, and a new system was established. But this new system did not remain stable, for humanity multiplied too rapidly because limits had not been placed upon reproduction.

> Twelve hundred years had not yet passed
> When the land extended and the peoples multiplied.
> The land was bellowing like a bull,
> The god got disturbed with their uproar.[2]

Unable to sleep because of the uproar of humanity, Enlil decided to limit the number of humans by means of a pestilence, then a partial drought, and, finally, a complete drought. When these attempts failed, he decided to bring the Flood. However, Enki, the god who had created humankind, tried to save his creation. He addressed Atraḫasīs and instructed him to build an ark and save himself, his family, and the animals from the anticipated Flood. With the onset of the Flood, the people were destroyed, and the gods themselves retreated before its terror. Moreover, they found that in the absence of their human servants they were starving for lack of food. They regretted the Flood, however, not only because of their own physical needs, but also because of the destruction of their human creation. Enlil, by contrast, was outraged that anyone should have survived the Flood; nevertheless, he was forced to accept the fact.

But now a new order had to be established, for if it were not, reproduction would continue without limit, and every twelve hundred years there would be a new crisis. Therefore, a compromise had to be reached between two sets of gods: gods of power, rule, and order, and gods of reproduction—or, if you will, between human reason or control and human passion. The compromise that was reached was to set limits on human reproduction, for both sides were right—both those who represented power and organization and those who

2 *Atraḫasīs* I 352–355 // II 1–4. Translation: W. G. Lambert and A. R. Millard, *Atra-ḫasīs: The Babylonian Story of the Flood* (Oxford: Clarendon, 1969), 67, 73.

represented the interests of birth and humanity. In the future, there would be cloistered women who were not permitted to bear children, women who were sterile, and children who would die in infancy. Moreover, natural death was added to violent death. From the Mesopotamian point of view, we live in the new order that was established. Humanity exists to serve the gods—for this reason it was created, but it must not burden them; that is, it must not overproduce and overwhelm the earth with excessive numbers of people.

## 3 Biblical Sources

Turning back to the biblical material, we note that there was no single biblical view, as there was no single Mesopotamian view. In fact, the biblical account is made up of two sources, the Yahwistic or J source and the Priestly or P source. In Gen 2–4, the J source presents the story of Adam and Eve, the events in the Garden of Eden, the expulsion from the garden, and the story of Cain and his descendants. An account of the Flood follows in chapters 6–8; chapter 8 concludes with God's acceptance of humankind and his promise that he will never again destroy the natural order. The P source comprises chapter 1, which tells of the creation of the world, and chapter 5, which gives the genealogical line of Adam through Noah. Then, in chapters 6–8 we have a parallel account of the Flood. In this source, too, there follows an acceptance of humankind, for in chapter 9, God introduces innovations, imposes limits on human activity, and promises never again to bring a Flood. Here, I offer an interpretation of the individual sources and of their interaction, and, while these sources may contain some preexisting units that originally had a somewhat different meaning, my focus here is the documentary source in its present form.

In my estimation, there are three issues that are central to both the J and P sources; the treatment and resolution of these three issues inform these accounts and will inform our discussion. The text addresses the questions of reproduction, work and food, aggression and death. Overshadowing all is the question of natural death. By treating these questions, the writers deal with the nature and fate of humankind. The relationship of the J and P accounts of prehistory is interesting and complex, for I believe that in the section treating human prehistory these two sources were not two wholly independent documents. To be more precise, I would suggest that, whereas J had an existence prior to and independent of P, the P account of prehistory took its present form in response to J. That is, P was not a fully independent source that a later redactor or editor happened to put together with J in an effort to include in the Torah the creation account of both sources. Rather, P was composed or revised in reaction to J's treatment of basic human issues. Each source deals with the same issues, but each source deals with these issues in diametrically opposed ways. J's presentation may be regarded as representative of his position. What P really believes is not as clear, for P's purpose is to counteract and neutralize J. We will see how these documents represent diametrically opposed positions and how they interact with each other. Neither source presents a picture that does justice to the complexity of human beings. Each source or story presents only one aspect of human nature, but together, the two sources provide a complex and true-to-life picture of human nature. In contrast to Mesopotamia, the main interaction is between humans and God. The model for the interaction is the relationship between a parent and a child. The representation of human beings as active participants as well as the use of this model allow for the presentation of the several aspects of human nature.

### 3.1 *J Source*

We turn first to the J story. The story is, first of all, a story of ever-increasing spatial areas of human activity: the garden; the area outside the garden; Cain's wanderings; his entrance into the land of Nod, which is the land of wanderers east of Eden; the return from the east to the plain of Shinar, the city of Babylon; and then the dispersion over the whole world. Moreover, in addition to a series of geographical areas, we have a series of successively more complex social situations: a husband and wife who are food gatherers, then brothers, a shepherd and a farmer, then nomads, city builders, and wanderers. Overall, the movement is from simple to complex, but we are not dealing with a straight-line progression, for built into the story are a number of conflicts. The text moves forward and then backward, and then again forward and backward.

The story tells of conflicts between humans and God. The first conflict that we shall address here takes the form of a conflict between nature and culture. According to J, God intended humans to live in a state of impotence—impotence in nature and then powerlessness in nomadism. Humans found such a state to be intolerable, for they sought self-expression and safety; they did not wish to be at the mercy of God or nature. I shall begin, then, with the story of the Tower of Babel, for although it stands outside the first nine chapters, the conflict of nature and culture can be most readily observed and understood there. (In any case, this story follows upon and is thematically related to the preceding account and may even have formed a continuation of an early part of the J story, prior to the insertion of the Flood account.)

In this story, men migrate from the east; apparently, the purpose of their movement is to spread over the earth. When they come to the plain of Shinar, they recognize that although God wishes them to spread over the earth they would be vulnerable if they did so, they would be powerless. So they stop and build a city, not to vie with God or to reach the heavens, but for reasons of self-expression and self-preservation: "Then they said, 'Come, let us build ourselves a city, and a tower with its top in the sky, to make a name for ourselves; else we shall be scattered all over the world'" (Gen 11:4). When the people say, "Come, let us build ourselves a city, and a tower with its top in the sky," they are not seeking to reach the heavens; rather, they are simply talking in terms drawn from Babylonian city structure and architecture. They are seeking to build a base from which they can create and build and can thus prevent their power from being dissipated and their numbers dispersed. Their desire "to make a name for ourselves; else we shall be scattered all over the world," does not suggest that they are rebelling against God; rather, they are attempting to protect themselves and to use power in a creative way. God views this as a threat; he scatters the human race.

We have here a conflict of urbanism and nomadism, of culture and nature. What are the connotations of these concepts for our author? In this text, nature represents human powerlessness and vulnerability, while civilization represents power. For this author, there are two sets of extremes: nature and impotence on the one hand, city and power on the other. But the author is ambivalent about cities and about the human use of power. In contrast to Mesopotamia, the city does not exist under the aegis of God. The result is a polarization that leads the author to present humanity as either bereft of all power or as possessing too much power, of being almost omnipotent: "And Yhwh said, 'If this is how they have started to act, while they are one people with a single language for all, then nothing that they may presume to do will be out of their reach'" (Gen 11:6). The poles are concretized in the conflicting figures of God and human, nature and city. The nomadic state is the divine order, but humans have no power in that natural state. Power as well as the internal, that is, psychological, and external, that is, natural forces inhibiting the human being from using power, are projected onto God; God, thus, has all the power. So, for this composer, the human use of power and simple self-expression amount to depriving God of his power, for in this author's mind all power belongs to God. Self-expression, creativity, building is seen as rebellion.

In more general terms, then, when humankind takes action and uses or overuses its power in response to feelings of powerlessness and vulnerability, it is seen as acting in an extreme fashion, as overreacting, for it was meant to be without power. In the J account, human beings fluctuate between weakness and power, between submissiveness with feelings of helplessness and mastery with feelings of competence. God is self-protective and punitive; he retaliates. Each time humans act, God reacts and sets humanity into a new position, into a new relationship. Humans are placed in a new situation in which they are again vulnerable, yet the situation allows them to create and build a new modality if they so desire. Herein the author explains the emergence of such cultural institutions as languages, cities, nations, and so forth.

In the new setting, humanity can succumb and be powerless, or it can exploit the situation and create a new modality of existence. An example of this can be seen very clearly in chapter 4, the story of Cain and Abel. Instead of being mere grubbers, as Adam was to have been, men have now become farmers and shepherds. Cain is a farmer, Abel a shepherd. By presenting God with sacrifices or offerings, Cain and Abel draw God into their arena, but they also make themselves vulnerable to his response. Having entered their world, God takes advantage of the situation, for humans have attained more independence and power than God had intended. God undermines both of them by rejecting Cain's offering and accepting Abel's, for he wishes to deprive both of them of their achievements and to set humanity again into a condition of powerlessness and dependence.

A conflict between two brothers, between a farmer and a shepherd, is a commonplace of ancient literature that here serves to concretize this author's attitude toward human culture. Cain used his power to become a farmer. God accepted the shepherd's sacrifice so that the farmer—the representative of sedentary culture—would kill the shepherd and then be stripped of his power. Cain kills his brother. His action in response to God's calculated favoritism of the shepherd is an overreaction, an overreaction that takes the form of killing, of aggression.

At this point, God reenters the story and takes control. He takes advantage of Cain's new vulnerable position as a killer. He strips him of his power, telling Cain that he can no longer be a farmer but instead must be a wanderer. Cain is powerless and vulnerable. He recognizes that as a wanderer he may be killed. God responds by giving him a mark of protection; to be sure, the mark protects Cain, but it also establishes his dependence on God.

Cain is forced to give up being a farmer and goes into the land of Nod, the land of wanderers. But notice what he does there. Instead of giving in to powerlessness, here in the land of wanderers he marries, has a child, builds a city, and thus creates a new modality of expression. Cain, the murderer, is also the first city builder. And now the pattern repeats itself. The text recites Cain's genealogy. The highlight of the genealogy is Lamech, who is an aggressor par excellence and talks about how he maims and kills.

> Lamech said to his wives,
> "Adah and Zillah, hear my voice;
> O wives of Lamech, give ear to my speech:
> I have slain a man for wounding me,
> And a boy for injuring me.
> If Cain be avenged sevenfold,
> Then Lamech seventy-sevenfold."
>
> Gen 4:23–24

Notice who Lamech's sons are. They, too, are wanderers: herdsmen, musicians, metalworkers. In other words, in the story of Cain and his descendants, we again find the pattern of humans creating a new modality (the city) but then overextending themselves by becoming excessively aggressive and again being placed in the vulnerable position of wanderers.

We now move beyond the social formulation to the existential one, to the story of the Garden of Eden. That story takes up the issue of mortality/immortality. Thus, in addition to nature and culture, impotence and potency, we deal now with death and life. We may assume that in this story God originally intended Adam to live forever. He neither forbade Adam to eat of the Tree of Life nor intended that he reproduce. Woman was created only to be a companion to Adam, not a sexual mate; hence, we find that God first created the animals to see if any of them might satisfy Adam's need for companionship. When that attempt failed, a woman was created. Man and woman possessed no sexuality; they were unaware of each other sexually even though they were naked.

God originally planned to allow humans to eat of the Tree of Life and be immortal. But he forbade them to eat from the Tree of Knowledge, the tree of awareness and sexuality. He was working on the assumption that there would be no human reproduction because reproduction is only necessary when there is mortality—when children are needed to replace those who have died. So the story starts from the premise that humans would live forever in a dependent, impotent, sterile state in the garden; such was God's intention. But Adam and Eve rejected this option, ate of the Tree of Knowledge, and gained sexual awareness and desire. They now possessed power and creativity. They had become a threat to God; for, if they remained in the garden, they might also eat of the Tree of Life, that is, the tree of immortality, and become as gods, the equal of God. Hence, they were expelled from the garden. Death was called into existence, and its existence gives meaning to life.

The issues dealt with in the story are seen most clearly in the curses. The curses represent essential human characteristics; these features of human life are presented as emerging from the conflict of humanity and God. Three curses or destinies are established: the curses of the snake, the woman, and the man. (1) The curse on the snake is the curse of aggression: he will fight the descendant of woman; the descendant of woman will fight him. Herewith, we have the introduction of aggression into life. (2) The curse on the woman is not that now she will have pain in childbirth, whereas previously she gave birth without pain; rather, from now on she will give birth to children, an act which is physically painful, although she will still desire her husband. (3) The curse on the man is that he will have to work, to eat by grubbing, and finally to die. God says:

> Condemned be the soil on your account!
> In anguish shall you eat of it
> All the days of your life.
> Thorns and thistles
> Shall it bring forth for you,
> As you feed on the grasses of the field.
> By the sweat of your face
> Shall you earn your bread,
> Until you return to the ground,
> For from it you were taken:
> For dust you are
> And to dust you shall return!
>
> Gen 3:17–19

But, of course, the curses on the individual characters serve the more general purpose of accounting for the existence of such defining characteristics of human life as aggression, sex and birth, labor and death.

Now that we have examined the antediluvian section of J, let us look back at the J source and articulate a more general sense of it. The central concern is not sin. The emergence of human life is not a consequence of ever-recurring sin and of the accumulation of evil. Nor is it a story of the dissolution of communion with God and God's just judgment and punishment of a sinner. In our text, God is not just; humans are not necessarily sinners. Rather, the J source has dealt with the emergence of human self-expression in the face of adversity and has provided an explanation for the human way of life—the things that are part of our lives, the how and why of food, death, reproduction, aggression, and killing. The picture is one-sided. Humans are presented either as essentially powerless or as overly powerful. In an attempt to protect themselves, to gain a sense of value, and to gain God's favor, they act in an overly aggressive manner, using whatever power they have. To obey God was to remain sterile, uncreative, and in a position of dependence. In this text, the attainment of some autonomy involves immediate punishment and the imposition of limits. Autonomy and limits are part of human life. But in this story, the introduction of limits comes about in the context of conflict and punishment. In other words, the human is not simply told that he will die; rather, death comes about because he has tried to assert himself. Human nature and human destiny emerge out of the conflict of man and God—that is, of man and reality.

Let us look more closely at the nature of the divine–human relationship here in J; the simplest way to do so is to use human metaphors—family metaphors. God is a father, a punitive father who fears his own children; he is afraid of being supplanted and abandoned. He wishes to keep humans dependent and weak. God fears that if humans become strong they will vie with him and possibly abandon him. But humans do become strong, and God is forced to reject and eject them. He thus carries out his threat and brings about his own worst fear. Man is set on an independent course, and God has created the very situation that he tried to prevent. J conceives of God as a punitive *superego* and of the human will to achievement as split and in conflict with itself.

Adam and Eve, Cain and Abel, Lamech, the sons of God and the daughters of man—all overstep limits and produce a situation that God finds intolerable. The situation goes from bad to worse, and finally, God brings the Flood, for "Yhwh saw how great was man's wickedness on earth, and how every scheme that his mind devised was nothing but evil all the time" (Gen 6:5). Yet, after the Flood, God realizes that he must treat the surviving human beings differently, and he states, "Never again will I doom the world because of man, since the devisings of man's mind are evil from the start" (8:21). That is to say, "I will never again bring a Flood, because man is evil by nature."

But human evil was the very reason that God gave prior to the Flood to explain his decision to destroy humanity. Here, by saying that he accepts man's evil, God is now saying that he has changed and that he accepts humanity. God's utterance of contradictory statements reflects more than just the fact that two gods who held opposing positions in a polytheistic myth (recall Enlil and Enki in *Atraḫasīs*) have been compressed into one actor in a monotheistic story. A compression such as this may well be a necessary condition for the development of the biblical story, but the J author is doing more. He is playing on the paradox—that man is evil, and that God both destroys and preserves man because he is evil—in order to show that at first God did not accept man but that finally he did. J's God now realizes that he has no reason to fear humanity, for the destructiveness of the Flood has brought home to him how great is his own strength. He also realizes that he needs humans:

> Then Noah built an altar to Yhwh and, choosing from every clean animal and every clean bird, offered burnt offerings on the altar. As Yhwh smelled the soothing odor, he said to himself, "Never again will I doom the world because of man, since the devisings of man's heart are evil from the start; neither will I ever again strike down every living human being, as I have done."
>
> Gen 8:20–21

God comes to the realization that he needs humanity when he smells the soothing odor of the sacrifice. The metaphor for God's need for humanity is food, an image which is, in fact, the basic theme in the Mesopotamian material. Thus, God recognizes that not only need he not fear man but actually he requires his existence.

### 3.2 *P Source*

Let us now take up the P version of prehistory. As noted earlier, the P source is not a wholly independent story; rather, it is an editorial framework. P also uses Mesopotamian material and treats the same issues as J, but it does so from a position diametrically opposed to that of J.

P's story begins in chapter 1 with the creation of the world. There, God is presented as separate from the world and as creating humans in his own image.

> And God created man in his image;
> In the divine image created he him,
> Male and female created he them.
>
> Gen 1:27

We learn immediately that human maleness and femaleness are inherent in creation. The emergence of the two sexes and of sexuality is not a result of conflict; it is free from conflict. And, in fact, the two sexes are part of and derive from the image of God.

Immediately following the creation of human beings in the divine image, God commands humanity to reproduce, to multiply, and to eat vegetation: "God blessed them, saying to them, 'Be fertile and increase, fill the earth and subdue it; subject the fishes of the sea, the birds of the sky, and all the living things that move on earth.' God further said, 'See, I give you every seed-bearing plant on earth and every tree in which is the seed-bearing fruit of the tree; they shall be yours for food'" (Gen 1:28–29). And the same kind of food is given to the animals: "And to all the animals on land, all the birds of the sky, and all the living creatures that crawl on earth [I give] all the green plants as their food" (1:30). Thus, humans are to reproduce, but they and the animals are to eat only plants, not meat; that is, not other animals, not each other.

Let us now note that the two very issues that are conflict-ridden in J—sex and eating—here in P derive from and are imposed by God. But still everything degenerates, and P also contains a Flood story. What caused the God of P to bring the Flood? What was the problem or flaw in God's creation? Allow me to anticipate my answer: according to P, the problem was excessive autonomy without limitation. The clue to the identification of the problem is to be found in its solution, which is found in God's speech after the Flood (Gen 9:1–6). In chapter 9, God resolves the problem as follows: "God blessed Noah and his sons and said to them, 'Be fertile and increase and fill the earth. Dread fear of you shall possess all the animals of the earth, all the birds of the sky—everything with which the ground is astir—and all the fishes of the sea: they are placed in your hand'" (9:1–2). So again, as in chapter 1, humans are intended to reproduce and to have power over nature; but in addition, "Every creature that is alive shall be yours to eat; I give them all to you as I did with the grasses of the field" (9:3). That is, humans may now eat not only vegetation, as before, but also animals. But now a limitation is introduced; notice the effect of the additional statement in the next verse: "Only flesh with its lifeblood still in it shall you not eat" (9:4). The P author has again addressed the topic of reproduction and food, but now he wants to introduce another point. He knows that there is hostility, aggression, and killing in the world, something of which we were not informed in chapter 1. He now introduces blood because he wants to use it as a jumping-off point to assert something new:

> So, too, will I require an accounting for your own lifeblood:
> I will ask it of every beast;
> and of man in regard to his fellow man will I ask an accounting for human life.
> He who sheds the blood of man,
> By man shall his blood be shed;
> For in the image of God
> Was man created.
> Be fertile, then, and increase,
> Abound on earth and subdue it.
>
> Gen 9:5–7

In this manner, the P text has God say: multiply, eat animals, but bloodshed and killing are forbidden. We have here an acceptance of man's nature as one who kills as well as an attempt to regulate the killing. The passage recognizes, moreover, that humans kill each other as well as animals and that also animals kill humans as well as other animals. By recognizing the existence of killing and imposing execution on killers, limitations are built into the natural and human order. Population is thus curtailed, and chaos is prevented.

What, then, was the problem that led to the Flood? The problem seems to be reflected in the verses in chapter 6 that state that the earth was full of *ḥāmās* (Gen 6:11, 13), full of violence. In this statement, I understand the author to be playing on the earlier "reproduce and fill the earth": humans have filled the earth, and the earth is full of violence. What did the violence result from? The conflict of man and man, man and beast, beast and man, and beast and beast. Thus far, the problem of aggression had gone unrecognized in P. Conflicts emerged because at creation, in chapter 1, no limit had been placed on human reproduction, and no attempt had been made to limit animals. Moreover, natural aging and death had not been established, as indicated by the long lifespans in chapter 5. But now, limits are set. Humans may kill animals, thus acquiring food and limiting the animal population, but animals may not kill humans, and humans may not kill each other. But, as we all know, men and beasts do, in fact, kill men. The killing and the punishment reduce both population and the competition for food. And setting the limit serves as a recognition of the existence of that which is being limited but had previously gone unrecognized: aggression.

The issues in P, then, are the same as in J: reproduction, food, aggression. But here in P, they are linked not only to each other but also to God. Thus, in both chapters 1 and 9, we are told that humans were created in the image of God; in chapter 1, they are then divinely mandated to reproduce and eat vegetation and, in chapter 9, to reproduce and to eat meat as well. In chapter 9, the existence of the killing of humans is then mentioned and thereby acknowledged, and God further mandates that men and animals guilty of that act are to be punished, because humankind is created in the image of God.

On the surface, the meaning is clear: human nature is good, for it is divinely derived and, in the main, derived without conflict. This understanding is correct but insufficient. We attain a better understanding of the text by seeking a metaphor that allows us a fuller and more concrete appreciation of God's behavior in P and of the image of humanity that is there presented. In J, God was represented as a punitive parent, the human as an immature child; God was, effectively, the *superego*. The metaphor that I suggest for understanding

P's account, a metaphor that allows our story to cohere, is that of a parent who absents himself and leaves his children in charge, with the mandate to be adults: reproduce and rule the earth. He is a parent who creates children and leaves them before giving them a chance to grow up. The parent—God here—assumes that his children are his equals, for they are created in his image and can presumably take charge of the situation. God withdraws and humans are all-powerful. But neither humankind nor God is prepared for the situation. For P, the human is not split as in J; he is not in conflict with himself, for humankind is allegedly in the form of God. But God is an absent parent who has abandoned his children. He is not a *superego*; rather, he is here a *divorced ego ideal*. P's approach to humanity is no less unrealistic than J's. In J, humans are powerless; in P, they are all-powerful. Neither picture is true. In P's story, humanity is asked to live up to an unrealistic ego ideal, for God has imposed adult life on a child well before the child is ready. God has asked humanity to be like God. Humanity is betrayed; God is disappointed. Thus, he brings the Flood but then recognizes that he can no longer abandon the world, for humans are not his equals and cannot function perfectly in his stead. He must impose limits on chaos.

## 4 Summary and Conclusions

Having reviewed each of our two biblical sources, we have noticed that each one treats the same three issues—reproduction, food, killing—but in very different ways. The J source reflects a psychic conflict within man, and thus the human activities of reproduction, eating, and aggression are depicted as resulting from a conflict between man and God; in the P source, on the other hand, these basic activities are seen as mandated by an external source, God.

P takes up the same themes as J in order to neutralize J. The P account of creation was created (more likely just modified) to serve as a framework to be placed around J. As a frame, it causes, nay, compels the reader to read J through the eyes of P. P thus overshadows J, and because P lays out assumptions and sets up expectations that are opposite to J's, it counteracts many of J's approaches and positions.

In J, God is a punitive father, and humans are asked to submit and to remain helpless. God is a parent who tries to keep his children immature. Humans assert their own will; God retaliates. The process repeats itself, and eventually a crisis is reached. In P, God is a parent who withdraws soon after the birth of children and imposes an unrealistic demand: Be perfect because

I am perfect. The child cannot do this. Disorder leads to a crisis and causes the parent to reengage. More precisely, the disorder caused by humans acting without limitations, along with God's own needs, draw God back. In J, God deprived humanity of power; in P, God gave humanity too much power. In J, God rejected humanity when it became powerful; in P, God withdrew from humanity after having made it too powerful.

Acceptance of humanity is accomplished differently in J, in P, and in the Mesopotamian sources. One can even see how the different sources relate to each other in the way they resolve this problem. After the Flood, an attempt is made to create a new balance that allows humankind as we know it to be rooted in the world, that allows the integration of the child into the adult world. God recognizes that he needs humanity, and a code of coexistence is established. Just as a parent and child must create a pattern of coexistence, else one or the other may be killed, so here, the two must learn to coexist. The imbalance prior to the Flood brings God back, and after the Flood a permanent relationship is established.

J's God is no longer threatened by the human propensity to overstep limits and to seek autonomy and creativity. God accepts humans for what they are and returns to them, and humans accept the fact that they will serve God. Man offers and God accepts. Contrast this with God's reaction to the offering of Cain and Abel in chapter 4. For their part, humans recognize that they need God and can coexist with him in a relationship of respectful interaction.

In P, the Flood was brought because of violence due to overpopulation and to the resulting competition among both humans and animals. After the Flood, P's God recognizes that he must remain engaged and cannot again absent himself, for humanity is not perfect. In order to avert recurring chaos, he limits man's numbers by accepting killing but also by regulating the killing and the killers; he thus creates an ecological balance.

In both sources, humanity and God are alienated until they are reconciled. First, however, the situation becomes intolerable, and there is a crisis reaction—the Flood. Following the Flood, there must be a resolution of the problem that led God to bring the Flood. And the changes can only come when God changes his attitude toward people and they acquiesce. God must accept humanity and the world, and humans must accept limits. Humanity is accepted after the Flood, and there is the establishment of a balance—a balance between God and man.

In the biblical account, there is only one God. The conflict is in the heart of God and between God and man. The real and important relationship is between man and God; hence, a parent–child model underlies the biblical account of creation. In the Mesopotamian materials, the problem is resolved by the creation of a balance not between god and man but among the gods themselves. The interaction is not between god and man as parent and child but among the gods themselves, a group of adults; the model for Mesopotamia is the interaction of adult peers. Man is a passive participant; both he and the original worker-gods represent a servant population.

Interestingly, both J and P keep an element of the Mesopotamian solution, and each rejects an element of that solution. J rejects the notion of the goodness of cities but keeps the notion that man is created to serve God by providing food. P rejects the notion that man was created to serve the gods—for, in contrast both to the Mesopotamian source and to J, from the beginning, P commands man to go out and control the world; but he accepts the notion that there must be a limitation placed on numbers. In the end, a balance is struck: man and God accept limits and each other.

Looking at the biblical text, then, as a composite, we find that, while the text is not logical, it is coherent and provocative in that contradictory aspects are treated and balanced along a temporal scheme. The two sources present contradictory scenarios that ultimately complement each other, for we get to see two opposite sides of the human being—man as powerless, man as powerful—as well as the manner in which these sides must be balanced and integrated in the world. Each source is dependent on Near Eastern material, yet each conveys its own special notion by the nuances it lends the text and the images it creates and evokes.

The biblical account is very attractive because it is complex. Instead of presenting the human being's complexities, contradictions, and conflicts through a unitary story or a unitary theory, the text presents two contradictory sides of man and each in an extreme fashion. The writer can do this in ways that we cannot, simply because the writer can use God as an actor and God may represent man, the world, reality, whatever. In humanistic theories of man, the conflicts and the resolutions are within us. For J, humans are in constant conflict with the world. The world is destructive and punitive, yet humans can overcome. For P, humans are an extension of the world. The world is orderly and protective, and humans can rule it and organize it. However, it sometimes becomes chaotic. Both are true; neither is exclusively true. The human being is not always in conflict. He is not always hurt by the world. Nor is he simply an extension of the world. The world is not orderly. Yet, by these two absolute and contradictory statements and approaches to life, the composer manages to set out, to formulate the complexity of human life.

But, although the middle is touched on by the dialectic of the two extremes, the middle is really missing. What is the middle? God, nature, reality as a nurturing parent that helps children to attain a sense of autonomy and limits and does so in a loving, gradual way so that the child does not feel isolated, rejected, betrayed. Thus, even if man's independence is comprehended in J and/or P, man is left to feel rejected and abandoned in J, betrayed, inadequate, and out of control in P.

We find the story moving partly because the story, by presenting two opposite points of view, presents the complexity of human nature and life; it also is moving, even existentially gripping, because of the empty middle. We are forced to confront the existential dilemma, the gap, the emptiness that represents the dilemma for humankind, for all of us: the fact the we are alone and not yet fully integrated into our world.

CHAPTER 19

# Two Passages in the Biblical Account of Prehistory

Elsewhere, I have presented my overall understanding of the biblical account of prehistory.*[,1] Here, I wish to pick up on that topic and present some additional thoughts on two of the passages treated there.

## 1 The Creation of Man and Woman

Genesis 1–2:4a is the Priestly (P) account of creation. Here, God stands at some distance from his creation. Among other creations, the passage describes God's creation of humanity. In the earlier J account (Gen 2), man and woman were not created at the same time; first man was created from earth, and only later woman was created from the body of man—and neither was created initially for the purpose of sexual reproduction. By contrast, in P, man and woman are created together in the image of God and are expected to reproduce.

The text of Gen 1:26–27 reads:

> 26 וַיֹּ֣אמֶר אֱלֹהִ֔ים נַֽעֲשֶׂ֥ה אָדָ֛ם בְּצַלְמֵ֖נוּ כִּדְמוּתֵ֑נוּ וְיִרְדּוּ֩ בִדְגַ֨ת הַיָּ֜ם וּבְע֣וֹף הַשָּׁמַ֗יִם
> וּבַבְּהֵמָה֙ וּבְכָל־הָאָ֔רֶץ וּבְכָל־הָרֶ֖מֶשׂ הָֽרֹמֵ֥שׂ עַל־הָאָֽרֶץ׃ 27 וַיִּבְרָ֨א אֱלֹהִ֤ים ׀ אֶת־הָֽאָדָם֙
> בְּצַלְמ֔וֹ בְּצֶ֥לֶם אֱלֹהִ֖ים בָּרָ֣א אֹת֑וֹ זָכָ֥ר וּנְקֵבָ֖ה בָּרָ֥א אֹתָֽם׃

> 26 And God said, "Let us make man in our image, after our likeness. They shall rule the fish of the sea, the birds of the sky, the cattle, the whole earth, and all the creeping things that creep on earth." 27 And God created man in His image, in the image of God created He him; male and female created He them.

We may begin with the obvious question: Why does God speak in the plural and state, "Let us make man …"? Explanations for the plural, such as the writer's use of the "royal we" as God's mode of speech, or the background of

---

* Professor Raymond Scheindlin is a master of language and poetry. It is a special pleasure to dedicate these two notes, one on poetic form, the other on the theme of language, to Ray, an old friend with whom I first bonded over glasses of hot coffee.

1 T. Abusch, "Biblical Accounts of Prehistory: Their Meaning and Formation," in *Bringing the Hidden to Light: The Process of Interpretation. Studies in Honor of Stephen A. Geller*, ed. K. F. Kravitz and D. Sharon (Winona Lake, IN: Eisenbrauns, 2007) [[238–254]].

 | DOI:10.1163/9789004435186_020

the text in Near Eastern mythological tales set in the divine council have been offered. It seems to me that a solution is rooted in the overall thought of the passage and can be inferred from the linguistic/poetic form of the two verses.

The writer believed that man and woman were created together and that both were formed in the image of God. But how was the writer to shift from the man made in the image of God (ויברא אלהים את האדם בצלמו) to male and female (זכר ונקבה ברא אתם), both in the image of God? That is, how was he to convey the fact that the two sexes were made in the image of the one God while maintaining both their inherent duality as well as the oneness of God? He solved (or perhaps only sidestepped) a logical problem by linguistic legerdemain of a most elegant sort.

A careful examination of the two verses should make this clear. Let us look first at v. 27. This verse begins with the statement that God made (singular) "man" (האדם) in his own image. The author then restated his position but shifted from the use of nouns to the use of pronouns and stated that God created "him" (אתו) in his own image. Following this, the author split "him" into two, male and female, and transformed the singular pronoun "him" into the plural pronoun "them" (אתם): זכר ונקבה ברא אתם, "male and female created he them."

The writer made this transformation seem natural by beginning v. 26 not with the singular, "Let me make man in my image," but rather with the plural, "Let us make man in our image." The existence of the literary tradition of the divine council provided the writer with the means to have God speak in the plural and thus allowed him to open the passage in the plural. The author then shifted to the singular in v. 27. But by means of the final transformation of the singular pronoun "him" into plural "them" at the end of v. 27, he brought back the plural and thus rounded off the passage. A circle had been created that opened with the plural "Let us make …" of v. 26 and concluded with the plural "them."

Thus, the plural in v. 26 prepared the reader for the transformation of the singular human into the dual man and woman, both created in the image of God. By creating a chiastic structure (plural–singular–singular–plural), the writer has solved his logical and theological problem.[2]

2 Some months after submitting this article and many years after working out the analysis of Gen 1:26–27, I discovered that some of my arguments had been anticipated by P. Trible, *God and the Rhetoric of Sexuality* (Philadelphia: Fortress, 1978), 12–21.

## 2 The Tower of Babel

Genesis 11:1–9, the account of the tower of Babel, recounts the story of a migrating humanity that spoke one language. In concise terms, the story runs as follows: migrating from the east, mankind settled in the land of Shinar and there built a city. Threatened by what they were doing, Yhwh confounded their speech and dispersed them over the earth.

When I first analyzed this passage, I assumed that it was an old Yahwistic (J) account and reflected an early Israelite anti-urban strain. This remains true, I think, but some years later I realized that I could not just assume that the Babylon tradition was brought to Israel with the patriarchs and therefore represented second-millennium BCE traditions. Rather, I had to look for a context that might explain the choice of the name of the city as Babylon, and thus it occurred to me that the text may owe some elements to a late revision of J.

It now seems to me that one should imagine the text as comprising two strata and treating two separate themes: city life and language. In the base text, an early Israelite anti-urbanism came to expression. This text would not—and, in any case, need not—have dealt with Babylon; the city could remain nameless. At a later stage, the language stratum and the name "Babylon" were brought in. If we imagine this text as having been revised in the exilic age, we can identify a very distinct purpose served by this addition. The purpose of the revision could have been to persuade the exiles not to settle in an urban metropolis like Babylon, for there they would lose their linguistic and ethnic distinctiveness. Rather, so the argument would have gone, they should settle in separate communities, as most of the Babylonian Jews of that era actually did, and thus maintain their group identity. Apparently, then, an original anti-urban text was transformed into a polemic against living in a metropolis like Babylon characterized as a melting pot that assimilated diverse communities by means of a common language.

The basic anti-urban text would have been vv. 2–5, 8, and perhaps 9b, to which were added the elements that presume that people were settling in the city of Babylon and spoke only one language: vv. 1, 6–7, 9a. Using the NJPS translation, we may lay out the two strata of the texts.

### *A. The Original Anti-Urban Text*

> 2And as they migrated from the east, they came upon a valley in the land of Shinar and settled there. 3They said to one another, "Come, let us make bricks and burn them hard."—Brick served them as stone, and bitumen served them as mortar.—4And they said, "Come, let us build us a city,

> and a tower with its top in the sky, to make a name for ourselves; else we shall be scattered all over the world." [5]The Lord came down to look at the city and tower that man had built.... [8]Thus the Lord scattered them from there over the face of the whole earth; and they stopped building the city.... [9b]and from there the Lord scattered them over the face of the whole earth.

### *B. The Babylon/Language Addition*

> [1]Everyone on earth had the same language and the same words.... [6]and the Lord said, "If, as one people with one language for all, this is how they have begun to act, then nothing that they may propose to do will be out of their reach. [7]Let us, then, go down and confound their speech there, so that they shall not understand one another's speech." ... [9]That is why it was called Babel, because there the Lord confounded the speech of the whole earth.

Only later, after having worked out this analysis, did I recall Hermann Gunkel's brilliant analysis of this story in which he argued that the text was made up of two separate and independent sources that had been joined.[3] One source, a Babel recension, involved the issue of language and presumed that people were already dispersed over the world and spoke only one language; the other source, a tower recension, involved a nomadic population that stopped to build a tower but then was scattered.

However drawn I am to his analysis, it still seems to me that the assumption of an early anti-urban source overlaid by an anti-Babylon source has the advantage of placing the material into a historical context, and that in a short text of this sort, a rewriting of a base text by expansion seems more reasonable than a conflation of two independent sources. Still, Gunkel's analysis is sufficiently elegant and compelling for us to leave the matter as an open question.

---

3 H. Gunkel, *Genesis*, trans. M. E. Biddle (Macon, GA: Mercer University Press, 1997), 94–102. Biddle's English translation is based on the third German edition; I have before me the second German edition: H. Gunkel, *Genesis*, HKAT (Göttingen: Vandenhoeck & Ruprecht, 1902), 81–89.

CHAPTER 20

# Jonah and God: Plants, Beasts, and Humans in the Book of Jonah

The biblical book of Jonah ends on a rather strange note (4:10–11).[*,1] The text reads:

---

* The central argument presented here regarding the meaning of the last verses of the biblical book of Jonah—in particular, the underlying analogy and the significance of the "beasts" of Nineveh—was worked out as part of a more general presentation on the book that I originally gave as a public lecture in 1983. In preparing that lecture, I found the following studies particularly helpful for understanding the form and structure of the book: G. M. Landes, "Jonah, Book of," in *Interpreter's Dictionary of the Bible: Supplementary Volume*, ed. K. Crim (Nashville: Abingdon, 1976), 488–491, esp. 489b–490a, on structure; J. Magonet, *Form and Meaning: Studies in Literary Techniques in the Book of Jonah*, BBET 2 (Bern: Herbert Lang, 1976), 13–28, on language; T. S. Warshaw, "The Book of Jonah," in *Literary Interpretations of Biblical Narratives*, ed. K. R. R. Gros Louis et al. (Nashville: Abingdon, 1974), 191–207, as an example of a literary approach to the book. The present essay is a humanistic-literary endeavor, not a historical-philological one. While my argument draws on elements of these earlier discussions, I arrived on my own at what I believe is a novel interpretation of the book and especially of its conclusion. In summer 2012, at my request, my student Bronson Brown-deVost made a search of recent literature. As far as I can tell, my interpretation has not been rendered obsolete, nor have I seen anything to suggest that it should be discarded. See n. 1 below.

With a few exceptions, the English translation of passages in Jonah follows the NJPS. I render Hebrew חָרָה (*ḥārā*) as "to be angry" rather than as "to be grieved," remove "yet" from 4:11, and add a question mark at the end of that verse.

Raʿanan Boustan, Bronson Brown-deVost, Molly DeMarco, Stephen Geller, Kathryn Kravitz, Tina Sherman, and Jeffrey Stackert read drafts of the present essay; I am grateful to them for their helpful suggestions.

I would particularly draw attention to T. M. Bolin's remark regarding the end of the book: "in spite of the best efforts of scholars ancient and modern, the hanging end of Jonah and the precarious nature of human existence which it metaphorically represents remain a haunting biblical witness to a theology that defies easy expression or analysis"; see T. M. Bolin, *Freedom beyond Forgiveness: The Book of Jonah Re-Examined*, JSOTSup 236 (Sheffield: Sheffield Academic Press, 1997), 178.

1 I would here mention that in this study, my focus is on the dialogue and on the main character's psychological reactions to the developing situation and to the questions and responses of his interlocutor; the relationship of plant, animal, and human is treated in a series of statements of proportions meant to change Jonah's attitude toward other human beings. This essay stands on its own; however, I include here a few bibliographical notes that draw upon the literature search mentioned in the previous note, and comments of the reviewers.

 | DOI:10.1163/9789004435186_021

10וַיֹּאמֶר יְהוָה אַתָּה חַסְתָּ עַל־הַקִּיקָיוֹן אֲשֶׁר לֹא־עָמַלְתָּ בּוֹ וְלֹא גִדַּלְתּוֹ שֶׁבִּן־לַיְלָה
הָיָה וּבִן־לַיְלָה אָבָד׃ 11וַאֲנִי לֹא אָחוּס עַל־נִינְוֵה הָעִיר הַגְּדוֹלָה אֲשֶׁר יֶשׁ־בָּהּ הַרְבֵּה
מִשְׁתֵּים־עֶשְׂרֵה רִבּוֹ אָדָם אֲשֶׁר לֹא־יָדַע בֵּין־יְמִינוֹ לִשְׂמֹאלוֹ וּבְהֵמָה רַבָּה׃

10Then the Lord said: "You cared about the plant, which you did not work for and which you did not grow, which appeared overnight and perished overnight. 11And should not I care about Nineveh, that great city, in which there are more than a hundred and twenty thousand persons who do not know their right hand from their left, and many beasts as well?"[2]

In order to understand the meaning of God's pointed reply to Jonah in the last two verses of the book, we should focus on two questions raised by the passage: What is the force of the equation of the plant and the Ninevites? What is

---

Hierarchy of beings has been observed by others, thus for example: "Animals are closer to human beings than plants, as the Priestly writing shows in the clearest possible way; cf. Gen. 1:11–12* with vv. 24–25*. So, to the very end the final question proceeds from the lesser (pity for the castor oil plant) to the greater, trying to conquer Jonah's resistance through convincing arguments"; see H. W. Wolff, *Obadiah and Jonah* (Minneapolis: Augsburg, 1986), 175. See more recently, e.g., E. Ben Zvi, "Jonah 4:11 and the Metaprophetic Character of the Book of Jonah," *JHebS* 9/5 (2009): 5.

A discussion of the difficulties of the comparison of the plant and the Ninevites can be found in P. P. Jenson, *Obadiah, Jonah, Micah* (New York: T&T Clark, 2008), 91; Jenson does not bring the mention of animals in v. 11 into the equation.

There has been much discussion of the animals in Jonah 4:11; see, for example, T. M. Bolin, "Eternal Delight and Deliciousness: The Book of Jonah after Ten Years," *JHebS* 9/4 (2009): 10; L. K. Handy, *Jonah's World: Social Science and the Reading of Prophetic Story*, Bible World (London: Equinox, 2007), 91–92; J. A. Miles, "Laughing at the Bible: Jonah as Parody," *JQR* 65 (1974–1975): 168; R. F. Person, "The Role of Nonhuman Characters in Jonah," in *Exploring Ecological Hermeneutics*, ed. N. C. Habel and P. Trudinger, SBLSymS 46 (Atlanta: Society of Biblical Literature, 2008), 85–90; J. Sasson, *Jonah: A New Translation with Introduction and Commentary*, AB 24B (New York: Doubleday, 1990), 315; P. Trible, *Rhetorical Criticism: Context, Method, and the Book of Jonah*, GBS (Minneapolis: Fortress, 1994), 185; U. Simon, *The JPS Bible Commentary: Jonah* (Philadelphia: Jewish Publication Society, 1999), 47; Y. Shemesh, "'And Many Beasts' (Jonah 4:11): The Function and Status of Animals in the Book of Jonah," *JHebS* 10/6 (2010): 23–25; Wolff, *Obadiah and Jonah*, 175.

2 I understand v. 11 as a question directed to Jonah, a rhetorical question that reflects God's position that he would not destroy Nineveh if it repented. I see no difficulty in understanding the verse this way and have added a question mark to the NJPS translation to make this point clear. For the understanding of the verse as an assertion, see P. Guillaume, "The End of Jonah and the Beginning of Wisdom," *Bib* 87 (2006): 243–250, with references, and P. Guillaume, "Rhetorical Reading Redundant: A Response to Ehud Ben Zvi," *JHebS* 9/6 (2009); for the understanding of the verse as an interrogative, see Ben Zvi, "Jonah 4:11," with references (see esp. n. 24). For the import of the question, see the discussion below.

the point of the mention of animals alongside the description of the Ninevites (both here and in 3:7–8)?

To answer these questions, we should first state clearly that the book deals neither with prophetic issues nor with Nineveh as such; instead, we would set the passage into its context in the narrative (in this essay, I deal only with portions of the narrative and dialogue and do not take any account of the poetic psalm of ch. 2).

This passage is not intended as an explanation of God's actions, a theodicy as it were. Rather it is part of a dialogue and is the climax of an attempt to educate or transform the main character in the narrative, Jonah. Jonah is angry, but can only express his anger in a self-destructive fashion (4:1, 3–4, 8–9); he is suicidal, a trait that comes to overt expression in Jonah's several wishes for death in both chapter 1 and chapter 4. (Thus, for example in 1:13, Jonah asks the sailors to throw him overboard. Were he not suicidal, he might have asked them to carry him back to shore, something that they then actually try to do; alternatively, he could have simply jumped into the sea, thereby taking responsibility for the act and not forcing the sailors to do something that they clearly did not want to do and that elicited strong feelings of guilt in them.) This characterization is also apparent in his overall behavior in chapter 1 (e.g., his falling asleep during the storm [v. 5]—an act deemed abnormal not only by a modern reader but also by a character in the ancient narrative itself [v. 6][3]), as well as in the downward movement that is central to much of that chapter and is expressed by the repeated use there of the verb יָרַד (*yārad*), "to go down." Jonah's character is that of a depressive.[4]

When Jonah finally goes to Nineveh and declares God's decision to destroy the city, the Ninevites repent in the hope that God may relent and turn back from his anger (3:9). When God sees them "turning back from their evil ways," he renounces "the punishment he had planned to bring upon them" (3:10). God has given up his anger against the Ninevites, as they had hoped (3:9). But instead of being pleased, Jonah takes on the "evil" and becomes deeply angry (4:1), for he does not accept the notions of compassion and forgiveness (cf. 4:2)—justice must rule supreme, for Jonah neither expects nor gives compassion.

3 The sleep into which Jonah falls (√רדם [*rdm*] in the *niphal*) is a deep sleep, but it is surely not a prophetic sleep; in any case, cf. the uses of √רדם in the *niphal* (e.g., Judg 4:21) and תרדמה (*tardēmā*; e.g., Gen 2:21).

4 For an example of a psychological study of Jonah, see J. More, "The Prophet Jonah: The Story of an Intrapsychic Process," *American Imago* 27, no. 1 (1970): 2–11. For Jonah as suicidal and depressive, see, e.g., A. Lacocque and P.-E. Lacocque, *The Jonah Complex* (Atlanta: John Knox, 1981), 48.

Jonah cares neither for himself nor for others; neither he nor other humans are worthy of love or are lovable. Hence, the perspective from which he assesses and relates to other humans is that of fairness—right behavior is required; wrong behavior is punished—there are no other options. Jonah abides by absolute rules. Humans can only be judged, not loved. But whereas Jonah does not feel any connectedness to other human beings, he is able to relate to non-humans, something that the author observes in chapter 2 (the fish) and emphasizes in chapter 4 (the plant).

How, then, are Jonah's position regarding change and forgiveness and, even more, his underlying disposition to be addressed? The answer to this is provided by chapter 4, where Jonah is forced into a dialogue and confronted by his relationship to the non-human; in this chapter, moreover, חָרָה (*ḥārā*) and חוּס (*ḥûs*), anger and compassion, are central to both the narrative and the dialogue.

Whereas previously in the book there had been no dialogue between Jonah and God, by the beginning of chapter 4 Jonah is so upset by God's pardon of the Ninevites that he finally enters into such a dialogue. He now states what he could not or would not say directly when he received the initial command to go to Nineveh, namely, that he knew that God would surely forgive the Ninevites if they repented (v. 2). He found such forgiveness unacceptable, and at that time, flight was his only recourse. He reiterates his desire to die (v. 3). God responds and asks Jonah whether he is "that deeply angry" about the saving of the people (v. 4). Jonah does not answer; perhaps he is again unable to answer. Instead, he leaves the city and settles down nearby to see what will happen. He makes a shelter to protect himself (v. 5). God now provides a plant to give shade to Jonah; but Jonah had not asked for assistance. As with the fish before, Jonah does not ask here for a plant to protect him. At the end of chapter 1, he expected and wished to die; the intervention of the fish was unexpected and undeserved. Here, too, Jonah does not expect outside assistance. The text makes it clear that he himself had erected a booth for shade (v. 5). But the appearance of the plant makes him happy because its bestowal and services are unearned. He cares for this non-human object precisely because he did not ask for it, did not think that he needed it, did not expect it, and did not feel that he deserved it. The protection bestowed by these non-human entities—here a plant, earlier a fish—was a gift that was given gratuitously.

But, then, God destroys the plant. Jonah feels its loss and again seeks death (4:8). As earlier, God responds and asks Jonah whether he is "so deeply angry about the plant?" "'Yes,' he replied, 'so deeply that I want to die'" (v. 9). Jonah can now answer the very question that he did not answer earlier, for now it is not about people but about the plant. God now provides his response to Jonah in vv. 10–11, and here we return to the verses with which we began. Verses 10–11 do not simply mean to say that, of course, God would care about the Ninevites, whom he had created, seeing that Jonah cares about the plant, which he did not plant. Rather, the statement in v. 10 and the question in v. 11 imply a proportion, a complex set of equations that must be filled out by Jonah (and by the audience).

Let us try to grasp the logic of the formula as it emerges from the text. The key to understanding the proportion is provided by the last half of v. 11, which emphasizes the obtuseness of the Ninevites and their interconnectedness with beasts. This connection was already forged in chapter 3, where it was stated that not only human beings but also beasts were to fast, were not to drink, and were to be covered with sackcloth—a truly absurd and therefore noteworthy situation. What is the purpose of this association?

The aim of the underlying argument of vv. 10–11 is not to justify God and to explain why God would forgive the Ninevites. The object of Jonah's dialogue with God and of his overall experience is to try to persuade Jonah to care for others, in this case, the Ninevites. This could not be achieved by invoking a sense of identification with other human beings, for such a sense is lacking in Jonah. But Jonah does have the capacity to care for living things other than humans (i.e., non-humans), and this capacity is brought to the fore by God's arranging for a non-human being to provide Jonah with gratuitous protection. The writer hopes that the evocation of Jonah's feeling for the non-human might then serve as a way of bringing about a change of attitude and of getting him to care about other humans. Hence, once the engagement and identification with the non-human has been established by means of the plant (vv. 7–10, esp. v. 10), the Ninevites are associated with non-humans by their description as (if they were) beasts and their juxtaposition with beasts (v. 11b). The beasts stand between the plant and the human and serve as a transition from one to the other. Thus, the last half-verse is meant to help bridge the gap between the non-human and the human. This association allows for a psychological slippage whereby compassion for non-humans may carry over to compassion for humans.

God's point is not made explicitly in his response in vv. 10–11. He does not tell Jonah what to feel but tries to lead him toward new feelings and behavior by means of a question. An attempt at moral and psychological suasion is better served by a question than by an assertion. God's final utterance contains an incomplete analogy. The equation is intentionally not satisfying and would leave Jonah confused and open to some form of psychological change. For the challenge contains a set of analogies that invoke proportions, some of which are left unstated; certainly, the final element in the proportion is left open or unknown.

Here, then, we would set out the relationships contained in vv. 10–11 as we understand them (there seem to be other ways as well) and would try to work out the reasoning as best we can. To lay out the logic underlying God's speech in diagrammatic symbolic form, let us represent Jonah with *a*, God with *b*, non-humans with *c*, and humans with *d*. Accordingly:

| | |
|---|---|
| Given | $a : c :: b : d \,\&\, c$ |
| And since | $b : d :: b : c$ |
| Then should not | $a : d :: a : c$ |

Turning our proportion into prose terms, we may say: If Jonah cares for (חוס) non-humans (v. 10, קיקיון) as God cares for (חוס) both humans (v. 11, נינוה ... אדם) and non-humans (v. 11, בהמה), and since God cares for humans as God cares for non-humans, then should not Jonah also care for humans as Jonah cares for non-humans?

In more general terms, the text establishes a proportion, then expands the set by adding another element (i.e., the equation of God's relationship to both the human and the non-human), and thus points to the possibility of a further relationship should Jonah (or the audience) choose to carry the progression to its logical conclusion. That is, the text first equates two sets of relationships—God's caring for Nineveh (human), Jonah's caring for the plant (non-human). It then introduces another relationship, namely, the association/equation of the Ninevites with the beasts (also non-human). Given the similarity of God and Jonah and the similarity of the object of God's caring and of Jonah's caring (both objects partake of the non-human), the question then becomes whether Jonah will relate to the Ninevites as he relates to the non-human and will imitate God's behavior.[5]

Here we have remained focused on 4:10–11, but the analogies and connections we have noted in these verses are strengthened by the larger narrative, where anger draws together the several entities: both Jonah and God share a relationship of displeasure toward Nineveh (see, e.g., the recurrence of √רעע [*r*ʿʿ] in 3:8–4:1), and Jonah is angry both about the non-destruction of the Ninevites and about the destruction of the plant.

5 The nature of the relationship between *a* (Jonah) and *d* (humans) is the unknown variable that is to be inferred from the proportion.

In any case, the book ends with God's question. Whether or not God's attempt at moral and psychological suasion was effective is left up in the air. Jonah is as silent at the end as he was in the beginning. Thus, the book ends as it began—in silence and with the question intentionally left open. God has the last word, and Jonah simply disappears at the end of the text. He disappears so that the audience can take his place, for the question and message are really directed at the ancient audience and are not aimed at the literary character. The lack of an answer on the part of Jonah is meant to give the audience space to decide whether and how Jonah might have responded to God's challenge and to provide its own answer to the central question of the book (4:11).

# PART 3

## *Comparative Studies*

CHAPTER 21

# *alaktu* and *halakhah*: Oracular Decision, Divine Revelation

לזכר נשמת אבי מורי ר׳ אברהם משה אבוש ז״ל למלאות עשר שנים לפטירתו
(נולד בגאליציה בכ״ח בתמוז תרס״ג והלך לעולמו בארץ ישראל בי״ד בסיון תשל״ו)

This paper contains some thoughts about words. It is a modest undertaking and is meant to do no more than elaborate upon and set forth the reasoning underlying a proposal that I advanced some years ago regarding the meaning of Akkadian *alaktu* and its relation to the Jewish terms Hebrew *hălāḵā* and Aramaic *hilḵĕṯā*.[1] In preparing this paper, I have had before me two distinct goals and have, accordingly, divided the paper into two separate sections. First, I try to establish an additional (and thus far unnoticed) set of meanings for *alaktu* (= Sumerian a.rá) and to track this meaning especially when *alaktu* appears in combination with the verb *lamādu*. Then, turning to *halakhah*, I set out some of the implications of our inner Assyriological examination for the

1 A version of this paper was first presented before the Annual Meeting of the Association of Jewish Studies, Boston, December 1977. The proposal was originally advanced in T. Abusch, "Studies in the History and Interpretation of Some Akkadian Incantations and Prayers Against Witchcraft" (Ph.D. diss., Harvard University, 1972), 225 n. 94. While writing the version for the AJS I consulted with Moshe Bar-Asher and William L. Moran. I am grateful to them for their questions and advice. I wish also to thank J. C. Greenfield, T. Jacobsen, S. A. Kaufman, S. J. Lieberman, J. Strugnell, H. Tadmor, and F. Talmage for reading or discussing that version with me, as well as M. Fox and N. M. Sarna for their recent comments; none of these scholars is responsible for the ideas expressed in this paper. Although I recognize the conjectural nature of some of my arguments and conclusions, I early came to the conclusion that I could better advance the study of the terms and related cultural issues by presenting my arguments with a minimum of equivocation. I have tried to incorporate some of Jonas Greenfield's cautions. Overall, I have retained the original form of the oral presentation; notes have been held to a minimum.

Although I arrived at my understanding of *alaktu* and *alakta lamādu* on the basis of a consideration of *Maqlû* I 14 and my own collection and assessment of *alaktu* / *alakta lamādu* in prayers and medical texts, I wish to emphasize my indebtedness to the dictionaries; I have drawn heavily on the material collected in *CAD* A/1, s.v. *alaktu*.

 | DOI:10.1163/9789004435186_022

origin of the Hebrew and Aramaic terms *hălāḵā* and *hilḵĕṯā*. In doing so, I register my dissent from a previous proposal of a particular Akkadian term (*ilku*) as the source of the word *halakhah*, and present a set of alternative hypotheses as to the derivation of the Jewish terms. The opinions expressed about even *alaktu* are tentative and in need of further refinement, and our thoughts on the relation of *alaktu* and *halakhah* remain perforce in the realm of conjecture. Still, an attempt, however limited, to establish one more meaning for a word, to trace a semantic development, and to speculate about cultural contacts is nonetheless a worthwhile and productive endeavor. Certainly, in view of the important place that divination occupies in Mesopotamian culture and that law occupies in Judaism, a discussion of a possible Babylonian analogue or source of the word *halakhah* should be of some use not only to those who study words and their history, but also to those who recognize that words, no less than icons, may reflect the thought and religious sentiments of a civilization.

## 1 *alaktu*: Mesopotamian Sources

The Akkadian noun *alaktu* derives from the verb *alāku*, "to go," a cognate of the Hebrew verb *hālaḵ*. *Alaktu* has been translated "way," "path," "course," "behavior," and the like.[2] The word, indeed, does have these meanings. However, these renderings have also been applied to passages where such translations seem to be less than apt. To cite one example, we note that the request

> *izizzānimma ilī rabûti šemā dabābī*
> *dīnī dīnā alaktī limdā* (*Maqlû* I 13–14)[3]

in an address to the gods of the night sky[4] has been repeatedly translated

> Step forth O great gods, give heed to my suit.
> Judge my case, *learn about my behavior.*[5]

2 See *CAD* A/1, 297–300 and *AHw*, 31.

3 Meier, *Maqlû*, 7.

4 For a detailed analysis of this incantation, see Abusch, "Studies," 128–231.

5 K.L. Tallqvist, *Die assyrische Beschwörungsserie "Maqlû,"* 2 vols., ASSF 20/6 (Leipzig: E. Pfeiffer, 1895), 1:33: "schaffet mir recht, nehmt kenntniss von meinem wandel"; B. Landsberger, "Babylonisch-assyrische Texte," in *Textbuch zur Religionsgeschichte*, ed. E. Lehmann and H. Haas (Leipzig: Deichert, 1912), 125; 2nd ed. (Leipzig: Deichert, 1922), 322: "verschaffet mir Recht, erfahret mein Handeln"; A. Ungnad, *Die Religion der Babylonier und Assyrer* (Jena: Diederichs, 1921), 243: "Schafft mir Recht, lernt mein Ergehen kennen"; Meier, *Maqlû*, 7: "Schafft mir Recht, vernehmt meinen Wandel"; I. Mendelsohn, *Religions of the Ancient Near East* (New York: Liberal Arts Press, 1955), 216: "Judge my case, give heed to my procedure";

The occurrence of *dīna dânu*, “to provide a judgment,” “to render a verdict,” and similar phrases alongside *alakta lamādu* in this passage and in similar passages, as well as the fact that in this instance an examination of the petitioner’s conduct is unexpected, indicate that the translation “to learn about the behavior (of a petitioner)” for *alakta(šu) lamādu* is inadequate. This inadequacy points up the need for a more fitting rendering of *alaktu* and *alakta lamādu*.

This is not to say that the standard translations of the terms under consideration are not often times correct; rather it indicates the necessity of supplementing the already recognized meanings of *alaktu* with a new meaning. This new meaning is “oracular decision,” “divine revelation.” In our opinion, *alaktu* in this meaning belongs to the divine sphere and refers to the divine ruling revealed by means of signs. These signs, we believe, are of an astral character. *Alaktu* in the sense of a message manifest in the heavens appears alongside and is to be compared with the related *têrtu*, the designation of the signs and messages revealed by extispicy. *Alaktu* may refer, then, not only to the divine oracle or decision but also to the astral course or celestial movement from which is inferred or which makes known the divine decision.[6] Accordingly, *alakta lamādu* denotes not a secular juridical activity but rather an act carried out by divine beings. The action described by *alakta lamadu* does not involve a looking backward toward the past, an examination of past behavior; rather it is an action performed for the purpose of determining the future and should be taken to mean something akin to: “to clarify or understand a course (of signs) and/or reveal (by means of the same signs or oracles) a divine ruling or prediction regarding the destiny of a supplicant or petitioner,” or sometimes perhaps only “to infer and make known a ruling which will govern the destiny of the one affected.”

Translations based upon this understanding render a number of passages more intelligible and thus draw out their meaning. In the address to the gods of the night sky cited above, we would now translate *dīnī dīna alaktī limdā* as “judge my case, grant me an (oracular) decision.” This passage suffices to create a presumption in favor of the new rendering. However, since the new

*CAD* A/1, 297: “judge me (gods), learn about my behavior”; L. Cagni, *Crestomazia accadica*, Sussidi Didattici 4 (Rome: Istituto di Studi del Vicino Oriente, 1971), 241: “Giudicate la mia causa, apprendete il mio agire”; M.-J. Seux, *Hymnes et prières aux dieux de Babylonie et d’Assyrie*, LAPO 8 (Paris: Cerf, 1976), 376: “Rendez un jugement pour moi, prenez connaissance de ma conduite.” [I might mention that this passage was, in fact, the starting point for this study. I do not deny that “the speaker felt himself to have been accused of an unspecified but serious crime, accused, that is, of having in some way violated societal norms, thus becoming the object of shame in the opinion and judgment of the public.” T. Abusch, *Babylonian Witchcraft Literature: Case Studies*, BJS 132 (Atlanta: Scholars Press, 1987), xii.]

6 I do not exclude the possibility that *alaktu* also refers to the course of life prefigured or announced by the signs.

translation is intended to replace in more than a few texts translations that are commonly accepted, we shall cite several additional passages in which *alaktu* and *alakta lamādu* appear in the meaning here suggested. Besides, an examination of several such passages will illustrate the usage and provide an insight into the world of thought behind it. We begin, therefore, with the presentation of a few passages that exemplify the meaning (divine) "message," "decision," "oracle." Once this meaning has been rendered credible, we shall refine our analysis and tell a somewhat more nuanced story; that is, we shall attempt to set out a few of the constructions in which *alaktu* in the meaning "divine decision" occurs. We hope thereby to trace the development of the term and formulate in a reasonable fashion a hypothesis regarding the cultural and theological context of this usage.

### 1.1 *Occurrences*

A meaning (divine) "oracle," "decision," "decree," for *alaktu*[7] is suggested by the fact that this word occurs in association with words for "directive," "decision," "order"; *alaktu* is equated with and used as a synonym, equivalent, replacement, or complement of these other words. Often these other words also refer to divine decisions. *Alaktu* occurs with some frequency in the inscriptions of the Neo-Babylonian king Nebuchadnezzar II (604–562 BCE). This in itself may be of some significance, since *alaktu* is not often used in royal inscriptions. Here we need only take note of an instance in which a similar line occurs in two inscriptions but with one interesting difference:

> *Nabûkudurriuṣur šar Bābili … [ša] … ana <u>ṭēmu</u> ilūtišunu bašâ uznāšu*
> Nebuchadnezzar, king of Babylon, … who … heeds the decree of their godhead. (Wadi Brisa)[8]

> *Nabûkudurriuṣur šar Bābili … ša ana <u>alkakāt</u> ilī rabûti bašâ uznāšu*
> Nebuchadnezzar, king of Babylon, … who heeds the rulings of the great gods. (Borsippa)[9]

Whereas *ṭēmu* "decree," occurs in the Wadi Brisa inscription, *alaktu*[10] is used in the one from Borsippa. The treatment of *ṭēmu* and *alaktu* as equivalents or

7 In this section of the paper I shall use "decision," "oracle," more or less interchangeably for *alaktu*.

8 VAB 4, 150: NbK 19A, i 14–15.

9 Ibid., 98: NbK 11, i 4–5.

10 *Alaktu* appears here in the plural form *alkakāt* because of the following plural *ilī rabûti*; *ṭēmu*, on the other hand, is construed on the basis of the singular *ilūti*. For further discussion of the equivalence of *alaktu* and *ṭēmu* in these texts, see n. 62 below.

replacements by Nebuchadnezzar's scribes argues in favor of the contention that *alaktu* denotes a divine ruling. The occurrence of *alaktu* where one might have expected *ṭēmu* is not surprising; in lexical texts *alaktu* is equated or associated with words denoting order/directive/plan: *alaktu* is equated with *ṭēmu*[11] (and *ṭēmu* with *milku*[12]).

Further support for the use of *alaktu* in the sense of "divine decision," "oracle," is provided by the occurrence of *alaktu* in parallelism with *têrtu*, "extispicy," "sign," "order," in literary texts.[13] This, too, is not particularly surprising, since both *alaktu* and *têrtu* derive from verbs meaning "to go" (*alāku, wa'āru*), and *alaktu* and derivatives of *wa'āru* (*ûrtu, mûrtu*) are listed, moreover, alongside each other in a synonym list as equivalents of *ṭēmu*.[14] Here we should mention also the possible support provided by the statement *pî lā kīni alakti lā ṭābti*, "an unfavorable oracle and an unpropitious decision," and the like in apodoses of astrological reports,[15] if *pû* may at least sometimes refer to a divine pronouncement or oracle.[16]

The meaning here suggested for *alaktu* seems to be intended in a number of passages. Having just mentioned the association of *alaktu, ṭēmu,* and *milku*, we may at least note that the meaning "decision" may perhaps be considered

11 a.rá = *ṭēmu* and *alaktu*; *alaktu* = *ṭēmu*. See *CAD* A/1, s.v. *alaktu*, 297, lexical section, esp. references there to Kagal E par. 1: 15–16 (subsequently reassigned to Proto-Kagal [bilingual version] = M. Civil, *Materials for the Sumerian Lexicon*, vol. 13 [Rome: Pontificum Institutum Biblicum, 1971], 84: 15–16), and *Malku* IV.

12 For *ṭēmu* = *milku*, see *CAD* M/2, s.v. *milku*, 66–67, lexical section. By implication, *alaktu* = *milku* in *Enūma eliš* VII 97–98: ᵈa.rá.nun.na *mālik* ᵈ*Ea bān ilī abbī*[*šu*] *ša ana alakti rabûtisu lā umaššalu ilu ayyumma*. Here ᵈa.rá.nun.na is explicated etymologically by *mālik* ᵈ*Ea* and by *ana alakti rabûtišu*. The commentary to these lines (for which see now J. Bottéro, "Les noms de Marduk, l'écriture et la 'logique' en Mésopotamie ancienne," in *Essays on the Ancient Near East in Memory of Jacob Joel Finkelstein*, ed. M. de Jong Ellis, MCAAS 19 [Hamden, CT: Archon, 1977], 10: 97–98) then equates a.rá of the name with *milku* (line 97) and *alaktu* (line 98). Note [a.rá]= *milku* (Diri), cited in *CAD* M/2, 66–67. For a recent discussion of *ṭēmu*, esp. in its meaning "plan," "proposal (of a plan)," see W. W. Hallo and W. L. Moran, "The First Tablet of the SB Recension of the Anzu-Myth," *JCS* 31 (1979): 97.

13 For a discussion of the relevant passages, see below, section 1.3.

14 See *CAD* A/1, s.v. *alāktu*, 297, lexical section, and *AHw*, 1498–1499, s.v. *wu''urtum*.

15 R. C. Thompson, *The Reports of the Magicians and Astrologers of Nineveh and Babylon*, 2 vols. (London: Luzac, 1900), vol. 1, nos. 24: 5–6; 120: 3–4; vol. 2, nos. 85A: 4–5; 115D: 1–2: *pû lā kīnu alaktu lā ṭābtu ina māti ibašši*; vol. 1, nos. 122: 2; 123: 2: *pû lā kīnu alakti māti lā iššer.* [See now H. Hunger, *Astrological Reports to Assyrian Kings*, SAA 8 (Helsinki University Press, 1992).]

16 G. Pettinato, *Die Ölwahrsagung bei den Babyloniern*, 2 vols., StSem 21–22 (Rome: Istituto di Studi del Vicino Oriente, 1966), 1:202; 2:21; 2:29: 45; 2:39; 2:64; 2:70: 37; 2:78; and *AHw*, 873, s.v. *pû* I, 8) understand *pû* in apodoses as referring to human utterances (*AHw:* "meist v. Menschen?"). But see CT 20, 33: 115 and CT 5, 5: 45 = Pettinato, *Ölwahrsagung*, vol. 2, 21: 45(!), as read by *CAD* K, 390, s.v. *kīnu* 1. a).

for the famous passage *Ludlul bēl nēmeqi*[17] (the so-called Righteous Sufferer) II 36–38, where *alaktu* appears in parallelism with *ṭēmu* and *milku*. To this passage has often been imputed a philosophical meaning that may perhaps not be warranted. It has been treated as if it gives voice to an anguished and profound reflection on the incomprehensibility of the divine and of the world. These lines should be understood in the context of the statements at the beginning and end of the tablet: in the parallel complaints[18] II 4–9 and II 108–113, the speaker states that his gods have not helped him and that various diviners and sources of divine information have not provided the requisite information. Lines 36–38 mean to say, I think, that the gods do not provide reliable omens or that one cannot trust the experts' reading of omens. If these lines are not actually an indictment of divination by one who is in despair, they do at least contain the realization that we cannot depend upon signs. The speaker is saying that we are unable to interpret natural phenomena in a manner that will allow us to predict the future.[19] We would translate lines 36–38 as follows:

*ayyu ṭēm ilī qereb šamê ilammad*
*milik ša anzanunzê ihakkim mannu*
*ekâma ilmadā alakti ili apâti*[20]

Who can ascertain the gods' decree in the midst of heaven?
Who can read out the gods' order in the abyss?

17 *BWL*, 21–62, and D. J. Wiseman, "A New Text of the Babylonian Poem of the Righteous Sufferer," *AnSt* 30 (1980): 101–107 (cf. W. L. Moran, "Notes on the Hymn to Marduk in *Ludlul Bēl Nēmeqi*," *JAOS* 103 [1983]: 255–260).

18 For a similar opinion regarding the parallelism of the first and last part of this tablet, see E. Reiner, *Your Thwarts in Pieces, Your Mooring Rope Cut: Poetry from Babylonia and Assyria*, Michigan Studies in the Humanities 5 (Ann Arbor: University of Michigan Press, 1985), 110–111.

19 This interpretation would seem to be supported by the following lines where the speaker points to the consequences of the statement made in lines 36–38 (that is, lines 39–43 are not intended as an explanation of lines 36–38 or as a statement of the underlying cause behind the situation described in lines 36–38); for in lines 39–43, he seems to develop his earlier thought by pointing to the rapidity and unexpectedness of change in our lives (he who was alive yesterday is dead today, and so forth). Cf. Heracles's statement in Euripides, *Alcestis*, lines 782–786: "Death is an obligation which we all must pay. There is not one man living who can truly say if he will be alive or dead on the next day. Fortune is dark; she moves, but we cannot see the way nor can we pin her down by science and study her." R. Lattimore, trans., *Euripides I*, in D. Grene and R. Lattimore, eds., *The Complete Greek Tragedies* (Chicago: University of Chicago Press, 1955), 38.

20 *BWL*, 40: 36–38.

> Where (in the whole physical world) can mankind ascertain the divine ruling?[21]

Lines 36–38 form a tristich. The first two lines stand in complementary parallelism to each other and thus create a balanced representation of the "Above" and the "Below." This duality implicitly conveys a sense of the totality of the universe. This totality is rendered explicit by the last line of the triplet, which draws together the earlier two statements, with the divinities of lines 36–37 now becoming the generic *ili* of line 38 and the heaven and abyss becoming the indefinite *ekâma*.

Turning to prayers[22]—our original point of departure—we cite a few occurrences of *alaktu* + verb. With one exception, the verbal complement is *lamādu*. The examples show *alaktu* + verb semantically coupled with phrases denoting the rendering of a (divine) decision, verdict, or judgment, or the signaling or determination of destiny. Usually *alaktu* + verb occurs in final position in the sequence. In view of the frequent use of forms of synonymous parallelism in these texts, there will certainly be some overlap in meaning between *alaktu* + verb and these other idioms. At the very least, *alakta lamādu* stands in a relationship of repetition, complementarity, or consequentiality with the preceding clauses. Furthermore, based on this evidence, it is even safe to say that *alaktu* / *alakta lamādu* may sometimes belong to the same conceptual category as *dīnu* / *dīna dânu*. Even granting that a variety of semantic relationships come under the heading of synonymous parallelism, we would go so far as to state that *alakta lamādu* is similar in meaning to, and may even be an approximate synonym of, the idioms with which it is coupled; accordingly, *alaktu* will denote a (divine) decision, and *alakta lamādu* the rendering or publicizing of that decision.

21 The related bilingual proverb *BWL*, 265, rev. 7–8 may perhaps be treated in a similar fashion. The text is broken (perhaps read n[u].un.zu for n[u].x.x, and restore [*alakti ili ul* ...]), and our translation is less than assured: "The divine decree (umuš: *ṭēmu*) does not become known / the divine ruling (a.rá: [*alaktu*]) is not made known / the divine prerogative is not given to man to know." For different translations of *Ludlul* II 36–38, see, e.g., *BWL*, 41; R. D. Biggs, "I Will Praise the Lord of Wisdom," in *ANET*, 597; T. Jacobsen, *The Treasures of Darkness: A History of Mesopotamian Religion* (New Haven: Yale University Press, 1976), 162.

22 For collections of translations of Akkadian prayers, including many of those cited in this paper, see A. Falkenstein and W. von Soden, *Sumerische und akkadische Hymnen und Gebete* (Zurich: Artemis, 1953), and Seux, *Hymnes*. W. Mayer, *Untersuchungen zur Formensprache der babylonischen "Gebetsbeschwörungen,"* StPohl, series maior 5 (Rome: Biblical Institute Press, 1976), 218–222, cites many of the same examples from the prayers that I do; his book, however, was not yet available to me when I drafted this paper.

For *šīmtu* // *alaktu*:

> *šīmtī šīmā alaktī limdā*
> Decree my destiny, grant me an (oracular) decision. (*LKA* 139, rev. 25; gods of the sky)

> *šīmtī šīm alaktī dummiq*
> Decree my destiny, make my oracular decision/ruling favorable (or, perhaps, render a favorable fate for me). (*BMS* 6: 113;[23] Šamaš)

Here *alakta lamādu* and *alakta dummuqu*, "to make *alaktu* favorable," are coupled with *šīmta šâmu*. This latter phrase denotes the setting or assigning of an allotment or the disposal of a disposition. Here it denotes the determination of fate and seems to refer to the decreeing of a verdict regarding the destiny of a human by the gods. When, as here, *alaktu* occurs in parallelism with *šīmtu*, and *alakta lamādu* is coupled with *šīmta šâmu*, the translations "behavior" and "to learn about the petitioner's behavior," or the like, for *alaktu* and *alakta lamādu*, respectively, are clearly not intended. It is less clear, however, whether *alaktu* in these passages denotes the future course of events (the outcome) determined by the divine ruling or, rather, the divine ruling itself. Both may be intended.[24] But if we must choose between them, we tend to suppose that the divine ruling or oracle itself is meant. This is suggested by the surrounding lines in *BMS* 6 and dupls. Lines 110–116[25] read:

> *ina libbi immeri tašaṭṭar šērē tašakkan dīna*
> *dayyān ilī bēl igigi*
> …………[26]
> *šīmtī šīm alaktī dummiq*
> *līšira idātū'a*
> *lidmiqā šunātū'a*
> *šutti* / *šunāt aṭṭulu ana damiqti šukna*

> In the innards of the sheep you inscribe signs, you set down judgment.

23 *BMS* 6: 113 = *AGH* 48: 113 = Mayer, *Untersuchungen*, 507: 114.

24 Cf. R. Caplice, "Namburbi Texts in the British Museum. III," *Or* NS 36 (1967): 273: 4′: *ana dīniya qūlānimma šīmātīya šīmā*.

25 *BMS* 6: 110–116 and dupls. = *AGH* 48: 110–116 = Mayer, *Untersuchungen*, 505–506: 111–117.

26 The various mss. have different readings for this line (see Mayer, *Untersuchungen*, 506: 113); all contain a form of *šīmtu*. The original reading would have included $^{d}$*šamaš bēl uṣurāti mušīm šīmāti attāma*. Note that KUR (: *māti*) of some mss. should not be dissociated from the sign KUR = *mat* of *šīmāt*(*i*).

O judge of the gods, lord of the igigi,
............
Decree my destiny, make my ruling favorable / provide me with a favorable oracle.
May my omens turn out well,
May my dreams be favorable,
Make the dream(s) I dreamt favorable for me.

In this passage, Šamaš is called upon as a judge who makes known his decisions by means of signs, and is asked to render a favorable decision and to make known his oracular decision through the medium of auspicious signs. The supposition that *alakta dummuqu* refers to the revelation of the divine decision is supported by the lines which follow upon *alaktī dummiq*. These lines treat the theme of auspicious signs and continue or elaborate upon the idea already stated by *alaktī dummiq*. That *alaktu* should be linked with these signs is suggested not only by contiguity but even more by the conspicuous and exceptional use of the verb *damāqu* with *alaktu*. This verb is used here not only with *alaktu* in line 113 but also in the following lines with ominous dreams which transmit oracular rulings by means of their manifest contents and the emotions these evoke in the dreamer: *lidmiqā šunātū'a, šutti / šunāt aṭṭulu ana damiqti šukna*. Our supposition, furthermore, is supported by the next group of passages to be considered.

The following passages exemplify the use of *alakta lamādu* with terms denoting the rendering and decree of a decision. In these citations, *alakta lamādu* is coupled with such terms as *dīna dânu*, "to provide a judgment," and *purussâ parāsu*, "to render a verdict," terms denoting the very act of ruling itself.

*dīnī dīnā alaktī limdā*
Judge my case, grant me an (oracular) decision. (*Maqlû* I 14; gods of the night sky)

*dīnī dīnı purussâya pursı alaktı lim[dī]*
Judge my case, render my verdict, grand me an (oracular) decision. (*BMS* 4 and dupls.: 30;[27] Gula[28])

*[d]īnī dīnā alaktī limdā*
*[šem]â qabâya purussâya pursā*

27 = *AGH* 30b: 8 = Mayer, *Untersuchungen*, 456: 16.
28 The astral nature of Gula here is evident from the first line of the prayer: $^{d}$*Gula bēltu šurbūtu āšibat šamê* $^{d}$*Anim* (Mayer, *Untersuchungen*, 455: 10).

Judge my case, grant me an (oracular) decision.
Hear my plaint, render my verdict. (82–5–22, 532: 3–4)[29]

*dayyānāti dīnī dīn[ī]*
*muštēširāti alaktī li[mdī]*
You are one who judges, judge my case.
You are one who gives correct decisions, grant me an (oracular) decision. (*BMS* 30: 8–9;[30] Ištar)

There are other passages in which *alaktu* and *alakta lamādu* occur in the meaning here proposed. A few of these will be cited in a later section of this paper. Others are best not considered at this time because a judicious decision is not yet possible. Still, I believe that the small number of examples cited thus far[31] document and establish the meaning "oracular decision," "divine revelation," and "to render or reveal such a decision" for *alaktu* and *alakta lamādu*, respectively.

Before we proceed further we must digress and say a few words about the Akkadian verb *lamādu*; for the many occurrences cited in this paper are in the *Grundstamm* (G) or *qal*. That the Akkadian G-stem of *lamādu* may mean not only "to learn," "study," "understand," but also "to infer," "deduce," "conclude," "decide," "rule," "propound," may perhaps not surprise one familiar with the use of Hebrew *lāmad* in rabbinic literature. But especially considering that even *CAD*, volume L, does not seem to recognize these meanings, some

29 Copy F. W. Geers: *[d]i-ni di-na a-lak-ti lim-da* / *[še-m]a-a qa-ba-a-a* EŠ.BAR-*a-a pur-sa*.

30 = *AGH* 120: 8–9 (without the reading *limdī*) = Mayer, *Untersuchungen*, 458: 13′–14′. Already *CAD* A/1, 297b seems to have read *limdī*; so, too, Seux, *Hymnes*, 326, and Mayer: *li[m!-di]*.

31 The passages cited thus far derive generally from late texts. Here I should mention, therefore, that an examination of the references in *CAD* A/1, s.v. *alaktu* suggests that there may also be instances of *alaktu* = "decision," "oracle," "sign," in Old Babylonian Akkadian. I have in mind especially the mythological hymn *Agušaya* Tablet B I = B. Groneberg, "Philologische Bearbeitung des Agušayahymnus," *RA* 75 (1981): 126 i 5–9: *idat dunniša(,) arkassa pursa, ašrātaša litammad, leqeam ittātiša, šunnia alkāssa*. In view of the usages cited throughout my paper, I note the occurrence and uses here of *idātu* (? // *arkatu*) // *ašrātu*; *ittātu* // *alkātu*; *arkata parāsu*; *lamādu*; and cf. *ašrāta litammudu … alkāta šunnû* with the command *alkakāti sibittišunu lamādu ašrātīšunu šite*"*â hišamma* (CT 16, 45: 123–124), cited below. The cluster of usages in *Agušaya* is striking. Is the object of the examination a heavenly body or being? In *Agušaya*, cf. further Tablet A vi = Groneberg, "Agušayahymnus," 111 vi 38–41 (*ittu* // *alaktu*) and other passages. Possibly also G. Boyer, *Contribution à l'histoire juridique de la 1*[re] *dynastie babylonienne* (Paris: Geuthner, 1928), pl. VII, Text 119: 29ff., and J. van Dijk, *LUGAL UD ME-LÁM-BI NIR-ĞÁL: Le récit épique et didactique des Travaux de Ninurta, du Déluge et de la Nouvelle Création*, 2 vols. (Leiden: Brill, 1983), 1:107: 435–437 (= 2:122–123: 435–437); in line 436 a.rá: *alaktu* at least of the late version seems to denote a decree pronounced or a ruling enjoined by Ninurta: *qarrādu ana* $^{na4}$*šê* $^{na4}$*kasurrê izzizma išassi* / *bēlu alakta itammišunūti* / $^{d}$*Ninurta bēlu mār* $^{d}$*Enlil irraršunūti*.

explanation is necessary. *Lamādu* in the G occurs in the meaning "to reveal," "make known," "rule," or "pronounce" with *alaktu* and apparently also with other words for decision. An example of this usage is provided by a passage drawn from a prayer to the star Sirius at the time of the rising of the sun, a passage that we shall have occasion to cite once again when we discuss *warkata parāsu*:

> *u anāku mār bārî pāliḫu aradka* /
> *urrī dalḫūma aše''e marušti dīnu šupšuqma ana lamāda ašṭu* /
> *parās arkatu nesânni* ᵈ*šamš*[*i*] *aššušamma ina mūši uqa''a rēška* /
> *ana lamāda arkati attaziz maharka ana šutēšuru dīnu* / *nīš qāti rašâku* …[32]

> And as for me, the diviner, your reverent servant,
> The signs are confused and whatever I examine portends evil;
> The decision is difficult and it is therefore hard to ascertain.
> Revealing the future is far from me, O Sun;
> I have become worried and wait for your rising all night.
> To reveal the future (*ana lamāda arkati*) I stand before you;
> To give a right decision I pray with uplifted hands (to you).

It is not hard to imagine how *lamādu* can have taken on these new meanings. One explanation for the change might be to regard it as a secondary passive–active transformation whereby the N ingressive "to become known" became a G factitive "to make known." But I prefer a different explanation. *Lamādu* is a verb of perception, and a stative one to boot; one can therefore easily conceive of some such development in the G whereby *lamādu* went from the meaning "to understand," "become aware," "come to the knowledge of," to the meaning "to call to mind," "clarify," "conclude," "reveal," "make known," "pronounce a decision." Another verb of perception, Akkadian *amāru*, the cognate of Hebrew *ʾāmar* and Arabic *ʾamara*, provides us with an example of a similar change. Its primary meaning in Akkadian is "to see," and this may be presumed to have been its original meaning in Semitic. The change posited for *lamādu* should help us understand how *amāru* may have assumed the meaning it has in West Semitic; such a development can even be documented in Akkadian itself where the meaning "to decide," "pronounce a decision," for *amāru* is attested, albeit rarely,[33] and we may posit the semantic development "to observe," "find"

32 E. Burrows, "Hymn to Ninurta as Sirius (K 128)," *JRAS Centenary Supplement* (1924): 35: 2–36: 6 (pl. III); cf. Seux, *Hymnes*, 482.

33 Cf. *CAD* A/2, 23: *ṭēmu* b). For the verb *ʾmr*, cf. J. Barr, "Etymology and the Old Testament," in *Language and Meaning: Studies in Hebrew Language and Biblical Exegesis*, OTS 19 (Leiden: Brill, 1974), 5–6.

→ "to decide," "make known," "say," "command." A comparable development, but this time from West to East, occurs with *zakāru*: Hebrew *zāḵar*, "to remember" (*hizkîr*, "to mention") → Akkadian *zakāru*, "to mention." In English, the verb "find" in its legal usage "to find for" comes close to exemplifying the kind of change we have in mind.

### 1.2 *Constructions and Development*

Having cited some examples of *alaktu* and *alakta lamādu*, we may now attend to their behavior in Akkadian literature. We recall that *alaktu* is an oracular term and refers to a divine decision and that *alakta lamādu* refers to the revelation of that decision. These terms were limited to the divine sphere and to the institutions of divination. In this respect, they contrast with a number of other terms referring to divine rulings, such as *dīnu*, *purussû*, *dīna šutēšuru*, *warkata parāsu*, etc. Regardless of whether these judicial terms are regarded as intrusions from the legal domain into that of divination or from divination into law,[34] these terms became the common property of the law court and of the divination priest. Consequently, divine deliberation came to be seen as a judgment, and the revelation of the divine decision by means of signs as the handing down of a verdict.[35] The literary consequences are striking, for with the introduction of legal images and courtroom metaphors, prayers for divine guidance are modified and even transformed into addresses to divine judges, and divination procedures take on the guise of a hearing. And legal formulations serve as complements of and alternatives to prayer and oracular formulae. It should suffice to compare the beginning of Codex Ḫammurabi §5: *šumma dayyānum dīnam idīn purussâm iprus*, "If a judge judged a case and rendered a verdict," with the common *dīnī dīn purussâya purus*, "provide my judgment, render my verdict," of the prayers of the individual as well as with such phrases drawn from the rituals of the *bārû* priest as *dīnu u purussû*, "divine judgment and verdict," *dīnu u bīru*, "divine judgment and oracular answer (extispicy)," and *bīru u purussû*, "oracular answer and divine verdict."[36]

34 It should not be forgotten that divination may be used to settle legal matters when normal "human" juridical processes are unable to resolve the problem.

35 For the use of judicial terms and images in divination, cf., e.g., A. Walther, *Das altbabylonische Gerichtswesen*, LSS 6/4–6 (Leipzig: Hinrichs, 1917), 89 n. 1, 219 n. 2, 222 n. 2; J. Bottéro, "Symptômes, signes, écritures en Mésopotamie ancienne," in *Divination et rationalité*, ed. J. P. Vernant (Paris: Seuil, 1974), 139–143; I. Starr, *The Rituals of the Diviner*, BMes 12 (Malibu, CA: Undena, 1983), 57–58.

36 Cf. *BBR* 2, no. 25: 4; Langdon, VAB 4, 150: NbK 12, iii 21; *BBR* 2, no. 24, obv. 29 = W. G. Lambert, "Enmeduranki and Related Matters," *JCS* 21 (1967 [1969]): 132: 29 (for the join *BBR* 2, nos. 24 and 25, see Lambert, "Enmeduranki," 127).

The opposite or a reversal of this trend is to be associated with the introduction of *alakta lamādu*. This phrase came into contact with and competed with judicial terms and brought about a change of imagery and emphasis in prayers to astral deities and in descriptions of divination procedures. In factual terms, *alakta lamādu* either supplemented, eliminated, or combined with standard legal terms and thus effected the change. We may illustrate this development by examining several prayers to astral deities and descriptions of divination procedures.

Prayers

1) *dīnī dīnī purussâya pursī alaktī lim*[*dī*] (*BMS* 4: 30; Gula 1b).[37] Here *alakta lamādun* is simply added to the standard legal stereotype *dīna dânu, purussâ parāsu*. That *alaktī limdī* in this prayer to Gula is an addition is evident from a comparison of this text with the genetically related prayer to Gula, *BMS* 6 and dupls. (// Bēlet-ilī, *BMS* 7 and dupls.).[38] Whereas *aššu*(*m*) *dīni dâni purussâ parāsi* is found in Gula 1a (*BMS* 6 // Bēlet-ilī, *BMS* 7),[39] *alakta lamādu* is absent there. The secondary nature of *alaktī limdī* is further suggested by the poetic clumsiness and unnecessary length of the chain in *BMS* 4: 30.
2) *Maqlû* I 14: Here *alakta lamādu* has simply replaced the second half of the stereotype *dīna dânu purussâ parāsu*, and we now have *dīnī dīnā alaktī limdā*.
3) *Šamaš dayyān šamê u erṣeti dayyān mīti u balāṭi attāma*
*ana nīš qāt<ya> qūlamma alaktī limad*.[40]

37 = Mayer, *Untersuchungen*, Gula 1b, 456: 16.

38 *BMS* 6 = *AGH* 46–49; *BMS* 7 = *AGH* 54–57. For a new edition of the combined prayer, see Mayer, *Untersuchungen*, 450–454. [For a comparison of these Gula prayers, see now pp. 206–214 in this volume.]

39 Mayer, *Untersuchungen*, 451: 74. However, I must admit that this line in *BMS* 6 // 7 seems to have been subjected to revision/corruption. It lacks a predicate (contrast the following two lines in both *BMS* 6 // 7 and *BMS* 4) and shows excessive textual fluidity (an earlier form of the line might have been **dīnī dīnī purussâya pursī*). [But see above, pp. 212–213.]

40 *BAM* 214 [[*CMAwR* 1, no. 8.1, A]] ii 10–13: $^{d}$UTU DI.KUD AN *u* KI-*ti* / DI.KUD BA.ÚŠ *u* TI.LA *at-ta-ma* / *ana* ÍL ŠU *qu-lam-ma* / *a-lak-ti li-mad*. Similar lines are found on the edge of *KAR*, no. 92 [[*CMAwR* 1, no. 7.7, B]]. Duplicates of the ritual *KAR* 92, obv. 1–29 (// K 9334 [identified by F. W. Geers] // 9082 [identified by T. Abusch] // 15055 [identified by T. Abusch] [[*CMAwR* 1, no. 7.7, Ac]]) link the prayer with *KAR* 92, obv. and allow us to insert it between *KAR* 92, obv. 17 and 18, with the section ÉN $^{d}$UTU ... as the beginning of the prayer and *a-ta-nam-da-ru* ... as the end. The opening lines of the prayer are on *KAR* 92 // K 9082 // 15055. The lines in *KAR* 92 of interest to us read: ÉN $^{d}$UTU MAN (var. LUGAL) AN-*e u* KI-*ti* DI!.KUD $^{d}$[*í*]-⌜*gì-gì*⌝ (?) (E. Ebeling, *Quellen zur Kenntnis der*

O Šamaš, the judge of the heavens and the netherworld,
the judge of the dead and of the living are you.
Pay heed to my prayer and grant me an (oracular) decision.

The request "Pay heed to my prayer and grant me an (oracular) decision" seems to have no legal overtones and to represent a simple request for an oracle. Here the expected legal stereotype *dīna dânu purussâ parāsu* does not even occur in vestigial form and may be regarded as having been ousted.

Descriptions

The following citations derive from therapeutic texts and provide us with a statement of some of the purposes of the treatment:

*itti bārî u šā'ili*[41] *dīnšu adi sibittišu lā iššer*
*qabû lā šemû šaknūšu*
*ana purussêšu parāsimma dīnšu ana šutēšuri*
*šunātūšu ana damiqti alaktašu ana lamādi*[42]
*ubān damiqti arkišu ana tarāṣi*

As many as seven times the divination for him does not work out well with the diviner and dream interpreter.
He is beset by speaking and not being heeded.
So that a verdict be rendered for him, that a successful judgment be given him,
that his dreams become favorable, that an oracle be manifest for him,
that a favorable finger be stretched out after him. (*BAM* 316 [[*CMAwR* 2, no. 3.6, A]] ii 12′–16′)[43]

*ilšu u ištaršu ina qaqqadišu ana uzuzzi itti bārî u šā*[*'ili dīnšu ana šutēšuri*]
*alaktašu*[44] *ana lamādi dīnšu purussû* ... [ ]

*babylonischen Religion*, vol. 2, MVAG 23/2 [Leipzig: Hinrichs, 1919], 35, reads [*šamê*]$^{e}$) *at*-⌈*ta*⌉-[*ma*] / *ana* ÍL ŠU$^{II}$-*iá*! (var. MU) *qu-lam-ma a*-[*l*]*ak-ti* ⌈*li*⌉-[*mad*].

41 I have interpreted LÚ.DINGIR.RA as *ša*(LÚ)-*ili*(DINGIR.RA).

42 For parallel passages without *alakta lamādu*, cf., e.g., *STT*, nos. 95 iii + 295 [[*CMAwR* 2, no. 3.7, B]]: 136–137, and *SpBTU* 2, no. 22, p. 109 [[*CMAwR* 2, no. 3.4, a]]: 22–25.

43 [K]I LÚ.ḪAL *u* LÚ.DINGIR.RA *di-in-šú* EN 7-*šú* NU SI.SÁ / [D]UG$_4$.⌈GA⌉ NU ŠE.GA GAR-*nu-šú* / *ana* EŠ.BAR-*šú* TAR-*si-im*-⌈*ma di*⌉-[*i*]*n*-⌈*šú* ⌉ *ana* SI.SÁ / MÁŠ.GI$_6$.MEŠ-*šú ana* SIG$_5$-⌈*tì*⌉ A.RÁ-*šú ana* ZU-*di* / ŠU.SI SIG$_5$-*tì* EGIR-*šú ana* LAL-*ṣi*.

44 It is possible that the occurrence of [*a-lak*]-*ta-šu* GIG-*at* (cf. the duplicate line in *BAM* 326 [[*CMAwR* 2, no. 3.7]] ii′ 7′: A.RÁ-*šú* GIG): *alaktašu marṣat* in the first line of the text (446, obv. i) should be taken into account.

> In order that his god and goddess stand at his head, that an efficacious divination judgment be provided him by diviner and dream interpreter, that an oracle be manifest for him, that his judgment and verdict be …
> (*BAM* 446 [K 2562] [[*CMAwR* 2, no. 3.8]], obv. 8–9)[45]

In these therapeutic texts *alakta lamādu* refers to a form of divination and has been added to or included with a series of other divination procedures or methods. Their successful operation/application is one of the goals of the magical treatment.

### 1.3 alaktu *and* têrtu

Our results thus far suggest a solution to a well-known crux of Akkadian literature; in turn the passages provide support for our interpretation of *alaktu*.

> *dalḫā têrētū'a nuppuḫū uddakam*
> *itti bārî u šā'ili alaktī ul parsat*
> *Ludlul* I 51–52[46]

> *ušabri bārâ têrtī dalḫat*
> *ašāl šā'ila alktī ul parsat*
> K 2765 = *BWL*, 288: 8–9

> *itti bārî šā'ili alaktu ul parsat attīlma / ina šāt mūši šutti pardat*
> Nabonidus[47]

In these passages we notice that *alaktu* is joined to the verb *parāsu*, stands in parallelism with *têrtu* (in the first two), and occurs together with other types of omens (e.g., dreams).[48]

*Alaktī ul parsat* of *Ludlul* I 52 has puzzled Assyriologists. Several translations of this line have been considered. None are satisfactory. One need only study W. G. Lambert's presentation of alternative translations and the objections

---

45 DINGIR-*šú u* $^{d}$XV *šú ina* SAG.DU *šú ana* GUB-*zi* KI LÚ ḪAL *u* E[NSI DI-*šú ana* SI.SÁ] / ⌜Á.⌝RÁ-*šú ana* ZU-*di di-in-šú* EŠ.BAR ⌜xx(x)⌝ [ ]. (The space between EŠ.BAR and the traces prevents me from restoring -⌜*šú* ⌝.)

46 *BWL*, 32. Lambert (*BWL*, 33) translates: "The omen organs are confused and inflamed for me every day. / The omen of the diviner and dream priest does not explain my condition." Biggs (*ANET*, 596) translates: "The omens concerning me are confused, daily there *is inflammation.* / I cannot stop going to the diviner and dream interpreter."

47 C. J. Gadd, "The Harran Inscriptions of Nabonidus," *AnSt* 8 (1958): 62: 1–2, as cited and read by Lambert, *BWL*, 284, in his discussion of *Ludlul* I 52 and K 2765: 9.

48 *BWL*, 284. *Ludlul* I 54; K 2765: 7; Gadd, "Harran Inscriptions," 62: 1–2.

to each (*BWL*, 284)[49] to understand the difficulties that this usage has posed. *Alaktī* (*ul*) *parsat* has been misunderstood because it was not recognized that *alaktu* here is used in the meaning that we have tried to establish for this word and because the true significance of the joining here of *alaktu* with *parāsu* escaped notice. Previously, we encountered *parāsu* in the legal/divination phrase *purussâ parāsu* and also found this phrase coupled with *alakta lamādu*. In *Ludlul* as well as in the two other passages cited above, *alaktu* and *parāsu* have the same force that they have in *alakta lamādu* and *purussâ parāsu*, respectively. *Alaktu* (*ul*) *parsat* in these three passages is nothing more than a (newly coined) conflation, a cross between *alakta lamādu*, "to grant an (oracular) decree" and *purussâ parāsu*, "to render a verdict." Accordingly we would now translate *dalḫā têrētū'a* / *têrtī dalḫat ... alaktī ul parsat* as

> My extispicy-omens are confused;
> My oracular decision is not rendered.

What has happened in these passages is quite simple. The noun *alaktu* has suppressed *purussû*, the cognate accusative of *parāsu*, and has become fused with the verb *parāsu* to form a new idiom *alaktu parsat*.[50] Substitutions comparable to that of *alakta parāsu* for *purussâ parāsu* are observable elsewhere. Thus we find *milku* with the meaning "decision of a deity" serving as the object of *parāsu* in *ina qibītika rabīti milikšina taprus*,[51] "By your great decree you render their decision." Similarly *purussâ* or *warkata parāsu* is replaced by *awāta parāsu* in an Old Babylonian prayer to the gods of the night.[52]

Our analysis and translation of *alaktī ul parsat* fit the general divination context of the passages cited above. That they are correct is proved by the fact that *alaktī ul parsat* is used in these passages in parallelism with *dalḫā têrētū'a* / *têrtī dalḫat*. And the parallelism here of *alaktu* and *têrtu*, "extispicy omen," in

49 After weighing several alternatives, Lambert chose the last of the alternatives and translated the line as "The omen (*itti*) of the diviner and dream priest does not explain my condition (*alaktī ul parsat*)." In any case, *it-ti* here must be the preposition *itti* in view of *itti*(KI) *bārî u šā'ili* of the therapeutic texts cited above. Biggs, *ANET*, 596, and *CAD* A/1, 299, follow Lambert's second alternative.

50 The occurrence of *alaktu* with *parāsu* in a different meaning (see, e.g., *CAD* A/1, 299) may have facilitated the formation of this neologism.

51 W. G. Lambert, "Fire Incantations," *AfO* 23 (1970): 43: 27, cited in *CAD* M/2, 68. The replacement of *purussû* by *milku* may be due perhaps to the association of these two words in parallelism; cf. *CAD* M/2, 68, 1c) 1'.

52 G. Dossin, "Prières aux 'dieux de la nuit' (AO 6769)," *RA* 32 (1935): 180a: 8 // b: 8–9: *ul idinnū dīnam ul iparrasū awâtim*, "They (the gods Šamaš, Sîn, etc.) are not providing judgment, are not deciding cases."

a divination context confirms our interpretation of *alaktu* as denoting some form of oracular decision.

The occurrence of the older *têrtu* and the later *alaktu* in poetic parallelism should not surprise us.[53] Such an association of similar phenomena was almost to be expected; certainly the association is illuminating. *Têrtu* and *alaktu* are approximate synonyms. As stated earlier, both derive from verbs of motion: *alaktu* from *alāku*; *têrtu* from *wa'āru*. Accordingly, neither is the derivation of a noun referring to an "oracular decision," *alaktu*, from a verb of motion, *alāku*, strange, nor is such a development limited to *alaktu*. We now have the proportion: *alāku* : *wa'āru* :: *alaktu* : *tertu*.[54]

## 1.4 *Context and Meaning*

We must still define more closely the meaning of *alaktu* and *alakta lamādu*. First, though, we should acknowledge that we have simplified matters thus far and have not drawn the desired distinctions, passage by passage, between objects which may, however, not always be distinguishable: sign, oracle, course. *Alaktu* and *alakta lamādu* deserve more nuanced treatments than I have provided. I have stated the case in a rather bald manner because it seemed necessary, first of all, to establish for the contexts examined here that *alaktu* does not simply mean "procedure," "behavior," "way," but refers, rather, to a form of divine revelation/oracle through which is manifested a message regarding the future, and that the activity designated *alakta lamādu* is oriented to the future rather than to the past.

All the more reason, therefore, to mention the well-known idiom *warkata parāsu* before moving ahead with our treatment. For this idiom underwent a semantic development strikingly similar to the one we observed with *alakta lamādu* and provides further confirmation. A basic meaning of *warkata parāsu* is "to look into a matter," "investigate or learn a situation or background," just as a basic meaning of *alakta lamādu* is "to learn/perceive a course." Several scholars noticed that this meaning of *warkata parāsu* did not fit all contexts and suggested that *warkata parāsu* could also refer to the prediction of the future (thus providing an example of the development or perhaps just the association of "to investigate/look into a matter" and "to decide a matter").[55] We find

53 Cf. the association of *alaktu* with *wu''urtu* noted above, section 1.1.

54 I have been careful not to state *alāku* : *alaktu* :: *wa'āru: têrtu*.

55 See A. Goetze, "Reports on Acts of Extispicy from Old Babylonian and Kassite Times," *JCS* 11 (1957): 96 n. 41; R. Borger, "Die Inschriften Asarhaddons (AfO Beiheft 9). Nachträge und Verbesserungen," *AfO* 18 (1957–1958): 117; E. Reiner, "Fortune-Telling in Mesopotamia," *JNES* 19 (1960): 26 n. 7; cf., already, Zimmern, *BBR* 2, pp. 87–88. Even B. Landsberger (*Brief des Bischofs von Esagila an König Asarhaddon* [Amsterdam: N.V.

that the past perspective of *warkata parāsu* shifts to a future one in divination contexts, and we notice that *warkata parāsu,* then, takes on the added meaning "to reveal the future," "send an oracle." What is striking here are, first, the occurrence of a semantic shift comparable to the one we witness with *alakta lamādu* (to learn/investigate a course → to reveal the course/sign/decision) and, second, the occurrence of that shift in similar social contexts: the institutions of divination. One is almost tempted to suppose mutual contact and influence, a suggestion that finds explicit support in the interchange of *parās* and *lamāda* with (*w*)*arkati* in a passage previously quoted: *parās arkatu nesânni* ᵈ*šamši ... ana lamāda arkati attaziz maḫarka,*[56] and in the substitution of *parāsu* for *lamādu* (or, if you wish, the substitution of *alaktu* for *purussû*) in the usage *alaktī ul parsat.*

As regards *alaktu* our understanding is not yet sufficiently precise or concrete. We stated earlier that *alaktu* refers to a divine ruling revealed by means of signs and to the ominous course itself. In light of such analogies as *warkata parāsu* we are now perhaps in a better position to understand how "a course" came to mean "an oracular decision" and "to learn a course" came to be used in the meaning of "to reveal a divine decision." But clearly we must also specify the means by which the oracular decision was given, the signs and forms to which *alaktu* refers and through which the course manifested itself. In fact, these questions are not unrelated; for by determining the kind of signs intended, we will also see how "course" could come to mean "decision."

The evidence is not really sufficient, but what there is suggests to me that *alaktu* is an astrological term and refers to the manifestations, movements, or configurations of heavenly bodies. The gods are sometimes powers that are separate from the heavenly bodies, and sometimes they are the heavenly bodies themselves; thus, depending on whether the gods observe the heavenly bodies or are identical with them, "to learn the course," said of the gods, may mean either that the gods learn the course or that they themselves experience and reveal the actual course.[57] *Alaktu* is explicitly used of the course of the stars

Noord-Hollandsche Uitgevers Maatschappij, 1965], 21 n. 28) concurred, albeit with the caveat that *warkatu* in the past use derives from *warkatu,* "das Dahinterliegende," whereas *warkatu* in the future use derives from *warkiātu,* "Zukunft." But see C. Wilcke's interesting remarks on the Babylonian association of the notions "back" and "future" in C. Wilcke, "Zum Geschichtsbewusstsein im alten Mesopotamien," in *Archäologie und Geschichtsbewusstsein,* Kolloquien zur allgemeinen und vergleichenden Archäologie 3 (Munich: Beck, 1982), 31–32.

56 See above, section 1.1.

57 Part of the modern and even ancient confusion of terminology and images may be due to the existence separately as well as in combination of two distinct attitudes: gods are identical with natural phenomena, here the heavenly bodies, and the activities of heavenly

(*alkāt kakkabī*) in *Enūma eliš*.[58] This is in line with the use elsewhere of *alāku* and its derivatives, *mālaku* and *tāluku*. The existence of an astral signification for *alaktu* need not surprise us; we may presume that this meaning resulted from a transfer or extension of terrestrial meanings of *alāku*/*alaktu* to the heavens, and may compare, for example, the extension of terrestrial meanings of *uzuzzu* "to stand," and derivatives (e.g., *mazzaz*/*ltu*) to heavenly contexts.[59] Assuming, moreover, that the beings found among the stars in the bilingual incantation CT 16, pls. 42–46, are, or may be treated as if they were, celestial bodies,[60] we might also cite here imin.bi a.rá ba.an.zu ki.bi in.kin.kin.gá

bodies are manifestations of the divine; gods are separate from, but in control of, heavenly bodies. Hence, gods examine but also reveal themselves through heavenly bodies and movements. A carry-over of this duality may perhaps be seen in the identification and differentiation of the roles of diviner and god: sometimes the human, sometimes the divine, and sometimes both are seen as judges who investigate and make decisions. (When the divine and the phenomenon are identical, the diviner investigates and decides; when the divine and the phenomenon are separate, the god or both the god and the diviner investigate and decide.) For a different explanation of the functioning of both diviner and god as judges, see Bottéro, "Symptomes," 142.

58 See *AHw*, s.v. *alaktu*, 31, 6 a) v, "Sternen," citing *Enūma eliš* VII 130. [d]*nēbiru nēbiret šamê u erṣeti lū tameḫma* / … / [d]*nēbiru kakkabšu ša ina šamê ušāpû* / … / *ša kakkabī šamāmī alkāssunu likīnma* (*Enūma eliš* VII 124, 126, 130). Text: W. G. Lambert and S. B. Parker, *Enūma Eliš: The Babylonian Epic of Creation: The Cuneiform Text* (Oxford: Clarendon, 1966), 45–46. Translation: B. Landsberger and J. V. Kinnier Wilson, "The Fifth Tablet of Enūma Eliš," *JNES* 20 (1961): 173: "Nebiru shall hold the passages of Heaven and Earth … Nebiru is his star, that he had made appear in the sky … He shall stablish the roads of the stars of heaven …" See also [d]*Tutu* … / *ša ukinnu ana ilī šamê ellū*[*ti*] / *alkāssunu iṣbatuma u'addû* [*manzāssun*] (*Enūma eliš* VII 15–17). Text: Lambert and Parker, *Enūma Eliš*, 41. Translation: "Tutu … who established the bright heavens for the gods, who took control of their (celestial) courses, assigned them their (celestial) positions."

59 See *CAD* A/1, s.v. *alāku*, 309, 3. a); *CAD* M/1, s.v. *mālaku*, 159, end of first paragraph; *AHw*, 1312, s.v. *tāluku* 4), "Gestirnbahn." See also R. Borger, *Die Inschriften Asarhaddons, Königs von Assyrien*, AfO Beih. 9 (Graz: Ernst Weidner, 1956), 18: Episode 14b 6–7: *kakkabū šamê ina manzāzišunu illikūma* (DU.MEŠ-*ma*; but see Landsberger and Kinnier Wilson, "Fifth Tablet," 171 n. 8, who read *izzizzūma* [i.e., GUB.MEŠ-*ma*]) *ḫarrān kītti iṣbatū umaššerū uruḫ la kitti*. "Die Sterne des Himmels zogen in ihren (normalen) Stationen dahin; sie zogen den richtigen und verliessen den unrichtigen Weg." For other examples of the projection of terrestrial forms into the heavens, cf., e.g., B. A. Levine, "From the Aramaic Enoch Fragments: The Semantics of Cosmography," *JJS* 33 (1982): 311–326.

60 For the close association of demons and stars, see R. Caplice's important statement, "É.NUN in Mesopotamian Literature," *Or* NS 42 (1973): 304–305. As regards the demons of CT 16, pls. 42–46, Caplice (305) observes: "In other instances, demons seem to be even more closely associated with stars …, and the seven evil demons, having spread destruction, 'went off to the heavens on high, departed to the unapproachable heavens; they cannot be recognized among the stars of heaven (Sum.: the stars of heaven do not reveal their sign) in their three watches.'"

sağ.na.an.gi ù.mu.un.na.an.sum: *alkakāt sibittišunu lamādu ašrātīšunu šite''â ḫīšamma*,[61] "Quickly examine the course of the seven and seek/search out oracles/omens from them." This line calls to mind Nebuchadnezzar's statement *ašrāti ilī ašten''e / alakti ilī erteneddi*,[62] "I repeatedly seek oracles of the god(s), I repeatedly follow after the (celestial) course of the god(s)."

---

61 CT 16, 45: 122–124.

62 Langdon, VAB 4, 122: NbK 15, i 28–29. For the meaning "to seek/inquire for an oracle" (from the god's temple) for *ašra* DN *site''û*, see H. Tadmor, "The Inscriptions of Nabunaid: Historical Arrangement," in *Studies in Honor of Benno Landsberger on His Seventy-fifth Birthday, April 21, 1965*, ed. H. G. Güterbock and T. Jacobsen, AS 16 (Chicago: University of Chicago Press, 1965), 357 n. 36. See also A. Goetze, "An Inscription of Simbar-Šīḫu," *JCS* 19 (1965): 129–131, and M.-J. Seux, "*šite''û ašrāt*(*i*) (À propos d'un article récent)," *RA* 60 (1966): 172–174. Note M.-J. Seux, *Épithètes royales akkadiennes et sumériennes* (Paris: Letouzey et Ané, 1967), 323 n. 309 on *mušte''û asrāt* DN, "qui examine les lieux d'DN": "Il s'agit ici de l'examen des lieux où les dieux manifestent leur volonté par des signes ou des oracles." Or as he states in "*šite''û ašrāt*(*i*)," 174, *ašrāt* DN *šite''û* means "'soumettre à investigation les lieux (où cette divinité manifeste sa volonté par des signes),' 'examiner les lieux (omineux),'" or even "'examiner (*ou*: soumettre à investigation, analyser) ce qui a lieu, la conjoncture.'" In VAB 4, 122: NbK 15, i 28–29, I am uncertain whether to read *ilī* (cf., e.g., *CAD* A/1, 298: *ilī* and Langdon's translation [VAB 4, 123], "Götter") or *ili* (1*R* records only DINGIR, and this agrees with the use of *alaktu* in the singular). I 1–50 treat Nebuchadnezzar's relation to both Marduk and Nabû.

Note also the mention of *alaktu* before and after the lines cited above, NbK 15, i 28–29. Thus among the introductory epithets, Nebuchadnezzar is *migir* ᵈ*Marduk* ... *narām* ᵈ*Nabû*(*m*) ... *ša alakti ilūtišunu ištene''û* (pp. 120 and 122: 4, 6, 8–9), and following lines 28–29, the internally balanced double clause says of him: *ša* ᵈ*Marduk bēlu rabû ilu bāniya epšētūšu naklāti eliš attanâdu* // *ša* ᵈ*Nabû apilšu kīni*(*m*) *narām šarrūtiya alakti ilūtišu ṣīrti kīniš uštenêdu* (122: 30–36). (Note the use of rare forms—Gtn, Št—of *nâdu* here with both Marduk and Nabû.) Here in NbK 15, *alaktu* (NbK 19, i 6, *alkakāt*) of Marduk + Nabû refers to decrees made known by the movements of the heavenly bodies of Marduk and Nabû; cf. *ina qibīti ṣīrti ša* ᵈ*Nabû* ᵈ*Marduk ša ina manzāz kakkabī ša šutbê kakkiya iṣbatū tāluku* / *u idat dumqi ša* ... (F. Thureau-Dangin, *Textes cunéiformes du Louvre*, vol. 3 [Paris: Geuthner, 1912], lines 317–318). Note also that VAB 4, 150: NbK 19, i 14–15: *ana ṭēmu ilūtišunu basâ uznāšu* (// [= parallel] VAB 4, 98: NbK 11, i 4–5: *ša ana alkakāt ilī rabûti bašâ uznāšu* [the use of *bašâ uznāšu* is original to *ṭēmu* and is carried over to *alaktu*]) is preceded by *ša alkakāt* ᵈ*Marduk bēlu rabiu*(*m*) *ilu bānišu u* ᵈ*Nabû aplišu kīni*(*m*) *narām šarrūtišu ištene''û kayyānam* (150: NbK 19, i 6–10). Far from indicating that *ṭēmu* and *alaktu* are not synonyms in that text or undercutting our argument that *alaktu* in NbK 11 denotes an oracle, the use of both *alaktu* and *ṭēmu* in NbK 19—when taken together with the functional equivalence of NbK 19, i 14–15 and NbK 11, i 4–5 and with the pattern of use of *alaktu* in NbK 15—suggests that even for the writer of NbK 19 *alaktu* and *ṭēmu* are already synonyms, and shows us how easily a scribe could replace *ṭēmu* with *alaktu*.

That the manifestation designated *alaktu* is of an astral character is also suggested by the fact that, as far as I can recall, the Akkadian prayers in which *alakta lamādu* occurs are apparently all addressed to celestial deities.[63] The suggestion is supported by considerations of a circumstantial nature. The two major types of divination are extispicy and astrology. The practice of astrology and astral speculation increase in importance during the latter part of Mesopotamian history. While *alaktu* may already have been used earlier in the meaning here posited,[64] it is in this late period that *alaktu* is used with some frequency in its oracular sense. Clusters of datable examples occur precisely in documents from the seventh and sixth centuries: astral reports sent by astrologers to the late Assyrian court[65] and the inscriptions of Nebuchadnezzar II. Moreover, the other major form of divination, extispicy, is already covered, for the ominous signs in the exta of a sacrificial lamb, the scrutiny of the exta, and the divine intention thus revealed are designated by the term *têrtu*, and the companion term *alaktu* need therefore not be pressed into the service of extispicy.

The use of *alaktu* as an astrological term for celestial movements should explain how "course" came to mean "divine decision." The course of the planets and stars, the signs or writing of the heavenly gods, represent the cosmic will. These signs, especially when properly examined or rendered especially conspicuous, reveal the intention of heaven and provide man with the ruling of the gods. This, then, is the *alaktu*. Like *dīnu*, *alaktu* denotes a medium or source, an act, and an outcome. The course of the stars is the vehicle by which, or the canvas upon which, the divine or natural will manifests itself. The examination undertaken and the decision announced by astral gods and divination priests constitute the act of drawing out and making known that will. And the way of life one leads as a consequence of the decision is the final outcome. *Alakta lamādu* is, then, coming to know the revelation and announcing its ruling.[66]

---

63 Even *alakta dummuqu* occurs in a prayer to the sun.

64 See above, n. 31. It is possible that a.rá was used with this meaning in Sumerian (cf., e.g., the bilingual texts cited in this paper) or even that the development had its starting point in Sumerian. The latter does not seem likely. I have not conducted a proper investigation of the use of a.rá in Sumerian (my thanks to S. J. Lieberman for providing me with a list of references from the files of the Pennsylvania Sumerian Dictionary) and would leave these questions to others.

65 See above, section 1.1.

66 Hence it is possible for *alaktu* in this meaning to refer not only to the course of the stars, but also to the course that the individual will take in the future.

## 2 *halakhah*: Jewish Sources and Mesopotamian Influence

Turning to the question of *halakhah*, we may now seek to extend our earlier proportion to include *torah* (*tôrā*) and *halakhah* (*hălāḵā*), for *têrtu* and *alaktu* are probably their respective antecedents or analogues: *waʾāru* : *alāku* :: *têrtu* : *alaktu* :: *tôrā* : *hălāḵā*. Recalling the lines cited above: *ašrāti ilī aštene*ʾʾ*e* / *alakti ilī erteneddi* and *alkakāt sibittišunu lamādu* / *ašrātīšunu šite*ʾʾ*â*, where *ašrāt DN šite*ʾʾ*û* actually means to seek an oracle or a sign of the god and is comparable to the semantic range of Hebrew *dāraš* (דרש) or *biqqēš* (בקש),[67] we are reminded of the remark in b. Shabbat 138b on Amos 8:12: לבקש את דבר ה׳ דבר ה׳ זו הלכה, "'to seek the word of the Lord': 'the word of the Lord'—this refers to *halakhah*," and of Rashi's astute comment on this Talmudic remark: זו הלכה כדכתיב להגיד לכם את דבר ה׳ דהיינו תורה, "'this refers to *halakha*': as it is written 'to tell you the word of the Lord,' that is, Torah."

### 2.1 *Information*

Let us now set out some pertinent information regarding *halakhah*.[68]

1. In Hebrew, the earliest certain occurrences of *hălāḵā* (הלכה), "law," known to me are in the Mishna. It seems to have meant: a normative religious law, a ruling the human derivation of which was not witnessed by those party to the discussion, a traditional or anonymous law, a ruling which occasionally even derived from a divine revelation to Moses on Sinai. *Hălāḵā* belongs to a pattern used for judicial/exegetical terms. The pattern differs from that used to form terms of a general nature derived from the same root; thus

הלכה—הליכה; דרשה—דרישה; ראיה—ראייה

2. Jewish Aramaic (JA) *hilḵēṯā* (הלכתא) first appears in Talmudic Aramaic and perhaps earlier in the Targum to 2 Kgs 11:14. The word is not Common Aramaic. It occurs in JA and Syriac[69] and in both it has the meaning "going,"

67 For *še'û* // Hebrew *dāraš*, cf. Tadmor, "Inscriptions," 357 n. 36; for *še'û* // Hebrew *biqqēš*, cf. M. Held, "Two Philological Notes on Enūma Eliš," in *Kramer Anniversary Volume: Cuneiform Studies in Honor of Samuel Noah Kramer*, ed. B. L. Eichler, AOAT 25 (Kevelaer: Butzon & Bercker; Neukirchen-Vluyn: Neukirchner Verlag, 1976), 233 and n. 23.

68 Cf. the standard lexicons (Bacher, Dalman, Jastrow, Levy) and concordances of rabbinic literature.

69 Syriac *helkĕtā* / *helaḵtā*: "going, walking, treading, marching, way"; cf. *helkā*: "going, way, walk"; see R. Payne Smith, *A Compendious Syriac Dictionary*, ed. J. Payne Smith (Oxford: Clarendon, 1903), 104. The transcription JA *hilḵēṯā* follows the traditional Jewish pronunciation of the word.

"walk," "way." The more usual meaning of *hilk̲ĕt̲ā* in JA is, of course, "norm," "rule," "decision," etc., the meaning it shares with Hebrew *hălāk̲ā*. Thus *hilk̲ĕt̲ā* covers the same ground as Hebrew *hălîk̲ā* + *hălāk̲ā*. Of special interest to us is the fact that the juridical meaning is limited to Jewish Aramaic. Dictionary entries notwithstanding, the consonantal verb *hlk* does not seem to appear in Aramaic in the *peʿal* (*qal*).[70] In its stead, we have the suppletive verbs *hwk* and *ʾzl*; *hlk* does appear in the *paʿel* (denominative[?]).

3. *Lāmad* (למד), "to learn," is a common Hebrew word. In rabbinic Hebrew it also means "to infer," "conclude," "decide," etc. The usual word for *lāmad* in JA is *yĕlaf* (ילף ← אלף). Generally speaking, *lāmad* is alien to Aramaic except in mixed Hebrew-Aramaic Jewish texts, and then it occurs usually in a Hebrew clause.

4. Finally, the idiom *lāmad hălāk̲ā* (למד הלכה) [cf. *alakta lamādu*] is not uncommon. For example, b. Baba Batra 130b: למדין הלכה לא מפי למוד ולא מפי מעשה, "One decides a ruling neither from theoretical considerations nor from action," or b. Niddah 7b: אלא הא קמ"ל שאין למדין הלכה מפי תלמוד.

## 2.2 *Hypotheses*

It is possible that *halakhah* is the result of an inner Hebrew development. A parallel and independent semantic development would then have taken place in both Akkadian and Hebrew, a fact of no little importance. If such is indeed the case, then we have reconstructed and partially documented the stages of development in Akkadian and have provided a model which can be carried over to explain the development of *halakhah* in Hebrew: courses of the stars →

70 Note that M. Jastrow himself observed that of the two examples of *peʿal* that he cites, one has *paʿel* in ms. and the other *paʿel* in some editions; see M. Jastrow, *A Dictionary of the Targumim, the Talmud Babli and Yerushalmi, and the Midrashic Literature*, 2 vols. (1926; repr., New York: Pardes, 1950), 1:353, s.v. *hălak̲* Ch[aldaic] verb. Generally speaking, the few examples cited by C.-F. Jean and J. Hoftijzer, *Dictionnaire des inscriptions sémitiques de l'ouest* (Leiden: Brill, 1965), 65, of an Aramaic *peʿal* with the consonants *hlk* are better treated as *paʿel* (Nab. *qal* pf. 3fs *hlkt* can be *paʿel*; so, too, Palm. *qal* pf. 3ms *hlk*; the only other Palm. form cited is a *paʿel* partic.). The occurrence of *hlk* in the *qal* at Deir ʿAlla may be ignored, since the language seems to be Canaanite rather than Aramaic; cf., e.g., J. C. Greenfield, review of J. Hoftijzer and G. van der Kooij, eds., *Aramaic Texts from Deir ʿAlla*, *JSS* 25 (1980): 250–251, and J. A. Hackett, "The Dialect of the Plaster Text from Tell Deir ʿAlla," *Or* NS 53 (1984): 57–65, esp. 64. For *hlk* in the Genesis Apocryphon, see J. A. Fitzmyer, *The Genesis Apocryphon of Qumran Cave I*, BibOr 18 (Rome: Pontifical Biblical Institute, 1966), 134, on col. 21: 13. W. R. Garr (*The Dialect Geography of Syria-Palestine, 1000–586 B.C.E.* [Philadelphia: University of Pennsylvania Press, 1985], 144–146) has now reviewed the evidence and reconfirmed the observation that the root *hlk* is not attested in Old Aramaic: "In short, Aramaic stood apart from the other NWS dialects which attest a verb 'to go,' since it alone used the root **hwk* instead of **hlk* / **wlk*" (145).

divine oracle → path of action. Certainly, this explanation seems preferable to the common explanation whereby one derives "law" from "walk." For example: "Halakah, from *halak* 'to go, follow' means literally 'going, walking,' then figuratively: the teaching which one follows, the rule or statute by which one is guided, the categorial religious law" (Strack);[71] "הלכה ... Ein dem Aramäischen entnommenes Wort, aus dessen Grundbedeutung—Gang, Schritt, Weg,—sich die Bedeutung: Brauch, Sitte, Satzung entwickelte" (Bacher);[72] "Im späteren Hebräisch ist *hᵃlākā*, ursprünglich 'Wandel' 'Sitte', dann 'Gesetz', ... von grosser Bedeutung" (Landsberger).[73]

But even if the possibility of such coincidence in both Hebrew and Akkadian is accepted, it should also already be obvious that the data lend themselves to different interpretations and do not point unambiguously in one direction. Here we should start then by emphasizing how unlikely it is for Hebrew *hălāḵā*, "law," to be a consequence of a purely Aramaic development, for *hilḵĕṯā* itself is probably not an inner Aramaic development. *hlk* does not seem to be a particularly productive root in Aramaic (an Aramaic creation would more likely have been some such form as *ʾaziltā*); and *hilḵĕṯā* may best be regarded as some form of loan. Certainly, JA *hilḵĕṯā*, "law," must be a loan or calque from either Akkadian or Hebrew.[74]

There is much to be said for the position that Hebrew *halakhah* was borrowed from or influenced by Akkadian either directly or via Aramaic. Perhaps the very use in Hebrew of the word *halakhah* with the meaning "law" when there were already other suitable words such as *minhāg*, which also derives from a verb of motion (*nāhag*, "to lead"), can best be explained on the assumption that *halakhah* is a foreign import. Even the noted Talmudist Saul Lieberman thought that the word *halakhah* was derived from Akkadian. But he chose *ilku*, "tax," as the point of origin and assumed that the borrowing took place via Biblical Aramaic *hălāḵ* (הלך).[75] His suggestion is not convincing despite the

71 H. L. Strack, *Introduction to the Talmud and Midrash* (repr., New York: Meridian; Philadelphia: Jewish Publication Society of America, 1959), 6.

72 W. Bacher, *Terminologie der Tannaiten*, vol. 1 of *Die exegetische Terminologie der jüdischen Traditionsliteratur* (Leipzig: Hinrichs, 1899; repr., Hildesheim: Georg Olms, 1965), 42.

73 B. Landsberger, "Die babylonischen Termini für Gesetz und Recht," in *Symbolae ad iura orientis antiqui pertinentes Paulo Koschaker dedicatae*, ed. J. Friedrich et al., Studia et documenta ad iura orientis antiqui pertinentia 2 (Leiden: Brill, 1939), 223 n. 20.

74 It is of course possible that the word *hilḵĕṯā* always existed in Aramaic in the meaning "going." This need not affect our conclusion.

75 S. Lieberman, *Hellenism in Jewish Palestine*, 2nd ed., Texts and Studies of the Jewish Theological Seminary of America 18 (New York: JTSA, 1962), 83–84 n. 3. Below I shall modify my position and state that *halakhah* is more probably a calque than a loan. Here I would emphasize, therefore, that the fact that the Aramaic and Hebrew words show *heh*

neat Roman–Jewish parallel that Lieberman thereby created. The derivation is immediately suspect because were *ilku* the word from which *hălāḵā* derived, *hălāḵā* should have had a totally different form; suffice to note that *ilku*, a masculine noun, should not have generated the feminine *hălāḵā* or *hilḵĕṯā*. Furthermore, if we accept the possibility that *hălāḵā* derives from Akkadian, then a far more promising candidate is *alaktu* in the meaning "divine decision," "oracle," "ruling," advanced in this paper. In contrast to *ilku*–*hălāḵā*, *alaktu* and *hălāḵā* are semantically parallel, and they share the following: a common meaning, etymon, root metaphor, gender, and morphological structure, as well as a verbal complement *lāmad*/*lamādu*.

Most Akkadian words found in late Hebrew entered the language through the medium of Aramaic. Accordingly, one might suppose that the linguistic medium of transmission for *hălāḵā* was also Aramaic, that is, that JA *hilḵĕṯā* in the meaning "law" came directly from Akkadian and then generated Hebrew *hălāḵā*, and that Aramaic *yĕlaf* was a loan translation of Akkadian *lamādu* and was then turned back into *lāmad* in Hebrew. But this does not seem to be the best or even the simplest solution. For the coincidence of the use of Akkadian *lamādu* and Hebrew *lāmad* with both *alaktu* and *hălāḵā*, respectively, is suspicious. And the fact that *hilḵĕṯā* in the meaning "going" is shared by Syriac and JA, whereas the meaning "law" is limited to JA, requires in any case that we posit no fewer than two stages of borrowing into Aramaic. Even then, there are two different ways of construing these stages of borrowing: either the word entered Syriac and JA at different times, or more likely, it entered general Aramaic from Akkadian in the meaning "going," and the JA meaning "law" was taken over separately by Jewish speakers of Aramaic.

Since a simple solution is not readily available, a more convincing, if daring, solution, one which dissents from the common Akkadian–Aramaic–Hebrew route, may be considered. I would venture the following guesses: (1) *hilḵĕṯā* in the meaning "going" entered general Aramaic from Akkadian. (2) Akkadian *alaktu*, "divine revelation," "decision," and *alakta lamādu*, "to infer such a decision," entered into or affected Hebrew directly. Here it should be recalled that direct contact between Akkadian and Hebrew during the exile means that the possibility of an Akkadian word entering into or influencing Hebrew directly cannot be excluded.[76] (3) The meaning "law" was then transferred by the Jews

rather than *aleph* does not prove that they are not loans from Akkadian. Even in the case of *hălāḵ*, "tax," from *ilku* (cf., e.g., S. A. Kaufman, *The Akkadian Influences on Aramaic*, AS 19 [Chicago: University of Chicago Press, 1974], 58), the *heh* appears (perhaps as a result of etymological consciousness).

76 See Kaufman, *Akkadian Influences*, 156–157 nn. 79–80.

themselves from Hebrew *hălāḵā* to Aramaic *hilḵĕṯā*, and Hebrew *lāmad* was translated by Aramaic *yelaf*. If, as seems likely, the Jewish meaning "law" was taken over separately by Jewish speakers of Aramaic, it could have entered Aramaic as easily (if not more easily) from Hebrew as from Akkadian. It is not at all surprising to find Hebrew influencing Aramaic[77] rather than the reverse, especially if the contact takes place within the Jewish community itself.

It is possible to regard *halakhah* as the result of an internal Hebrew development. But we prefer to treat it as if it had developed under the influence of Akkadian *alaktu*. The phenomenon of loans is complex;[78] in the absence of decisive evidence that *halakhah* is a simple loan word, it is best to be cautious and to entertain the possibility of a view intermediate between independent development and outright loan. We have already made use of the notion of loan translation. The possibility that we are dealing with some form of loan translation even allows us to make our case more credible. Certainly in the case of cognate languages such as Akkadian, Hebrew, and Aramaic, words in one language may be modeled on those of the other, and meanings may be transferred from one language to the other. The word *hălāḵā* may already have existed in Hebrew as a gerund, "going," or it may have been created on the basis of the existing formation *qĕṭālā* by Hebrew speakers familiar with Akkadian *alaktu* (my preference). This question may be left open. In either case, under the impact of Babylonian–Jewish linguistic and cultural contact, the special meaning of Akkadian *alaktu*—divine/heavenly revelation, oracular decision—was carried over from Akkadian into Jewish *hălāḵā* (and *hilḵĕṯā*). Metaphors such as ללכת בדרכי ה׳, ללמד אורחות / דרכי ה׳ and the astral usage of הליכות עולם[79] prepared the ground for either the transference or extension of meaning.

77 For Hebrew influences on Aramaic, cf., e.g., J. A. Fitzmyer, *A Wandering Aramean: Collected Aramaic Essays*, SBLMS 25 (Missoula: Scholars Press, 1977), 42–43.

78 For loanwords and loan-translations, see, esp., U. Weinreich, *Languages in Contact* (New York: Linguistic Circle of New York, 1953; repr., The Hague: Mouton, 1963), 47–53.

79 Cf. *HALAT*, 236, s.v. *hălîḵā* and reference there to W. F. Albright, "Two Letters from Ugarit (Ras Shamrah)," *BASOR* 82 (1941): 49. Albright translates the phrase in Hab 3:6 as "The everlasting roads (of the stars)" and compares Ugaritic *hlk kbkbm* and Akkadian *alkāt kakkabī* ("the orbits of the stars"). In fact, the Rabbis themselves already made the connection between *hălîḵôṯ* of Hab 3:6 and *halakhah*; cf. b. Niddah 73a (// b. Megillah 28b): תנא דבי אליהו כל השונה הלכות בכל יום מובטח לו שהוא בן העולם הבא שנאמר הל(י)כות עולם לו אל תקרי הל(י)כות (*hălîḵôṯ*) אלא הלכות (*hălāḵôṯ*).

### 2.3 *Further Questions and Refinements*

Several serious questions remain as regards our suggestion that *halakhah* derives from Akkadian *alaktu*.[80] In contrast to many Akkadian loan words, *alaktu* in the meaning that I have tried to establish is not a legal term and would not have entered Hebrew through legal or commercial channels. Moreover, while the fact that the meaning "law" of Aramaic *hilḵĕṯā* is limited to JA and may derive from Hebrew does not disqualify Akkadian *alaktu* as the ultimate source of this meaning, it does require us to acknowledge that the Akkadian word would not have affected Hebrew through Aramaic speech or letters. In light of these observations, we must ask: why did *alaktu* influence or enter the Jewish lexicon? And through what channels might it have entered Jewish life and had an impact on the Jews? Furthermore, if *halakhah* is some form of Akkadian loan or loan translation, why does it not appear in pre-Mishnaic documents? In truth, these questions do not constitute objections. If anything, they are leading questions which force us to set aside stereotyped and general responses and to think through the implications of our suggestion. They require us to seek out and help us to consider very specific answers to the questions: why, how, and when was Babylonian *alaktu* borrowed by the Jews as a word for normative law? If we can answer these questions in a reasonable way, we can hope to have provided some further support for the position that *halakhah* derives from *alaktu*.

In the Babylonian view, the king[81] or other human agency was the source of law and judgment; civil and criminal law were regarded as having a secular character. In Judaism, on the other hand, both the Written Law and the Oral Law, which encompass civil, criminal, ethical, and ritual legislation, were regarded as divine revelation. God was the ultimate source of the law.[82] A secular term for law would not be entirely suitable for religious law because of its secular overtones. A term drawn from the realm of divination and denoting an oracular decision revealed by the heavens themselves would be suitable because the source of the decision was the divinity. Hence, it was precisely

---

80 In the following section, I use such terms as "borrowing" and "loan" as convenient ways of referring to the complex situation described above.

81 This statement is not invalidated by the fact that the king's mandate to rule justly and his discriminating ability to make just laws and judgments may derive from the gods.

82 This notion finds expression in many statements. Suffice it to cite Rashi's remark ad Gen 18:1: "The Holy One, blessed be He, said to him [Abraham], 'Sit and I will stand, so that you may serve as a sign to future generations that I will be present [lit., stand] in the assembly of judges when they sit in judgment.'" God's presence at, and involvement in, the juridical process provide inspiration and lend authority to judgment. This is one more mythic way of drawing together the human and the divine and expressing the idea that law and judgment derive from God.

because *alaktu* and *alakta lamādu* had no secular juridical meaning, were not part of the cuneiform legal formulary, and were not used in legal documents, that they could be chosen to designate laws that were considered to be divinely ordained. So, perhaps, it is not a coincidence that just as in the earlier period the divination term *têrtu* was possibly taken up into Hebrew as *torah*, so in the later period, *alaktu*, another divination term for decision, was "borrowed" and became the standard term for Jewish law.

If *alaktu* was not part of the cuneiform legal formulary that entered Aramaic and Hebrew through standard legal channels and documents, how did the Jews come into contact with *alaktu*? Because *hilk̠ĕṯā* in the meaning "law" is restricted to Jewish Aramaic, we have decided that we cannot rely on Aramaic channels; hence, while there are indications that Arameans carried Mesopotamian astrological lore westward in the second half of the first millennium BCE, we are not able at this time to credit them with passing on this word. It would seem that we are at an impasse, because Akkadian itself seems not to have been the daily language of speech in seventh–sixth century BCE Babylonia. But precisely because we cannot utilize Aramaic or spoken Akkadian, we can look to traditional Babylonian sources and institutions for a solution. Although Akkadian was dying out as a spoken language during the seventh or sixth century, cuneiform texts were written at least as late as 75 CE, and native schools and a Babylonian intelligentsia/literati survived and flourished in Babylonia of the Neo-Babylonian, Persian, and Hellenistic periods. Scholars studied and copied Sumerian and Akkadian literature, prepared numerous commentaries on these works, and pursued the study of astrology and astronomy. I would suggest, therefore, that the borrowing took place in Babylonia itself. There would have been, I surmise, contact between the Jewish exiles and the Babylonian literati and their schools. There was knowledge within some Jewish intellectual circles of what was being studied in Babylonian schools. It might have been through these intellectuals, then, that *alaktu* "(oracular) decision," affected Hebrew and Jewish thought.[83]

It is difficult to specify a date for the "borrowing" of *halakhah*, beyond saying that it was probably no earlier than the Babylonian exile (under

83 Such a surmise is in agreement with the fact that learned Akkadian words and divination terms seem to have entered directly into Jewish technical language during the Late Babylonian period; cf., e.g., W. L. Moran, "Some Akkadian Names of the Stomachs of Ruminants," *JCS* 21 (1967 [1969]): 178–179. Note also the Mesopotamian origins of speculative lore in Enoch literature; cf. M. E. Stone, "Apocalyptic Literature," in *Jewish Writings of the Second Temple Period*, ed. M. E. Stone (Assen: Van Gorcum; Philadelphia: Fortress, 1984), 392, 438, and literature there.

Nebuchadnezzar II) and certainly no later than the redaction of the Mishna. I am impressed by what may be no more than a coincidence. *Alaktu* seems to have taken on new life and flourished in the seventh and sixth centuries, as witnessed by the reports of the astrologers of the late Assyrian court and by the inscriptions of Nebuchadnezzar II. And I should like to suggest a date as close as possible to the time of Nebuchadnezzar and the exile.

To be sure, *hălāḵā* first appears as a significant term in the Mishna. This does not constitute an objection either to an Akkadian origin or to an early date for the "borrowing." The appearance of *hălāḵā* in the Mishna agrees with the nature of the documentation of Hebrew and accords with the introduction of this word into spoken Hebrew as a result of the Babylonian exile. The dialect of Mishnaic Hebrew extends back to the Babylonian exile and represents the vernacular Hebrew speech form. But only with the destruction of the Second Temple did Mishnaic Hebrew succeed Biblical Hebrew as the standard literary language. Usages that entered the vernacular as early as the exile might only surface in the literary idiom hundreds of years later.[84]

• • •

I have tried to establish one more meaning for Akkadian *alaktu*, and to provide cogent reasons for believing that *alaktu* influenced Hebrew *hălāḵā*. There are

84 It has been suggested that *ḥălāqôṯ* in the DSS phrase דורשי החלקות is a pun on *hălāḵôṯ*; see J. Strugnell apud J. T. Milik, *Ten Years of Discovery in the Wilderness of Judaea*, trans. John Strugnell, SBT 26 (London: SCM; Naperville, IL: Allenson, 1959), 73 n. 1; cf., e.g., G. W. E. Nickelsburg, *Jewish Literature between the Bible and the Mishnah* (Philadelphia: Fortress, 1981), 131. If this suggestion is correct, the wordplay assumes and points to the existence of the word *hălāḵā* in the spoken language at this time, and accords with (and is partially due to [?]) the fact that the word was not yet regarded as part of the standard literary lexicon. In a discussion of the nominal form *qĕṭālā*, E. Y. Kutscher, "Studies in the Grammar of Mishnaic Hebrew according to Ms. Kaufmann" (in Hebrew), in *Hebrew and Aramaic Studies*, ed. Z. Ben-Ḥayyim et al. (Jerusalem: Magnes, 1977), p. קיח, expressed the view that apparently *hălāḵā* was originally a gerund and noted the possibility of two such occurrences in the *Rule of the Community*. However, both forms seem to be construct infinitives rather than gerunds: (1) For בהלכתנו (1:25) read בלכתנו; the letter between the ב and ל was erased (see J. C. Trevor, *Scrolls from Qumrân Cave I* [Jerusalem: Albright Institute of Archaeological Research and The Shrine of the Book, 1972], 126–127, line 25, and cf., e.g., A. M. Habermann, *Megilloth Midbar Yehuda: The Scrolls from the Judean Desert* [in Hebrew; Jerusalem: Machbaroth Lesifruth, 1959], 184 ad א,24; and J. Licht, *The Rule Scroll: A Scroll from the Wilderness of Judaea: 1QS, 1QSa, 1QSb* [in Hebrew; Jerusalem: Bialik Institute, 1965], 68 nn. 24–25). (2) להלכת (3:9) might be a mixed *qal-piʿēl* form or a *piʿēl* infinitive (cf. Licht, *Rule Scroll*, 80 n. 9). I prefer treating it as a *piʿēl* infinitive construct להלך and would explain the final *-t* as a dittography (להלכת תמים); see 9:19 (להלך תמים), and cf., e.g., 2:2 and CD 2:15.

differences in the way these words were used. These differences help us gain some further understanding of the differences between Babylonian and Jewish cultures and mentalities. Yet these words also belong together. And suggesting a medium through which the Akkadian term entered or influenced Hebrew helps us imagine the intellectual milieu in which some groups of Babylonians and Jews studied and thought.

CHAPTER 22

# Blood in Israel and Mesopotamia

My paper will focus on the significance of blood in Israel and Mesopotamia.* I begin with Israel or, rather, with the biblical text. That blood plays an important role in biblical cultic ritual is well known and hardly requires documentation. It is not an exaggeration to state that blood "is sprinkled, splashed, poured, and smeared on altars, persons, on the veil of the Holy of Holies, even, once a year, on the Ark of the Covenant itself."[1] Many passages could be cited as examples, but here, let me simply quote a well-known passage from the Holiness Code that contains important reflections on blood and expresses some of the beliefs regarding the significance of animal and human blood.

> And if anyone of the house of Israel or of the strangers who reside among them partakes of any blood,[2] I will set My face against the person who partakes of the blood, and I will cut him off from among his kin. For the life of the flesh is in the blood, and I have assigned it to you for making expiation for your lives upon the altar; it is the blood, as life, that effects expiation.[3]

Many scholars have studied the significance of blood in the Israelite cult.[4] Among others, B. A. Levine has contributed significantly to our understanding of this topic. He maintains that blood is life and serves as a representation of the human person. Because it is the life force, blood can substitute for a life, *pars pro toto*. God accepts the blood of the sacrifice in lieu of human blood. Accordingly, Levine understands a verse such as Lev 17:11 just quoted as meaning that blood is a ransom for life. He translates *kî haddām hûʾ bannep̄eš yəḵappēr* there as "it is the blood that effects expiation in exchange for life,"

---

* It is a great pleasure to dedicate this paper to Emanuel Tov and thereby to celebrate Emanuel's great contribution to biblical scholarship as well as a personal friendship that has been sustained and developed over thirty-five years on three continents.

1 S. A. Geller, *Sacred Enigmas: Literary Religion in the Hebrew Bible* (London: Routledge, 1996), 64.

2 For the prohibition against eating blood, see also Gen 9:4, Deut 12:16, and 1 Sam 14:32–34.

3 Lev 17:10–11; translation: NJPS.

4 E.g., D. J. McCarthy, "The Symbolism of Blood and Sacrifice," *JBL* 88 (1969): 166–176; D. J. McCarthy, "Further Notes on the Symbolism of Blood and Sacrifice," *JBL* 92 (1973): 205–210; Geller, *Sacred Enigmas*, 62–86, 205–207.

 | DOI:10.1163/9789004435186_023

taking the *beth* in *bannep̄eš* as the *beth* of price, and not of means. Similarly, when used with the phrase *ləḵappēr ʿal nep̄eš*, the blood serves as a ransom for human life. Thus, the offering of animal blood on the altar as part of the sacrifice serves to give a substitution, or ransom, for the human life. The sprinkling of blood thus protects the human being who has sinned or who needs protection. The blood is given to God, but it is a development of the earlier offering of blood to chthonic deities.[5] The aforementioned use of blood protects human beings from divine anger, but of course, this is not the only use of blood, and Levine also recognizes that in certain circumstances it also functions to protect the divine from contamination (e.g., Lev 16).[6]

In any case, I find Levine's interpretation attractive and accept the idea that blood as a representation of life may serve as a substitute for the person and that this is one of its functions in the cult. But blood as a representation of life can also be used to create relationships between persons. And, thus, it is unfortunate that Levine sets up his interpretation as an alternative to W. Robertson Smith's well-known ideas propounded in his *Lectures on the Religion of the Semites* (1889),[7] as if substitution and communion could not be two complementary aspects of the use of sacrificial blood but need rather be mutually exclusive.

Levine notes Robertson Smith's proposal that "the predominant factor in 'Semitic' sacrifice was the experience of communion actualized in the blood rites of the animal sacrifice,"[8] that is, communion through blood, but then contends that a weak point in Robertson Smith's argument is that "if the blood rite was an expression of kinship, the kinship of covenant brothers, then the covenant should, in itself, represent a kinship arrangement."[9] Levine states that Robertson Smith sensed this weakness in his own position[10] and seems to feel that he can dismiss Robertson Smith's position on the grounds that the latter believed "that the covenant between Yahweh and Israel was a relationship

5 B. A. Levine, "Prolegomenon," in G. B. Gray, *Sacrifice in the Old Testament: Its Theory and Practice* (New York: Ktav, 1971), xxvii–xxviii; B. A. Levine, *In the Presence of the Lord*, SJLA 5 (Leiden: E. J. Brill, 1974), 67–69; B. A. Levine, *The JPS Torah Commentary: Leviticus* (Philadelphia: Jewish Publication Society, 1989), pp. 115–116 on Lev 17:11 and pp. 6–7 on Lev 1:4.

6 See Levine, "Prolegomenon," xxviii; Levine, *Presence*, 73–78, cf. 103.

7 Reprinted as *The Religion of the Semites: The Fundamental Institutions* (New York: Schocken, 1972).

8 Levine, "Prolegomenon," xxiii.

9 Levine, "Prolegomenon," xxv.

10 In my reading, I do not find that Robertson Smith recognized as a weakness that which Levine ascribes to him (*Religion of the Semites*, 312–320; cf. Levine, "Prolegomenon," xli, n. 48, where he cites *Religion of the Semites*, 319 n. 2 and additional note H).

created artificially, an adoptive relationship."[11] For Levine believes that "The fatherhood of Yahweh, like his kingship, was not based on blood kinship, but on a type of contract in which the terminology of kinship was proverbially metaphorical,"[12] and thus concludes that since Israelite religion is based on a covenant with a vassal lord or king, a covenant that is thus artificial, the cult cannot be understood in terms of a commensality model or as an expression of the kinship of blood.[13]

In my opinion, this argument is somewhat misleading. First of all, kinship may be artificially constructed by legal and/or metaphorical means. In this context, we note that a relationship is no less powerful for being metaphorical. Moreover, one may mix types of metaphor—the Israelite God may be both kin and king. Second, in a clan context, he may, in fact, be a kin. For example, in the patriarchal accounts of Genesis, God is presented as a kin with whom the patriarch and his family bear a family relationship. In fact, in a tribal context, the relationship between man and god created by sacrifice may be one of kinship.[14] Let us also not forget that the blood-covenant between Israel and God as found, for example, in Exod 24 is not only retributive but also creates ties of consanguinity between man and god. In this context, I need hardly remind the reader of the rite of circumcision. In Exod 4, for example, the blood of circumcision turns Yhwh into a *ḥātān dāmîm*, a kinsman (v. 25).

Finally, and perhaps most important, the kinship established by sacrifice is not simply between man and god.[15] For sacrifice is also a social act that brings

11 Levine, "Prolegomenon," xxv. Actually, this constitutes a form of kinship relationship. Cf. now, e.g., F. M. Cross's discussion of kinship-in-law in "Kinship and Covenant in Ancient Israel," in his *From Epic to Canon: History and Literature in Ancient Israel* (Baltimore: Johns Hopkins University Press, 1998), 3–21, esp. 7–11.

12 Levine, "Prolegomenon," xxv.

13 Levine, "Prolegomenon," xxv–xxvi.

14 Cf. N. Jay, *Throughout Your Generations Forever: Sacrifice, Religion, and Paternity* (Chicago: University of Chicago Press, 1992), 33: "It is on the father-son relation that the sacrificial relation of deity to worshiper is founded, although it was later expanded to include ... king-subject."

15 In fact, social bonds in the Bible are often translated into kinship relationships (e.g., the people Israel are described as the descendants of one father); some of these relationships derive from actual kinship relationships, others are created. Cf. Cross, "Kinship and Covenant," 3–21, esp. 7–13. On the creation of kinship, I may repeat Robertson Smith's comment in his *Kinship and Marriage in Early Arabia* (1903), recently quoted by Cross, "Kinship and Covenant," 8: "The commingling of blood [in the oath and covenant ritual] by which two men became brothers or two kins allies, and the [legal] fiction of adoption by which a new tribesman was feigned to be the veritable son of a member of the tribe, are both evidences of the highest value, that the Arabs were incapable of conceiving any absolute social obligation or social unity which was not based on kinship; for a

men into relationship with each other. Through blood covenants, human parties artificially create a tie of consanguinity between themselves by mixing their blood, blood that represents themselves. That is, sacrifice and the use of blood may also establish or reaffirm blood brother-ship; it is a form of commensality between blood kin, but it sometimes creates the relationship itself. If anything, blood sacrifice, in and of itself, actually stands in opposition to the natural relationship created by birth. It creates relations between men, and places these artificial relationships on a higher level than the natural relationship of mother and child created in the blood of birth.[16]

The insight that blood sacrifice is an artificial means of creating relationships has been developed recently by Nancy Jay in her posthumously published

legal fiction is always adopted to reconcile an act with a principle too firmly established to be simply ignored.... We see that two groups might make themselves of one blood by a process of which the essence was that they commingled their blood, at the same time applying the blood to the god or fetish so as to make him a party to the covenant also. Quite similar is the ritual in Exodus 24 where blood is applied to the people of Israel and to the altar."

16 Thus, Levine's contention that "Once the artificiality of the Israelite covenant is acknowledged, we can no longer maintain that the cult, as the supposed actualization of the covenant, expresses the kinship of blood" ("Prolegomenon," xxvi) seems not to be true. Actually, Levine's argument may be more complex than this summary indicates, but is perhaps also self-contradictory. Levine denies the kinship aspect of covenant and asserts its political nature (cf. "Prolegomenon," xxv–xxvi; *Presence*, 78). He then claims that covenant and sacrificial systems belong to different categories, and he argues that blood functions differently in covenant and in the sacrificial system ("Prolegomenon," xxvi; *Presence*, 78–79). But initially interpreting the basis of the sacrificial system as a relationship between master and servant, he then notes that the same terminology is used for vassal relationships and implicitly acknowledges the equation of God the master and man the servant with God the suzerain and man the vassal (cf. "Prolegomenon," xxviii–xxix), and thus brings together what he had claimed to separate, the covenantal and sacrificial systems. He also acknowledges the connections between the covenantal and sacrificial systems (cf. *Presence*, 37, 41: "The covenant (or covenants) merely served as the charter, or commission under the terms of which the cult, as well as the other establishments within Israelite society operated"; 103: "The covenant ... represent[s] the larger framework within which the *ḥaṭṭā't* sacrifice functioned"). Note further that while dismissing the kinship dimension of covenant as merely metaphorical, he acknowledges the communal or bonding function of blood in the covenant ceremony and relationship of Sinai (*Presence*, 78).

I accept the expiatory function of the sacrificial cult but cannot understand why, especially in view of the connections between the covenantal and sacrificial systems, both the expiatory and communal functions of blood cannot be present in the sacrificial system, especially in view of the communal function of the *zeḇaḥ* and/or *šəlāmîm*. Hence, for example, the blood of *ḥaṭṭā't* is expiatory, and that of the *šəlāmîm* may also serve a binding function.

book *Throughout Your Generations Forever: Sacrifice, Religion, and Paternity*.[17] Jay argues that "sacrifice is at home in societies where families are integrated into extended kin groups of various kinds,"[18] and that "sacrificing identifies, legitimates, and maintains enduring structures of intergenerational continuity between males that transcend their absolute dependence on women's reproductive powers."[19] Jay notes that while sacrifice may serve to define both matrilineal and patrilineal descent systems, it is especially prevalent and significant in patrilineal societies, where "sacrificing orders relations within and between lines of human fathers and sons, between men and men, at least as effectively as it does relations between men and their divinities."[20] Sacrifice establishes blood-ties among men that supersede the natural blood-ties produced through women's childbirth.[21]

Thus, it is not sufficient to take a phenomenological approach to blood; rather, we must also look for its cultural or social functions. But to understand why I believe that a social explanation derived in some way from Robertson Smith provides a productive approach, we must place the question into a comparative context. We should examine blood and sacrifice in Mesopotamia, whose culture undoubtedly influenced Israel in many ways, but where there seems to be little use of blood in the cult, and we should ask: Why does blood play such an important role in the Israelite cult but hardly any role in the Mesopotamian?

First, then, some background and context about Mesopotamian sacrifice. When we think of sacrifice we tend to think of slaughtering animals or consuming an offering by means of fire. But to approach the topic of sacrifice in Mesopotamia we must look at things a bit differently, for our Mesopotamian

---

17 See n. 14 above.

18 So K. E. Fields in the foreword to Jay, *Generations*, xxiv.

19 Fields, foreword to Jay, *Generations*, xxvii. That is, in Jay's words (*Generations*, 32), "sacrificing produces and reproduces forms of intergenerational continuity generated by males, transmitted through males, and transcending continuity through women."

20 Jay, *Generations*, 34. Cf. p. 36: "When membership in patrilineal descent groups is identified by rights of participation in blood sacrifice, evidence of 'paternity' is created which is as certain as evidence of maternity, but far more flexible."

21 In sum, according to Jay: "The twofold movement of sacrifice, integration and differentiation, communion and expiation, is beautifully suited for identifying and maintaining patrilineal descent. Sacrifice can expiate, get rid of, the consequences of having been born of woman (along with countless other dangers) and at the same time integrate the pure and eternal patrilineage. Sacrificially constituted descent, incorporating women's mortal children into an 'eternal' (enduring through generations) kin group, in which membership is recognized by participation in sacrificial ritual, not merely by birth, enables a patrilineal group to transcend mortality in the same process in which it transcends birth" (*Generations*, 40).

religious sources emphasize neither the slaughter of animals nor the process of consumption. Rather, they usually focus on the presentation of the offering.

To understand the Mesopotamian view of sacrifice, we do well to understand the culture's view of the gods.[22] The purpose of human life, the purpose of the community, was to serve the gods, to provide them with whatever care a powerful ruling class, a landed aristocracy, would require. Paramount among these needs are shelter and food. This represents the developed or classical form of Mesopotamian theology and was probably not the original ideology or theology of god and temple. But certainly by the early part of the third millennium BCE, the characteristic and defining forms of classical Mesopotamian theology had emerged. This new ideology was part of the evolution of early civilization and of the development of hierarchical structures within the cities.

Originally temples may have served as communal storehouses, but by the classical period, we have moved from storage to presentation. Gods formerly understood as naturalistic forces were now seen as manorial lords, as the divine equivalents to the newly emerging human chieftains and kings. Along with a human form, the gods were given families and households. Most importantly, their homes were now seen as manors or palaces, that is, the temples were now treated as the divine equivalent of the human ruler's abode. Hence, older cultic centers now became the classic Mesopotamian temples in which the god and his family were treated by his subjects as the ruling class of the city. For its part, the city and its inhabitants were required to care for these anthropomorphized deities.

The central act of the daily cult was not sacrifice in the sense of giving the food over to be consumed by fire, nor was it acts of slaughter and pouring out of blood. Food was placed before the god and consumed by him through that mysterious act that characterizes Babylonian religiosity. After being placed on the god's table and somehow magically eaten by the god, it was distributed to the temple personnel and to the king.

The act of killing the animal is almost hidden behind the construct of feeding the god, a construct which emerges out of a combination of the earlier offering and storage and the later image of feeding a divine king in his palace.

The temple is the center of an urban world. The temple and the feeding and care of its gods define the primary community of the dwellers in the land between the two rivers. To serve the god by supporting and participating in

22 My understanding of earliest Mesopotamian religious history follows in the tradition of several scholars, notably that of Thorkild Jacobsen; see especially T. Jacobsen, *The Treasures of Darkness: A History of Mesopotamian Religion* (New Haven: Yale University Press, 1976).

the economy of the temple constitutes the mark of membership in the urban community, a community which thus replaces or, at least, overshadows membership in one or another kinship community such as the family or clan.

We return now to the question of blood.[23] A. Leo Oppenheim observed that a "difference that separates the sacrificial rituals in the two cultures [scil. Mesopotamia and the West, "represented best by the Old Testament"] is the 'blood consciousness' of the West, its awareness of the magic power of blood, which is not paralleled in Mesopotamia."[24] This observation seems to be correct so far as the major urban temples of Mesopotamia are concerned. And yet one can find an important place where blood does play a role in Mesopotamia, and this place may provide a clue to the significance of the emphasis on blood at least in the Semitic West and its apparent absence in Mesopotamia.

This clue can be found, I think, in texts that tell the story of the creation of man for the service of the gods. For example, in the *Atraḫasīs* epic, the god who led the rebellion was slaughtered and his flesh and blood mixed together with clay in order to create the human creature whose service was necessary for the welfare of the gods. The use of flesh and blood in addition to clay in the formation of humanity represents a *novum*. In this mythic tradition, the original model for the creation of humanity was that of a potter who creates statues by forming them out of wet clay.[25] The killing of a god and the use of his flesh and blood to create humanity are an intrusion into the Mesopotamian system of thought. This intrusion affects the two major early Mesopotamian mythological traditions, those of Eridu and of Nippur,[26] and is probably due to western

23 An earlier version of this discussion is contained in T. Abusch, "Sacrifice in Mesopotamia," in *Sacrifice in Religious Experience*, ed. A. I. Baumgarten, SHR 93 (Leiden: Brill, 2002), 39–48 [[56–64]].

24 A. L. Oppenheim, *Ancient Mesopotamia: Portrait of a Dead Civilization*, rev. ed. (Chicago: University of Chicago Press, 1977), 192.

25 Compare the earlier Sumerian myth "Enki and Ninmah," which, like *Atraḫasīs*, describes the discontent of the divine workers and the subsequent creation of human beings by means of clay. But see now W. G. Lambert, "The Relationship of Sumerian and Babylonian Myth as Seen in Accounts of Creation," in *La circulation des biens, des personnes et des idées dans le Proche-Orient ancien, XXXVIII^e R.A.I.*, ed. D. Charpin and F. Joannès (Paris: Editions Recherche sur les Civilisations, 1992), 129–135. Basing himself upon a bilingual version of "Enki and Ninmah," Lambert argues that Enki created man by mixing clay and blood. If Lambert's understanding also applies to the original Sumerian text, the episode in "Enki and Ninmah" would then represent an earlier example of the mixing of blood and clay.

26 Thus gods are killed in order to create human beings not only in *Atraḫasīs* and texts related to it, like *Enūma eliš*, but also in the Nippur text *KAR* 4. For these texts and traditions, see G. Pettinato, *Das altorientalische Menschenbild und die sumerischen und akkadischen Schöpfungsmythen* (Heidelberg: Carl Winter, 1971), esp. 29–32 and 39–46,

Semitic influences. The killing of a god seems to be depicted already on seals dating to the Akkadian period,[27] but it enters the literary tradition in the Old Babylonian period possibly as a consequence of the settlement of the tribal Amorites in Mesopotamia.

In the new construct, the clay still serves to form the physical person, while the flesh and blood of the slaughtered god add qualities to the clay and to the human who was created therefrom. While the flesh is the source of the human ghost, the blood, as I have argued elsewhere,[28] is the origin of an ability to plan, that is, of human intelligence, and is ultimately the source and etiology of the personal god. The personal god is not simply the god of an isolated individual; rather, he is the god of the individual as a social being. He is both the divine personification of individual procreation and achievement as well as the god of the tribal or family group who is passed down from generation to generation by the male progenitor. The god is the blood or is in the blood, and his transmission from father to son creates a relationship of kinship between generations of men by the emphasis on the tie of blood.[29]

For the Semites it was the family, the tribe, and the wider tribal territory that defined identity and power. This remained true even of the Semites of northern Babylonia and northeastern Syria who absorbed the culture of urban Mesopotamia, for they did not fully give up their own identities, but instead transformed the culture that they had assimilated and introduced new images. One of these images was that of blood, but this image could not dominate the Mesopotamian cultic landscape, whose form was and remained fundamentally urban.

The classical Mesopotamian city defined itself not as a community of kinsmen, but rather as a community of service which had grown out of and around a female center, the fertility of the earth. Its admission rules were based on a willingness to serve the city god, not on family ties. In Mesopotamia the basic form was created in Sumer: That society seems to have descended directly from

as well as M. Dietrich, "Die Tötung einer Gottheit in der Eridu-Babylon-Mythologie," in *Ernten, was man sät: Festschrift für Klaus Koch zu seinem 65. Geburtstag*, ed. D. R. Daniels et al. (Neukirchen-Vluyn: Neukirchener-Verlag, 1991), 49–73; W. G. Lambert, "Myth and Mythmaking in Sumer and Akkad," in *CANE* 3:1832–1834.

27 See F. A. M. Wiggermann, "Discussion," in E. Porada, *Man and Images in the Ancient Near East* (Wakefield, RI: Moyer Bell, 1995), 78–79.

28 T. Abusch, "Ghost and God: Some Observations on a Babylonian Understanding of Human Nature," in *Self, Soul and Body in Religious Experience*, ed. A. I. Baumgarten et al., SHR 78 (Leiden: Brill, 1998), 363–383 [[67–86]].

29 It is not a coincidence that in Gen 9:6, we read that "He who sheds the blood of man, by man shall his blood be shed; for in the image of God was man created"; that is to say, the shedding of human blood is prohibited because man is created in the image of God, or put differently, human blood is equated with the god.

the Neolithic villages of the same area where the Sumerians lived in historical times, and saw itself as indigenous to the land. Hence, the central forms of the Mesopotamian temple had little use for blood. They emphasized offerings, first to natural forces and then to the divine owners of the city. And in any case, in contrast to the West, the distribution and consumption of meat were several steps removed from the process of slaughter.

By contrast, the tribal shepherds and herdsmen who spread out over the ancient Near East and entered Palestine and Mesopotamia during the Middle and Late Bronze Age were primarily organized according to family and clan. It is the Semites for whom the family god is important, a god represented by blood; it is they who created and cemented alliances by means of the bloody splitting of animals, a splitting evident, for example, in the "Covenant of Parts" of Gen 15; and it is the Semites to whom we owe the image of divine blood in the *Atraḫasīs* epic. Especially in light of our earlier citations from Nancy Jay, I think that we should give serious consideration to the possibility that for these Semites the systems of sacrifice that emphasize blood served to maintain family groups, groups that were organized along common blood lines that were usually tribal and patrilineal. That is, blood sacrifice maintains a relationship of kinship between men by the emphasis on a tie of blood and would be consonant with the emphasis on blood in a clan context.

Thus, it is difficult to escape the conclusion that it is in the context of the contrasting forms of social organization of Semitic/Israelite tribal society and Mesopotamian urban society that we should view the blood-consciousness in the Israelite cult and its apparent absence in the Mesopotamian temple. The importance of blood in the West would seem to reflect the fact that an important element in Israelite society derived from a pastoral semi-nomadic element which defined itself in tribal terms. And it is significant, moreover, that the livelihood of this group was involved in the flesh and blood of animals of the herd. Moreover, at least in the case of the Israelites, this semi-nomadic element saw itself as different from the indigenous, autochthonous element of the population and tried to maintain that separateness by means of blood rituals. For, in the main, Israel did not see itself as indigenous dwellers of the land of Canaan; rather, it defined itself by means of its distinctiveness from the Canaanites and asserted that its origin lay elsewhere.

Israelite communities defined themselves as communities of kinsmen. The "Children of Israel" thought of themselves as bound together by ties of blood. Blood served many purposes in the Israelite cult. Surely one of them was that of creating or maintaining bonds of kinship which were defined in terms of covenant.

We recognize that our solution is a speculative and tentative one. It is really no more than a suggestion intended to provoke further discussion.

CHAPTER 23

# Cultures in Contact: Ancient Near Eastern and Jewish Magic

While ancient Jewish magic was indigenous and influenced cultures around it, its literary remains betray the strong influence of the magic and mythology of surrounding cultures, most notably those of Mesopotamia. Actually, Israel and Mesopotamia share many commonalities even when these are not due to any direct influence or when, at least, no influence is discernible. For at least the first thousand years of their existence, Jews and ancient Judaism should be seen and studied as part of the ancient Near East rather than as an outside entity that may have absorbed some cultural elements due to influences from foreign bodies.

There is a minimum of testimony and usable information in our earliest Judaic source, the Hebrew Bible, as regards the topic of magic. To assess the significance of this and to understand the scope and nature of magical thought and action in Judaic antiquity, we must broaden our purview and examine the most amply documented and influential culture of the ancient Near East, that of ancient Mesopotamia. Thus, we would begin our essay with remarks about the cuneiform record of magic in Mesopotamia; this will be followed by reflections on the nature of the record of magic preserved in the Hebrew Bible (my remarks draw upon the written remains; they do not treat material remains[1]). Finally, I will give a few cursory examples of magical forms and practices shared by Jews in antiquity and other cultures of the Near East, especially Mesopotamia.

Magic is here defined as those activities involving supernatural forces that are undertaken to serve the needs of the individual member of society and to deal with his/her difficulties. In Mesopotamia, as elsewhere, magic treats illness and other personal crises, crises that may play out on the physical, psychological, psychosomatic, or social plane. Therefore, our focus is on those magical activities that are directed against evil, that is, the elimination of

1 But cf. D. Rittig, *Assyrisch-babylonische Kleinplastik magischer Bedeutung von 13.–6. Jh. v. Chr.*, Münchener vorderasiatische studien 1 (Munich: Verlag Uni-Druck, 1977); E. A. Braun-Holzinger, "Apotropaic Figures at Mesopotamian Temples in the Third and Second Millennia," in *Mesopotamian Magic: Textual, Historical, and Interpretive Perspectives*, ed. T. Abusch and K. van der Toorn, AMD 1 (Groningen: Styx, 1999), 149–172.

 | DOI:10.1163/9789004435186_024

harmful demonic forces and the protection against future attack, rather than on other uses of magic, such as love magic.

In ancient Mesopotamia, magical acts may be undertaken either by an individual on his own behalf or by an exorcist (*āšipu*).[2] The exorcist tries to determine the cause of distress and finds this cause in either personalistic or mechanistic powers within the supernatural universe. Distress is the result of the action or inaction of supernatural powers or agencies. Some of these agencies are: gods, demons, ghosts, tutelary gods, witches, evil omens, curses, and sins.

Having defined the causal agents and chains of causation, the exorcist will then undertake magical acts, that is, manual rites, and utter magical speeches, that is, oral rites. The ritual may be either a relatively simple one or an extensively elaborate performance. The *āšipu* recited one or more oral addresses (incantations or prayers); the ceremony itself often involved purification, food and drink offerings to the gods, the burning of incense, a central operation directed toward significant objects or symbols such as the burning of images, the tying and untying of knots, washing, the setting up of protective devices, and the application of amulets.

In the main, the reconstruction of Mesopotamian magical activity is based upon prescriptive texts written, transmitted, and adapted by professionals either as part of their professional education or, more often, as sources to be consulted in their service of the upper classes of society. This type of material leaves some major gaps in our knowledge, such as the magic of the rural population and lower classes. The texts were composed as guides for practicing magicians; hence, the fullest texts usually present in varying combinations and patterns the main ritual activities as well as statements describing the circumstance and purpose of the ceremony. To be sure, prayers and incantations may occasionally appear alone. At first, only the incantation was committed to writing; subsequently, instructions regarding the time, place, and manner of ritual performance as well as such other types of information as an objective description of the problem, a diagnosis, and a statement of purpose were added.

The fullest written record comes from the first millennium BCE. A comparison of the materials from this later period with those from the earlier

2 For Mesopotamian magic, see W. van Binsbergen and F. Wiggermann, "Magic in History: A Theoretical Perspective, and Its Application to Ancient Mesopotamia," in Abusch and van der Toorn, *Mesopotamian Magic*, 3–34; T. Abusch, *Mesopotamian Witchcraft: Toward a History and Understanding of Babylonian Witchcraft Beliefs and Literature*, AMD 5 (Leiden: Brill/Styx, 2002).

periods indicates that the texts from the later period are significantly greater in number and much fuller, more explicit, and more systematic. This difference reflects the growing tendency to transmit magical materials in writing, and once in written form to reorganize, systematize, and expand the corpus. While this disparity between early and late is true of prayers and incantations, it is particularly the case with ritual instructions and handbooks, materials that are rarely recorded in the earlier period and begin to appear in significant amounts only in the late second millennium.

Turning back to the Hebrew Bible, we notice immediately that the biblical sources are of a different order from those from Mesopotamia and that the picture we get of magic is different as well.[3] Of course, there should be some differences between a literature reflecting the emergence of Yahwistic monotheism in a society that sees itself as newly formed and marginal and the literature of a polytheistic, cosmopolitan society. But this does not mean that magic was of little consequence in ancient Israel, nor is it the reason why we find few straightforward magical prescriptions in the Hebrew Bible. For whether the evaluations of magic in the Hebrew Bible are negative or positive, there are enough indications there that magic was a significant activity in ancient Israel.

For example, in stories about Elijah and Elisha, we find the man of God performing miraculous cures (1 Kgs 17:17–24 [Elijah]; 2 Kgs 4:17–37 [Elisha]; 2 Kgs 5:1–14 [Elisha]), as well as miraculously multiplying or purifying food (1 Kgs 17:10–16 [Elijah]; 2 Kgs 4:1–7 [Elisha]; 2 Kgs 4:38–41 [Elisha]). Many of the biblical Psalms were laments of the individual and served as petitions. Many of them would originally have been recited as part of a ceremony for a sick individual. They were originally recited in household contexts similar to those in which their Mesopotamian parallels were recited.[4] Psalms 6, 13, 38, 69, and 88 provide examples of this type of prayer. The Elijah and Elisha cycles and the Psalms show enough of the kind of activity that we find organized in Mesopotamia as *āšipūtu* that we cannot doubt the existence of magic in ancient Israel. Given, moreover, the extensive record of magical activity in the contemporary ancient Near East, on the one hand, and in Judaism of late

3 As regards biblical magic I have come to conclusions similar to those reached by Gideon Bohak in his recent volume *Ancient Jewish Magic: A History* (Cambridge: Cambridge University Press, 2008).

4 E. S. Gerstenberger, *Der bittende Mensch: Bittritual und Klagelied des Einzelnen im Alten Testament*, WMANT 51 (Neukirchen-Vluyn: Neukirchener Verlag, 1980); E. S. Gerstenberger, *Psalms: Part 1, with an Introduction to Cultic Poetry*, FOTL 14 (Grand Rapids, MI: Eerdmans, 1988); E. S. Gerstenberger, *Psalms: Part 2 and Lamentations*, FOTL 15 (Grand Rapids, MI: Eerdmans, 2001).

antiquity, on the other, I think that it is absurd (and religiously or philosophically partial) to claim significantly less magic for ancient Israel.

More to the point, the difficulty with reconstructing the magical life of ancient Israel is due to the nature of the biblical record. The Hebrew Bible does not provide an accurate portrayal of the religious life of ancient Israel, generally, and of its magical practices, specifically. Rather, in the main, it reflects the beliefs of "biblical" religion, that strain of Israelite/Judean religion that emphasized the exclusive monotheistic worship of Yhwh. Writing in the biblical period represented not Israelite/Judean culture, but rather "biblical" religion with its emphasis on prophets or cultic priests as well as its anti-magician attitude. Because magic is often identified with foreign culture in the Bible, it is sometimes portrayed negatively or ambiguously, especially in legal texts (e.g., Deut 18:9–14; Lev 19:26, 31; 20:6, 27) and in historiographic texts.

Ancient Israel did not transmit its magical expertise in writing. In ancient Israel magical practices used to help the individual were generally neither written down nor organized into handbooks. For when writing and handbook genres were taken up in the seventh century BCE and later, they were first applied to biblical cultic religion and were used to set down the practices of the sanctuary or temple priesthood, not those of private magic utilized by magicians who catered to the needs of the individual. This would happen later.

Perhaps the phenomenon of recording only a small portion of its magical practices that obtained for the early periods of Mesopotamia has a parallel in the absence of written magical prescriptions in ancient Israel. So, perhaps, the very process of gradually writing down magical practices observed in the comparison of materials from early and late Mesopotamia was also operative in ancient Israel, and could provide at least a partial explanation for the difference between the amount of magic recorded in the Bible, on the one hand, and that found in the literary corpora of Judaism in late antiquity, on the other. For already in the Second Temple period we encounter numerous examples of magical thought and activity in Jewish sources. Magic is an important element in Jewish culture, and a significant written record of this is found in our sources from late antiquity and the Middle Ages.

I turn now to a few examples of magical forms and practices shared by ancient Israel and the other cultures of the Near East, especially Mesopotamia.

Mention has already been made of biblical laments of the individual that serve as petitions. These laments contain themes and sections comparable to those found in Mesopotamian petitionary prayers (e.g., Akkadian *šuilla* prayers).[5] Actually, the two types—the biblical laments and the Akkadian

5 For a more detailed discussion of the Akkadian general *šuilla* prayers and their relationship to the biblical laments of the individual, see T. Abusch, "Prayers, Hymns, Incantations,

general *šuilla* prayers—seem to be genetically related. Each of the two supplication types has gone through its own development, but they both derive particularly from prayers to the god of the family. Both types were parts of ceremonies meant to heal or protect an individual, were originally recited in household contexts (rather than in temple ones), and were intended to heal a rupture between the head of a household and his god. Of course, many of these prayers make mention of enemies, and some are actually a victim's imprecations against his enemies, their evil actions, and their unjust accusations (e.g., Ps 109 and "special" *Gebetsbeschwörungen* found in the anti-witchcraft ceremony *Maqlû*[6]).

The mention of enemies leads us to our second example: witches. Witches are known from both cultural spheres. In Mesopotamia, where magic was regarded as legitimate and as part of the established religion, witchcraft refers not to magical behavior as such, but to inimical behavior, that is, to the practice of magic for antisocial and destructive purposes.[7] In the Bible, witches often appear alongside diviners, and both are treated as representatives of foreign and, therefore, dangerous and hostile cultures. In both instances, the witch is usually a woman—the enemy of the *āšipu* in Mesopotamia and of the prophet and jurist in Israel. Incantations and rituals are directed against her—there are many examples in cuneiform literature in Sumerian and especially Akkadian,[8] and not a few from Israel, especially if we accept Sigmund Mowinckel's argument that the *poʿale ʾaven* of the Psalms were malevolent magicians similar to the Mesopotamian witches.[9]

Our third example: certain themes regarding dreams are common to Mesopotamia and early Judaism. Here I would begin by mentioning the common notion that while the dreamer might not know or remember a dream, a divine being could still make sure that an unpleasant dream should not have any effect, but that a favorable dream should issue in a positive result. A. L. Oppenheim, in his study of a Mesopotamian dream book, compared parts of a Babylonian prayer with what he called "a curious echo in a prayer

---

and Curses: Mesopotamia," in *Religions of the Ancient World: A Guide*, ed. S. I. Johnston (Cambridge, MA: Belknap Press of Harvard University Press, 2004), 353–355 [[111–117]].

6 For a recent edition, see T. Abusch, *The Magical Ceremony "Maqlû": A Critical Edition*, AMD 10 (Leiden: Brill, 2016).

7 For the witch and witchcraft in Mesopotamia, see T. Abusch, *Mesopotamian Witchcraft: Toward a History and Understanding of Babylonian Witchcraft Beliefs and Literature*, AMD 5 (Leiden: Brill/Styx, 2002).

8 For Sumerian and Akkadian incantations and rituals against witchcraft, see *CMAwR*.

9 See S. Mowinckel, *ʾÅwän und die individuellen Klagepsalmen*, vol. 1 of *Psalmenstudien* (Oslo: Dybwad, 1921).

quoted in the Babylonian Talmud."[10] The relevant lines of the Babylonian text in Oppenheim's translation read:

> He shall say as follows: "You are the judge, judge (now) my case. This dream which … was brought to me and which you know but I do not know—if (its content predicts something) pleasant, may its pleasantness not escape me—if (it predicts something) evil, may its evil not catch me."[11]

The Talmudic prayer that Oppenheim cited as a parallel, which is still part of the traditional Jewish liturgy, is worth quoting in full:

> If one has seen a dream and does not remember what he saw, let him stand before the priests at the time when they spread out their hands, and say as follows: "Sovereign of the Universe, I am Thine and my dreams are Thine. I have dreamt a dream and I do not know what it is. Whether I have dreamt about myself or my companions have dreamt about me, or I have dreamt about others, if they are good dreams, confirm them and reinforce them like the dreams of Joseph, and if they require a remedy, heal them, as the waters of Marah were healed by Moses, our teacher, and as Miriam was healed of her leprosy and Hezekiah of his sickness, and the waters of Jericho by Elisha. As Thou didst turn the curse of the wicked Balaam into a blessing, so turn all my dreams into something good for me." He should conclude his prayer along with the priests, so that the congregation may answer, Amen![12]

---

10 I should note that I do not find it "curious." See A. L. Oppenheim, *The Interpretation of Dreams in the Ancient Near East. With a Translation of an Assyrian Dream-Book*, TAPS NS 46/3 (1956): 298–299; cf. 232. The Babylonian prayer is quoted from K 8583; this fragment has now been edited by S. A. L. Butler, *Mesopotamian Conceptions of Dreams and Dream Rituals*, AOAT 258 (Münster: Ugarit-Verlag, 1998), as part of K 3333 + K 8583 + Sm 1069 = plates 3–4.

11 Oppenheim, *Interpretation of Dreams*, 398, for Oppenheim's transliteration, see 340, Fragment III; it is transliterated and translated by Butler, *Mesopotamian Conceptions of Dreams*, 314–315, 317, and translated by B. R. Foster, *Before the Muses*, 3rd ed. (Bethesda, MD: CDL, 2005), 719.

12 b. Berakhot 55b; this and all subsequent English translations of b. Berakhot are taken from the Soncino edition: *Seder Zera'im*, ed. I. Epstein, vol. 1 of *The Babylonian Talmud* (London: Soncino Press, 1948). b. Berakhot 55–57 is largely devoted to the topic of dreams. For discussions, see, e.g., A. Weiss, *Studies in the Literature of the Amoraim* (New York: Yeshiva University Press, 1962), 264–270 (in Hebrew); R. Kalmin, *Sages, Stories, Authors, and Editors in Rabbinic Babylonia* (Atlanta, GA: Scholars Press, 1994), 61–80; P. S. Alexander, "Bavli Berakhot 55a–57b: The Talmudic Dreambook in Context," *JJS* 46 (1995): 230–248.

This is an excellent example of a prayer that in a Jewish milieu has been loaded/overlaid with biblical references and allusions but can be stripped back to what could easily pass for a Mesopotamian statement.

Here, moreover, I would draw attention to the belief common to Babylonians and to Jews that one can turn the outcome of a dream (whether a good or even an "evil" or frightening dream) into a result that is favorable. On the Babylonian side, note the following incantation from *Maqlû* VII 162–169:

> Incantation. At dawn my hands are washed.
> May a propitious beginning begin (the new day) for me,
> May happiness (and) good health ever accompany me,
> Whatsoever I seek, may I attain,
> May [the dre]am I dreamt be made favorable for me,
> May everything evil, everything unfavorable,
> The spittle of warlock and witch, [not appro]ach me, not touch me—
> [By] the command of Ea, Šamaš, Marduk, and the princess Bēlet-ilī. TU$_6$ ÉN[13]

On the Jewish side, we would again cite a passage from b. Berakhot 55b:

> If one has a dream which makes him sad he should go and have it interpreted in the presence of three.... Say rather then, he should have a good turn given to it in the presence of three. Let him bring three and say to them; I have seen a good dream; and they should say to him, Good it is and good may it be.

There are, of course, other examples in b. Berakhot 55–57 of ways to make sure that a dream's outcome is good. Note, for example, the first in a series of similar statements made by R. Joshua ben Levi (56b):

> If one sees a river in his dreams, he should rise early and say: "Behold I will extend peace to her like a river" (Isa 59:19), before another verse occurs to him, viz., "for distress will come in like a river."

13 For further examples, cf. Šamaš 1, lines 115–117 (text: W. Mayer, *Untersuchungen zur Formensprache der babylonischen "Gebetsbeschwörungen,"* StPohl, series maior 5 [Rome: Pontifical Biblical Institute, 1976], 507; translation: Foster, *Before the Muses*, 745). See also the examples and references cited by Butler, *Mesopotamian Conceptions of Dreams*, 166–167, under the heading "To make a bad dream favorable."

Thus far I have noticed topics that I have treated as areas of (cultural) commonality between Mesopotamia and Judaism, though it is not impossible that some of these "commonalities" reflect Babylonian influence. In any case, I should like to conclude this essay with an example of direct Mesopotamian influence not on ritual or prayer but rather as regards worldview. The early chapters of 1 Enoch present us with an ideological reflection on the nature of magic in mythological form. The myth (or rather the myths) of the Watchers in 1 Enoch presents a view of magic as well as an explanation of the origin of magical lore. First Enoch 6–11[14] contains a conflation of at least two accounts of rebellious angels (i.e., the "Watchers") who descend to earth to take human wives. These Watchers teach humans various arts and are the source of human knowledge of magic and divination. In any case, 1 Enoch presents a negative take on the human institution of magic (as well as on other institutions, such as metallurgy), for this art derives from divine beings ("angels") who have assumed a demonic quality by virtue of their rebellion against the divine order. The mythological formulation may owe much to borrowing from Mesopotamia. Recently, Amar Annus has argued that the story of the Watchers derives from the Mesopotamian mythology of the antediluvian *apkallu*-sages, who came from the world of the gods and brought knowledge of major arts to humanity.[15] Annus contends, among other things, that since the *apkallu* had already been demonized in Mesopotamian literature, the negative character of the Watchers is a continuation of existing trends in Mesopotamian theology.

I desist from adding more examples. This essay has taken for granted the existence of contact between two major cultures, but it has also noted similar phenomena and developments. Moreover, we have utilized a major development in the way Mesopotamian magic was recorded to explain the character of the biblical record. I conclude by reiterating my earlier point that just as the Jews were part of the ancient Near East, so too ancient Jewish magic was part of the wider world of ancient Near Eastern magic.

14 For a source-critical analysis of the chapters and the myth(s) they contain, see, e.g., G. W. E. Nickelsburg, *A Commentary on the Book of 1 Enoch, Chapters 1–36; 81–108*, vol. 1 of *1 Enoch*, Hermeneia (Minneapolis: Fortress, 2001), 165–173.

15 A. Annus, "On the Origin of Watchers: A Comparative Study of the Antediluvian Wisdom in Mesopotamian and Jewish Traditions," *JSP* 19 (2010): 277–320.

## PART 4

# *Ancient Near Eastern Legal Practices and Thought*

CHAPTER 24

# A Shepherd's Bulla and an Owner's Receipt: A Pair of Matching Texts in the Harvard Semitic Museum

The purpose of this note is to share the results of an examination of the inscribed and sealed clay container SMN 1854 (HSS 16, no. 449; Museum Reg. No. 2000.3.277) and the related tablet SMN 2096 (HSS 16, no. 311; Museum Reg. No. 2000.3.192).[*,1] The results are given in the form of a transliteration and translation of the documents. In view of the various readings that have been suggested previously[2] and of the constructions that have been built on or supported by one or both of the texts,[3] a new edition hardly needs justification. The present edition is accompanied by two observations—one relating to the writing, the other to the seal impressions and function of the documents. Drawings of the seal impressions and photographs of the tablets are appended (Fig. 1 and Pls. 1 and 2).[4]

---

* These notes have benefitted substantially from discussions with Gernot Wilhelm; my warmest thanks to him. I also wish to thank Alan Wachman for drawing the seal impressions, Sharon White for preparing the photographs, and Martha Morrison for sharing her knowledge of Nuzi. My thanks to the officers of the Harvard Semitic Museum (now the Harvard Museum of the Ancient Near East): Frank M. Cross, Director; Carney Gavin, Curator; and William L. Moran, Curator of Tablets, for inviting me to work on the Nuzi tablets in 1977; this work was made possible by a grant from the National Endowment for the Humanities. Permission to republish the tablets was granted by William L. Moran.

1 That the two texts are related was observed by R. F. S. Starr, *Texts*, vol. 1 of *Nuzi* (Cambridge, MA: Harvard University Press, 1937), 316–317; see also A. L. Oppenheim, "On an Operational Device in Mesopotamian Bureaucracy," *JNES* 18 (1959): 121–128, at 127.

2 For previous editions and suggested readings, see, e.g., HSS 16; Oppenheim, "Operational Device," 123, 127; D. O. Edzard, review of *Excavations at Nuzi VII*, by E. R. Lacheman, *BO* 16 (1959): 136.

3 See, e.g., Oppenheim, "Operational Device"; O. Eissfeldt, *Der Beutel der Lebendigen*, BSGW Phil.-hist. Klasse 105, no. 6 (Berlin: Akademie Verlag, 1960); D. Schmandt-Besserat, "An Archaic Recording System and the Origin of Writing," *Syro-Mesopotamian Studies* 1 (1977): 31–70; D. Schmandt-Besserat, "The Invention of Writing," *Discovery: Research and Scholarship at the University of Texas at Austin*, 1, no. 4 (June 1977): 4–7; D. Schmandt-Besserat, "The Earliest Precursor of Writing," *Scientific American* 238, no. 6 (June 1978): 50–59, etc.

4 A drawing of the container and a copy of its inscription were published by Oppenheim, "Operational Device," 122; a photograph of the container by Schmandt-Besserat, "Earliest Precursor," 52; translations of the texts by Starr, *Texts*, 127, and Oppenheim, "Operational Device," 123, 127.

 | DOI:10.1163/9789004435186_025

Texts 311 and 449 record a transaction between a sheepowner Puḫišenni, son of Mušapu, and a shepherd Ziqarru, son of Šalliya. Both documents were found in the same room, S112, a room which was part of an area occupied by five generations of the family to which Puḫišenni belonged.[5]

| | SMN 1854 = Bulla 449 (Museum Reg. No.2000.3.277) | | | SMN 2096 = Tablet 311 (Museum Reg. No.2000.3.192) |
|---|---|---|---|---|
| 1. | NA$_4$.MEŠ *ša* UDU.MEŠ | | | |
| 2. | 21 UDU.MEŠ MUNUS *ša* Ù.TU | obv. | 1. | 21 UDU.MEŠ MUNUS *ša* Ù.TU |
| 3. | 6 *ka*$_4$*-lu-mu* MUNUS.MEŠ | | 2. | 6 *ka*$_4$*-lu-mu* MUNUS.MEŠ[6] |
| 4. | 8 UDU.MEŠ NITA.GAL | | 3. | 8 UDU.MEŠ NITA.GAL |
| 5. | 4 *ka*$_4$*-lu-mu* MEŠ! NITA![7] | | 4. | 4 *ka*$_4$*-lu-mu* MEŠ NITA |
| 6. | 6 *en-zu* MEŠ MUNUS *ša* ⌜Ù⌝.[TU] | | 5. | 6 *en-zu* MEŠ MUNUS *ša* Ù.TU |
| 7. | 1 M[ÁŠ.GAL] ⌜3⌝ ⌜*la*⌝*-li-ú* MUNUS.ME[Š] | | 6. | ⌜1⌝ MÁŠ.GAL |
| | | | 7. | ⌜3⌝ *la-li-ú* MUNUS.MEŠ |
| | | lo. edge | 8. | [ŠU.N]ÍGIN 49 UDU.MEŠ *ù en-za* |
| | | | 9. | [*š*]*a* ᵐ*pu-ḫi-še-en-ni* |
| | | rev. | 10. | [D]UMU *mu-ša-pu-ù* ⌜*ša*⌝ |
| | | | 11. | *a+na* ŠU ᵐ*zi-qar-ru* |
| | | | 12. | DUMU *šal-li-ia* LÚ.SIPA |
| | | | 13. | *na-ad-nu* |
| 8. | ⌜NA$_4$⌝ ⌜ᵐ⌝*zi-qar-ru* ⌜LÚ⌝.⌜SIPA⌝ | | 14. | NA$_4$ ᵐ*pu-ḫi-še-en-ni* (mistake for: NA$_4$ ᵐ*zi-qar-ru* LÚ.SIPA[8]) |
| | | l. edge | 15. | *i+na* ŠÀ-*šu-nu* |
| | | | 16. | 8 UDU.MEŠ *ṣa-ri-p*[*u*] |

| | | | |
|---|---|---|---|
| 1. | Counters representing small cattle: | | |
| 2. | 21 ewes that lamb; | 1. | 21 ewes that lamb; |

5 See Starr, *Texts*, 316–317, and HSS 16, viii and n. 11. Starr states that the texts were found in Room S112; the room assignment of SMN 1854 and 2096 in HSS 16, x should be corrected accordingly.

6 MEŠ written over partially erased MUNUS.

7 Text: ⌜MUNUS.MEŠ⌝.

8 See Observation 2, below.

3. 6 female lambs;
4. 8 full grown male sheep;
5. 4 male![9] lambs;

6. 6 she-goats that kid;
7. 1 he-goat; 3 female kids.

8. The seal of Ziqarru, the shepherd.

2. 6 female lambs;
3. 8 full grown male sheep;
4. 4 male lambs;

---

5. 6 she-goats that kid;
6. 1 he-goat;
7. 3 female kids:
8. Total: 49 sheep and goats
9. belonging to Puḫišenni,
10. the son of Mušapu, and which
13. were given
11. over to the care of Ziqarru,
12. the son of Šalliya, the shepherd.
14. The seal of Puḫišenni. (mistake for: The seal of Ziqarru, the shepherd.)
15. Among them are
16. 8 red-colored sheep.

## 1 Observation 1

The reading of each document is facilitated by the occurrence of corresponding entries in the other and by the scribe's note that the total number of animals enumerated was 49 (311: 8). Thus the numbers in each text should correspond to those in the other and should total 49. Here mention must be made of Oppenheim's emendation of 49 in 311: 8 to 48—and his restoration of missing numbers in accordance with this emendation—on the evidence of a slip of paper attached to 449 which stated that 449 "when found contained 48 little stones."[10] However, the explicit testimony of a tablet carries more weight than a modern note.[11] And even if 449 could be shown to have contained only 48 pebbles, one could demonstrate without too much difficulty that the statement ŠU.NÍGIN 49 UDU.MEŠ *ù en-za* (311: 8) is still to be reckoned with. Such demonstration is unnecessary in view of Starr's observation that "Inside the tablet were forty-nine pebbles."[12]

9 Text: female.

10 See HSS 16, 134; Oppenheim, "Operational Device," 123, 127.

11 The note was written in the early 1930s by an assistant who removed the stones. Ernest Lacheman told me that when he first saw 449 ca. 1930 it contained pebbles, but these had been removed and the note affixed when he next saw 449 several years later.

12 Starr, *Texts*, 316. The volume of the container is approximately 19 milliliters (of sand).

We begin, therefore, with the evidence of the texts and try to work out the readings accordingly. With the exception of 311: 6–7 // 449: 7, all numbers are well enough preserved and total 45. Thus 311: 6–7 // 449: 7 must record four animals. A first examination of 311 is unsatisfactory, for, if anything, traces of too many "heads" seem to be visible in lines 6–7. Fortunately, the number in 449: 7a is preserved; accordingly, 311: 6 // 449: 7a yields: 1 MÁŠ.GAL. Since the difference between the total arrived at thus far (46) and the summary total 49 is three, the number in 311: 7 // 449: 7b must be three: 3 *la-li-ú*. A reexamination of the traces in 311: 6–7 and a comparison with well-preserved signs clears up the mystery of the "extra heads" in 311 (and shows that the traces can accommodate the readings "1" and "3"), for in the inside of the impress of well-preserved signs there is an extra line running through the upper part of the head—a mark comparable to the double line produced by a pencil with a split point—which in a broken sign might create the impression that two or three heads had been inscribed where in actuality no more than one had been. The tablet 311 was written with a stylus with a hairline crack. A glance at the signs on the bulla 449 confirms what we would have expected from the parallel content of the two texts: the signs in 449 show the same defect as those in 311. Both documents were written with the same split stylus and—we may infer—by the same scribe. This observation accords well with the finding of both texts in the same room but does not account for it. Below we shall consider this archaeological datum and suggest that it explains why only one bulla has thus far been found.

## 2 Observation 2

The clay container (449) is covered with multiple rollings of a seal identified as "the seal of Ziqarru, the shepherd" (line 8). This is as expected. There is one seal impression on the tablet (311): on the reverse immediately beneath the identifying notation "the seal of Puḫišenni" (line 14). An examination of the seal impressions (see Fig. 1) is most instructive. The impression on the tablet and those on the container are identical: the same seal was used on both documents. We may safely assume that the seal belonged either to Puḫišenni or to Ziqarru.

On the face of it, it would seem that each of the parties sealed one of the records of the transaction and had his name inscribed alongside the sealing: the sheepowner, the tablet recording the receipt of animals by the shepherd; the shepherd, the filled and inscribed clay bulla. Further thought, however, shows this explanation to be fallacious. It is unlikely that two parties to a transaction would use the same seal. This aside, texts such as the tablet serve to document the number and type of animals handed over by a sheepowner to a shepherd and to record the shepherd's acknowledgment of receipt of the animals. The tablet is intended to protect the owner; it is his receipt and, therefore, would be sealed by the shepherd[13] and kept by the owner. This accords with the archaeological findspot of the tablet: a room occupied by the family of Puḫišenni. Accordingly, the notation NA$_4$ $^{m}$*pu-ḫi-še-en-ni* in 311: 14 may be regarded as a mistake for NA$_4$ $^{m}$*zi-qar-ru* LÚ.SIPA and the seal treated as the property of the shepherd. This conclusion is not contradicted by other sealings of Puḫišenni; to the best of my knowledge, the seal 311 // 449 is elsewhere not ascribed to him.[14]

Having stated that the seal belonged to the shepherd and that he used it to seal both the receipt (311) and the bulla (449), we are required to take account of three related problems: what is the function of the bulla; why is it the only such container found thus far at Nuzi; why was it stored in the same room as the tablet? A. L. Oppenheim proposed answers to the first two questions; he interpreted the bulla as a container used to send counters from one accounting department into another and thought that this "procedure may well represent an exceptional case, which would explain why only one such 'egg-shaped tablet' has been found in Nuzi."[15] I prefer different answers to these questions. Although Oppenheim deemed it unacceptable, he also stated another possible explanation of the bulla, one which I find more convincing: "It seems to be a simple device to control the transfer of animals entrusted to illiterate shepherds, to whom the number of pebbles was meant to suggest tangibly the number of sheep and goats in their care. Such pebbles, inclosed (and sealed) in their container, would serve well to protect the shepherd, no less than the officials who handed out or received the animals, against fraud or error."[16]

13 Cf. J. N. Postgate, "Some Old Babylonian Shepherds and Their Flocks," *JSS* 20 (1975): 2; regarding Nuzi, Gernot Wilhelm informs me that the tablets of Šilwa-Teššup recording similar transactions are sealed by his shepherds.

14 I have checked references to Puḫišenni *mār* Mušapu and Ziqarru *mār* Šalliya cited in *NPN* and E. Cassin and J.-J. Glassner, *Les anthroponymes*, vol. 1 of *Anthroponymie et anthropologie de Nuzi* (Malibu, CA: Undena, 1977). Seals of Puḫišenni are found on HSS 16, no. 322 and HSS 19, no. 111; they are different from each other and from HSS 16, no. 311 // 449. AASOR 16, no. 62 and HSS 15, no. 300 are unsealed. SMN 2122 and 2680 are published by D. I. Owen in his dissertation ("The Loan Documents from Nuzi," Ph.D. diss., Brandeis University, 1969); I have not seen them. The only references to Ziqarru are HSS 16, no. 311 // 449.

15 Oppenheim, "Operational Device," 127.

16 Oppenheim, "Operational Device," 123. Starr (*Texts*, 316–317) already suggested what amounts to essentially the same explanation; cf. E. Cassin, review of *Economic and Social*

We need only add that the writing on the bulla itself—a text authenticated and protected by multiple rollings of the shepherd's seal in the empty spaces between the lines of text—attested to the number and type of animals in his care. The bulla was intended to serve and protect the shepherd; it was his way of handling the transaction.

The tablet and bulla were intended to fulfill different functions, to serve different people, and to be kept in different places. Receipts would be placed among the documents of the sheepowners; bullae would be held by the shepherds or stored with their possessions apart from the archives of the sheepowners. Our bulla was the only one found precisely because it was stored together with the tablet of the sheepowner. A possible explanation of this irregular arrangement may even be provided by the earlier observation of the erroneous character of the notation "the seal of Puḫišenni." The bulla may have been kept with the tablet because of the error; perhaps the error was caught and both documents rendered inoperative, or the bulla was kept to allow redrafting of the tablet or to provide confirmation of the authenticity of the flawed receipt.

The finding of only this bulla is due, then, to an accident of history and of archaeological excavation. Bullae were used by shepherds around Nuzi. This use may be inferred from references to stones in the Nuzi texts.[17] Normally when sheep were handed over by or given to the shepherd, the appropriate number of counters were, respectively, removed from or deposited in the bulla.

---

*Documents*, vol. 7 of *Excavations at Nuzi*, HSS 16, by E. R. Lacheman, *RA* 53 (1959): 164. In view of some of Oppenheim's stated objections ("Operational Device," 124), I note the following: The bulla served the needs of the shepherd: the pebbles inside gave testimony to the total number of animals given over to his care; the inscription on the outside—writing which was protected from tampering by multiple rollings—attested to the types of animals received and the number of each. The sealed inscription and the sealed contents supplement each other and supply full information. In its own way, the shepherd's bulla provides the same information as the sheepowner's tablet; and just as the tablet did not have to be accompanied by a pouch of pebbles, so the bulla did not have to provide a total on the outside. The bulla and tablet are parallel documents and serve as checks on each other. Furthermore, it is also possible that the writing on the bulla was meant to allow an official to check the document. Such a perusal would be sufficient for certain purposes and would eliminate the necessity of breaking the covering. (The Nuzi bulla may be regarded as having the form of a double document; see S. J. Lieberman, "Of Clay Pebbles, Hollow Clay Balls, and Writing: A Sumerian View," *AJA* 84 [1980]: 339–358, at 352.) Finally, the tablet, and not the bulla, protects the owner and prevents the shepherd from substituting less valuable animals. The fact that our bulla is the only one discovered in Nuzi is discussed below. For a different explanation of the bulla, see Edzard, review of *Excavations at Nuzi VII*, 136; as noted above, protection of the owner was provided by the herding contract and not by the bulla.

17 See Oppenheim, "Operational Device," 125–127; *CAD* A/1, 60.

There was no need to record the withdrawal, deposit, or transfer of counters; the new number of counters in the bulla and, when appropriate, the drafting of a new text were record enough. Only when the procedure deviated from this norm was this fact recorded: hence references to stones almost always mention the fact that stones were not deposited, not removed, not transferred. The small number of references is due to the fact that the texts record exceptions.[18] To be sure, the bulla and receipt tablet were intended to protect, respectively, the shepherd against unfounded claims and the owner against loss. But full protection was not always necessary; the two parties could agree to a transfer without going through the bother of breaking the covering and changing the count and text of the bulla; one simply registered the new situation and the fact that the number of stones had not been altered. Trust based on sustained relationships and common interest may be presumed to have existed between owner and shepherd.

On this note I may draw this discussion to a close. I have perhaps said too much already about a city in which I am only a visitor. But having spent some time working on the Nuzi tablets of the Harvard Semitic Museum, I could not but welcome an opportunity to dedicate a note to Professor E. R. Lacheman; I would thus celebrate a scholar's lifelong devotion to the decipherment and publication of an important corpus of cuneiform tablets.

18 The exceptional character of the references is noted by Oppenheim, "Operational Device," 125–128; his explanation is different and consonant with the system of recording that he envisioned.

RIGHT EDGE

OBVERSE

LOWER EDGE

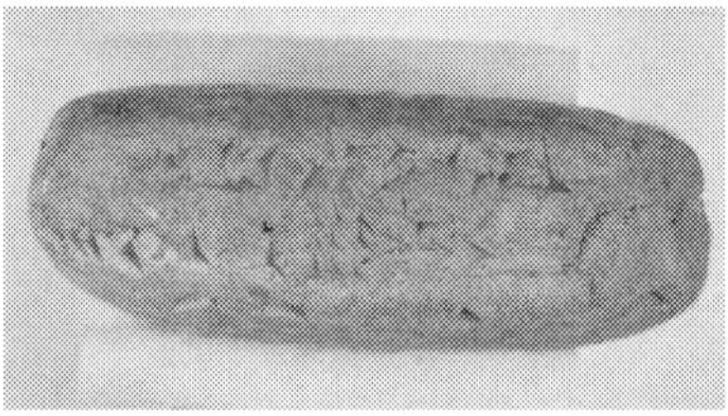

REVERSE

LEFT EDGE

PLATE 1 *SMN* 2096 = Tablet HSS 16, 311 (museum reg. no. 2000.3.192). Width of obverse: 6.0 cm; height of obverse: 5.6 cm; depth from obv. to rev.: 2.1 cm. Scale: 1:1. For color images, see https://cdli.ucla.edu/search/archival_view.php?ObjectID=P409311.

FIGURE 1 Seal impression from Tablet 311. Width: 5.4 cm; height: 1.7 cm; Scale: 2:1 (top). Composite drawing of seal impressions taken from seven rollings on the bulla 16–449 (bottom).

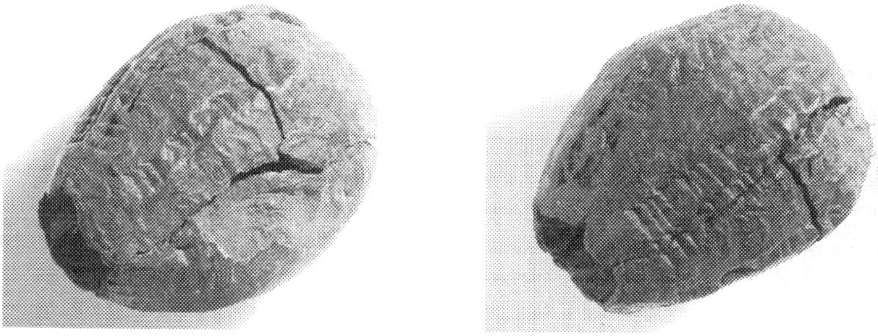

PLATE 2 *SMN* 1854 = Bulla HSS 16, 449 (museum reg. no. 2000.3.277). Height: 6.0 cm; circumference: 15.0 cm. Not to scale. For color images, see https://cdli.ucla.edu/search/archival_view.php?ObjectID=P409396.

CHAPTER 25

# "He Should Continue to Bear the Penalty of That Case": Some Observations on Codex Ḫammurabi §§3–4 and §13

The purpose of this paper is to suggest an explanation for *aran dīnim šuāti ittanašši* in §§4 and 13 of Codex Ḫammurabi (hereafter CḪ).[1] More specifically, we wish to reconsider the function of the *-tan-* form of the G(rundstamm)tn durative *ittanašši* in §4, and secondarily in §13, and to reconstruct the legal situation, thought, and intent of the relevant legal cases. My concern here is to understand "the conceptual framework and moral standards implied in the normative prescriptions which these law collections explicitly set out."[2] I have paid little attention to the relationship of the relevant paragraphs to actual practice. This procedure is valid under any circumstance; it is especially valid since the nature of the "Code" has not yet been finally determined nor has it been decided whether the individual cases are statutory law, exemplary precedents or reforms, or scholastic speculation. Perhaps our reflections will provide further support for one or another position.

A study of the wording and thought of legal cases in a collection that forms an early part of a tradition that eventually included biblical and rabbinic legal collections is surely a fitting presentation in honor of the person and achievements of Professor Marvin Fox. For one of the areas nearest to his heart and central to his scholarship is the close reading of legal texts and the recovery of their underlying values and conceptions. Marvin has been a dear friend and respected colleague since we first met, and I take very great pleasure in dedicating this study to him on this occasion.

1 A version of this paper was read before the 198th meeting of the American Oriental Society, Chicago, March 1988. I have benefited from the questions and observations of several friends, most recently Marvin Fox and Stephen Kaufman. I am especially grateful to Kathryn Kravitz for her assistance and for a number of helpful suggestions.

2 J. J. Finkelstein, *The Ox That Gored*, TAPS 71/2 (Philadelphia: American Philosophical Society, 1981), 16.

 | DOI:10.1163/9789004435186_026

## 1 Introduction

The first part of the Code (§§1–5) sets out selected procedures to be followed by the courts. Opening the Code in this way seems to have been intentional, for such an introduction highlights the importance of proper judicial procedure for the administration of justice and suggests Ḫammurabi's concern for the rule of law. §4 treats the testimony of a witness in a case involving a dispute over property, probably silver or barley loans. Actually, the division into paragraphs is modern,[3] and §4 is not a separate unit. Rather, it is related to §3 and forms the second segment of a unit comprising §§3 and 4. The text of §§3–4 reads:

(3) *šumma awīlum ina dīnim ana šībūt sarrātim ūṣiamma awāt iqbû lā uktīn*
*šumma dīnum šū dīn napištim awīlum šū iddâk*
(4) *šumma ana šībūt še'im u kaspim ūṣiam aran dīnim šuāti ittanašši*

As we shall see, the protasis of §4 is parallel to the opening protasis of §3 and should be construed as if it read *šumma* (*awīlum ina dīnim*) *ana šībūt še'im u kaspim ūṣiam* (*ma awāt iqbû lā uktīn*), "If he (a man) came forward (in a case) to bear witness to (a claim for) barley or silver, (but then has not proved the statement that he made)." But how shall we translate the apodosis: *aran dīnim šuāti ittanašši*, and what nuance of meaning does the /*tan*/ iterative lend to the verb?

G. R. Driver and J. C. Miles have translated this phrase in §§4 and 13 as "he shall remain liable for the penalty for that suit."[4] Other scholars have been unwilling to work with the standard repetitive-habitual-continuous meaning for *ittanašši* here, perhaps because they felt that no sense was conveyed by this kind of iterative. Thus, while some have ignored the /*tan*/ here,[5] others have attributed a distributive meaning to it. A. Falkenstein correctly rejected the translation "he shall bear" for *ittanašši*, arguing that this translation "unterdrückt die hier vorliegende distributive Bedeutung der Gtn Form," and

3 The designation of the text as a "code" is also modern. Cf., e.g., Finkelstein, *Ox That Gored*, 15–16, for the problems inherent in using this conventional designation as well as those inherent in the use of the modern division into paragraphs.

4 G. R. Driver and J. C. Miles, *The Babylonian Laws*, 2 vols. (Oxford: Oxford University Press, 1952–1955), 2:15, 19. Cf. *CAD* A/2, 298: CḪ §13: "That man is guilty, he will remain liable for the penalty (involved in) that suit."

5 E.g., T. J. Meek, "The Code of Hammurabi," *ANET*, 166, §4: "he shall bear the penalty of that case."

followed W. Eilers's earlier translation.[6] In his translation of the Code, Eilers rendered *aran dīnim šuāti ittanašši* as "so lädt er sich die jeweilige Strafe dieses Rechtsstreites auf."[7] A similar translation and analysis were accorded a somewhat authoritative status when W. von Soden cited our passage as one of several examples of a distributive meaning for the */tan/*.[8] And this understanding has been followed by others such as D. O. Edzard,[9] R. Borger,[10] and G. Steiner[11] in their grammatical studies and translations of the Code. Finally, another twist was given to the */tan/* form here by A. Finet in his translation of the Code. He translates *aran dīnim šuāti ittanašši* in §§4 and 13 as "il supportera dans sa totalité la peine de ce procès," and glosses the word "totalité" with the note that "C'est le sens exprimé ici par la forme à infixe *-tana-*."[12]

For a while I, too, was content to accept the interpretation of the */tan/* in §§4 and 13 as a distributive largely because I had some difficulty imagining a situation that would suit a repetitive or habitual meaning. But, then, also the interpretation as a distributive seemed somewhat forced. In view of the limited number of alleged distributives and in response to a student's question,

6 A. Falkenstein, review of *The Babylonian Laws*, vol. 1, by G. R. Driver and J. C. Miles, *ZA* 51 (1955): 262.

7 W. Eilers, *Gesetzesstele Chammurabis: Gesetze um die Wende des dritten vorchristlichen Jahrtausends*, *AO* 31/3–4 (Leipzig: Hinrichs, 1932), 17, §4; 19, §13.

8 "Bisweilen haben Iterativstämme auch eine Art von distributiver Bedeutung, die am besten durch unser 'jeweils' wiedergegeben wird (z.B. aB *ittanašši* 'er tragt (die jeweils vorgesehene Strafe)' KH vi 5 ..." (*GAG*, §91f).

9 D. O. Edzard, "Die Stämme des altbabylonischen Verbums in ihrem Oppositionssystem," in *Studies in Honor of Benno Landsberger on His Seventy-fifth Birthday, April 21, 1965*, ed. H. G. Güterbock and T. Jacobsen, AS 16 (Chicago: University of Chicago Press, 1965), 112, cites "*aran dīnim šuāti ittanašši*, 'er wird die für diese Rechtssache jeweils (vorgesehene) Strafe erleiden' (KH vi 3–5)," and notes that the Gtn "drückt hier das ... distributiv gedachte ... Vorkommen der durch G beschriebenen Handlung aus." It may not be irrelevant that in this instance Edzard deviates from his standard operating procedure of citing only Old Babylonian examples and draws on Middle Assyrian *inašši* as the example of a contrastive form to the Gtn.

10 R. Borger translates "(die jeweils vorgesehene Strafe, *arnu*) tragen (KH §§4, 13)." R. Borger, *Babylonisch-assyrische Lesestücke*, 3 vols. (Rome: Pontifical Biblical Institute, 1963), 1:lxix; 2nd ed., 2 vols., AnOr 54 (Rome: Pontifical Biblical Institute, 1979), 2:262 s.v. *našû* Gtn. This formulation appears as well in R. Borger, "Der Codex Hammurapi," in *Rechtsbücher*, ed. O. Kaiser, TUAT NF 1/1 (Güttersloh: Gerd Mohn, 1982), 45, §4: "muss er die jeweilige Strafe dieses Prozesses tragen." Cf. 46, §13.

11 G. Steiner, "Die sog. tan-Stämme des akkadischen Verbums und ihre semitischen Grundlagen," *ZDMG* 131 (1981): 24, notes that "bezeichnet die Präsensform der Iterativstämme ... das Eintreten eines Vorgangs ... unter verschiedenen Umstanden, z.B. ... *aran dīnim šuāti it*[*t*]*anašši* 'er soll jeweils die entsprechende Strafe in diesem Rechtsfall auf sich nehmen.'"

12 A. Finet, *Le Code de Hammurapi*, LAPO 6 (Paris: Cerf, 1973), 45–46, §4; 48–49, §13.

I decided to go back to the common basic meaning of /*tan*/ (*GAG*, §91e: "Die Grundfunktion der *tan*-Stämme ist die eines Iterativs zu den zugehörigen einfachen Hauptstämmen.... Nicht selten ist die Bedeutung der Iterativstämme zugleich habitativ"), and see if I could make sense of the passage on the basis of the /*tan*/'s standard temporal meaning of repetition, habituality, continuity, permanence. What I should like to do here is to set out an alternative interpretation of *aran dīnim šuāti ittanašši* that satisfies, I believe, the philological and juristic requirements of the passage.

## 2 Analysis and Translation

Driver and Miles's translation assumes that /*tan*/ here operates within a temporal dimension and conveys a sense of continued or repeated action. In the philological commentary on §4, Driver and Miles note as follows:

> the infixed -*tan*- ... in *ittanašši* implies continued or repeated action ... as the addition of *adi balṭat* elsewhere shows (CḪ 148 81). Verbs denoting responsibility, such as *našû* and *apālu*, often take it to show that it continues so long as any actual or potential claims remain to be settled ... especially so long as the person to whom they are due is alive or when the obligation is lifelong.[13]

I do not know whether there is always a meaningful distinction between the G and Gtn of *apālu* and *našû*; that question remains to be investigated. But it is obvious from its uses elsewhere in the Code, for example in §148, that in the Code the Gtn of *našû* conveys a standard temporal iterative meaning of repetition, regularity, and habit. True, *ittanašši* in §§4 and 13 could refer to bearing responsibility for all claims that might arise in the future. But this, too, is an insufficient explanation of *aran dīnim šuāti ittanašši*, because §4 seems to be dealing not so much with real estate, which might require a permanent responsibility from the seller—*ittanappal*,[14] but rather with a loan, or the like, whose claim can be settled with a one-time payment and need not require a lifelong obligation. Surely, *aran dīnim šuāti ittanašši* does not mean that he pays the amount of his fine repeatedly, or even more than just once. It seems, then, that

13 Driver and Miles, *Babylonian Laws*, 2:149.
14 Cf., e.g., S. D. Simmons, "Early Old Babylonian Tablets from Ḥarmal and Elsewhere," *JCS* 13 (1959): 91–92; 14 (1960): 23, no. 46: 21–25.

standard situations do not convincingly or completely account for the iterative /*tan*/ form of the verb here.

Assuming that we are not dealing with a frozen form, we must wonder what specialized meaning or nuance of the standard sense of iteration or continuity is conveyed here by the /*tan*/ form of *našû* in combination with *arnu*. Why should someone be repeatedly or continuously penalized?

I, too, would now translate *aran dīnim šuāti ittanašši* as "he shall continue to bear the penalty in that case," and would suggest that the iterative in §4 conveys the notion that the witness always remains liable for testimony that he gave, that having paid the amount due in that case, he bears the guilt—for the duration of his life and even under changed circumstances—for not having been able to prove his testimony; the penalty will never be rescinded. Such absoluteness and irrevocability are compatible with the penalties stipulated in the apodoses of §§3 and 5: in §3 the witness is to be killed—nothing is more absolute or irrevocable than death; in §5 a guilty judge is to be expelled from his judge's seat in the assembly and may never resume that office. But the question remains: why should the witness of §4 remain liable, and what can that mean?

Some scholars have understood the law as being directed against a lying witness who has come forward with false testimony. They have based this interpretation on the translation of *šībūt sarrātim* in §3 as "false testimony"[15] and on the assumption that "false testimony" characterizes the nature of the testimony in both §§3 and 4.[16] I believe that this translation and interpretation are incorrect. The aforementioned translation and interpretation take for granted that the protasis at the beginning of §3 serves as an overall introduction to both §§3 and 4, and that the second protasis and the apodosis of §3 are parallel to §4. But this construction is wrong. For neither is §3b, *šumma dīnum*

15 Cf., e.g., Eilers, *Gesetzesstele Chammurabis*, 17: "Wenn ein Bürger vor Gericht zu falschem Zeugnis aufgetreten ist"; A. Pohl and R. Follett, *Codex Ḫammurabi* (Rome: Pontificium Institutum Biblicum, 1950), 12: "Si (ali)quis pro tribunali ad testimonium falsitatis exierit"; Meek, *ANET*, 166: "If a seignior came forward with false testimony in a case"; W. J. Martin, "The Law Code of Hammurabi," in *Documents from Old Testament Times*, ed. D. Winton Thomas (Edinburgh: Nelson, 1958), 29: "If a citizen in a case has borne false witness"; Finet, *Code de Hammurapi*, 45: "Si quelqu'un a paru dans un procès pour (porter) un faux témoignage"; Borger, "Codex Hammurapi," 45: "Wenn ein Bürger zu falschem Zeugnis auftritt." Our line is also treated this way in the dictionaries: *AHw*, 1031, s.v. *sartu* 4a ("falsches Zeugnis"); *CAD* S, 179, s.v. *sarrātu* ("false testimony").

16 E.g., Meek, *ANET*, §3: "If a seignior came forward with false testimony in a case, and has not proved the word which he spoke, if that case was a case involving life, that seignior shall be put to death"; §4: "If he came forward with (false) testimony concerning grain or money, he shall bear the penalty of that case."

*šū dīn napištim*, "If that case is a capital case," the counterpart of §4a, *šumma ana šībūt še'im u kaspim ūṣiam*, "If he came forward to bear witness to (a claim for) barley or silver," nor does §3a, *šumma awīlum ina dīnim ana šībūt sarrātim ūṣiamma*, "If a man came forward in a case to bear *šībūt sarrātim*," provide the common background of §§3 and 4.

To understand why this translation is incorrect and to grasp more fully the meaning of §§3 and 4, we must set out the structure of this text in a little more detail. *šumma awīlum ina dīnim ana šībūt sarrātim ūṣiamma* (§3a) introduces only §3. §3 contains a split protasis; *šumma dīnum šū dīn napištim* (§3b) forms a second delimiting protasis and presents the only—if most extreme—subcategory of *šībūt sarrātim* given in the text. §3a, *šumma* (...) *ana šībūt sarrātim ūṣiamma*, and §4a, *šumma ana šībūt še'im u kaspim ūṣiam*, are on the same syntactic and logical level, and each may serve as a replacement for the other; *ana šībūt sarrātim* and *ana šībūt še'im u kaspim* are parallel to each other. Thus, §4a is functionally equivalent or parallel to §3a. Hence, while §§3 and 4 are surely related, they are not a single integrated legal unit that opens with an introduction (§3a) laying out a common background, followed by two parallel sets (§3b–c, §4) of subsidiary protases (§3b, §4a) and concluding apodoses (§3c, §4b). Rather, §4 is parallel to §3; they set forth two parallel but independent cases.

To understand why this must be so, we must take note of some of the different ways of setting out related laws that are used in the Code. For example, there are those adjoining cases for which the beginning portion of the text provides the initial situation that serves as the starting point for several possible cases; this background situation is not repeated as each case is described, and the individual case only consists of a secondary protasis with its apodosis, and therefore cannot stand on its own (e.g., §§9–11, §§17–20, §§138–140, §§163–166, §§229–231). §§9–11, §§229–231, and §§17–20 provide very good examples of this type. The beginning of §9 (vi 70–vii 17) lays out the situation that forms the common background for and introduces each of the three cases that follow. These three then examine various possibilities. Each one picks up at the point where the common background of §9a ends, and, in each case, the first principal verb of the main clause is a perfect—not a preterite—form of the verb *wabālu*: (*lā*) *itbalam*. Thus, §9a: vi 70–vii 17 introduces (1) §9b: vii 18–47 // (2) §10: vii 48–61 // (3) §11: vii 62–viii 3. Less complicated and therefore perhaps more clear are §§229–231 and §§17–20. §229: 64–70 describes a situation in which a house that a builder has built collapsed (*imqutma*). This situation is then followed by three instances of different people being killed by the collapsing house. Each of the three alternative delimiting protases simply repeats the verb *uštamīt*, "has killed," in the perfect—not the preterite—form and is then followed by an apodosis. Thus, §229a: 64–70 introduces (1) §229b: 71–72 // (2) §230: 73–76 // (3) §231: 77–81. §§17–20 treat situations that arise from the capture of a runaway slave. §17: 49–53 provides this background. This common protasis is followed by four separate protases presenting different situations that may then arise, each with its own apodosis: §17a: 49–53 introduces (1) §17b: 54–58 // (2) §18: 59–67 // (3) §19: 68– ix 4 // (4) §20: 5–13. In contrast to the preterite verb form of the common protasis (*iṣbatma*, "seized"), the verbs in each of the four delimiting protases are in the perfect form.

Different are adjoining legal cases that repeat from the initially stipulated legal situation all or most of the details that apply to the following cases and make whatever necessary change and insert whatever additional information is required (e.g., §§162–163). Each individual case contains a primary protasis and, on the whole, each case can stand on its own. §§3 and 4 are an example of this latter type of formulation. Actually, §§3–4 are part of a group comprising §§1–4, which group presents cases of unproved (*lā uktīn*) accusations (§§1–2) and testimony (§§3–4).

Having observed, moreover, that a subsidiary protasis, whether parallel to other subsidiary protases (as in the examples noted above) or as part of a single split protasis (e.g., §136), would usually begin not with a preterite, but with a perfect form of the verb or its equivalent, we find therein additional support for our conclusion that §4a (*šumma ana šībūt še'im u kaspim ūṣiam*) is not a subsection of §3 that stands in parallelism with §3b (*šumma dīnum šū dīn napištim*) but rather is itself a primary protasis that stands in parallelism to the previously occurring primary protasis §3a (*šumma awīlum ina dīnim ana šībūt sarrātim ūṣiamma*). For if §4 were parallel to §3b, it should have read *šumma ana šībūt še'im u kaspim *ittaṣi* (cf., e.g., §136: 64–67) rather than the attested *ūṣiam*. Hence, §4 // §3, and *šībūt sarrātim* and *šībūt še'im u kaspim* are parallel to each other.

And the relationship which obtains between §§4 and 3 is similar to that between §§2 and 1 (§4 : §3 :: §2 : §1). As the first of the two legal cases dealing with accusation, §1 gives a full version of its protasis; relying on §1, §2 can then state its protasis in a slightly abbreviated and less explicit form. Thus, where §1 has the fuller text: *šumma awīlum awīlam ubbirma nērtam elišu iddima lā uktīnšu*, "If a man accused another man and charged him with murder but then has not proved it against him," §2 states only: *šumma awīlum kišpī eli awīlim iddima lā uktīnšu*, "If a man charged another man with witchcraft but then has not proved it against him," and this is to be understood as an abbreviated form of **šumma awīlum awīlam ubbirma kišpī elišu iddima lā uktīnšu*, "If a man accused another man and charged him with witchcraft but then has not proved it against him." Similarly, §4 is to be understood as if it read **šumma* (*awīlum ina dīnim*) *ana šībūt še'im u kaspim ūṣiam*(*ma awāt iqbû lā uktīn*), "If a man came forward in a case to bear witness to a claim for barley or silver but then has not proved the statement that he made." The words *awīlum ina dīnim* and *-ma awāt iqbû lā uktīn* of §3 are suppressed in §4, but are surely implicit there.[17] The wording of §3 that applies to both §§3 and 4 but is not repeated in §4 is not *ana šībūt sarrātim*, but rather wording that need not be rendered explicit and can be abbreviated without loss.

The word *sarrātu* here in §3 means "wrongdoing," "crime," or the like.[18] *šībūt še'im u kaspim* in §4 presents a case comparable to the one involving the testimony about a crime (*šībūt sarrātim*), but involving instead testimony about barley and silver. §§3–4 are to be translated:

> If a man came forward in a case to bear witness to a wrongdoing but then has not proved the statement that he made, if that case is a capital case, that man should be put to death.
>
> If he came forward to bear witness to (a claim for) barley or silver (but then has not proved the statement that he made), he should continue to bear the penalty of that case.

§§3–4 take up the problem of unconfirmed testimony, with §3 addressing this problem in legal cases involving wrongdoing, generally, and capital cases, specifically, and §4 addressing this problem in cases involving disputes over contractual obligations, notably payment. The writer probably has in mind a situation such as that described in the Laws of Ur-Nammu §26 where the witness to a lawsuit declined to testify on oath.[19] Both §§3 and 4 stipulate that

17 These abbreviations of §§2 and 4 are stylistic and should not be confused with what we find in those laws where the initial situation is set out only once at the beginning of a series of cases.

18 The meaning "wrongdoing" or "crime" is certainly one of the meanings of *sarrātu*. For this meaning, see, e.g., *AHw*, 1031, s.v. *sartu*, "Falsches, Lüge, *Verbrechen*" (italics mine); *CAD* S, 187–188, s.v. *sartu*, mng. 2 ("fraud, misdeed, criminal act"); 182, s.v. *sarru*, mng. 3 ("[in substantival use] criminal, thief, liar"). Note the translation of *šībūt sarrātim* of CḪ §3 as "witness to a felony" in Driver and Miles, *Babylonian Laws*, 2:15 (cf. 2:148), and as *ad testimonium de crimine* in A. Deimel, *Codex Ḫammurabi: Textus Primigenius* (Rome: Pontifical Biblical Institute, 1930), cited by Driver and Miles, *Babylonian Laws*, 2:148.

19 J. J. Finkelstein, "The Laws of Ur-Nammu," *JCS* 22 (1969): 70: 41–46; cf. O. R. Gurney and S. N. Kramer, "Two Fragments of Sumerian Laws," in *Studies in Honor of Benno Landsberger on His Seventy-fifth Birthday, April 21, 1965*, ed. H. G. Güterbock and T. Jacobsen, AS 16 (Chicago: University of Chicago Press, 1965), 17. While I will not take up here in detail the relationship of the laws of Ur-Nammu §§25–26 and of Lipit-Ištar §17 to our laws, I would simply note that at least Ur-Nammu §26 clearly supports my assumption that *lā uktīn* in CḪ §§3(–4) means that the witness has refused to take an oath in support

the witness who is unable to substantiate his testimony by oath or the like is to suffer the same punishment or pay the same amount that would have been required of the accused. The principle of talion before the fact is applied. Thus, §3 focuses on the extreme instance of wrongdoing, namely cases involving the death penalty, and stipulates that our witness should suffer the death penalty. §4 requires of our witness that he pay the same amount that a party found liable would have been obliged to pay.

Many scholars have been deceived by the alleged falseness of the testimony and have treated false testimony as the central issue of §§3 and 4. Perhaps they defined the issue in this manner because they were influenced by such laws as Deut 19:16–19, where, by contrast, however, the testimony is explicitly designated as a lie (v. 18). Even Driver and Miles, who saw the parallelism of *šībūt sarrātim* and *šībūt še'im u kaspim*, understood the meaning of *sarrātim* as wrongdoing or felony, and correctly translated our text,[20] persisted in seeing false evidence as the issue, and, distracted by the supposed falseness of the testimony, interpreted *aran dīnim šuāti ittanašši* almost as if it did not contain an iterative:

> The distinction in §§3–4 is between giving false witness of which the subject is *sarrātum* and giving false evidence of which it is grain or silver.... Here the phrase [scil. *aran dīnim šuāti ittanašši*] means that the false witness must pay the penalty applicable to the case in which he has given the false evidence, and what this means is quite obvious: the principle is that he must suffer what he has tried by his false evidence to bring upon another person.[21]

of his testimony rather than that he could not prove his testimony because it was a lie. The fact that the related law Lipit-Ištar §17 has -íl-e (and not íl-íl) may provide further support for our contention that the /*tan*/ of *našû* in CḪ §4 was intentionally introduced and carries special meaning. W. F. Leemans, "Le faux témoin," *RA* 64 (1970): 65–66, also concludes that the witness in CḪ §§3–4 did not take the oath: "Dans ce cas aussi, il n'est pas dit que le témoin a juré son témoignage; il a simplement paru en portant témoignage devant les juges et n'a pas prouvé son témoignage, mais il ne l'a pas juré" (cf. Finkelstein, "Laws of Ur-Nammu," 79–80). The death penalty stipulated in §3, while probably theoretical (see below), may also have been intended to warn a witness in a capital case that if he were required to take the oath, he would not be able to refuse and pay a fine instead. For the oath, see S. E. Loewenstamm, "The Cumulative Oath of Witnesses and Parties in Mesopotamian Law," *Comparative Studies in Biblical and Ancient Oriental Literatures*, AOAT 204 (Kevalaer: Butzon & Bercker; Neukirchen-Vluyn: Neukirchener Verlag, 1980), 341–345 (reference courtesy R. Westbrook).

20 Driver and Miles, *Babylonian Laws*, 1:66–67, 2:15.

21 Driver and Miles, *Babylonian Laws*, 1:66–68.

But as we have seen, *šībūt sarrātim* and *šībūt še'im u kaspim* are parallel to each other, and *šībūt sarrātim* of §3 denotes and connotes false testimony no more than does *šībūt še'im u kaspim* of §4. Here in §3, *sarrātu* does not mean falsehood, and *šībūt sarrātim* does not mean false testimony or perjury.[22] Certainly it does not mean false testimony that had been intentionally contrived. There is no unambiguous proof that the witness in §§3–4 intentionally lied. For the text of §3a does not state that the witness has come forward intentionally for

22 While some scholars have understood *šibūt sarrātim* as explicitly denoting "false testimony" (see above), several others have not translated the phrase this way but still seem to have understood false testimony as the issue at stake (e.g., Driver and Miles, who seem to confuse the nature of the case under discussion with the kind of testimony). Whether because of biblical and other legal parallels or because of the associations of the word *sartu/sarrātu* (Hebr. *sārā*), they seem to have equated unsubstantiated testimony with false testimony. As stated, the issue is not falsehood but proof, not so much intent as objective result. The failure of testimony to convince or convict may lead to the labeling of that testimony as false—that is, unproved testimony may be regarded as false testimony—but only after the fact and only as one limited way of construing such testimony. But in the absence of very clear distinctions, such reasoning in the study of CḪ and other Mesopotamian law collections only serves to confuse the issues. (As an aside, I should perhaps mention that Deut 19:16 should probably not be translated "If a man appears against another to testify maliciously and gives false testimony against him" [NJPS] but rather something like "If a witness [in a case] of violence comes forward to testify against a man that he had committed a crime.")

Not surprisingly, several scholars have noted correctly that the main issue in CḪ §§1–4 was the absence of proof (though even here some equate absence of proof with falseness). See the following: A. Walther, *Das altbabylonische Gerichtswesen*, LSS 6/4–6 (Leipzig: Hinrichs, 1917), 223 n. 1 on *lā uktīn* in CḪ §§1–4 and 127: "vielmehr ist der einfache Grundsatz: wer etwas nicht beweist, hat Unrecht." M. San Nicolò, "Anschuldigung, falsche," *RlA* 1 (1928): 112: "Dem Anzeiger liegt der Wahrheitsbeweis ob, bei dessen Misslingen er straffällig wird. Auf seinen eventuellen guten Glauben wird, wie auch nicht anders zu erwarten, keine Rücksicht genommen." (Followed by H. P. H. Petschow, "Altorientalische Parallelen zur spätrömischen calumnia," *ZSS, Romanistische Abteilung* 90 [1973]: 18–19; cf. H. P. H. Petschow, "Zur Systematik und Gesetzestechnik im Codex Hammurabi," *ZA* 57 [1965]: 148.) D. Nörr, "Zum Schuldgedanken im altbabylonischen Strafrecht," *ZSS, Romanistische Abteilung* 75 (1958): 22: "§3 betrifft das falsche Zeugnis in Kapital-, §4 dasselbe in Vermögenssachen. In keinem Falle wird auf das Wissen des Täters um die Unrichtigkeit seiner Anschuldigung oder seiner Zeugenaussage Rücksicht genommen. Kann er den Wahrheitsbeweis nicht führen, der ihm auferlegt ist, so wird er bestraft." C. H. Gordon, *Hammurapi's Code: Quaint or Forward-Looking?* (New York: Rinehart, 1957), 4: "The first law (§1) states that a man who accuses another of murder and cannot prove it shall be put to death. The code shows no interest in the possible sincerity of the accuser or in the possible guilt of the accused. Unprovable claims have no place in the code. Moreover, he who makes unprovable accusations must bear the penalty that he would impose on the accused. An unproved accusation entailing the death penalty means death for the accuser (§3); one entailing the payment of goods imposes that payment on the accuser (§4)."

the purpose of giving false testimony, and in any case, §4a and not §3a provides the background for the apodosis in §4b. In this connection and as regards *aran dīnim šuāti ittanašši*, I should note that properly speaking, a lying witness can do nothing but bear his penalty forever; hence, it seems gratuitous to use the Gtn when a simple G should have sufficed. The text states neither that the testimony is necessarily false nor that the witness has intentionally lied. Hence, the punishment of death in §3 and the permanent liability in §4 cannot be accounted for by the intentional giving of false testimony.

## 3 Meaning and Significance

We are dealing, here, not with false testimony but with unconfirmed testimony. What is at stake is not the absence of truth but the absence of proof. If §§3–4, then, are not dealing, explicitly at least, with falsehood or lies, why should the witness continue to bear the penalty? A correct translation of *aran dīnim šuāti ittanašši* must be connected with an appropriate situation. We must reformulate our understanding of these legal cases and derive therefrom an explanation or justification for the permanent liability of the witness in §4.

The opening section of the Code constitutes an attempt to establish guidelines for the proper working of a just and orderly judicial process. The jurist's goal in §§3–4 is to define and discourage irresponsible or improper testimony. Responsible testimony is testimony that can be proved and upon which one can rely. Accordingly, the jurist stipulates that a person may not voluntarily come forward in a judicial context for the purpose of making a statement for which he is unable or unwilling to provide confirmation (by means of an oath or the like), for such behavior is of no utility and is actually harmful to all concerned.

The intention of the witness is of no consequence. The value or assessment of the testimony is in no way dependent on whether the witness himself believed the testimony or whether he fabricated it. Nor is it dependent on his motivation—whether it be concern for the public good or selfishness and malice. Our writer wishes to know only whether the witness is able and willing to prove his accusation or testimony. He is interested only in objective or external results, not in the witness's reasons or intentions. Actually, whether or not the witness is lying is of no interest whatsoever to the jurist. He does not even assume that an irresponsible witness is necessarily falsifying testimony. But irrespective of intentions, a witness must bear absolute responsibility and liability for his acts and their results. And an irresponsible witness must bear the responsibility for bringing unproven testimony.

Accordingly, testimony for which the witness is penalized is not necessarily untrue. It is simply unproven or unsubstantiated. And for bringing this kind of testimony he is to be subjected to the punishment that would have been meted out to the accused: death in capital cases, payment in cases involving dispute over contractual obligations. But if the witness was not lying, his testimony would sometimes be true. It is important that we remember this, for herein lies the rub. For especially in cases of unproven but true testimony, proof substantiating the penalized witness's testimony may turn up at a later date. How should the system react in the instance where evidence turns up subsequent to the imposition of the penalty? Should the case be reopened and the witness absolved and perhaps even rewarded? This is one of the questions which the jurist wished to answer in §§3–4.

These two cases envision and address themselves to this eventuality. They treat the very act of bringing unsubstantiated testimony as an unqualified crime. They tell us that this act is and remains a crime and that its penalty may not be revoked. In a capital case, the witness is to be killed: capital punishment cannot be undone—the witness perforce remains dead. In a case involving a dispute over payment, the witness pays the appropriate penalty; and if afterward, evidence substantiating his testimony turns up, he remains liable for the earlier act of bringing unconfirmed testimony and does not receive restitution. Hence, *aran dīnim šuāti ittanašši* and the use of the */tan/* form of the verb; he bears the liability for that case whenever and however the case comes up again.

Some may think it harsh of the jurist not to revoke a penalty that can be undone, especially when the penalized witness might actually have been telling the truth and acting in good faith. But in fairness to the writer, I must note, first of all, that such criticism is off the mark if the writer's concern is not actual practice but rather the formulation of legal principles. Our reading of §4 provides further support for the idea that at least some of the laws in the Code are of a theoretical character. Along with B. L. Eichler and others, I would argue that some of the law cases in the Code are the result of scholastic activity and represent casuistic investigation and exposition of legal principles.[23] The writer presumably did not expect that the rules we have been examining would serve as actual judicial regulations. (Additionally, the death penalty in the Code should often be construed as meaning that the offender is deserving

23 See B. L. Eichler, "Literary Structure in the Laws of Eshnunna," in *Language, Literature, and History: Philological and Historical Studies Presented to Erica Reiner*, ed. F. Rochberg-Halton, AOS 67 (New Haven: American Oriental Society, 1987), 71–84, and references there. Note especially the conclusions regarding the scholastic nature of the laws of Eshnunna and Hammurabi (81–84). Cf. also T. Abusch, "Hammurabi," in *Harper's Bible Dictionary*, ed. P. J. Achtemeier et al. (San Francisco: Harper & Row, 1985), 370–371.

of death and not be taken literally. It is an evaluation of the act and not a judicial sentence.) In any case, our witness may well be a prosecuting witness, that is, an accuser, and not simply a bystander, and is therefore deserving of punishment for initiating a charge.

Moreover, to revoke the penalty or fine would be counterproductive from our writer's point of view, for it would subvert his purpose. The writer wishes to make clear the rule that a witness should not come forward except when he is able and willing to prove his testimony. He stipulates this rule because he believes that an accusation and testimony carry objective results; they adversely affect the accused regardless of later qualification or outcome. His purpose is not to penalize but rather to ensure that witnesses in judicial (and perhaps even in pre- or extrajudicial) settings give strong weight to the rules of evidence and only come forward with testimony (*ana šībūtim waṣû*)[24] when they can expect to prove it. By stipulating formal objective guidelines, the writer helps the court and the witness understand what it means to initiate or volunteer testimony. He wishes to discourage unfounded and possibly malicious accusations. Perhaps he wants to lay out these principles and guidelines in the belief that more objective procedures are needed by an urban society that is becoming increasingly less cohesive and more diverse and anonymous, a society in which people are less able to render judgment on the basis of personal knowledge and where the accused (even more perhaps than in a simpler society) is at the mercy of public declarations—formal or informal—made against him. To revoke the penalty and make restitution would effectively go against our jurist's belief that what is done in court has permanent effects and is, in some cases, absolute and irrevocable and would undercut the principle upon which he bases his reasoning: the absoluteness of the legal act. Neither the original action nor the outcome can be reversed: hence, the absoluteness and irrevocability of the actions described in the protases of §§3 and 5 and of the penalties of these cases. Similarly, by excluding restitution in §4, the writer emphasizes this absoluteness and also conveys the idea that the legal act should be undertaken only with great care and assessed only on the basis of objective guidelines.

To revoke a punishment imposed originally to discourage unfounded testimony, when evidence later turns up confirming that testimony, would only serve to contradict and render useless the original purpose and act of imposing

24 I have in mind a witness who comes forward voluntarily in contrast to one who is summoned. Cf. A. Falkenstein, *Einleitung und systematische Darstellung*, vol. 1 of *Die neusumerischen Gerichtsurkunden*, ABAW NS 39 (Munich: Bayerischen Akademie der Wissenschaften, 1956), 68–69 n. 4.

the punishment. Such an absolutist approach to testimony is especially valid in the present instance where the jurist is operating with a theoretical system of state-sanctioned punishment and determining the nature of the punishment on the basis of the rule of talion. In §3, it is actually true that what is done cannot be undone, for while this is always true to some extent, it is absolutely true in a capital case. The punishment in §4 must remain in force to exemplify the insight and precept that what is done cannot be undone. To revoke the punishment would be tantamount to saying that one need not operate with care and according to objective criteria in the first place. Such a lack of care is undesirable in any case; it is unthinkable in a capital case.

In this context, I should mention yet another reason why the jurist should not allow the penalty to be revoked. He must exclude the return of property in order to protect the underlying principle of the rule of talion. In theory, at least, a system of talion that imposes penalties, such as capital punishment, that cannot be reversed or compensated may not revoke or undo others of its penalties that are capable of revocation. To do so would expose the system to major contradictions and to the possibility of breakdown. Our writer is a purist and holds to the principle. Both the act and the penalty cannot be undone. One can revoke a penalty no more than one can undo a legal act.

## 4 Confirmation: Variant Readings and §13

The phrase *aran dīnim šuāti ittanašši* is a specific rule of jurisprudence and describes the situation as seen from the perspective of the judiciary. From that perspective, the liability is held to be permanent—*ittanašši*. This interpretation actually finds support in the variant reading *rugummânê* [*dīnim šuāt*]*i ippal*, "he shall pay the claims in that case," which replaces *aran dīnim šuāti ittanašši* in a late Old Babylonian copy of the Code.[25] J. J. Finkelstein, who published this text, was of the opinion that "Exactly the same sense is given by both versions, and there is no way of deciding which is the 'superior' text. It is likely that both readings were already current in Hammurapi's own time."[26] Here I must disagree with Finkelstein. There is a difference in meaning between the readings. The variant highlights the approach of the jurist who wrote *aran dīnim šuāti ittanašši*; it emphasizes that writer's courtroom orientation by showing us what happens once that orientation is changed and the

25 J. J. Finkelstein, "A Late Old Babylonian Copy of the Laws of Hammurapi," *JCS* 21 (1967 [1969]): 44.

26 Finkelstein, "Late Old Babylonian Copy," 44.

penalty is looked at not from the point of view of the abstract judicial system but from the practical perspective of litigants who need to be satisfied. From the perspective of claimants, not permanent liability but actual payment is of interest; hence, the shift to a simple G durative of *apālu*.[27] Moreover, the reading *aran dīnim šuāti ittanašši* seems to be the better reading because it appears more consonant with the overall perspective and intention of these laws and their concrete expression of abstract principles of justice. While it is not easy to decide which is the more original of the two readings, I would favor *aran dīnim šuāti ittanašši*.

Further support for our understanding of *aran dīnim šuāti ittanašši* in §4 is provided by §13, where this phrase recurs. §13 reads:

> *šumma awīlum šū šībūšu lā qerbū dayyānū adānam ana šeššet warḫī išakkanūšumma šumma ina šešet warḫī šībīšu lā irde'am awīlum šū sār aran dīnim šuāti ittanašši*
>
> If that man's witnesses are not at hand, the judges shall grant him a period of up to six months, and if he has not brought his witnesses hither within six months, that man is guilty; he should continue to bear the penalty of that case.

The judges grant him an extension because they recognize that he may be telling the truth but needs more time to produce his witnesses. He does not produce his witnesses within six months. This fact, however, does not in itself prove that he does not have witnesses or that he is a criminal. He may still be telling the truth and be able to produce witnesses in the future. Moreover, the judges who accorded him the presumption of truthfulness in the first place may still even believe him and accept the possibility that witnesses will eventually appear. But the judges must bring the case to a close within a reasonable period. The question of truth must be deemed irrelevant at some point because an orderly judicial process requires limits and closure. A time period must be designated and a decision made. And the ruling must remain binding whether or not he brings witnesses. He is punished not because he was lying but because he has not been able to produce the witnesses who could confirm his claim. To overturn the decision were he to bring witnesses after six

27 I would also note here the interesting shift of the notion of plurality from the verb (*ittanašši*) to the noun (*rugummānê* [cf. A. Poebel, *Studies in Akkadian Grammar*, AS 9 (Chicago: University of Chicago Press, 1939), xi–xii, 140]). Also the shift from the objective *arnam našû* to the subjective *rugummānê apālu* is of interest.

months would not only contradict the rule of responsibility but would, moreover, undercut the justice of using a time period in the first place as a limit and as a basis for a legal decision.

This use of *aran dīnim šuāti ittanašši* in §13 clarifies its meaning in §4 and confirms our interpretation. By granting the man an extension, the judges in §13 indicate their belief that he may well be speaking the truth and have witnesses. And by setting a limit of six months, they indicate that, regardless of his truthfulness, they will have to impose the penalty permanently should he not bring witnesses in the time stipulated. Here, then, the judges impose a permanent penalty on a man although he may be telling the truth, and here, the writer conveys this by means of the formulation *aran dīnim šuāti ittanašši*. Similarly, *aran dīnim šuāti ittanašši* in §4 indicates that although the witness may be telling the truth, he must permanently bear the penalty of the case. Even if evidence is eventually produced in support of his testimony, he remains liable because initially he was not able to prove his testimony.

Here, we should say a word about the identity of the *awīlum šū*, "that man," of §13, for his identity defines his place in the legal situation (e.g., plaintiff vs. defendant) and determines the kind of proof he is required to bring in support of his claim; his identity, therefore, may allow us to understand better the connection between §13 and §4 and may even increase the usefulness of §13 for an understanding of *aran dīnim šuāti ittanašši*. Students of the Code have puzzled over which of the parties to the suit is referred to by *awīlum šū* and have come to different conclusions. For example, Driver and Miles think that *awīlum šū* designates the original owner, seller, and purchaser of the lost property contested in §§9 ff.;[28] P. Koschaker[29] and A. Finet[30] think it the owner and purchaser; E. Szlechter[31] and R. Westbrook and C. Wilcke[32] think it the purchaser.

The very real confusion over the identity of *awīlum šū* of §13 is due to the redactional history of §§9–13. Thus, we should be able to determine his identity by taking into account the history of the text. There can be no doubt that §13 is some form of addition to this section. Koschaker suggested that §12

28 Driver and Miles, *Babylonian Laws*, 1:101–104.

29 P. Koschaker, *Rechtsvergleichende Studien zur Gesetzgebung Hammurapis, Königs von Babylon* (Leipzig: Veit, 1917), 99.

30 Finet, *Code de Hammurapi*, 49, §13, note c.

31 E. Szlechter, "L'interprétation des lois babyloniennes," *Revue internationale des droits de l'antiquité*, 3rd ser., 17 (1970): 103–106.

32 R. Westbrook and C. Wilcke, "The Liability of an Innocent Purchaser of Stolen Goods in Early Mesopotamian Law," *AfO* 25 (1974–1977): 113. In the context of our discussion of the theoretical character of the laws, see their remarks on pp. 118–119.

is an early interpolation and that §13 was a later accretion or addition to §12.[33] But the subject of §11 is the owner while the subject of §12 is the buyer. §13, on the other hand, seems to be a direct continuation of §11 (cf., e.g., the use of *sār* [§§11: 1; 13: 21–22]) and, like §11, only deals with witnesses. I would, therefore, suggest that §13, not §12, was added directly to §11 (§12, which treats a problem related to §10, would subsequently have been inserted between §§11 and 13[34]). Accordingly, the subject of §13, like that of §11, should also be the owner. Note that §13 deals exclusively with witnesses and seems to make the outcome of the case dependent solely on their testimony; according to §§9–13, the owner brings only witnesses for the confirmation of his claim, while the buyer brings the seller as well. Therefore, a case such as §13 describes the situation of the original owner but not that of the buyer, and we conclude that the referent of *awīlum šū* is only the owner. The immediate unavailability of the witnesses in §13 fits best with this identification, for the owner may well have gone in search of his lost property and found it in a community other than his own.

This identification of the referent of §13 agrees with the nature of the act underlying and the penalty prescribed in that law and, thus, confirms and is supported by our understanding of the intent of *aran dīnim šuāti ittanašši*. The penalty—he shall permanently bear the liability—suggests that we regard the *awīlum* of §13 as one who came forward of his own volition and initiated an accusation and proceedings, for such a penalty is imposed not on one who is summoned, but on one who voluntarily brought forward an accusation or testimony and who then could not prove his contention. Therefore, this party must bear absolute responsibility and permanent liability even if he should be telling the truth. Of the three possible referents—owner, seller, purchaser—only the owner may be regarded as one who came forward of his own free volition, without constraint, and volunteered an accusation or claim; the others are reacting directly or indirectly to the original owner's accusation.

Here we should follow up one further implication of our historical scheme. We note that the phrasing in §12 (*rugummê*[35] *dīnim šuāti adi 5-šu ileqqe*) matches the aforementioned variant reading of §4 and that also the phrasing of §13 matches the reading *aran dīnim šuāti ittanašši* of §4. Should the

33 Koschaker, *Rechtsvergleichende Studien*, 98–100.

34 Although §12 was added to the text later than §13, it was placed before §13. This position may be explained as follows: whereas §13 treats a problem related to the owner (= §11), §12 treats a problem related to the buyer (= §10). It was not inserted immediately after §10 because §§9–11 form a tight unit. §12 was added after this unit, but before §13 so as to maintain the relative order of topics in §§9–11. Cf. also Finet, *Code de Hammurapi*, 49.

35 Note that the Late Old Babylonian copy containing the variant *rugummānê* ... in §4 also reads here *ru-gu-um-ma-*⸢*né*⸣(?)-⸢e⸣(?) (see Borger, *Babylonisch-assyrische Lesestücke*, 2nd ed., 1:12).

chronology that we have posited be correct (§§9–11 + §13 + §12), then *aran dīnim šuāti ittanašši* of §13 would be earlier than *rugummê dīnim šuāti* of §12. Perhaps this temporal sequence would explain the change in §4 from *aran dīnim šuāti ittanašši* to *rugummānê dīnim šuāti ippal* and provide the additional evidence necessary to confirm the originality of *aran dinim šuāti ittanašši* in §4 and its priority over its later replacement *rugummānê dīnim šuāti ippal*. This reconstruction would confirm the connection of §13 and §4,[36] insofar as both use the same terminology in similar situations, and both are affected by the same later development which carried with it both the addition of §12 and the rewriting of §4.

The connections between §4 and §13 are not unexpected if, as we have argued, the referent of §13 is the party who initiated the accusation and the legal proceeding. In any case, this would explain why a permanent penalty is imposed on him—as on the witness of §4—for not producing his witnesses, for regardless of his truthfulness, it is the accuser and/or witness who came forward who must bear the burden of the principle of absolute legal responsibility. He remains liable even if witnesses confirming his claim eventually appear.

## 5 Conclusion

To conclude, then, *aran dīnim šuāti ittanašši* means that the person who has initiated or supported a legal claim in a dispute over property but has not been able to prove his claim must bear his punishment permanently—a revocable penalty will not be revoked—regardless of whether his claim is eventually proved by the appearance of witnesses or of other kinds of proof. This provides at least part of the explanation for the use of the /*tan*/ form of *našû* in CḪ §§4 and 13.

We have observed the ancient Babylonian student as he worked out and applied his legal principles in a systematic way. It is especially revealing, I think, to study this reasoning when it operates in a manner that is both logical and impractical, when—divorced from reality—the scholar applies his understanding of justice to the formulation of basic rules for proper judicial procedure. As do other sections of the Code, §§3–4 represent a statement of a principle, and this principle is formulated in terms that are logical but seem, in practice, to contradict rules of fairness and common sense.

36 I am intrigued by the possibility that originally §13 was the direct continuation of §4. Both deal with procedure; note the similarity: *šumma awīlum šū šībūšu lā qerbū ... aran dīnim šuāti ittanašši* // *šumma (awīlum) ana šībūt ... ūṣiam ... aran dīnim šuāti ittanašši.*

Rather than discuss other examples of this scholastic procedure in Mesopotamian legal collections,[37] I should prefer to conclude this study in honor of a scholar of mishnaic jurisprudence and ethics by citing a mishnaic parallel as a partial illustration of some of the themes that we have examined in §§3–4 and 13. I have in mind m. Sanhedrin 3:8.

Sanhedrin, chapter 3, sets out procedures of the court in commercial cases. Mishna 8, sections 1–2 read:

> 1. So long as [a litigant] brings proof, he may reverse the ruling. [If] they had said to him, "All the evidence which you have, bring between this date and thirty days from now," [if] he found evidence during the thirty-day period, he may reverse the ruling. [If he found evidence] after the thirty-day period, he may not reverse the ruling. Said Rabban Simeon b. Gamaliel, "What should this party do, who could not find the evidence during the thirty-day period, but found it after thirty days?"
>
> 2. [If] they had said to him, "Bring witnesses," and he said, "I don't have witnesses," [if] they had said, "Bring proof," and he said, "I don't have proof" and after a time he brought proof, or he found witnesses—this is of no weight whatsoever. Said Rabban Simeon b. Gamaliel, "What should this party do, who did not even know that he had witnesses on his side, but found witnesses? Or who did not even know that he had proof, but who found proof?"[38]

I have no intention of analyzing this text, but I would simply note that in the first section of m. Sanhedrin 3:8, the unnamed jurist opines, like CḪ §13, that evidence cannot be considered if it is brought after the expiration of a time period set by the judges. And in the second section, this mishna resembles CḪ §4 (or, at least, our interpretation thereof) insofar as this jurist stipulates that witnesses or proof that only appear after the ruling should not be considered, even if they had not been brought forward originally because of the litigant's ignorance of their existence. Notice here the objections of R. Simeon b. Gamaliel, whose point of departure seems to be the apparent practical injustice of the rulings. Cuneiform and Talmudic scholasticism may take different literary forms but intellectually they are probably not very far apart.

37 E.g., CḪ §§229–232; see Finkelstein, *Ox That Gored*, 33–35.

38 J. Neusner, *The Mishnah: A New Translation* (New Haven: Yale University Press, 1988), 589. For the sake of an unbroken reading, I have omitted the translator's sentence designations.

# Bibliography


Abusch, T. "Alternative Models for the Development of Some Incantations." Pages 223–234 in Van Buylaere et al., *Sources of Evil*. [[AMD 17, 146–156]]

Abusch, T. *Babylonian Witchcraft Literature: Case Studies*. BJS 132. Atlanta: Scholars Press, 1987.

Abusch, T. "Biblical Accounts of Prehistory: Their Meaning and Formation." Pages 3–17 in *Bringing the Hidden to Light: The Process of Interpretation. Studies in Honor of Stephen A. Geller*. Edited by K. F. Kravitz and D. Sharon. Winona Lake, IN: Eisenbrauns, 2007. [[238–254]]

Abusch, T. "Blessing and Praise in Ancient Mesopotamian Incantations." Pages 1–14 in *Literatur, Politik und Recht in Mesopotamien: Festschrift für Claus Wilcke*. Edited by W. Sallaberger, K. Volk, and A. Zgoll. OBC 14. Wiesbaden: Harrassowitz, 2003. [[AMD 17, 94–109]]

Abusch, T. "Comments on the Opening Session: Ancient Mesopotamia and Egypt." Pages 65–68 in *The Body of the King: The Staging of the Body of the Institutional Leader from Antiquity to Middle Ages in East and West. Proceedings of the Meeting Held in Padova, July 6th–9th, 2011*. Edited by G. B. Lanfranchi and R. Rollinger. HANE/M 16. Padua: S.A.R.G.O.N. Editrice e Libreria, 2016.

Abusch, T. "Considerations When Killing a Witch: Developments in Exorcistic Attitudes to Witchcraft." Pages 191–210 in *The Dynamics of Changing Rituals: The Transformation of Religious Rituals within Their Social and Cultural Context*. Edited by J. Kreinath, C. Hartung, and A. Deschner. Toronto Studies in Religion 29. New York: Peter Lang, 2004. [[AMD 5, 65–78]]

Abusch, T. "The Demonic Image of the Witch in Standard Babylonian Literature: The Reworking of Popular Conceptions by Learned Exorcists." Pages 27–58 in *Religion, Science, and Magic in Concert and in Conflict*. Edited by J. Neusner, E. Frerichs, and P. Flesher. New York: Oxford University Press, 1989. [[AMD 5, 3–25]]

Abusch, T. "Etemmu אטים." Pages 309–312 in *Dictionary of Deities and Demons in the Bible*. Edited by K. van der Toorn, B. Becking, and P. W. van der Hoorst. 2nd ed. Leiden: Brill, 1999. [[87–92]]

Abusch, T. "The Form and History of a Babylonian Prayer to Nabû." Pages 169–182 in *"The Scaffolding of Our Thoughts": Essays on Assyriology and the History of Science in Honor of Francesca Rochberg*. Edited by C. Jay Crisostomo, E. A. Escobar, T. Tanaka, and N. Veldhuis. AMD 13. Leiden: Brill, 2018. [[149–162]]

Abusch, T. "The Form and Meaning of a Babylonian Prayer to Marduk." *JAOS* 103 (1983): 3–15. [[126–148]]

Abusch, T. "Fortune and Misfortune of the Individual: Some Observations on the Sufferer's Plaint in *Ludlul bēl nēmeqi* II 12–32." Pages 51–57 in *Fortune and Misfortune in the Ancient Near East (Proceedings of the 60th Rencontre Assyriologique Internationale, Warsaw, 2014)*. Edited by O. Drewnowska and M. Sandowicz. Winona Lake, IN: Eisenbrauns, 2017. [[217–224]]

Abusch, T. *Further Studies on Mesopotamian Witchcraft Beliefs and Literature*. AMD 17. Leiden: Brill, 2020.

Abusch, T. "Ghost and God: Some Observations on a Babylonian Understanding of Human Nature." Pages 363–383 in *Self, Soul and Body in Religious Experience*. Edited by A. I. Baumgarten, J. Assmann, and G. G. Stroumsa. SHR 78. Leiden: Brill, 1998. [[67–86]]

Abusch, T. "Hammurabi." Pages 370–371 in *Harper's Bible Dictionary*. Edited by P. J. Achtemeier et al. San Francisco: Harper & Row, 1985.

Abusch, T. "Hunting in the Epic of Gilgamesh: Speculations on the Education of a Prince." Pages 11–20 in *Treasures on Camels' Humps: Historical and Literary Studies from the Ancient Near East Presented to Israel Eph'al*. Edited by M. Cogan and D. Kahn. Jerusalem: Magnes, 2008. [[*Gilgamesh*, 166–176]]

Abusch, T. "Illnesses and Other Crises: Mesopotamia." Pages 456–459 in Johnston, *Religions of the Ancient World*. [[AMD 17, 203–208]]

Abusch, T. "Ishtar's Proposal and Gilgamesh's Refusal: An Interpretation of the *Gilgamesh Epic*, Tablet 6, Lines 1–79." *HR* 26 (1986): 143–187. [[*Gilgamesh*, 11–57]]

Abusch, T. "Kingship in Ancient Mesopotamia: The Case of *Enūma Eliš*." Pages 59–64 in *The Body of the King: The Staging of the Body of the Institutional Leader from Antiquity to Middle Ages in East and West. Proceedings of the Meeting Held in Padova, July 6th–9th, 2011*. Edited by G. B. Lanfranchi and R. Rollinger. HANE/M 16. Padua: S.A.R.G.O.N., 2016. [[225–232]]

Abusch, T. *The Magical Ceremony "Maqlû": A Critical Edition*. AMD 10. Leiden: Brill, 2016.

Abusch, T. *Male and Female in the Epic of Gilgamesh*. Winona Lake, IN: Eisenbrauns, 2015.

Abusch, T. "*Maqlû*." *RlA* 7 (1987–1990): 346–351.

Abusch, T. "Marduk." Pages 543–549 in *Dictionary of Deities and Demons in the Bible*. Edited by K. van der Toorn, B. Becking, and P. W. van der Horst. 2nd ed. Leiden: Brill, 1999. [[99–107]]

Abusch, T. "Mesopotamian Anti-Witchcraft Literature: Texts and Studies. Part I: The Nature of *Maqlû*: Its Character, Divisions, and Calendrical Setting." *JNES* 33 (1974): 251–262. [[AMD 5, 99–111]]

Abusch, T. *Mesopotamian Witchcraft: Toward a History and Understanding of Babylonian Witchcraft Beliefs and Literature*. AMD 5. Leiden: Brill/Styx, 2002.

Abusch, T. "A Paean and Petition to a God of Death: Some Comments on a *Šuilla* to Nergal." Pages 15–28 in *From the Four Corners of the Earth: Studies in Iconography and Cultures of the Ancient Near East in Honour of F. A. M. Wiggermann*. Edited by D. Kertai and O. Nieuwenhuyse. AOAT 441. Münster: Ugarit-Verlag, 2017. [[163–175]]

Abusch, T. "Prayers, Hymns, Incantations, and Curses: Mesopotamia." Pages 353–355 in Johnston, *Religions of the Ancient World*. [[111–117]]

Abusch, T. "The Reconciliation of Angry Personal Gods: A Revision of the Šuillas." In "Approaching a Critique of Mesopotamian Reason," ed. G. Gabriel, special issue, *JANEH* 5 (2018): 57–85. [[176–205]]

Abusch, T. "The Revision of Babylonian Anti-Witchcraft Incantations: The Critical Analysis of Incantations in the Ceremonial Series *Maqlû*." Pages 11–41 in *Continuity and Innovation in the Magical Tradition*. Edited by G. Bohak, Y. Harari, and S. Shaked. JSRC 15. Leiden: Brill, 2011. [[AMD 17, 51–80]]

Abusch, T. "Sacrifice in Mesopotamia." Pages 39–48 in *Sacrifice in Religious Experience*. Edited by A. I. Baumgarten. SHR 93. Leiden: Brill, 2002. [[56–64]]

Abusch, T. "A Shuilla: Nergal 2." Pages 339–349 in Lenzi, *Reading Akkadian Prayers and Hymns*.

Abusch, T. "The Socio-Religious Framework of the Babylonian Witchcraft Ceremony *Maqlû*: Some Observations on the Introductory Section of the Text, Part I." Pages 1–34 in *Riches Hidden in Secret Places: Ancient Near Eastern Studies in Memory of Thorkild Jacobsen*. Edited by T. Abusch. Winona Lake, IN: Eisenbrauns, 2002. [[AMD 5, 219–247]]

Abusch, T. "Studies in the History and Interpretation of Some Akkadian Incantations and Prayers Against Witchcraft." Ph.D. diss., Harvard University, 1972. Published as Abusch, *Babylonian Witchcraft Literature*.

Abusch, T. "Witchcraft and the Anger of the Personal God." Pages 83–121 in Abusch and van der Toorn, *Mesopotamian Magic*. [[AMD 5, 27–63]]

Abusch, T. *The Witchcraft Series "Maqlû."* WAW 37. Atlanta: Society of Biblical Literature, 2015.

Abusch, T., and D. Schwemer. "Das Abwehrzauber-Ritual *Maqlû* ('Verbrennung')." Pages 128–186 in *Omina, Orakel, Rituale und Beschwörungen*. Edited by B. Janowski and G. Wilhelm. TUAT NF 4. Gütersloh: Gütersloher Verlagshaus, 2008.

Abusch, T., and K. van der Toorn, eds. *Mesopotamian Magic: Textual, Historical, and Interpretive Perspectives*. AMD 1. Groningen: Styx, 1999.

Abusch, T., et al. *Corpus of Mesopotamian Anti-witchcraft Rituals*. 3 vols. AMD 8/1–3. Leiden: Brill, 2011–2019. Vol. 1 coauthored with D. Schwemer; vol. 2 coauthored with D. Schwemer with the assistance of M. Luukko and G. Van Buylaere; vol. 3 coauthored with D. Schwemer, M. Luukko, and G. Van Buylaere.

Abushihab, I. "The Role of Lexical Cohesion and Coherence in Promoting Reading Comprehension." *Ekev Akademi Dergisi* 12/35 (2008): 333–342.

Albertz, R. "*Ludlul bēl nēmeqi*—eine Lehrdichtung zur Ausbreitung und Vertiefung der persönlichen Mardukfrömmigkeit." Pages 25–53 in *Ad bene et fideliter seminandum:*

*Festgabe für Karlheinz Deller zum 21. Februar 1987*. Edited by G. Mauer and U. Magen. AOAT 220. Kevelaer: Butzon & Bercker; Neukirchen-Vluyn: Neukirchener Verlag, 1988.

Albertz, R., and R. Schmitt. *Family and Household Religion in Ancient Israel and the Levant*. Winona Lake, IN: Eisenbrauns, 2012.

Albright, W. F. "Two Letters from Ugarit (Ras Shamrah)." *BASOR* 82 (1941): 43–49.

Alexander, P. S. "Bavli Berakhot 55a–57b: The Talmudic Dreambook in Context." *JJS* 46 (1995): 230–248.

Ambos, C. *Der König im Gefängnis und das Neujahrsfest im Herbst: Mechanismen der Legitimation des babylonischen Herrschers im 1. Jahrtausend v. Chr. und ihre Geschichte*. Dresden: Islet, 2013.

Ambos, C. "Rites of Passage in Ancient Mesopotamia: Changing Status by Moving Through Space: *Bīt rimki* and the Ritual of the Substitute King." Pages 39–54 in *Approaching Rituals in Ancient Cultures*. Edited by C. Ambos and L. Verderame. *RSO* NS 86, Supplement 2. Pisa: Fabrizio Serra, 2013.

Ankerloo, B., and S. Clark, eds. *Witchcraft and Magic in Europe*. 6 vols. Philadelphia: University of Pennsylvania Press, 1999–2002.

Annus, A. "On the Origin of Watchers: A Comparative Study of the Antediluvian Wisdom in Mesopotamian and Jewish Traditions." *JSP* 19 (2010): 277–320.

Annus, A. *The Standard Babylonian Epic of Anzu: Introduction, Cuneiform Text, Transliteration, Score, Glossary, Indices and Sign List*. SAACT 3. Helsinki: Neo-Assyrian Text Corpus Project, 2001.

Annus, A., and A. Lenzi. *"Ludlul bēl nēmeqi": The Standard Babylonian Poem of the Righteous Sufferer*. SAACT 7. Helsinki: Neo-Assyrian Text Corpus Project, 2010.

Bacher, W. *Terminologie der Tannaiten*. Vol. 1 of *Die exegetische Terminologie der jüdischen Traditionsliteratur*. Leipzig: Hinrichs, 1899. Repr., Hildesheim: Georg Olms, 1965.

Barr, J. "Etymology and the Old Testament." Pages 1–28 in *Language and Meaning: Studies in Hebrew Language and Biblical Exegesis*. OtSt 19. Leiden: Brill, 1974.

Baumgartner, W., et al. *Hebräisches und aramäisches Lexikon zum Alten Testament*. 5 vols. 3rd ed. Leiden: E. J. Brill, 1967–1996.

Bayliss, M. "The Cult of Dead Kin in Assyria and Babylonia." *Iraq* 35 (1973): 115–125.

Beaulieu, P.-A., and W. R. Mayer. "Akkadische Lexikographie: CAD $Š_2$ und $Š_3$." *Or* NS 66 (1997): 157–180.

Ben Zvi, E. "Jonah 4:11 and the Metaprophetic Character of the Book of Jonah." *JHebS* 9/5 (2009). doi:10.5508/jhs.2009.v9.a5.

Biggs, R. D., trans. "I Will Praise the Lord of Wisdom." Pages 596–600 in Pritchard, *Ancient Near Eastern Texts*.

Biggs, R. D. "Medizin. A. In Mesopotamien." *RlA* 7 (1987–1990): 623–629.

Biggs, R. D. *ŠÀ.ZI.GA: Ancient Mesopotamian Potency Incantations*. TCS 2. Locust Valley, NY: J. J. Augustin, 1967.

Binsbergen, W. van, and F. A. M. Wiggerman. "Magic in History: A Theoretical Perspective, and Its Application to Ancient Mesopotamia." Pages 3–34 in Abusch and van der Toorn, *Mesopotamian Magic*.

Black, J. A. "The New Year Ceremonies in Ancient Babylon: 'Taking Bel by the Hand' and a Cultic Picnic." *Religion* 11 (1981): 39–59.

Böck, B. *Das Handbuch Muššu'u "Einreibung": Eine Serie sumerischer und akkadischer Beschwörungen aus dem 1. Jt. vor Chr.* BPOA 3. Madrid: Consejo Superior de Investigaciones Científicas, 2007.

Bohak, G. *Ancient Jewish Magic: A History*. Cambridge: Cambridge University Press, 2008.

Bolin, T. M. "Eternal Delight and Deliciousness: The Book of Jonah after Ten Years." *JHebS* 9/4 (2009). doi:10.5508/jhs.2009.v9.a4.

Bolin, T. M. *Freedom beyond Forgiveness: The Book of Jonah Re-Examined*. JSOTSup 236. Sheffield: Sheffield Academic Press, 1997.

Borger, R. *Babylonisch-assyrische Lesestücke*. 3 vols. Rome: Pontifical Biblical Institute, 1963.

Borger, R. *Babylonisch-assyrische Lesestücke*. 2nd ed. 2 vols. AnOr 54. Rome: Pontifical Biblical Institute, 1979.

Borger, R. "Der Codex Hammurapi." Pages 39–80 in *Rechtsbücher*. Edited by O. Kaiser. TUAT NF 1/1. Gütersloh: Gerd Mohn, 1982.

Borger, R. "Die Inschriften Asarhaddons (AfO Beiheft 9). Nachträge und Verbesserungen." *AfO* 18 (1957–1958): 113–118.

Borger, R. *Die Inschriften Asarhaddons, Königs von Assyrien*. AfO Beih. 9. Graz: Selbstverlag des Herausgebers, 1956.

Borger, R. "*Šurpu* II, III, IV und VIII in 'Partitur.'" Pages 15–90 in *Wisdom, Gods and Literature: Studies in Assyriology in Honour of W. G. Lambert*. Edited by A. R. George and I. L. Finkel. Winona Lake, IN: Eisenbrauns, 2000.

Bottéro, J. "Antiquités assyro-babyloniennes." Pages 93–149 in *École pratique des hautes études. 4e section, Sciences historiques et philologiques. Annuaire 1976–1977*. Paris: La Sorbonne, 1977.

Bottéro, J. "La création de l'homme et son nature dans le poème d'*Atraḫasîs*." Pages 24–32 in *Societies and Languages of the Ancient Near East: Studies in Honour of I. M. Diakonoff*. Edited by M. A. Dandamayev, I. Gershevitch, H. Klengel, G. Komoróczy, M. T. Larsen, and J. N. Postgate. Warminster: Aris & Phillips, 1982.

Bottéro, J. "La mythologie de la mort en Mésopotamie ancienne." Pages 25–52 in *Death in Mesopotamia*. Edited by B. Alster. Mesopotamia 8. Copenhagen: Akademisk, 1980.

Bottéro, J. "Les morts et l'au-delà dans les rituels en accadien contre l'action des 'revenants.'" *ZA* 73 (1983): 153–203.

Bottéro, J. "Les noms de Marduk, l'écriture et la 'logique' en Mésopotamie ancienne." Pages 5–28 in *Essays on the Ancient Near East in Memory of Jacob Joel Finkelstein*. Edited by M. de Jong Ellis. MCAAS 19. Hamden, CT: Archon, 1977.

Bottéro, J. *Mesopotamia: Writing, Reasoning, and the Gods*. Chicago: University of Chicago Press, 1992.

Bottéro, J. "Symptômes, signes, écritures en Mésopotamie ancienne." Pages 70–197 in *Divination et rationalité*. Edited by J. P. Vernant. Paris: Seuil, 1974.

Bowie, F. *The Anthropology of Religion: An Introduction*. Oxford: Blackwell, 2000.

Boyer, G. *Contribution à l'histoire juridique de la 1re dynastie babylonienne*. Paris: Geuthner, 1928.

Braun-Holzinger, E. A. "Apotropaic Figures at Mesopotamian Temples in the Third and Second Millennia." Pages 149–172 in Abusch and van der Toorn, *Mesopotamian Magic*.

Bremmer, J. M. *The Early Greek Concept of the Soul*. Princeton: Princeton University Press, 1983.

Bremmer, J. M. "The Soul, Death and the Afterlife in Early and Classical Greece." Pages 77–106 in *Hidden Futures: Death and Immortality in Ancient Egypt, Anatolia, the Classical, Biblical and Arabic-Islamic World*. Edited by J. M. Bremmer, T. P. J. van den Hout, and R. Peters. Amsterdam: Amsterdam University Press, 1994.

Brettler, M. Z. "The 'Coherence' of Ancient Texts." Pages 411–419 in *Gazing on the Deep: Ancient Near Eastern and Other Studies in Honor of Tzvi Abusch*. Edited by J. Stackert, B. N. Porter, and D. P. Wright. Bethesda, MD: CDL, 2010.

Brothwell, D., and A. T. Sandison, eds. *Diseases in Antiquity*. Springfield, IL: C. C. Thomas, 1967.

Burkert, W. *Creation of the Sacred: Tracks of Biology in Early Religions*. Cambridge, MA: Harvard University Press, 1996.

Burrows, E. "Hymn to Ninurta as Sirius (K 128)." *JRAS Centenary Supplement* (1924): 33–40.

Butler, S. *Mesopotamian Conceptions of Dreams and Dream Rituals*. AOAT 258. Münster: Ugarit-Verlag, 1998.

Cagni, L. *Crestomazia accadica*. Sussidi Didattici 4. Rome: Istituto di Studi del Vicino Oriente, 1971.

Caplice, R. I. *The Akkadian Namburbi Texts: An Introduction*. SANE 1/1. Los Angeles: Undena, 1974.

Caplice, R. I. "The Akkadian Text Genre Namburbi." Ph.D. diss., University of Chicago, 1963.

Caplice, R. I. "É.NUN in Mesopotamian Literature." *Or* NS 42 (1973): 299–305.

Caplice, R. I. "Namburbi Texts in the British Museum I." *Or* NS 34 (1965): 105–131.

Caplice, R. I. "Namburbi Texts in the British Museum II." *Or* NS 36 (1967): 1–38.

Caplice, R. I. "Namburbi Texts in the British Museum. III." *Or* NS 36 (1967): 273–298.

Cassin, E. "Le mort: valeur et représentation en Mésopotamie ancienne." Pages 355–372 in *La mort, les morts dans les sociétés anciennes*. Edited by G. Gnoli and J.-P. Vernant. Cambridge: Cambridge University Press; Paris: Éditions de la Maison des sciences de l'homme, 1982.

Cassin, E. Review of *Economic and Social Documents*, vol. 7 of *Excavations at Nuzi*, HSS 16, by E. R. Lacheman. *RA* 53 (1959): 162–164.

Cassin, E., and J.-J. Glassner. *Les anthroponymes*. Vol. 1 of *Anthroponymie et anthropologie de Nuzi*. Malibu, CA: Undena, 1977.

Civil, M. *Materials for the Sumerian Lexicon*. Vol. 13. Rome: Pontificum Institutum Biblicum, 1971.

Clay, A. T. *Epics, Hymns, Omens, and Other Texts*. BRM 4. New Haven: Yale University Press, 1923.

Clines, D. J. A. "Mordechai." *ABD* 4:902–904.

Cohen, H. R. *Biblical Hapax Legomena in the Light of Akkadian and Ugaritic*. SBLDS 37. Missoula, MT: Scholars Press, 1978.

Cohen, M. E. *Balag-Compositions: Sumerian Lamentation Liturgies of the Second and First Millennium B.C.* SANE 1/2. Malibu, CA: Undena, 1974.

Cohen, M. E. *The Canonical Lamentations of Ancient Mesopotamia*. 2 vols. Potomac, MD: CDL, 1988.

Cohen, M. E. *Sumerian Hymnology: The Eršemma*. HUCASup 2. Cincinnati: Hebrew Union College Press, 1981.

Cooper, J. S. *Presargonic Inscriptions*. Vol. 1 of *Sumerian and Akkadian Royal Inscriptions*. AOSTS 1. New Haven: American Oriental Society, 1986.

Cooper, J. S. "A Sumerian ŠU-ÍL-LA from Nimrud with a Prayer for Sin-šar-iškun." *Iraq* 32 (1970): 51–67.

Cooper, J. S. "Symmetry and Repetition in Akkadian Narrative." *JAOS* 97 (1977): 508–512.

Cross, F. M. "Kinship and Covenant in Ancient Israel." Pages 3–21 in *From Epic to Canon: History and Literature in Ancient Israel*. Baltimore: Johns Hopkins University Press, 1998.

Cryer, F. H., and M.-L. Thomsen. *Biblical and Pagan Societies*. Vol. 1 of *Witchcraft and Magic in Europe*. Edited by B. Ankerloo and S. Clark. Philadelphia: University of Pennsylvania Press, 2001.

Cunningham, G. *"Deliver Me From Evil": Mesopotamian Incantations, 2500–1500 BC*. StPohl, series maior 17. Rome: Pontifico Istituto Biblico, 1997.

Dalley, S. *Myths from Mesopotamia: Creation, The Flood, Gilgamesh, and Others*. Rev. ed. Oxford: Oxford University Press, 2000.

Dalley, S. "Statues of Marduk and the Date of Enūma Eliš." *AoF* 24 (1997): 163–171.

Deimel, A. *Codex Ḫammurabi: Textus Primigenius*. Rome: Pontifical Biblical Institute, 1930.

Delcor, M. "Allusions à la déesse Ištar en Nahum 2,8?" *Bib* 58 (1977): 73–83.

Delitzsch, F. *Assyrische Lesestücke mit grammatischen Tabellen und vollständigem Glossar: Einführung in die assyrische und babylonische Keilschriftliteratur bis hinauf zu Hammurabi*. 5th ed. Assyrische Bibliothek 16. Leipzig: Hinrichs, 1912.

Dietrich, M. "Die Tötung einer Gottheit in der Eridu-Babylon-Mythologie." Pages 49–73 in *Ernten, was man sät: Festschrift für Klaus Koch zu seinem 65. Geburtstag*. Edited by D. R. Daniels, U. Glessmer, and M. Rösel. Neukirchener-Vluyn: Neukirchener Verlag, 1991.

Dijk, J. van. *LUGAL UD ME-LÁM-BI NIR-ĜÁL: Le récit épique et didactique des Travaux de Ninurta, du Déluge et de la Nouvelle Création*. Leiden: Brill, 1983.

Dossin, G. "Prières aux 'dieux de la nuit' (AO 6769)." *RA* 32 (1935): 179–187.

Driver, G. R., and J. C. Miles. *The Babylonian Laws*. 2 vols. Oxford: Clarendon, 1952–1955.

Durand, J.-M. "Le mythologème du combat entre le dieu de l'orage et la mer en Mésopotamie." *MARI* 7 (1993): 41–61.

Ebeling, E. "Beiträge zur Kenntnis der Beschwörungsserie Namburbi." *RA* 49 (1955): 32–41, 137–148.

Ebeling, E. *Die akkadische Gebetsserie "Handerhebung" von neuem gesammelt und herausgegeben*. Berlin: Akademie-Verlag, 1953.

Ebeling, E. *Keilschrifttexte aus Assur religiösen Inhalts*. 2 vols. WVDOG 28, 34. Leipzig: Hinrichs, 1915–1923.

Ebeling, E. *Literarische Keilschrifttexte aus Assur*. Berlin: Akademie-Verlag, 1953.

Ebeling, E. *Quellen zur Kenntnis der babylonischen Religion*. Vol. 2. MVAG 23/2. Leipzig: Hinrichs, 1919.

Ebeling, E., et al., eds. *Reallexikon der Assyriologie und vorderasiatischen Archäologie*. Berlin: de Gruyter, 1928–.

Edzard, D. O. "Die Stämme des altbabylonischen Verbums in ihrem Oppositionssystem." Pages 111–120 in Güterbock and Jacobsen, *Studies in Honor of Benno Landsberger*.

Edzard, D. O. Review of *Excavations at Nuzi VII*, by E. R. Lacheman. *BO* 16 (1959): 133–137.

Eichler, B. L. "Literary Structure in the Laws of Eshnunna." Pages 71–84 in *Language, Literature, and History: Philological and Historical Studies Presented to Erica Reiner*. Edited by F. Rochberg-Halton. AOS 67. New Haven: American Oriental Society, 1987.

Eilers, W. "Altpersische Miszellen I." *ZA* 51 (1955): 225.

Eilers, W. *Gesetzesstele Chammurabis: Gesetze um die Wende des dritten vorchristlichen Jahrtausends*. *AO* 31/3–4. Leipzig: Hinrichs, 1932.

Eissfeldt, O. *Der Beutel der Lebendigen: Alttestamentliche Erzählungs- und Dichtungsmotive im Lichte neuer Nuzi-Texte*. Berichte über die Verhandlungen der

Sächsischen Akademie der Wissenschaften zu Leipzig, Phil.-hist. Klasse 105/6. Berlin: Akademie Verlag, 1960.

Epstein, I., ed. *Seder Zeraʿim*. Vol. 1 of *The Babylonian Talmud*. London: Soncino Press, 1948.

Falkenstein, A. *Die Haupttypen der sumerischen Beschwörung literarisch untersucht*. LSS NF 1. Leipzig: Hinrichs, 1931.

Falkenstein, A. *Einleitung und systematische Darstellung*. Vol. 1 of *Die neusumerischen Gerichtsurkunden*. ABAW NS 39. Munich: Bayerischen Akademie der Wissenschaften, 1956.

Falkenstein, A. Review of *The Babylonian Laws*, 2 vols., by G. R. Driver and J. C. Miles. *ZA* 52 (1957): 324–328.

Falkenstein, A., and W. von Soden. *Sumerische und akkadische Hymnen und Gebete*. Zurich: Artemis, 1953.

Farber, W. *Beschwörungsrituale an Ištar und Dumuzi: Attī Ištar ša Ḫarmaša Dumuzi*. Wiesbaden: Franz Steiner, 1977.

Farber, W. *Lamaštu: An Edition of the Canonical Series of Lamaštu Incantations and Rituals and Related Texts from the Second and First Millennia B.C.* MC 17. Winona Lake, IN: Eisenbrauns, 2014.

Farber, W. "Witchcraft, Magic, and Divination in Ancient Mesopotamia." In Sasson, *Civilizations of the Ancient Near East*, 3:1895–1909.

Fields, K. E. Foreword to *Throughout Your Generations Forever: Sacrifice, Religion, and Paternity*, by Nancy Jay. Chicago: University of Chicago Press, 1992.

Finet, A. *Le Code de Hammurapi*. LAPO 6. Paris: Cerf, 1973.

Finkel, I. L. "Adad-apla-iddina, Esagil-kīn-apli, and the Series SA.GIG." Pages 143–159 in *A Scientific Humanist: Studies in Memory of Abraham Sachs*. Edited by E. Leichty, M. de Jong Ellis, and P. Gerardi. OPSNKF 9. Philadelphia: The University Museum, 1988.

Finkel, I. L. "Necromancy in Ancient Mesopotamia." *AfO* 29–30 (1983–1984): 1–17.

Finkelstein, J. J. "A Late Old Babylonian Copy of the Laws of Hammurapi." *JCS* 21 (1967 [1969]): 39–48.

Finkelstein, J. J. "The Laws of Ur-Nammu." *JCS* 22 (1969): 66–82.

Finkelstein, J. J. *The Ox That Gored*. TAPS 71/2. Philadelphia: American Philosophical Society, 1981.

Finn, J. *Much Ado about Marduk: Questioning Discourses of Royalty in First Millennium Mesopotamian Literature*. SANER 16. Boston: de Gruyter, 2017.

Fitzmyer, J. A. *The Genesis Apocryphon of Qumran Cave I*. BibOr 18. Rome: Pontifical Biblical Institute, 1966.

Fitzmyer, J. A. *A Wandering Aramean: Collected Aramaic Essays*. SBLMS 25. Missoula, MT: Scholars Press, 1977.

Flynn, S. *YHWH Is King: The Development of Divine Kingship in Ancient Israel*. VTSup 159. Leiden: Brill, 2014.

Fossey, C. *La magie assyrienne: Étude suivie de textes magiques transcrits, traduits, et commentés*. Paris: Ernest Leroux, 1902.

Foster, B. R. *Before the Muses: An Anthology of Akkadian Literature*. 3rd ed. Bethesda, MD: CDL, 2005.

Frahm, E. "Counter-texts, Commentaries, and Adaptations: Politically Motivated Responses to the Babylonian Epic of Creation in Mesopotamia, the Biblical World, and Elsewhere." *Orient: Reports of the Society for Near Eastern Studies in Japan* 45 (2010): 3–33.

Frahm, E. "The Exorcist's Manual: Structure, Language, *Sitz im Leben*." Pages 9–47 in Van Buylaere et al., *Sources of Evil*.

Frahm, E. "A Tale of Two Lands and Two Thousand Years: The Origins of Pazuzu." Pages 272–291 in *Mesopotamian Medicine and Magic: Studies in Honor of Markham J. Geller*. Edited by S. V. Panayotov and L. Vacín. AMD 14. Leiden: Brill, 2018.

Frame, G. *Rulers of Babylonia from the Second Dynasty of Isin to the End of the Assyrian Domination, 1157–612 BC*. RIMB 2. Toronto: University of Toronto Press, 1995.

Frankfort, H. *The Birth of Civilization in the Near East*. 1951. Repr., Garden City, NY: Doubleday, 1956.

Frankfort, H., H. A. Frankfort, J. A. Wilson, T. Jacobsen, and W. A. Irwin. *The Intellectual Adventure of Ancient Man: An Essay on Speculative Thought in the Ancient Near East*. Rev. ed. Chicago: University of Chicago Press, 1977.

Frayne, D. R. *Presargonic Period (2700–2350 BC)*. RIME 1. Toronto: University of Toronto Press, 2008.

Frechette, C. *Mesopotamian Ritual-prayers of "Hand-lifting" (Akkadian Šuillas): An Investigation of Function in Light of the Idiomatic Meaning of the Rubric*. AOAT 379. Münster: Ugarit-Verlag, 2012.

Frechette, C. "A Shuilla: Nisaba 1." Pages 351–366 in Lenzi, *Reading Akkadian Prayers and Hymns*.

Frechette, C. "Shuillas." Pages 24–35 in Lenzi, *Reading Akkadian Prayers and Hymns*.

Frechette, C., and I. Hrůša. "The Ritual-Prayer Nisaba 1 and Its Function." *JANER* 11 (2011): 70–93.

Freedman, D. N., ed. *The Anchor Bible Dictionary*. 6 vols. New York: Doubleday, 1992.

Frymer-Kensky, T. "The Atrahasis Epic and Its Significance for Our Understanding of Genesis 1–9." *BA* 40 (1977): 147–155.

Frymer-Kensky, T. *In the Wake of the Goddesses*. New York: Fawcett Columbine, 1992.

Gabbay, U. *The Eršema Prayers of the First Millennium BC*. HES 2. Wiesbaden: Harrassowitz, 2014.

Gabbay, U. *Pacifying the Hearts of the Gods: Sumerian Emesal Prayers of the First Millennium BC*. HES 1. Wiesbaden: Harrassowitz, 2014.

Gabriel, G. *enūma eliš—Weg zu einer globalen Weltordnung: Pragmatik, Struktur und Semantik des babylonischen "Lieds auf Marduk."* ORA 12. Tübingen: Mohr Siebeck, 2014.

Gabriel, G. "An Exemplificational Critique of Violence: Re-Reading the Old Babylonian Epic *Inūma ilū awīlum* (a.k.a. *Epic of Atramḫasīs*)." In "Approaching a Critique of Mesopotamian Reason," ed. G. Gabriel, special issue, *JANEH* 5 (2018): 179–213.

Gabriel, G. "Introduction." In "Approaching a Critique of Mesopotamian Reason," ed. G. Gabriel, special issue, *JANEH* 5 (2018): 1–14.

Gadd, C. J. "The Harran Inscriptions of Nabonidus." *AnSt* 8 (1958): 35–92.

Garr, W. R. *The Dialect Geography of Syria-Palestine, 1000–586 B.C.E.* Philadelphia: University of Pennsylvania Press, 1985.

Gelb, I., P. Purves, and A. A. MacRae. *Nuzi Personal Names.* OIP 57. Chicago: University of Chicago Press, 1943.

Geller, M. J. *Ancient Babylonian Medicine: Theory and Practice.* Chichester: Wiley-Blackwell, 2010.

Geller, M. J. *Evil Demons: Canonical* Utukkū Lemnūtu *Incantations.* SAACT 5. Helsinki: Neo-Assyrian Text Corpus Project, 2007.

Geller, M. J. *Forerunners to Udug-ḫul.* FAS 12. Stuttgart: Franz Steiner Verlag Wiesbaden GMBH, 1985.

Geller, M. J. "Incipits and Rubrics." Pages 225–258 in *Wisdom, Gods and Literature: Studies in Assyriology in Honour of W. G. Lambert.* Edited by A. R. George and I. L. Finkel. Winona Lake, IN: Eisenbrauns, 2000.

Geller, M. J., with the assistance of L. Vacín. *Healing Magic and Evil Demons: Canonical Udug-hul Incantations.* Boston: de Gruyter, 2016.

Geller, S. A. *Sacred Enigmas: Literary Religion in the Hebrew Bible.* London: Routledge, 1996.

Geller, S. A. "Some Sound and Word Plays in the First Tablet of the Old Babylonian *Atramḫasīs* Epic." Pages 63–70 in vol. 1 of *The Frank Talmage Memorial Volume.* Edited by B. Walfish. Haifa: Haifa University Press, 1993.

George, A. R. *The Babylonian Gilgamesh Epic.* 2 vols. Oxford: Oxford University Press, 2003.

Gerstenberger, E. S. *Der bittende Mensch: Bittritual und Klagelied des Einzelnen im Alten Testament.* WMANT 51. Neukirchen-Vluyn: Neukirchener Verlag, 1980.

Gerstenberger, E. S. *Psalms: Part 1, with an Introduction to Cultic Poetry.* FOTL 14. Grand Rapids, MI: Eerdmans, 1988.

Gerstenberger, E. S. *Psalms: Part 2 and Lamentations.* FOTL 15. Grand Rapids, MI: Eerdmans, 2001.

Glucklich, A. *The End of Magic.* New York: Oxford University Press, 1997.

Goetze, A. "An Inscription of Simbar-šīḫu." *JCS* 19 (1965): 121–135.

Goetze, A. "Reports on Acts of Extispicy from Old Babylonian and Kassite Times." *JCS* 11 (1957): 89–105.

Gordon, C. H. *Hammurapi's Code: Quaint or Forward-Looking?* New York: Rinehart, 1957.

Grayson, A. K. *Babylonian Historical-Literary Texts*. Toronto: University of Toronto Press, 1975.

Greenfield, J. C. Review of *Aramaic Texts from Deir 'Alla*, edited by J. Hoftijzer and G. van der Kooij. *JSS* 25 (1980): 248–252.

Greenfield, J. C. "Un rite religieux araméen et ses parallèles." *RB* 80 (1973): 46–52.

Greenwood, K. "A Shuilla: Marduk 2." Pages 313–324 in Lenzi, *Reading Akkadian Prayers and Hymns*.

Groenewegen-Frankfort, H. A. *Arrest and Movement: An Essay on Space and Time in the Representational Art of the Ancient Near East*. Chicago: University of Chicago Press, 1951.

Groneberg, B. "Die sumerisch-akkadische Inanna/Ištar: Hermaphroditos?" *WO* 17 (1986): 25–46.

Groneberg, B. "Philologische Bearbeitung des Agušayahymnus." *RA* 75 (1981): 107–134.

Groneberg, B. "Zu den mesopotamischen Unterweltsvorstellungen: Das Jenseits als Fortsetzung des Diesseits." *AoF* 17 (1990): 244–261.

Guillaume, P. "The End of Jonah and the Beginning of Wisdom." *Bib* 87 (2006): 243–250.

Guillaume, P. "Rhetorical Reading Redundant: A Response to Ehud Ben Zvi." *JHebS* 9/6 (2009). doi:10.5508/jhs.2009.v9.a6.

Gunkel, H. *Genesis*. 2nd German ed. HKAT. Göttingen: Vandenhoeck & Ruprecht, 1902.

Gunkel, H. *Genesis*. Translated by M. E. Biddle from the 3rd German edition, 1910. Macon, GA: Mercer University Press, 1997.

Gurney, O. R., J. J. Finkelstein, and P. Hulin. *The Sultantepe Tablets*. 2 vols. Occasional Publications of the British Institute of Archaeology at Ankara 3, 7. London: British Institute of Archaeology at Ankara, 1957–1964.

Gurney, O. R., and S. N. Kramer. "Two Fragments of Sumerian Laws." Pages 13–20 in Güterbock and Jacobsen, *Studies in Honor of Benno Landsberger*.

Güterbock, H., and T. Jacobsen, eds. *Studies in Honor of Benno Landsberger on His Seventy-fifth Birthday, April 21, 1965*. AS 16. Chicago: University of Chicago Press, 1965.

Habermann, A. M. *Megilloth Midbar Yehudah: The Scrolls from the Judean Desert*. In Hebrew. Jerusalem: Machbaroth Lesifruth, 1959.

Hackett, Jo Ann. "The Dialect of the Plaster Text from Tell Deir 'Alla." *Or* NS 53 (1984): 57–65.

Hallo, W. W. Review of *Hymnes et prières aux dieux de Babylonie et d'Assyrie*, by M.-J. Seux. *JAOS* 97 (1977): 582–585.

Hallo, W. W., and W. L. Moran. "The First Tablet of the SB Recension of the Anzu-Myth." *JCS* 31 (1979): 65–115.

Handy, L. K. *Jonah's World: Social Science and the Reading of Prophetic Story*. Bible World. London: Equinox, 2007.

Harris, R. "Inanna-Ishtar as Paradox and a Coincidence of Opposites." *HR* 31 (1991): 261–278.

Heeßel, N. P. "The Babylonian Physician Rabâ-ša-Marduk: Another Look at Physicians and Exorcists in the Ancient Near East." Pages 13–28 in *Advances in Mesopotamian Medicine from Hammurabi to Hippocrates*. Edited by A. Attia and G. Buisson. CM 37. Leiden: Brill, 2009.

Heeßel, N. P. "Neues von Esagil-kīn-apli." Pages 139–187 in *Assur-Forschungen*. Edited by N. P. Heeßel and S. M. Maul. Wiesbaden: Harrassowitz, 2010.

Heeßel, N. P. *Pazuzu: Archäologische und philologische Studien zu einem altorientalischen Dämon*. AMD 4. Leiden: Brill/Styx, 2002.

Heeßel, N. P. "'Sieben Tafeln aus sieben Städten': Überlegungen zum Prozess der Serialisierung von Texten in Babylonien in der zweiten Hälfte des zweiten Jahrtausends v. Chr." Pages 171–195 in *Babylon: Wissenskultur in Orient und Okzident*. Edited by E. Cancik-Kirschbaum, M. van Ess, and J. Marzahn. Berlin: de Gruyter, 2011.

Heimpel, W. "A Catalog of Near Eastern Venus Deities." *SMS* 4 (1982): 59–72.

Held, M. "Two Philological Notes on Enūma Eliš." Pages 231–239 in *Kramer Anniversary Volume: Cuneiform Studies in Honor of Samuel Noah Kramer*. Edited by B. L. Eichler. AOAT 25. Kevelaer: Butzon & Bercker; Neukirchen-Vluyn: Neukirchener Verlag, 1976.

Hunger, H. *Astrological Reports to Assyrian Kings*. SAA 8. Helsinki: Helsinki University Press, 1992.

Hunger, H. *Spätbabylonische Texte aus Uruk*, Teil 1. ADFU 9. Berlin: Mann, 1976.

Jacobsen, T. "Babylonia and Assyria, Part V. Religion." *Encyclopedia Britannica* (1963) 2:972–978. Repr., T. Jacobsen. "Mesopotamian Gods and Pantheons." Pages 16–38 in *Toward the Image of Tammuz*. Edited by W. L. Moran. HSS 21. Cambridge, MA: Harvard University Press, 1970.

Jacobsen, T. "The Battle between Marduk and Tiamat." *JAOS* 88 (1968): 104–108.

Jacobsen, T. "The lil$_2$ of $^{d}$En-lil$_2$." Pages 267–276 in *DUMU-E$_2$-DUB-BA-A: Studies in Honor of Åke W. Sjöberg*. Edited by H. Behrens, D. Loding, and M. T. Roth. Philadelphia: University of Pennsylvania Museum of Archaeology, 1989.

Jacobsen, T. "Mesopotamia: The Cosmos as a State." Pages 125–219 in *The Intellectual Adventure of Ancient Man: An Essay on Speculative Thought in the Ancient Near East*. Edited by H. Frankfort, H. A. Frankfort, J. A. Wilson, T. Jacobsen, and W. A. Irwin. Rev. ed. Chicago: University of Chicago Press, 1977.

Jacobsen, T. "Mesopotamian Religions." *Encyclopedia of Religion* 9:458–461. New York: Macmillan; London: Collier Macmillan, 1987.

Jacobsen, T. "Religious Drama in Ancient Mesopotamia." Pages 65–97 in *Unity and Diversity*. Edited by H. Goedicke and J. J. M. Roberts. Baltimore: Johns Hopkins University Press, 1975.

Jacobsen, T. "Some Sumerian City-Names." *JCS* 21 (1967): 100–103.

Jacobsen, T. *The Treasures of Darkness: A History of Mesopotamian Religion*. New Haven: Yale University Press, 1976.

Janowski, B., and G. Wilhelm, eds. *Omina, Orakel, Rituale und Beschwörungen*. TUAT NF 4. Gütersloh: Gütersloher Verlagshaus, 2008.

Jaques, M. *Mon dieu qu'ai-je fait? Les diĝir-šà-dab*$_{(5)}$*-ba et la piété privée en Mésopotamie*. OBO 273. Fribourg: Academic Press; Göttingen: Vandenhoeck & Ruprecht, 2015.

Jastrow, M. *Dictionary of Targumim, Talmud and Midrashic Literature*. 1926. Repr., New York: Pardes, 1950.

Jay, N. *Throughout Your Generations Forever: Sacrifice, Religion, and Paternity*. Chicago: University of Chicago Press, 1992.

Jean, C. *La magie néo-assyrienne en contexte: Recherches sur le métier d'exorciste et le concept d'āšipūtu*. SAAS 17. Helsinki: Neo-Assyrian Text Corpus Project, 2006.

Jean, C.-F., and J. Hoftijzer. *Dictionnaire des inscriptions sémitiques de l'ouest*. 2nd ed. Leiden: Brill, 1965.

Jenson, P. P. *Obadiah, Jonah, Micah*. New York: T&T Clark, 2008.

Johnston, S. I., ed. *Religions of the Ancient World: A Guide*. Cambridge, MA: Belknap Press of Harvard University Press, 2004.

Kalmin, R. *Sages, Stories, Authors, and Editors in Rabbinic Babylonia*. BJS 300. Atlanta: Scholars Press, 1994.

Kämmerer, T. R., and K. A. Metzler. *Das babylonische Weltschöpfungsepos Enūma eliš*. AOAT 375. Münster: Ugarit-Verlag, 2012.

Katz, D. *The Image of the Netherworld in the Sumerian Sources*. Bethesda, MD: CDL, 2003.

Kaufman, S. A. *The Akkadian Influences on Aramaic*. AS 19. Chicago: University of Chicago Press, 1974.

Kearney, M. *World View*. Novato, CA: Chandler and Sharp, 1984.

Kilmer, A. D. "The Mesopotamian Concept of Overpopulation and Its Solution as Reflected in the Mythology." *Or* NS 41 (1972): 160–177.

Kilmer, A. D. "Notes on Akkadian *uppu*." Pages 129–138 in *Essays on the Ancient Near East in Memory of Jacob Joel Finkelstein*. Edited by M. de Jong Ellis. MCAAS 19. Hamden: Archon Books, 1977.

King, L. W. *Babylonian Magic and Sorcery*. London: Luzac, 1896.

King, L. W. *Babylonian Religion and Mythology*. London: K. Paul, Trench, Trübner, 1899.

King, L. W. "Magic (Babylonian)." Pages 253–255 in vol. 8 of *Encyclopaedia of Religion and Ethics*. Edited by J. Hastings. Edinburgh: T&T Clark; New York: Scribner, 1910.

Kinnier Wilson, J. V. "An Introduction to Babylonian Psychiatry." Pages 289–298 in Güterbock and Jacobsen, *Studies in Honor of Benno Landsberger*.

Kinnier Wilson, J. V. "Mental Diseases of Ancient Mesopotamia." Pages 723–733 in Brothwell and Sandison, *Diseases in Antiquity*.

Kinnier Wilson, J. V. "Organic Diseases of Ancient Mesopotamia." Pages 191–208 in Brothwell and Sandison, *Diseases in Antiquity*.

Klein, J. "'Personal God' and Individual Prayer in Sumerian Religion." Pages 295–306 in *Vorträge gehalten auf der 28. Rencontre Assyriologique Internationale in Wien 6.–10. Juli 1981*. AfO Beih. 19. Horn: Berger, 1982.

Köcher, F. *Die babylonisch-assyrische Medizin in Texten und Untersuchungen*. 6 vols. Berlin: de Gruyter, 1963–1980.

Köcher, F., A. L. Oppenheim, and H. G. Güterbock. "The Old Babylonian Omen Text VAT 7525." *AfO* 18 (1957–1958): 62–80.

Koschaker, P. *Rechtsvergleichende Studien zur Gesetzgebung Hammurapis, Königs von Babylon*. Leipzig: Veit, 1917.

Kugel, J. L. "Topics in the History of the Spirituality of the Psalms." Pages 113–144 in *Jewish Spirituality I: From the Bible through the Middle Ages*. Edited by A. Green. New York: Crossroad, 1986.

Kunstmann, W. G. *Die babylonische Gebetsbeschwörung*. LSS NF 2. Leipzig: Hinrichs, 1932.

Kutscher, E. Y. "Studies in the Grammar of Mishnaic Hebrew according to Ms. Kaufmann." In Hebrew. Pages 51–77 in *Hebrew and Aramaic Studies*. Edited by Z. Ben-Ḥayyim, A. Dotan, and G. Sarfatti. Jerusalem: Magnes, 1977.

Kutscher, R. *Oh Angry Sea (a-ab-ba hu-luh-ha): The History of a Sumerian Congregational Lament*. YNER 6. New Haven: Yale University Press, 1975.

Labat, R., A. Caquot, and M. Sznycer. *Les religions du Proche-Orient asiatique: Textes babyloniens, ougaritiques, hittites*. Paris: Fayard-Denoël, 1970.

Lacheman, E. R. *The Administrative Archives*. Vol. 6 of *Excavations at Nuzi*. HSS 15. Cambridge, MA: Harvard University Press, 1955.

Lacheman, E. R. *Economic and Social Documents*. Vol. 7 of *Excavations at Nuzi*. HSS 16. Cambridge, MA: Harvard University Press, 1958.

Lacheman, E. R. *Family Law Documents*. Vol. 8 of *Excavations at Nuzi*. HSS 19. Cambridge, MA: Harvard University Press, 1962.

Lacocque, A., and P.-E. Lacoque. *The Jonah Complex*. Atlanta: John Knox, 1981.

Laessøe, J. *Studies on the Assyrian Ritual and Series "bît rimki."* Copenhagen: Munksgaard, 1955.

Lambert, W. G. *Babylonian Creation Myths*. MC 16. Winona Lake, IN: Eisenbrauns, 2013.

Lambert, W. G. *Babylonian Wisdom Literature*. Oxford: Clarendon, 1960.

Lambert, W. G. "The Cult of Ištar of Babylon." Pages 104–106 in *Le Temple et le Culte: Compte rendu de la vingtième Rencontre Assyriologique Internationale, organisée à Leiden du 3 au 7 juillet 1972*. Istanbul: Nederlands Historisch-Archeologisch Instituut, 1975.

Lambert, W. G. "Dingir.šà.dib.ba Incantations." *JNES* 33 (1974): 267–322.

Lambert, W. G. "Donations of Food and Drink to the Gods in Ancient Mesopotamia." Pages 191–201 in *Ritual and Sacrifice in the Ancient Near East: Proceedings of the International Conference Organized by the Katholieke Universiteit Leuven from the 17th to the 20th of April 1991*. Edited by J. Quaegebeur. OLA 55. Leuven: Peeters, 1993.

Lambert, W. G. "Enmeduranki and Related Matters." *JCS* 21 (1967 [1969]): 126–138.

Lambert, W. G. "Fire Incantations." *AfO* 23 (1970): 39–45.

Lambert, W. G. "The Great Battle of the Mesopotamian Religious Year: The Conflict in the Akītu House." *Iraq* 25 (1963): 189–190.

Lambert, W. G. "Myth and Mythmaking in Sumer and Akkad." In Sasson, *Civilizations of the Ancient Near East*, 3:1832–1834.

Lambert, W. G. "Ninurta Mythology in the Babylonian Epic of Creation." Pages 55–60 in *Keilschriftliche Literaturen*. Edited by K. Hecker and W. Sommerfeld. BBVO 6. Berlin: Dietrich Reimer, 1986.

Lambert, W. G. "The Reign of Nebuchadnezzar I: A Turning Point in the History of Ancient Mesopotamian Religion." Pages 3–13 in *The Seed of Wisdom: Essays in Honour of T. J. Meek*. Edited by W. S. McCullough. Toronto: University of Toronto Press, 1964.

Lambert, W. G. "The Relationship of Sumerian and Babylonian Myth as Seen in Accounts of Creation." Pages 129–135 in *La circulation des biens, des personnes et des idées dans le Proche-Orient ancien, XXXVIII*[e] *R.A.I.* Edited by D. Charpin and F. Joannès. Paris: Éditions Recherche sur les Civilisations, 1991.

Lambert, W. G. "Studies in Marduk." *BSOAS* 47 (1984): 1–9.

Lambert, W. G., and A. R. Millard. *Atra-ḫasīs: The Babylonian Story of the Flood*. Oxford: Clarendon, 1969.

Lambert, W. G., and S. B. Parker. *Enūma Eliš, The Babylonian Epic of Creation: The Cuneiform Text*. Oxford: Clarendon, 1966.

Landes, G. M. "Jonah, Book of." Pages 488–491 in *Interpreter's Dictionary of the Bible: Supplementary Volume*. Edited by K. Crim. Nashville: Abingdon, 1976.

Landsberger, B. "Babylonisch-assyrische Texte." In *Textbuch zur Religionsgeschichte*. Edited by E. Lehmann and H. Haas. 1st ed., Leipzig: Deichert, 1912, pp. 73–134; 2nd ed., Leipzig: Deichert, 1922, pp. 277–330.

Landsberger, B. *Brief des Bischofs von Esagila an König Asarhaddon*. Amsterdam: N. V. Noord-Hollandische Uitgevers Maatshappij, 1965.

Landsberger, B. "Die babylonischen Termini für Gesetz und Recht." Pages 219–234 in *Symbolae ad iura orientis antiqui pertinentes Paulo Koschaker dedicatae*. Edited by

J. Friedrich et al. Studia et documenta ad iura orientis antiqui pertinentia 2. Leiden: Brill, 1939.

Landsberger, B., and J. V. Kinnier Wilson. "The Fifth Tablet of *Enuma Eliš*." *JNES* 20 (1961): 154–179.

Langdon, S. *Die neubabylonischen Königsinschriften*. VAB 4. Leipzig: Hinrichs, 1912.

Langdon, S. *Sumerian and Babylonian Psalms*. Paris: Geuthner; New York: G. E. Stechert, 1909.

Laroche, E. *Catalogue des textes hittites*. Paris: Klincksieck, 1971.

Lattimore, R., trans. *Euripides I*. In *The Complete Greek Tragedies*. Edited by D. Grene and R. Lattimore. Chicago: University of Chicago Press, 1955.

Leemans, W. F. "Le faux témoin." *RA* 64 (1970): 63–66.

Lenzi, A. "Dingirshadibbas to Personal Deities." Pages 431–445 in Lenzi, *Reading Akkadian Prayers and Hymns*.

Lenzi, A. "Invoking the God: Interpreting Invocations in Mesopotamian Prayers and Biblical Laments of the Individual." *JBL* 129 (2010): 303–315.

Lenzi, A., ed. *Reading Akkadian Prayers and Hymns: An Introduction*. ANEM 3. Atlanta: Society of Biblical Literature, 2011.

Lenzi, A. "Scribal Revision and Textual Variation in Akkadian *Šuila*-Prayers: Two Case Studies in Ritual Adaptation." Pages 63–108 in *Empirical Models Challenging Biblical Criticism*. Edited by R. F. Person and R. Rezetko. AIL 25. Atlanta: SBL Press, 2016.

Lenzi, A. "A Shuilla: Marduk 4." Pages 291–311 in Lenzi, *Reading Akkadian Prayers and Hymns*.

Lenzi, A. "A Shuilla: Sin 1." Pages 385–402 in Lenzi, *Reading Akkadian Prayers and Hymns*.

Levack, B. P., ed. *Anthropological Studies of Witchcraft, Magic, and Religion*. Vol. 1 of *Articles on Witchcraft, Magic, and Demonology: A Twelve-Volume Anthology of Scholarly Articles*. New York: Garland, 1992.

Levine, B. A. "From the Aramaic Enoch Fragments: The Semantics of Cosmography." *JJS* 33 (1982): 311–326.

Levine, B. A. *In the Presence of the Lord*. SJLA 5. Leiden: Brill, 1974.

Levine, B. A. *The JPS Torah Commentary: Leviticus*. Philadelphia: Jewish Publication Society, 1989.

Levine, B. A. "Prolegomenon." Pages vii–xliv in *Sacrifice in the Old Testament: Its Theory and Practice*, by G. B. Gray. New York: Ktav, 1971.

Licht, J. *The Rule Scroll: A Scroll from the Wilderness of Judaea: 1QS, 1QSa, 1QSb*. In Hebrew. Jerusalem: Bialik Institute, 1965.

Lieberman, S. *Hellenism in Jewish Palestine*. 2nd ed. Texts and Studies of the Jewish Theological Seminary of America 18. New York: Jewish Theological Seminary of America, 1962.

Lieberman, S. J. "Of Clay Pebbles, Hollow Clay Balls, and Writing: A Sumerian View." *AJA* 84 (1980): 339–358.

Limet, H. *Les légendes des sceaux cassites*. Brussels: Palais des Académies, 1971.
Linssen, M. J. H. *The Cults of Uruk and Babylon: The Temple Ritual Texts as Evidence for Hellenistic Cult Practice*. CM 25. Leiden: Brill/Styx, 2004.
Livingstone, A. *Court Poetry and Literary Miscellanea*. SAA 3. Helsinki: Helsinki University Press, 1989.
Loewenstamm, S. E. "The Cumulative Oath of Witnesses and Parties in Mesopotamian Law." Pages 341–345 in *Comparative Studies in Biblical and Ancient Oriental Literatures*. AOAT 204. Kevalaer: Butzon & Bercker; Neukirchen-Vluyn: Neukirchener Verlag, 1980.
Löhnert, A. "Manipulating the Gods: Lamenting in Context." Pages 402–417 in Radner and Robson, *Oxford Handbook of Cuneiform Culture*.
Löhnert, A. *"Wie die Sonne tritt heraus!" Eine Klage zum Auszug Enlils mit einer Untersuchung zu Komposition und Tradition sumerischer Klagelieder in altbabylonischer Zeit*. AOAT 365. Münster: Ugarit-Verlag, 2009.
Loretz, O., and W. R. Mayer. *ŠU-ILA-Gebete: Supplement zu L. W. King, "Babylonian Magic and Sorcery."* AOAT 34. Kevalaer: Butzon & Bercker, 1978.
Lutz, H. F. *Selected Sumerian and Babylonian Texts*. PBS 1/2. Philadelphia: The University Museum, 1919.
Magonet, J. *Form and Meaning: Studies in Literary Techniques in the Book of Jonah*. BBET 2. Bern: Herbert Lang, 1976.
Malmkjaer, K. "Text Linguistics." Pages 461–471 in *The Linguistics Encyclopedia*. Edited by K. Malmkjaer. London: Routledge, 1991.
Martin, W. J. "The Law Code of Hammurabi." Pages 27–37 in *Documents from Old Testament Times*. Edited by D. Winton Thomas. Edinburgh: Nelson, 1958.
Maul, S. M. *The Art of Divination in the Ancient Near East: Reading the Signs of Heaven and Earth*. Translated by B. McNeil and A. J. Edmonds. Waco, TX: Baylor University Press, 2018.
Maul, S. M. "How the Babylonians Protected Themselves against Calamities Announced by Omens." Pages 123–129 in Abusch and van der Toorn, *Mesopotamian Magic*.
Maul, S. M. *Zukunftsbewältigung: Eine Untersuchung altorientalischen Denkens anhand der babylonisch-assyrischen Lösrituale (Namburbi)*. BaF 18. Mainz am Rhein: Phillip von Zabern, 1994.
Maul, S. M., and R. Strauss. *Ritualbeschreibungen und Gebete I*. KALI 4, WVDOG 133. Wiesbaden: Harrassowitz, 2011.
Mauss, M. "A Category of the Human Mind: The Notion of Person, the Notion of 'Self.'" Pages 57–94 in *Sociology and Psychology: Essays*. Translated by B. Brewster. London: Routledge & Kegan Paul, 1979.
Mayer, W. R. "Das Bussgebet an Marduk von *BMS* 11." *Or* NS 73 (2004): 198–214.
Mayer, W. R. Review of *Hymnes et prières aux dieux de Babylonie et d'Assyrie*, by M.-J. Seux. *Or* NS 46 (1977): 386–392.

Mayer, W. R. "Sechs Šu-ila-Gebete." *Or* NS 59 (1990): 449–490.

Mayer, W. R. *Untersuchungen zur Formensprache der babylonischen "Gebetsbeschwörungen."* StPohl, series maior 5. Rome: Pontifical Biblical Institute, 1976.

McCarthy, D. J. "Further Notes on the Symbolism of Blood and Sacrifice." *JBL* 92 (1973): 205–210.

McCarthy, D. J. "The Symbolism of Blood and Sacrifice." *JBL* 88 (1969): 166–176.

Meek, T. J., trans. "The Code of Hammurabi." Pages 163–180 in Pritchard, *Ancient Near Eastern Texts*.

Meier, G. *Die assyrische Beschwörungssammlung "Maqlû."* AfO Beih. 2. Berlin: Selbstverlag E. F. Weidner, 1937.

Meier, G. "Die zweite Tafel der Serie *bīt mēseri*." *AfO* 14 (1941–1944): 139–152.

Meier, G. "Studien zur Beschwörungssammlung *Maqlû*: Zusammengestellt nach hinterlassenen Notizen." *AfO* 21 (1966): 70–81.

Mendelsohn, I. *Religions of the Ancient Near East*. New York: Liberal Arts Press, 1955.

Metcalf, C. "New Parallels in Hittite and Sumerian Praise of the Sun." *WO* 41 (2011): 168–176.

Metcalf, C. "Old Babylonian Religious Poetry in Anatolia: From Solar Hymn to Plague Prayer." *ZA* 105 (2015): 42–53.

Miles, J. A. "Laughing at the Bible: Jonah as Parody." *JQR* 65 (1974–1975): 168–181.

Milik, J. T. *Ten Years of Discovery in the Wilderness of Judaea*. Translated by John Strugnell. SBT 26. London: SCM; Naperville, IL: Allenson, 1959.

Miller, R. D. II. *The Dragon, the Mountain, and the Nations: An Old Testament Myth, Its Origins, and Its Afterlives*. Explorations in Ancient Near Eastern Civilizations 6. University Park, PA: Eisenbrauns, 2018.

Moore, C. A. "Esther, Book of." *ABD* 2:633–643.

Moran, W. L. "Atrahasis: The Babylonian Story of the Flood." *Bib* 52 (1971): 51–61.

Moran, W. L. "The Babylonian Job." Pages 182–200 in *The Most Magic Word: Essays on Babylonian and Biblical Literature*. Edited by R. S. Hendel. CBQMS 35. Washington, DC: Catholic Biblical Association of America, 2002.

Moran, W. L. "The Creation of Man in Atrahasis I 192–248." *BASOR* 200 (1970): 48–56.

Moran, W. L. "Notes on the Hymn to Marduk in *Ludlul Bēl Nēmeqi*." *JAOS* 103 (1983): 255–260.

Moran, W. L. "Some Akkadian Names of the Stomachs of Ruminants." *JCS* 21 (1967): 178–182.

More, J. "The Prophet Jonah: The Story of an Intrapsychic Process." *American Imago* 27, no. 1 (1970): 2–11.

Mowinckel, S. *ʾÅwän und die individuellen Klagepsalmen*. Vol. 1 of *Psalmenstudien*. Oslo: Dybwad, 1921.

Mullo-Weir, C. J. "Four Hymns to Gula." *JRAS* 1 (1929): 1–18.

Mullo-Weir, C. J. "Fragment of an Expiation-Ritual against Sickness." *JRAS* 2 (1929): 281–284.

Myhrman, D. W. *Babylonian Hymns and Prayers*. PBS 1/1. Philadelphia: The University Museum, 1911.

Neusner, J. *The Mishnah: A New Translation*. New Haven: Yale University Press, 1988.

Nickelsburg, G. W. E. *A Commentary on the Book of 1 Enoch, Chapters 1–36; 81–108*. Vol. 1 of *1 Enoch*. Hermeneia. Minneapolis: Fortress, 2001.

Nickelsburg, G. W. E. *Jewish Literature between the Bible and the Mishnah*. Philadelphia: Fortress, 1981.

Nörr, D. "Zum Schuldgedanken im altbabylonischen Strafrecht." *ZSS, Romanistische Abteilung* 75 (1958): 1–31.

Noth, M. *Die israelitischen Personennamen im Rahmen der gemeinsemitischen Nemengebung*. Stuttgart: Kohlhammer, 1928.

Nougayrol, J., E. Laroche, C. Virolleaud, and C. F. A. Schaeffer, eds. *Ugaritica* 5. Paris: Paul Geuthner, 1968.

Oberhuber, K. "Ein Versuch zum Verständnis von Atra-Hasīs." Pages 279–281 in *Zikir Šumim: Studies Presented to F. R. Kraus on the Occasion of His Seventieth Birthday*. Edited by G. van Driel, T. J. H. Krispijn, M. Stol, and K. R. Veenhof. Leiden: Brill, 1982.

O'Keefe, D. L. *Stolen Magic: The Social History of Magic*. New York: Random House, 1983.

Oppenheim, A. L. *Ancient Mesopotamia: Portrait of a Dead Civilization*. Rev. ed. Chicago: University of Chicago Press, 1977.

Oppenheim, A. L. "Divination and Celestial Observation in the Last Assyrian Empire." *Centaurus* 14, no. 1 (1969): 97–135.

Oppenheim, A. L. *The Interpretation of Dreams in the Ancient Near East. With a Translation of an Assyrian Dream-Book*. TAPS NS 46/3. Philadelphia: American Philosophical Society, 1956.

Oppenheim, A. L. "On an Operational Device in Mesopotamian Bureaucracy." *JNES* 18 (1959): 121–128.

Oppenheim, A. L., et al., eds. *The Assyrian Dictionary of the Oriental Institute of the University of Chicago*. Chicago: The Oriental Institute of the University of Chicago, 1956–2006.

Oshima, T. *Babylonian Poems of Pious Sufferers*. ORA 14. Tübingen: Mohr Siebeck, 2014.

Oshima, T. *Babylonian Prayers to Marduk*. ORA 7. Tübingen: Mohr Siebeck, 2011.

Owen, D. I. "The Loan Documents from Nuzu." Ph.D. diss., Brandeis University, 1969.

Parpola, S. *Letters from Assyrian Scholars to the Kings Esarhaddon and Assurbanipal*. 2 vols. AOAT 5/1–2. Kevelaer: Butzon & Bercker; Neukirchen-Vluyn: Neukirchener Verlag, 1970–1983.

Parpola, S. "The Murder of Sennacherib." Pages 171–182 in *Death in Mesopotamia*. Edited by B. Alster. Mesopotamia 8. Copenhagen: Akademisk Forlag, 1980.

Payne Smith, R. *A Compendious Syriac Dictionary*. Edited by J. Payne Smith. Oxford: Clarendon, 1903.

Person, R. F. "The Role of Nonhuman Characters in Jonah." Pages 85–90 in *Exploring Ecological Hermeneutics*. Edited by N. C. Habel and P. Trudinger. SBLSymS 46. Atlanta: Society of Biblical Literature, 2008.

Petschow, H. P. H. "Altorientalische Parallelen zur spätrömischen calumnia." *ZSS, Romanistische Abteilung* 90 (1973): 14–35.

Petschow, H. P. H. "Zur Systematik und Gesetzestechnik im Codex Hammurabi." *ZA* 57 (1965): 146–172.

Pettinato, G. *Das altorientalische Menschenbild und die sumerischen und akkadischen Schöpfungsmythen*. Heidelberg: Carl Winter, 1971.

Pettinato, G. *Die Ölwahrsagung bei den Babyloniern*. 2 vols. StSem 21–22. Rome: Istituto di Studi del Vicino Oriente, 1966.

Pfeiffer, R. H., and E. A. Speiser. *One Hundred New Selected Nuzi Texts*. AASOR 16. New Haven: American Schools of Oriental Research, 1936.

Poebel, A. *Studies in Akkadian Grammar*. AS 9. Chicago: University of Chicago Press, 1939.

Pohl, A., and R. Follett. *Codex Ḫammurabi*. Rome: Pontificium Institutum Biblicum, 1950.

Pomponio, F. "Nabû. A. Philologisch." *RlA* 9 (1998): 16–24.

Pomponio, F. *Nabû: Il culto e la figura di un dio del Pantheon babilonese ed assiro*. StSem 51. Rome: Istituto di Studi del Vicino Oriente, Università di Roma, 1978.

Postgate, J. N. *Early Mesopotamia: Society and Economy at the Dawn of History*. Rev. ed. London: Routledge, 1994.

Postgate, J. N. "Some Old Babylonian Shepherds and Their Flocks." *JSS* 20 (1975): 1–21.

Pritchard, J. B., ed. *Ancient Near Eastern Texts Relating to the Old Testament*. 3rd ed. Princeton: Princeton University Press, 1969.

Radner, K., and E. Robson, eds. *The Oxford Handbook of Cuneiform Culture*. Oxford: Oxford University Press, 2011.

Rathus, S. A., and J. S. Nevid. *Abnormal Psychology*. Instructor's ed. Englewood Cliffs, NJ: Prentice Hall, 1991.

Rawlinson, H. C. *The Cuneiform Inscriptions of Western Asia*. Vol. 1. London: E. E. Bowler, 1861.

Rawlinson, H. C., G. Smith, and T. G. Pinches. *The Cuneiform Inscriptions of Western Asia*. Vol. 4. 2nd ed. London: [British Museum], 1891.

Redfield, R. *The Primitive World and Its Transformations*. Ithaca, NY: Cornell University Press, 1953.

Reiner, E. *Astral Magic in Babylonia*. TAPS NS 85/4. Philadelphia: American Philosophical Society, 1995.

Reiner, E. "Fortune-Telling in Mesopotamia." *JNES* 19 (1960): 23–35.

Reiner, E. *A Linguistic Analysis of Akkadian*. The Hague: Mouton, 1966.

Reiner, E. "Lipšur Litanies." *JNES* 15 (1956): 129–149.

Reiner, E. *Šurpu: A Collection of Sumerian and Akkadian Incantations*. AfO Beih. 11. Graz: Im Selbstverlage des Herausgebers, 1958.

Reiner, E. *Your Thwarts in Pieces, Your Mooring Rope Cut: Poetry from Babylonia and Assyria*. Michigan Studies in the Humanities 5. Ann Arbor: University of Michigan Press, 1985.

Rendu Loisel, A.-C. "Gods, Demons, and Anger in the Akkadian Literature." *SMSR* 77, no. 2 (2011): 323–332.

Riemschneider, K. K. *Lehrbuch des Akkadischen*. Leipzig: VEB Verlag Enzyklopaedie, 1969.

Ritter, E. K. "Magical-Expert (= *āšipu*) and Physician (= *asû*): Notes on Two Complementary Professions in Babylonian Medicine." Pages 299–321 in Güterbock and Jacobsen, *Studies in Honor of Benno Landsberger*.

Rittig, D. *Assyrisch-babylonische Kleinplastik magischer Bedeutung von 13.–6. Jh. v. Chr*. Münchener vorderasiatische Studien 1. Munich: Verlag Uni-Druck, 1977.

Roaf, M. "Palaces and Temples in Ancient Mesopotamia." In Sasson, *Civilizations of the Ancient Near East*, 1:423–441.

Roberts, J. J. M. *The Earliest Semitic Pantheon*. Baltimore: Johns Hopkins University Press, 1972.

Roberts, J. J. M. "Nebuchadnezzar I's Elamite Crisis in Theological Perspective." Pages 183–187 in *Essays on the Ancient Near East in Memory of Jacob Joel Finkelstein*. Edited by M. de Jong Ellis. Hamden, CT: Archon, 1977.

Robertson Smith, W. *Kinship and Marriage in Early Arabia*. 2nd ed. Edited by S. A. Cook. London: Adam and Charles Black, 1903.

Robertson Smith, W. *The Religion of the Semites: The Fundamental Institutions*. Reprint of W. Robertson Smith, *Lectures on the Religion of the Semites* (1889). New York: Schocken, 1972.

Rollin, S. "Women and Witchcraft in Ancient Assyria." Pages 34–45 in *Images of Women in Antiquity*. Edited by A. Cameron and A. Kuhrt. Detroit: Wayne State University Press, 1983.

Römer, W. H. P. "Religion of Ancient Mesopotamia." Pages 115–194 in vol. 1 of *Historia Religionum: Handbook for the History of Religion*. Edited by C. J. Bleeker and G. Widengren. Leiden: Brill, 1969.

Sachs, A. "Daily Sacrifices to the Gods of the City of Uruk." Pages 343–345 in Pritchard, *Ancient Near Eastern Texts*.

San Nicolò, M. "Anschuldigung, falsche." *RlA* 1 (1928): 112–113.

Sasson, J., ed. *Civilizations of the Ancient Near East*. 4 vols. New York: Scribner, 1995.

Sasson, J. *Jonah: A New Translation with Introduction and Commentary*. AB 24B. New York: Doubleday, 1990.

Scheftelowitz, I. *Arisches im Alten Testament, I*. Königsberg: Hartungsche Buchdruckerei, 1901.

Schmandt-Besserat, D. "An Archaic Recording System and the Origin of Writing." *SMS* 1 (1977): 31–70.

Schmandt-Besserat, D. "The Earliest Precursor of Writing." *Scientific American* 238, no. 6 (1978): 50–59.

Schmandt-Besserat, D. "The Invention of Writing." *Discovery: Research and Scholarship at the University of Texas at Austin* 1, no. 4 (1977): 4–7.

Schramm, W. *Bann, Bann! Eine Sumerisch-Akkadische Beschwörungsserie*. GAAL 2. Göttingen: Seminar für Keilschriftforschung, 2001.

Schramm, W. *Ein Compendium sumerisch-akkadischer Beschwörungen*. Göttinger Beiträge zum Alten Orient 2. Göttingen: Universitätsverlag Göttingen, 2008.

Schuster-Brandis, A. *Steine als Schutz- und Heilmittel: Untersuchung zu ihrer Verwendung in der Beschwörungskunst Mesopotamiens im 1. Jt. v. Chr.* AOAT 46. Münster: Ugarit-Verlag, 2008.

Schwemer, D. *Abwehrzauber und Behexung: Studien zum Schadenzauberglauben im alten Mesopotamien (Unter Benutzung von Tzvi Abuschs Kritischem Katalog und Sammlungen im Rahmen des Kooperationsprojektes Corpus of Mesopotamian Anti-witchcraft Rituals)*. Wiesbaden: Harrassowitz, 2007.

Schwemer, D. *The Anti-Witchcraft Ritual "Maqlû": The Cuneiform Sources of a Magic Ceremony from Ancient Mesopotamia*. Wiesbaden: Harrassowitz, 2017.

Schwemer, D. "Evil Helpers: Instrumentalizing Agents of Evil in Anti-witchcraft Rituals." Pages 173–191 in Van Buylaere et al., *Sources of Evil*.

Schwemer, D. "'Forerunners' of *Maqlû*: A New *Maqlû*-Related Fragment from Assur." Pages 201–220 in *Gazing on the Deep: Ancient Near Eastern and Other Studies in Honor of Tzvi Abusch*. Edited by J. Stackert, B. N. Porter, and D. P. Wright. Bethesda, MD: CDL, 2010.

Schwemer, D. "Hittite Prayers to the Sun-God for Appeasing an Angry Personal God: A Critical Edition of *CTH* 372–74." Pages 349–393 in M. Jaques, *Mon dieu qu'ai-je fait? Les diĝir-šà-dab₍₅₎-ba et la piété privée en Mésopotamie*. OBO 273. Fribourg: Academic Press; Göttingen: Vandenhoeck & Ruprecht, 2015.

Schwemer, D. "Magic Rituals: Conceptualization and Performance." Pages 418–442 in Radner and Robson, *Oxford Handbook of Cuneiform Culture*.

Schwemer, D. "The Ritual Tablet of *Maqlû*: Two New Fragments." *JCS* 63 (2011): 105–109.

Scurlock, J. "Magical Means of Dealing with Ghosts in Ancient Mesopotamia." Ph.D. diss., University of Chicago, 1988.

Scurlock, J. *Magico-Medical Means of Treating Ghost-Induced Illnesses in Ancient Mesopotamia*. AMD 3. Leiden: Brill/Styx, 2006.

Scurlock, J. *Sourcebook for Ancient Mesopotamian Medicine*. WAW 36. Atlanta: SBL Press, 2014.

Scurlock, J., and B. R. Andersen. *Diagnoses in Assyrian and Babylonian Medicine: Ancient Sources, Translations, and Modern Medical Analyses*. Urbana: University of Illinois Press, 2005.

Seri, A. "The Fifty Names of Marduk in *Enūma eliš*." *JAOS* 126 (2006): 507–519.

Seux, M.-J. *Épithètes royales akkadiennes et sumériennes*. Paris: Letouzey et Ané, 1967.

Seux, M.-J. *Hymnes et prières aux dieux de Babylonie et d'Assyrie*. LAPO 8. Paris: Éditions du Cerf, 1976.

Seux, M.-J. "*šite*"*û ašrāt*(*i*) (À propos d'un article récent)." *RA* 60 (1966): 172–174.

Shaffer, A. "Sumerian Sources of Tablet XII of the Epic of Gilgameš." Ph.D. diss., University of Pennsylvania, 1963.

Shemesh, Y. "'And Many Beasts' (Jonah 4:11): The Function and Status of Animals in the Book of Jonah." *JHebS* 10/6 (2010). doi:10.5508/jhs.2010.v10.a6.

Simmons, S. D. "Early Old Babylonian Tablets from Ḥarmal and Elsewhere." *JCS* 13 (1959): 105–119; 14 (1960): 23–32.

Simon, U. *The JPS Bible Commentary: Jonah*. Philadelphia: Jewish Publication Society, 1999.

Simons, F. "Burn Your Way to Success: Studies in the Mesopotamian Ritual and Incantation Series *Šurpu*." Ph.D. diss., University of Birmingham, 2017.

Singer, I. *Hittite Prayers*. WAW 11. Atlanta: Society of Biblical Literature, 2002.

Smith, J. Z. *Imagining Religion: From Babylon to Jonestown*. Chicago: University of Chicago Press, 1982.

Soden, W. von. *Akkadisches Handwörterbuch*. 3 vols. Wiesbaden: Harrassowitz, 1958–1981.

Soden, W. von. "Bemerkungen zu einigen literarischen Texten in akkadischer Sprache aus Ugarit." *UF* 1 (1969): 189–195.

Soden, W. von. "Der altbabylonische Atramchasis-Mythos." Pages 612–645 in *Mythen und Epen II*. Edited by O. Kaiser. TUAT NF 3/4. Gütersloh: Gütersloher Verlagshaus, 1994.

Soden, W. von. "Der Mensch bescheidet sich nicht: Überlegungen zu Schöpfungserzählungen in Babylonien und Israel." Pages 349–358 in *Symbolae Biblicae et Mesopotamicae Francisco Mario Theodoro de Liagre Böhl Dedicatae*. Edited by M. A. Beek, A. A. Kampman, and C. Nijland. Leiden: Brill, 1973.

Soden, W. von. "Der Urmensch im Atramḫasīs-Mythos." Pages 47–52 in *Mésopotamie et Elam: Actes de la XXXVI*ème *Rencontre Assryriologique Internationale*. Edited by L. de Meyer and H. Gasche. Mesopotamian History and Environment, Occasional Publications 1. Ghent: Universiteit Ghent, 1991.

Soden, W. von. "Die erste Tafel des altbabylonischen Atramḫasīs-Mythus. 'Haupttext' und Parallelversionen." *ZA* 68 (1978): 50–94.

Soden, W. von. "Die Igigu-Götter in altbabylonischer Zeit und Edimmu im Atramḫasīs-Mythos." Pages 339–349 in *Aus Sprache, Geschichte und Religion Babyloniens: Gesammelte Aufsätze*. Edited by L. Cagni and H.-P. Müller. Dipartimento di studi asiatici Series Minor 32. Naples: Istituto Universitario Orientale, Dipartimento di Studen Asiatici, 1989.

Soden, W. von. *Grundriss der akkadischen Grammatik*. AnOr 33. Rome: Pontifical Biblical Institute, 1952.

Sommerfeld, W. *Der Aufstieg Marduks: Die Stellung Marduks in der babylonischen Religion des zweiten Jahrtausends v. Chr.* AOAT 213. Kevalaer: Butzon & Bercker; Neukirchen-Vluyn: Neukirchener Verlag, 1982.

Sommerfeld, W. "Marduk." *RlA* 7 (1987–1990): 360–370.

Speiser, E. *Genesis: A New Translation with Introduction and Commentary*. AB 1. Garden City, NY: Doubleday.

Spronk, K. *Beatific Afterlife in Ancient Israel and in the Ancient Near East*. AOAT 219. Kevalaer: Butzon & Bercker; Neukirchen-Vluyn: Neukirchener Verlag, 1986.

Stackert, J. "Pentateuchal Coherence and the Science of Reading." Pages 253–268 in *The Formation of the Pentateuch: Bridging the Academic Cultures of Europe, Israel, and North America*. Edited by J. C. Gertz, B. M. Levinson, and D. Rom-Shiloni. Tübingen: Mohr Siebeck, 2016.

Starr, I. *The Rituals of the Diviner*. BMes 12. Malibu, CA: Undena, 1983.

Starr, R. F. S. *Texts.* Vol. 1 of *Nuzi*. Cambridge, MA: Harvard University Press, 1937.

Steiner, G. "Die sog. tan-Stämme des akkadischen Verbums und ihre semitischen Grundlagen," *ZDMG* 131 (1981): 9–27.

Steinert, U. *Aspekte des Menschseins im Alten Mesopotamien: Eine Studie zu Person und Identität im 2. und 1. Jt. v. Chr.* CM 44. Leiden: Brill, 2012.

Steinert, U. "Catalogues, Texts, and Specialists: Some Thoughts on the Aššur Medical Catalogue and Mesopotamian Healing Professions." Pages 48–132 in Van Buylaere et al., *Sources of Evil*.

Steinert, U. "Fluids, Rivers, and Vessels: Metaphors and Body Concepts in Mesopotamian Gynaecological Texts." *JMC* 22 (2013): 1–23.

Steinert, U. "K. 263+10934, A Tablet with Recipes against the Abnormal Flow of a Woman's Blood." *Sudhoff's Archive* 96 (2012): 64–94.

Steinkeller, P. "The Reluctant En of Inana—or the Persona of Gilgameš in the Perspective of Babylonian Political Philosophy." In "Approaching a Critique of Mesopotamian Reason," ed. G. Gabriel, special issue, *JANEH* 5 (2018): 149–177.

Stol, M. *Birth in Babylonia and the Bible: Its Mediterranean Setting*. CM 14. Groningen: Styx, 2000.

Stol, M. *Epilepsy in Babylonia*. CM 2. Groningen: Styx, 1993.

Stol, M. "Ghosts at the Table." Pages 259–281 in *From the Four Corners of the Earth: Studies in Iconography and Cultures of the Ancient Near East in Honour of F. A. M. Wiggerman*. Edited by D. Kertai and O. Nieuwenhuyse. AOAT 441. Münster: Ugarit-Verlag, 2017.

Stol, M. *Letters from Yale*. AbB 9. Leiden: Brill, 1981.

Stone, M. E. "Apocalyptic Literature." Pages 383–441 in *Jewish Writings of the Second Temple Period*. Edited by Michael E. Stone. Assen: Van Gorcum; Philadelphia: Fortress, 1984.

Strack, H. L. *Introduction to the Talmud and Midrash*. Repr., New York: Meridian; Philadelphia: Jewish Publication Society of America, 1959.

Szlechter, E. "L'interprétation des lois babyloniennes." *Revue internationale des droits de l'antiquité*, 3rd ser., 17 (1970): 81–115.

Tadmor, H. "The Inscriptions of Nabunaid: Historical Arrangement." Pages 351–363 in Güterbock and Jacobsen, *Studies in Honor of Benno Landsberger*.

Tallqvist, K. L. *Die assyrische Beschwörungsserie "Maqlû."* 2 vols. ASSF 20/6. Leipzig: E. Pfeiffer, 1895.

Talmon, S. "Conflate Readings (OT)." Pages 170–173 in *Interpreter's Dictionary of the Bible: Supplementary Volume*. New York: Abingdon Press, 1976.

Talmon, S. "Double Readings in the Massoretic Text." *Textus* 1 (1960): 143–184. Repr., S. Talmon, *Text and Canon of the Hebrew Bible: Collected Studies*, pp. 217–266. Winona Lake, IN: Eisenbrauns, 2010.

Talmon, S. "Synonymous Readings in the Textual Traditions of the Old Testament." *Scripta Hierosolymitana* 8 (1961): 335–383. Repr., S. Talmon, *Text and Canon of the Hebrew Bible: Collected Studies*, pp. 171–216. Winona Lake, IN: Eisenbrauns, 2010.

Talmon, S. "The Textual Study of the Bible: A New Outlook." Pages 19–84 in Talmon, *Text and Canon of the Hebrew Bible: Collected Studies*. Winona Lake, IN: Eisenbrauns, 2010.

Talon, P. *The Standard Babylonian Creation Myth Enūma Eliš*. SAACT 4. Helsinki: Neo-Assyrian Text Corpus Project, 2005.

Thompson, R. C. *The Reports of the Magicians and Astrologers of Nineveh and Babylon*. 2 vols. London: Luzac, 1900.

Thompson, R. C. *Semitic Magic*. London: Luzac, 1908.

Thomsen, M.-L. *Zauberdiagnose und schwarze Magie in Mesopotamien*. CNIP 2. Copenhagen: Museum Tusculanum Press, 1987.

Thureau-Dangin, F. *Textes cunéiformes du Louvre*. Vol. 3. Paris: Geuthner, 1912.

Toorn, K. van der. *Family Religion in Babylonia, Syria, and Israel: Continuity and Change in the Forms of Religious Life*. SHCANE 7. Leiden: Brill, 1996.

Toorn, K. van der. *Sin and Sanction in Israel and Mesopotamia: A Comparative Study*. SSN 22. Assen: Van Gorcum, 1985.

Toorn, K. van der. "The Theology of Demons in Mesopotamia and Israel. Popular Belief and Scholarly Speculation." Pages 61–83 in *Die Dämonen: Die Dämonologie der israelitisch-jüdischen und frühchristlichen Literatur im Kontext ihrer Umwelt*. Edited by A. Lange, H. Lichtenberger, and D. Romheld. Tübingen: Mohr Siebeck, 2003.

Tov, E. *Textual Criticism of the Hebrew Bible*. 3rd ed. Minneapolis: Fortress, 2012.

Trevor, J. C. *Scrolls from Qumrân Cave I*. Jerusalem: Albright Institute of Archaeological Research and The Shrine of the Book, 1972.

Trible, P. *God and the Rhetoric of Sexuality*. Philadelphia: Fortress, 1978.

Trible, P. *Rhetorical Criticism: Context, Method, and the Book of Jonah*. GBS. Minneapolis: Fortress, 1994.

Tropper, J. *Nekromantie: Totenbefragung im Alten Orient und im Alten Testament*. AOAT 223. Kevelaer: Butzen & Bercker; Neukirchen-Vluyn: Neukirchener Verlag, 1989.

Tsukimoto, A. *Untersuchungen zur Totenpflege (kispum) im alten Mesopotamien*. AOAT 216. Kevelaer: Butzen & Bercker; Neukirchen-Vluyn: Neukirchener Verlag, 1985.

Turner, J. H. *The Structure of Sociological Theory*. Rev. ed. Homewood, IL: Dorsey, 1978.

Unger, E. "Aššur, Stadt." *RlA* 1 (1928): 170–195.

Ungnad, A. *Die Religion der Babylonier und Assyrer*. Jena: Diederichs, 1921.

Van Buylaere, G. "CTN 4, 168." *ORACC*. 2010. http://oracc.museum.upenn.edu/cams/gkab/P363582/html (accessed September 6, 2016).

Van Buylaere, G., M. Luukko, D. Schwemer, and A. Mertens-Wagschal, eds. *Sources of Evil: Studies in Mesopotamian Exorcistic Lore*. AMD 15. Leiden: Brill, 2018.

Van De Mieroop, M. "Theses on Babylonian Philosophy." In "Approaching a Critique of Mesopotamian Reason," ed. G. Gabriel, special issue, *JANEH* 5 (2018): 15–39.

Vanstiphout, H. L. J. "Inanna/Ishtar as a Figure of Controversy." Pages 225–238 in *Struggles of Gods: Papers of the Groningen Work Group for the Study of the History of Religions*. Edited by H. G. Kippenberg, H. J. W. Drijvers, and Y. Kuiper. Religion and Reason 31. Berlin: Mouton, 1984.

Vernant, J.-P. "A 'Beautiful Death' and the Disfigured Corpse in Homeric Epic." Pages 50–74 in Vernant, *Mortals and Immortals*.

Vernant, J.-P. "India, Mesopotamia, Greece: Three Ideologies of Death." Pages 75–83 in Vernant, *Mortals and Immortals*.

Vernant, J.-P. *Mortals and Immortals: Collected Essays*. Edited by F. Zeitlin. Princeton: Princeton University Press, 1991.

Vernant, J.-P. "Psuche: Simulacrum of the Body or Image of the Divine?" Pages 186–192 in Vernant, *Mortals and Immortals*.

Vorländer, H. *Mein Gott: Die Vorstellungen vom persönlichen Gott im Alten Orient und im Alten Testament*. AOAT 23. Kevelaer: Butzon & Bercker; Neukirchen-Vluyn: Neukirchener Verlag, 1975.

Walker, C., and M. Dick. *The Induction of the Cult Image in Ancient Mesopotamia: The Mesopotamian "Mīs Pî" Ritual.* SAALT 1. Helsinki: Neo-Assyrian Text Corpus Project, 2001.

Wallace, A. F. C. *Religion: An Anthropological View*. New York: Random House, 1966.

Walther, A. *Das altbabylonische Gerichtswesen*. LSS 6/4–6. Leipzig: Hinrichs, 1917.

Warshaw, T. S. "The Book of Jonah." Pages 191–207 in *Literary Interpretations of Biblical Narratives*. Edited by K. R. R. Gros Louis, J. S. Ackerman, and T. S. Warshaw. Nashville: Abingdon, 1974.

Wasserman, N. *Akkadian Love Literature of the Third and Second Millennium BCE*. LAOS 4. Wiesbaden: Harrassowitz, 2016.

Weiher, E. von. *Spätbabylonische Texte aus Uruk*. Vol. 2. ADFU 10. Berlin: Mann, 1983.

Weinreich, U. *Languages in Contact*. New York: Linguistic Circle of New York, 1953. Repr., The Hague: Mouton, 1963.

Weiss, A. *Studies in the Literature of the Amoraim*. In Hebrew. New York: Yeshiva University Press, 1962.

Weissert, E. "Creating a Political Climate: Literary Allusions to *Enūma Eliš* in Sennacherib's Account of the Battle of Halule." Pages 191–202 in *Assyrien im Wandel der Zeiten: XXXIX$^{e}$ Rencontre Assyriologique Internationale, Heidelberg 6.–10. Juli 1992*. Edited by H. Waetzoldt and H. Hauptmann. HSAO 6. Heidelberg: Heidelberger Orientverlag, 1997.

Westbrook, R., and C. Wilcke. "The Liability of an Innocent Purchaser of Stolen Goods in Early Mesopotamian Law." *AfO* 25 (1974–1977): 111–121.

Westenholz, A. "*berūtum, damtum*, and Old Akkadian KI.GAL: Burial of Dead Enemies in Ancient Mesopotamia." *AfO* 23 (1970): 27–31.

Wiggermann, F. A. M. "Discussion." Pages 77–92 in *Man and Images in the Ancient Near East*, by E. Porada. Anshen Transdisciplinary Lectureships in Art, Science, and the Philosophy of Culture 4. Wakefield, RI: Moyer Bell, 1996.

Wiggermann, F. A. M. "The Four Winds and the Origins of Pazuzu." Pages 125–165 in *Das geistige Erfassen der Welt im Alten Orient: Sprache, Religion, Kultur und Gesellschaft*. Edited by C. Wilcke. Wiesbaden: Harrassowitz, 2007.

Wiggermann, F. A. M. "Lamaštu, Daughter of Anu. A Profile." Pages 217–252 (= ch. 10) in *Birth in Babylonia and the Bible: Its Mediterranean Setting*, by M. Stol. CM 14. Groningen: Styx, 2000.

Wiggermann, F. A. M. "The Mesopotamian Pandemonium. A Provisional Census." *SMSR* 77, no. 2 (2011): 298–322.

Wiggermann, F. A. M. *Mesopotamian Protective Spirits: The Ritual Texts*. CM 1. Groningen: Styx, 1992.

Wiggermann, F. A. M. "Nergal." *RlA* 9 (1998): 215–226.

Wiggermann, F. A. M. "Some Demons of Time and Their Functions in Mesopotamian Iconography." Pages 103–116 in *Die Welt der Götterbilder*. Edited by B. Groneberg and H. Spieckermann. Berlin: de Gruyter, 2007.

Wiggermann, F. A. M. "Theologies, Priests, and Worship in Ancient Mesopotamia." In Sasson, *Civilizations of the Ancient Near East*, 3:1857–1870.

Wilcke, C. "Inanna/Ištar." *RlA* 5 (1976–1980): 74–87.

Wilcke, C. "Vom göttlichen Wesen des Königtums und seinem Ursprung im Himmel." Pages 63–83 in *Die Sakralität von Herrschaft: Herrschaftslegitimierung im Wechsel der Zeiten und Räume*. Edited by F.-R. Erkens. Berlin: Akadamie, 2002.

Wilcke, C. "Zum Geschichtsbewusstsein im alten Mesopotamien." Pages 31–52 in *Archäologie und Geschichtsbewusstsein*. Kolloquien zur allgemeinen und vergleichenden Archäologie 3. Munich: Beck, 1982.

Wilhelm, G. "Ein neues Lamaštu-Amulett." *ZA* 69 (1979): 34–40.

Wilhelm, G. "Zur Struktur des hethitischen 'Kantuzzili-Gebets.'" Pages 33–40 in *Kulte, Priester, Rituale: Beiträge zu Kult und Kultkritik im Alten Testament und Alten Orient* (*Festschrift für Theodor Seidl zum 65. Geburtstag*). Edited by S. Ernst and M. Häusl. Arbeiten zu Text und Sprache im Alten Testament 89. Erzabtei St. Ottilien: EOS, 2010.

Wiseman, D. J. "A New Text of the Babylonian Poem of the Righteous Sufferer." *AnSt* 30 (1980): 101–107.

Wiseman, D. J., and J. A. Black. *Literary Texts from the Temple of Nabû*. CTN 4. London: British School of Archaeology in Iraq, 1996.

Wolff, H. W. *Obadiah and Jonah*. Minneapolis: Augsburg, 1986.

Wyatt, N. "Arms and the King: The Earliest Allusions to the *Chaoskampf* Motif and their Implications for the Interpretation of the Ugaritic and Biblical Traditions." Pages 834–882 in *"Und Mose schreib dieses Lied auf": Studien zum Alten Testament und zum alten Orient. Festschrift für Oswald Loretz zur Vollendung seines 70. Lebensjahres*. Edited by M. Dietrich and I. Kottsieper. AOAT 250. Münster: Ugarit-Verlag, 1998.

Yahuda, A. S. "The Meaning of the Name Esther." *JRAS* 8 (1946): 174–178.

Zgoll, A. *Die Kunst des Betens: Form und Funktion, Theologie und Psychagogik in babylonisch-assyrischen Handerhebungsgebeten zu Ištar*. AOAT 308. Münster: Ugarit-Verlag, 2003.

Zimmern, H. "Babylonians and Assyrians." Pages 309–319 in vol. 2 of *Encyclopaedia of Religion and Ethics*. Edited by J. Hastings. Edinburgh: T&T Clark; New York: Scribner, 1910.

Zimmern, H. *Beiträge zur Kenntnis der babylonischen Religion*. 2 vols. Assyriologische Bibliothek 12. Leipzig: Hinrichs, 1896–1901.

Zomer, E. *Corpus of Middle Babylonian and Middle Assyrian Incantations*. LAOS 9. Wiesbaden: Harrassowitz, 2018.

# Index of Passages Quoted

The index lists texts that were quoted rather than merely cited. The numbering of prayers follows Mayer, *Untersuchungen zur Formensprache der babylonischen "Gebetsbeschworungen."*

## 1 Prayers, Incantations, and Rituals

### *šuillas*


Adad 1b
lines 34–36 196

Anu 1
*AGH* 36: 18–25 121
lines 9–13 182
lines 10–11 197

Ea, Šamaš, Marduk 9
*LKA* 86, rev. 4 // *LKA* 88, obv. 32 203
*LKA* 86, rev. 13–15 // *LKA* 88, rev. 9–11 203

Enlil 1a
PBS 1/1, 17 // BMS 19 193–195

Enlil 1b
*KAR* 68 // *KAR* 25 col. iii 21′–iv 2′ 193–195

Gula 1a
passim 206–214
line 74 281
lines 81–82 198
lines 87–89 198

Gula 1b
passim 206–214
line 10 277 n. 28
line 14 281
line 16 277 n. 27, 281
lines 22–23 198
lines 31–33a 198

Ištar 1
*AGH* 62: 37b–38 120 n. 8
line 21 199
lines 22–25 199

Ištar 2
lines 67–78 190–191
lines 75–78 190–191
lines 85–90 190–191

Ištar 4
lines 13′–14′ (= *BMS* 30: 8–9) 278
line 15′ 189, 199

Ištar 25
lines 9–10 203

Madānu 1 (= Nusku 1)
lines 13–19 189

Marduk 2
passim 20–21, 126–148, 149–162
lines 1–9 181
lines 22b–27 (*AGH* 64: 21–25) 120

Marduk 16
line 12 204

Nabû 1
lines 9–10 199 n. 59

Nabû 3
lines 1–29 149–162

Nabû 6
lines 14–17 (*AGH*, 110: 14–17) 130

Nergal 2
passim 19–20, 112–113, 163–175
lines 1–10 180
lines 19–24 182

Ninurta 1
line 24 204
line 40 204

Sîn 1
20b–24b 186
21–24b 183

Sîn 3
55–60 187
64–66 188
66–68 187

Šamaš 1
*BMS* 6: 110–116 276–277

Šibzianna 1
line 24 204

Tašmētu 1
CTN 4, no. 168,
rev. i 3–43 189, 202

Zarpanītu 1
*AGH* 68: 5–6 133 n. 17

Zarpanītu 2
*AGH* 140a, rev. 5 204

***
82–5–22, 532: 3–4 277

Assyrian Dream Book (ed. Oppenheim)
Fragment III 313

*CMAwR* 1, no. 7.8.2: 14′–45′ 30
*CMAwR* 1, no. 8.1: 26′–29′
= *BAM* 214 ii 10–13 281 n. 40
*CMAwR* 1, no. 8.2: 115–116 =
*LKA* 154 rev. 14′–15′ 122–123
*CMAwR* 2, no. 3.6: 8–12 =
*BAM* 316 ii 12′–16′ 282
*CMAwR* 2, no. 8.23:
47′–56′ 31
*CMAwR* 2, no. 8.28: 90–91 =
BMS 12 (= Marduk 5) 121 n. 9
*CMAwR* 2, no. 9.8: 24
(= Šibzianna) 204
*CMAwR* 2, no. 10.8: 19
(= Ninurta 4 = Kaksisa 2) 189, 201

CT 16, 45: 122–124 278 n. 31, 287–288, 290
CT 23, 15: 6–9 17, 38

Dingirshadibbas
*JNES* 33: 274–277: 23–39 40
*JNES* 33: 276–277: 40–54 40–41

Hymn to Ninurta as Sirius (K 128)
*JRAS Centenary Supplement*
(1924): 35: 2–36: 6 279, 286

*KAR* 228: 7 (= Šamaš 6) 204, 204–205 n. 71
*KAR* 228: 12–14 (= Šamaš 6) 204, 204–205 n. 71

Lamaštu
II 152–166 37

Lamaštu amulet
*ZA* 69 (1979): 34–40 133 n. 17

*Lipšur* litanies (*JNES* 15 (1956): 129–149)
Type I 81–95 47
Type II 7′–22′ 46–47

*LKA* 139, rev. 25
(Gods of the Sky) 275

*Maqlû*
I 13–14 270–271
I 14 277, 281
I 140–143 // V 152–155 78 n. 26
II 98–103 122
II 136–148 33–34
II 183–204 43

*Maqlû* (cont.)
III 1–16 18, 42
VI 119″–126″ 34, 113
VII 29–46 34
VII 162–169 314
VIII 124″″–127″″ 78

Marduk 24
lines 35–36 200

Marduk Kiutukam
4*R*² 29/1, obv. 27–30 //
*STT* 182 (+) 183, obv. 6′–7 132 n. 16

*namburbis*
SANE 1/1, no. 6 (against a monstrous birth) 33
SANE 1/1, no. 7, obv. 10–rev. 3 44
Šamaš 23 (Ebeling *RA* 49 (1955): 35–40, no. 20) 201
*Or* NS 36 (1967): 273: 4′ 276

Prayer to the Gods of the Night (AO 6769)
*RA* 32 (1935): 180a: 8 // b: 8–9 284 n. 52

Šamaš 48 (Against Ghosts)
AMD 3, no. 10: 1–7 39

Šamaš 73
AMD 3, no. 226, obv. 28 205

*Šurpu*
V–VI 1–16 45
V–VI 144–172 45–46

Udug.ḫul
V 1–20 36–37
V 167–181 16
V 167–182 36

*Ugaritica* 5
no. 162, lines 28′–31′ 218

## 2. Mythological and Other Literary Texts

### Mythological Texts

*Agušaya*
Tablet B I = *RA* 75 (1981): 126: i 5–9 278 n. 31

*Atraḫasīs*
I 192–226 68–75
I 352–355 // II 1–4 240
I 378–383 // 393–398 83

Descent of Ištar
lines 3–11 89

*Enūma eliš*
passim 225–232
V 117–VI 120 233–237
VI 5–6 80 n. 28
VII 15–17 287 n. 58
VII 124, 126, 130 287 n. 58

Gilgamesh, Enkidu, and the Netherworld
Shaffer, 121:3–4 78

Lugal ud me-lám-bi nir-g̃ál
van Dyke, vol. 1, 107: 436 278 n. 31

### Literary Texts

*Ludlul bēl nēmeqi*
I 41–48 172–173
I 51–52 283, 284
II 4–20 15
II 12–32 217–224
II 36–38 274

Lambert, *BWL* 227: 23–26 83
Lambert, *BWL* 288: 8–9 (= K2765) 283

## 3. Mesopotamian Legal Texts

Codex Ḫammurabi
§1 334
§2 334
§§3–4 328–346

§13 341–345
rev. xxvii, 34–40 90

Harvard Semitic Museum
SMN 1854 = Bulla 449 319–325
SMN 2096 = Tablet 311 319–325

Vassal Treaties of Esarhaddon
476–477 90


**4. Historical Inscriptions and Miscellaneous Texts**

**Historical Inscriptions**


RIME
1.9.3.1: iv 9–v 17 228

*TCL* 3
lines 317–318 288 n. 62

Esarhaddon inscriptions, AfO Beih. 9
18: Episode 14b 6–7 287 n. 59

Neo-Babylonian Royal Inscriptions
VAB 4, NbK 11, i 4–5 288 n. 62, 272
VAB 4, NbK 15, i 4 288 n. 62
VAB 4, NbK 15, i 6 288 n. 62
VAB 4, NbK 15, i 8 288 n. 62
VAB 4, NbK 15, i 9 288 n. 62
VAB 4, NbK 15, i 28–29 288, 290
VAB 4, NbK 15, i 30–36 288 n. 62
VAB 4, NbK 19, i 6–10 288 n. 62
VAB 4, NbK 19, i 14–15 288 n. 62
VAB 4, NbK 19A, i 14–15 272
*AnSt* 8 (1958): 62: 1–2 283


**Miscellaneous Texts**


AbB 9
no. 141 186

Thompson, *Reports of the Magicians and Astrologers*
vol. 1, no. 24: 5–6 273 n. 15
vol. 1, no. 120: 3–4 273 n. 15
vol. 1, no. 122: 2 273 n. 15
vol. 1, no. 123: 2 273 n. 15
vol. 2, no. 85A: 4–5 273 n. 15
vol. 2, no. 115D: 1–2 273 n. 15

BRM 4
no. 32, obv. 2–3 84 n. 41

*SpBTU* 1
no. 49, 36–37 73

Euripides, *Alcestis*
lines 782–786 274 n. 19


**5. Bible and Rabbinic Literature**


Hebrew Bible
Gen 1–11 238–254
Gen 1:26–27 255
Gen 9:6 306 n. 29
Gen 11:1–9 257–258
Gen 18:1 295 n. 82
Lev 17:10–11 299
Num 14:15–17, 20 125
1 Kgs 18:26–27 119
Ezek 44:7 7 n. 2
Jon 4:10–11 259–265

Mishnah
Sanhedrin 3:8, 1–2 344

Babylonian Talmud
Baba Batra 130b 291
Berakhot 55b 313, 314
Berakhot 56b 314
Niddah 7b 291
Niddah 73a // Megillah 28b 294 n. 79
Shabbat 138b 290

Rashi
ad Gen 18:1 295 n. 82
ad b. Shabbat 138b 290

Printed in the United States
By Bookmasters